Gilbert and Sullivan

GENDER AND CULTURE

Carolyn Williams

Gilbert and Sullivan

GENDER • GENRE • PARODY

Columbia University Press *New York*

COLUMBIA UNIVERSITY PRESS
Publishers Since 1893
New York   Chichester, West Sussex

Copyright © 2011 Columbia University Press
Paperback edition, 2012
All rights reserved

Library of Congress Cataloging-in-Publication Data
Williams, Carolyn, 1950–
Gilbert and Sullivan : gender, genre, parody / Carolyn Williams.
p. cm. — (Gender and culture)
Includes bibliographical references and index.
ISBN 978-0-231-14804-7 (cloth : alk. paper)
ISBN 978-0-231-14805-4 (pbk. : alk. paper)
ISBN 978-0-231-51966-3 (e-book)
1. Sullivan, Arthur, 1842–1900. Operas. 2. Gilbert, W. S. (William Schwenck), 1836–1911.
3. Opera—England—19th century. 4. Parody in music. 5. Sex role in music. I. Title. II. Series.

ML410.S95W45   2010
782.1'20922—dc22   2010018859

Columbia University Press books are printed on permanent and durable acid-free paper.
This book is printed on paper with recycled content.
Printed in the United States of America

c 10 9 8 7 6 5 4 3
p 10 9 8 7 6 5 4 3 2 1

Designed by Lisa Hamm

References to Internet Web sites (URLs) were accurate at the time of writing.
Neither the author nor Columbia University Press is responsible for URLs that
may have expired or changed since the manuscript was prepared.

For Michael and Lucy

Contents

Part II. Genders

Part III. Cultures

Illustrations

FIGURES

PLATES

Following page 234

Preface

Gilbert and Sullivan: Gender, Genre, Parody describes William S. Gilbert and Arthur Sullivan's formation of an innovative genre, English comic opera, which they created through parodies of older works, genres, and traditions, both British and Continental. Indeed, as we will see, the parodies sometimes refer to a specific work, but more often they allude to an entire theatrical or literary genre.

The Gilbert and Sullivan operas "recollect" these older genres within their novel, and characteristically late Victorian, parodic form. In the chapters to come, I pay special attention to the parodies of extravaganza and melodrama, but I'm also concerned with grand opera, opéra bouffe, the minstrel show, and the music hall.

We can see Gilbert and Sullivan's formula for English comic opera emerge in their third collaboration, *The Sorcerer* (1877), and their new genre was fully formed by the time of *The Mikado* (1885), the ninth of their fourteen collaborations. But the operas after *The Mikado* continued to develop genre parodies and to investigate familiar themes and parodies of social types, behaviors, lines of thought, and institutions. Common stereotypes—such as "the angel in the house," "the strong-minded woman," "the aesthete," and "the separate spheres"—are good examples of such cultural formations, which may be regarded as forms of typecasting in the theater of popular culture.

In other words, in addition to genre parody, *Gilbert and Sullivan* is concerned with various figures and forms of social parody. In both genre parody and social parody, the practice of twisting and playing with convention is central. The conventions of a genre, like the conventions of social life, may be seen as signs of its historical formation—and this is one reason that genre is such a powerful analytic lens, because through it we can consider both literary or theatrical form and cultural formations simultaneously. I don't attempt to prove the existence of common conventions and stereotypes, nor do I dwell on current critical discussions of them (many of which debate the extent to which they operated in fact and the extent to which they must be regarded as ideological constructs). Instead, I assume that my readers will grant their existence in discourse, so I treat conventions as given and proceed to analyze the way Gilbert and Sullivan used them for parodic purposes.

Obviously, parody keeps cultural stereotypes in circulation even while holding them up for ridicule or critique. This is so because the imitative and critical functions of parody are always closely intertwined. We should think of parody involving a spectrum of attitudes on the part of its creators and its audiences. At one extreme of the spectrum lies critique, but at the other lies a kind of homage. In any particular instance, these attitudes can be mixed, and thus a parody can make fun of its object, humorously indicating that it is old-fashioned or long past, while affectionately, ruefully—or with any other attitude—preserving its memory. The fragmentary preservation of old-hat, easily recognizable things, within a new aesthetic and historical context, can create quite preposterous effects, which this book enjoys recounting. Indeed, by parodying older genres, the Savoy operas effectively push them even more securely into the past while recollecting them in the present. Through this aesthetic dynamic, these characteristically late-nineteenth-century artifacts trenchantly and humorously comment on the century-long preoccupation with historical, literary, and art-historical revival.

We are accustomed to the Savoy operas' treatment of class and nationality, but questions of gender have been given short shrift in the commentary tradition. *Gilbert and Sullivan* redresses that imbalance by examining the importance of gender in each of the Savoy operas. Indeed, gender is structurally fundamental to the form of the operas from *Trial by Jury* (1875) to *The Yeomen of the Guard* (1888), for these operas rely on a Chorus that is graphically divided into masculine and feminine cohorts, stereotypically conceived as oppositional. After *Yeomen*, when the divided Chorus is no longer central to the representation of gender stereotypes, gender often remains a central thematic concern nonetheless.

Ian Bradley once remarked that "Gilbert and Sullivan is very much a male taste." If this has ever been the case, it certainly need not be, and I hope that my book will show why. I regard the treatment of gender in Gilbert and Sullivan's operas from a feminist point of view, and, indeed, I frequently find that the operas themselves advance a feminist argument. In this respect, I hope to offer a particularly refreshing contribution to ongoing discussions of the work. The misogyny that is sometimes attributed to aspects of these operas is often parodic and critical; in any case, "misogyny" is too blunt an instrument with which to approach them. For one thing, misogyny comes in many forms and flavors; for another, in these works it is often turned against itself.

A further aim of this book is to embed the Savoy operas in the milieu of late Victorian culture. Such a treatment can never be exhaustive, since the sheer number of cultural contexts that could be usefully adduced would far exceed the range of any one book. I have chosen some that I hope will be surprising and illuminating. This book is not only about Gilbert and Sullivan, in other words. When I discuss other works of literature, theater, or art, however, I do so for one of two reasons: (1) to illustrate the conventions of a genre or a figure in the opera under discussion, or (2) to establish a wider cultural context in which to place the works of Gilbert and Sullivan, in order better to understand their significance in the late Victorian period.

I see the operas as falling into three phases, indicated by this book's three parts: (1) the formation of the genre of English comic opera through parodies of older genres; (2) the consideration of gender and parodies of it; and (3) the examination of cross-cultural and autoethnographic thinking and parodies of it. I want to say, here at the beginning, that these phases are not mutually exclusive; their concerns overlap, and most of the operas treat all three concerns. This division is useful, nevertheless, as a matter of emphasis, proportion, or degree, and I hope, using these three phases, to show a rational development in the unfolding of the Savoy canon. Therefore, I have followed the chronological order of the operas. So although this book does pursue a sequential argument, I've written a separate chapter on each opera, with the hope that readers who may not want to read the entire book might still enjoy reading chapters on single works.

But there are two important points at which my discussion is devoted to features that are crucially important throughout the Savoy canon: the section on the patter song, which appears in chapter 3 (on *The Sorcerer*), and the section on the Dame figure, which appears in chapter 7 (on *Iolanthe* [1882]).

One last word. Although *Gilbert and Sullivan* is not a musicological study, I do explain, in the last section of the introduction, how Sullivan's music is relevant to my arguments about gender, genre, and parody. In the fourteen chapters that follow, I discuss the music incidentally from time to time.

Acknowledgments

Many thanks to the John Simon Guggenheim Memorial Foundation for a fellowship that afforded me precious time to write. At Rutgers University, support from the School of Arts and Sciences allowed for a well-timed sabbatical leave.

A few sections of *Gilbert and Sullivan: Gender, Genre, Parody* appeared in earlier and substantially different forms. "Making Fun of Victorian Poetry," a section of chapter 6, was published in a longer version: "Parody and Poetic Tradition: Gilbert and Sullivan's *Patience*," *Victorian Poetry* 46, no. 4 (2008): 375–403. My thinking about *Topsy-Turvy* in chapter 9 began with "Intimacy and Theatricality: Mike Leigh's *Topsy-Turvy*," *Victorian Literature and Culture* 28, no. 2 (2000): 471–76. And, finally, chapter 13 was prefigured by "*Utopia, Limited*: Nationalism, Empire and Parody in the Comic Operas of Gilbert and Sullivan," in *Cultural Politics at the Fin de Siècle*, ed. Sally Ledger and Scott McCracken (Cambridge: Cambridge University Press, 1995), pp. 221–47. Thanks to the editors of these publications.

The memory of Cecil Y. Lang stays with me, and I wish he could read this book. I miss Eve Kosofsky Sedgwick, too, so much, and I know that she would have been glad to see it coming out.

Fredric Woodbridge Wilson, formerly curator of the Gilbert and Sullivan Collection at The Pierpont Morgan Library, New York, and late curator of the Harvard Theatre Collection, Houghton Library, Harvard University, provided me with expert guidance to those collections and to his own. Ric's generous spirit is most prominently demonstrated in this book's illustrations, but his influence may be felt throughout.

I owe a great deal, too, to Jonathan Strong. His wonderful novel *Secret Words* (Cambridge, Mass.: Zoland, 1993) envisions a local production of *Utopia, Limited* that showed me, in captivating, concrete terms, the present-day cultural, political, racial, gendered, and global resonances of that opera. Later, Jonathan read the manuscript of *Gilbert and Sullivan* in its entirety and offered valuable encouragement, suggestions, and corrections, for all of which I'm truly grateful—but for the bracing inspiration of his fiction, most of all.

Most of all, thanks to Nancy K. Miller, who is responsible for the work taking shape as this particular book. Her friendship and her editorial vision are always in full force, and I thank her sincerely for both. Thanks, too, to Victoria Rosner, Nancy's co-editor. Two excellent readers for Columbia University Press later identified themselves to me as Robyn Warhol and Adrienne Munich. This book assumed its final—and much improved—form in response to their acute questions and comments. Bill Germano provided inescapably good and timely advice at an even earlier stage. Jennifer Crewe welcomed the book to Columbia University Press with enthusiasm and carefully guided it to completion. Irene Pavitt at Columbia University Press beautifully copyedited the manuscript, improving it greatly. For research assistance, I would like to thank Manuel Betancourt. Anna Witek graciously helped me with the images. And for proofreading, I would like to thank Naomi Levine and Greg Ellermann.

Three fabulous chairs of the Department of English—Barry V. Qualls, Cheryl Wall, and Richard E. Miller—made support and encouragement seem a natural part of the Rutgers landscape. I've been lucky to have their intellectual companionship along the way, as well as their institutional support. With his characteristic combination of good humor and sharp judgment, Barry read countless pages and turned them in a better direction. What a pleasure, always, to hear his far-ranging comments on all things (including this book)! George Levine and I worked productively together for fifteen years at the Center for the Critical Analysis of Contemporary Culture (now the Center for Cultural Analysis) at Rutgers, a remarkable environment for interdisciplinary scholarship and exchange. Many thanks to him for that collaboration and for the collegial network it afforded so many of us. The center's seminar on "The Performance of Culture," which I directed, contributed a great deal to my sense of this book's argument, and I would like to thank the seminar members who had an especially strong influence on my thinking: Matt Buckley, Chris Chism, Elin Diamond, Brent Edwards, Jonathan Goldberg, Caroline Levine, Ray Ricketts, Jeffrey Shandler, Brian Walsh, and

Yael Zerubavel. Elin Diamond got the conversation going in the best possible way through her wonderful Classes for Colleagues on performance theory.

I want to thank my colleagues in Victorian studies at Rutgers for steadily providing the sense of an ongoing conversation in an exciting, expanding field: Matt Buckley, Kate Flint, John Kucich, David Kurnick, Dianne Sadoff, Jonah Siegel, and Barry Qualls. Other colleagues in nineteenth-century studies at Rutgers have been great friends and steady interlocutors; I would like to thank, especially, Billy Galperin and Meredith McGill. Many inspiring friends and colleagues, whom I first met when they were graduate students at Rutgers, have contributed immeasurably to my thinking: Tanya Agathocleous, Hillary Chute, Matthew Kaiser, Vincent Lankewish, Rick Lee, April Lidinsky, Ankhi Mukerjee, Carrie Preston, and Jason Rudy. Tanya, Vincent, and Jason responded to parts of this work in progress with wonderful critical generosity.

Outside Rutgers, I've been enlivened by the Nineteenth-Century Historical Poetics working group, which brings a searching urgency to every topic of our study; thanks to Max Cavitch, Michael Cohen, Virginia Jackson, Meredith Martin, Meredith McGill, Yopie Prins, Eliza Richards, and Jason Rudy. The Dickens Universe, sponsored by the Dickens Project at the University of California, Santa Cruz, has become increasingly important to me, ever since I first entered its busy hive of thinking, learning, and collegial exchange with Carolyn Dever, Jonathan Grossman, the late Sally Ledger, Tricia Lootens, Teresa Mangum, Elsie Michie, Helena Michie, Rob Polhemus, Catherine Robson, and Rebecca Stern. In particular, I would like to thank the director of the Universe, John Jordan.

Essential sustenance far beyond the boundaries of institutional life has been generously proffered all along by Marcia Ian, Barry Qualls, Marianne DeKoven (who also carefully read several chapters), Rachel Jacoff, Jim Richardson and Connie Hassett, Eviatar and Yael Zerubavel, Rosemarie Bodenheimer, Eve Sedgwick, and Peggy Carr. I've depended on them for their gifts of intimacy, interrogation, companionship, and mutual narration. The ID 450 Collective, a feminist working group in Boston, has had a lasting effect on my life, as well as on my work.

These words—and the thanks they attempt to express—can never be enough! But thanks, always, to my family: Mary and James Williams, Nancy Williams, Matt Mancini, and Philip Mancini. Above all to Michael McKeon and Lucy McKeon, to whom I've dedicated this book. So much love to Lucy, who is gorged with existence and pouring from the sky! To my husband and colleague, Michael, excruciatingly felt thanks for steady, uncompromising support and unfailing intellectual companionship. I remain happy with the thought that my debt to him will continue to appreciate as time passes.

Gilbert and Sullivan

Introduction

etween 1871 and 1896, William Schwenck Gilbert (1836–1911) and Arthur Sullivan (1842–1900) wrote and composed fourteen important works of musical theater. By the time they staged *The Sorcerer* (1877), they had developed a novel genre, English comic opera, with the invaluable leadership of Richard D'Oyly Carte (1844–1901), who succeeded in his dream of establishing a school of native English comic opera by bringing Gilbert and Sullivan together and keeping them together, in an almost unbroken contractual relation.[1] The Savoy operas—as they are called, after the theater that Carte built to house them—span the last quarter of the nineteenth century (1871–1896) and are important documents of late Victorian culture.

Because this book focuses on the Savoy operas, with incidental examinations of other works by Gilbert and Sullivan, it is important to note, at the outset, that the accomplishments of the librettist and the composer were by no means limited to their collaborations with each other. Before, during, and after their partnership, Gilbert and Sullivan were highly acclaimed for work in their separate fields. Their careers were consolidated in the 1860s, and when they came together, each was already at the top of his game.

For more than a decade before he began his collaboration with Gilbert, Sullivan was regarded as the foremost English composer of his age, the personification of hope for an English national music. Sullivan's genius showed itself early. In 1856, the Royal Academy of Music awarded him the Mendelssohn Scholarship and then extended the award for an unprecedented second and third year, so Sullivan could continue his studies in Leipzig, where he mastered the full range of European musical styles, past and present. His incidental music for *The Tempest*, originally written as a graduation piece, was performed at the Crystal Palace in 1862 and immediately made Sullivan's name. He presented major orchestral works, large choral pieces, and oratorios throughout the 1860s and 1870s. Most of his composition of hymns and parlor songs took place during this period as well, including "Onward Christian Soldiers," his best-known hymn (1872, with text by Sabine Baring-Gould), and "The Lost Chord," his best-known song (1877, with text by Adelaide Procter). Most important for our purposes, in the 1860s, Sullivan also began to write music for the theater, most notably his first opera, *The Sapphire Necklace* (1863–1864), which has largely been lost, and the ever-popular *Cox and Box* (1866, with a libretto by F. C. Burnand), an adaptation of *Box and Cox* (1847), a farce by John Maddison Morton.

During his collaboration with Gilbert, Sullivan continued to write incidental music for the theater (*Henry VIII* [1877] and *Macbeth* [1888]). Apart from the Savoy operas, however, his most significant achievements during those years were two large-scale choral works, *The Martyr of Antioch* (1880, with a libretto partly adapted by Gilbert) and *The Golden Legend* (1886, based on Longfellow's poem). After Sullivan was knighted in 1883, he was frequently needled in the press for not devoting himself entirely to serious music. Perhaps this public criticism contributed to his increasing feeling, from the mid-1880s on, that his partnership with Gilbert was somehow holding him back. Nevertheless, he continued to compose comic operas, and the music for *The Mikado* (1885) and *The Yeomen of the Guard* (1888) is among his best in any genre. During a hiatus in his collaboration with Gilbert, Sullivan composed his only grand opera, *Ivanhoe* (1891), significantly English in theme and story. After his association with Gilbert ended in 1896, he continued to write both light and serious music until his death in 1900.[2]

Before his long collaboration with Sullivan, Gilbert was a well-known comic journalist, poet, and playwright. After a couple of careers that came to nothing (nonprofessional military service, training in the law), Gilbert began in 1861 to contribute to *Fun*, an eclectic comic periodical that was, for a while, the chief competitor to *Punch* (plate 1). From 1865 to 1871, he published "parodistic playlets" almost weekly. Both "trenchant and hilarious," these one-page illustrated reviews commented on specific dramatic productions, but also took off on various conventional forms and figures of drama.[3] For *Fun*, Gilbert wrote under several pseuedonyms—the Comic Physiognomist, the Comic Mythologist, A. Dapter, Desiderius Erasmus, A Trembling Widow, R. Ditty, A. Pittite, Animal Carraccio, R. Chimedes, and Snarler—but his most famous and lasting signature was Bab, short for Babby (that is, baby), his infant nickname.[4] Over this signature, Gilbert wrote the so-called Bab Ballads, accompanying them with his own whimsical drawings, and it was with these illustrations that Bab was first chiefly associated.[5] The Bab Ballads are, by turns, grisly and grotesque, hyperlogical, sentimental, satirical, and parodic. Their humor is quirky and light; the versification is impressive. They prefigure the Savoy operas in two ways, for Gilbert later mined the Bab Ballads for ideas and story lines, and in their variety we can observe the early development of the lyricist. First published in book form in 1869, the Bab Ballads are still in print.

In the 1860s, Gilbert also embarked on his career as a dramatist, with humor and parody uppermost in mind. His first play, a *comedietta* called *Uncle Baby*, was produced as a curtain-raiser at the Lyceum in 1863. From 1866 to 1869, he wrote opera burlesques on well-known operas from the 1830s and 1840s, beginning with *Dulcamara! or, The Little Duck and the Great Quack* (1866), a parody of Gaetano Donizetti's *L'elisir d'amore* (*The Elixir of Love*, 1832). Four other opera burlesques followed. Notably less vapid than the usual midcentury burlesque, "they reveal how a playwright may begin by making burlesque of opera and end by making opera of burlesque."[6] Gilbert's only pantomime was produced in 1867, and the excesses of its title show his sense of genre parody well at work: *Harlequin Cock Robin and Jenny Wren! or, Fortunatus and The Water of Life, The Three Bears, The Three Gifts, The Three Wishes, and the Little Man Who Woo'd the Little Maid* (plate 2). Starting in 1868, Gilbert wrote dramatic entertainments for the German Reeds' Royal Gallery of Illustration, a small theater so named in order to evade antitheatrical prejudice with titular claims to be educational and artistic.[7] These entertainments include a genre parody of supernatural melodrama, *Ages Ago* (1869), in which the paintings in a family portrait gallery come to life; a genre parody on nautical themes, *Our Island Home* (1870), which involves a pirate apprentice; and a genre parody of sensation fiction, *A Sensation Novel: In Three Volumes* (1871). Gilbert's first serious comedy appeared in 1869, but further humorous and parodic works followed in 1870: a burlesque of Tennyson's *The Princess*; a supernatural tale of identity, *The Gentleman in Black* (with music by Frederic Clay); and his first fairy comedy, *The Palace of Truth*, based very loosely on Madame de Genlis's novel *Le palais de la vérité*, a good example of the so-called lozenge plot, in which transformation is wrought by a magical agent.

By the time of his first collaboration with Sullivan in 1871, Gilbert was already a successful playwright, and he continued rapidly to establish himself during the 1870s, with two more fairy comedies, *Pygmalion and Galatea* (1871) and *The Wicked World* (1873); the social-problem plays *Charity* (1874) and *Ought We to Visit Her?* (1874); and the comedy *Sweethearts* (1874). He published the first volume of *Original Plays* in 1875,[8] the year in which his first collaboration with Sullivan and Carte, *Trial by Jury*, was produced. His greatest play, *Engaged*, a parody of comedy and a satire on mercenary motivations for marriage that are supported by absurd conventions of courtship, was produced in 1877.[9] Gilbert is widely regarded as the best comic dramatist between Richard Brinsley Sheridan and Oscar Wilde or George Bernard Shaw; he is the most notable English playwright of any sort between T. W. Robertson and the late-nineteenth-century renaissance of English drama wrought by Arthur Wing Pinero, Wilde, and Shaw. Gilbert was knighted in 1907, and he continued to write until his death in 1911.

The Formation of Genre

English comic opera—the genre created by Gilbert, Sullivan, and Carte—was formed through parody of older theatrical genres. Because of the emphasis on genre parody in the Savoy operas, their representations of social conventions must never be taken "straight." Continental genres like Italian and French grand opera, French opéra bouffe and Italian opera buffa, and German supernatural melodrama were one resource for Savoy parody. But English precursors were also important to the creation of English comic opera: ballad opera, music hall, adaptations of the American minstrel show, melodrama, pantomime, and extravaganza. These "illegitimate" theatrical genres flourished in the first three-quarters of the nineteenth century in England and were ripe for parody by the time Gilbert and Sullivan came together. From this rich historical field, I focus mainly on two traditions that were most important to the development of Savoy parody: extravaganza and melodrama.

The representation of gender is treated differently in these two formative traditions, and the Savoy parodies of extravaganza and melodrama reflect that difference. While extravaganza trades in travesty, transgression, and fantasy, melodrama prefigures social realism, in part by representing and meditating on the gendered "separate spheres." Indeed, along with the novel, melodrama played a significant role in constructing those polarized and separate spheres of social life. Much of the figural parody in the Savoy operas—parody of particular conventional figures like the Jolly Jack Tar from nautical melodrama, the Dame from pantomime, and the fairy from fairy extravaganza—carries a burden of both gender and genre. But the links between gender and genre are deeper and more pervasive than these stock figures could, on their own, convey.

Extravaganza and melodrama accomplish the resolutions of their plots in markedly different ways—and this is important, for the logic of their conventional plot resolutions helps to reveal the aims of the genres. Extravaganza ends with an elaborate "transformation scene," in which the stage set slowly opens up and turns inside out, like a bloom unfolding, to reveal a formerly hidden world of enchantment. Melodrama, on the contrary, specializes in a sudden, purportedly realistic ending, in which a document is produced or a secret is confessed, revealing social identities and relations that have been hidden or unknown. Through the melodramatic happy ending, social justice and upward mobility are suddenly achieved. The world does not change—as it certainly does at the end of extravaganza—but the transformation in social relations changes everything within it. These quick and fortuitous melodramatic reversals are imitated and parodied in *H.M.S. Pinafore* (1878), *The Pirates of Penzance* (1879), and *Ruddigore* (1887), while the extravaganza transformation is parodied in *Thespis* (1871), *Trial by Jury* (1875), and *Iolanthe* (1882). Through Savoy opera genre parodies, both of these characteristic resolutions are shown to be absurd. In their intertwining of extravaganza and melodrama, and their parodies of each, Gilbert and Sullivan ground their humor in a profound sense of theater history.

Through parodies of English classical extravaganza, French opéra bouffe, seduction melodrama, and supernatural melodrama, Gilbert and Sullivan began the development of English comic opera in their first three collaborations. The Gilbert and Sullivan "formula" was fully achieved with their third opera, *The Sorcerer* (1877). With the addition of nautical melodrama to the foundational parodies, the genre continued to evolve steadily through the next six operas, the development of each turning on its genre parodies and its treatment of gender. After *The Mikado* (1885), however, the process of genre formation was essentially complete, and the remaining five Savoy operas ring the changes on the established formula. They continue to meditate on issues of genre, gender, and culture, especially devoting themselves to exploring cross-cultural thinking and parodies of it. After *The Mikado*, one might say that "Gilbert and Sullivan" itself became "generic" and subject to parody as a genre in its own right.

Genre formation is not only an aesthetic and historical, but also an economic, process, and genre was important to Gilbert and Sullivan's effort to carve out their own market niche. They distinguished their productions from other theatrical fare through their genre parody and their particular treatments of gender. Their success at capital accumulation supported unusually high production values, which led, in turn, to further capital growth. Acknowledging the sine qua non of capital accumulation, in other words, does not reduce the aesthetic dimension of their success. The operas reflect an acute awareness of the conditions of their own production. For example, a meditation on the double meaning of "company"—both theatrical and financial—forms the scaffolding of the plot in *Thespis*. Likewise, *The Pirates of Penzance* suggests several senses of "piracy," tacitly reflecting on theatrical piracy, especially in America. *The Gondoliers* (1889) and *Utopia, Limited* (1893), return to the philosophical and material paradoxes of incorporation and limited liability. But because the story of Gilbert and Sullivan has been told many times, I focus on only a very few nodal points in the material history of the D'Oyly Carte Opera Company, choosing only episodes that contribute to my analysis of gender or of genre formation.

Advancing an explicitly nationalistic agenda, English comic opera also explicitly makes fun of the English. This is a familiar hallmark of Gilbert and Sullivan's humor, yet some critics still take the nationalism "straight," as if the patriotic anthems were seriously patriotic, rather than parodic. Through their internalization, amalgamation, and parody of both European and English precursors, then, the Savoy operas lampoon English insularity, respectability, and national fervor. Savoy opera became a specifically *English* comic opera, in large part, by launching its critique of what it means to be English. Demonstrating Victorian fin-de-siècle attitudes *avant la fin*, the comic operas of Gilbert and Sullivan focus on the denaturalization of gender, the analysis of social class, and the critique of nation, empire, and global capitalism. This book explores this dimension of their work through the lens of their particular forms of genre parody, but it also argues that these generalized forms of culture are like genres, exhibiting their own histories of cultural formation. This book, then, considers two kinds of parody: parody of genres and parody of social types, behaviors, and institutions. Parody is always based on imitation, unlike satire, although its forms of imitation are exaggerated, twisted, and preposterous. Thus I choose the term "parody" rather than "satire" to emphasize the formal feature of the types, behaviors, and institutions that are represented.

Parody

This book advances an expansive view of parody—which, nevertheless, can be specified. Let us begin with a few general principles:

1. Parody is both mimetic and critical. It comes in all tonalities, from affectionate to scathing, but it always looks (or sounds) like what it criticizes.

Thus it can be easily mistaken for its object and taken for a "straight" representation. This feature of its form often causes it to be misrecognized and misinterpreted.

2. Parody is both serious and comic—or, rather, its comedy ranges across a spectrum from entertaining silliness to serious reflection and critique.

3. Parody blurs the distinctions between inside and outside—of the body, the nation, the theater, the parodic work itself—in order to make it clear that both aesthetic and historical formations can be treated as *forms*.

4. Parody can be—and often simultaneously is—both conservative and progressive, since it preserves the memory of past forms while turning away from them into its own, more highly valued, present. Parody takes a knowing, present-day perspective on past forms of art and social life, which are, from the parodic point of view, seen to be old and outworn.

Another good way to look at parody in the Savoy operas is to think of the parodic dynamic moving in three directions. Parody turns things upside down, inside out, and backward. Parody inverts social hierarchies, perverts the representation of the world outside the theater (and the very idea of representation itself), and preposterously recollects older forms within its present moment. Most treatments of Gilbert and Sullivan have focused on the first, or "topsy-turvy," aspect of parody, whereby social hierarchies are turned upside down, or on the "inside-out" perversions of reference in a no-longer-real, but often elaborately real-looking theatrical world. Indeed, I see the deadpan Gilbertian acting style as a generalized parody of high Victorian "natural acting." Within this context, the Savoy operas seem not so much unrealistic as *antirealistic*. But for this study, the most important aspect of parody is its complex temporal dynamic, which includes its play of recollection, its knowing re-formation of past genres, and its dependence on preposterous logics.

An essay published in the *Westminster Review* in 1845 makes it clear that the ancient history of parody was a matter of interest to its mid-nineteenth-century readers.[10] Arguing that parody "appears to have been the most ancient form of comicalities," the anonymous reviewer takes a historical, cross-cultural, and ultimately autoethnographic point of view toward his subject. In order to characterize parody through the particularities of its historical emergence, he reminds his readers of the ancient Greek itinerant rhapsodist, who would travel from place to place reciting epic, followed by another sort of itinerant entertainer, who would imitate the high style of the rhapsodist with an "air of mock solemnity." The reviewer names Hegemon of Thasos as the original parodist, speaking of his works with the tacit assumption that they would be familiar to readers of the *Westminster Review*. Parody literally follows—comes after and takes after—its model, in space, in time, and in tone.

The writer offers this history of parody merely as context, for under review were several nineteenth-century works that, he claims, might vie for a place in this history of parody: *Punch*, the *Rejected Addresses* (1812) of James and Horace Smith, and the *Ballads* (1845) of Bon Gaultier (the nom de plume of William Edmonstoune Aytoun and Sir Theodore Martin). In a remark particularly delicious for our purposes, he compares the ancient Hegemon with the contemporary Charles Mathews, surely thinking of his famous pattering show, *Patter versus Clatter* (1838), Mathews's chief claim to fame. At another point, he compares the ancient parodies with afterpieces in the nineteenth-century theater, entertainments that allowed the audience to come down from the heights of serious drama. The writer appreciates the ephemerality, currency, and topicality of parody, comparing the function of ancient parody with the eclectic comic journalism of his own day. "Let us imagine," he writes, "how well a volume of 'Punch' would be understood, in the fortieth century, by a future antiquary, in some distant land." As part of this exercise, he points out the usefulness of parody for diagnosing social types; in his hypothetical fortieth-century culture, "the fine distinctions between the 'snob,' the 'gent,' and the 'swell,' would inevitably be lost." Finally, the writer analyzes the mutually dependent relation between parody and journalism, pointing out that news of disasters in Sicily interrupted Hegemon's performance of "The Battle of the Giants," while, similarly, during "the first revolution in France," people rushed out of the theaters to see victims pass on their way to the guillotine and then went back inside to forget the dark tragedy of outside events again.[11]

As this review makes clear, parody focuses on temporality by mobilizing the difference between a "now" and a "then." Its play depends not only on something putatively outside itself, but on something before itself in time. The word "parody" ultimately derives from the Greek *paroidia* (*para* + *oide*), the name for the mock-epic and mock-rhapsodic songs themselves; Aristotle first uses the word *paroidia* (as a term for the mode of performance) with reference to Hegemon, a near contemporary of Aristophanes (*Poetics* 2); and the term was developed by the commentary tradition on Aristophanes "to cover all sorts of comic quotation and textual re-arrangement."[12] Most classical etymologists interested in this question have commented on the ambivalence of the prefix *para-*, which ranges across a full spectrum of meanings—"like, resembling, changing slightly, imitating, replacing, spurious"— through which similarity gradually shades into difference, likeness into substitution, and originality into spuriousness.[13] In this ambivalence, we can detect all the familiar Platonic suspicions of imitation. For definitions of *para-*, the *Oxford English Dictionary* gives "by the side of," "beside," and "whence alongside of, by, past, beyond," showing that *para-* implies both spatial juxtaposition and the temporal and critical consequences of that juxtaposition. In other words, the difference that is inextricably involved in imitation is also—and most especially—a matter of time.

Parody, then, is a rhetoric of temporality, projecting the difference between a "before" and an "after" as part of its structure.[14] When a present is differentiated from a past, that relation can be specified or concretized in any way imaginable; in writing history or autobiography, for example, the past can be made to seem better or worse, happier or sadder, more or less admirable than the present. But when parody activates this structure of temporal difference, it tips the scales of value toward the present, for it always represents itself (whether implicitly or explicitly) as inhabiting the later, more knowing, more comprehensive, and more up-to-date perspective. Parody produces the sense of temporal difference that it then proceeds to turn on and play with. A parody "takes after" its model, succeeding and imitating it, but it is also a "takeoff" on its model, stripping and exposing its secrets, seeing it afresh in a new, present context.

Thus parody, although by no means a modern mode, is a powerfully *modernizing* one. In taking up its models, parody implicitly leaves them behind or, rather (to put the same point more actively), casts them back into the past, treating them as outmoded relics compared with itself. Parody turns on its models, but also internally turns against them and away from them, moving beyond them into the novelty of the present, recasting them as outworn and old-fashioned. Depending on the particular blend of imitation and critique, past forms may be regarded as dangerous, stupid, and mistaken or as simply old hat, exhausted, and passé. And yet, however much they are dismissed or put in their place, those former objects of critique and imitation also remain formative.

The modernizing effects of parody, therefore, are conservative as well as progressive, preserving the forms of the past even while mocking, overturning, twisting, or updating them. We must understand the terms "conservative" and "progressive" here in a strictly neutral or literal sense.[15] Parody performs the conservative function of historical preservation, effectively creating repaired continuity while making a break from the past. In this way, parody becomes the negative moment of a historical dialectic in tradition building. For the late nineteenth century in particular, parody is the other side of the century's historicist concern for revival. The Savoy operas act out an awareness that tradition cannot be understood simply as continuity, an awareness that the past does not "live" in the present except in ghostly, fragmentary form. In order to build on the past, the parodic present takes it apart and stands on its fragments. Parody inventively re-creates the past by projecting it into the background of its own present achievement, taking off on it and moving quickly beyond it, leaving it behind like a discarded costume turned inside out.[16]

Aristophanes—with whom Gilbert is often compared—provides a classic example of this point, for his comedy represents precisely such a modernizing genre, founded on its relentless parody of Euripides in particular and of tragedy in general. In the very effort to parody Euripides, Aristophanes inevitably preserves allusions to and fragments of Euripides' plays in his own plays. This is not the point most often made in comparisons between Gilbert and Aristophanes. When Max Keith Sutton argues that the Savoy "parodies of melodrama and grand opera have a function that parallels Aristophanes' continual ridicule of Euripides," he means to call attention to the deflation of grand passion in comic opera, like the deflation of tragic grandeur in Aristophanic comedy. In other contexts, Aristophanes' admiration for Euripides is often cited to make the point that parody does not necessarily (or not only) ridicule its model or target, but may also admire it.[17]

But my point here is different: Aristophanic parody preserves Euripides, making his principles and styles a matter of current perception even while turning away from them and treating them as if they were outmoded or outlandish. Aristophanic comedy constitutes itself—and becomes traditional—by engaging dialectically with a projected generic other. This point hits home especially when we realize that some of the lost plays of Euripides are now known only through fragmentary allusions and quotations in the comedies of Aristophanes.

It may seem a parodic deflation on my part to compare the relation between Aristophanes and Euripides with that between the Savoy operas and their various precursor genres. But the point is a theoretical one: what is remembered is often remembered in the mode of negation or critique. If, in any present time, parody defends against the overwhelming vastness or grandeur of the past, then, from a retrospective point of view, parody reviews past objects as they recede into invisibility. And thus parody serves a historical function, for often it is the best way to learn about something now estranged, invisible, or unrecognizable, one of those "now-disappeared performances" that might not otherwise be recalled.[18] Genre parody serves the same function for whole genres of performance, and so we might say that Savoy opera helps us to remember a host of "now-disappeared genres."

These days, there is no better—and, indeed, there is practically no other—way to learn about the fairy extravaganza than to see a good production of *Iolanthe*. Likewise, there is no better way to learn about nautical melodrama than to see *H.M.S. Pinafore* or *The Pirates of Penzance*. In other words, parody's modernizing negation serves a constructive historical function as well.[19]

The Savoy operas thematize this dynamic, evaluative relation between present and past, once again highlighting their own anthological, parodic, and dialectical form. *Utopia Limited* jokes with a metatheatrical jab at the censor, who is said to have "declined to license any play that is not in blank verse and three hundred years old." And Ko-Ko's "little list" of "society offenders who . . . never would be missed" includes "the idiot who praises, with enthusiastic tone, / All centuries but this, and every country but his own." Bunthorne in *Patience* advises that an aesthete should "be eloquent in praise of the very dull old days which have long since passed away." But because the opera is critical of the aesthete, we know that it privileges the everyday present, represented as "fresh and new." Through their stereotypical characters, too, the Savoy operas conserve, in twisted and fragmentary form, what otherwise is passing out of fashion and memory. In this way, parody marks itself simultaneously as "late" and as "novel," producing its relative newness with a backward glance at older genres, gathered up into a more compendious form.

This differential relation between present and past is mobilized to represent the individual, psychological subject as well. In the autobiographical songs, Gilbert and Sullivan love to show that retrospection is often a manner of self-fashioning, reinvention, impersonation, or downright lying. Present need always dominates the past in revisionary rationalization. From Wordsworth to Freud, the nineteenth century was engaged in trying to understand the novel premise that the past persists, distorted, in the present—that "the child is father to the man," but that the route from child to adult is by no means direct. So it is that the great age of the biography, autobiography, and bildungsroman was also the great age of nonsense verse, boasting Lewis Carroll and Edward Lear as well as Gilbert. Regression is another form of preposterous, parodic temporality that turns back the clock, allowing the integrated authority of the adult to be temporarily overturned in favor of immaturity. Like Carroll's parody of Southey ("You are old father William"), parodic temporality poses the supposedly venerable—but actually ridiculous—old man standing on his head.

Gilbert takes this cluster of notions—the formative influence of childhood, the nonsensical extremes of rationality, the refreshment offered by regression, and the adult's complacent pride in maturity—quite literally. His

Bab eponym immortalizes his playful infantilism, as does the title of his first play, *Uncle Baby*; the frequency of infant betrothals in his libretti; and—as scores of people have pointed out—the Savoy flagship that takes its name from the costume of childhood, the *Pinafore*. Making fun of adult rationality through recourse to forms of reasoning more familiar during "childhood's happy hour," the Savoy operas expose adult competence as fabricated, theatrical nonsense. But these Bab regressions are not precisely nostalgic; indeed, they are minutely, rigorously critical and controlled.[20]

The capacity of the Savoy operas to entertain both children and adults, or both highly educated and relatively uneducated audience members, has often been remarked. Stephen Jay Gould could write appreciatively that his pleasure at Gilbert and Sullivan matured with time, as he matured. Hooked in childhood by the operas' spectacle and fun, Gould remembers being refreshed again and again by their novelty as he learned more and more about what the words really mean, how the plots really work, and how the operas refract their historical milieu. His story of his own history of spectatorial pleasure speaks directly to my point.[21] Parodic "re-creation" involves the serious, yet preposterous, reversion to the past—whether historical or personal—along with the bracing attempt to re-create that past for the purposes of the present.

Genre Parody

Parody is a mode, not a genre, and it can operate in any genre. Moreover, as we have seen, parody is a primary mode of genre formation, for new genres are never entirely new, but emerge from the assimilation and critique of older genres. That is why English comic opera must be regarded as a "novel" genre, not a "new" one. As Mikhail Bakhtin uses the term, "novelization" describes a modern shift in the organization of genres, which are no longer held to be ideal and prescriptive, but are understood as constantly mixing and re-forming. Bakhtin's concept of "novelization" does not mean that modern genres are becoming like the novel, but that the process of modern genre formation is like the process that created the novel, a process of mixing, critically re-forming, and sublating many different precursor genres within a novel form. Parody plays a crucial role in this process, as George Levine, analyzing the dynamics of realism, points out when he emphasizes the crucial way in which parody is involved in the continuing genre formation of the nineteenth-century novel. Like Bakhtin, Levine clarifies the relative values of mimesis and parody in the modern understanding of genre.[22] The result is not pure but mixed, not absolutely but only relatively new.[23]

What particular effects can be generated when the object of parody is not a particular work but a genre?[24] Concentrating parody on the level of genre offers several critical advantages.

Some of the Savoy operas are parodies of particular works—as *The Sorcerer* is a parody of Donizetti's *L'elisir d'amore*. But far more important for understanding the form of the operas is their use of genre parodies—as *H.M.S. Pinafore* is a parody of nautical melodrama and *Iolanthe* is a parody of the fairy extravaganza. Even when the Savoy operas include parodies of individual works, the specific parody is usually employed for its general value. While *The Sorcerer* can be regarded as a particular parody of *L'elisir d'amore*, its real humor lies in its more general parody of the conventional magic potion, here served in an English teapot by a professional sorcerer. It is very important for audiences to grasp the parody of the conventional love potion—so they can enjoy the funny English version of the elixir, served in a teapot—but it is not especially important that they recognize the specific reference to Donizetti's opera. Every one of the Savoy operas offers examples of this sort. In *Thespis*, audiences might or might not recognize the parody of Jacques Offenbach's *Orphée aux enfers* (*Orpheus in the Underworld*, 1858), but they must recognize the general parody of descent to an underworld and of topsy-turvy misrule. Similarly, *The Pirates of Penzance* may be regarded as a particular parody of Offenbach's *Les brigands* (1869), but much more important is the way it engages the enormous general popularity of pirate operas, nautical melodramas, and burlesques of both.

Therefore, on the practical level, the first advantage of genre parody is that it allows for, encourages, and facilitates differential reception. Any individual spectator can be satisfied with simple amusement at the absurd situations, can go further to grasp topical references and allusions, or can go even further to enjoy the operas' engagement with precursor traditions of music, literature, art, and theater. The operas' invitation to different sorts of spectators works in their parodies of class and gender, too. Focusing their parody at the level of genre provides a democratic hospitality, an invitation to relax and enjoy the operas as superficial or profound—for they make both claims.

In the second place, their interest in genre parody shows that the Savoy operas are invested in the consideration of a modern and relative form of originality that acknowledges the claims of adaptation and partial derivation as legitimate forms of authorship.[25] Focusing on genre allows the operas to play within their theatrical-historical situation in a singularly late Victorian way. If the claim to be "new and original" seems humorous when applied to Gilbert's extravaganzas—each of which is a parody of a well-known opera— the same claim for the Savoy operas is utterly different and serious. They play with (and against) notions of originality, a vexed issue in the worlds of music and theater at the time. Both Gilbert and Sullivan were sensitive about their claims to it. Genre parody allowed them to recycle all sorts of conventions while creating original plots, original lyrics, and original music. There was no resetting of old tunes, as in burlesque and extravaganza, and no episodic feel of numbers being strung together by pattering filler, as in the music hall. And yet genre parody entertains deeply familiar character types, old jokes, and plot conventions whose very familiarity is a large part of the point. This is "re-creation" with a vengeance, involving the blatant re-creation of old elements in a novel, overarching whole.

The play of these recognition effects can be quite hilariously intoxicating. For example, take the old joke about recognition itself. A staple of melodrama, the recognition scene often features the sudden discovery of a legible sign on the body—a scar, for example, or a birthmark such as a "strawberry mark." In *La Vivandière; or, True to the Corps* (1867), Gilbert's "operatic extravaganza" on Donizetti's *La fille du régiment* (*The Daughter of the Regiment*, 1840), Gilbert wreaks havoc with this convention. Sergeant Sulpizio says to Lord Margate:

> Say, are you covered, pardon the allusion,
> With strawberry marks in prodigal confusion?
> Two on each shoulder, on your bosom four;
> Twelve on your back, on each arm seven more;
> Three on your left foot, nine upon each knee;
> Five on your calves, upon each elbow three,
> Just sixty-six in all . . . ?

Lord Margate rapidly counts his strawberry marks and answers yes, "exactly so." To which Sulpizio replies: "Then you are *not* the Earl of Margate! . . . No peer of Margate, young, old, short or tall, / Had any strawberry marks at all!" The peasant hero, Tonio, then exclaims: "I have no strawberry marks!" To which Sulpizio responds: "Ha! Then I see / The rightful Earl of Margate you must be!"

The humor of this scene depends first on the hyperbolic proliferation of strawberry marks, an apt reminder that this sort of recognition scene has been staged many, many times. But the logic of melodramatic recognition turns out to be a red herring, and the joke further inflates its hilarity with the illogical notion that recognition—and the inversion of social hierarchy that inevitably follows—could depend on the *absence* of legible markings. Furthermore, this is an example of a joke for which a specific allusion cannot be pinpointed with any certainty. Fredric Woodbridge Wilson has made the point that it is difficult or impossible to determine exactly what source Gilbert had in mind. Sullivan's first comic opera, *Cox and Box* (written with F. C. Burnand), features the joke, when one of the "long-lost brothers" identifies the other by means of the absence of a strawberry mark on his arm, but *Cox and Box* was not performed until a few months after *La Vivandière*, so it cannot be considered as a source. The play on which *Cox and Box* was based, *Box and Cox* by John Maddison Morton, shows that the joke was already an "old staple." But the joke was not original to *Box and Cox* either, as it had been adapted from *Une chambre à deux lits* (1846), a French farce by Charles Varin and Charles Lefèvre that also was probably not original.[26]

That neither an original source nor a specific model can be ascertained is precisely the point of genre parody.[27] There *is* no immediate precursor available for recognition, but only the general aura of familiarity mediated by a long series of works, during which both forms and themes become recognizable in relation to one another. Again, this sort of humor offers something to a wide variety of audience members, from those who love the joke for its exaggerated silliness to those who appreciate it in a more intellectual frame of mind. The *Westminster Review* essay on parody dilates on precisely this range of interests, noting the appeal of parody for philosophical and historical scholarship, and making an elaborate joke about how parody can foster an absurdly pedantic antiquarianism.[28] The best critical reception is the most comprehensive, of course, and this study strives to do justice to both silly and scholarly points of view.

The third critical advantage—perhaps the greatest advantage—of genre parody has to do with the way historical processes of generalization provide an argumentative link between the theater and social life outside the theater. Genre parody promotes an awareness of social forms of life precisely as *formations* that have been precipitated as general forms in historical time and are then recognizable as such.[29] This is one reason that the social satire in the Savoy operas is so closely related to their parodies; the operas treat social formations as a variety of "preformed material," available to parody insofar as they may be seen as forms already mediated by representation. Cultural stereotypes, conventional behaviors, and collective social groups may be seen in this light; even, as Caroline Levine has suggested, "separate spheres" may be seen as one such social formation that may be treated as a form.[30] The Savoy operas, indeed, treat social conventions as if they were theatrical conventions, social roles as if they were theatrical roles, social group formations as if they were representations, and cultural stereotypes as if they were easily recognizable figures from theatrical tradition. Conventional behavior becomes conventional, after all, because processes of socialization teach their malleable subjects to act this way and no other. Conventional behavior makes for recognition, of course, whether inside or outside the theater. By the same token, as the late Savoy operas will show, the conventional behaviors of a "foreign" culture are so estranging as to seem absurd. This intertwining of metatheatrical and sociological critique lends the Savoy operas their distinctively late-nineteenth-century flavor.

One of the easiest ways to grasp this point is to remember that the Savoy operas are populated by two very different types of type. There are the ostentatiously conventional literary or theatrical types—Arcadian shepherds, for example, Olympian gods, court jesters—familiar from long traditions of representation. There are also cultural types, representatives of present-day social life: lawyers, judges, various specific sorts of military men, bureaucrats, aesthetes, "Sisters, Cousins, and Aunts," a Major-General, and even a Lord Chancellor. When the Savoy operas juxtapose conventional literary or theatrical types with recognizable types of social life, they make the point that both these types of type are the result of historical formation. And as if to drive this point home, many of their typified characters fall somewhere between the social and the literary, representing "real" social figures from the historical past whose characterizations have already been thoroughly processed by theatrical representation—for example, the fairies, the pirates, or the true-blue Jolly Jack Tars.

To present social types within such a densely textured theatrical context forces attention not only on the "content" of the types (the particular characteristics of an aesthete, say, or a sailor) but also on their forms and on the principles of their formation, including the genres and discourses through which these types have been precipitated in social life (the popular journalistic discourse on aestheticism, say, or the genre of nautical melodrama). Both theatrical types and social types are "generic," in other words, and like genres can be recognized by their generalized and conventional aspects in both form and content. On its most profound level, genre parody thus reflects on the process of historical generalization itself. This viewpoint makes the twisted stereotypes of Savoy opera much more critically interesting than they otherwise would be. Even the recognizable types of modern social life must be seen as aesthetic creations, while the conventional literary and theatrical types must be associated with their histories of formation. In this respect, Savoy opera—despite its refusal to be overtly argumentative, consistent, or sometimes even coherent about a political agenda—can be credited with provoking real cultural critique. Thinking through genre, the Savoy operas provoke their audiences to see that social formations are created and re-created through performative repetition, within a densely woven fabric of cultural recognition.

Genre parody therefore invites and sustains critical reflection. Not everyone will accept this invitation, of course. Savoy opera does not offer the explicitness of radical theater, but a more subtle indirection whose critical value should be taken seriously nevertheless. It aims to re-form the critical awareness of its audience, offering them serious recreation—in both senses of that word.

Gender and Genre: The Savoy Chorus

Gender roles, stereotypes, behaviors, and forms of socialization provide a prime example of this sort of historical generalization and recognition, through parody, of conventions that are both theatrical and cultural. Gilbert and Sullivan's operas intensely inhabit and perform Victorian gender conventions and stereotypes in order to demonstrate their absurdity. Exactly how they do so is a central focus of this book. But let us begin with Gilbert's use of the Chorus, for it will allow us to consider many aspects of their treatment of gender through a formal feature that was also definitive for the genre of English comic opera.

Gilbert's greatest formal innovation, his treatment of the Chorus, is already germinating in *Thespis*, develops in *Trial by Jury* and *The Sorcerer*, and comes into full flower from *H.M.S. Pinafore* through *The Yeomen of the Guard*. From *Pinafore* to *Yeomen*, the divided Chorus supports the operas' analysis of gender. Before establishing its central place in that analysis, however, Gilbert changed the role of the Chorus as a whole. As Sullivan later put it:

> Until Gilbert took the matter in hand choruses were dummy concerns, and were practically nothing more than a part of the stage setting. It was in "Thespis" that Gilbert began to carry out his expressed determination to get the chorus to play its proper part in the performance. At this moment it seems difficult to realize that the idea of the chorus being anything more than a sort of stage audience was, at that time, a tremendous novelty.[31]

Indeed, as Sullivan points out, it is hard to appreciate precisely how "tremendous" this novelty was. But we must focus on it if we are to understand the way these operas contribute to the discussion of gender in late Victorian England.

No longer standing around like "extras" on the stage (as chorus members do in grand opera), the Savoy Chorus dances as well as sings, with strictly enforced precision far beyond the usual fare at the time.[32] Most important, the Chorus takes part in the dramatic action, and it thereby performs a critical parody of the conventions of grand opera. Gilbert's first opera burlesque, *Dulcamara! or, The Little Duck and the Great Quack* (1866), makes this intention clear, simultaneously lampooning both the hackneyed conventions of opera and the conventions of their burlesque parody, such as rhyming couplets and songs set to familiar music:

> You're in a village during harvest time,
> Where all the humblest peasants talk in rhyme,
> And sing about their pleasures and their cares
> In parodies of all the well-known airs.
> They earn their bread by going in a crowd,
> To sing their humble sentiments aloud
> In choruses of striking unanimity—
> (*aside*) The only rhyme I know to that is dimity.
> . . .
> Their dresses of *drawing rooms* is emblematic,
> Although their mode of life is *upper-atic!*[33]

This passage also calls attention to the musical parodies involved in burlesque and extravaganza. But my main point, for now, is that this joke about the "striking unanimity" of the operatic (*upper-atic*) chorus prefigures and announces Gilbert's development of his refreshing alternative.

On another level, the Savoy Chorus parodies the Chorus of classical Greek drama, speaking and singing as representative groups, commenting on the action, and sometimes taking sides with this or that principal character. Often the Chorus is directly tied into the plot through secondary characters who are of its number.[34] In these and other ways, the Savoy Chorus takes a fully characterized and dramatized part in the action—yet it also stands apart, fulfilling the ancient function of producing social commentary from the point of view of a particular group formation. (This dimension of the Savoy Chorus can be considered as an extension of the classical burlesque, which we will examine in connection with *Thespis*, for in that precursor genre, parodies of the classical Chorus are well known.)

Most important of all—although never before made the focus of critical analysis—is the formal subdivision and characterization of the Chorus according to gender. The separation of the Chorus into male and female Choruses cannot be overstressed, for it enables and embodies the Savoy operas' analysis of gender. In other words, this structural principle, which has often seemed merely to reflect the most reductive gender stereotypes prevalent in the Victorian period, instead exposes their absurdity, revealing them to be the repetitive and parodic stereotypes they are. Through this device, stereotypical masculine and feminine social positions, behaviors, and points of view are structurally differentiated, opposed, related to one another, and made available for critique.

Offering a graphically heightened picture, this articulation of gender positions shows up visibly in the differentiated color blocks made by the costumes and sounds out audibly in the voice registers, blending harmoniously or agitating and opposing one another, as the situation might demand (plate 3). Operating in a representational realm somewhere between realism, caricature, and fantasy, this strategy of group typification allows social relations to be clarified schematically, unmasked, highlighted, seen, and heard as blandly self-evident. It offers both aesthetic and sociological commentary on group formation, particularly on the systematic assignment of functions within a gendered division of labor. But if these representations are taken as simple rather than complex, as straight rather than twisted through parody, their purpose will have been doomed to misinterpretation.

We can see the full importance of this innovation in *Trial by Jury*, where the male Chorus portrays members of the Jury, while the female Chorus of Bridesmaids sweeps into the courtroom to support the Plaintiff. Insofar as women in 1875 were not full subjects under the law (and did not serve on juries), the all-male composition of the Jury is realistic. Likewise, the Jury's vacillations mimic the back-and-forth weighing of judgment required of a real jury. However, the sudden entrance of the Chorus of Bridesmaids, dressed entirely in wedding regalia, is completely fanciful—and registers the conventional assignment of fancy to the feminine. The particular blend of realism and fantasy in the opera, in other words, is parsed according to gender, with the male Chorus representing the real social world and the female Chorus representing a disempowered fancy (which, nevertheless, has its own shaping force in the real social world). Following Jane Stedman's influential analysis of the importance of the "invasion motif" in Savoy opera,[35] we can understand the Bridesmaids' entrance as a penetration—by the feminine—of the precincts of masculine law. They "back up" the Plaintiff (both argumentatively and musically) with their display of gender solidarity. This structural setup is a recognizable version of that old favorite topos of parody, which mocks the structures of social authority by imagining that women are in a position to overturn, invade, or replace them. *Trial by Jury* acknowledges that this scenario is a culturally poignant fantasy, and that recognition is part of the point, for its parody of the case for breach of promise turns on the fact that women are definitely not "on top."[36]

After *Thespis*, Gilbert and Sullivan famously outlawed cross-dressing in their productions—both female-to-male and male-to-female cross-dressing, two separate traditions in the nineteenth century.[37] By this means, they distinguished their novel genre from extravaganza and pantomime, both of which offer a more overt appeal to sexual fantasy. On the practical side, this decision to emphasize the respectability of the Savoy operas was a canny attempt at niche marketing. However, it is more complex, not—or, at least, not merely—evidence of their capitulation to bourgeois respectability. On the contrary, the absence of cross-dressing in the operas, like the gendered organization of the Chorus, enables the examination of gender relations, roles, and types, for without the blurring occasioned by cross-dressing, conventional gender arrangements show up clearly and schematically. The overt representations of normative gender allow a critique very different from the titillating spectacle of gender-bending enabled by extravaganza cross-dressing. This may seem counterintuitive today, when cross-dressing is often understood as a radical attempt to escape from or transform conventional gender assignments. And fantasy can, in some Victorian extravaganzas, be seen to work toward a productive unhinging of gender norms.[38] But in the Savoy operas, the critical reflection on gender becomes clear only after Gilbert and Sullivan rule out cross-dressing, for only then does their critique of gender as the systematic performance of social function pop clearly into view.

Thus their rejection of cross-dressing, which might seem at first to represent a reproduction of social norms, is nothing of the kind, but a critical choice that enables the Savoy operas simultaneously to imitate and to criticize the standards of bourgeois respectability, as they are expressed in the roles and rules of the separate spheres. In other words, this tactic is parodic as well as satiric. The formation of the Chorus shows that the Savoy operas treat *social formations* as if they were generalized, historically sedimented forms—analogous to genres in this respect. Gender is treated generically, as a conventional set of performances of social action and as a set of stereotypes that have been formulated in historical time and can now be easily recognized. Within the theatrical conventions of the day, Gilbert and Sullivan's blend of realism and fantasy expresses the Savoy parody of both Robertsonian "natural acting" and extravaganza transformation.[39] The realistic sets, along with Gilbert's famously deadpan style of direction, enable the trick whereby the most absurd antics are presented as if they were absolutely realistic. At the same time, those antics can be taken seriously, when they are perceived to represent an ideological or a social reality that is, in fact, absurd. As if the nineteenth-century social-problem play had been turned inside out, the Savoy operas twist serious social problems into a graspable knot of absurdity, all the while acting as if everything were perfectly normal; they expose the absurdity inherent in ideological contradictions.

In their actual business relations with female members of the Savoy Chorus, Gilbert, Sullivan, and Carte could be said to represent a paternalistic, late-nineteenth-century feminism. They were protective, and they advanced the material interests of their female performers while holding them to strict rules of conventional feminine conduct. Gilbert especially was scrupulous—even avuncular and fussy—about correct middle-class feminine behavior, insisting that the female members of the Chorus not be thought coarse in any way. To some extent, this fastidious attention to correct feminine behavior was a business matter (and thus, again, a matter of genre), for the women of the Savoy Chorus were marketed as exceptionally beautiful, but chaste—to be looked at, but not to be approached. In this sense, they were meant ostentatiously to differ from the widespread image of women who worked on the stage. If actresses were thought to be sexually available, much more so were the dancing girls of pantomime, extravaganza, and opéra bouffe. Gilbert firmly forbade the women of the Chorus to engage in illicit relationships outside the theater. Inside the theater, he discouraged "admirers" by threatening to have them thrown out or by returning their letters of solicitation himself.[40] But he was also sensitive to the economic plight of female performers and to the particular difficulties of their lives as working women. He therefore insisted on contractually steady work and good pay for Savoy Chorus members, knowing that only economic security could sustain feminine virtue.[41]

In other words, as a product on the market, the Savoy operas did claim respectable gender norms as an identifying feature of their genre. And this highly theatricalized appearance of respectability is as important to my argument as my assertion that these norms are often being parodied and challenged. Just as the active and gender-differentiated role of the Chorus distinguishes Savoy opera from grand opera, so the absence of cross-dressing distinguishes Savoy opera from pantomime, extravaganza, minstrelsy, and other forms of burlesque. These formal markers of differentiation, surely one dynamic way of carving out a novel genre, are never "merely formal."

The structural division of the Savoy Chorus according to gender is also historically expressive, a cultural marker of its time and place, when the tacit acceptance of the separate spheres began to give way to a more outspoken critique of gender. On the face of things, the divided Chorus reproduces the separate spheres of Victorian domestic ideology; however, through hyperbolic mimicry of gender conventions, parody tips the balance from reproduction toward critique. Especially when the male and female Choruses are set up in graphic opposition to each other, the absurdities of gender's systematic organization are clearly to be seen. Take, for example, the Sailors on board the *Pinafore*, paired against Sir Joseph's Sisters, Cousins, and Aunts; the Pirates of Penzance paired against Major-General Stanley's nubile Wards; or the incompetent Peers in *Iolanthe* paired against the powerful Fairies—in each of these operas, the setup of the divided Chorus is both a joke and a critical comment. In each of these operas, too, gender bears on the question of genre, as we shall see. By making the social divisions of gender highly theatrical, both visibly and audibly apparent, the Savoy operas align them with other mechanisms of social separation, bureaucratization, and classification—like social class and nationality, the two categories that will come up most frequently in this study.

Thus the operas of Gilbert and Sullivan belong with other late-nineteenth-century works that perform, encourage, or focus on the denaturalization of gender.[42] They demonstrate the function of gender as a structuring principle of social life, making the sex/gender system available for analysis specifically *as a system*.[43] In *Trial by Jury*, for example, one particular case in the ongoing battle of the sexes, both parties to the quarrel are lampooned for their conventionally gendered behavior. Not cross-dressed gender confusion, then, but the confusion that results from gender stereotypes is the point of the parody. Similarly, in *Iolanthe*, the Choruses of Peers and Fairies represent two systems of law and two forms of government, one incompetent and outworn, the other powerful enough to accomplish the extravaganza transformation to Fairyland at the end of the opera. With feminine and masculine thus coded as "high" and "low," *Iolanthe* performs a successful parodic inversion. These are only two examples of the gendered Savoy Choruses at their best.

In musical terms, the most powerful use of the gendered Chorus can be heard in the double Choruses, when first one Chorus sings, then the other, and finally the two sing together, blending and superimposing the two radically different melodies. Gervase Hughes describes this device as the "simultaneous presentation of two or more distinct melodies previously heard independently."[44] The witty contrapuntal surprise provides a great deal of listening pleasure. Sometimes a similar effect can be achieved with solo voices weaving around one another and singing different melodies, as in "I am so proud" from *The Mikado*; sometimes a similar effect can be achieved with solo voices poised against a Chorus, as in *The Pirates of Penzance*, when Frederic and Mabel's love duet poignantly soars above the chattering Chorus of girls in the background, who are acting out the need for respectable distraction from the scene of passion ("How beautifully blue the sky").

But the tour de force of this contrapuntal technique occurs in the double Choruses that use the two melodies to represent two distinctly gendered perspectives. Two of the best examples occur in *H.M.S. Pinafore* and *Patience*. In *Pinafore*, the Chorus of Sailors sings out their anticipation of Sir Joseph's barge, along with their anxious hope that Sir Joseph will find them "attentive to their duties." After their bluff masculine expression of submission, the female relatives appear to the tune of "Gaily tripping," a light feminine number (for "tripping" is as quintessentially feminine as "chatter" in musical characterization, as the Fairies' "tripping" music in *Iolanthe* will later make clear). When these two melodies are superimposed, the musical humor has everything to do with gender, for it focuses on the Sailors' polite welcome of the ladies, and the ladies' correlative love of "shipping." Their musical characterizations make a point of both their difference and their mutual attraction. In *Patience*, though, masculine and feminine groups are at odds with each other. Their strife is humorously characterized in the music, when the Chorus of Aesthetic Maidens sings their melancholy song of unrequited love ("Mystic poet, hear our prayer") while the Dragoon Guards express their outrage ("Now is not this ridiculous—and is not this preposterous?").

Even though this powerful device is merely residual in both *Ruddigore* and *The Yeomen of the Guard*, these operas still make use of the double Chorus. Near the beginning of act 2 of *Yeomen*, women taunt the Tower Warders while the Warders search for the missing prisoner "up and down, and in and out." *Ruddigore*'s encounter between the Professional Bridesmaids and the Bucks and Blades, although brief and of no consequence in the plot, is one of the best of the double Choruses. The Bridesmaids sing first, welcoming the "gentry," and then the Bucks and Blades announce their intention to dally with the village maidens. Their cross-class attraction, in other words, is staged as a particular sort of sexual encounter, conventional in seduction melodrama, in which rakish gentlemen irresponsibly engage with innocent, rural women. Thus, in this double Chorus, a point is made that speaks simultaneously to the opera's concerns with gender and genre. The gendered Choruses show that these social groups fit together as two aspects of a conventional seduction plot, one the moth to the other's flame. Singing and dancing together or against each other, the Savoy Choruses can embody gendered divisions of labor, the genders as warring factions, sexual attraction, or the genders interactively and systemically constructing each other—and many other relations as well.

This introduction would not be complete without a discussion of Sullivan's music and the way it figures in Savoy opera's treatments of gender, genre, and parody. Sullivan was a great dramatic composer who excelled at characterization, thematic development, and musical plotting. His act 1 finales are tours de force of suspense, variety, momentum, and climax. Sullivan surpassed all his contemporaries in skill of orchestration and sheer melodic fecundity, as Herman Klein, the music critic for the *Sunday Times*, pointed out on the occasion of the première of *Princess Ida*. Praising the music in general, Klein also makes a point of mentioning Sullivan's musical wit: "Humour is almost as strong a point with Sir Arthur Sullivan as with his clever collaborator."[45] Indeed, in Klein's review, the musical humor was taken to be greater than the verbal.

Sullivan's music often imitates a specific musical predecessor for comic purposes, and thus it is parodic in the strictest sense of that term. In *Patience*, for example, the Maidens' plaintive "Twenty lovesick maidens we" recalls "Alas those chimes so sweetly stealing" from Vincent Wallace's *Maritana* (1845). In *The Pirates of Penzance*, Mabel's "Poor wandering one!" employs Gounod-style "barnyard effects," as Sullivan called them, to suggest the excessive histrionics of the feminine reformer's zeal.[46] An old English air ("A Fine Old English Gentleman") supplies the tune for "Behold the Lord High Executioner!" in *The Mikado*. Many more examples can be given, but Sullivan's riff on the "Anvil Chorus" from Giuseppe Verdi's *Il trovatore* (*The Troubadour*, 1852) in *The Pirates of Penzance* ("With catlike tread") is perhaps the best known. The Verdian grand-opera celebration of hard work, good wine, and women turns to characterize Pirates in the process of deciding to pursue their lawlessness on land. The allusion recalls the unruly gypsies of *Il trovatore* while making fun of the Pirates:

> Come, friends, who plough the sea,
>   Truce to navigation,
>   Take another station;
> Let's vary piracee
> With a little burglaree!

This near-citation of the "Anvil Chorus" does not make fun of Verdi, but uses the higher operatic form to invest the Pirates with a sort of overweening boisterous boastfulness.

Similarly, Sullivan's parodies of the music of Handel employ this mock-heroic strategy, most often exaggerating the grandeur of ridiculous characters, such as the humorously self-important, casually corrupt Learned Judge in *Trial by Jury*, who is introduced with Handelian pomp, or Ida's brothers, whose song, "This helmet, I suppose," makes fun of their inability to tolerate the conventionally masculine costume of the warrior. Commenting on "This helmet, I suppose," Anthony Tommasini notes Sullivan's mastery at "evoking diverse musical styles" and goes on to point out that this "humorously ominous" music is a reference to the "sturdy solo arias from Handel oratorios."[47] In other words, the musical humor alludes to genre as well as to a particular composer. Sometimes the mock-heroic dynamic works in the other direction, deflating the pretensions of highly serious music. When Iolanthe emerges from the bottom of the stream to a parody of Wagner, for example, the music simultaneously deflates Wagner's grandiosity and inflates the mythic portentousness of Iolanthe's recovery. Because of the context, this music might remind us of the Rhine Maidens, but Iolanthe's entrance music, instead, directly quotes *Tristan und Isolde* (1859). In this case, Sullivan's parody of recent developments in grand opera supports the light humor of this "fairy opera." And, unlike Sullivan's takes on Verdi and Handel, this music *does* have fun with Wagner.

Often Sullivan's music is parodic in the broader sense in which not only individual works or composers, but also genres or musical styles are the objects of parody. Specific and general parodies are often linked together, for the imitation of a specific work or composer can carry generic implications; the representative case implies the genre. For example, the Fairy music in *Iolanthe* ("Tripping hither") recalls the whole genre of nineteenth-century fairy music, although it also may be seen as a particular reference to Mendelssohn.[48] Likewise, Sullivan's spoofs of Italian opera might be called Offenbachian, though Sullivan does them even better than Offenbach. The quartet in *Trial by Jury* ("A nice dilemma we have here") performs a wonderful parody of the early-nineteenth-century bel canto dilemma ensemble, although it also refers to Vincenzo Bellini in particular. The intricate involvement of voices in this number imitates several minds at work on the same legal problem, sometimes drifting toward, sometimes pulling away from one another—a musical situation, as well as a legal one, "that calls for all our wit." But frequently the genre parodies in the music do not refer to specific works or composers. Sullivan is a genius at suggesting generic styles of Italian opera, French opéra bouffe, gothic and nautical melodrama, the minstrel show, and the music hall. In addition to their function as characterization, he uses the semiotics of these musical styles, modes, and genres self-consciously to achieve clever mixtures of various "high" and "low," native and foreign, stylistic registers.

The temporal dimension of parody also works through the music, comprehending the past and claiming for itself the most up-to-date position in the present. In one sense, Sullivan's music is a virtuosic recollection of European musical traditions, carrying the tacit assertion that the Savoy operas can comprehensively sum up the musical past from their knowing, contemporary moment. From this point of view, the music can seem neutrally allusive rather than parodic, and it is here that parody shades into pastiche (a term that must be understood in a positive sense, naming a quality of historical texture). The music situates itself historically by recollecting previous composers and musical traditions, as well as contemporary forms of musical theater, high and low, often engaging in jokes about music history. At the time of the original productions of the operas, reviewers noticed that "the composer is never more happy than when he reproduces the mannerisms of former musical epochs."[49]

Sullivan's gift for musical characterization relates directly to his tendency toward genre parody. Hughes argues that Sullivan "had a definite gift for characterization, but rarely fastened it on individuals," instead focusing on "variegated *groups*."[50] In other words, Sullivan's music attends to forms of historical generalization other than the genres of musical history. Social categories are frequently represented in the music: social classes, nationalities, and, of course, genders. When the villagers drink the potion in *The Sorcerer*, we hear their "Mummerset" accents while they fall into pairs during a country dance. When Josephine agonizes about her marriage choice in *H.M.S. Pinafore*, the parody of recitative conveys a critique of middle-class (and feminine) considerations in the marriage choice. National group characterization is even easier to hear. To set "A British Tar is a soaring soul" as a glee carries nationalistic implications. "He is an Englishman!" should be heard as a parody of patriotic anthems in the music halls, like "Macdermott's War Song" (from which the term "jingoism" derives). And while Englishness is thematized in the earlier operas, it is musicalized in the later ones, where the madrigals of *The Mikado*, *Ruddigore*, and *The Yeomen of the Guard* may serve as a good marker of Sullivan's citations of an "Early English" style. Other national styles are also featured, such as the Japanese music in *The Mikado* and the Viennese (or pan-European) flavor of *The Grand Duke* (1896). In sum, Sullivan's musical characterizations of social groups testify to the historical formations through which such groups are recognized. Hughes even credits Sullivan with the "even more remarkable" ability to characterize historical forces themselves. He praises in particular the "*impersonal*" characterization of the Tower of London in *The Yeomen of the Guard*, which hovers over that opera like a brooding historical presence.[51]

Most important for the argument of this book, the generalized force of social categorization comes into play around conventional characterizations of gender. Musical parodies—both of individual composers and of genres—often support the operas' analysis of gender. For example, the "Defendant's Song" in *Trial by Jury* imitates a minstrel number in order to make fun of his masculine self-importance, his defense of men's "natural" tendency toward faithlessness. Josephine's histrionic scena and Ida's brothers' song ("This helmet, I suppose") are also relevant in this context. But more powerful than these individual moments of musical wit are the aggregate musical characterizations of conventional masculine and feminine attitudes. As Hughes points out, "There is as much difference between Sullivan's yokels and his gondoliers as there is between the Warwickshire Avon and the Grand Canal; the Fairies of *Iolanthe* bear no more resemblance to the girl graduates of *Princess Ida* than Arcadia does to the popular conception of Girton in the eighteen-eighties."[52] As I have suggested, the most important musical characterizations of gender occur in the divided Chorus, central to the operas' organization from *Trial by Jury* through *The Yeomen of the Guard*.

The music also pursues the operas' analysis of gender through its self-conscious wit about the conventional ensemble of voice registers. Sullivan often gives to the high soprano, the powerful contralto, or the tenor hero parts that exaggerate the role of gender in sound production. Jeffrey Shandler suggests that Savoy performance styles are meant as a subtle parody of the ensemble itself, each voice register teased into a slight exaggeration of itself from time to time. Anna Russell's parody of Gilbert and Sullivan implies this point, too, making fun of "the British piercing type soprano that is always connected with these operations."[53] From time to time, the Savoy libretto makes this humor explicit—in *Princess Ida*, for example, when the cross-dressed men are recognized as men by their voices, which therefore represent that opera's argument for the essential, natural grounding of sexual identity, taken to be telling even when visual gender cues are obscured by costume. In addition to participating in the opera's conservative argument about gender, this moment in *Princess Ida* offers a self-conscious comment, akin to Ralph's "I know the value of a kindly Chorus" in *H.M.S. Pinafore*, Mad Margaret's accusation in *Ruddigore* that the villagers "are all mad—quite mad . . . they sing choruses in public," and Captain Fitzbattleaxe's "A tenor all singers above" in *Utopia, Limited*. In the last—a comic opera in which King Paramount has written a comic opera—the ostentatiously English name of the celebrated English tenor, "Mr. Wilkinson," makes a joke about English singers affecting Italian pseudonyms in the Victorian theater, while "A tenor all singers above" dilates on the paradoxes of this particular role in the ensemble.

In all these ways, the music participates in the parody as much as the words do. But the music also interrupts the parody with moments of deep feeling that completely overthrow the humor. Even using an expansive definition of parody, in other words, we could never characterize the whole of Sullivan's music as either parodic or generic. Every student and fan of the Savoy operas has noticed that "Sullivan's music always tends to give 'heart' to Gilbert's words," as Andrew Crowther has put it.[54] The music cuts across the grain of plot and situation, interrupting the parody (and even the humor) with moments of great emotional fervor, seriousness, idealism, piercing sentiment, and sheer beauty. Perhaps this three-way tug-of-war—among absurd premises, tenaciously pursued; a deadpan acting style that pretends these premises are nothing out of the ordinary; and the emotional depth and variety of the music—would be the best characterization of Savoy opera.

One example should suffice, although there are many more. Think of the moment in *The Pirates of Penzance* when Mabel and Frederic realize that they must part until 1940, while he works off an apprenticeship whose length is determined by the hyperlogical calculation of his age by leap years. The situation is preposterous, although meaningful, for it thematically emphasizes not only Frederic's exaggerated devotion to "Duty's Name," but also the regression played out in this numerical logic chopping. The absurdity of the situation is interrupted and transcended, however, when they sing, each in turn, the two verses of the beautiful ballad "Ah, leave me not to pine / Alone and desolate." Even in its nonsensical context, the ballad is impossible to hear without being moved. What moves the listener is not only the spectacle of the lovers parting, but the music itself, with its grieving, dignified simplicity—her passionate desire for his presence ("He loves thee—he is here"), answered by his dutiful determination that he must leave ("He loves thee—he is gone"). The music forcibly lifts us out of the context of the plot and into another realm altogether, a realm of fundamental affect. When the ballad is over, we have been moved to another place, from which the dialogue picks up again.

These moments do not always have to do with love, although they often do have to do with gender. *Topsy-Turvy* (1999), Mike Leigh's film about the original production of *The Mikado*, makes a similar point in its conclusion, using "The sun whose rays are all ablaze / With ever-living glory" as its example. Yum-Yum introduces the song with her absurdly naïve self-centeredness:

Yes, I am indeed beautiful! Sometimes I sit and wonder, in my artless Japanese way, why it is that I am so much more attractive than anybody else in the whole world. Can this be vanity? No! Nature is lovely and rejoices in her loveliness. I am a child of Nature, and take after my mother.

The song then lifts itself entirely away from the gender parody implied in this introductory remark. Leigh ends his film with the singer alone on stage, dignified, ravishing, poignant, and sublime. Here, again, many examples might be adduced of music interrupting humor with feeling that is associated with the opera's argument about gender. My favorite is Princess Ida's lament following the disappointment of her feminist idealism: "I built upon a rock." Even though the burlesque text makes fun of her feminist separatism, the passion of that song is unmistakably anti-ironic.

At moments like this, the music "subverts the very subversiveness of Gilbert's libretti" with "an overflow of affect that *must* be taken straight."[55] The structure of English comic opera—like the ballad opera before it and "the musical" after it—lends itself particularly to these effects, for its generic signature is this strategic cutting between spoken dialogue and musical "numbers." The serial interruption provides a specific sort of narrative and dramatic structure. In other words, the music does not always work along with the text. Sometimes it works off the text, and sometimes it works against the text. From this perspective, the Savoy operas might be characterized as parody interrupted by feeling. The lyrics carry the plot forward while their musical settings often interrupt its mood, lifting the opera into another register of feeling and then dropping it back to earth again. There, on the ground, the libretto will again pursue the momentum of an overarchingly parodic form. Until that time, music bears the burden of feeling that cannot sufficiently be put into words.

Part I. Genres

1

Outmoding Classical Extravaganza, Englishing Opéra Bouffe

Thespis

hespis; or, The Gods Grown Old (1871), the first collaboration between Gilbert and Sullivan, makes it clear that the parodic intertwining of two genre traditions—English extravaganza and French opéra bouffe— was fundamental to the formation of English comic opera. In addition, each of these genre parodies highlights conventions of gender. But at the outset, an act of imagination is necessary to recover a sense of this piece, for the modern text is riddled with omissions. Worse still, Sullivan's original music has been lost—or perhaps was intentionally destroyed. While these circumstances can explain why *Thespis* is so rarely discussed (and even more rarely performed), they cannot justify it. *Thespis* has never been given the attention it deserves.[1] No one has fully explored its thematic and formal coherence or its rich cultural resonance. Indeed, some critics go out of their way to dismiss its importance entirely.[2] Despite its anomalous status in the Savoy canon, however, *Thespis* clearly illuminates the process through which Gilbert and Sullivan's novel genre came into being by incorporating, mixing, and parodically turning away from precursor genres.

In particular, *Thespis* should be understood as a parody of the classical extravaganza, an important subgenre whose conventions were extremely familiar in 1871, when *Thespis* was produced. At the same time, *Thespis* is an ostentatiously English appropriation of the discernibly risqué "French" humor of opéra bouffe, a genre most easily identified, then and now, with the works of Jacques Offenbach. *Thespis* turns on—and also overturns—these genre traditions with its own complex blend of homage and critique, as all good parody is wont to do. Genre parody always has a modernizing effect, valuing its own present moment while implying that its precursors are exhausted and old-fashioned. In *Thespis*, the exhaustion is embodied explicitly in "the gods grown old," whereas the modernizing effect of genre parody is worked out through an explicit thematic concern with modernity in general, especially with characteristically contemporary organizations of work and play. After highlighting the boredom, exhaustion, and mismanagement that prevail in the working world, *Thespis* proposes itself as a perfect, although temporary, solution—a well-managed, up-to-the-minute holiday relief.

A Brief Introduction to *Thespis*

Since *Thespis* is so little known, a brief plot summary might be in order. Its subtitle, *The Gods Grown Old*, announces the opera's main theme. Act 1 opens on the summit of Mount Olympus, in the ruined Temple of the Gods, where a spectacular Chorus of Stars emerges through a thick fog to sing the opening number. These Stars are characterized as workers coming off duty, exhausted from their nightly business of shining in the sky. The lunar Diana, "*an elderly goddess*," peels off her cloaks, shawls, and galoshes while complaining of the cold night air. Apollo does not feel much like shining, for (as he puts it) he is much more quickly fatigued than "when [he] was a younger sun."[3] Now "*an elderly 'buck' with an air of assumed juvenility*," Apollo shirks his duty by sending a "fine, thick wholesome fog" to substitute for the blazing sun. Thus, in its opening, *Thespis* turns outward toward its London audience, humorously acclimatizing them to the play's premise while offering a mock explanation of the weather.

All the play's central themes—the decline of the Olympian gods, modern work and its management, and the logic of performative substitution—are deftly established in this opening scene and are reinforced when Mercury enters, also complaining of overwork. Mercury calls himself a "celestial drudge," since he performs tasks for all the other gods while they get all the credit. His role as agent, substitute, and general go-between focuses the thematic joke about performance that links the theater to the workplace in this play. Returning from a fact-finding mission, Mercury dutifully reports to his boss, Jupiter, that the power of the Olympian gods is steadily diminishing on earth.

Suddenly, the gods are interrupted by a band of mortals. These humans turn out to be the members of a theatrical troupe, climbing Mount Olympus to attend a wedding picnic for two of their number: Sparkeion and Nicemis. Like the Olympian gods, these thespians bicker fretfully among themselves, arguing about their professional roles and working relations.

The two groups decide to exchange places. For one year, the theatrical company, under the management of Thespis, will assume all the roles and functions of the gods, while the gods will travel down to earth, hoping to restore their waning reputations. Only Mercury is left behind, providing a point of exchange between high and low, heaven and earth, gods and humans.

Of course, everything goes terribly wrong. In the end, the gods return to Mount Olympus and hear about the absurd acts of mismanagement perpetrated by the humans during their absence. When the substitute ("acting") gods are ousted and order is restored in the end, *Thespis* concludes by turning outward to its audience again, with the complimentary gesture that is conventional in extravaganza, praising them for coming to the play and letting them know that *they* are the truly important "gods" in the modern theater. Thus when the topsy-turvy inversion is set right again, the play turns itself inside out, acknowledging its own artifice and determination to entertain.

Outmoding the Classical Extravaganza

Thespis includes incidental riffs on pantomime and melodrama, but the central organizing force of the piece derives from burlesque and extravaganza, as many critics have pointed out.[4] Commissioned by John Hollingshead, the manager of the Gaiety Theatre—who was thus the first manager to join Gilbert and Sullivan in collaboration—*Thespis* was written to feature several performers already well known on the burlesque and pantomime stage. J. L. Toole, who created the role of Thespis, was renowned as a "notorious gagger," while Fred and Harry Payne, who played Stupidas and Preposteros, were the reigning Harlequin and Clown of their day.[5]

The most important star attraction, however, was Nellie Farren, who created the role of Mercury. Extravaganza specialized in female-to-male cross-dressing, and Farren was famous for her version of the arch, provocative, innocent yet "cheeky" performance style that characterized these roles. Hollingshead, appreciating her value, called her "my priceless burlesque boy" and praised her respectable styling of gender ambiguity, for "without the slightest tinge of offensive vulgarity, she was the brightest boy-girl or girl-boy that ever graced the stage."[6] Farren's costume was a short skirt made of a flowing, clinging "quicksilver" material that deftly characterized Mercury while prominently displaying her famous legs, as these roles in extravaganza were designed to do (figure 1.1; plate 4). Since Gilbert and Sullivan would never again feature travesty roles, *Thespis* is notable for its use of this convention. As Hollingshead later commented, the form of burlesque

FIGURE 1.1 Playing Mercury in *Thespis*, Nellie Farren (*far right*) wore a flowing skirt of "quicksilver" material. Illustration by D. H. Friston, in *Illustrated London News*, January 6, 1872. (Wikimedia Commons)

that appeared "in short clothes at the Gaiety" was later re-dressed in "long clothes at the Savoy."[7]

In this first work, Gilbert and Sullivan played along with genre conventions, performance styles, established stars, and production values that they would soon seek to transform. Even Hollingshead admitted that "neither Mr. J. L. Toole nor Miss Nelly Farren could be called 'singers' even in the most elastic English."[8] Thus we can imagine that Sullivan's music was not particularly well supported in this first collaboration. Soon Gilbert and Sullivan would gather an ensemble skilled in both acting and singing; rule out cross-dressing of any kind; forbid clowning, gagging, broad and low humor, and all unscripted stage business; and emphasize the smooth working of the company as a whole over individual star turns. Both librettist and composer would insist on the most rigorously precise standards in rehearsal. In short, later collaborations were marvels of company management. The production arrangements for *Thespis*, though, were decidedly slipshod. By all accounts, the work was drastically under-rehearsed on opening night, and it ran much too long, although it did become a success after cutting, shaping, and further rehearsal.

Because of its featured stars, the season of its launch, and the particular house in which it was produced, audiences at the time would certainly have viewed *Thespis* as an extravaganza. For *Thespis* premièred at the Gaiety on Boxing Night, the traditional opening night for the Christmas pantomimes and extravaganzas staged all over town. The Gaiety was a relatively new theater, having opened its doors only three years before, in 1868, and was most famous for burlesque. Sexy yet free of "offensive vulgarity," silly yet intelligent, raucous yet spectacularly beautiful, extravaganza was a relatively "high" form of burlesque, intended for an urbane adult audience.[9]

Advertising "extravaganza" while being associated with burlesque, the Gaiety represents the close relation of these genres at this time. Ever since the 1830s, when Madame Vestris employed James Robinson Planché to develop their signature form of "elegant burletta similar to French vaudeville" at the Olympic Theatre, extravaganza was taken to be "higher," more delicate, and more dedicated to sheer gorgeousness than the usual burlesque.[10] The two main subgenres of extravaganza—classical extravaganza and fairy extravaganza—specialized in a sophisticated mix of musical styles, elegant costumes (not the clown-like garb worn in burlesque), and spectacular special effects. Audiences especially loved the culminating "transformation scene," which unfolded slowly, revealing wonder after wonder, as the stage set almost literally turned itself inside out, transforming the world of the story into another, even more fantastic world. Emphatically contemporary topical allusions peppered the text, but gave way, in the end, to a profound realm of fantasy. One might say that extravaganza's most fundamental structure depended on this juxtaposition of the present-day metropolis with a world elsewhere—whether Fairyland or the mythical realms of classical story. In historical retrospect, then, extravaganza can be seen clearly to emphasize both modern urbanity and the escape from it.

The foundational work in the genre was Planché's *Olympic Revels* (1831), a classical extravaganza starring Madame Vestris as Orpheus. *Olympic Revels* was quickly followed by *Olympic Devils* (Olympic, 1831) and then by many, many more. *The Golden Fleece; or, Jason in Colchis and Medea in Corinth* (Haymarket, 1845) was probably the most influential classical extravaganza written by Planché, for its parody turns not only on classical stories and characters, but also on the formal conventions of classical drama and stagecraft. Influenced by Edward Blanchard's *Antigone Travestie* (Covent Garden, 1845), Planché used a raised stage to evoke the high style of classical tragedy. But surely his greatest stroke of parodic genius was to cast a single actor, Charles Mathews, as the Chorus. Mathews was known for his "monopolylogues," a humorous style of pattering in which he successively took all the parts. In other words, Mathews's individual history as a contemporary performer was part of the wit of having one person portray the quintessentially communal group of the classical Chorus.[11] Twenty-five years after Blanchard's *Antigone Travestie* and Planché's *Golden Fleece*, *Thespis* depended on the profound familiarity with classical extravaganza that could be assumed on the part of the audience by 1871.[12]

Both the form and the content of classical extravaganza place it in the main line of modern burlesque poetry, which originated in and developed through parodies of the classics. English burlesque verse, influenced by the seventeenth-century French poets Scarron and Boileau, often took up the later, five-beat line, since it handily mocks the high seriousness of English blank-verse heroic drama, but the earlier, octosyllabic rhymed couplet also provides a rich vein of rhythmic humor. Mostly end-stopped in order to emphasize the rhyme, the lines of early-nineteenth-century theatrical burlesque were relished for their doggerel jogtrot. These lines of English burlesque developed many tricks of their own, exaggerating faux-classical stichomythia, for example, tossing the line back and forth among several characters without missing a beat, until someone would finally complete the anticipated rhyme. Ostentatious rhyming was allied to the other notorious feature of extravaganza: blatant and copious punning. Overdoing the use of puns can produce a rising sense of giddy, knowing hilarity to accompany the deflating pleasure of the wince. Like the rhymes, the puns operated as a form of punctuation, forming the points in a pointed style with its topsy-turvy dynamic of mock-heroic inflation and deflation. The puns were italicized in playbills, in lists of dramatis personae, and in extravaganza play texts, so that they would pop out visually and be easily grasped.

The music for extravaganza was derivative and allusive. Borrowed from opera arias and street ballads alike, familiar melodies were set with new lyrics. This comic refunctioning of the music enhanced the dynamic of mock-heroic elevation, deflation, and mismatching. Too, the ironic juxtaposition of high and low registers, operating between the music and the words, created a dynamic disjunction that was analogous to the oddly dislocated topical jokes on metropolitan current events, uttered within the context of Fairyland or classical antiquity. In another world, zany reminders of this world burst through. Needless to say, these musical conventions capitalized on recognition rather than originality. Sullivan's original music turns this feature of the precursor genre on its head. On its own, the presence of original music raises *Thespis* from burlesque toward opera. Meyer Lutz, who took over as conductor of *Thespis* after Sullivan's opening-night performance, believed that the music was too "ultra-classical" for its intended audience.[13] Like Sullivan's music, Gilbert's libretto provides a coherent, overarching two-act dramatic plot, significantly less episodic than the usual extravaganza.

After *Thespis*, Gilbert and Sullivan would leave the formal conventions of the extravaganza behind, while also suggestively transforming—and therefore recollecting—them. For example, Gilbert brilliantly recast the function of the pun. Drastically reducing its blatancy and frequency, he nevertheless retained its logic; but instead of appearing as merely an incidental point, it serves a fundamental, structural purpose. Thus the pun becomes less—but also more—important, absorbed within the plot and thematic arguments of the play, rather than frequently punctuating the dialogue with diversionary linguistic wit. In *Thespis*, Gilbert orients the plot around the double meaning of "company," linking the theatrical and economic senses of the word in order to engage in a critique of the functionalist segregation of roles demanded by an efficiently working capitalist enterprise. (The theme of company management is explored later in this chapter.)

Thus *Thespis* should be seen both as a late classical extravaganza and as a first step away from extravaganza toward comic opera. *Thespis* updates and, at the same time, outmodes this popular precursor genre. For in 1871, when Gilbert and Sullivan took it up, the classical extravaganza was quite a familiar old thing, rapidly receding into the past. Even the stage set for Mount Olympus—"*Picturesque shattered columns, overgrown with ivy, etc.*"—makes the point (in the "*etc.*") that the ruins of the classical past have been humorously recycled and staged many times before. In the course of *Thespis*, all the familiar elements of classical extravaganza are trotted out: pseudo-Greek comic names like Tipseion, Preposteros, and Nicemis; young women in short skirts and tights impersonating Greek gods; jokes on Jupiter's many love affairs; a recitation from Lemprière's *Classical Dictionary*; anachronistic juxtapositions between the mythic past and the urban present; and other humorous engagements in mock erudition.[14]

In order to make sure that *Thespis* is understood as a genre parody, the central character, Thespis, makes the point quite explicitly. When consulted as "an expert judge of what the public likes," Thespis pans Jupiter's performance of his own role. "You don't come up to my idea of the part," he tells Jupiter, adding, "Bless you, I've played you often." Thespis further suggests that the role itself is outmoded. "In fact," he tells Jupiter, "we don't use you much out of burlesque." This is a metageneric point—a deflation of the classics, of course, but also an assertion that the classics are by now most familiarly preserved in burlesque. At one point, Thespis even mistakes Jupiter for an aspiring actor who would like to *play* Jupiter. "When we do our Christmas piece, I'll let you know," Thespis quips dismissively, thus cueing audience members to recognize the reflexive humor (since they themselves are sitting in a theater and watching an actor play Jupiter in a Christmas piece).

As a genre, extravaganza specializes in this sort of sophisticated reflection of the current moment, along with a running commentary on its own conventions. In one sense, then, *Thespis* simply extends these conventions.

But they are reflexively developed ad absurdum. Thus *Thespis* pushes the extravaganza's modernizing, sophisticating impulses to the point where they become parodic. In other words, the content of *Thespis*—its story about how the gods have grown old and have been replaced by human actors—offers an allegory of its own form of genre parody.

"The Gods Grown Old"

Why might a work that makes fun of classical extravaganza as an exhausted and outmoded genre be especially appealing in 1871? I suggest two answers: first, because many Victorians worried that their gods, too, had perhaps grown old; and, second, because a parody of the classics could appeal to audience members from diverse social classes.

The topsy-turvy parodic exchange of high and low in *Thespis* is scripted as the substitution of humans for gods and earth for heaven. The Olympian gods have fallen, come down in the world, been brought down to earth. Indeed, their loss of prestige derives from their having become too much like humans, with their aging, their internecine squabbling, and their complaints about overwork. When the thespians mistake the ruined Temple of the Gods for the dilapidated palace of a mighty king who must be hiding to avoid his creditors, this parodic secularization is clear. The gods, in turn, fail to recognize the thespians, wondering whether they represent a government survey, an Alpine club, or a "Cook's Excursion." Thus the meeting of gods and humans is overlaid with references to modern bureaucracy, tourism, and the decline of the aristocracy. Their mutual misrecognition emphasizes the cross-cultural foreignness of the two realms to each other while suggesting how very much alike they have already become.

The idea that the Olympian gods have grown old suggests the disturbing possibility that whole regimes of divinity can be superseded and displaced. Some informed audience members may have recalled the mythic displacement of the Titans, which had established the regime of the Olympian gods in the first place. But a great many late Victorians had pondered the later, historical displacement of the Olympians, who had been relegated to the status of mere "pagan" deities after the rise of Christianity. Examples of this troubling idea abound in the literature of the period, some taking up the notion that the Olympian gods survive in exile, cloaked and disguised in cold, northern European climates; some dilating on the incongruity of classical art among the artifacts of Victorian culture; and some focusing on the shocking historical impermanence of whole dispensations of faith.[15] In the history of musical theater, Wagner's "Twilight of the Gods" is the most memorable—and serious—evocation of this last idea, and to some extent *Thespis* can be seen as a parodic comment on the sort of high seriousness expressed in *Götterdämmerung.*[16]

Needless to say, *Thespis* takes a light view of these serious issues, but it does suggest them. If the Olympian gods can be reduced to tired, limping, cold, and disgruntled day laborers, then perhaps the same thing could happen to another deity. The idea that Christianity itself might be displaced— or the more radical idea that Christianity was, in the nineteenth century, already in the process of being displaced—seemed a disturbing possibility to many Victorians. Could a parody of the classical extravaganza suggest even this off-limits issue? I think so. When Thespis berates the gods for being out of date and "behind [the] age," he suggests that all historical eras have their popular fashions, even in matters of religion. When Jupiter complains that "the sacrifices and votive offerings have fallen off terribly of late" and are now "dwindled down to preserved Australian beef," he makes present-day, "down-under" Australia a sign of the world's lowering, democratic, and secularizing tendencies.

The very idea that human actors could substitute for the gods suggests a dangerous absurdity, paradox, or contradiction in terms. Of course, that paradox happens to be precisely the principle on which ritual theater is founded. But it is also the particular paradox on which Christianity is founded, the notion that divinity can be not only represented in human form (as in theater, including *Thespis*), but also fully incarnated as human. In this sense, the Christian incarnation can be seen in the light of performative substitution, or even of parodic deflation, since the human God "comes down" to represent a prior, more distant, and sterner image of divinity. Theological argument through the ages, articulating the three persons (or roles) taken by the one God, attempts to analyze this paradox, treating it as a mystery rather than an absurdity. But the troubling effects of bringing God down to earth were reaching a critical level of explicitness in the nineteenth century.[17] Of course, the church and its beliefs were beyond the reach of theatrical parody at this time.[18] But this historical collapse of the firm distinction between God and human can be felt hovering behind the inversion of gods and humans in *Thespis*.

I am not the first to suggest that the waning reputation of the Olympian gods is recognizable as an analogy for (and a humorous displacement of) the Victorians' own struggles with the loss of faith. Alan Fischler, for example, argues that the play suggests the necessity for a bracing, humanistic self-reliance. The moral of *Thespis*, Fischler suggests, is that humanity must face the fact that the gods have disappeared and thus must assume control.[19] I think the implications of *Thespis* go further—and are funnier—than that. When absolute distinctions between high and low collapse—whether between gods and humans or between aristocrats and commoners—then the human world is securely fixed within the realm of theatrical substitution, where humans can act like gods or ordinary people can act up, playing whatever role they might like. Modern social mobility involves acting. That is Gilbert's sharpest point, one shared by some sociologists, who recognize the importance of the idea of theatricality in the development of their discipline.[20]

This association of secularization with democratization suggests another answer to our pending question: Why might a parody of classical extravaganza have been especially appealing in the late nineteenth century? As Edith Hall argues, the attraction depended on the wide range of class-inflected attitudes toward classical education among those in the audience for classical extravaganza.[21] Classically educated theatergoers could find relief from the memory of school discipline in the spoof, laughing at the easy simplicity of the jokes, while those not educated in the classics could enjoy the comic deflation of an elite tradition. As Hall points out, the major extravaganza writers were bohemians, elegant and educated, but rebellious, disaffected, and sometimes radical in their political sentiments.[22] She further argues that the very popularity of classical burlesque (from its inception in 1831 until *Thespis* in 1871) shows that "working-class and lower middle-class theatergoers of both sexes must have been much more familiar" with the classics "than they have been given credit for hitherto."[23] At the same time, the classical references in extravaganza may have served a loose pedagogical purpose. Providing ready information in a journalistic, fragmentary, modern style, the classical extravaganza perhaps was a sort of primer, even though the information comes across in bits and pieces, like the form of modern journalistic information itself.

According to this interpretation, the topical references characteristic of extravaganza would have been received by audience members in multiple and complex ways, cutting across the audience and differentiating it from within, while binding it together in common enjoyment. Since their humorous mock erudition often turns on rudimentary problems of translation, classical extravaganzas worked across the difference between those who knew Greek and Latin and those who knew only English. At the same time, these mock-scholarly jokes provided enough clues for all sorts of audience members to follow.[24] Greek and Latin tag phrases can be taken as evidence of *both* a carefree attitude toward the memory of classical education (which some audience members may have adopted) *and* the autodidactic, upwardly mobile attention to bits and pieces of classical learning (which other audience members may have brought to bear). This dynamic of differentiation may be seen, for example, in *The Golden Fleece*, where Charles Mathews's opening speech as the Chorus concludes with the following joke:

> At the end of each scene I shall sing you some history,
> Or clear up whatever is in it of mystery,
> But I can't tell you *why*—unless English I speak,
> For this very plain reason—there's no *Y* in Greek.[25]

This conventionally italicized pun on the word "*why*" and the letter "*Y*" humorously presents a bit of classical trivia, while also humorously justifying the translation of the classical story into English. Within this framework, English insularity can simultaneously be parodied, justified, and enjoyed.

So, in other words, we could read *Thespis* as one symptom of the great democratizing shift in education during the second half of the nineteenth century, which saw not only the broader dissemination of classical learning among some women and working-class men, but also the rise of English studies (the vulgar tongue treated as a subject of higher education). Regarded from a certain balefully "high" point of view, this cultural development was regarded as the dilution, fragmentation, and even demise of real learning. Classical extravaganza always makes fun of that high point of view. In other words, the genre registers a gradual, general shift in the perceived value of classical education, which may have begun to seem a thing of the past, even at the same time that it was becoming a more widely owned common coin of present-day exchange. Owing to its implied critique of classical education, displayed before a cross-class audience, classical extravaganza adopts an implicitly subversive attitude in general, Edith Hall argues. Indeed, she claims that the genre posits a broad cultural opposition between classical education and popular theater, implicitly championing the latter.[26] I agree. Within the dynamics of parody, cutting up the classics goes hand in hand with the gusto and power of democratic cultural appropriation. Thus for *Thespis*, as for all parody, in-crowd enjoyment may be felt both in tacit familiarity or recognition and in the excitement of "getting it" for the first time and "catching on." The parody of classical extravaganza is a particularly trenchant cultural tool, excavating the past while clearing the way for more modern forms of cultural exchange and common coin. Intensifying the holiday commingling of high and low, *Thespis* deftly involves the classics with the social classes.

If gods can be brought low, how might humans be elevated? Another genre parody takes up this other direction of parodic inversion in *Thespis*. If holiday extravaganza is purpose-built to elicit fantasy, evoke pleasure, and imagine the relaxation of rules, opéra bouffe offers an explicitly "French" set of conventions for relaxation, involving intoxication and risqué sexual explicitness, both of which *Thespis* turns to its advantage.

Offenbach had taken up these issues in *Orphée aux enfers* (*Orpheus in the Underworld*, 1858), perhaps the best-known work in the French tradition of opéra bouffe. *Thespis* is deeply indebted to *Orphée aux enfers*, and in its relation to the earlier work, *Thespis* processes risqué French content, converting it into a more respectable, acceptably English form of suggestiveness. Insofar as *Thespis* translates a decidedly French genre into pointedly English terms, it practices genre parody. Still current when *Thespis* was produced in 1871, *Orphée* parodies its own classical sources; in this respect, *Thespis* is a further parody of a parody, offering both homage to and critique of Offenbach in general and *Orphée aux enfers* in particular.

Several contemporary critics immediately recognized the fact that *Thespis* participates in this cross-channel cultural exchange, and they welcomed Sullivan's original music as the English answer to Offenbach.[27] Sullivan's earlier *Cox and Box* (1866, with a libretto by F. C. Burnand) had been directly inspired by Offenbach's *Les deux aveugles* (*The Two Blind Men*, 1855). Gilbert, too, was clearly involved in this particular genre parody, for *Orphée aux enfers* was his favorite Offenbach opera. He had reviewed Offenbach for *Fun*; had used several Offenbach melodies in his first (burlesque) version of Tennyson's *The Princess* (1870); and had published his English translation of the libretto for *Les brigands* (1869) in 1871. Thus it is clear that when Gilbert wrote the libretto for *Thespis*, Offenbach was very much on his mind.[28]

Thespis preserves, but tones down, two risqué topics highlighted in *Orphée aux enfers*: intoxication and sexual transgression. In this assimilation and transformation of opéra bouffe, we can see an important element of the formation of English comic opera. In *Orphée*, drink is proposed as one cure for the exhaustion and boredom that gods and humans suffer alike. "This regime is boring!" the gods chant in their "Rebellion Chorus." One reason for their descending into the underworld is its spicier diet, especially its replacement of nectar and ambrosia with wine and "fire-water." Even the waters of Lethe become a vehicle for intoxication. "I drink to forget," says John Styx, who has come down in the world. Here the inebriate's conventional excuse becomes an explanation of his downward mobility, which itself is a metaphor for the deflating aspect of parodic inversion. In other words, intoxication is an explicit marker of parody, as the gods descend into the underworld. *Orphée* concludes down there, with Eurydice dressed as a bacchante, backed up by the "Infernal Chorus" of gods, all singing the praises of intoxication.

Thespis plays on this bouffe topic while turning it upside down. The lowly thespians get "high" by climbing Mount Olympus, for its thin mountain air is "intoxicating" and "elating," but they are also drinking wine as they climb. As with the gods in *Orphée*, once the actors have achieved the heights, the regime becomes boring and routine. Thus *Thespis* alludes directly to *Orphée* when the thespians complain that ambrosia "cheers but don't inebriate us." As in *Orphée*, the conclusion of *Thespis* turns on the playful embrace of intoxication, but in *Thespis* that embrace is given an exaggeratedly English twist.

Tipseion, the thespian acting for Bacchus, turns out to have been a most inadequate substitute, for he has "taken the pledge." No longer true to his name, Tipseion is self-divided by virtue of his role, and he must ask himself: Which is the higher duty, his professional duty as an actor to play Bacchus well or his personal pledge not to drink? "When the functions clash," he says, everything must give way to "the pledge." Terence Rees discerns in this a satire of the temperance movement, always at its height during the Christmas season.[29] A tee-totaling fanatic in the role of Bacchus is funny in several respects: as a figure for an era of all-too-human misrule; as a figure for the inadequacy of dramatic substitution in general; but most especially as a figure for the particular English cultural resistance to a light-headed, bouffe encouragement of intoxication. Tipseion promotes the production of ginger beer instead of wine, a particularly English alternative. This dig at Victorian sobriety is also a critique of performative substitution. For one "moral" of the story is that "substitutes are nothing like the real thing," and, of course, ginger beer is no more likely to replace nectar, ambrosia, or wine as an intoxicant than respectable bourgeois values are likely to produce the high, intoxicated feeling of temporarily being godlike.

Like those of intoxication, themes of sexual transgression express the commitment of the genre to press against the limits of Victorian propriety. Classical parody, in general, is associated with a literary form of infidelity. Thus the risqué treatment of sexual infidelity in *Orphée aux enfers* cleverly dovetails with the opera's parodic infidelity to the classical version of the story, for Orpheus and Eurydice detest each other and are engaged in adulterous affairs. Offenbach's Orpheus absolutely does *not* want to reclaim his Eurydice. Only the stern figure of Public Opinion can convince him to pretend devotion, "pour servir d'exemple à la postérité [in order to serve as an example to posterity]."[30] This lack of respect for the classical story apparently shocked many of Offenbach's contemporaries, including Flaubert—which may seem shocking in its own way to twenty-first-century readers, who will recall that Flaubert treated marital infidelity with his own commitment to an antibourgeois critique. The links between social conventions and genre conventions—especially those circulating around marriage—are always strong.

The parodic dalliance with themes of sexual transgression was shaped differently in England than in France, of course. *Thespis* exaggerates the English refusal to raise risky topics, while raising them all the same: loose behavior during courtship, marital infidelity, even incest. For example, the betrothed couple (Sparkeion and Nicemis) pursues a tedious argument about whether he might properly kiss her yet, since they are only partway through their marriage ceremony. Later, the thespians consult Lemprière's *Classical Dictionary*, with pseudo-classical pedantry, about "the exact connubial relation of the different gods and goddesses." Following the long list of women to whom Apollo was "married," a tongue-in-cheek dispute breaks out among the thespians about whether he was actually *married* to them. This question is squelched with an exclamation of mock horror: "Sir! This is the Family Edition!" While ostentatiously identifying the work as English, this joke cuts against the notorious prudery of Victorian editors. Meanwhile, the suggestion of extramarital sexual relations provides a mild titillation, although remaining well within the limits of respectability.

While some critics have felt that Gilbert is squeamish about the sexual explicitness of opéra bouffe,[31] it seems to me that the opposite must be the case. He imitates French suggestiveness as much as possible within the conventions of the English stage, while making fun of excessive English propriety. Comparing Gilbert's libretto with French opéra bouffe, the reviewer for the *Era* said: "He ventures into fields where no previous dramatists have entered. . . . He says things which many of us may have thought, but which no one has dared to express."[32] Opéra bouffe might treat marital infidelity as routine, but Gilbert raises the issue with his own form of delectation. While Sparkeion and Nicemis jealously threaten each other with an infidelity they never enact, they keep the issue in the air. But a variety exemplum in act 2, the song about the "little maid of Arcadee," provides a more pointedly immoral moral. This fable clearly argues that inconstancy and change of sexual partners is only natural, even for women. The little maid was happily engaged to Cousin Robin, but he "did as Robins do" and jilted her. After mourning him for a while, however, she happily settles afresh on

Cousin Richard. Thus, sequestered within this little number, the question of sexual inconstancy is de-idealized, treated in bouffe fashion as perfectly to be expected, even likely to produce a happy outcome. This sort of implied argument against the prescriptions of Victorian gender ideology is not at all unusual in Savoy opera; my point is that we have to feel its dynamic being formed in response to extravaganza and opéra bouffe.

Thespis even jokes about incest. Pretteia, playing Venus, points out that the actor playing Mars is her father, while the one playing Vulcan is her grandfather. "I can't throw myself into a part . . . when I have to make love to my father," she protests. Along similar lines, when Daphne and Nicemis bicker about who is "really" married to Sparkeion, Daphne argues that Nicemis cannot be married to her own brother (since Nicemis is playing Diana and Sparkeion is playing Apollo). Daphne, playing Calliope, insists, instead, that *she* is married to Apollo: "By the rules of this fair spot / I'm his wife and you are not." But Nicemis replies out of her role, in propria persona as Sparkeion's betrothed: "By this golden wedding ring, / I'm his wife and you're a 'thing.'" This scene is all the more piquant since the character of Sparkeion is played *en travesti*, and thus all three parts in this bouffe erotic triangle are played by women (figure 1.2). Thus, again, extravaganza cross-dressing and fantasy assist in suggesting forms of transgression that are not explicitly being played out.

Raising the risqué topics of adultery and incest enables *Thespis* to satirize priggish, petit-bourgeois, respectable people who refuse to entertain such topics. During the discussion of whether Venus is married to Mars or Vulcan, Nicemis pipes up with: "If she isn't married to Mars, she ought to be!" This gives rise to a pseudo-pedantic axiom that the "exact connubial relation of the different gods and goddesses is a point on which we must be extremely particular" (where "particular" means both "precise" and "euphemistic"). Nicemis is a prig. (Her name is "Nice-miss," where "nice" means both "amiable" and "excessively precise.") As she says, quite absurdly, given the fact that she is acting: "I hope the original Diana is no rule for *me*." Because the "original Diana" goes out at night, Nicemis, playing Diana, must be unfaithful to the classical original in order to remain a respectable contemporary young lady.

All the female thespians worry about the relation of their "real," personal characters to the parts they are playing; for each, "fidelity" and "convention" are concerns of both genre and gender. Here we see, too, that playing a role—whether in a play or in social life—precipitates self-division. When *acting* properly—or when acting *properly*—one is never oneself. Amusingly, and very much according to bouffe conventions, the issues of performance

FIGURE 1.2 In the erotic triangle of Diana (Nicemis), Calliope (Daphne), and Apollo (Sparkeion)—clustered around Thespis—all three parts were played by women. Illustration by H. Woods. (Wikimedia Commons)

and self-division are raised for the female characters in *Thespis* around gender role-playing and sexual fidelity while, as we shall soon see, the same issues are raised for the male characters around professional role-playing. Thus the questions of gender, for women, and professional duty, for men, are signs of the much more pervasive problem of performance.

The extravaganza convention of female-to-male transvestism points up this difference in gender conventions by playfully confusing the genders. In this respect, the cross-dressed role of Mercury is particularly interesting. As the "brightest boy-girl or girl-boy" in John Hollingshead's Gaiety pantheon, Nellie Farren played the point of exchange—the "junction" we might say— between high and low, divine and human, but also female and male bodies. Aptly, the traditional figure of Mercury depends on the paradoxical function of crossing, going-between, and posing as both-at-once, while Farren's female body in male costume enacted these multiple transgressions. Certainly extravaganza transvestism suggests a play of homo- and hetero-erotic fantasy, in the audience at large and perhaps within any individual audience member, whether male or female.[33] In *Thespis*, gender transgression both embodies (as a symbol) and represents (as a metaphor) other social problems, for Mercury is also the exemplary figure of the worker-subject, exhausted and conflicted, divided among multiple roles.

The god's many "aspects" are wittily represented as modern, distracted multitasking. Thus the demands of modern social life—both the need to work and the self-division caused by work—are figured in Mercury's complaint that he is a "celestial drudge" who must perform in place of all the other gods.[34] Once again, Gilbert's particular transformation of opéra bouffe demands attention. Whereas in *Orphée aux enfers*, the role of the funny factotum is divided between Mercury and John Styx ("mon domestyx," as Jupiter fondly calls him), in *Thespis*, that role is united in Mercury, "the slave of the gods." In *Orphée*, Mercury recites a long list of his roles and titles, quoting from Bouillet's classical dictionary. He is facilitator of love affairs, master of eloquence, protector of commerce and thieves. Offenbach's Mercury even predicts his instrumentalized modern role: in a barometer. Gilbert adopts all these jokes, turning each of them in a slightly new direction. "I've made thunder for Jupiter, odes for Apollo, battles for Mars, and love for Venus," says Gilbert's Mercury, employing an amusingly elaborate zeugma. He must "go down" every evening and "rise" in the morning, bringing back to Mount Olympus all the things he has stolen ("a set of false teeth and a box of Life Pills" for Jupiter, and so on). In short, Mercury is simultaneously a disgruntled worker and a per-sonification of parodic inversion. Leaning on a rhyme with "futurity," he sings in protest: "Though noodles are baroned and earled / There's nothing for clever obscurity!" All the gods are workers, and none of them gets any respect; but because he works for all the other gods, Mercury represents the quintessence of the common, human worker.

Company Management

Critics have failed to see that the idea of company management—in both the capitalist and theatrical senses of the word "company"—provides the thematic coherence of *Thespis*. In this story of modern work and modern play, theatrical substitution and hierarchical inversion wreak havoc in every company—the company of Olympian gods, the company of actors, and a railway company whose ineffective management provides the humor in the central novelty song of *Thespis*. In this respect, *Thespis* creates relief and diversion by concentrating on bureaucratically divided functions, company management, and right relations between managers and workers.

The central variety number of act 1, about the North South East West Diddlesex junction, focuses these issues. The "Junction Song," as it is often called, is the crux of *Thespis*. As if to nudge us into apprehending its crucial importance, the song is framed by a blazon of clues to its exemplary significance. In the scene from which the "Junction Song" emerges, Thespis bemoans the difficulties of his managerial role, crying, "Oh why did the gods make me a manager?" The troupe treats this question as if it were the proposition of a riddle. They repeat it again and again, emphasizing a different word each time, as in a juvenile guessing game: "*Why* did the gods make him a manager? . . . Why did the *gods* make him a manager? . . . Why did the gods make *him* a manager? . . . Why did the gods make him a *manager*?" This silly device has a serious purpose, for it allows the question to be repeated so many times that its thematic importance loudly sounds out and must sink in—before the song. Then, closing the frame on the "Junction Song" after it concludes, Thespis again suggests its thematic relevance to the plot of the whole, for it is then that he drives his bargain with the Olympian gods, to become the temporary "manager" of Olympus. Notably, the agreement is formulated in the language of company business, when Thespis says: "I've a very good company, used to take long parts on the shortest notice. Invest us with your powers and we'll fill your places till you return." Rees's research shows that the original version also included an invitation from Jupiter to Thespis "to confer with a brother manager."[35]

The "Junction Song" is also preceded by Thespis's refusal to flirt with Nicemis, since (as he puts it) an association with her might impair his influence "before [his] company." Here we should notice that sexual "association" is related to the unruly cross-class associations that will be detailed in the song. Thespis rejects her advances with an outburst: "Don't you know the story of the gentleman who undermined his influence by associating with his inferiors?" Almost everybody replies, "Yes, yes,—we know it," but of course it will be sung anyway. This emphasis on its familiarity suggests that it is meant as a commonplace (even though the song is original to *Thespis*). Variety numbers like this would become a staple device in Savoy plot construction, with their giddily displaced, yet exemplary condensation of a serious point. (Think of the fable of "The Magnet and the Churn" in *Patience* or the song about "Darwinian Man" in *Princess Ida*.) These songs, which seem to be distractions at the time of their presentation, are little fables twisting the moral of the story around themselves—tiny, crazy allegories of the larger plot within which they are situated. This diversionary tactic explicitly points out the thematic coherence of the piece without making it overly "heavy" or serious.

The "Junction Song" tells the story of a railway company's Chairman of Directors, whose habit of "associating with his inferiors" makes him a very bad manager indeed:

> I once knew a chap who discharged a function
> On the North South East West Diddlesex junction,
> He was conspicuous exceeding,
> For his affable ways and his easy breeding.
> Although a Chairman of Directors,
> He was hand in glove with the ticket inspectors,
> He tipped the guards with brand-new fivers,
> And sang little songs to the engine drivers.

This managerial style backfires, of course, for his workers ignore their assigned functions and "[give] themselves up to a course of joking." The trains start behaving quite absurdly, "stopp[ing] all night in the middle of a tunnel," going to the wrong destination at the wrong time, and so forth. In the end, the results are disastrous. The company fails on the market, for "the general Public did not like" this rampant irregularity, and so "receipts fell, . . . [and] shares went down to a nominal figure." In a final flurry of worldly absurdity, the "Junction Song" explains that the railway line is eventually sold to marine store dealers (a company precisely *not* well suited to manage a railway, and a lower-middle-class kind of trade, at that). All the shareholders end up in the workhouse, and the Chairman of Directors ends up on the street, selling "pipe-lights in the Regent Circus." And the moral of the story?

> These are the sad results proceeding
> From his affable ways and his easy breeding!

Directly following the song, Thespis emphasizes the moral with his sympathetic commentary:

> It's very hard. As a man, I am naturally of an easy disposition. As a manager, I am compelled to hold myself aloof, that my influence may not be deteriorated. As a man, I am inclined to fraternize with the pauper—as a manager, I am compelled to walk about like this: Don't know yah! Don't know yah! Don't know yah!

Like Trabb's boy mocking Pip in *Great Expectations*, Thespis imitates the snubbing behavior of those who act better than their fellows. To be a proper manager, it seems that one has to "rise" to the occasion and "act" the part. Again, *Thespis* drives home the double point that social roles involve performance and that their performative pressure causes a painful self-division. A professional, it seems, is always an actor, while an actor is always a worker. With this knot of metatheatrical argument, the play equates social stratification with the bureaucratic assignment of separate functions in modern life. Thus the moral of the "Junction Song" points out the disciplined assignment of "function" in modern labor relations.[36]

As was so often the case in extravaganza (and will be the case in the Savoy operas), the "Junction Song" alludes to a topic in current circulation. The failed manager of the railway was supposedly intended as a reference to the Duke of Sutherland, the director of the London North Western Railway, who had a reputation for riding along on the footplates of his company's engines.[37] But the specific journalistic content of the reference is much less important than its form. Glancing, scattershot, and concretely related to the world outside the theater, such references attach the play's realm of fantasy to the world of reality, as if each topical reference were a tack, a nail, or a pushpin. Audience members can pick up on the concrete reference or not, for the song's humor will work either way.

The "Junction Song" also serves as a witty case of the medium being an apt vehicle for its message. The exuberant "musical onomatopoeia" of its railway orchestration included a station bell, a train whistle, and "some new instrument of music imitating the agreeable sound of a train in motion."[38] These sound effects were enormously popular with audiences. In the lyrics, an emphasis on the word "function" relentlessly sustains the railway onomatopoeia throughout the song, through the feminine rhymes of its chugging refrain ("compunction . . . unction . . . function . . . junction" and so on). While Thespis sang, the company was choreographed to imitate the motions of a railway train. The performers, "led by Mr. F. Payne [the famous Harlequin] whose arms represent[ed] a flying wheel," conveyed the "tremulous energy of the locomotives that 'rush and roar through all the shires.'" As the *Era* reported, this "screaming, whistling and shouting chorus fairly brings down the house."[39]

The mechanical sounds of the "Junction Song" express the thematic crux of the play, imitating the properly functioning parts of a modern social machine. Many decades in advance of Meyerhold and other dramatic modernists dedicated to showing that the human body had become part of the mechanism of modern life, this novelty number expresses the hopeful notion that modern automatism and mechanization can be homeopathically alleviated with a dose of playful imitation. Like Charlie Chaplin caught in the machinery in *Modern Times*, this number both belabors and lightens the burden of modernity's exaggerated discipline.

Again, the significance of the "Junction Song" depends on the multiple meanings of the word "company." The association of an acting company with a capitalist company now comes clearly into focus. This is Gilbert's first experiment in transforming the burlesque and extravaganza pun, raising a diversionary bit of verbal humor into an overarching principle of coherence. Although still tacit, an idea is forming—the idea that a pun can become a coherence-making engine, a thematic gear, a "junction" that links the parts of the working machine. The virtuosity of the coordinated performance also helps us see that producing a successful piece of theatrical relief is actually hard work, demanding the functional precision and capital consolidation of a modern machine.

Much has been made of the fact that Gilbert and Sullivan wrote *Thespis* for an "alien company" of actors who were neither trained as vocal artists nor disciplined to accept precise direction of the sort for which Savoy productions would become known. In fact, the performers in *Thespis* were not really a "company" at all, but a disparate group of individuals, brought together for this particular production. Since many were already famous for their own performance styles, they would have expected to create their parts themselves, relying on their signature styles of flirting, capering, clowning, mugging, or improvising business. Soon Gilbert and Sullivan would exercise their aesthetic control by prohibiting these unruly outbursts of individualistic grandstanding in favor of a coherent company style; pay relatively high salaries for performers' labor, thus stabilizing the company; and enforce rigorous rehearsal procedures. Therefore, we can also see the theme of company management in *Thespis* as a symptom of Gilbert and Sullivan chafing within the conditions they would soon transform, working under production constraints they would soon seek to transcend. *Thespis* can be read, in other words, as a metatheatrical critique of contemporary production values, an expression of the desire for a well-managed company that could be precisely disciplined to form an ensemble of stars who would agree to shine in chorus, who would work together like a well-functioning machine.[40]

When, at the conclusion of *Thespis*, Jupiter dismisses the actors for their gross mismanagement, Thespis complains that his company has been unfairly treated. His closing number, a reprise of the "Junction Song," brings back the wonderful clanging, puffing, and chugging of the railway music, while blaming Jupiter, who

. . . sends us home in a mood avengin',
In double quick time, like a railroad engine.
And this he does without compunction,
Because I have discharged with unction
A highly complicated function,
Complying with his own injunction.

The "unction" Thespis claims is the sure sign of an underling, pleading that he has only followed the orders of his manager. However, although the moral of the story does seem to be about the bad management of the thespians, another cluster of inversions must be undone for the restoration of order. Take Tipseion's substitution of ginger beer for wine as an example of mismanagement that must be set right. His sobriety has caused terrible problems in the world's economy, driving all the wine merchants out of business. Thus the ginger beer must go, and the wine must return. In other words, even in the restitution of order, not sobriety but intoxication is affirmed, in a truly fitting, tipsy moral for a holiday play. In the end, too, the light genres are affirmed above the heavy, when *Thespis* turns itself inside out, with a sly version of the extravaganza "tag" that appeals to the audience for approval. *Thespis* plays with this convention, implying that the very presence of the audience self-evidently confirms that the theater's management has expertly "discharged its function." Jupiter makes this clear when he sends Thespis and his company packing:

Away to earth, contemptible comedians,
And hear our curse, before we set you free;
You shall all be eminent tragedians,
Whom no one ever goes to see!

Thus are the comedians validated and the hierarchies of genre overturned again. *Thespis* ends by confirming the good taste of its audience, for they did not attend a tragedy that "no one ever goes to see." They chose, instead, to see *Thespis*, a spectacular example of the holiday entertainment that absolutely everyone goes to see.

2

Gender in the Breach

Trial by Jury

Trial by Jury (1875) is a satire on the law in general, but it is also a parody of one specific legal genre: the suit for breach of promise of marriage. The divided Savoy Chorus appears in this opera for the first time—the Chorus of Jurors backing up the Defendant, and the Chorus of Bridesmaids supporting the Plaintiff—as the scaffolding for an argument about gender. This short piece builds its critique of gender and the law on a set of brilliant genre parodies—of the cantata, the minstrel show, the seduction melodrama, the extravaganza transformation scene, and the case for breach of promise, which, by 1875, could certainly be understood as a genre in its own right.

Fred Sullivan, the older brother of the composer, created the role of the Learned Judge in the original production. Made up to resemble the Lord Chief Justice at the time, Sir Alexander Cockburn, Sullivan's impersonation lent the frisson of illegitimacy to the production.[1] Similarly, all the Jurymen appeared at the first dress rehearsal made up to resemble Dr. Edward Kenealy, Q.C., the counsel for the plaintiff in the famous case of the Tichborne Claimant, a lengthy and popular suit for imposture that had been tried before Lord Chief Justice Cockburn himself.[2] Arthur Sullivan "used to go and sit on the Bench with [the Lord Chief Justice] . . . at the time of the trial of the Claimant,"[3] and Sullivan reciprocated by taking him to a performance of Trial by Jury. The Lord Chief Justice was not amused. As he explained, "[T]he piece was calculated to bring the Bench into contempt."[4] His conventional personification of "the Bench" is itself funny, since it abstracts the judge's function from the person who discharges it, and Trial by Jury satirizes precisely that: an individual takes on the role as a matter of imposture. This work makes it blatantly clear that a judge is merely a representative of the law, calls attention to the inevitable disparity between the law and its individual agents, and points to the theatrical nature of social roles. Within the range of social roles, the performative reiterations of gender are shown to be even more powerful than the law itself.

Trial by Jury was the first Gilbert and Sullivan collaboration to have been masterminded by Richard D'Oyly Carte, the impresario who launched the triumvirate and kept them working together from 1875 until 1896. It appeared as an afterpiece to a production of Jacques Offenbach's *La Périchole* (1868) at the Royalty Theatre, where Carte was manager for Selina Dolaro. For years, Carte had been dreaming of creating a native English comic opera, and the huge success of *Trial by Jury* was the first real step toward realizing that goal.

Some journalists at the time worried that *Trial by Jury* might pale next to *La Périchole*, with its ultra-French, risqué representation of a tipsy heroine. However, the reviewer for the *Times* reported that "to judge by the unceasing and almost boisterous hilarity" of the audience, *Trial by Jury* suffered not at all in comparison with Offenbach, but, "on the contrary, it may fairly be said to have borne away the palm."[5] Also weighing the relative merits of the two works, the reviewer for the *Era* praised Gilbert's new English style of outspokenness: "He ventures into fields where no previous dramatists have entered. . . . He says things which many of us may have thought, but which no one has dared to express."[6] Again, as in *Thespis*, attacking risky topics in a particularly English way, *Trial by Jury* raises issues of sexual boredom, greed, professional ambition, and gender-specific rationalizations for social action.

For the libretto, Gilbert revised and expanded a piece of his own comic journalism that had appeared in *Fun*, "Trial by Jury—An Operetta."[7] Its genre parody explicitly turns on the humorous equation of courtroom drama with operetta. Only with Sullivan's music, then, is the full comic potential of Gilbert's parody realized, for the music sets the lively, arch mood, mobilizing parodies of several genres of musical theater—light and heavy, low and high—to point up the absurdity of gender arrangements and the futile, ritual attempt of the law to process them in an orderly way. Unlike the two- and three-act comic operas to follow, *Trial by Jury* is perfectly compressed into one short act. Billed as a "Dramatic Cantata," it has no spoken dialogue— unlike all the other Savoy operas—but was through-composed and is sung from start to finish of its short playing time (about half an hour).

Much more elaborate than the typical afterpiece, *Trial by Jury* featured original music and libretto, both male and female Choruses, and a stage set depicting the "SCENE—*A Court of Justice.*" Much has been made of this set, for it staked a claim for the high production values that would become one hallmark of the Savoy operas. The realism of the set created the sense that a real-life theater of social action—very different from the extravagant, fantastic setting of *Thespis* on Mount Olympus—could be the scene of zany and extravagant doings. Jane Stedman claims that these realistic sets "provide a right-side-up for topsy-turvydom."[8] But the situation is more complicated than that. These sets pretend that "real life" is stable and "right-side-up," while showing that it is actually characterized by parodic inversion. Ordinary social life *really is* topsy-turvy and crazily perverse. The generic stability of rule-bound legal procedure fails entirely to rule out the passions, deceptions, and absurdities that make life outside the courtroom so unruly. It is a crazy court, and yet—like the courtroom scene in *Alice's Adventures in Wonderland*, like Kafka's *The Trial*—its madness is strangely familiar, perhaps peculiarly English.[9] The fact that the Chorus of Bridesmaids sweeps into the courtroom is the most fantastic—that is to say, unrealistic—thing of all. In this case, the metatheatrical comparison of courtroom and theater implies that legal action is a cultural ritual, purporting to resolve ideological contradictions while actually reinstating them. Popular narratives of social engagement are stronger than the law, and they exert their own powerful shaping force on the legal proceedings. Chief among these is the familiar melodrama of the "broken flower," the "cheated maid" who has been jilted by a "regular cad . . . a shocking young scamp of a rover." She sues for breach of promise, hoping that the court will redress her loss with an award of monetary damages.

It is true enough that this familiar story refers to real social problems of seduction, abandonment, and gender inequity under the law, problems whose specific nineteenth-century forms were precipitated out of the long and wrenching shift from a traditional society to a modern, class-based one. *Trial by Jury* takes these social realities into account by making it absolutely clear that the Defendant is guilty—and so, too, are the Jury and the Judge. (In a serious sense, the plethora of guilty men seems to suggest that this script of seduction and abandonment is acted out all the time; but in a parodic sense, what we see is the hyperbolic multiplication of the already familiar.) Thus *Trial by Jury* exposes the network of male power relations that determines the endless repetition of gender inequities in the law.

In *Trial by Jury*—and in many of the later Gilbert and Sullivan collaborations—social action is regarded precisely in terms of its genres, the forms through which it is produced and reproduced in the repetitive performances of everyday life. Therefore, within the Savoy aesthetic, social actions and formations are every bit as susceptible to genre parody as any literary or theatrical genre might be. Furthermore, they are recognized and mediated through literary and theatrical genres that are also seen to be overly familiar, repetitive, and mechanical. If *Trial by Jury* pokes fun at the generic shaping force at work in all culture, it does so in a spirit of critical analysis. That analysis turns on the stereotypical performances of gender.

Masculine Will, Feminine Wiles

Keeping in mind that *Trial by Jury* is the first collaboration to feature a Chorus divided according to gender stereotypes, we should pay attention to the way the Chorus represents the polarized opposition of genders and interacts with individual characters. The humor of this piece turns on the social chaos that ensues when the genders clash and on the question of how that chaos may be processed, reorganized, and resolved. The suit for breach of promise is a brilliant choice for crystallizing this dramatic conflict around a point of law.

Edwin (the Defendant) and Angelina (the Plaintiff) are conventionally named, blatant stereotypes of the couple who have fallen out. James Ellis reminds us that this naming convention dates back at least to Oliver Goldsmith, but "Gilbert was more immediately thinking of a pair of newlyweds, Edwin and Angelina Brown, who had appeared in a long series in *Fun* entitled 'Letters from a Young Married Lady.'"[10] Thus the list of dramatis personae immediately forecasts the gendered conflict to come, while evoking a sense of critical detachment in the audience, since these roles refer to a joke both familiar and up-to-date.

Despite its lightness, *Trial by Jury* is ambitious in the scope of its critique. Portraying the social organization of gender specifically *as a system*, the piece demonstrates that masculine and feminine performances are constituted in relation to each other—like parts within a theatrical ensemble— and perpetuated, along with the inequities they represent, through cultural institutions, discourses, and genres.[11] The ensemble stereotypes represent the pattern of social relations at its most schematic, and they tacitly suggest that both the gender-specific plot and the gender relations sketched in *Trial by Jury* have been repeated to the point of easy familiarity. Both Edwin and Angelina play up their roles, acting out a cultural narrative that has been rehearsed for decades in advance of this particular trial, in the melodramatic theater and the novel. The utter familiarity of the roles, in other words, is a large part of the joke.

Thus the metatheatrical humor is not merely analogical, for not only is the courtroom *like* a theater, but action in the courtroom is *determined by* the theater. Composed of recognizable roles, plots, and rationales, the trial for breach of promise is a ritualized cultural performance, thoroughly understood as such by all its participants. We see this when the Counsel for the Plaintiff introduces Angelina's claim. He disingenuously pretends that this case is extraordinary, while revealing its humdrum familiarity:

> ... I never had a notion
>   That a man could be so base,
> Or deceive a girl, confiding,
>   Vows, *etcetera*, deriding!

His *"etcetera"* blandly gestures to the formulaic nature of this narrative, which falls well within the audience's horizon of expectations. Only this shorthand is needed to conjure the familiar story, which exerts its generic force so suddenly that the Usher and Jury immediately side with the Plaintiff. This is the central comic notion of *Trial by Jury*—that the narrative of seduction and the suit for breach of promise exert a conventional force so powerful that impartial judgment is simply impossible. This genre of trial *will always* be prejudged, for the story is already written. Instantly assuming the guilt of the Defendant, the Jury greets him, *"shaking their fists"* and threatening, "Monster, dread our damages!"

Edwin protests against this reaction, since the Jury has not yet heard his side of the story. They jovially agree to hear it now, and, gathering around the Defendant, they listen as he sings his autobiographical confession while strumming a prop guitar. The "Defendant's Song" is a parody of a minstrel number, with a vocal refrain that employs nonsense syllables to suggest the plucking of guitar strings: "Tink-a-Tank, Tink-a-Tank, Tink-a-Tank!" During Edwin's song, the Jury assumes the characteristic arc-like pose of the minstrel lineup, literally backing up the defendant physically and musically, to signify that they also back him up ideologically (plate 5, lower half).[12] One promptbook for *Trial by Jury* confirms this intention in a telling annotation to the "Defendant's Song": "At 'Tink-a-Tank' the Jury affect to be playing a guitar. The man on the right affects to be playing a taborine [*sic*] & the one on the left to be playing the bones."[13] But even without recourse to this evidence, we can hear the minstrel parody in the rolling, tumbling musical figure in the woodwinds following each choral echo. The aura of condescending mimicry from the minstrel show transfers itself to the Defendant, exposing his absurd self-justifications as a parody of conventional masculinity. In other words, the comment on gender is conveyed through a genre parody, for minstrelsy is itself a genre of burlesque, and the courtroom is one of its favorite settings.[14] Thus the "Defendant's Song" is a genre parody of a broader and "lower" form of burlesque. *Trial by Jury*, therefore, blends the minstrel show into its generic mix, prefiguring English comic opera by positioning itself as higher than the minstrel show, yet lower than the cantata.

The Defendant blandly confesses that he did indeed jilt Angelina ("When first my old, old love I knew"). As he explains, when his passion cooled, she "became a bore intense," at which point he "became / Another's love-sick boy." Later, in his second song ("Oh, gentlemen, listen, I pray"), he justifies his inconstancy by arguing that it is only natural to change partners ("Of nature the laws I obey, / For nature is constantly changing"). Some critics have called this self-justification "Rabelaisian," emphasizing its appetitive gusto.[15] But I see it as part of the critique of gender and the law. In the Defendant's self-justification, in other words, "nature" is proposed as a system of law, while it has also been reduced to—and made the euphemism for—roving male sexual appetite.

That the Jurymen are swayed "as a body" in their opinion is indicated in performance by their swaying to the music, first to the Plaintiff's and then to the Defendant's. Although their vacillations can be rationalized as the usual back-and-forth vicissitudes of a Jury making up its mind, they also reveal the powerful force of convention, shaping collective judgment. While listening to the "Defendant's Song," for example, the Jury identifies with him, but then disavows that very identification; at first they relish the Defendant's rakish bravado, conspiratorially murmuring ("Ah, sly dog!") while fondly recalling their own wilder days, but then they affirm their grown-up respectability instead:

> Oh! I was like that when a lad!
> A shocking young scamp of a rover,
> I behaved like a regular cad;
> But that sort of thing is all over.
> I'm now a respectable chap
> And shine with a virtue resplendent
> And, therefore, I haven't a scrap
> Of sympathy with the defendant!

Their recognition of their identification fuels their reaction against it. Here *Trial by Jury* cagily suggests that in a representative group of males ("a jury of his peers"), all will be implicated in the Defendant's crime. At the same time, all will want to deny that implication in the name of respectability. When the Jury does its next about-face and returns to support the Plaintiff, in other words, they are motivated by the desire to purify themselves of their own past behavior, now ruled out of order. In this humorous staging of the swaying vicissitudes of sympathy and judgment, we can see a satire on the sexual double standard (and on Victorian respectability in general), characterized as the product of denial and disavowal. These arguments are theatrically embodied in the swaying of the male Chorus, their choral murmuring, and their conspiratorial "asides" to the audience.

The punch line of *Trial by Jury* comes early in the piece, when the Learned Judge reveals that he, too, is guilty of breach of promise. The dynamic of complicity and disavowal that we have observed in the Jury is writ large in the autobiographical confession of the Learned Judge ("When I, good friends, was called to the bar"). Like the Jury, but much more explicitly, he is guilty of the crime being tried; like the Defendant and the Jury, he glibly confesses. This parody of professional autobiographical confession would become a staple in Savoy opera. As one critic has aptly put it, the characters who sing these autobiographical lyrics confess to things usually kept under wraps, as if they were "under some compulsion to speak the truth."[16] Like the Jury's confession, the "Judge's Song" shows that the process of becoming a successful professional may be nothing more than the disavowal of past behavior—venal at best, criminal at worst, and definitely gender based.

The Judge enters to a musical parody of Handel, as the joined Choruses welcome him ("All hail great Judge!"). This sets the scene for the comic deflation that follows in the "Judge's Song." Elaborating on an imitation of English oratorio, the Choruses repeatedly beg him to tell the story of how he came to be a judge. Frustrated with their seemingly endless repetition of their request—which is part of the Handel parody—the Judge interrupts with a petulant demand: "Let me speak." Then another great Handelian flourish is punctured by the humorously nonoperatic voice of the comic baritone. This is funny on the face of things—or in the ear of things—but its abstract point is more important. For the Judge, associated with greatness by the Handelian entrance music, is in fact small, unimpressive, and peculiar. This radical disparity between the embodied social actor and the role he is given to perform must be played to the hilt, for it conveys an important aspect of the political satire, whose mockery is not so much aimed at *this* particular Judge, but at the corruption of the profession, undermined from within by individuals falling short of their exalted roles.

His characterization is, just as Lord Chief Justice Cockburn feared, "calculated to bring the Bench into contempt."

Very much like Gilbert himself, who was a failed barrister before he became a comic journalist and playwright, this Judge was formerly "an impecunious party" who feared that he "should never hit on a chance / Of addressing a British Jury." His eventual success demonstrates that pecuniary motives for romantic engagement belong to men as well as to women. He reports matter-of-factly on his stratagem for professional advancement: "So I fell in love with a rich attorney's / Elderly, ugly daughter."

> The rich attorney, he jumped with joy,
>   And replied to my fond professions:
> "You shall reap the reward of your pluck, my boy
>   At the Bailey and Middlesex Sessions.
> You'll soon get used to her looks," said he,
>   "And a very nice girl you'll find her!
> She may very well pass for forty-three
>   In the dusk, with a light behind her!"
> . . .
> At length I became as rich as the Gurneys—
>   An incubus then I thought her,
> So I threw over that rich attorney's
>   Elderly, ugly daughter.
> The rich attorney my character high
>   Tried vainly to disparage—
> And now, if you please, I'm ready to try
>   This Breach of Promise of Marriage!

With a pun on "fond professions" (professions of love, profession in the law), the song emphasizes the illicit overlap of romantic engagement and professional advancement. "It was managed by a job," he confesses pianissimo, to which the Chorus echoes, "And a good job, too!" For audiences in 1875, "a job" indicated the betrayal of public trust for individual gain. Rhyming "job" with "mob" and "nob," Gilbert's "Bab" humor continues its simplistic, bobbing rhythm. Finally, the "Judge's Song" reaches the height of its mock-heroic grandeur when he boasts—with fatuous, childish, bravado—"now I am a Judge!" and the Chorus echoes, "And a good Judge too!"

Even the gross misogyny with respect to the "elderly, ugly daughter" must be understood as part of a critique that has a distinctly feminist edge. The misogyny belongs to the Judge's voice, so the exposure of his self-serving

FIGURE 2.1 Angelina makes her feminine appeal to the Counsel for the Plaintiff in *Trial by Jury*, watched by the Chorus of Jurors on one side and the Chorus of Bridesmaids on the other. Engraving by D. H. Friston, in *Illustrated Sporting and Dramatic News*, May 1, 1875. (Collection of Fredric Woodbridge Wilson)

character encompasses that misogyny in its critique. The Judge's confession makes it plain that the middle-aged female figure has been ill-used by father and suitor alike, who seal a professional pact through the exchange of her hand.[17] Drawing this comparison among the Defendant, the Jury, and the Judge, *Trial by Jury* argues for their collusion in an unspoken system of male power, arising from the masculine wish, or even will, to make personal inclination into law.

The mercenary motives of the male professional exceed those of the abandoned Plaintiff, in other words, which goes directly to the heart of the parody of the suit for breach of promise, as we shall see. But the feminine position is lampooned as well. For the Plaintiff is not without her own resources—beauty, a seductive dependence, and her impeccable performance of "the cheated maid," a performance demanded in this genre. The stage directions emphasize her role-playing, as she appeals with flirtatious vulnerability first to one man and then to another. First she "*falls sobbing on* COUNSEL'S *breast and remains there*" (figure 2.1). Then, while she is being installed in the witness box, she *"reels as if about to faint,"* whereupon the foreman of the Jury offers her solace, and she *"falls sobbing on to [his] breast."* *"Kissing her,"* the foreman of the Jury interprets his attraction as paternalistic ("Just like a father / I wish to be"). At this point, the Judge, *"approaching her,"* offers his own support ("Or, if you'd rather, / Recline on me!"). She quickly *"jumps on to Bench, sits down by the* JUDGE, *and falls sobbing on his breast."*[18] This feminine act is surely meant to be regarded as another form of special pleading, as humorous in its own way as the Defendant's absurd self-justifications. An abandoned woman in search of a new protector creates a palpable sense of chaos, where there should be "order in the court." Thus *Trial by Jury* provides a little allegory of the legal system attempting to process the systematic disorder of gender inequity, as male profligacy and female dependence are so clearly related.

Melodrama and the Breach of Promise

The suit for breach of promise represents—and purports to solve—a set of difficult social problems. As the double senses of "suit" and "courtship" suggest, love shades into law during the delicate period leading up to marriage. The promise is a telling example of performative language, but it performs only when specified consequences are subsequently enacted. In this sense, the performative "I do" of the marriage ceremony seals a pact that is prefigured by a previous promise, the engagement.[19] In the suit for breach of promise, an award of monetary damages attempts to cover the breach that opens when another kind of suit is left unfulfilled.

The case for breach of promise both reveals and conceals the evidence of gender inequity at the heart of the law. Susie Steinbach has described this paradox: by interpreting the promise to marry as a contractual obligation, the law attempts to hide—while at the same time to redress—the severe disability engendered on the woman as a contracting party.[20] In the nineteenth century, since a woman could not enter into a legal contract, she was never an active party to the pseudo-contract of the marriage promise, but only the passive recipient of it. If the promise was broken, the woman was without recourse under the provisions of contract law. In other words, the suit for breach of promise was a sort of nonce spin-off, deriving from an analogy with contract law. Without explicit acknowledgment of its function, the legal procedure for breach of promise negotiated a few ideological gaps, conceptualizing man and woman, individual and family, love and money in relation to one another in a newly modern way.

Breach of promise evolved in order to address inequities of gender at a time when gender itself was in transition, coming into the foreground that it would occupy in the mid-nineteenth century. Put very simply, the historical emergence of companionate marriage (marriage based on affection as opposed to family alliance) accompanied the rise of the middle classes (and, in the history of genres, the rise of the novel and melodrama). During this long transition, marriage became more individualized and romanticized, yet also rationalized as a market phenomenon. While the premium put on female chastity remained in force, individual women were gradually accorded more responsibility for their choice of a mate. This emergent freedom of choice for the woman was hardly free, however, insofar as it depended on residual forms of honor in the man ("honorable intentions") that could not be enforced. As middle-class women passed from father to husband, they were particularly vulnerable. But women in the lower and working classes were more vulnerable still, to rape or seduction and abandonment. The nineteenth-century literary and discursive obsession with the figure of the "fallen woman" represents one long imaginative attempt to mediate this seemingly intractable social problem. The suit for breach of promise represents another.

In the background (both psychologically and historically) of the breach of promise suit lurked the possibility of the other, unmentionable, and more physical sort of breach. If a woman had actually been "seduced"—if her virginity had been breached, whether by rape or by her own willingness—she was from that time irrevocably "fallen." However, if she had simply been jilted, she could recover her status. In other words, "seduction" and, to some extent, even "engagement" are euphemisms for sexual entanglement, and the breach of promise existed to cover a wide variety of these situations.[21]

In the early decades of the nineteenth century, melodramas of seduction and abandonment routinely depicted a rapacious male aristocrat and his unwilling female victim—a village girl, servant, ward, or wife of a commoner—any "helpless and unfriended" woman whose vulnerable femininity could stand in for the vulnerabilities of an outraged and rising working class.[22] In these early days of the genre's development, in other words, the melodramatic opposition between good and evil was highlighted as a graphic difference in class as well as gender. The sheer repetition of this melodramatic plot makes it clear that early melodrama existed in part to mediate the decline of the aristocracy and the rise of class consciousness through the representative figures of gender. In one respect, then, the history of melodrama is a history of considering, attempting to come to terms with, and actively constructing the modern cultural categories of class and gender (as well as nation, which we will consider in later chapters).

The helpless, victimized woman was often the epicenter of melodrama. By the mid-nineteenth century, when middle-class values clearly had come to dominate, melodrama tended to focus its politics around this center, and class yielded to gender as the central term of analysis. Similarly, seduction yielded to breach of promise as the dominant version of the story. However, the earlier, even more dangerous plots were still very palpably felt in the background.[23] Thus the suit for breach of promise represents a link between class and gender disparities in the law. In *Trial by Jury*, the ideological contradictions inherent in this situation are suggested. When is a contract not a contract? When one of the principal parties is a woman. Can virginity be reconstructed and chastity restored? Yes, through certain forms of ritual (legal) theater. These absurdities are gathered up in *Trial by Jury* and generalized as an overarching contradiction between Love and Law, but actual, historical law is saddled with the task of rationalizing the irrational impulses of sexual attraction and the irrational absurdities of ideological contradiction.

Purportedly, the monetary damages sought in a breach of promise suit were meant to repair the damage to the woman's reputation. Sullied by previous engagement and rejection, a jilted woman was "damaged goods" on the marriage market. She was "ruined," and her chances for future marriage were nullified. According to this logic, the award of damages in court restored the virtuous victim to the ranks of the eligible, transforming her into a marriageable innocent again. Figuratively speaking, the monetary damages symbolically reversed the damage to her reputation—and, by implication, to her body. The monetary award healed the hymeneal breach and restored virginity after the fact. The attribution of virtue was granted retroactively, the result of a successful performance that unfolds in and through the legal proceeding itself.[24] This uncanny ritual of restoration virtually turned back the clock—and was therefore literally preposterous—in order to endow the plaintiff with a new beginning.

In order to achieve this result, the woman had to present a persuasive performance of feminine virtue, signified conventionally through her heartbroken abjection. "Heartbreak," in other words, was the guarantor of—and the euphemism for—her damaged virtue (itself a euphemism). The compensation for acting sincerely heartbroken was the "heart balm" of monetary damages. Thus in assessing its award of damages, the jury had to decide precisely how "heartbroken" the plaintiff was. To what extent had she been misled in her engagement? How irreparably wounded was she? How inconsolable? These factors had to be taken into account, along with the question of the defendant's lost value—financial and relational—as a potential husband. Thus the conundrum of how to put a monetary value on romantic attachment clearly covered—and covered for—the issue of female economic dependence. This nineteenth-century notion of heartbreak and mental suffering was the romantic side of a coin whose obverse was a tough-minded focus on the financial value of the promise and its power (or lack of it) to seal a deal on the marriage market.

By 1875, when *Trial by Jury* was produced, its scenario was extremely familiar, "as close to contemporary life as the morning newspaper."[25] Indeed, upcoming trials for breach of promise were announced in local newspapers. These trials were so common that their outcome seems to have been determined in advance: the woman would win, especially if she was beautiful and charming, and she would be awarded monetary damages.[26] The historical record clearly supports this contemporary assumption. As Steinbach's research shows, the breach of promise suit "worked well for women for the first two-thirds of the nineteenth century." Her data demonstrate that from 1780 to 1869, the cases that reached trial had a success rate of 87 percent.[27] It is important to see that the utter familiarity of the suit bespeaks the generic, shaping pressure that this conventional story exerted on each individual case.

Steinbach shows that the success or failure of any breach of promise suit depended to a great extent on how close the performances in the courtroom conformed to roles familiar from the melodramatic theater. Furthermore, the participants in a breach of promise case fully recognized that they were engaged in staging a performance and following a conventional script. It was well understood that the outcome of the trial depended not so much on the facts of the case as on the skill with which counsels could manipulate their narratives of the courtship in order to approximate or refute the stock melodramatic plot of seduction and abandonment.[28] Steinbach puts the point this way: "[T]he breach of contract suit worked structurally, independent of the particularities of a case. The suit encompassed contractual and romantic notions of marriage in ways that allowed women who seemed sincerely in love to triumph without being of perfect virginity or virtue." In a profound sense, the theatrical appearance of virtue was much more important than the facts of the case.

The year 1869 marked a "turning point in the history of breach of promise," as Steinbach's research has shown.[29] That year Parliament passed a law, the Evidence Further Amendment Act, which expanded the kinds of evidence allowable in court. Previously considered too interested to be eligible to give evidence, now the parties to a breach of promise suit could testify, as long as their evidence was "corroborated by some other material evidence." This change in the law was explicitly designed to make it easier for plaintiffs to sue. And it accomplished that goal: "Around the country, newspapers report significantly more accounts of breach of promise cases, local and otherwise, in 1869 and 1870 than in previous years. . . . [S]uddenly breach of promise cases were much more in the public eye than they had been before." But although the number of cases increased, the percentage of winning plaintiffs and the size of their awards decreased. Most important for my argument, there were widespread attacks on the principle of breach of promise itself, suggesting that the expansion of the law's coverage had called forth a popular reaction against it. Steinbach's analysis shows that the hostility to breach of promise from 1870 to 1900 went far beyond criticism of weak cases and was aimed at the action in general. Between 1879 and 1890, five bills were introduced to abolish breach of promise altogether. (It was finally abolished in 1970.)

Trial by Jury participated actively in this cultural conversation, and it is notable for engaging on the woman's side of the debate. In *Charity* and *Ought We to Visit Her?* (both produced in 1874), the social-problem plays he wrote just before *Trial by Jury*, Gilbert vehemently attacked the sexual double standard. Soon, in his best comedy, *Engaged* (1877), he would expose romance as the flimsiest cover for financial and social competition and greed. As in *Trial by Jury*, the principal women in *Engaged* are conniving and mercenary. But also as in *Trial by Jury*, *Engaged* parodies the elaborate act demanded of women who strive for a middle-class future. *Engaged* does not single out the female part for critique, in other words, but coolly analyzes the entire, systematic sham of courtship. Similarly, Gilbert saw both sides of the case for breach of promise—its absurdly overdetermined, repetitive familiarity, as well as the inequities that enforced its seemingly endless reiteration. Gilbert was sympathetic to the woman's position in actual cases of breach of promise and was known to have backed his Chorus members in suits of this kind.[30]

Of course, Gilbert was by no means the first writer to parody the suit for breach of promise. Charles Dickens vividly conjured the ever-present danger to his male characters, using the familiar joke about scheming women entangling innocent men in the suit for breach of promise. Most audience members at *Trial by Jury* would have recalled the humorously absurd characterization of Mr. Pickwick as a "ruthless destroyer" and the demand against him for "damages, gentlemen, . . . heavy damages!" In the case of *Bardell v. Pickwick*, the innocent Pickwick is required to pay £750 to Mrs. Bardell—a huge award.[31] Although the suit depicted in *The Pickwick Papers* (1836–1837) is the best-known example of Dickens's comic use of the breach of promise, it is by no means the only one.[32]

The focus of the absurdity in *Trial by Jury* is strikingly different from that in Dickens's novels. I agree with Andrew Goodman, who argues emphatically that its treatment of breach of promise was more daring at the time than Gilbert has been given credit for.[33] But it was not audacious because it was introducing a new topic. Indeed, its relentless focus on the utterly conventional familiarity of the case is a large part of what was daring about it. But more striking is its revision of the popular gender politics of the conventional suit. Dickens highlights the danger to men. His humor depends for its intelligibility on his comic inversion of the commonsense understanding—and, indeed, the social fact—that courtship is more dangerous for women than for men. Gilbert overturns Dickens's satirical critique while preserving its logic. In *Trial by Jury*, he outdoes—or at least updates—Dickens by exposing the old-boys' network of male power relations. In his characterizations of the Defendant, Judge, and Jury, Gilbert finds a less conventional and more contemporary villain than the rapacious melodramatic seducer of old or the innocent, victimized male of Dickens's novels. He twists the plot of seduction and abandonment inside out to expose another sort of social problem in the systematic abuse of power within a network of men that cements their relations with one another through the exchange of women.

In other words, *Trial by Jury* is not the complacent representation it is sometimes taken to be, but an exposure of the force of generic conventions in theatrical and social life. The systematic relation of male characters, with their absurd rationalizations for their actions, is the comic villain of the piece. Caught within their network, the Plaintiff's only weapons are her beauty and her willingness to play the hackneyed female role of the "broken flower," the "cheated maid," the "helpless and unfriended" melodramatic heroine. Her feminine act of solicitation and dependence, while also parodied, is comprehended as a necessary response of the weaker party to a nonbinding pseudo-contractual engagement. Furthermore, the law is lampooned for lubriciously covering male "nature"; after all, the "elderly, ugly daughter" is discarded as part of the back story, and the plot's resolution is achieved with the Judge's "rapture" as he claims the Plaintiff for his own. That these familiar facts of life cannot be seen for what they are highlights the daring of the piece, which insists on exposing what the law attempts to cover up. The Usher's demand—"Silence in court!"—is a joke with a serious double meaning.

Thus *Trial by Jury* comes to its crisis in the legal bickering about the award of monetary damages. True to type, the Plaintiff argues that she is inconsolable:

I love him—I love him—with fervour unceasing
    I worship and madly adore;
My blind adoration is always increasing,
    My loss I shall ever deplore.
Oh, see what a blessing, what love and caressing
    I've lost, and remember it, pray,
When you I'm addressing, are busy assessing
    The damages Edwin must pay!

To these plaintive words, sung while *"embracing him rapturously,"* the Defendant offers his plea in abatement. While *"repelling her furiously,"* he argues that he would have been worthless as a husband:

I smoke like a furnace—I'm always in liquor,
    A ruffian—a bully—a sot;
I'm sure I should thrash her, perhaps I should kick her,
    I am such a very bad lot!
I'm not prepossessing, as you may be guessing,
    She couldn't endure me a day;
Recall my professing, when you are assessing
    The damages Edwin must pay!

This song stresses the oddity of the modern attempt to equate love and money, taking it to its reductio ad absurdum. The Plaintiff's loss of love is even humorously equated with her capital outlay during courtship, when it is discovered that the Defendant abandoned her quite late in the game:

Doubly criminal to do so,
For the maid had bought her *trousseau!*

The Jury, shaking their fists at the Defendant, promises "substantial damages, / Dam"—a truncated judgment, reduced to a curse, which the Usher interrupts with his characteristically repressive refrain: "Silence in Court!"

Grand Transformation Scene

A parodic justice does emerge in the end. Like most comic endings, the resolution of *Trial by Jury* turns on marriage, which in this case repairs the breach of promise. But the resolution is hilariously sudden, suggesting just how irrational it is. In the end, that very irrationality is wonderfully expressed in a parody of the extravaganza transformation scene.[34]

Rapidly winding up, *Trial by Jury* reels through a sequence of three different ways to resolve the legal issue, each of them absurd. (As in *Thespis*, the three-part crescendo of absurd suggestions both postpones and prepares for closure.) First, the Defendant offers to "marry this lady to-day / And . . . marry that lady to-morrow!" Counsel objects, citing legal precedent:

> In the reign of James the Second,
> It was generally reckoned
> As a rather serious crime
> To marry two wives at a time.

He hands a law book to the Judge, to prove this obvious point, while the female Chorus rapturously admires the "man of learning!" Second, the quartet ("A nice dilemma we have here") enacts a parody of legal reasoning through its musical parody of the Italian operatic "dilemma" ensemble. The intricate involvement of voices in this number imitates several legal minds at work on the same complex problem. Of course, the content is itself absurd, as if breach and bigamy were two horns of a legal dilemma, but the form makes it all the funnier. Third, as we have seen, the Defendant argues that he would have been a drunken wife beater instead of a good husband. But the Judge takes it seriously as a legal argument, and proposes an experiment:

> The question, gentlemen—is one of liquor;
>   You ask for guidance—this is my reply:
> He says, when tipsy, he would thrash and kick her,
>   Let's make him tipsy, gentlemen, and try!

Suddenly, *Trial by Jury* threatens to become an opéra bouffe, with this proposal of trial by intoxication. Not surprisingly, both the Plaintiff and her Counsel object. At this point, the Judge throws up his hands, both figuratively and literally. "*Tossing his books and papers about*," he offers his resolution of the dilemma:

> Put your briefs upon the shelf,
> I will marry her myself!

He then lifts Angelina up to the high seat of authority on "the Bench." Thus has Angelina managed her upward mobility into the protective bosom of the law.

In 1875, the audience would have recognized a parody of the extravaganza transformation scene in the visual humor of *Trial by Jury*'s conclusion. Suddenly, the courtroom set is transformed into a wedding cake, with the Plaintiff and the Learned Judge posing on top as the conventional figurines of bride and groom. A contemporary sheet-music cover gives us an idea of how this transformation was accomplished—simply by raising the Judge's bench and festooning it with the Bridesmaids' floral garlands (plate 5, upper half).[35] The promptbook for *Trial by Jury* in the British Library confirms that this closing scene was meant as a parody, for a handwritten notation enthusiastically exclaims, "GRAND TRANSFORMATION SCENE!"[36] The stage directions in the first-edition libretto elaborate:

> JUDGE and PLAINTIFF *dance back, hornpipe step, and get on to the Bench—the* BRIDESMAIDS *take eight garlands of roses from behind the* JUDGE'S *desk, and draw them across floor of Court, so that they radiate from the desk. Two plaster Cupids in bar wigs descend from flies. Red fire.*

The "trick change to Fairyland" was even more elaborate in the two promptbooks that Ian Bradley examined from the D'Oyly Carte archives, which include further details of a wild mélange of genre parodies (the Bridesmaids "clap their hands à la Minstrels," and the "Plaintiff gets on Judge's back à la fairy") as well as further special stage effects, using revolving pieces, fan pieces, a canopy, cloths coming down, and a rise coming up—all employed to transform the realistic courtroom into another realm altogether.[37] Alluding to this transformation scene, the opening-night program pictures Gilbert and Sullivan as the tutelary cupids, in bar wigs, hovering around Selina Dolaro, "directress" of the Royalty Theatre, where *Trial by Jury* was performed (figure 2.2).

Parody is notoriously ambivalent, characterized always by both imitation and critique. And, indeed, this parody of the extravaganza transformation scene cuts both ways, simultaneously enchanting and disenchanting, inflating and deflating its object. As critique, this parody of an extravaganza transformation scene comments on the real world in all its lowly disenchantment, suggesting that love is nothing more than mercenary roleplaying and that law is only a form of theater. As imitation of the extravaganza transformation, however, the same parody suggests that marriage is an effective form of ritual renewal and that the comic happy ending transforms the social world as if by magic. That the realistic courtroom of *Trial*

FIGURE 2.2 Gilbert (*right*) and Sullivan figure as cupids flanking Selina Dolaro, "directress" of the Royalty Theatre, an allusion to the finale transformation scene, when cupids hover over the Learned Judge's bench, turned into a wedding cake (see plate 5). Detail from the first-run program for *Trial by Jury* (1875). (Collection of Fredric Woodbridge Wilson)

by Jury could transform itself into a wedding cake suggests that marriage provides the only fairy-tale happy ending available in the real, modern world. Thus (within the logic of this parody) marriage replaces Fairyland, as the ensemble celebrates ("To castle moated / Away they go"). Indeed, when their love was new, Edwin and Angelina experienced its power to transform the real social world:

> Camberwell became a bower,
> Peckham an Arcadian Vale,
> Breathing concentrated otto!—
> An existence *à la* Watteau.

Now the realm of Law has been transformed into the realm of Love. Of course, this is not realistic; the ending depends on fantasy, like its generic precursor.

Through its parody of the transformation scene, *Trial by Jury* escapes from its own critical arguments into a realm of happy fantasy. No damages are awarded, but neither has the Plaintiff been damaged herself. She is explicitly defined as "designed for Capture," and in the end she is willingly recaptured by male desire. The rhyming moral of that story is the Judge's "one word—Rapture." There is no longer any hint of rapacity in this "rapture," for the Judge, too, has been transformed through the topsy-turvy inversion of realms. When the courtroom is transformed into a wedding cake, he is recast as another kind of judge—a judge of female beauty. These new, frivolous standards of judgment are visual, theatrical, and conventionally gendered, as the Usher points out when he sings:

> It seems to me, sir,
> Of such as she, sir,
> A judge is he, sir,
> > And a good judge too!

Once the standards of judgment themselves have been parodically inverted and transformed, the Judge really *is* a "good Judge, too." In the end, sex appeal takes precedence over law as an organizing principle of social life, with an ethical shrug that is the essence of extravaganza:

> Though homeward as you trudge,
> You declare my law is fudge,
> Yet of beauty I'm a judge.

At this point, the entire company agrees, with their triumphant, concluding reprise: "And a good Judge too!"

3

English Magic, English Intoxication

The Sorcerer

The "formula" for the novel genre created by Gilbert and Sullivan falls into place with *The Sorcerer* (1877).[1] Some of the important ingredients can already be tasted in both *Thespis* and *Trial by Jury*. But only in *The Sorcerer* is the recipe set out in the form that would become known as English comic opera, Savoy opera, or simply Gilbert and Sullivan. Before exploring how *The Sorcerer* identifies itself as quintessentially English, I want to highlight the defining elements of that formula. In light of *The Sorcerer*'s plot, which features a magical elixir sold by a successful company, we might consider the following list as a product's secret formula or as a catalogue of items for sale. Hence the word "formula" aptly conveys both the transformative effect of combining certain reactive ingredients—as in chemistry, cookery, or a magical elixir—and its popular, commercial nature, its aim to fulfill audience expectations again and again. In both cases, the whole is more than the sum of its various parts.

From *The Sorcerer* on, Savoy opera will be known for

- An ensemble of specifically typed characters
- Unusually lavish costumes and set designs
- Exceptionally precise performance standards in the acting, singing, and dancing, achieved through unusually rigorous rehearsal
- Alternation of prose dialogue with musical numbers
- Musical numbers that emerge from and contribute to the dramatic action (rather than merely illustrating or interrupting the plot)
- A new and enhanced role for the Chorus, which becomes a full and characterized participant in the dramatic action

- A Chorus divided into male and female cohorts
- An emphasis on choruses and ensembles in the musical structure, especially in the elaborate finales to act 1
- Great variety in song styles and rhythms (like a catalogue, an anthology, or a "songbook")
- Parodies of past literary, theatrical, and musical genres
- Social satire and parodies of gender, class, and national identities (gentle or cutting, depending on directorial choice and individual spectator response)
- Plots that depend on absurdity, yet are coherently governed by internal consistency
- A new style of acting that highlights the parody with its deadpan pretense of naturalism, no matter how absurd the dramatic situation
- An absence of broad, crude, or indecent humor; like the exaggerated pretense of natural acting, the elaborately chaste nature of the humor could sometimes itself appear as patently absurd[2]

Some of these formal characteristics would themselves have been recognized as particularly English. For example, the alternation of spoken dialogue and musical numbers was a native English format for opera, starting at least as early as English ballad opera of the early eighteenth century, of which John Gay's *The Beggar's Opera* (1728) will always be the canonical example. The mock-heroic intent of *The Beggar's Opera* works in two ways, as it elevates low figures of English life by making them the focus of an opera, while its formal dynamics, as everybody immediately realized, deflate the pretensions of Italian opera with an alternative English form. The tradition of English ballad opera after the era of Gay includes the pastoral strain exemplified in Isaac Bickerstaffe's *Love in a Village* (1763), as well as the so-called English Ring—composed of Michael Balfe, William Wallace, and Julius Benedict—whose operas kept the form popular in the decades before the Savoy collaborations. In other words, the form of the Savoy operas seems in part to continue this domestic tradition and form.

But the specifically English character of English comic opera is even more strongly felt through its parodic assimilation of styles, topics, stories, and music from other traditions, both native and foreign. If a sense of nationalism may be created through—and, in turn, creates—an "imagined community," the very imagination of community depends on the opposition, implicit or explicit, of an inside to an outside, a national identity to its external, thereby "foreign," competitors.[3] In the nineteenth century, the English keenly felt their national identity damaged by the absence of a national music. A great deal of worried journalistic attention was devoted to this supposed lack, so much that only now is the assumption that Victorian England was "das Land ohne Musik" beginning to be reexamined.[4] The Savoy operas jest with that concern, while creating a national style at the same time. Their fundamental dynamic of parodic assimilation and critique makes each opera part of a cosmopolitan conversation.

Like the Victorian culture of exhibition, the musical-theatrical genre imports artifacts from elsewhere, displaying them in the metropolitan center of England and offering a sort of stay-at-home tourism.[5] Its form of accumulating cultural capital is closely aligned with capital accumulation of the economic kind, and Savoy opera should be regarded as a late Victorian, imperial collection that exhibits a dynamic of consumption and digestion. While absorbing so much, like an overfilled Victorian parlor or an over-stuffed Victorian sofa, the Savoy operas were also aware of precisely their own sort of cultural formation. They make fun of cultural pastiche, thus elevating their whole above the sum of its parts. In short, the results are both works of art and commercial products on the market, produced by a successful company. Late-nineteenth-century theatrical genres were increasingly purveyed through specific theaters that came to be known for the kind of fare they offered, and the Savoy operas, while a consummate example of this trend, also transcend it.[6] Enabled by the entrepreneurial vision of Richard D'Oyly Carte, the collaboration between Gilbert and Sullivan was stabilized and well supported enough that the librettist and the composer could work at the height of their creative powers. Their business success, high production values, and aesthetic values developed hand in hand.

Carte often said that creating and sustaining "English comic opera in a theatre devoted to that alone was the scheme of my life."[7] Although the purpose-built theater he envisioned would have to wait until 1882, when the Savoy Theatre opened its doors, Carte could imagine that he might realize his ambition after the huge success of *Trial by Jury* in 1875. He secured contracts with Gilbert and Sullivan that, because of their generous terms, became significant milestones in the history of dramatic authors' rights. The artists demanded a substantial payment for their intellectual labor when the manuscript words and music were delivered and before the work was produced, as well as a set amount of the box-office receipts each night during the run of the piece (minus the amount of the initial payment).[8] Carte, in turn, had the business acumen (and vision) to meet their demands, believing that the unprecedented terms, which entailed an obvious financial risk to him, would turn out to be an investment well rewarded, both for himself and for the cause of native comic opera. In order to raise the capital necessary to launch the project, and in order to divide the risk, Carte persuaded a group of investors to join in a limited-liability company, the Comedy Opera Company, incorporated in 1876. Finally, he leased a serviceable theater, the London Opera Comique, which was centrally located, although inconvenient (practically underground, accessible by means of a tunnel from the Strand).[9]

Why had English comic opera failed to develop until then? In seeking investment capital for his venture, Carte proposed a few reasons.[10] He explained that the best English singers were almost always whisked away from England and drafted onto the Italian stage, whereas the libretti supplied to English composers (Balfe and Wallace, for example) were usually feeble and uninteresting. There was no dearth of English talent in singing, writing, or composing, he argued, but those talents had yet to be joined and produced effectively. Noting the "recent agitation against the more pronounced forms of *opéra bouffe* and burlesque," he argued that the time was now right to support English authors and composers. A fine native composer was already popular, he pointed out, stressing that Sullivan's songs were far more likely to be heard in English drawing rooms than were tunes by Jacques Offenbach or Charles Lecocq. Thus from the start, Carte's enterprise displayed its nationalistic, competitive drive against French and Italian forms of opera. "If it is a great success," Sullivan promised, "it is another nail in the coffin of Opera Bouffe from the French."[11]

Establishing the Comedy Opera Company marked one step forward, but another important step was taken by forming a special company of performers made up of comic actors who could sing well and excellent singers who could act. Again, *The Sorcerer* marks a beginning in this respect, for several of the chief stars of later Savoy operas were first assembled for this production: Richard Temple, Rutland Barrington, and especially George Grossmith—the great comic baritone whose impish capering and droll singing style was first heard in the role of the Sorcerer. As Isaac Goldberg points out, the Savoy ensemble of correlated, typed characters can also be seen in *The Sorcerer* for the first time: "The elderly lady, the elderly admirer, the parted and united pair of youthful lovers, the responsive chorus, the Vicar or Major General or Captain—these were to become as stereotyped as any villain, hero or heroine in an Adelphi melodrama."[12]

Barrington recalled later in life that the "great initial idea was that every soul and every thing connected to the venture should be English." Two choristers even "renounced their Italian titles [that is, their Italian stage names] and became Englishmen for the express purpose of being associated with such an enterprise." Barrington humorously recollected that one chorister was very nearly not hired at all because his name was "Parris." He continues:

"This sentiment inspired us all with a kind of patriotic glow combined with a determination to show other nations (and *inter alia* our own) what we could do." As part of this effort, Temple had to be trained out of his habit of using the "Italian production" (or singing style).[13] To make it clear that a new, national style was being proposed, act 1 of *The Sorcerer* was originally meant to end in an elaborate parody of Italian grand opera, with all the singers stretching their hands toward the audience.[14] Sullivan exhorted his performers in rehearsal: "Don't you understand? I want you to think you are at Covent Garden Opera, not at the Opera Comique. I want you, Miss— , to imagine you are Adelina Patti; and you, my dear Grossmith, are dreadful; there is not enough Mario about you." Grossmith understood what he meant and leaned even farther over the footlights. "Capital!" said Sullivan. "Do even more! You needn't consider your safety."[15] So much for the Italian manner. As for French matter, Gilbert once again cleverly pushed against English limits of propriety, all the while acting out a rejection of the risqué subjects familiar in opéra bouffe. All the Savoy operas remain ostentatiously correct while poking fun at English hypercorrectness.

Even an exceedingly brief plot summary will suggest immediately why *The Sorcerer* is an important piece of national musical drama. A magical elixir causes everyone in the village of Ploverleigh to fall into a deep sleep. Upon waking, the villagers fall in love with the first person they see, despite "ill-assorted" differences of age, rank, and class. Needless to say, everyone falls in love with a most unsuitable mate. The magical elixir, administered by the "professional sorcerer," is served from the quintessentially English vehicle of a steaming teapot.

English Magic, English Intoxication

Sullivan's objection to the so-called lozenge plot is now legendary in the commentary tradition on Gilbert and Sullivan. According to Sullivan, Gilbert relied too frequently on the plot device of a magical lozenge—or any other such magical device that could cause a sudden transformation. Of the many versions of this story, I like Mike Leigh's best, represented in a scene from his film *Topsy-Turvy* (1999). The scene is set in 1884, when Gilbert and Sullivan have reached an impasse in their collaboration. Sullivan rejects the new plot that Gilbert has sent him (which later, in 1892, was produced as *The Mountebanks*, with music by Alfred Cellier). Throughout the following scene, their legendary disagreement is represented as personal and temperamental, yet also as entirely principled, abstract, and even theoretical:

GILBERT: . . . Now, would you care for me to read this to you or not? (*He takes out a large bound notebook, which he opens.*)

SULLIVAN (*unenthusiastically*): Where's it set?

GILBERT: In the Sicilian mountains. Plenty of scope there for gypsy music, one might suggest. Now the local alchemist is killed in an explosion, and there, among his effects, a chorus of villagers discover a potion.

SULLIVAN: A magic potion, no doubt.

GILBERT: Indeed.

SULLIVAN: I thought as much.

GILBERT: Now, the effect of this magic potion is to transform the character who takes it into whatever he or she is pretending to be.

SULLIVAN: Oh, Gilbert! You and your world of topsy-turvydom. (*Gilbert laughs.*) In 1881, it was a magic coin; and before that it was a magic lozenge; and in 1877 it was an elixir.

GILBERT: In this instance it is a magic potion.[16]

Sullivan's reference to 1877, of course, is to *The Sorcerer*, which was running in revival (in a slightly revised version) during their stalemate. Sullivan was probably worried that the new opera might seem too much like the older one. Gilbert's use of the lozenge plot in *The Sorcerer* was not a compulsive gesture, however, but a pivotal moment in the formation of the genre. It should be reinterpreted as a kind of manifesto, a sign of the genre's claim to its own English novelty. Alluding to, while transcending, both extravaganza and opéra bouffe, *The Sorcerer* parodies bouffe intoxication and extravaganza transformation, turning those conventions against themselves and combining twisted elements of those precursor genres into a new whole.

In other words, in *The Sorcerer* the fact that a magical elixir is traditional—indeed, conventional, readily recognizable by anyone, even hackneyed as a plot device—is a very large part of the point. Then and now, critical response sometimes misses this point, describing the plot as conventional without seeming to notice that it harps on the convention in order to make fun of it—and to make serious arguments from it as well. Yet some discerning critics, such as the reviewer for the *Times* of November 19, 1877 (two days after opening night), did seize on this point: "The idea of the love potion exists from time immemorial, from Tristan and Iseult, the fate-struck lovers whom Wagner has resuscitated, to the *Philtre* of Auber and the *Elisir d'Amore* of Donizetti. Mr. Gilbert's treatment of the subject, nevertheless, is quite original."[17] This is a particularly modern understanding of parodic "originality," which always depends on citation, allusion, and partial reproduction to make its models recognizable. The critic's awareness of Wagner's version is notable, since *Tristan* had not yet had its English première, and he clearly caught the fact that *The Sorcerer* places itself within several Continental (French, Italian, German), as well as native English, traditions. For the humor of *The Sorcerer* to work, in other words, the device of the magical elixir absolutely must be recognized as hyperconventional, familiar, and even overused.

Insofar as *The Sorcerer* is an English takeoff on Gaetano Donizetti's *L'elisir d'amore* (*The Elixir of Love*, 1832), its sharpest parodic point is that an English elixir has replaced Italian, French, and German ones—for *L'elisir d'amore* itself already participates in the traditional parody of the love potion. When the peasants urge Adina to read them a story, she offers "Della crudele Isotta," the tale of Tristan and Isolde drinking their magical love potion. This scene of reading inspires Nemorino, who asks Dr. Dulcamara if he sells the elixir of love described in Adina's book. Dr. Dulcamara, a mountebank peddling his spurious wares, sells Nemorino a bottle of Bordeaux, which makes him so tipsy that Adina almost marries someone else. Obviously, Donizetti's opera disenchants the story of Tristan and Isolde by transforming the elixir into common wine, sold by an itinerant quack.[18]

In *The Sorcerer*, Gilbert takes the idea of parodic disenchantment one fabulous step further by placing the elixir in an ordinary pot of tea. Tea is the English "national beverage"—much more clearly identifiable as such than the ginger beer that serves a similar function at the end of *Thespis*.[19] In both operas, the joke inheres in ostentatiously turning away from bouffe intoxication toward sober English values, while making fun of the English addiction to sobriety.[20] Neither the red wine of Donizetti nor the "fire-water" of Offenbach will do for an English comic opera.

Twice before *The Sorcerer*, *L'elisir d'amore* had supplied the foundation for Gilbert's parodic treatment. His first opera burlesque, *Dulcamara! or, The Little Duck and the Great Quack*, was performed at the St. James's Theatre in 1866. At that time, Gilbert's career in the theater was only beginning, and *Dulcamara* offers a simple parody of one specific, familiar work. (*The Sorcerer* shows how far Gilbert had come from his opera burlesques, for it blends indebtedness to and difference from several traditions: Italian opera buffa, French opéra bouffe, German melodrama, and English opera burlesque and extravaganza.) A further parody of *L'elisir d'amore* appeared in story form in 1869. "An Elixir of Love" is, then, the most proximate source for *The Sorcerer*'s original plot.[21] In this story, the curate of Ploverleigh rails obsessively against the class system. Wanting to spread this gospel of equality by fostering universal love, he orders a nine-gallon cask of "Oxy-Hydrogen Love-at-first-sight Philtre" from the black-magic firm of Baylis & Culpepper, planning to administer the philter to the entire village. The story highlights the similarity between magical transformation and intoxication, for the housekeeper believes that the cask holds sherry and that the curate is about to give himself up to a "steady course of drinking." His plan backfires, of course. Much of the plot and dialogue of this story also appear in the libretto for *The Sorcerer*. But *The Sorcerer* tones down the anticlerical humor and develops a more hyperbolic comic resolution, multiplying the loving couples, differentiating them by class, and seeing them through their romantic difficulties.

Constance Partlet, the seventeen-year-old daughter of a pew opener, loves the vicar, Dr. Daly, even though he is unsuitably older. She suffers passionately, imagining that he could never love her, while, in turn, he believes himself to be unloved. The aristocratic older characters, Sir Marmaduke Pointdextre and Lady Sangazure, have loved each other for more than fifty years, but their upper-class reticence prevents them from openly acknowledging their mutual passion. By contrast, the young betrothed couple—Sir Marmaduke's son, Alexis, and Lady Sangazure's daughter, Aline—love each other with a modern, flagrantly romantic expressiveness. In *The Sorcerer*, it is Alexis (not the clergyman, as it is in "An Elixir of Love") who envisions a democratic experiment and who hires the Sorcerer to administer his "Patent Oxy-Hydrogen Love-at-first-sight Philtre" to the villagers. Crafting his metaphor in the language of tea preparation, Alexis expresses his plan "to steep the whole village up to its lips in love."

Conveying the boundary-dissolving spell through the vehicle of an English teapot, *The Sorcerer* self-consciously participates in nationalistic genre formation. The Incantation Scene, during the ensemble finale of act 1, makes this very clear. This scene is the apotheosis of Gilbert and Sullivan's efforts to turn both the magical-lozenge plot and the bouffe theme of intoxication toward their new, parodic roles in English comic opera. But the Incantation Scene also pours a Teutonic ingredient into the mix, along with the French, Italian, and English flavors already discussed. When the Sorcerer, John Wellington Wells, announces that "we will proceed at once to the Incantation," the "*stage grows dark*" (plate 6). Appealing to "sprites of earth and air," as well as "fiends of flame and fire," "noisome hags of night," "imps of deadly shade," and "pallid ghosts," the Sorcerer conjures them to "Appear, appear, appear!" Three times he utters the summons, and three times he pours the love potion into the teapot. Each time the potion mixes with the tea, there is a sudden "*flash*."

The special effects are meant to be thrilling, but also humorously cheesy and conventional. Most members of the audience would have recognized this scene as genre parody, for the Summoning of the Spirits was a stock scene in supernatural melodrama, popular since the first two decades of the nineteenth century, whose effects were "more widely copied than any other in the whole range of the genre."[22] Ian Bradley notes the similarity of *The Sorcerer*'s incantation to the prologue of Heinrich Marschner's opera *Der Vampyr* (1828), while Frank Rahill recalls a more proximate model from James Robinson Planché's *The Vampire; or, The Bride of the Isles* (1819–1820).[23] Both prologues, summoning spirits and immediately placing these plays within their supernatural frameworks, recall the prologue of Goethe's *Faust* (1808). Indeed, the most influential examples of this German Romantic folk demonology were *Faust* and Carl Maria von Weber's *Der Freischütz* (*The Marksman*, 1821), whose "carnival of special effects" made it enormously popular throughout the nineteenth century. There were innumerable imitations, revisions, and spinoffs of Weber's opera, including Edward Fitzball's *The Flying Dutchman* (1826) and *The Devil's Elixir* (1829), from a tale by E. T. A. Hoffmann, as well as, in the Incantation Scene, *The Sorcerer*.

Sullivan set the Incantation Scene to a musical parody of the eerie, atmospheric episode in the Wolf's Glen from *Der Freischütz*, a landmark in the history of German Romantic opera that significantly influenced Wagner. In the Wolf's Glen, the eponymous hero watches while an agent of the devil molds seven magic bullets. Rahill describes this scene very well, with its

> sinister mountain defile where the action passes with its moonlight, its flapping bats and hooting owls; the apparition of the Black Huntsman (surrounded by blue fire) from a trap; the bargaining for a human soul while the demonic fire spits and glows; and the bloodcurdling climax when the final bullet is cast amid the flashing of lightning, the plunging of meteors, and the darting of flames from the bowels of the earth.[24]

It was this sort of over-the-top *son et lumière* to which the parody in *The Sorcerer*'s Incantation Scene alludes. The evocation of the Wolf's Glen episode was to have marked the beginning of a "grand-opera" finale.[25]

Instead, as it is, the villagers drink to the "Tea-Cup Brindisi." Since a *brindisi* is a rousing drinking song, conventional in Italian grand opera, we should again hear in the music Sullivan's joking transformation of bouffe sexuality and intoxication.[26] But these risqué, cosmopolitan forces are twisted into a parody of the English temperance movement, too, especially the attempts to reform alcoholics using rousing songs in praise of tea, water, and other nonintoxicants.[27] Thus the "Tea-Cup Brindisi" gathers up parodic ingredients from French, Italian, and English culture, mixing them up to form a sober English potion, "brewed by the vicar." This English humor about a "pretty stiff jorum of tea" continues as the love philter begins to take effect, and the villagers struggle against its intoxicating effects. They worry that their lack of self-control might lead to unrespectable behavior:

> I must regain my senses,
>   Restoring Reason's law,
> Or fearful inferences
>   Society will draw!

Considering its conversion of risqué material into a sober English form, we can see in this scene a great example of the ambivalence of parody, for it engages in both imitation and critique of both convention and impropriety.

Having explored the conventional aspects of the parody, it is time to ask: What still seemed risky? In 1877, the figure of Dr. Daly, the Vicar of Plover-leigh, hovered on the verge of offending. It was unusual to treat a clergyman with any humor, especially to focus on his love life in anything but the mild-est sentimental vein. Also risky was his "ill-assorted" May–December union, sustained and valorized in the opera's conclusion. Indeed, some observers at the time felt that the character represented a rude satire on the clergy. It may seem strange to us, but one reviewer took Gilbert to task for making "the ear-nest, hard-working, and serious clergy" the subject of a "sneering caricature."[28]

The Reverend Charles Dodgson (Lewis Carroll) was notoriously outraged. Dodgson, who had unsuccessfully attempted to collaborate with Sullivan on a musical version of *Alice's Adventures in Wonderland*,[29] wrote a scathingly vengeful essay for the *Theatre*, waxing so righteous in his indignation that he sounds like a veritable parody of Victorian respectability:

> That clever song, "The Pale Young Curate," with its charming music, is to me simply painful. I seem to see him as he goes home at night, pale and worn with the day's work, perhaps sick with the pestilent atmosphere of a noisome garret where, at the risk of his life, he has been comforting a dying man—and is your sense of humor, my reader, so keen that you can *laugh* at that man?

And so forth, to a near-hysterical crescendo, comparing the "pale young curate" with the "pale young doctor" and the "pale young soldier" who "red-dens the dust with his life-blood for the honor of Old England!"[30] In Dodg-son's rant, we can clearly perceive the co-implication of bourgeois respecta-bility, church piety, and exhortations to national defense. Without Dodgson's self-righteous projection, however, some twentieth-century commentators nevertheless agree that a parody of the clergy was intended.[31]

The reviewer for *Figaro*, however, praised Gilbert's tact in the characterization of Dr. Daly: "By his good taste and freedom from exaggeration, he preserved the character of the Vicar from any suspicion of impropriety."[32] Certainly the portrait of Dr. Daly—the only clergyman represented in the fourteen Savoy operas—represents a complex balancing act. The vicar's sentimentality is appealing, although also the butt of a gentle joke. Dr. Daly is "pastoral" in both senses of the word; his attitudes seem as old-fashioned as the literary resonance of his habit of *"playing on a flageolet."* Indeed, his activities are characterized not by spiritual leadership, but by the regular round of respectable social duties—like pouring tea. In the end, the plot deals kindly with him, for he is rewarded with love and marriage. Thus the ultimate reach of this parodic elixir turns on its highly attenuated association of sensual intoxication with the English Church.

Thus the parody, which mixes so many Continental elements, returns on English attitudes and conventions. The humor of a vicar presiding over the scene of mass intoxication is deliciously English.

The "Professional Sorcerer"

The plot of *The Sorcerer* cleverly divides the labor of administering the elixir between Dr. Daly and John Wellington Wells, the "professional sorcerer." The one represents an old-fashioned type of access to the supernatural, while the other represents a secular form of access to modern magic. As usual with tropes of secularization, change is accompanied by continuity. In this case, the parodic deflation of the elixir—from Tristan's magical potion, to Dulcamara's red wine, to English tea—strongly emphasizes the continuity of an ineffable force, even while its identity is changing. Somehow, even in the modern world, the intoxication of magic lives on. Similarly, the parodic deflation of the person who administers the elixir—a quack doctor, a vicar brewing the magic potion, a "professional sorcerer"—does not negate, but actively conserves, the idea of a magical agent still at work in the modern world.

The figure of the sorcerer reaches back through English supernatural melodrama and German Romanticism to *Faust*. In this tradition, summoning spirits and trading the soul in exchange for supernatural power suggests an evil, overweening heritage for the Sorcerer, while very gently hinting at the Christian lineage on which this parody depends and from which it departs. Gilbert thought that *Faust* was the greatest philosophical poem ever written, and he wrote *Gretchen* (1878), his blank-verse drama "suggested" (as he put it) by Goethe's poem, the year after *The Sorcerer*. But played by George

Grossmith, who created the role, the Sorcerer was parodically spooky during the Incantation Scene, but otherwise predominantly funny. Interviewing for the part, the "wispy, nervous" Grossmith said to Gilbert, "I should have thought you required a fine man with a fine voice." And Gilbert answered, "No, that is just what we don't want."[33] For the physical comedy that characterizes the Sorcerer, Grossmith invented a famous piece of stage business, which Jane Stedman describes as his "chugging round the stage in an absurd crouch with the enchanted teapot." *Punch* called the posture Grossmith's "squatter's-run." And Isaac Goldberg says that he held "the sizzling, charm-brewing tea pot" over his body "like the chimney of a steaming locomotive" (figure 3.1).[34] (Here we might want to imagine Groucho Marx later striding around in his own version of the crouching walk, cigar held high.)

The Sorcerer's crouching walk alludes to the "walk around," an ensemble finale to the minstrel show; indeed, a cartoon of this posture from the *Illustrated Sporting and Dramatic News* is titled "A Walk Round by Mr Grossmith" (figure 3.2). Furthermore, the famous illustration in which the Sorcerer's crazy bug-eyed facial expression frightens the lovers during the Incantation Scene surely alludes not only to gaslight melodrama but also to minstrel black-face makeup (figure 3.3). Gayden Wren, taking this illustration as his starting point, traces through a series of representations of the Sorcerer from 1877 to 1971, arguing that this series shows "graphic evidence of the century-long transformation of an evil figure into a sideshow barker."[35] But, of course, the sorcerer has been a parody of the modern salesman all along, as is Dr. Dulcamara, the mountebank quack. Gilbert and Sullivan's Sorcerer is poised a bit "higher" than Dulcamara because he is ostentatiously billed as a "professional," but he is still directly in the line of "low" tradesmen as well.

Thus the agent of magic is a professional man of trade, a social oxymoron of an interesting sort. The comic brilliance of this character's conceptualization is hard to overemphasize. The figure of the "professional sorcerer" embodies two sorts of historical transition—on the one hand, showing how magic can be preserved in the modern world, and, on the other hand, offering a witty analysis of the class system as a form of classification, with all sorts of paradoxical blends of high and low making up a new middle.

Marx offers one answer to the question of where magic might be preserved in the modern world. In the commodity, Marx argues, the present-day form of talismanic object, or fetish, the consumer feels the promise of more than its use-value, more even than its exchange-value. But Max Weber offers another answer to the question, more apt for our consideration of *The Sorcerer*. For Weber, a sense of magic is preserved in professional expertise, a contemporary form of occult knowledge. The modern professional thus

FIGURE 3.1 George Grossmith as the Sorcerer, John Wellington Wells, in position for his crouching walk. Cabinet photograph by Barraud (London, 1884). (Collection of Fredric Woodbridge Wilson)

FIGURE 3.2 The title of this cartoon alludes to conventions of the minstrel show. Detail from Alfred Bryan, "A Walk Round by Mr Grossmith," *Illustrated Sporting and Dramatic News*, 1877. (Collection of Fredric Woodbridge Wilson)

FIGURE 3.3 This representation of the Incantation Scene in *The Sorcerer* suggests gaslight melodrama and perhaps the minstrel show. *Illustrated London News*, February 23, 1878. (Collection of Fredric Woodbridge Wilson)

replaces the ancient guild craftsman in a weird way, for what he sells has a value apart from questions of how (or even whether) it works in use. The fact that the "professional sorcerer" actually *does* work magic makes him a figure for this historical transition from ancient occultism to modern professional charisma, a "most ingenious paradox" of ideology, holding together the self-contradictory figures of olden and newer days.

The song in which John Wellington Wells introduces himself features these elements of modern magic:

> My name is John Wellington Wells,
> I'm a dealer in magic and spells,
>   In blessings and curses
>   And ever-filled purses,
> In prophecies, witches, and knells.

The song is at once a novelty number, which presents a fable about the foibles of modern life; a patter song, the genre that Grossmith would make so famous across the history of Savoy opera; a professional confession, like the

"Judge's Song" in *Trial by Jury*; and the first of the catalogue, or "list," songs that will increasingly display the Savoy operas' intense concentration on the culture of consumerism:

> If anyone anything lacks,
> He'll find it all ready in stacks.

This is the magical thinking of modern consumerism, to imagine that the lack can be supplied from the storehouse of consumer goods. The repetition of "prophet" in this context makes it inevitable for the audience to hear a pun on "profit":

> We've a first-class assortment of magic;
> And for raising a posthumous shade
> With effects that are comic or tragic,
> There's no cheaper house in the trade.
> Love-philtre—we've quantities of it;
> And for knowledge if any one burns,
> We keep an extremely small prophet, a prophet
> Who brings us unbounded returns.

John Wellington Wells's sorcery consists in not only his specialized trade, but also his professional expertise. That sorcery could be called a "profession" is funny in the same way it is funny that Frederic is an "apprentice" Pirate in *The Pirates of Penzance*. In both those examples of Savoy social humor, the emphasis falls on the historical difference between guilds, with their secret skills and career paths, and professions, with their occult expertise, specialized jargons, and divisions of labor. *The Sorcerer* especially makes fun of the modern, disciplinary division of knowledge, with its fussy taxonomic distinctions between specializations. Boasting of his company, the modern Sorcerer claims, "We practice Necromancy in all its branches."

> Barring tautology,
> In demonology,
> 'Lectro-biology,
> Mystic nosology,
> Spirit philology,
> High-class astrology,
> Such is his knowledge, he
> Isn't the man to require an apology!

This is a parody of Faust's first monologue, when he details the variety and extent of his knowledge. John Wellington Wells, unlike Faust, is smugly self-satisfied. Although the many branches of his study are humorously deflated by the repetitive rhyme on "-ology" (like all the "-ologies" that overwhelm Mrs. Gradgrind in *Hard Times* [1853]), they are humorously arcane, distinctly not "common knowledge." Furthermore, this expertise is for sale—classified, catalogued, and advertised, like commodities in a warehouse.

Modern class formations, as distinguished from inherited status formations, constitute a difficult and complex system of classification, since they involve such criteria as education and "inner virtue." Not given, like birth, these markers of worth are often hard to mark or identify. Within this system, the professional is a particularly modern social type, who represents a paradoxical middle ground between high status (formerly aristocratic, now expert) and low trade. The professional associations, as well as corporate and state bureaucracies, are allied with the rise of class as a novel system for registering a hierarchy within a democratic social order, registering stratification within a fluid middle ground. The development of a professional-managerial class highlights these issues, making it clear that various "middle"-class formations are themselves paradoxical blends of high and low.

All the Savoy operas reflect on the rise of the professional middle classes, dilating especially on absurdly unmerited promotion and absurdly proliferating subdivisions within "the middle." In this respect, it is important that J. W. Wells & Co. is a firm of "old-established Family Sorcerers." Here the combined values of family and trade yield a middle ground of some complexity, where professional respectability is associated with both inherited status and earned distinction. Thus it is important that the Sorcerer's manners—a particular blend of aggressive hawking and deferential delicacy—mark the professional as a tradesman who attempts to cover his trading with gestures of serviceable attention to old-fashioned family distinctions. John Wellington Wells does aggressively dedicate himself to protecting the respectability of his superiors. When the love philter takes effect, it works only on the peasantry, for the Sorcerer has put all the upper-crust characters to bed, in order to protect them from the social mixing that is bound to occur. Alexis condescendingly commends him in this:

> Sir, you have acted with discrimination,
> And shown more delicate appreciation
> Than we expect in persons of your station.

In other words, the modern professional class defines itself specifically *in relation to* old-fashioned (traditional, residual, archaic) notions of high and low. The oxymoron "professional sorcerer" is a joke about this complex middle ground, for John Wellington Wells represents a higher form of the lower middle class, as well as a lower form of the upper middle class. Thus the honor of the tradesman and the honor due to family blend in the professional, who knows how to sell that most modern of commodities—himself.

A Short Digression on the Patter Song

We are introduced to the patter song—an important feature of the Gilbert and Sullivan operas—by a "dealer in magic and spells," who makes it clear that his services are as marketable as his goods. John Wellington Wells's catalogue begins a long run of lyrics in the form of lists, each of which marks its attention to commerce and its understanding that personal identity is not formed in isolation from market forces. Like the Sorcerer, Little Buttercup introduces herself in *H.M.S. Pinafore* through a list of her wares, while the rival poets in *Patience* identify themselves through their objects, vendors, and venues. In *Pinafore*, Josephine's anguish about her marriage choice becomes a list of things she would not possess if she married Ralph, while the Dragoon Guards in *Patience* illustrate their group identity through a jumble of topical references from current popular culture. Patter is the perfect song style for conveying the pastiche formation of popular culture, for its "fascinating rattle" bespeaks both the patchwork knowingness and the superficiality of this sort of collection.

Like the extravaganza tradition, which also features the patter song, Savoy opera calls attention to its own place in the market, binding itself to current popular culture through its circulation of current topics, events, names, and trends. Edith Hall records the importance of the patter song to classical extravaganza, which itself owes a debt to earlier burlesque traditions.[36] However, the patter song predates extravaganza. For example, the famous solo variety acts by Charles Mathews featured a form of patter. Beginning in 1819 in his "monopolylogues," he imitated a series of other actors or characters. Mathews's later role as Captain Patter in *Patter versus Clatter* (1838) solidifies his association with the genre.[37] Isaac Goldberg argues for patter's more venerable antecedents as well, for it is found in ancient comedy—in Aristophanes, for example—as well as in the European classical music tradition from Haydn and Mozart on.[38] Given our present interests, we might point especially to Dr. Dulcamara's patter song, "Udite, udite, O Rustici," from *L'elisir d'amore*, as well as to "La vendetta, oh, la vendetta" from Mozart's *The Marriage of Figaro* (1786) and "Largo, al factotum" from Rossini's *The Barber of Seville* (1816).

Despite this complex genealogy, in the nineteenth century patter was most commonly associated with selling. Street vendors who hawked their wares using appealingly individualized refrains were known as "patterers," their clever patter distinguishing them from the costermongers, the other denizens of the marketplace at its most demotic. Patterers lived by their wits, not just by their wares, according to Henry Mayhew, who notes that they were intellectuals, "the aristocracy" of the street sellers.[39] In one sense, then, a patter song offers a little allegory of competition in the marketplace.[40] One particularly well-known type of patterer was the seller of broadside ballads, who circulated current "ballad songs and snatches" on the street. In this respect, the conventional presence of the patter song in extravaganza emphasizes its generic mandate to recycle old tunes, resetting them with new words in their new context. Musical entertainment is itself a kind of marketplace, a site of exchange for cultural currency of a certain sort. For variety formats like vaudeville, in venues like dinner rooms, public houses, and music halls, "patter" refers to the spoken interludes between acts and musical numbers. This kind of patter continually sells the show to the members of the audience, keeping their attention fixed, during the short interludes between acts.

Goldberg further suggests that patter can be heard as an anglicized, allusive abbreviation of the opening to the Paternoster. This idiosyncratic idea is tantalizingly relevant to our purposes, since it implies that frequent automatic repetition can bleed the meaning even out of prayer.[41] In this sense, patter names a performance style that responds to all sorts of modern mechanical activities and distractions: the sound of the street vendor; the rote-learned chant of the church or the schoolroom; the worker's repetitive movement on the assembly line. If modern life has become mechanical, then singers and actors can homeopathically imitate the machinery. Thus in the "Junction Song" from *Thespis*, as we have seen, dancing and singing bodies join together to represent a railway train, imitating and making fun of modern, mechanical discipline, exaggeratedly running on time.

Thus, I would argue, Savoy patter is a response to the ills and anxieties of modern life, a dose of a remedy that imitates the problem itself—like parody. The patter song answers to the pastiche form of contemporary culture, too, with its disparate elements circulating rapidly on the surface of metropolitan life. Thus the jumble of topical information in the patter song reflects a concern about the ragtag quality of journalistic information, while it redresses that anxiety with a form of middlebrow pedagogy. The apprehension that knowledge might be reduced to pastiche knowingness—rote, disparate, and superficial—becomes most acute when turned toward the interior world of mental processes. Popularized associationist theories of psychology give rise to the worry that mechanical association might make nonsense of mental life. The Lord Chancellor's "Nightmare Song" in *Iolanthe* expresses all these anxieties bundled together. When his pattering dream sequence parodically imagines the nightmare of corporate capitalism as natural cultivation, its products growing on human trees, it is clear that the dream allegory portrays modern culture as the frantic activity of consuming—in both senses of the word:

> And he and the crew are on bicycles too—which they've somehow or
> other invested in—
> And he's telling the tars all the parti*culars* of a company he's interested
> in—
> It's a scheme of devices, to get at low prices all goods from cough mix-
> tures to cables
> (Which tickled the sailors), by treating retailers as though they were all
> vege*tables*—
> You get a good spadesman to plant a small tradesman (first take off his
> boots with a boot-tree),
> And his legs will take root, and his fingers will shoot, and they'll blossom
> and bud like a fruit-tree—
> From the greengrocer tree you get grapes and green pea, cauliflower,
> pineapple, and cranberries,
> While the pastrycook plant cherry brandy will grant, apple puffs, and
> three-corners, and Banburys—
> The shares are a penny, and ever so many are taken by Rothschild and
> Baring,
> And just as a few are allotted to you, you awake with a shudder
> despairing—

Freud's *The Interpretation of Dreams* was still more than a decade in the offing, but Gilbert attended to the sense-making tactics of the dream work's supposed nonsense. The song's tumbling sequence of investment schemes, the catalogue of products (most of them edible), the cultivation of trade, and the fluid transformation of identities all evoke the nightmare of modern social life.

Thus in the Savoy operas, it is often the professional man who patters. Anxiously or smugly playing his professional role, this character type is meant to seem mechanical, as anyone knows who has enjoyed the rattle of Major-General Stanley's song: "I am the very model of a modern Major-General." His manic recitation of irrelevant expertise characterizes the modern bureaucrat, promoted beyond his capacity, a figure of fun familiar in Gilbert and Sullivan. This pattering professional man sings in the register of the comic baritone, emphasizing his worldly nature in the near-slippage between song and ordinary speech.

But patter has its feminine correlative: chatter. Chatter is cheerful, empty, high-spirited talk characteristic of young women whose minds have not yet been sullied with desire or resentment—or, indeed, for that matter, with anything of serious worldly import at all. The best example from Savoy opera is surely the chattering female Chorus in *The Pirates of Penzance*, singing excitedly about the weather in order to distract attention from Frederic and Mabel, who are engaged in their love duet. In the burlesque tradition, where misogynist splitting is a generic convention, the contrast can be quite graphic between chatter *in bono* (the mark of innocent, feminine good spirits) and chatter *in malo* (the mark of the overbearing virago of a certain age who, to the misogynist's ear, just will not stop talking).[42] Both these aspects of the feminine have been toned down in the Savoy operas, where both the too-innocent girl and the virago are subject to parody.

The performance style of patter demands elocutionary finesse, for words tumble out in a mad, mechanical rush, inviting feats of memory, breath control, tongue twisting, and rapid, rhythmic pronunciation. These songs have always been among the most popular in the repertoire. In the Savoy performance tradition, these numbers are encored repeatedly, accelerating with each reiteration, until spectators and performer are overwhelmed and exhausted. (Twenty-first-century audiences may seem merely to suffer the many encores, but nineteenth-century theatergoers enthusiastically demanded them.) Thus the Lord Chancellor's conclusion to the "Nightmare Song" offers an apt commentary on the song style itself: "[T]he night has been long—ditto ditto my song—and thank goodness they're both of them over!"[43]

Going Down to Ahrimanes

Like professional expertise, love preserves some residual magic even in the modern commercial world. In *The Sorcerer*, love is characterized as an intoxicating, transformative force that mixes people up and turns the social hierarchy upside down. Marriage offers the antidote to love's most radical power, providing the stable form that can be recognized as closure. Early on, when the Sorcerer explains that "this philtre is compounded on the strictest principles. On married people it has no effect whatever," we can see that marriage represents the opposite of unruly love. Before the opera's comic order can fall into place, with its hyperbolically multiplied marriages, the magical agent must be expelled.

As it stands, this dimension of the libretto remains incoherent. The Sorcerer's sudden remorse for all the "evil" he has done makes no sense in an opera that has not portrayed him as evil. Furthermore, his abrupt proposal of the "one means" of reversing the spell—either he or Alexis must "yield up his life to Ahrimanes"—comes out of nowhere. The debate that ensues, about which one of them will be sacrificed, cannot keep the audience from wondering what is going on. After some byplay, it is decided by popular opinion that the Sorcerer must die. Thus the expulsion of the supernatural agent from the modern, rationalized world is staged as a ritual scapegoating.[44] But who is Ahrimanes? Is he the devil (as in *Faust*)? If so, it seems important that the distant allusion to Mephistopheles has been displaced, precisely through the Persian name Ahrimanes.[45] When he "goes down to Ahrimanes," does the Sorcerer descend into hell or, more neutrally, into Hades (as some commentators have put it, hedging their bets)?[46]

To answer these questions, recourse to a previous version of the libretto shows that a second Incantation Scene had been planned for act 2. That scene, unfortunately, was cut[47]—and should be restored in future productions of *The Sorcerer*. It called for the grand figure of Ahrimanes himself to appear through a transparency. In that deleted scene, Ahrimanes, who turns out to be the Sorcerer's master spirit, explicitly demands that either John Wellington Wells or Alexis be sacrificed. As the libretto now stands, however, "Ahrimanes" is left stranded and unexplained, the result of hasty and careless revision.[48] Yet the revised libretto does gain one advantage in not explaining who Ahrimanes is, since lack of clarity on this point supports the vague notion that magic must exist somewhere in the secularizing, modern world. In this reading, the ending of *The Sorcerer* is meant to seem parodic, ostentatiously fictive, suddenly posited, and abruptly "tacked-on." As the Sorcerer himself puts it, in his last words: "I go—it matters not with whom—or where!"

The ending, when the Sorcerer "*sinks through the trap, amid red fire*," parodies supernatural melodrama, extravaganza, and grand opera. Both the trapdoor and the red fire highlight the genre parody, with their pyrotechnic display of supernatural special effects. Nineteenth-century audiences would immediately have recognized the extravaganza transformation, especially when a gong announces the change (a convention familiar from pre-extravaganza pantomime). The trap, in turn, suggests the trappings of gothic melodrama, especially since the "vampire trap," which allows a body to rise above or sink below the stage, was invented for Planché's *Vampire*. Then and now, the Sorcerer sinking below the stage also recalls the final scene of Mozart's *Don Giovanni* (1787), in which a fiery pit opens and the protagonist is dragged down by demons. Christopher Marlowe's *Dr. Faustus* (1604) also ends with the mouth of hell opening to swallow the modern seeker of knowledge and experience. Even Don Giovanni is a modern comedown from that titanic transgressor, for Don Giovanni offends against human law, while Faust attempts to reach beyond the limits of the human.

While this parodic sacrifice is unfolding, everyone pairs up correctly—Lady Sangazure with Sir Marmaduke, Aline with Alexis, Constance with Dr. Daly, and Mrs. Partlet with the Notary. The young couple, who had fallen out, and the older couple, who had parted long ago, are reunited, and a mass outburst takes precisely the form that Sir Marmaduke has rejected as "indelicate":

GENTLEMEN: Oh, my adored one!
LADIES: Unmingled joy!
GENTLEMEN: Ecstatic rapture!
LADIES: Beloved boy!

Present-day expressiveness trumps the reticence of the past, and thus conventional social forms like marriage, which have been seen to limit passion, are now also seen to express it. Sir Marmaduke seals the unions by inviting everyone to another feast, featuring (of course) more tea and a quintessentially English menu:

Now for the tea of our host—
    Now for the rollicking bun—
Now for the muffin and toast—
    Now for the gay Sally Lunn!

During this festive finale, the Sorcerer makes his self-sacrificial exit, sinking out of sight through the trapdoor "*amid red fire*," "while winding his watch, cleaning his glasses, putting on his gloves, and brushing his hat." When the curtain rose for the final picture, he tossed a handful of business cards toward the audience, professional to the last.[49]

4

"Never Mind the Why and Wherefore"

The Parody of Nautical Melodrama in *H.M.S. Pinafore*

The early Gilbert and Sullivan collaborations parodically recollect the main theatrical genres of the early nineteenth century. In this sense, the parody of nautical melodrama in *H.M.S. Pinafore; or, The Lass That Loved a Sailor* (1878) follows logically on the parody of supernatural melodrama in *The Sorcerer*, for early English melodrama was dominated by these two main subgenres. A popular dramatic revue by James Robinson Planché makes it clear that this assumption was widely shared. When a personification of "Melodrama" is summoned to the stage, by means of a parodic incantation—very much like that in *The Sorcerer—two* figures answer the command to "Appear!" One is a gothic monster, and the other a true-blue Jolly Jack Tar, identified specifically as William, the sailor-hero of Douglas Jerrold's immensely popular nautical melodrama, *Black-Ey'd Susan*.[1]

H.M.S. Pinafore and *The Pirates of Penzance* form a diptych, for both are concerned with the parody of nautical melodrama, but they approach that parody from two different directions. Thus this chapter and the next should be read together, for both place the Savoy operas within a larger theater history while examining the parody of nautical melodrama. Unlike extravaganza or supernatural melodrama, nautical melodrama is a proto-realistic genre, concerned with the real world of social relations. Yet, as these two operas show, its forms of resolution seem as irrational as the extravaganza transformation scene. *Pinafore* uses its parody of the particular absurdity found in melodrama to comment on the social conventions that underlie the genre.

Cues to the genre parody are blatantly obvious in *H.M.S. Pinafore*. In addition to conventional costumes, sets, and musical styles, the opera rolls out a veritable blazon of nautical clichés: alliterative names like Dick Dead-eye and Ralph Rackstraw; the "strong right arm" and "honest brown right hand" of the hero; the heroine under siege from an unsuitable suitor; the nautical metaphors peppering the Sailors' speech on board ship; the cheerful shipboard rallying cries; the jokes about the hornpipe and the Sailors' bad language; and, of course, the Sailors' exaggerated patriotism. Most of all, Little Buttercup's histrionic "remorse" floats the entire plot with its melodramatic suspense. The eventual revelation of her dark secret sets up the opera's conclusion, which turns on a parody of the melodramatic transformation scene. To go beyond a superficial rehearsal of these signs, however, in the effort to understand the scope, depth, and significance of the genre parody, we must consider nautical melodrama itself, for *H.M.S. Pinafore* engages its social logic and historical force.

Nautical Melodrama

An authentically English, popular, and often radical genre, nautical melodrama flourished especially in the 1820s and 1830s. Developing from a native mixture of naval and military spectacles performed at Astley's Amphitheatre and Sadler's Wells, dumb shows at the Royal Circus, and melodrama itself (which was performed in England from the 1790s), nautical plays often alluded to specific historical events—reenactments of Horatio Nelson's naval victories, for example, or the famous mutinies at Spithead and the Nore.[2] Melodrama's characteristic attention to class, gender, and national relations intensified in the aftermath of the Napoleonic Wars; in retrospect, we can see that melodrama, as much as the novel, was involved in the formulation of those social categories. Nautical melodrama focuses its attention through particular theatrical types and figures—like the Tar and the pirate—as well as through such thematic obsessions as the hierarchical structure of absolute authority on board ship and the traumatic disruptions of the family left on shore. Melodramatic images of piracy and smuggling were invested with a new sense of national urgency during the Napoleonic conflicts, while various attempts to regulate trade and police the borders can also be read as palpable signs of the developing nation-state. In the exaggerated patriotism of melodrama, we can feel the defensiveness involved in national defense. In other words, nautical melodrama clearly displays its commitment to loyal service and national pride, but it also emphasizes the oppressive inequalities engendered on the common man and woman. Sometimes both attitudes can be found in the same play.

Considered as a genre, nautical melodrama must be seen *both* as opposi-tional *and* as complicit in the disciplining of the populace.

J. T. Cross's *The Purse; or, The Benevolent Tar* (1794) is generally taken to be the first nautical melodrama, but Douglas Jerrold's *Black-Ey'd Susan; or, All in the Downs* (Surrey, 1829) is always considered to be the canonical example of the genre, as Planché's revue makes clear.[3] A brief look at that play, therefore, will give us a better idea of exactly how the genre parody works in *H.M.S. Pinafore*.

Generally speaking, the social critique in *Black-Ey'd Susan* may be seen in the way it displays particular forms of suffering engendered in the com-mon man and woman by the fact of national service. In this context, the Jolly Jack Tar becomes a new kind of hero, a particularly fit mate for the heroine of melodrama. Melodrama presents feminine suffering as the state of being "helpless and unfriended," whether poverty-stricken, cast out of house and home, in danger of being ruined, or already fallen. In *Black-Ey'd Susan*, the eponymous heroine has been left to fend for herself at home, while her hus-band, William, fulfills his naval service. Her virtue is beset from all sides: by an evil landlord who is also her uncle; by a smuggler in cahoots with the landlord-uncle; and by the captain of her husband's ship. These vari-ous threats to her virtue are socially significant. Through the figure of the landlord-uncle, Susan's plight alludes to the perilous economic situation of non-property-owning commoners. Through the figure of the smuggler, Susan's body comes to represent the nation endangered by trade outlaws. And through the figure of Captain Crosstree, whose drunken and ungovern-able desire suggests a frightening corruption of authority, Susan represents the common woman under threat of ruin at the hands of a man higher in the social hierarchy. In other words, the threads of class, nation, and gender are tied very tightly in this plot. The heroine under duress becomes densely representational—here suggesting the economic plight of commoners, the permeable borders of the island nation, and the corruption of national authority in general.

Masculine suffering, in melodrama, is portrayed as the potential divi-sion between public and private duties. Defending his wife, William knocks down his captain, and, for the crime of striking his superior officer, he is court-martialed and sentenced to die. The play relentlessly meditates on William's intractable self-division. He begs, at his trial, that the law might "condemn the sailor" but "respect the husband." As a parable of modern sub-ject formation, William's dilemma is the dilemma of every common man, formed by the state, but striving to express a freer world of personal feeling. William has literally been conscripted, written into his social role and forced to perform it. His dramatic speech, chock-full of nautical metaphor, shows how deeply inhabited he is by his social role; in this respect, the sailor's "salt sea lingo," a "peculiarity of the English theatre," sounds out its social significance.[4] Yet when he speaks sentimentally to his wife, William rises to a manly eloquence that is unblemished by the specialized language of his profession. This audible self-division in his speech embodies the ideological contradictions that issue in his death sentence.

As a parable of the changing nation, *Black-Ey'd Susan* condenses complex historical transition into a domestic framework. Since Susan remains unravished, the sailor-hero has successfully defended the domestic front—in both the familial and the national senses of the word "domestic."[5] After the play's happy ending, William and Susan plan to move from the country to the town, where they will keep a shop. This plot, in other words, transfers William and Susan from their rural origins, sentimentally remembered, to the mercantile economy of a town, precisely poised on the shoreline border; the period of William's naval service transfers him from one world to another. Representative figures for the massive population shift occurring in the first decades of the nineteenth century, William and Susan are also upwardly mobile in terms of class; he will retain his naval past by selling marine wares, while he rises into the lower middle classes of tradesmen.

No plot can directly represent such long-term historical transitions, nor can it resolve the intractable social conflicts they create. The problems taken up reach far beyond the dramatic scope of any one time, place, hero, and heroine. In this fact lies the key to the melodramatic happy ending, which is sudden and far-fetched *because* the problems it addresses are so complex and intractable. Only the willing suspension of disbelief in sociological probability can provide for justice and a happy ending, the sine qua non of melodrama. In *Black-Ey'd Susan*, the far-fetched happy ending comes about because a document is discovered in the nick of time, dragged up from under the sea on the dead body of the smuggler. That document is William's discharge from the navy, and it is "dated back." Suddenly it turns out that William was no longer a sailor when he struck Captain Crosstree. In other words, their social relation is suddenly—and retroactively—transformed. This re-creation of social identity releases William from his crime, as well as from his service to the state; in place of hierarchy, it establishes equality; and it provides the platform for his upward mobility. But the "sheer contingency" of this happy outcome must be keenly felt. Justice easily might *not* have been done.[6]

Melodrama is famous for these sudden and highly improbable resolutions—"Never mind the why and wherefore"—which *H.M.S. Pinafore* parodies in its own dénouement.[7] Given melodrama's vast project of imagining how justice might prevail and how common virtue might be recognized in the end, its happy endings should be regarded not only as willful and utopian, but also as socially constructive.[8] Among other genres (most notably the novel), melodrama registers the difficulty of creating new forms of social organization. If melodramatic resolutions seem far-fetched and improbable, they show, by that very measure, how hard it was to imagine that justice could be done, villainy defeated, and common virtue rewarded in the modern world.

For our purposes, it is important to see that melodramatic resolutions are every bit as transformative as any elixir-induced transformation in the theater of extravaganza. Unlike the magical transformations of extravaganza, however, the transformations of melodrama are elaborately rationalized in sociocultural terms, usually through the confession of a crime, the revelation of a secret, the discovery of a document, or the clever unraveling of a legal nicety. They come about through the sudden disclosure of a truth or reality that had been waiting to be discovered and recognized all along. It is the great genius of *H.M.S. Pinafore* not only to parody these conventions of the genre, but to take account of their historical logic, for the resolution of *H.M.S. Pinafore* goes to the heart of the opera's critique of class relations; government bureaucracy and its disregard for merit; the theatricality of patriotism and national pride; and indeed, the performative quality of all social roles.

For now, the crucial point is simply this: the transformations of melodrama can be as sudden and implausible as the magical transformations of pantomime and extravaganza. They imagine a retroactive reconstruction of social identity that is illogical, impossible, or, at the very least, highly improbable, as we have seen in the brief examination of *Black-Ey'd Susan*. (We saw the same preposterous logic at work in the figurative reconstruction of virginity imagined by the resolution of a suit for breach of promise, as parodied in *Trial by Jury*.) Both *H.M.S. Pinafore* and *The Pirates of Penzance* parody these features of the melodramatic resolution.

Melodramatic Legibility

Despite its far-fetched endings, melodrama aims to represent the structure of social relations, however typified and abstract its characters might seem. Likewise, the setting for melodrama aims to represent the real world. Thus *H.M.S. Pinafore*, like *Trial by Jury*, sets the stage for its parody with elaborate visual verisimilitude. The set reproduces the quarterdeck of Lord Nelson's famous ship, HMS *Victory*, which lay idle in Portsmouth, where Gilbert traveled with Sullivan to do research.[9] But the realism of the set only emphasizes the play's absurdities. The *Pinafore* is emphatically *not* the *Victory*, in other words, and there is no one like Lord Nelson on board (although in the early days of the production, Sir Joseph Porter was made up to look like him).

As in *Trial by Jury*, the mixture of realism and fantasy is crucial. The name *Pinafore* announces a zany regression, referring both to the "uniform of childhood" and to Victorian children's favorite theatrical genre.[10] While every audience member (then and now) will know that a pinafore is a dress-like over-garment worn by children, theater historians would add that "a pinafore all besmeared with lollipops" is a familiar costume in the pantomime.[11] Thus the opera signals its fantasy element, its entertainment of juvenile nonsense, and its nostalgia for both childhood and the theatrical past.[12] Although the full logic of its regressive playfulness is not revealed until the end, when we discover that Buttercup was a nursemaid, it begins to be felt when Sir Joseph's Sisters, Cousins, and Aunts come on board. The stage picture graphically illustrates the division of the Chorus according to gender. As in *Trial by Jury*, when the Bridesmaids sweep into the courtroom, the separate spheres are zanily brought together in a normatively male space. Sir Joseph's Female Relatives act out a fussy femininity that is allied to his bureaucratic discipline, but even more reminiscent of the nursery and schoolroom, where the principle of discipline is normatively female.

With this mixture of realism and fantasy, various sorts of recognition are mobilized and mixed up. Against the melodramatic premise of legibility—whereby the looks and sounds of characters reveal immediately who is villainous and who is virtuous—a more skeptical attitude, focusing on the deceptive nature of appearances, alerts us to the parody. The parodic system of recognition plays with stereotypes to upend them, turning both melodramatic credulity and realistic skepticism on their heads. In other words, *Pinafore* takes melodrama's commitment to legibility at face value, so to speak, reproducing it and making fun of it at the same time.

Take Dick Deadeye, for example, whose character embodies and voices the opera's parody of melodramatic legibility and recognition (figure 4.1). His name, with its alliterative reference to his calling, follows a convention of melodramatic characterization. This convention is writ large in nautical melodrama, with such heroes as Harry Hallyard, from J. T. Haines's *My Poll and My Partner Joe* (1835), which also mentions a "Dan Deadeye."[13] Dick Deadeye's name identifies him with his ship, for a deadeye is a shipboard

FIGURE 4.1 Richard Temple as Dick Deadeye, who embodies the ugly truth of social inequality in his twisted, parodic figure. Cabinet photograph by Barraud (London, 1878). (Collection of Fredric Woodbridge Wilson)

instrument, "a wooden block with three holes, used for tightening or extending the shrouds of a sailing ship."[14] His name also advertises the deadeye aim he takes in his sociological observations. However, his looks inform against him. With his distorted, twisted appearance and his squinting "dead eye," he would be clearly bad (or mad) in any melodramatic ensemble—a villainous, sinister, untrustworthy fellow. Alerting us to the parody, Dick himself acknowledges this convention as if it were a fact of life:

> I say—it's a beast of a name, ain't it—Dick Deadeye? . . . I'm ugly, and they hate me for it. . . . From such a face and such a form as mine the noblest sentiments sound like the black utterances of a depraved imagination. It is human nature—I am resigned.

The joke is far from trivial, for it speaks to the politics of equality at the center of the opera's concern. Dick Deadeye cuts alike through Ralph's romantic idealism and Sir Joseph's pretension, but no one welcomes his incisive commentary. When he warns that "captains' daughters don't marry foremast hands," he merely repeats what has just been said. But when Dick says it, everyone recoils. When his fellow Sailors fall for Sir Joseph's sham democracy, he reminds them: "When people have to obey other people's orders, equality's out of the question." And again they recoil, pronouncing him "Horrible! Horrible!" This belief in equality wound together with the realistic acknowledgment that it does not yet exist in the real world is at the heart of nautical melodrama, as we have seen.

Like his person, Dick's message *is* ugly. What the opera subjects to critique, however, is the fact that no one will believe it, choosing instead to believe in stock protestations of equality. The Boatswain finds Dick's skepticism "a disgrace to our common natur." Dick's sentiments, like the more radical nautical melodramas, *are* revolutionary because they insist on pointing out injustice and showing the world for what it is, a place where principles of equality may be loudly bruited, but are not practiced. Thus more than any other character, Dick Deadeye speaks for the opera as a whole. He represents its social critique as well as its twisted and parodic form. He may look like a villain, but with his deadeye aim, he is the one whose points hit their mark, dead-on.

The Jolly Jack Tar

Unlike Dick Deadeye, who calls the melodramatic principle of recognition into question, the figure of our hero, Ralph Rackstraw, supports it to such an extent that his characterization, too, is parodic, an exaggerated representation of a conventional figure. A handsome, romantic, idealistic sailor, the tenor in the vocal ensemble, he fulfills every promise of the heroic masculine type (figure 4.2). Ralph takes his place at the apogee of a long tradition of Jolly Jack Tars who morph through serious and silly, dramatic and narrative literature for over a century before *Pinafore*. Like the magical elixir in *The Sorcerer*, the utter conventionality of the Tar is at the heart of the parody.

The figure of the true-blue Jolly Jack Tar predates nautical melodrama by more than a hundred years.[15] In William Congreve's *Love for Love* (1695), Ben is the first stage sailor "with a gay heart and a strange vocabulary," although he is not a romantic hero. Neither are the salty, picaresque protagonists of Tobias Smollett's alliteratively named *Roderick Random* (1748) and *Peregrine Pickle* (1751). David Garrick famously proclaimed the prologue for David Mallet's masque, *Britannia* (1755), in the character of a drunken sailor, while Isaac Bickerstaffe's entertainment *Thomas and Sally; or, The Sailor's Return* (1760) contributes the now-legendary description of the happy sailor, who

FIGURE 4.2 J. G. Robertson as Ralph Rackstraw, the hyper-virtuous British Tar in *H.M.S. Pinafore*. Cabinet photograph by Barraud (London, 1887 or 1888). (Collection of Fredric Woodbridge Wilson)

finds "a wife in every port" and "in every land a home." Sentimental ballads and rough street songs alike took the sailor's life as one of their favorite topics.

Nautical melodrama advances a sentimental version of the Jolly Jack Tar, who becomes an iconic representation of the common man. Indeed, the Enlightenment topos of the "natural man" hovers about the figure.[16] He could be comic and self-deprecating, a sort of trickster figure, and then become seriously heroic, in turn. J. S. Bratton, writing the history of the romantic hero emerging from this seriocomic figure, explains that contemporary audiences were aware of the development, perceiving that a novel, sentimental, and particularly nineteenth-century Jack Tar had appeared and caught hold around the naval victories of Edward Hawke, George Rodney, Richard Howe, and Nelson.[17] In addition, those audiences recognized the shift as "the genius of T. P. Cooke and Douglas Jerrold coming together to create William in *Black Ey'd Susan*." Cooke was credited with giving new "thoughtfulness and mystery . . . deep-toned passion and romance" to the figure of the Jolly Jack Tar.[18] No longer a roving rogue, no longer "random," picaresque, promiscuous, and comic, the Jack Tar of nautical melodrama is a sentimental, domesticated, and patriotic man—faithful alike to wife, home, and country.

The Tar's hyperbolic virtue allowed him to become not only the docile servant of the nation, but also a weapon in the developing arsenal of revolutionary class consciousness. Before nautical melodrama, the Jolly Jack Tar extols the freedom of the sailor's life; now he laments its bondage, expressing the politically complex question of how to reconcile the ideals of national service with its realities (where "equality is out of the question"). In both respects, his stereotypicality is a large part of the point, for the complex potentialities of the figure must be immediately recognizable by the audience. V. C. Clinton-Baddeley, focusing on the burlesque tradition, complains that the Jolly Jack Tar was the "custodian of the nation's virtue" and that a "character has been converted into a type. A man has been exchanged for a prig."[19] For our understanding of *H.M.S. Pinafore*, however, the fact that the Tar has become a type is exactly the point, for the hyperbolically virtuous Tar invites parody. Ralph Rackstraw bears the marks of this hyper-virtuous Tar, especially in his credulous trust of Sir Joseph's false radicalism.

Literary parody of the Tar's hyperbolic virtue predates theatrical parody by several decades. It seems to have been noticed first by Frederick Reynolds in *The Life and Times of Frederick Reynolds. Written by Himself* (1826), followed by Charles Dickens in *Nicholas Nickleby* (1838) and Gilbert à Beckett in *George Cruikshank's Table Book* (1845).[20] The popular nautical novels of Captain Frederick Marryat, roughly contemporaneous with the heyday of nautical melodrama, are especially relevant. In *Mr. Midshipman Easy* (1836), for example, are many of the jokes that Gilbert would employ in *Pinafore*: unexpectedly polite Sailors; a Dick Deadeye figure, whose shocking appearance belies his good sense; Cockney "Hinglish" patriotism; the formative figure of a wet nurse; a bluff and innocent hero; and an elaborate demonstration of the absurdity of radical politics. Although Marryat was concerned—as Gilbert would be—to show that the pretense of equality is absurd in a place that demands hierarchy, Mr. Midshipman Easy is a genial, admirable fellow, as Sir Joseph certainly is not. In attributing falsely democratic principles to a bureaucrat (rather than true democratic feelings to a Tar, as Marryat does), Gilbert revises the critique and places the burden on the bureaucratic governance of the navy.[21]

The first real nautical burlesques did not come until the 1860s, with Thomas Gibson Bowles's *The Port Admiral; or, The Mysterious Mariner, the Child of Destiny, and the Rightful Heir* (1863) and *The Tyrant! The Slave!! The Victim!!! and the Tar!!!!* (1864), and F. C. Burnand's *The Very Latest Edition of Black-Eyed Susan; or, The Little Bill that Was Taken Up* (1866).[22] Burnand was praised in the *Times* for opening this subject matter to theatrical burlesque, and it is notable that Burnand's parody was staged over a decade before *H.M.S. Pinafore* and was credited at the time for marking a formal change in extravaganza (away from rhymed couplets and so many puns).[23] Perhaps Gilbert was inspired to create something better.

Neither the nautical melodramas nor the burlesques are much remembered today. Nautical melodrama as a genre survives in the popular cultural memory in only a few narratives—*Mutiny on the Bounty*, for example, or *Billy Budd*—in pirate operas and their cinematic heirs, and on the musical stage, especially in *H.M.S. Pinafore*. Thus *Pinafore* shows that genre parody can be a powerful instrument of literary and theatrical history, since it prompts the partial recovery of a past genre that has been largely lost; yet the recovery is emphatically only partial, parodic, and twisted.[24] Like the magical elixir—although less mythic and more historically inflected—the Jolly Jack Tar was a convention, ripe for parody in the theater of the 1860s and 1870s. Thus *H.M.S. Pinafore* must be seen as the culmination of a parodic tradition, its "apotheosis," as Clinton-Baddeley has rightly claimed (plate 7).[25]

Manly Eloquence, Manly Attitudes

The figure of the Jolly Jack Tar is complex and self-divided. To show that he is a man of the people, absorbed by his social role in national service, he speaks the nautical jargon of his calling. To show that he is innately virtuous and therefore upwardly mobile, destined to rise in social class, he soars into eloquence when speaking of his feelings.[26] Ideal masculinity is riven by these divided loyalties in nautical melodrama, as we have seen. Confessing his love for Josephine in a perfect mixture of nautical jargon and manly eloquence, Ralph declares: "She is the figurehead of my ship of life—the bright beacon that guides me into my port of happiness—the rarest, the purest gem that ever sparkled on a poor but worthy fellow's trusting brow!" The other Sailors approve Ralph's sentimental rhetoric ("Verry pretty!"), rolling their *r*'s in the Tar's distinctive growl ("arrr!"). Speaking directly to Josephine, however, Ralph drops the nautical metaphors; his inflated rhetoric becomes opaque, "uncommon," and "poetic":

> RALPH: I am poor in the essence of happiness, lady—rich only in never-ending unrest. In me there meet a combination of antithetical elements which are at eternal war with one another. Driven hither by objective influences—thither by subjective emotions—wafted one moment into

blazing day, by mocking hope—plunged the next into the Cimmerian darkness of tangible despair, I am but a living ganglion of irreconcilable antagonisms. I hope I make myself clear, lady?

JOSEPHINE: Perfectly! (*Aside*) His simple eloquence goes to my heart.

This eloquence is anything but simple, and that is the joke. Perhaps a parodic whiff of Coleridge wafts through this passage, for Ralph's use of "objective" and "subjective" seemed abstrusely German for decades, before it became common coin. The Tar's manly eloquence situates him in the sentimental tradition, for like the late-eighteenth-century "man of feeling," whose tears transgress the usual bounds of masculine gender conventions, the nautical hero is affirmed in his masculinity by his access to feminine signs of strong emotion.[27] The language of the heart guarantees his nobility, which is a matter of innate character, not of inheritance or socialization. This emphasis on the masculine distinguishes Gilbert's parody from that of Burnand, whose nautical burlesque featured a Tar played by a "young girl in blue satin trousers," dancing breakdowns and singing comic songs; thus, Percy Fitzgerald argues, Burnand created no true burlesque humor, for he failed to focus on style, missing the opportunity to make the Tar's "heroic sentiments" and elevated diction the point of the parody.[28]

Swearing is another linguistic register of passionate feeling, the low correlative of the high outbursts of manly eloquence. Even William, the hero of *Black-Ey'd Susan*, swears throughout the play, but his "Damme" never undermines his role as a paragon of virtue. In other words, the Tar's virtue is carefully distinguished from genteel respectability. Against this convention of nautical melodrama, Gilbert floats his parodic figure of the polite sailor, an inversion of the type. The idea appears in his Bab Ballad "The Bumboat Woman's Story" (1870), in which the *Pinafore* is prefigured in the *Hot Cross Bun*:

When Jack Tars growl, I believe they growl with a big big D—
But the strongest oath of the Hot Cross Bun was a mild "Dear me!"[29]

Captain Corcoran's outburst in act 2 of *Pinafore*, when he finds that his daughter has eloped with a common sailor ("Yes, damme, it's too bad!") derives its humor from the unconventional politeness that reigns in this parodic inversion of the nautical world.

The injunction to polite restraint is associated with both women and bureaucracy, represented as the dual forces of domestic discipline (again, in both the familial and the national senses of "domestic"). At the Captain's mild, but climactic oath, Sir Joseph's Sisters, Cousins, and Aunts sing out their feminine sense of outrage, chattering and murmuring like reproving gossips:

> Did you hear him—did you hear him?
>   Oh, the monster overbearing!
> Don't go near him—don't go near him—
>   He is swearing—he is swearing!

This moment underscores the parodic opposition of masculinity and femininity, bolstered by the division in the Chorus between Sailors and Female Relatives (see plate 3). Swearing affirms the male-separatist shipboard culture, away from women and the constraints of the genteel society they encourage. But this male bastion—like the courtroom in *Trial by Jury*—has been invaded by women. Certainly one powerful dramatic rationale for bringing the Female Relatives on board is to have them act out this Grundyesque reprimand, parodying the guardians of middle-class propriety and the conventionally feminine hope of civilizing the brute "natural" man.

Like fussy female officiousness, Sir Joseph's "official utterances" are forms of repression, directly opposed to the passionate outbursts both of swearing and of manly eloquence. Sir Joseph's requirement that all commands be followed with "if you *please*" links national authority and discipline with bourgeois standards of conduct. To serve as "the bulwarks of England's greatness," the Sailors must use "no strong language of any kind." Likewise, the "official utterance" is opposed to the language of love. In wooing Josephine, Sir Joseph uses only "as much eloquence as is consistent with an official utterance." His prim and well-considered statements are bureaucratic, functional, and unfeeling, while the language of passion is always structured as an outburst. Humorously enough, Sir Joseph's "official utterance" works against itself, for when Josephine hears Sir Joseph state "officially" that "love is a platform upon which all ranks meet," she takes him to mean that she should marry Ralph.

Not at all effective in proclaiming love, "official utterances" are very effective in disciplining common sailors and inculcating their proper roles. As if to make it crystal clear that the opera understands its own implication in the circulation of these attitudes, Sir Joseph's instruction takes the form of a musical number sung by Ralph and members of the crew, the wonderful glee "A British tar is a soaring soul." And Sir Joseph explicitly acknowledges its ideological function; the song is "designed to encourage independence of thought and action in the lower branches of the service, and to teach the principle that a British sailor is any man's equal, excepting mine." Encouraging

Ralph and his fellows to "hum this at your leisure (*giving him MS. music*)," the actor playing Sir Joseph usually engages in some linguistic by-play to emphasize his superior class position (loudly pronouncing the *h* in "hum," while the common sailor drops it, saying "um"). The point is that "the British tar" results from a performance, as do all social roles.

"A British tar is a soaring soul" makes fun of the scripted process of socialization, the way all social roles are learned and enforced. The Sailors gullibly hope that the song will cause everyone to conform, even to "bring this here miserable creetur [Dick Deadeye] to a proper state of mind." As they sing, they illustrate the correct performance of the "British tar" with a series of choreographed poses.

> His nose should pant and his lip should curl,
> His cheeks should flame and his brow should furl,
> His bosom should heave and his heart should glow,
> And his fist be ever ready for a knock-down blow.
> . . .
> His foot should stamp and his throat should growl,
> His hair should twirl and his face should scowl;
> His eyes should flash and his breast protrude,
> And this should be his customary attitude— (*pose*).

Emphasizing the last point, the chorus manically repeats, crescendo: "His attitude! His attitude! His attitude!" (figure 4.3). By paying attention to the parody of nautical melodrama, we can see that the "customary attitude" of the British Tar is precisely the attitude that has been taught by decades of conventional representation and "official utterance." Of course, the effect is humorous, for the Tars seem like puppets of their profession, or "like the cut-out sailors of the Toy Theatre."[30]

The humor of this glee depends on its parody of a particular performance tradition as well. A technical term in theater history, the "attitude" is a momentary pose, struck in the midst of dramatic action, a pose that calls out to be recognized and interpreted. These attitudes were especially exaggerated in melodrama, where each sweeping gesture would come to a "point." But posing in attitudes was important before, after, and outside melodrama as well.[31] Victorian photography, deeply invested in the aesthetics of the pose, intertwined across the nineteenth century with the pervasive influence of tableaux vivants, with their technical necessity for lengthily held poses and their impulse toward narrative.

FIGURE 4.3 "And this should be his customary attitude." Drawing by Bab [W. S. Gilbert] to accompany "The British Tar," in *Songs of a Savoyard* (1891). (Collection of Fredric Woodbridge Wilson)

The history of Victorian posing on the stage is closely associated with gender, from the early days of the nineteenth century, when Emma Hamilton posed in a niche, garbed in "classical" drapery, to entertain her husband's guests, to the later days of the century, when Eugen Sandow made body-building a popular activity for the British upper-middle classes. Hamilton's subtle way of passing from one attitude to the next was praised as a form of art by visiting dignitaries, including Goethe; her practice can be seen to prefigure the serial dissolving views of the Victorian magic-lantern show, in which one still picture, projected onto a screen, dissolves into another that takes its place, creating the illusion of moving pictures.[32] Feminine posing in attitudes occupied high, middle, and low registers of cultural significa-tion. The genteel form of posing in tableaux vivants was an acceptable parlor entertainment in upper- and middle-class homes (as we know from *Vanity Fair*, *Daniel Deronda*, and a host of other novels). The *poses plastiques*, though, were risqué, allowing glimpses of the seemingly nude female form through clinging gauze and tight "fleshings" (body suits made to resemble white skin). Like Hamilton's, these less restrained exhibitions often claimed an educational purpose—and therefore a cover story—through their imitation of works of art.

Masculine poses, too, were appreciated from the early nineteenth century, especially in Andrew Ducrow's famous *poses plastiques équestres* at Astley's Amphitheatre, in which he struck attitudes from myth and legend while riding around a circus ring on horseback. Certainly his act emphasized physical strength, daring, and consummate skill, although hints of its erotic aspect were also clear. Circus and vaudeville performers who engaged in acts of strength were known for wearing scanty costumes (sandals, a leopard-skin loincloth) and for posing as Greek statuary. Thus the *poses plastiques* are an early generic precursor of the compulsory figures of competitive bodybuilding, launched by Sandow as early as the late 1880s.

"A British tar is a soaring soul" takes the theatrical practice of posing in attitudes and uses it as a model for the compulsory socialization to a masculine, nationalist ideal. Automatic, unquestioning patriotism is the butt of the joke. In other words, genre parody—of nautical melodrama, of the figure of the Jolly Jack Tar, of posing in attitudes—is used to point out and to criticize cultural and social formations. Gender identification and national identification are shown to be related, scripted performances, their repetitive figures required by tacit communal expectation, as well as by direct order from superior officers, and disguised as leisure activities: "[H]um this at your leisure." To be manly is to be British; to be outspoken about being British is to be manly.

This parodically facile reciprocity suggests the changing face of patriotism at the time of *Pinafore*'s production. The radicalism of Jerrold's melodramas died away in the 1840s, and, increasingly after that, the figure of the British Tar became a tool of imperialist ideology, negotiating "the acceptability of British imperialism to the people" and standing for the heroism of unquestioning national service.[33] Yet *H.M.S. Pinafore* hints at the rise of a critical attitude toward Britain's imperial role. Transitional and complex, *Pinafore* expresses both confidence in and rising skepticism about British expansion. In other words, its parody of nautical melodrama as a genre implies a critique of current attitudes as well, especially of manipulated zeal for national service.

Other scripts of nationalistic fervor were being staged in the music hall. The term "jingoism" entered the language at exactly this moment, a neologism adopted from the music hall in the year *Pinafore* was produced, which was also the year G. H. Macdermott (the "Great Macdermott") brought the audience at the London Pavilion to its feet to cheer his famous "War Song."[34] Macdermott was one of the "Lions Comiques" who in the 1860s and 1870s transformed the music hall from a folk- and street-based tavern culture into a site of political and cultural commentary (and exploitation). He "took the song very seriously as a contribution to British foreign policy," when Russia was threatening to advance into Turkey and capture Constantinople, thus challenging Britain's naval supremacy in the Mediterranean. Soon everyone knew the refrain to "Macdermott's War Song":

> We don't want to fight, but by jingo if we do,
> We've got the ships, we've got the men, and got the money too!
> We've fought the Bear before, and while we're Britons true,
> The Russians shall not have Constantinople![35]

Counter-jingoistic sentiment was expressed in parodies of this song. Henry Pettit, for example, blamed journalists and politicians for inflaming public opinion and demanding war, when in fact it would fall to the common soldier to do the job:

> I don't want to fight
> I'll be slaughtered if I do.
> . . .
> I'd let the Russians have Constantinople![36]

Both "A British tar is a soaring soul" and "He is an Englishman!" balance parodically between imitation and critique, sounding serious while making fun of an uncritical, knee-jerk, jingoistic group mentality. Wonderful examples of the music and words working at cross-purposes, these numbers sound and feel rousing, even though the Sailors' exaggerated attitudes—and the words to "He is an Englishman!"—establish a clear critical humor. Thus the tug-of-war between words and music advances the critique of socialization as well, which has been seen—in Sir Joseph's glee—to take place tacitly, through music and custom. The rousing music is ironic, set against words that put forth the ridiculous premise that national identity is the result of individual choice rather than an "accident of birth":

> He is an Englishman!
>   For he himself has said it,
>   And it's greatly to his credit,
> That he is an Englishman!
> . . .
> For he might have been a Roosian,
> A French, or Turk, or Proosian,

Or perhaps Itali-an!

. . .

But in spite of all temptations
To belong to other nations,
  He remains an Englishman!

The comic malapropism in the pronunciation of the names of "other nations" ("Roosian . . . Proosian") comes to a climax with "Eye-tal-eye-ann," stretched over several beats to emphasize the Sailors' unsophisticated, anti-cosmopolitan bravado. The performance signals a differential in language within the common boundaries of English, a differential that is meant to be heard (as we have seen in *Thespis* and *The Sorcerer*). Emphatically, we are *not* in the music hall, but in a place—and a genre—that can look critically on the music hall. In other words, the superior knowingness of the members of the *Pinafore* audience is affirmed *only if* they imagine themselves as less narrowly patriotic and more cosmopolitan than these "common" Sailors.[37]

By focusing on the Sailors' tacit ("customary") acceptance of their proper gender and national "attitudes" and their smug satisfaction in their nationality, the opera prepares the way for its meditation on other sorts of accidents of birth—those of social class. *H.M.S. Pinafore* takes the sociological premise of environmental determination and turns it on its head.

Upward Mobility, Accidents of Birth, and the Force of Circumstances

Josephine and Sir Joseph share a name, in feminine and masculine forms, so we are invited to notice their thematic entanglement. They throw a double light on the modern potential for social mobility. Josephine is the conventional "Lass That Loved a Sailor," self-divided by the feminine mandate to make a marriage choice that would entail either upward or downward mobility as its consequence.[38] While a man preserves his rank, a woman takes the rank of her husband, whether up or down in the social scale. Even though modern class allows for more mobility than traditional rank, this gender disparity remains in the relation of class to marriage. Thus Josephine is also a figure for the historical transition from traditional to companionate marriage, the one motivated by family alliance and the other by romantic love. Caught, on the one hand, between father and future husband, and, on the other, between rival lovers,

Josephine is structurally central to a plot whose conventionality hardly needs stressing.[39]

Josephine is not the typical melodramatic heroine, however, but a parodic twisting of that ideal. Even the romantic female lead does not escape the thrusts directed against conventional gender performances. Like *Engaged*, Gilbert's comedy of 1877, *Pinafore* (produced the following year) exposes the material concerns hovering behind feminine attitudes of romantic anguish. The critique is conveyed through a parody of recitative in the wonderfully histrionic scena.[40] Josephine dilates upon her romantic psychomachia:

> On the one hand, papa's luxurious home,
>   Hung with ancestral armour and old brasses,
> Carved oak and tapestry from distant Rome,
>   Rare "blue and white" Venetian finger-glasses,
> Rich oriental rugs, luxurious sofa pillows,
> And everything that isn't old, from Gillow's.
> And on the other, a dark and dingy room,
>   In some back street with stuffy children crying,
> Where organs yell, and clacking housewives fume,
>   And clothes are hanging out all day a-drying.
> With one cracked looking-glass to see your face in,
> And dinner served up in a pudding basin!

This catalogue, with its shopping list of all the things necessary for a proper middle-class interior, reduces high operatic emotions to the scope of a middle-class girl's concern for her material comforts. The rising middle classes preposterously imagine an ancient heritage for themselves, with "ancestral" trappings (just as Major-General Stanley in *The Pirates of Penzance* will buy an estate, complete with buried ancestors), retroactively creating a pseudo-aristocratic interior through a cosmopolitan, eclectic collection of objects from Italy and the Orient, both "antiques" and imports joined by furnishings bought new at the best local department store.[41]

If Josephine shows how far we have come from the heroine of melodrama, Sir Joseph shows how far we have come from nautical melodrama's personification of corruption in naval authority. Sir Joseph represents no brute, authoritarian sadist, but a distinctly later nineteenth-century figure: the bureaucrat. An example of social mobility gone wrong, Sir Joseph rose "to the top of the tree" without benefit of *either* birth *or* worth. The figure of Sir Joseph overturns the fundamental premise of poetic justice nurtured by novel and melodrama alike, for his life story is a parody of all the many upward-mobility narratives based on rewarding inner virtue and merit. *Pinafore* mixes parodies of figures from theatrical convention with the parody of a figure from social life.

Although George Grossmith—who created the role of Sir Joseph—was made up to look like Lord Nelson, his character was meant, instead, to suggest W. H. Smith, founder of the eponymous newsagent and bookselling firm. Smith provided a perfect model of unjustifiable upward mobility, for he had no experience at sea, yet had been appointed First Lord of the Admiralty in 1877, the year before *H.M.S. Pinafore* was produced. Smith had begun life as a hawker of newspapers, so he *was* a striking example of upward mobility by virtue of his economic success. Even so, his appointment was shocking, for the cabinet-level position of First Lord still usually went to an aristocrat. (The parody involved in Sir Joseph's caricature is conservative insofar as the new man is no better—indeed, he is worse—than the aristocrat he replaces.) With tongue in cheek, Gilbert denied that the characterization of Sir Joseph had anything to do with Smith. Writing to Sullivan in 1877, he explained: "I send you herewith a sketch plot of the proposed opera. . . . Of course there will be no personality in this—the fact that the First Lord in the opera is a radical of the most pronounced type will do away with any suspicion that W. H. Smith is intended."[42] But Sir Joseph is not a radical, and everyone suspected that Smith was intended. Indeed, a cartoon in *Punch* the year before *Pinafore* was produced shows the wide circulation of the joke about his inexperience (as well as the joke about seasickness and the need to "go below") (figure 4.4).

After *Pinafore*, Smith was inextricably associated with Sir Joseph. Thus can a character from the theater shape a historical figure.[43] Known popularly ever after as "Pinafore Smith," his official appearances were sometimes accompanied (against his will) by the musical strains of "When I was a lad." Popular humor at his expense was widespread. Playing on the homophone "stationery"/"stationary," one popular song, written by Sir Wilfrid Lawson, a radical member of Parliament, stressed the oddity of the First Lord of the Admiralty possessing an expertise in paper products rather than naval matters:

A paper fleet they say is ours,
If what we hear is true.
Let's hope the fleets of other powers
Are stationary too![44]

OUR NEW " FIRST LORD " AT SEA.

ADMIRAL SUPERINTENDENT PUNCH. " WELL, MR. SMITH, I BELIEVE YOU HAVE NOW SEEN EVERYTHING—
ARMOUR, TURRETS, TORPEDOES—EVERYTHING ! OF COURSE YOU UNDERSTAND IT ALL !! "
FIRST LORD. " QUITE SO, THANK YOU. AT LEAST I——" (A little "queer.") "IF YOU DON'T MIND, I THINK
I'LL NOW GO BELOW."

" The Lords of the Admiralty arrived at Portsmouth on their annual tour of inspection."—Morning Paper.

FIGURE 4.4 This cartoon, predating the production of *H.M.S. Pinafore*, demonstrates the popular circulation of jokes about W. H. Smith as First Lord of the Admiralty. John Tenniel, "Our New 'First Lord' at Sea," *Punch*, October 13, 1877. (Reproduced with permission of Punch, Ltd., www.punch.co.uk)

Samuel Butler alludes to *Pinafore* in *The Way of All Flesh* (1873–1884): "[T]he English nation entrusts the welfare of its fleet and naval defenses to a First Lord of the Admiralty, who, not being a sailor, can know nothing about these matters except by acts of faith."[45] And Gilbert, in the summary of *Pinafore* he wrote for children, explained: "You would naturally think that a person who commanded the entire British Navy would be the most accomplished sailor who could be found, but that is not the way in which such things are managed in England."[46]

Poetic justice prevails in the end, reversing Sir Joseph's unjust rise, when the plot of *Pinafore* is suddenly resolved in a parody of melodramatic transformation. In his emphatic use of the phrase "accident of birth" to indicate the arbitrary dispensation of rank, Sir Joseph prepares us early on: "That you are their captain is an accident of birth. I cannot permit these noble fellows to be patronised because an accident of birth has placed you above them and them below you." By the time of *Pinafore*, as is evident in its jokes about socialization, the idea of an "accident of birth" has been superseded by the idea of the "force of circumstances" as the popular catchphrase for social determinism. The latter phrase emphasizes environment and socialization, rather than inheritance, the ability (or inability) to acquire worth, not the luck of birth.[47] In both comic and sentimental veins, Gilbert expressed a strong sense of the injustice resulting from the "force of circumstances":

> Take a tipsy lout
>   Gathered from the gutter—
> Hustle him about—
>   Strap him to a shutter:
> What am I but he,
>   Washed at hours stated—
> Fed on filigree—
>   Clothed and educated?
>   He's a mark of scorn—
>   I might be another,
>   If I had been born
>   Of a tipsy mother!
>
>   Take a wretched thief
>   Through the city sneaking,
>   Pocket handkerchief
>   Ever, ever seeking:
> What is he but I
>   Robbed of all my chances—
> Picking pockets by
>   Force of circumstances?
>   I might be as bad—
>   As unlucky, rather—
>   If I'd only had
>   Fagin for a father!

This song was written later, for *Iolanthe*, and then cut; its political critique was thought to be too sharp.[48] Savoy opera audiences evidently preferred a more tacit awareness of the same phenomenon, such as we find in *Pinafore*. This lyric acknowledges what "He is an Englishman!" humorously disavows, the "force of circumstances" in determining character.

In its parody of melodramatic closure, *Pinafore* uses the genre parody to have fun with the logic of environmental thinking, the "force of circumstances." The agent of transformation is, of course, Little Buttercup. From early in act 1, it is clear that she harbors a melodramatic secret, since when she hears the name Ralph Rackstraw, she exclaims: "Ha! That name! Remorse! Remorse!" On this blatant outburst the entire plot begins to be suspended, for we know that the secret, whatever it is, will be revealed in the end. Her remorse, which has been "slowly but surely eating its way into [her] very heart" like "a canker-worm," is suddenly discharged in a melodramatic confession, a parody of the extreme lengths to which a melodramatic plot must often go in order to resolve itself. The "long concealèd crime / [she] would confess" was committed long ago, when Buttercup "practised baby-farming" in her younger days:

Two tender babes I nussed:
  One was of low condition,
The other, upper crust,
  A regular patrician.
. . .
Oh, bitter is my cup!
  However could I do it?
I mixed those children up,
  And not a creature knew it!
. . .
In time each little waif
  Forsook his foster-mother,
The well-born babe was Ralph—
  Your captain was the other!!!

In other words, this "accident of birth" had nothing to do with birth at all, but it really *was* an accident. Thus Buttercup's mistake both parodies and literalizes the contingencies of birth, shifting the focus to the determining force of nurture rather than nature. And yet, in the end, with topsy-turvy disregard for this sort of sociological insight, suddenly "accidents of birth" reign supreme once again, when the original class positions of Ralph and Captain Corcoran are suddenly restored.

The exchange is literally preposterous, in the way melodramatic resolutions often are, for Ralph and the Captain are retroactively endowed with class-inflected behaviors that would have taken a lifetime of environmental influence to acquire. When realistically imagined, such personal characteristics as dress, manners, and language use are deeply ingrained, habitual, and difficult to alter. (This is the logic of Shaw's *Pygmalion* [1913], which focuses on the lengthy training in new behavior that must underpin an upwardly mobile transformation.) But at the end of *Pinafore*, these socialized effects are transformed in an instant. This is melodrama's way of managing transformation, revealing social identities that have been abiding *in potentia* all along. As this transformation absurdly overturns sociological, environmental determination, so it emphasizes the performative quality of all social roles. *Pinafore* is getting at a rather precise (and profound) point here: the modern potential for social mobility depends on the notion that social roles are theatrical, that they can be put on and taken off like a costume or learned like a new accent.

When they reappear on stage after Little Buttercup's melodramatic revelation, Ralph is dressed in a captain's uniform and Captain Corcoran is dressed as a common sailor. The visual joke is followed by an audible one, for the two characters have exchanged habits of language use as well, the former Captain dropping his *h*'s like a common sailor, and Ralph suddenly issuing peremptory orders. This transformation in their speech is all the more humorous since Ralph has been speaking perfect English all along, his manly eloquence having alerted us from the beginning that he is destined to rise. He is a noble fellow, in the specifically modern sense in which the term "nobility" can now be used to describe the virtuous common man.

These questions of nature and nurture, of innate identity and performance, can be culturally contextualized through the figure of the nursemaid. Andrew Goodman notes that lawsuits regarding abuses of baby-farming were in the courts around the time of *Pinafore*'s composition.[49] It would be a mistake in critical tact to push the cultural significance of Buttercup's baby-farming very far, since the plot device of babies switched in their cradles is as conventional as strawberry marks or magical elixirs. Buttercup is, for example, a recognizably English version of Azucena from Giuseppe Verdi's *Il trovatore* (*The Troubadour*, 1852), with her gypsy blood, her dark sayings, and her baby switching.[50] Still, we can also see that the topic of baby-farming does suggest certain contemporary social anxieties swirling around questions of nature and nurture.

According to Jill Matus, a decades-long, class-inflected debate about wet-nursing peaked in the late 1850s and early 1860s. The debate centered on the nature of motherhood, as well as on the "nature" of other cultural categories, especially class. Is there a natural maternal instinct? If so, why did so many middle-class mothers farm their babies out to be nursed by lower-class or fallen women? Can the milk of fallen women contaminate a middle-class baby with disease or disreputable proclivities? What should be the role of illegitimate fathers? What is the responsibility of the state? Should foundling hospitals employ fallen women as wet nurses, thus helping them to support themselves and their children? Or would employing fallen women as wet nurses be tantamount to encouraging vice or even infanticide? The scandalous use of burial clubs (through which a mother might take out burial-insurance policies and thus profit from the death of her infant) added to the sensational horror of this popular debate.[51]

Although the topic is treated lightly, it is clear that the nursemaid is a powerful figure of fantasy in both *H.M.S. Pinafore* and *The Pirates of Penzance*. Her error in judgment is the origin of the hero's mistaken identity in both these parodies of nautical melodrama. In the regressive setting of *Pinafore*, it is apt that the wet nurse is the agent of a fantasy transformation; thus *Pinafore* implies that the melodramatic resolution is childish (and also, perhaps, that childhood is melodramatic). The parody of a melodramatic transformation in *Pinafore* argues *both* that modern social roles are theatrical *and* that melodrama (as a representation of social reality) is every bit as fantastic as extravaganza. Its transformations happen as if by magic, preposterously presuming to return Ralph and the Captain to social roles they had never performed before. Sir Joseph's question gives the audience time to grasp the humor: "Then I am to understand that Captain Corcoran and Ralph were exchanged in childhood's happy hour—that Ralph is really the Captain, and the Captain is Ralph?" The satire on bureaucracy is brought home by Buttercup's answer: "That is the idea I intended to convey, officially!"

In the end, Little Buttercup will marry Captain Corcoran, who is now a common sailor and, thus, an appropriate match for a bumboat woman. And Josephine will be upwardly mobile after all, since her father is now a common sailor, and her future husband is a captain. If they were at Buttercup's breast together, then Ralph must be approximately as old as Josephine's father. This conundrum further emphasizes the irrationality of the transformation—it is meant to be noticed for that reason alone: "Never mind the why and wherefore!" With a reprise of "He is an Englishman!" the opera ends in a summation of its parodies—not only of the sudden resolutions and the patriotic flourish characteristic of nautical melodrama, but also of the fortuitous "accident of birth" that endowed our nautical hero with his English "customary attitudes" in the first place.

5

Recollecting Illegitimacy

The Pirates of Penzance

Theatrical piracy forms an important context for understanding *The Pirates of Penzance; or, The Slave of Duty* (1880). Major-General Stanley's allusion to *H.M.S. Pinafore* in his famous patter song is the only overt textual suggestion of that fact, but it is a strong suggestion:

> I can hum a fugue of which I've heard the music's din afore,
> And whistle all the airs from that infernal nonsense *Pinafore*.

Breaking the frame with this self-conscious allusion to immediate production history, the Major-General reminds his audience of the enormous popularity accorded to the Savoy opera immediately preceding the one in which he appears. As Andrew Goodman has suggested, the huge domestic and international success of *H.M.S. Pinafore* was due partly to the great interest shown in the opera in the United States; yet the sheer extent of the American piracy is still astounding. By December 1878, eight pirated productions were playing in New York and six in Philadelphia, while "early in 1879 London newspapers announced that over a hundred companies were simultaneously playing unauthorized versions."[1]

At home, too, Gilbert, Sullivan, and Carte discovered the difficulty of controlling their intellectual property. Carte's struggle with the investors in his Comedy Opera Company over the ownership of *Pinafore* issued in a theater riot, when the investors hired thugs to invade the theater and make off with the costumes, props, and as much of the scenery as they could carry. The investors reasoned that the material objects were their property, even if the libretto and music were not. Consequently, they launched their own production of *Pinafore* at a rival venue, and thus two 375th performances of *Pinafore* took place on the same night, "the old cast in new costumes at the Opera Comique, and the new cast in old costumes at the Imperial."[2] The lawsuits pursuant to this absurd situation were not resolved until 1881, by which time Carte had long since established the D'Oyly Carte Opera Company, over which the three partners had total control. Surely the running joke in *The Pirates of Penzance*—that piracy is a business like any other—refers in part to these international and domestic struggles.

After the huge success of *H.M.S. Pinafore*, Gilbert, Sullivan, and Carte could count on popular reception for their next project. Everyone could "whistle all the airs from that infernal nonsense *Pinafore*." But the distortion of their work and the loss of revenue due to American piracy remained vexatious. As we know from the published libretto of *Thespis*, which contains a "Caution to American Pirates" on its title page, this issue had been troubling from the very beginning of the collaboration.[3] Now that the new company had been formed, the next phase of the partners' struggle to secure property rights and high production values began.[4] Domestic piracy of dramatic work had been a problem throughout the nineteenth century. When the Select Committee had heard testimony on the state of the theater in 1832, witnesses overwhelmingly complained of two things: the monopoly of the patent theaters and the absence of any sort of system for dramatic copyright protection.[5] As Douglas Jerrold put it, dramatic authors receive a "double injury" from the pirates: not only losing revenue, but also being "represented by the skeletons of their dramas," so they are "not only robbed but murdered."[6]

Dramatic copyright was slow to distinguish itself from print copyright in Britain.[7] In practice, however, customary stop-gap measures—such as the so-called copyright performance (or "stage-righting," as Shaw called it)—were employed to stabilize the situation.[8] A copyright performance was a stripped-down, token affair, sometimes no more than an on-stage reading of a play, offered at an out-of-the-way theater, with no advance notice. Shortly before the performance, a poster would suddenly appear, and a few audience members (often friends of the playwright) would pay to enter the theater. This limited public performance established stage rights to the play. It was necessary to establish stage rights before committing the play to print, for after the play text was published, it was immediately available to any manager who cared to produce it.[9] John Russell Stephens points out the "Gilbertian" absurdity of such a legal situation: "To the uninitiated, copyright performances had all the makings of Gilbertian burlesque, but they survived on custom and precedent."[10]

Difficult as it was to secure dramatic property within the domestic legal system, it was much more difficult within the transatlantic setting. At this time, American copyright law protected only American citizens. But American law and British law were at odds with each other in other fundamental ways as well. To secure stage rights in the United States, the première had to take place there; however, if a production opened in the United States, British copyright would be forfeited. Conversely, if the play was published in Great Britain, it would become fair game for piracy in the United States. In other words, as John Russell Stephens pithily puts it: "To publish in America was to be deprived of British copyright; to publish in Britain was effectively to lose all rights in America." In Britain, the discourse on dramatic copyright constantly returned to the "need to protect the income of English authors and publishers against depredations by foreign 'pirates,' specifically the Americans."[11]

Sullivan described this situation to his first biographer, Arthur Lawrence. In the United States, as he explained, an "author had a right in his unpublished work in the same way that he could lay claim to his own personal apparel or any other form of property," but he lost this prerogative as soon as the work was published: "The moment any portion of the opera appeared in print it was open to any one in the States to publish, produce, or do what he liked with it." Sometimes, American judges even interpreted performance as publication, thus opening the door to shorthand, longhand, and "memory pirates," who would try to steal the libretto and music from the vantage point of their seats in the audience. Recalling that the reception of *Pinafore* in the United States had "created a tornado-like *furore*," Sullivan dilated on the double result of piracy, which had deprived the authors and their manager of untold revenue, yet had granted them untold publicity. In planning their next venture, they determined to devise a scheme for thwarting "the piratical people." As Sullivan put it: "Our attempt to retain possession of our own property involved us in a guerilla warfare."[12]

In 1879, having announced that they would open their next opera in New York, Gilbert, Sullivan, and Carte traveled to that city well in advance of the première, which had been set for December 31, 1879, at the Fifth Avenue Theater. On the day before the opera opened in New York, however, a matinee copyright performance was staged at the Royal Bijou Theatre in Paignton, a small town in Devonshire not far from Penzance. Unlike the secret, stripped-down, and partially staged readings characteristic of most copyright performances, the Paignton production of *The Pirates of Penzance* was fully staged, with an orchestra and a professional cast. Also anomalously, it was highly publicized, seats were sold, and a full audience was gathered. The playbill announced "the first production *in any country*."[13] In staging this exceptionally public, fully produced performance, perhaps the partners simply hoped to gain more notice than usual for their nationalistic defiance of the American pirates. In addition, though, the production in a town near Penzance linked the themes of the opera to the situation of transatlantic piracy.

Thus the partners cannily managed to stage the "original" performance *both* in Great Britain *and* in the United States. As a practical matter, they made it possible to contend for dramatic copyright in both nations, despite their utterly contradictory laws. As a theoretical matter, this "Gilbertian" absurdity shows that an "original" performance *can* occur in two places—precisely the situation that the evolving law of dramatic copyright sought to regulate. If the uneven development of the law on dramatic copyright can seem absurd and open to parody, that is partly because parody itself engages the same vexed issues of temporal priority, the relation between author and work, and the relation between an original and its copies.

In this situation, at the intersection of art and business, an original and its copies can all be authentic, as long as the productions are controlled by the originating company. This, at least, is what Gilbert, Sullivan, and Carte sought to establish, by staging their authentic version of *Pirates* all over the United States. While in New York, the partners took precautions to secure their work, locking the manuscript score in a safe every night and expelling anyone from the theater audience who was discovered to be taking notes. In addition to securing their original text, they aggressively copied their own work, forming touring companies to take the authentic production to American cities from Boston to Atlanta and thereby attempting preemptively to destroy the commercial value of piracy. Thus they asserted their right to copy by copying. By the time *The Pirates of Penzance* finally opened in London at the Opera Comique several months later, it was already strangely familiar.

In retrospect, we can clearly see that transatlantic piracy benefitted Gilbert, Sullivan, and Carte as well as robbed them, but the struggle against it lasted throughout their collaboration.[14] Their aggressive litigiousness did help to clarify the law of dramatic copyright (and to clarify it in their favor).[15] Thus the D'Oyly Carte Opera Company plays an important role in histories of copyright law, histories of theatrical business practice, and histories of theatrical aesthetics in the nineteenth century. In Savoy opera, these three aspects of the struggle to control intellectual property are deeply intertwined. Thus for understanding *The Pirates of Penzance*, it is important to appreciate the fact that it was written and produced within the context of an ongoing struggle with the American pirates. In fact, the opera may be regarded as a wholesale allusion to theatrical piracy. In this respect, *Pirates* contributes to the operas' evolving wit about "company" practices, as well as their wit about

Law in the abstract. But theatrical piracy does not exhaust the forms of illegitimacy important to this opera, which also recollects illegitimate theater, illegitimate governmental authority, and illegitimate sexuality.

Illegitimate Theater

During the first third of the nineteenth century, the distinction between legitimate and illegitimate theater governed all forms of production and reception, although it was always contested.[16] The distinction follows from the Licensing Act of 1737, even though the specific terms ("legitimate" and "illegitimate") do not appear in its language. The act strengthened and codified earlier law and custom, dating back to at least 1662, when Charles II had granted patents to Covent Garden and Drury Lane, establishing them as the only two houses licensed to produce spoken drama. Thus the so-called patent theaters maintained a virtual monopoly, but they were also subject to regulation by the Lord Chamberlain, whose authority the act strengthened and codified as law.[17] Through his Examiner of Plays, the Lord Chamberlain could refuse to license a play for several reasons: subversive political commentary, especially during periods of unrest; unorthodox or skeptical religious views; and profanity or other offensive language. Furthermore, impersonation of the royal family (or of their ministers and official representatives) was forbidden. Due to the fear of a copycat effect, in order to control class disaffection, dramatic representations of notorious crimes were later disallowed as incendiary. Then, too, especially during the nineteenth century, codes of sexual propriety grew more and more stringent.[18] To what extent the Examiner of Plays followed public sentiment and to what extent he created it must remain a matter of debate in every historical period and in every particular case.

As Jane Moody demonstrates, a rich culture of illegitimate theater gradually grew up outside the purview of the patent theaters. Although the language of the patents stipulates that "all . . . entertainments of the stage" be performed only in the patent theaters, other houses did produce such entertainments, usually licensed by local magistrates. In direct opposition to the Licensing Act, managers attempted various creative evasions of its strictures. Challenging the part of the act that forbids playing "for gain, hire or reward," Henry Gifford charged a fee to listen to music, and then presented George Farquhar's *The Beaux' Stratagem* (1707) for free.[19] Challenging the "unwritten ban on spoken dialogue," Samuel Foote used puppets; his *Handsome Housemaid; or, Piety in Pattens*—a parody of Samuel Richardson's

Pamela; or, Virtue Rewarded (1740)—whose subtitle also makes fun of "piety in patents," used no human actors at all.[20] Certain spectacular scenes, such as the "blow up," in which a tyrant's or an aristocrat's castle explodes in flames of "red fire," were clearly perceived as metonymic displacements of explosive revolutionary feeling, likely to inflame their audiences.[21] While playing the hero of John Dent's *The Bastille* (Royal Circus, 1789), John "Plausible Jack" Palmer was prosecuted for "speaking Prose on the Stage" and committed to the Surrey jail as a rogue and a vagrant. In response to challenges like these, subsequent legislative acts introduced further regulations for places of "public entertainment," which were more and more associated with disorder, riotous enjoyment, sexual transgression, and even criminality. As Moody argues, it was "from this portmanteau category of public entertainments [that] illegitimate theatre would . . . evolve."[22]

Moody's focus on the "invention of illegitimate culture" helps us to see the relation of all sorts of theatrical genres within the category of the illegitimate.[23] She points out that the Licensing Act of 1737 itself "indirectly contributed to the emergence of an uncensored theatrical terrain beyond the control of the Lord Chamberlain." Within that "uncensored theatrical terrain" grew a popular culture of great energy and diversity.[24] In other words, the attempt to outlaw certain forms of theatrical entertainment instead created the conditions for them to proliferate within a relatively unregulated realm. Moody argues that the abolition of the distinction between "legitimate" and "illegitimate" (by the Theatre Regulation Act of 1843) can be seen to have had a deleterious effect. After 1843, exposed to the blue pencil of the Examiner of Plays, theatrical works that had been performed without scrutiny—"unlicensed," true, but at the same time unregulated—were now subject to censorship. Thus the nullification of the distinction became, ironically, a route toward more pervasive regulation in theatrical productions of all sorts.[25]

Before 1843, however, productions not based on dramatic speech were danced, acted in dumb show, declaimed to the accompaniment of music, spoken in verse, or sung. These illegitimate productions also used linen scrolls, banners, or flags with words printed on them, like captions or supertitles. Dramatic speech, in other words, was sometimes replaced with silence, sometimes with writing, sometimes with spectacle, and sometimes with music. Music soon became the dominant strategy for identifying a production that made no claim to legitimacy. The "*burletta* rule" stipulated that a performance could be exempt from the Licensing Act as long as it contained at least five pieces of incidental music. Thus it is no exaggeration to say that music itself was a mark of illegitimacy in the theater. For an understanding of Savoy opera, the importance of this fact cannot be overemphasized. Savoy opera's precursor genres came into being in relation to these strictures and the formal strategies for evading censorship and regulation; they bear the sedimented history of their relation to state control of the theater, both adhering to and pressing against the distinction between legitimate and illegitimate theater. The idea that music can express what cannot be expressed in words is no mere sentimental formulation, then, but a legal contingency, a historical fact conveyed in form.

The "illegitimate culture" that Moody describes is a culture of rebellion against authority, mixture rather than purity, bodies rather than texts, outlaws against the law, lower classes rather than upper, and inverted gender practices. All these characteristics of illegitimate theater are recollected in *The Pirates of Penzance*. Indeed, Savoy opera in general recollects the productive, generative effect of illegitimate theater, providing persistent allusions to the illicit within the well-established confines of legitimate theater. By the time of Gilbert and Sullivan's collaboration, the distinction between legitimate and illegitimate theater had long been a thing of the past. But the cultural memory of illegitimate theater remained, its various forms recalled in genre parodies. In *Pirates*, the recollected forms of illegitimacy include piracy itself, past genres of illegitimate theater, and various kinds of behavior. Needless to say, English comic opera recollects illegitimacy in an ostentatiously legitimate and respectable form. Genre parody allows this highly respectable genre to flirt with all sorts of risky material, preserving, while disavowing, illegitimate forms of theater and social life. Recollection—as memory, but also as re-mix—is a primary characteristic of the illegitimate genres, which "delighted in second-hand cultural property," sampling and mixing it all up in "monstrous medlies."[26] The mixed genre of Savoy opera continues this illegitimate mixture, while ostentatiously displaying its own integrity as a coherently overarching work, an *opera*. Savoy opera offers a parodic composite, a re-mix of already mixed forms.

Illegitimate Authority

As we have seen, nautical melodrama often implies a critique of naval (and, by extension, state) authority. Both *H.M.S. Pinafore* and *The Pirates of Penzance* base their parody on nautical melodrama, but they seize on its cluster of generic interests in different ways. *Pinafore* concentrates on the construction of national identity and the class conflicts inherent in naval hierarchy (analogous to those in society at large, for the ship represents a microcosm of social relations). *Pirates* concentrates on the opposition between law and lawlessness in general, represented as the conflict between Police and Pirates, land and sea, duty and freedom. Yet both focus on the figure of bureaucratic incompetence, an illegitimate authority figure particular to the later nineteenth century. Both *Pinafore* and *Pirates* base part of their humor on an anachronistic juxtaposition of conventional figures from the past (Jolly Jack Tar, pirates) with newer, illegitimate figures from the present.

The figure of the pirate was conventional long before 1880, when *The Pirates of Penzance* was produced, an even older stock character than the Jolly Jack Tar of nautical melodrama. Along with their generic confrères—corsairs, buccaneers, giaours, smugglers, robbers, highwaymen, brigands, and bandits—pirates are quintessential outlaws in both social and sexual terms. They abound in all the genres of musical theater, from pirate opera—Bellini's *Il pirata* (1827), for example, and Auber's *Fra Diavolo* (1830)—to the lighter, fantasy genres that offer Ali Baba or Captain Hook to fascinate children and adults alike. Melodrama depends on its villains to motivate the action, but those villains often are figures of fantasy and desire. Sometimes heroic criminals represent idealized figures of rebellion like Jack Sheppard, the famous prison breaker. Sometimes, though, melodramatic villains have turned criminal for a good reason, like the robbers of Friedrich Schiller's ur-melodrama *Die Räuber* (*The Robbers*, 1782), whose outlaw band gathers under the leadership of an angry disinherited son. Significantly, the working title of *The Pirates of Penzance* was *The Robbers*.[27] When we learn that the Pirates are "noblemen who had gone wrong," they are clearly being slotted into this venerable convention.

Like the eighteenth-century Tar, the pirate is a roving rogue, free from state control; in the nineteenth century, however, when the Jolly Jack Tar became a figure of national virtue, pirates and Tars parted company. The great age of the Mediterranean pirates ended in the eighteenth century, smugglers largely taking their place in the imagination of the nineteenth; by then, the pirate was a quaint, slightly old-fashioned figure. Pirates and smugglers are "shadow manifestations of the Tar," personifying the threat to legitimate authority at sea or on land at the borders of the nation.[28] Like two sides of a coin, the figures of the common sailor and the pirate show the genre's meditation on faithful national service and its opposite. The opposite of dutifulness is anti-authoritarianism, which is why a pirate who is "the slave of duty" is so funny a concept. But a pirate band has its own rules; it is a world elsewhere, organized as a parody of society on land. Needless to say, in both *Pinafore* and *Pirates*, these conventional figures of nautical melodrama are parodically exaggerated and inverted, yielding humorous figures of polite Sailors and sentimental Pirates.[29] And, unfortunately, the Pirates of Penzance follow the wrong rules, and they cannot make piracy pay. When the action of *Pirates* pauses for the anthem to poetry ("Hail, Poetry! . . . thou gildest e'en the pirate's trade"), the joke turns on anachronism; romantically harking back to a former time allows for sentimentalization. Thus *The Pirates of Penzance* is set on the coast of Cornwall, at the very edge of the island nation, offering the recollection of a former time and days of piracy long gone by.[30]

Pirates are central to literary history, too, from Aphra Behn and Daniel Defoe to Walter Scott and Byron. Scott's *The Pirate* (1822) provides a good example of Romantic literary history inspiring many a theatrical representation. Set in the late seventeenth century, during the great age of piracy, in a land occupied by many erstwhile and disguised pirates, the novel features Cleveland, a Byronic hero, and a young hero through whom (as always in Scott) complex historical forces act and who must learn to become his own man. *The Pirate* also contains a strain of light comedy, including a minor character who is an actor-pirate; Scott clearly understood the theatrical potential of his own novel. Indeed, three music dramas—by Thomas J. Dibdin, James Robinson Planché, and William Dimond—appeared in the same year the novel was published. James Fenimore Cooper, objecting to Scott's lack of realism, wrote a response five years later. His *Red Rover* (1827) features an eponymous character who has killed an English officer and is therefore forced to become a rover to escape hanging. An influential representation of the repentant pirate, whose restoration to orderly society is effected by his sister, *The Red Rover*, too, inspired many dramatizations in the same year (in London, Paris, and Philadelphia), followed by the most influential version, Edward Fitzball's in 1829.

At least since Byron's *The Corsair* (1814), women were supposed especially to enjoy pirates, thrilling to their dashing and dangerous sex appeal. Gilbert's *Princess Toto* (1876, with music by Frederic Clay) features an episode in which the ditzy Toto is eager to be captured by a Brigand Chief; when she becomes assimilated into the brigand band, however, she is magnificent in the cross-dressed attire of the extravaganza tradition (figure 5.1). This joke resurfaces in *The Pirates of Penzance*, when the Pirates try to "marry" the Wards. Parodied by Charlotte Brontë, this titillating vogue is featured in *Jane Eyre* (1847), where the stereotypical fashionable lady flirts by boasting: "I dote on corsairs!" By the middle of the nineteenth century, in other words, the fashionable interest in pirates could be parodied as an affectation of middle- and upper-class women who, it could be assumed, were interested in the thrill of pirate abduction, as long as it was represented at the safe distance of literature or theater. *The Pirates of Penzance* plays with this gendered appeal, as we shall see.

FIGURE 5.1 Kate Santley as Princess Toto, dressed as a female brigand. Autographed cabinet photograph (ca. 1876 or 1877). (Collection of Fredric Woodbridge Wilson)

The genre parody in *The Pirates of Penzance* also includes opéra bouffe, for the proximate source for *The Pirates of Penzance* was Jacques Offenbach's *Les brigands* (1869), whose libretto, by Henri Meilhac and Ludovic Halévy, Gilbert translated in 1871.[31] *Thespis* works toward English comic opera by crossing opéra bouffe with classical extravaganza, but *The Pirates of Penzance* crosses opéra bouffe with nautical melodrama. Thus into the parody of nautical melodrama initiated by *H.M.S. Pinafore*, the bouffe pirate comes to play, engaging fantasies of freedom from the law of the land, along with outlaw sexuality of various sorts. In other words, *Pirates* offers a bouffe array of illegitimacies as much as a melodramatic one.

Following *Les brigands*—and, indeed, many other melodramas and melodrama burlesques—*The Pirates of Penzance* treats stealing as a profession like any other.[32] Gilbert adapts the motto of Offenbach's brigands—"Il faut voler selon la position qu'on occupe dans le monde" (One must steal according to the position one occupies in the world)—in the opening song of the Pirate King. Like Offenbach's brigands, too, the Pirates of Penzance cannot make their business pay, although Gilbert brilliantly adds the running joke about orphans, which we will consider in a moment. Gilbert's libretto goes much further, too, into the absurdity of treating piracy as a career path like any other, imagining Frederic as an apprentice. A "tools of the trade" joke in act 2, when the Pirates decide to "vary piracee / With a little burglaree," is also indebted to *Les brigands*. The business in *Pirates*, when the Pirates receive the implements of burglary (crowbar, center bit, life preserver, silent matches, dark lantern, file, and skeleton keys) takes off on—and improves—a scene in *Les brigands* in which a character is sworn into brigand law while the mantel, hat, dagger, and gun are presented. In the comparable scene from *Pirates*, the musical parody of the "Anvil Chorus" implicitly equates these Pirates-turned-burglars with the gypsies of Verdi's *Il trovatore* (*The Troubadour*, 1852), who celebrate their hard work and its conventional reward: good wine, women, and song. Finally, the joke that piracy is a vocation like any other spills over into the romantic plot, as it does in *Les brigands*, where Falsacappa is reluctant to let his daughter marry the man she loves, a simple landowner. "Marry my daughter to an honest man? Never!" he protests. After all, "not just anyone can become a robber."[33] This joke, too, is sharpened in *Pirates*, in the exchange between the Major-General and the Pirate King. "I object to pirates as sons-in-law," says the Major-General, to which the Pirate King responds, "We object to Major-Generals as fathers-in-law." In sum, the humor of *Pirates* is denser and more complex, the genre parody effecting an improvement on *Les brigands*.

The idea that stealing may be regarded as a profession, like any other, is underscored by the Police, when they imagine the felon's employment and enjoyment, "just as great as any honest man's." In both *Les brigands* and *The Pirates of Penzance*, sentimental Pirates are structurally opposed to another parodic inversion of type: timid and incompetent Policemen. In both works, the forces of law are weak and ridiculous; both the timid Police in *Pirates* and the Mantuan carabinieri in *Les brigands* are known for their bluff, exaggerated marching. The sound of their boots announces their arrival in *Les brigands*, but they always arrive too late, whereas the Policemen in *Pirates* stomp around proclaiming their timidity: "*marching in single file . . . in line, facing audience,*" they sing:

> When the foeman bares his steel,
> > Tarantara! tarantara!
> We uncomfortable feel,
> > Tarantara!
> And we find the wisest thing,
> > Tarantara! tarantara!
> Is to slap our chests and sing,
> > Tarantara!

(Like the Peers in *Iolanthe*, these childish Policemen are inspired to imitate manliness by the chant of "the trumpet's martial sound, / Tarantara!")

Mabel possesses the bravery that the Police lack, and therefore she becomes a parodic figure of the feminine reformer. Trying to engender courage, she exhorts the Police to "Go ye heroes, go and die!" This feminine martial valor is clearly too easily adopted by someone who need not go herself. Thus the critique of gender yokes a fragile masculinity to a corelatively fierce and bloodthirsty femininity. Meanwhile, the Policemen cringe and gulp and repeat their resolve, yet famously delay. Like the Pirates, who weepingly forgive Frederic his wish to murder them, they reinterpret Mabel's words, determined to imagine that her intentions are sympathetic:

> We observe too great a stress
> On the risks that on us press,
> And of reference a lack
> To our chance of coming back.
>
> . . .
>
> Still to us it's evident
> These intentions are well meant.

In a parody of nautical melodrama, this representation of weak authority cleverly dovetails with piratical anti-authoritarianism.

Along with sentimental Pirates and cowardly Policemen, the incompetent bureaucrat is another personification of authority gone wrong. Like Sir Joseph Porter, Major-General Stanley personifies illegitimate authority at a time later than that of the figures of Tars and pirates, a time when the nation-state, with its increasingly centralized government and burgeoning bureaucracy, had prompted an awareness of illegitimate authority not outside, but inside the system. "I am the very model of a modern Major-General" is this opera's version of the professional confession, like the "Judge's Song" in *Trial by Jury* and "I am the monarch of the sea," Sir Joseph's description of his bureaucratic career path. Perhaps the most famous (and certainly the most frequently parodied) patter song in the entire Gilbert and Sullivan canon, the "Major-General's Song" makes it clear that his so-called expertise is only a patchwork of more or less irrelevant information, undigested and outdated. In his character, authority has degenerated into cheerful imbecility, shrunk to the size of an antic little man who boasts that his brain is "teeming with a lot o' news."

Like Reginald Bunthorne in *Patience*, the character of Major-General Stanley is formed as a journalistic bricolage, very much like his expertise.

After the near-impersonations of Sir Alexander Cockburn in the character of the Learned Judge in *Trial by Jury* and of W. H. Smith in the figure of Sir Joseph Porter in *H.M.S. Pinafore*, Major-General Stanley is a composite character, alluding to several real-world figures at once. *Pirates* does flirt with illegitimate impersonation, whose success as humor depends on the knowing access of the audience to a public sphere of discourse outside the theater. Clues to the interpretation of his character are offered in performance. George Grossmith, who created the role of Major-General Stanley, was given "the elegantly twirled moustache and the slightly imperious manner" of Viscount Sir Garnet Wolseley, who had recently led British troops against Coomassie in the Third Ashanti War (1873–1874).[34] Wolseley was enormously popular, yet was also commonly thought to possess only dated knowledge of military tactics.[35] Most productions of *Pirates* still outfit Major-General Stanley in African expeditionary garb, including the Wolseley pith helmet. (Wolseley is recollected again by Colonel Calverley in *Patience*, who recalls "the skill of Sir Garnet in thrashing a cannibal.") Perhaps Major-General Stanley's pretense at nobility also refers to Wolseley, who had bought property as a way to separate himself from his humble origins.[36] The Major-General buys an estate, including "the chapel and its contents," the dead bodies buried there, whom he adopts as "his ancestors," referring to himself as "their descendant by purchase (if I may so describe myself)." Thus his nobility is literally preposterous, a retroactive acquisition of something irreducibly inherited and non-material: a noble family line.

The character of Major-General Stanley also suggests cabinet matters, for the name Stanley echoes that of two other Stanleys: Sir Frederick Stanley, the Secretary of State for the Colonies, and Henry Morton Stanley, the journalist-explorer who found David Livingston in Africa in 1871. Frederick Stanley was associated in the cabinet with W. H. "Pinafore" Smith, so it is clear that Gilbert was still pursuing that game. In 1880, when *The Pirates of Penzance* was first performed, Henry Stanley had recently taken up a post in the Congo, where he was to spend five years in colonial administration.[37] Major-General Stanley's name, then, as well as his mustache and his pith helmet, are unmistakable references to the British colonial incursions into Africa. Thus his particular incompetence alludes to imperial expansion, ignorance in the prosecution of national defense, and colonial mismanagement. These allusive references, in other words, hint at a critique, but it is soft, oblique, and scattershot, exactly like extravaganza topicality. Veiled even at the time, this critique is almost inaccessible to audiences now (except to those who can interpret the cultural significance of the pith helmet).

Rife with figures of illegitimate authority, *The Pirates of Penzance* even more pointedly makes fun of its supposed opposite: duty. Like the Jolly Jack Tar, the opposite of the pirate in the lexicon of melodramatic types, Frederic displays the hyperbolic virtue whose very excess is the sign of parody. His self-division, unlike the Tar's, does not bespeak the struggle between private and public duty; instead, Frederic owes allegiance to two opposed systems of socialization, two opposed systems of law. The deep coherence of this opera's humor can be felt here, as the meditation on socialization, carried over from *H.M.S. Pinafore*, is joined to a nascent meditation on the conflict of cultures, which would begin to be articulated more particularly in *Iolanthe* and *The Mikado*. The parodic exaggeration of "duty" (to the point of slavery) formulates another critique of bourgeois respectability. Shaw, for example, points out that the theme of *Pirates* is the same as that of Henrik Ibsen's *The Wild Duck* (1884), but one treats the overestimation of duty as an absurdity while the other launches a "grimly serious attack."[38]

As the "slave of duty," Frederic is the quintessential figure of professional self-division, torn absurdly between his socialized identity as a Pirate and his respect for the law of the land. His address to the Pirates makes this clear:

Oh! pity me, my beloved friends, for such is my sense of duty that, once out of my indentures, I shall feel myself bound to devote myself heart and soul to your extermination!

His acquisition of his exaggerated "sense of duty" is preposterously portrayed as a matter of time. Half an hour before he reaches his majority, he offers the Pirates friendly professional advice, but at exactly noon, he leaves them to their fate at the hands of the law. This is essentially the same joke that governs the end of *Pinafore*, when Captain Corcoran and Ralph Rackstraw suddenly change places; in *Pirates*, it is as if moral reasoning and the sense of duty, supposedly internalized over time, could be acquired or applied instantaneously. Confused, one Pirate asks for elucidation: "You wouldn't have us absolutely merciless?" And Frederic replies: "There's my difficulty; until twelve o'clock I would, after twelve I wouldn't. Was ever a man placed in so delicate a situation?"

The word "delicate" is a clue to the absurdity, indicating the fastidious precision, the minute scruples engendered by the rituals of bourgeois socialization. As we all know, Frederic's "delicate situation" is eventually resolved in act 2 through a homeopathic dose of hyper-logical reasoning by clock and calendar. When challenged about the logic chopping that resolves the dilemma, the Pirate King *"produc[es a] document"* in true melodramatic fashion, showing that indeed Frederic was indentured not until his twenty-first "year" but until his twenty-first "birthday." Thus the formal parody of melodrama as a genre again involves the parody of sociological or environmental thinking, as it does in *Pinafore*. For where did Frederic get his exaggerated sense of duty? As in the revelation of Ralph's identity at the conclusion of *Pinafore*, Frederic's great "delicacy" seems to be the sign of innate virtue, not of the force of circumstances; yet Frederic's career shows him to be the quintessential victim of circumstance—again, as in *Pinafore*, at the hand of a nursemaid.

Illegitimate Sexuality: Nursemaids, Wards, and Orphans

It goes without saying that a nursemaid is absurdly out of place among pirates. After Ruth's nurture of Frederic is no longer required, she becomes a "piratical maid-of-all-work" to the sentimental pirate band. (Thus these Pirates are not "ruthless," for Ruth is on board their very ship!) Most important, Ruth is responsible for binding Frederic to the pirate band:

> I was, alas! his nurserymaid, and so it fell to *my* lot
> To take and bind this promising boy apprentice to a *pilot*—
> . . .
> Mistaking my instructions, which within my brain did gyrate,
> I took and bound this promising boy apprentice to a *pirate*.
> A sad mistake it was to make and doom him to a vile lot.
> I bound him to a pirate—you!—instead of to a pilot.

The premise that Ruth is hard of hearing rationalizes the near-pun that launches Frederic's career. As Richard Schoch has argued, the burlesque pun operates on the material surface of language, as pure sound, playing between sense and nonsense and leaning toward the latter.[39] In this case, sound does triumph over sense, and promiscuous language causes real trouble. This particular play on words does make sense, however, within the context of genre, since pilots are among the many conventional figures of nautical melodrama. The Savoy parody thus converts the convention of nonsensical sonic coincidence into a zany principle of reason. The "pilot"/"pirate" confusion presents us with a quintessential example of the pun playing a fundamental part in plot construction, rather than remaining an incidental sonic diversion. The "orphan"/"often" confusion, which we will examine shortly, is another such example.

Pushing hard on the absurdities of socialization developed in *H.M.S. Pinafore*, Gilbert shifts the mechanism from baby switching and "accidents of birth" to word switching (and an accident of career). The agent of confusion is the same, however: the nursemaid. In other words, Frederic's mistaken career is determined in the nursery, where parental authority is absent, having been delegated to "a stupid nurserymaid." Parental absence and surrogation, an important theme in melodrama, usually suggests the vulnerable modern subject, no longer covered by patriarchal protection. Thus Ruth is another figure of illegitimate authority, like Little Buttercup in *Pinafore*, with her displaced maternal control over the identities of Ralph and the Captain. In traditional parody, ruling women are the last word in illegitimate authority—"women on top," the ne plus ultra of the carnivalesque— but the Savoy operas consistently show their awareness of that literary and cultural convention.[40] Like Major-General Stanley, Ruth is a surrogate parent, an oblique and inadequate substitute for a grounding authority missing in the modern world.

Because she is a mother surrogate, Ruth also suggests the possibility of incest (a taboo, as we have seen in *Thespis*, very much alive in several of the Savoy operas). Her quasi-incestuous desire is overtly clear in the plot, "frighteningly fierce and explicitly sexual," as Adrienne Munich puts it.[41] Just before the parody rape scene, in which the Pirates attempt to "marry" all the Wards, Frederic is disillusioned to discover that Ruth is not, after all, the paragon of womanhood he has been taught to imagine her. Since he has been living in an exclusively male society on board the pirate ship, Ruth is the only woman he has ever seen, and thus he cannot evaluate her appearance. In their encounter, she becomes the butt of a misogynist joke about the sexual desire of a middle-aged woman, overly fervid and out of place because of its long frustration, "accumulating / Forty-seven year." But when Frederic catches sight of the nubile Wards, he suddenly realizes the extent of her quasi-maternal manipulation. "Oh, false one, you have deceived me!" he rages.

> And now I see you're plain and old.
> . . .
> Upon my innocence you play.
> . . .
> Your face is lined, your hair is grey.

Thus the extreme power of socialization trumps even sensory perception; he literally had not been able to see her before this moment.

In other words, the crisis of Frederic's majority is a sexual crisis as well as a professional one. It, too, is delineated as a matter of time, dividing his life into a pre-sexual before and an overtly heterosexual after. A moment ago *he* was the innocent one, played on (and almost preyed on) by the figure of a sexualized mother surrogate. The moment of incestuous danger at the hands of the older woman passes in a flash, and she is safely stereotyped as the ridiculous figure of the desiring middle-aged woman. Like other middle-aged female characters in the Savoy operas, Ruth is controversial.[42] Is she a misogynist figure or a fantastic figure of powerful gender-bending? My answer is that she is *both*. The shift in her characterization is very clear, for in act 2 she is recast as a female member of the pirate band (figure 5.2).[43]

Precisely at the moment of his revulsion at the body of the mother surrogate, Frederic undergoes the process of sexualization, condensed into a sudden, traumatic event. This is another joke about socialization, as if the transformative effects of a long process could take place with melodramatic suddenness; but it also registers the sense that sexualization itself is traumatic. The light-hearted boy's adventure does not disguise the fact that

FIGURE 5.2 Rosina Brandram as Ruth in act 2 of *The Pirates of Penzance*, dressed as a female pirate. Cabinet photograph by Alfred Ellis & Walery (London, 1900). (Collection of Fredric Woodbridge Wilson)

Frederic is simultaneously turning away from a cloying mother figure and renouncing the male homosocial band on board the pirate ship in favor of a heterosexual choice. True, homosociality need not imply homosexuality, but recent scholarship has shown that the sodomitical pirate was a well-established figure in the early eighteenth century, and, although veiled in the nineteenth, it was not forgotten.[44] Pirate life on the high seas afforded the fantasy of freedom from the law, from domestication, from women, and from all the normative restrictions of life on land, the model of what Hakim Bey terms the "temporary autonomous zone."[45] This polymorphous fantasy of escape into a world elsewhere is also characteristic of the extravaganza, with its Never Land of "pirate time," as Michael Warner calls it, with reference to J. M. Barrie's *Peter Pan*.[46] Of course, *Peter Pan* is a late pirate and fairy extravaganza, whose hero never grows up and whose world of "Lost Boys" might remind us of the regressive element we noticed in *Pinafore*. For even though Frederic attains his majority at the beginning of the opera, his access to manhood will be figuratively reversed in the end, and he will figuratively return to a time before sexual complications could rear their heads. At that point, he figuratively regresses to become a little boy of five and a quarter. For now, however, Frederic's heterosexuality suddenly occurs to him.

Seeing the girls frolicking on the shore, he suddenly recognizes his own manliness. Correlatively, the girls are ostentatiously feminine, for chatter is the feminine counterpart of masculine patter, conveying a gender-specific superficiality.[47] These graphically gendered groups face each other on stage (figure 5.3). Being "the slave of duty," however, Frederic no sooner feels his own sexual desire than he anxiously worries about the propriety of his piratical allure:

> What shall I do? Before these gentle maidens
> I dare not show in this alarming costume.
> No, no, I must remain in close concealment
> Until I can appear in decent clothing!

Thus Frederic simultaneously calls attention to his conventionally sexy costume, pants as tight as tights or the pirate "skirt" that would show his calves (a notable attraction in male as well as female sexual display at this time), while acting out his great delicacy in matters of sexual propriety (figure 5.4).[48] The girls respond to his "effective but alarming costume" and to his story: "How pitiful his tale! How rare his beauty!" Much rhyming of "beauty" with "duty" emphasizes the funny tug-of-war between sexual desire and propriety.

FIGURE 5.3 A graphic opposition of law and outlaws: (*upper half*) in act 1, the Chorus of Wards faces the Chorus of Pirates; (*lower half*) in act 2, the Pirate King and Ruth accost Major-General Stanley in his nightcap. Engraving by D. H. Friston, in *Illustrated Sporting and Dramatic News*, April 24, 1880. (Collection of Fredric Woodbridge Wilson)

A parody of middle-class feminine philanthropy, Mabel volunteers to rescue Frederic from his "unfortunate position," while the chattering girls pointedly suggest that her "sense of duty" is determined by the fact that he is "a thing of beauty." Mabel's feminine urge to reform an erring male matches Frederic's dutiful masculinity.

The relation between Ruth and Frederic is not the only suggestion of illegitimate sexuality in *Pirates*. Like Ruth, Major-General Stanley is a parent surrogate. In melodrama, the replacement of the father by an ineffectual surrogate often signals a wider and deeper social disorder, sometimes through illegitimate sexuality within the family.[49] Surrounded by a bevy of Wards, however, Major-General Stanley is not quasi-incestuously "susceptible," as is the Lord Chancellor in *Iolanthe*. The plot of *Pirates* turns his oblique relation to his Wards another way, raising the question of their origins. This question is often asked in commentary on *The Pirates*

FIGURE 5.4 The pirate "skirt" backed by the Jolly Roger: Richard Temple as the Pirate King. Engraving by M. Stretch, in *Illustrated Sporting and Dramatic News*, June 26, 1880. (Collection of Fredric Woodbridge Wilson)

of Penzance: Why does the Major-General have so many daughters (aside from the necessity of forming a female Chorus)? And if they are actually his daughters, why are they "Wards in Chancery" (aside from the necessity of rhyming with "caravanserai")? Ian Bradley helpfully points out that wards in Chancery are usually orphans. But he then undermines this helpful suggestion, reverting to the notion that the girls are actually Major-General Stanley's daughters and stretching to provide an explanation of why, then, they would be placed in wardship.[50] This is to seize the question by the wrong handle, as if the Major-General were a real person, whose motives and life story could be ascertained outside the information we are given in the opera. Instead, we should simply accept, as a given of the plot, that the girls are wards. In other words, *they are meant to suggest orphans*. This would make a great deal of sense, because it would knit the Major-General and the Wards more firmly to the opera's other humorous meditations on the figure of the orphan. According to my line of reasoning, Major-General Stanley refers to them as his "daughters," and they refer to him as "Father," as a matter of polite convention, not as a matter of actual relation. Given the importance of orphanage in *Pirates*, the suggestion that the girls are orphans could hardly be an accident.

During the nineteenth century, the figure of the ward was closely aligned to—and was often a euphemism for—the orphan, which itself carries a suggestion of possible sexual impropriety and illegitimacy in the past.[51] Both orphans and wards figuratively suggest the illegitimate child, whose origins have been obscured for respectable bourgeois representation. Think of Heathcliff in *Wuthering Heights* (1847), the uncertainty about his origin and the difficulty of assimilating him into the family. Or think of Adèle Varens in *Jane Eyre*, Rochester's ward and clearly his illegitimate daughter with Celine Varens. Or think of Esther Summerson in *Bleak House* (1852), the illegitimate child of Lady Dedlock, or Daniel Deronda, whose lifelong worry that he might be Sir Hugo's illegitimate son is eventually settled by the revelation of his true identity. Thus the orphan and the ward—these two figures of the nineteenth-century version of the "family romance"—form a symbolic pair, as do the foundling and the bastard in the eighteenth-century novel, as do second sons and governesses in the nineteenth-century novel, as do the disinherited sons and fallen women of melodrama.[52]

In other words, this suggestion of illegitimacy is also a matter of genre. Extravaganza and opéra bouffe have their own figures and styles of sexual suggestiveness, but the ward and the orphan belong most especially to the novel and to melodrama. In the history of the novel, the orphan is the quintessential figure of social mobility and self-making, the character who must devise an identity and a place in the social order. Abandoned to the vicissitudes of the world, the novelistic orphan testifies to the power of *Bildung* and to its fantasies of social self-creation. But in the history of melodrama, the orphan is often explicitly the sign of illegitimacy in the family; seduction and abandonment of the mother; rakish and irresponsible paternity; social disorder and disorganized inheritance. Denis Diderot's *Le fils naturel* (*The Natural Son*, 1757); August von Kotzebue's *Das Kind der Liebe* (*Lovers' Vows*, 1790); Guilbert de Pixérécourt's *Coelina* (1800), "the child of mystery"; and Edward Fitzball's *The Inchcape Bell; or, The Dumb Sailor Boy* (1828) all offer theatrical turns on this figure. Most relevant to *The Pirates of Penzance*, Harry Wilder in Fitzball's *The Red Rover* is a foundling, while "Frederic, an orphan" is one of the dramatis personae in his *Floating Beacon* (1824).[53] Thus these figures of illegitimacy—and their associated genres—embody the potential for a trenchant critique of newly forming class and gender relations. If narratives of upward mobility rehearse the hopefulness of the new order, narratives of illegitimacy convey its unruly side.

The centrality of illegitimate sexuality as a topos in melodrama is demonstrably clear—yet, as far as I know, no one has linked the notion of overtly represented illegitimacy in the family to the illegitimacy of the genre. In *The Pirates of Penzance*, that connection is firmly made, since its recollection of the illegitimate genres revolves around the figure of the orphan, thus joining its meditation on illegitimate authority to its meditation on illegitimate sexuality.

Within this context, we can more deeply appreciate the structuring force of the pun on "orphan" and "often." Together, the confusion of "pilot" and "pirate" and the confusion of "orphan" and "often" make *The Pirates of Penzance* the major example of Gilbert's transformation of the burlesque and extravaganza pun. No longer a moment of incidental wit, the pun becomes a principle of plot and thematic coherence, making sense out of nonsense. As we saw in chapter 2, *Thespis* is organized around the play on several senses of the word "company." Although *H.M.S. Pinafore* contains only a few puns, and their conventional nature is stressed to a wince-making and groan-inducing point, they point to the serious arguments of the plot. Even though "alas . . . a lass" might seem a throwaway, it emphasizes the conventionality of Josephine's gender position, while "birth . . . berth" recalls the conventional assumption that the ship is a microcosm of society.

But *The Pirates of Penzance* takes this principle to an extreme, often harping on the figure of the orphan. The Pirates "make a point of never molesting an orphan," for, as one of them explains, "we are orphans ourselves, and know what it is." In the fog of their sentimental gullibility, they cannot understand how it might be that "the last three ships we took proved to be manned entirely by orphans." Frederic attempts to unravel this mystery: "One would think that Great Britain's mercantile navy was recruited solely from her orphan asylums—which we know is not the case." The opera's obsession with orphans not only rationalizes the Pirates' sentimentality, but also secures its genre parodies of melodrama and the novel.

The scene of the Pirates' threatening to "marry" the Wards ("Against our wills, papa—against our wills!") is a euphemistic parody of piratical abduction and rape. Again, Gilbert found an immediate precursor in *Les brigands*, when Falsacappa leads unwitting peasant girls to the brigands' lair for the diversion of his men. The girls are excited, although they know they should be outraged; they find the attention flattering, although they know they should be frightened. Gilbert goes this one better, not only making fun of the supposed feminine attraction to dangerous sexuality, but also deflating sexuality itself by transforming a mass scene of abduction into an eventual mass marriage. Sudden domestication of the scene of sexual illegitimacy is the point of recasting the Pirates as "single gentlemen":

> Here's a first-rate opportunity
> To get married with impunity
> And indulge in the felicity
> Of unbounded domesticity.

The jingling feminine rhymes create a wonderful bouffe diversion. But the humorous domestication of the Pirates' illegitimate sexuality is a serious generic self-allegory, reminding us of the Savoy operas' domestication of all sorts of illicit and risqué material from the illegitimate genres they so lovingly and humorously recollect. That such a deflection of piratical rapaciousness would be demanded by bourgeois decorum is, of course, also part of the joke.

In this context, the inane proliferation of orphans in *The Pirates of Penzance* should become both more sexually suggestive and more deeply amusing. At first, the jokes about orphans seem only to be pressing the point of the Pirates' sentimentality. But soon the figure of orphanage proliferates across the plot, its very repetition making its importance clear. The Pirates are orphans; all their intended victims pretend to be orphans; the Major-General's Wards may be orphans; and the Major-General himself claims to be an orphan. Thus the punning exchange between the Pirate King and Major-General Stanley around their repeated confusion of "orphan" with "often," hilariously inane as it is, nevertheless coherently integrates other aspects of the opera's theme and form. It serves to remind us how repetitive and conventional the figure of the orphan has become, how often the orphan appears, not only in this opera but also in the literature and theater of the preceding hundred years. In other words, in this exchange the extravaganza pun is elevated to the level of a plotting function, while the figure of the orphan is parodied through the recollection of its utter conventionality in novel, melodrama, and journalism:

> GEN (*aside*): Hah! An idea! (*Aloud*.) And do you mean to say that you would deliberately rob me of these, the sole remaining props of my old age, and leave me to go through the remainder of my life unfriended, unprotected, and alone?
> KING: Well, yes, that's the idea.

GEN: Tell me, have you ever known what it is to be an orphan?

PIRATES (*disgusted*): Oh, dash it all!

KING: Here we are again!

GEN: I ask you, have you ever known what it is to be an orphan?

KING: Often!

GEN: Yes, orphan! Have you ever known what it is to be one?

KING: I say, often.

ALL (*disgusted*): Often, often, often. (*Turning away.*)

GEN: I don't think we quite understand one another. I ask you, have you ever known what it is to be an orphan, and you say "orphan." As I understand you, you are merely repeating the word "orphan" to show that you understand me.

KING: I didn't repeat the word often.

GEN: Pardon me, you did indeed.

KING: I only repeated it once.

GEN: True, but you repeated it.

KING: But not often.

GEN: Stop: I think I see where we are getting confused. When you said "orphan," did you mean "orphan"—a person who has lost his parents—or "often"—frequently?

KING: Ah! I beg pardon—I see what you mean—frequently.

GEN: Ah! You said often—frequently.

KING: No, only once.

GEN (*irritated*): Exactly—you said often, frequently, only once.

With plot-logic inextricably joined to homophonic silliness, this exchange offers an intellectual carrot at the end of a seemingly nonsensical schtick.

The Major-General—already suggestively and obliquely connected to the orphan plot through his Wards—is even more firmly connected through the melodramatic lie he tells here. He claims to be an orphan himself, knowing that the Pirates "cannot steel [their hearts] / Against the sad, sad tale of the lonely orphan boy!" In a magnificent ensemble, the girls react to his lie with shock, while the Pirates threaten him, should they find out that he is lying. But the Major-General justifies his lie:

I'm telling a terrible story,
But it doesn't diminish my glory;
For they would have taken my daughters
Over the billowy waters,
If I hadn't, in elegant diction,

Indulged in an innocent fiction;
Which is not in the same category
As a regular terrible story.

Pirates, Wards, and the Major-General all sing together, each with a different evaluation of the Major-General's "story." As the girls argue, his story *does* come "in the same category / As a regular terrible story!" They mean that it is a lie. (And, in fact, fraudulent stories of orphans passed off as "artistic fictions" had been exposed during the decade just preceding the composition of *Pirates*.)[54] Major-General Stanley's lie will provoke the Pirates to revenge, when they realize that he has taken advantage of their "credulous simplicity," while he himself will suffer melodramatic remorse, much like Little Buttercup's in *Pinafore*. Insomniac and "tormented with the anguish dread / Of falsehood unatoned," the Major-General wanders outside in his dressing gown, straight into the trap of the waiting Pirates and Police, and into the opera's dénouement.

Major-General Stanley's "terrible story" is a "regular terrible story" in another sense as well, insofar as it is an exceedingly familiar story. The ensemble's anxious logic chopping on the distinction between fiction and lie only serves to remind us once again how very common in Victorian fiction the story of the orphan is. Not only on the homophonic byplay, but also on that familiar convention, the "orphan" / "often" confusion depends.

"For all our faults, we love our Queen"

In the end, all suggestions of sexual illegitimacy are obliterated with the wholesale domestication of the Pirates. In both personal and national senses, every aspect of piratical danger is hilariously mooted. As we have come to expect, the opera's closure combines parodies of extravaganza and melodrama. While the regressive, polymorphous fantasy of transformation recollects extravaganza, the Pirates' sudden conversion and their exaggerated display of patriotism recollect nautical melodrama. As Kristie Allen has pointed out, "nautical melodrama represents the pirate as outside the law in order to reveal the necessity for law and order."[55] Thus pirate melodrama often ends with a tableau of the Union Jack being hoisted while the "great black flag," the Jolly Roger, is pulled down.[56] As in *H.M.S. Pinafore*, patriotic fervor is subjected to parodic critique through its very exaggeration, but the ending of *The Pirates of Penzance* goes further into zany, scattershot parody, veering wildly from one object of patriotic veneration to another.

When the Police finally find an effective incantation of the law, their magic words tame the Pirates into a tableau: "We charge you yield, in Queen Victoria's name!" And "*baffled*," the "PIRATES *kneel, [while the]* POLICE *stand over them triumphantly*" and the Pirate King submits:

> We yield at once, with humbled mien,
> Because, for all our faults, we love our Queen.

Most productions of *Pirates* take the opportunity of this final moment to roll out a portrait banner, an effigy, or even an impersonation of Queen Victoria. Thus the Pirates make their hyperbolic obeisance to the figure of a huge, matronly woman—the perfect Victorian figure for conjoined governmental and familial legitimacy. As Munich points out, the queen serves as a mother surrogate here, subsuming the orphaned Pirates and replacing Ruth's carelessness and inappropriate lust with a better model: "[I]n a script connecting the lack of mothering with lawlessness, the Queen represents the congruence of private maturation and public institutions."[57]

Ruth compounds the melodramatic transformation with her revelation that the Pirates are "all noblemen who have gone wrong!" This sudden, melodramatic disclosure of an original identity is managed even more capriciously than in *Pinafore*, without the usual confession or documentary rationalization that would ground the Pirates' nobility in a story of their past and how Ruth knows about it. As we know, the revelation of noble parentage is one conventional outcome within the story of the orphan. Eileen Cottis comments on the prevalence of this plot twist in the history of pirate melodrama, mentioning J. T. Haines's *The Wizard of the Wave* (1840), in which the Unknown Pirate repents and is revealed as the son of the Earl of Monteville, and Thomas J. Dibdin's *The Pirate: A Melo Dramatic Romance* (1822), a dramatic version of Scott's novel of the same name, in which Cleveland repents and is rewarded with a respectable marriage.[58] As in *Pinafore*, a sudden, retroactive transformation of identity, utterly regardless of the realistic logic of socialization, is announced by the oracular revealings of a mother surrogate. In this case, the wish-fulfilling transformation pokes fun at the Victorian taste for stories of repentance and reform. Like Frederic, who has been characterized by Mabel's feminine reformer's zeal as the "poor wandering one," the Pirates are suddenly reformed by the womanly influence of their queen.

To the revelation that the Pirates are really noblemen, the Major-General responds:

> No Englishman unmoved that statement hears,
> Because, with all our faults, we love our House of Peers.

His sudden, solemn devotion to the House of Lords echoes the Pirates' sudden capitulation to their queen, but in his case, patriotism goes hand in hand with satisfaction at the advantageous marriages of his Wards. Thus is the illegitimate melodramatically revealed to have been super-legitimate all along, noblemen having played as Pirates during an interlude of "pirate time."

Part II. Genders

6

New Light on Changing Gender Norms

Patience

atience; or, Bunthorne's Bride opened in 1881 and was running successfully at the Opera Comique when construction of the Savoy Theatre
reached completion. The splendid new theater, located between the
Thames Embankment and the Strand, was purpose-built by Richard D'Oyly
Carte to house the comic operas of Gilbert and Sullivan, afterward known
as the Savoy operas. Moved to the glorious new theater, *Patience* thereby
became, strictly speaking, the first "Savoy" opera.[1]

The interior of the Savoy was comfortably grand. More important, Carte
introduced several innovations in theater management, all designed to
appeal to an upscale audience. Programs were furnished, and coats were
checked free of charge. Neither ushers and program sellers nor refreshment
vendors were subcontracted; instead, they were paid fair wages by the theater's management, a practice that allowed Carte to establish new standards
for consistent courtesy. The system of queuing—now second nature to us—
was also a Savoy innovation. Unlike today's common practice, however, the
Savoy had separate entrances for different areas of the theater (with their
differentiated ticket prices), making segregation by social class a highly visible matter.[2] Thus the Savoy Theatre has become a historical touchstone
for the niche marketing of theatrical fare that had been escalating since the
1860s, as well as for the increasingly middle-class English theater audience.[3]

Carte's most important innovation was the theater's brilliant new lighting, for the Savoy Theatre was the first public building in the world to be lit
entirely by electricity. As part of the grand-opening ceremonies, he demonstrated the safety of the new technology on stage—by touching an illuminated bulb to show that it would not burn and by crushing another to show

that it would not burst into flames. Dimming and brightening the stage were more easily controlled with this steadier, cooler, whiter, sharper form of light. Outmoding the flickering of gaslight, the Savoy Theatre launched a new era in theatrical illumination, which often serves as an apt metaphor for modernity in general, as we shall see.[4] Certainly, the wedding of art and commerce that characterizes fin-de-siècle aestheticism was doubly on display, both in this fashionable venue and in its first production.

Beyond the "Serious Family"

Patience is cleverly schematic in its treatment of gender roles and relations. Three parodic types—characterized by facial expressions, body size and body language, costumes, attitudes, and gestures—represent each side of the gender divide and seem to characterize the limited range of positions available for male and female social actors. Through the characters' interactions, the opera builds its arguments about gender. Femininity is represented by Patience, the central object of desire, whose hyperbolic innocence parodies socialized femininity; by the Aesthetic Maidens, who are figures for aestheticism's trendiness, superficiality, and general wrong-headedness; and by Lady Jane, the strong-minded leader of the Aesthetic Maidens, an exemplary figure of female power and self-interest.[5] Masculinity, likewise, is parsed into three positions. On one level of conceptualization, Reginald Bunthorne and Archibald Grosvenor, the two poets, are structurally opposed to the Dragoon Guards, as literary men against military men, who display an old-fashioned manliness and group identity very well expressed by their love of their uniform. But on another level of conceptualization, the two literary men are also opposed to each other, the "aesthetic poet" pitted against the "idyllic poet" in both style and substance.

Patience, the character from whom the opera takes its name, is the linchpin of the opera's systematic representation of gender. The opening premise—that Patience "has never loved" and therefore "cannot tell what . . . love may be"—imagines a milkmaid simple to the point of simple-mindedness. Like so many simple-minded beauties, Patience exerts a strangely magnetic attraction on all the men around her. While represented as utterly sincere, her innocence is subject to parody for that very reason—because it is so clearly an unexamined form of behavior. In one respect, the figure of Patience mocks the traditional heroine of pastoral and idyll, the simple milkmaid or shepherdess who represents an earlier, rural way of life, seen from the perspective of later, urban nostalgia. But in another respect, the figure of Patience mocks the typical heroine of melodrama, the central object of desire, who provides the motive for the plot, yet remains oddly blank except when testifying to her own purity. Most of all, however, the figure of Patience mocks one particular strand in the texture of Victorian gender ideology: the expectation that young women remain relatively ignorant of bodily functions, sexual feelings, and strong emotions in order to be perceived as respectably feminine. Patience both personifies and parodies the Victorian cultural demand for a stupefied femininity (figure 6.1). Bunthorne's poem ("Oh, Hollow! Hollow! Hollow!") launches a critique of this sort of feminine inexperience. If, through its parody, the character of Patience exposes idyllic innocence as an old-fashioned form of femininity, the Dragoon Guards embody an equally old-fashioned, outmoded form of masculinity.

To see through the lens of gender critique is to see beyond the opera's more obvious parody of aestheticism, which itself was conventional at the time. As Jane Stedman points out, "few movements in literature or the fine arts have provoked such a concentrated popular sneer."[6] The reviewer for the

DISASTROUS RESULT OF BEAUTYMANIA.

The last new Beauty, having an innocent cast of Countenance, has been Painted, Sculptured, and Photographed with her Head on one side, Sucking her Thumb. (N.B.—The Gentlemen are joining the Ladies after Dinner.)

FIGURE 6.1 The infantile look of feminine innocence is a learned, fashionable pose. George du Maurier, "Disastrous Result of Beautymania," *Punch*, May 3, 1879. (Reproduced with permission of Punch, Ltd., www.punch.co.uk)

Illustrated London News, admitting that the topic was familiar, quipped: "By this time the stage is thickly sown all over with a crop of lilies and sunflowers."[7] Percy Fitzgerald criticized *Patience* because, as he put it, "this tide of fatuity has not even the merit of novelty."[8] Only a few months before *Patience* was completed, *Where's the Cat?* (1880), a new play by James Albery, made fun of the "lily-bearing poets" and included the first theatrical caricature of Oscar Wilde.[9] At that point, Gilbert had finished only about two-thirds of the libretto for *Patience*, but Albery's play received so much attention that Gilbert began to fear that his work would not be considered original.[10]

Of all the theatrical treatments of aestheticism, however, F. C. Burnand's *The Colonel* (1881), which opened several months before *Patience*, is most relevant to my argument. Burnand's three-act farce features the aesthetes Lambert Streyke and Basil Giorgione, who hope to gain control of a family fortune by manipulating the wife through their influence over her domineering mother.[11] With their pretentious "intensity" and "effeminate" sneakiness, they have converted both the wife and her mother to aesthetic dress, attendance at lectures, and refusal of ordinary enjoyment in general. Cowed by his aesthetic wife and her mother, the husband pretends to go on fishing expeditions in order to escape the constraints of his household. While supposedly fishing, however, he is actually in town, being entertained by a lively widow, who assumes that he is on the verge of proposing marriage. His old friend, the American colonel Woottwweell W. Woodd, intervenes, talks sense to the wife, and ends up marrying the widow.

The play's values are quite explicit. The wife should return to "mundane enjoyments," such as giving parties and dancing; she should throw off the influence of her mother, who has brought the aesthetes into her home; she should "consult [her] husband's tastes before everybody else's, and let him be master in his own house"; and she should change from aesthetic garb back into modern, fashionable dress, to please her husband.[12] In the end, wife and husband are reconciled within a renewed and explicitly conventional domestic harmony, making it clear that the aesthetes tampered not only with styles of courtship and male sexuality, but also with the family itself, represented as the bedrock of social stability.

The Colonel was an adaptation of Morris Barnett's three-act comedy *The Serious Family* (1849), itself a close English adaptation of Jean-François Bayard's *Le mari à la campagne* (*The Husband in the Country*, 1844). In these plays, the dangerous influence is wielded by a Tartuffe-like religious hypocrite. Barnett's religious fanatic, Aminadab Sleek, rules the Torrens family through the wife's mother. For relief from his domestic travails, Mr. Torrens pretends to go "out of town" from time to time "for several days of shooting," when he is actually visiting the lively widow in whose home he flirts, dresses fashionably, and in general behaves as the good-humored person he was before his marriage. His friend from youth, Captain Murphy Maguire, saves the marriage by teaching Mrs. Torrens that her "serious family . . . may be too serious." She must extricate herself from her mother and from Sleek in order to do her "superior duty" to her husband, the duty of being cheerful and light-hearted. Only when the wife fulfills her "first duty to obey [her] husband" can she expect her "husband's return to his duty."[13] In other words, the risqué element of the plot—the husband's close approach to adultery or, possibly, even bigamy—is thoroughly moralized in this piece of straightforward domestic ideology. Mr. Torrens almost strays into a serious affair because his wife has made their home unbearably unappealing. In this precursor to *The Colonel*, in other words, the threat to the family is made much more explicitly.

Burnand replaced the traditional religious imposters with aesthetic ones, clearly suggesting a modern kind of hypocrite.[14] This history of adaptation shows that there had been a significant shift in the popular representation of the force most likely to tempt women away from their conventional duties to home, family, and husband. As in *Patience*, these plays present the common-sense perspective through the figure of a military man. A naval officer in *Le mari à la campagne*, an Irish army captain in *The Serious Family*, and an American colonel in *The Colonel* guide the wives to see the danger into which they have plunged their families, and thus they restore the husbands to their rightful places as heads of their households. Bluff and upright, no-nonsense manly men, full of good humor, these appealing characters nevertheless do show that conventional gender norms are military-like in their discipline—or, at least, that they must be enforced by military guidance.

That Gilbert knew and worked within this lineage of adaptations is indisputable, for in the 1860s he formed a gentlemen's club for journalistic and theatrical friends, and he called his club The Serious Family. Members paid 2 guineas in annual dues, although "Gilbert was exempted as he undertook to supply a rump steak, a Stilton cheese, whisky and soda, and bottled ale every Saturday night for the term of his natural life." Tom Hood, the humorist and playwright who succeeded H. J. Byron as editor of *Fun*, was named "Head of the Family," while Gilbert was "l'enfant terrible."[15] *Patience*, in other words, was written directly within the ambit of this series of adaptations, which I call the "serious family tradition," for it not only cautioned against the too-serious aesthetic and religious families, dominated by women and their nefarious confidants, but also clearly worked to show how serious the maintenance of normative gender relations within the conventional family really was.

Oscar Wilde continued the tradition. Writing to George Grossmith (who created the part of Bunthorne), Wilde expressed the opinion that *Patience* would surely be much better than *The Colonel*, which he regarded as a dull farce.[16] We can deduce his interest in the serious family tradition, since *The Importance of Being Earnest* (1895) must be regarded as its culmination. Yet, in a familiar Wildean way, he twisted the moral of the serious family tradition away from its seriousness and toward a lightness that is quintessentially aesthetic.[17] This lineage adds significantly to our sense of the precursors for "Bunburying" in *The Importance of Being Earnest*. Wilde's chosen name for this form of masculine escape from domestic attachment braids the "Belvawneying" evil eye from Gilbert's *Engaged* (1877) with "Bunthorne" from *Patience* to form the possibly homoerotic double entendre.

Patience decidedly *is* much better than *The Colonel*, in large part because its engagement with family values is less explicit and more ambivalent. Even though styles of courtship are at issue, no one is already unhappily married; even though marriage rewards conversion to "every-day" conventionality, the alternatives are not so scathingly rendered as in *The Colonel*. Domestic ideology hovers in the background but does not move to center stage, as it does in the earlier plays in the serious family tradition. Before Wilde, Gilbert began to de-center the "serious family."

Significantly, *Patience* features its own military representation of common sense: Colonel Calverley and the Dragoon Guards. In addition to the importance of the military figure in the serious family tradition, both Burnand's and Gilbert's colonels were surely influenced by Our Gallant Colonel, who represents the common-sense perspective in George du Maurier's popular anti-aesthetic cartoons. Published in *Punch* from 1873 to 1882, the cartoons were almost precisely contemporaneous with the collaboration between Gilbert and Sullivan up to *Patience*.[18] As is well known, they provide clear evidence of a fascinated middlebrow hostility to aestheticism. In 1880, du Maurier introduced his most famous characters: Jellaby Postlethwaite, an aesthetic poet, and Maudle, a painter. Together, Postlethwaite and Maudle maintain an advisory sway over Mrs. Cimabue Brown, who, as her name indicates, trendily assimilates the primitive Italian to the present-day commonplace. In "Nincompoopiana.—The Mutual Admiration Society," Mrs. Cimabue Brown hosts Jellaby Postlethwaite, while the figure of Our Gallant Colonel stands to the left side, looking skeptical—a clear surrogate and stimulus for the common-sense reaction expected from *Punch*'s readership (figure 6.2).

NINCOMPOOPIANA.—THE MUTUAL ADMIRATION SOCIETY.

Our Gallant Colonel (who is not a Member thereof, to Mrs. Cimabue Brown, who is). "AND WHO'S THIS YOUNG HERO THEY'RE ALL SWARMING OVER NOW?"
Mrs. Cimabue Brown. "JELLABY POSTLETHWAITE, THE GREAT POET, YOU KNOW, WHO SAT FOR MAUDLE'S 'DEAD NARCISSUS'! HE HAS JUST DEDICATED HIS *LATTER-DAY SAPPHICS* TO ME. IS NOT HE *BEAUTIFUL*?"
Our Gallant Colonel. "WHY, WHAT'S THERE *BEAUTIFUL* ABOUT HIM?"
Mrs. Cimabue Brown. "OH, LOOK AT HIS GRAND HEAD AND POETIC FACE, WITH THOSE FLOWERLIKE EYES, AND THAT EXQUISITE SAD SMILE! LOOK AT HIS SLENDER WILLOWY FRAME, AS YIELDING AND FRAGILE AS A WOMAN'S! THAT'S YOUNG MAUDLE, STANDING JUST BEHIND HIM—THE GREAT PAINTER, YOU KNOW. HE HAS JUST PAINTED ME AS 'HÉLOÏSE,' AND MY HUSBAND AS 'ABÉLARD.' IS NOT HE *DIVINE*?" [*The Colonel hooks it.*
N.B.—Postlethwaite and Maudle are quite unknown to fame.

FIGURE 6.2 Our Gallant Colonel, the figure of common sense as spectator of aesthetic culture, stands to the far left. George du Maurier, "Nincompoopiana.—The Mutual Admiration Society," *Punch*, February 14, 1880. (Reproduced with permission of Punch, Ltd., www.punch.co.uk)

Du Maurier's anti-aesthetic cartoons, among many other popular representations, created the stereotype of the aesthete, who speaks in an erudite jargon, frequently punctuated by intensifiers like "precious," "intense," "consummate," "utter," "too-too," "quite," and "exactly so." The aesthete dresses in special costumes, loose draperies for women and suits of antiquated cut for men, in a palette of dull golds, grays, and the "dirty greens" that Bunthorne will confidentially disavow. Both male and female aesthetes wear their hair long and often unbound. In aesthetic iconography, they are associated with props like sunflowers, lilies, peacock feathers, and blue-and-white china. Their languid body language bespeaks aesthetic contemplation, as in du Maurier's famous cartoon "An Aesthetic Midday Meal" (figure 6.3). Bodily necessity—in this case, food—is a mere lowly irrelevance for the aesthete

AN ÆSTHETIC MIDDAY MEAL.

*At the Luncheon hour, Jellaby Postlethwaite enters a Pastrycook's and calls for a glass of Water,
into which he puts a freshly-cut Lily, and loses himself in contemplation thereof.*
Waiter. "SHALL I BRING YOU ANYTHING ELSE, SIR?"
Jellaby Postlethwaite. "THANKS, NO! I HAVE ALL I REQUIRE, AND SHALL SOON HAVE DONE!"

FIGURE 6.3 An iconic parody of aesthetic contemplation disregarding bodily needs. George du Maurier, "An Aesthetic Midday Meal," *Punch*, July 17, 1880. (Reproduced with permission of Punch, Ltd., www.punch.co.uk)

engaged in contemplation. Waiters and restaurant patrons stand around in the background looking shocked, as Our Gallant Colonel does in "Nincompoopiana," thus providing the template for middlebrow readers' reception.

Aesthetic body language flies directly in the face of conventional masculinity. Commenting on du Maurier's cartoon aesthetes, Ed Cohen argues that the male bodies draped over furniture seem literally "spineless," as if "they are about to slide off their chairs." This limp drooping, he argues, signifies the male aesthete's opposition to "somatic rectitude," the literal as well as metaphorical uprightness of conventional Victorian masculinity.[19] Burnand's Colonel Woodd speaks of the "effeminate invertebrate society" of the aesthetes.[20] What was called in the late nineteenth century the angular, "crooked" wrist (and would in the twentieth century be redefined as the "limp" wrist), the shyly in-turned knee and pointed toe, the "intense" postures of self-involved contemplation and gazing—all would be lampooned in *Patience*.

In one famous scene, the hyper-masculine Dragoon Guards attempt to look aesthetic in order to please the Maidens. But they cannot bend their upright manly bodies into the correct postures (plate 8). Formerly confident that no costume could be more attractive than their uniform—whose form and function emphasize the "uniform" nature of their masculinity—they lose their confidence when they are re-dressed. This scene plays in part on the "Early English" "stained-glass attitudes" that Bunthorne simultaneously acknowledges and disavows. Surely, though, the popularity of this scene owes most to its play on conventions of gender:

> It's clear that medieval art alone retains its zest,
> To charm and please its devotees we've done our little best.
> We're not quite sure if all we do has the Early English ring;
> But, as far as we can judge, it's something like this sort of thing:
> > You hold yourself like this (*attitude*),
> > You hold yourself like that (*attitude*),
> By hook or crook you try to look both angular and flat (*attitude*).
> > We venture to expect
> > That what we recollect,
> Though but a part of true High Art, will have its due effect.

As we saw with *H.M.S. Pinafore*, the "attitude" itself is a theatrical convention that is also parodied in *Patience*. Bunthorne can certainly pose, as he admits in his confession, linking aestheticism to a negative evaluation of theatricality, in which "acting" is equated with affectation and duplicity.[21] Unlike the aesthete, however, the Dragoon Guards cannot perform a body language other than their own. Committed to "natural" or "true" unconscious repetition, the manly body cannot contort itself into a shape not essentially its own (plate 9). Only unmanly men can perform these particular poses. The opera's tacit queer potential would unfold over time, but in 1881—since the Dragoons' performance is attempted in an effort to reclaim the Maidens—*Patience* explicitly identifies aesthetes as a threat to the heterosexual "serious family."

This parody cuts both ways, of course. That manly men simply cannot look or act effeminate signifies the supposed naturalness of gender identification. In this respect, the Dragoon Guards' clumsiness is meant to be understandable or even attractive; they appeal to and reinforce heterosexual spectatorship. Yet *Patience* makes the opposite, sharply critical point as well, poking fun at conventional masculinity for being self-evident, inflexible, untheatrical, old-fashioned, and proud of its uniformity; in this respect, the Dragoons' bumbling lack of theatricality admits the attraction of an alternative. If Bunthorne's confession and patter song offer a script for how to pose as an aesthete, Colonel Calverley's patter song ("If you want a receipt for that popular mystery") offers a recipe for dense conventional masculinity, a pastiche of popular references incoherently assembled and rattled off by rote.

Even devotion to the decorative craze was associated in popular representation with a perversion of marriage. Du Maurier's "The Six-Mark Tea-Pot," for example, notable for his first caricature of Oscar Wilde and for its reference to Wilde's youthful remark about living up to his blue-and-white china, depicts an Aesthetic Bridegroom and his Intense Bride, both admiring their "consummate" teapot and vowing to live up to it (figure 6.4). "Perils of Aesthetic Culture," another *Punch* cartoon of this period, advances the argument that "going in for High Art" has made it impossible for Edwin and Angelina (conventional names for the spatting couple, as seen in *Trial by Jury*) to recognize the old-fashioned good looks that should incite their heterosexual attraction. Instead of Our Gallant Colonel, the portly figure of Uncle John stands back, deploring the alienation of the young people and representing the normative point of view (figure 6.5). Although purportedly humorous, the implication that the "serious family" might be in jeopardy was no joke. In one famous *Punch* cartoon, "An Impartial Statement in Black and White," the aesthetic female is depicted as unattractive in two mutually incompatible and contradictory forms: skeletally lean and haggard, with lank hair, yet also fat and frizzy-headed (figure 6.6). Similarly, male aesthetes are mangy and unattractive, as in "Yᵉ Aesthetic Young Geniuses!" (figure 6.7). Associated with these representations of the outlandish perversion of normative gender, the threat of the degeneration of "the race" sometimes rears its ugly head.[22]

One astounding artifact of late Victorian material culture points up this threat quite sharply. The "aesthetic teapot," produced by the Royal Worcester Porcelain Company in December 1881 (on the occasion of the production of *Patience*), joins popular arguments against aestheticism to a growing popular (mis)understanding of Darwin's theory of natural selection (plate 10). One side of the teapot depicts an aesthetic man (with a sunflower on his breast), while the other portrays an aesthetic woman (with a lily on hers). Because they are two sides of the same teapot, they both cock their heads and show the effeminately crooked wrist, which forms the spout of the teapot. Their hat, hair, and pose are exactly alike; their costume is substantially so. On the bottom of the teapot, an inscription reads: "Fearful consequences, through the laws of Natural Selection and Evolution, of living up to one's Teapot." What might seem like clever gender-bending to us was interpreted by the Victorians as the dangerous eradication of gender

THE SIX-MARK TEA-POT.

Æsthetic Bridegroom. "It is quite consummate, is it not?"
Intense Bride. "It is, indeed! Oh, Algernon, let us live up to it!"

FIGURE 6.4 Caricatures of Oscar Wilde and Jane Morris as an aesthetic couple who aspire to "live up to" their blue-and-white china. George du Maurier, "The Six-Mark Tea-Pot," *Punch*, October 30, 1880. (Reproduced with permission of Punch, Ltd., www.punch.co.uk)

PERILS OF ÆSTHETIC CULTURE.

Uncle John (suddenly bursting on newly-wedded pair). "Hullo, my Turtle-Doves! What's the row? Not Quarrelled yet, I trust?"

Edwin. "Oh dear no. We've been going in for High Art, that's all."

Angelina. "And Drawing from Casts of the Antique."

Edwin. "And Angy's Nose turns up so at the end, and she's got such a skimpy Waist, and such a big Head, and such tiny little Hands and Feet! Hang it all, I thought her perfection!"

Angelina. "Yes, Uncle John; and Edwin's got a long Upper Lip, and a runaway Chin, and he c-c-can't grow a Beard and Moustache! Oh dear! Oh dear!" *[With difficulty restrains her sobs.*

FIGURE 6.5 Going in for "High Art" disrupts heterosexual attraction. George du Maurier, "Perils of Aesthetic Culture," *Punch*, May 10, 1879. (Reproduced with permission of Punch, Ltd., www.punch.co.uk)

ÆSTHETIC LADY AND WOMAN OF FASHION. | WOMAN OF FASHION AND ÆSTHETIC LADY.

FIGURE 6.6 Contradictory parodies of the unattractive "aesthetic lady." George du Maurier, "An Impartial Statement in Black and White," *Punch*, April 9, 1881. (Reproduced with permission of Punch, Ltd., www.punch.co.uk)

FIGURE 6.7 Unhealthy, emasculated "aesthetic geniuses." George du Maurier, "Yᵉ Aesthetic Young Geniuses!" *Punch*, September 21, 1878. (Reproduced with permission of Punch, Ltd., www.punch.co.uk)

THE COMING RACE.

While Mesdames Wilkins and Perkins are discussing grave School-Board matters and Parliamentary business, their respective Husbands are engaged on a topic more genial to their softer natures and weaker intellects.

"ISN'T SHE A DARLING PET, FRED! AND JUST FANCY—TWO FRONT TEETH, AND ONLY FOUR MONTHS LAST TUESDAY WEEK!"
"WELL, I NEVER!! WHY, MY DARLING ICKLE TOTTY HASN'T CUT A SINGLE TOOTH, AND HE'S SIX MONTHS TO-MORROW! HOW DO YOU FEED HER, TOM?"

FIGURE 6.8 A parodic inversion of gender roles. George du Maurier, "The Coming Race," *Punch*, September 14, 1872. (Reproduced with permission of Punch, Ltd., www. punch.co.uk)

difference. Du Maurier's cartoon "The Coming Race" makes a similar point, depicting a future society in which gender positions have been effectively switched (figure 6.8). If the separate spheres do not remain distinct, if the effeminate man and the masculine woman replace the manly man and the womanly woman, "fearful consequences" will ensue. The aesthetic teapot, in other words, bespeaks a conventionally late-nineteenth-century sexo-logical conception of the natural, essential fixity—yet threatened inversion—of the genders.[23]

Thus do middlebrow suspicions of high art spill over into, and help to construct, other anxieties. The idea that gender was not natural but cultur-ally determined and, worse, the idea that social behavior, including gender, might be merely theatrical—both gaining currency in the last quarter of the nineteenth century—were associated with the fear that the heterosexual, reproductive "serious family" might be seriously threatened. In fact, the very first cartoon in du Maurier's Chinamania series, "The Passion for Old China," suggests precisely that. It depicts a woman gently holding a teapot in her lap as if it were a baby. Her husband begs for a turn to nurse it, since she

THE PASSION FOR OLD CHINA.

Husband. "I think you might *let me* Nurse that Teapot a little *now*, Margery! You've had it to yourself all the *Morning*, you know!"

FIGURE 6.9 The displacement of procreative and nurturing urges into the "passion for old china." George du Maurier, "The Passion for Old China," *Punch*, May 2, 1874. (Reproduced with permission of Punch, Ltd., www.punch.co.uk)

has "had it to [herself] all the morning . . . !" (figure 6.9). Only in England, perhaps, could a teapot so suggestively replace a baby.[24]

The decisive role of du Maurier's cartoons in creating these stereotypes was widely recognized at the time. Gilbert himself acknowledged their importance to his inspiration for *Patience*, even hoping at one point to "get du Maurier to design the costumes."[25] In the end, he designed them himself, but it is clear that he wanted du Maurier's stereotype to be immediately recognizable, however elegantly turned out it might be.[26] Aside from the clear influence of du Maurier, however, it is notoriously difficult to tell who was copying whom on this topic. Parody in popular culture makes this question quite complex, for parody must re-create its object or model while presuming to reflect it. Thus parody, literally preposterous, makes the distinction between an original and its copies quite undecidable.

Critics and journalists at the time commented on this weird cultural effect. Percy Fitzgerald put the point succinctly: "This light persiflage seems to have created . . . the objects of its satire."[27] And Max Beerbohm reiterated:

"Ridicule is said to kill; and in France where it is wont to be fierce, it sometimes does so; but in England, . . . it rather tends to prolong life. The 'aesthetic craze' would belike have died away sooner than it actually did if 'Patience' had not been written."[28] In other words, parody exhibits its own creative force, not only because it re-creates its purported model in order to be recognized, but also because it causes real effects in history and social life. Parody plays a crucial role in the formation of certain historical figures, for example. In retrospect, the parody is taken to have been the copy, while in effect it may have been the original (so to speak). Understanding this theoretical conundrum, James Abbott McNeill Whistler tells the following anecdote: "Mr Du Maurier and Mr Wilde happening to meet in the rooms where Mr Whistler was holding his first exhibition of Venice etchings, the latter brought the two face to face, and taking each by the arm inquired: 'I say, which one of you two invented the other, eh?'"[29] The mutual reflection that makes Whistler's question unanswerable perfectly expresses the complex temporality of parody.

The re-creative effect of parody may vividly be seen in a transatlantic parable of cultural history, the story of the public emergence of Oscar Wilde. When a tour of the United States was planned for *Patience*, Carte perceived a marketing problem. Although the aesthetic movement was familiar (and even hackneyed) in England, the craze had not taken hold in America. Therefore, reasoned Carte, the phenomenon had to be produced, so that its parody might then be recognized in *Patience*. With his usual entrepreneurial acumen, Carte hired Wilde to conduct his now-famous lecture tour of North America, specifically so that regional groups of the American public could be exposed to an aesthete, before the touring production of *Patience* reached their nearest theater. A lecture tour is always a theatrical event in its own right, and Wilde's tour was highly so. Cohen puts it best: "Recognizing Wilde's potential as an aesthetic poster boy . . . D'Oyly Carte paid [him] to tour North America posing as the poseur he was supposed to be in order that the parody poseurs of *Patience* should pay off."[30]

In 1882, Wilde was known in only a limited way as a former Oxford prodigy, by no means yet the figure he would become. His *Poems* were published in 1881, the same year *Patience* was produced. However, Carte's marketing strategy created the semblance of temporal priority for the figure of Wilde. In relation to *Patience*, then, it has often been said that Wilde was the model for Bunthorne, while in fact the opposite was true. Bunthorne in *Patience* was the model that Wilde attempted both to imitate and to prefigure on his American tour. Wilde acted as Bunthorne's avatar. In cultural history, "Wilde" was in part a spin-off product. This transatlantic parable of parodic temporality highlights the aesthetic—and, in particular, the theatrical—formation of an actual historical figure. It suggests, too, that the temporal confusion of model and copy is a real historical phenomenon, not simply a theoretical point. Aestheticism was deeply embedded in commercial culture, but this parable also suggests that commercial capitalism can produce reality effects. Like parody, commercial publicity cites, recontextualizes, and theatricalizes everyday life. Bunthorne represents a jumbled-up and generalized stereotype that had been popularized primarily through the middlebrow, journalistic reaction against it; Wilde inhabited that stereotype, attempting to turn it to his own advantage. Finally, this parable suggests the perils and rewards of visibility and cultural recognition.

Wilde arrived in New York amid a great flurry of advance publicity and then appeared in several cities wearing his aesthetic garb: a double-breasted velvet jacket with a wide collar, velvet knee breeches, and silk stockings. This outfit, inscrutably both avant-garde and retro, was inspired by Bunthorne's costume in *Patience*, the costume designed by Gilbert. Although in *Patience* the fabric is described as a "cobwebby grey velvet, with a tender bloom like cold gravy," Wilde's costume now resonates with the deep pile of historical texture, looking luxurious and venerable under the retrospective light provided by decades of gay studies and queer theory. Immortalized in the cabinet photograph by Napoleon Sarony, the costume bespeaks Wilde's extravagantly brilliant nose thumbing at bourgeois respectability, his strength, and his beauty (figure 6.10).

In short, *Patience* was more involved in canonizing than in anathematizing Wilde. The trials would not come until later. Meanwhile, the American press caught on to the demand that he be treated as an oddity, but it did not always reproduce the effeminate type, by any means. For example, the *New York Tribune* emphasized Wilde's manliness: "The most striking thing about the poet's appearance is his height, which is several inches over six feet." This report goes on to describe other aspects of his appearance, noting that his eyes are not "'dreamy'" but "quick," and his hands are not delicate, "only fit to caress a lily," but powerful, for "his fingers are long and when doubled up would form a fist that would hit a hard knock."[31]

Yet the figure of Bunthorne, whom he represented, went far toward establishing the Wildean persona that the world would come to know. Like Whistler, we might well ask: "Which one of you two invented the other?" There is no uncomplicated answer to this question of cultural priority, so mutual was their influence, each in certain ways seeming to be the precursor of the other. Wilde was always mindful of these real-life dramatic ironies. Later, especially, he would discover the high stakes of trying to control the cross

FIGURE 6.10 Oscar Wilde in his aesthetic costume. Cabinet photograph by Napoleon Sarony (New York, 1882). (Bridgeman Art Library)

fire of recognition effects within which his fame increased. But during his lecture tour in America, we see an early Wilde, flirting brilliantly with the aesthetic stereotype as his fan, daring to inhabit a conventionally ridiculed type and to re-create it with the force of his character.

Patience, then, informed the public figure of Wilde more than the figure of Wilde informed *Patience*. In a real sense, Gilbert served as Wilde's dresser on the world-historical stage. Oscar Wilde emerged into the public spotlight with the figure of Reginald Bunthorne behind him.

Bunthorne in the History of Homosexuality

Patience concludes with a riot of marriages, exaggeratedly playing out the conventional ending of comedy. Like most Savoy operas, *Patience* wants to have it both ways in the end, availing itself of the conservatism of the marriage plot while undermining that very convention through absurd multiplication. Only Bunthorne is odd man out, repeatedly "crushed" and left uncoupled in the end. Thus the opera's subtitle, *Bunthorne's Bride*, turns out to be a red herring, since "Nobody [will] be Bunthorne's Bride." His exclusion from the happy ending has always presented a crux, if not an outright problem, for interpretation. Only in one other Savoy opera is a central character pointedly left alone in the end, when Jack Point falls devastated to the ground at the conclusion of *The Yeomen of the Guard*. Leaving Bunthorne out of the general celebration seems punitive, even if courtship and marriage—along with the conventional gender relations that prevail though them—have been subjected to parodic critique.

Many critics have felt that Bunthorne's conclusively unmarried state suggests other considerations. Although he is explicitly represented as heterosexual, Bunthorne's exclusion from the marriage plot seems to encode a homosexual subtext, especially coming as it does after so many references to his aesthetic effeminacy. Certainly, the history of the opera's reception bears out the suggestion. In other words, it is not necessary to argue that Bunthorne is meant to represent or "be" a homosexual in order to see the queer implications of the representation. Nor is it necessary to think that those implications were intentional on Gilbert's part; they can remain folded within the popular stereotype, and anyone, including Gilbert, could have deployed the stereotype without becoming critically conscious of them.

The best arguments for measuring the queer potential of *Patience* have been offered by Ed Cohen, Dennis Denisoff, Vincent Lankewish, and Tom Stoppard. The first three regard the exclusion of Bunthorne from the mass marriages as punitive, yet they also find hope in the promise of social change. As we have seen, Cohen argues that homosexuality was negatively associated then (as it often is now) with theatricality in general, with insincerity, and with posing. Along with Regenia Gagnier, however, he claims that this association had a beneficial effect, for the supposed theatricality of the aesthete exposed the theatricality of gender roles in general. Thus the negative characterization of the aesthete assisted in the general fin-de-siècle denaturalization of gender norms and supports the view that gendered behavior is never natural, but is always socialized and performative. Heaping irony on the earnestness of Victorian respectability, the stereotype of the aesthete moved beyond conventional gender, loosening its fixation.[32] Perhaps "the aesthete" was recognizable even in 1881 as a coded or veiled characterization of the homosexual, just as "the aesthete" now often suggests an old-fashioned style of homosexuality centered in tasteful connoisseurship. Perhaps recognition effects do not require an explicit unveiling.

Dennis Denisoff insists that even mainstream and middlebrow parodies can be "the catalysts for the denaturalization of gendered and sexual norms."[33] The character of Bunthorne, he argues, opens the possibility for "the formation of new identities defined by unconventional sexualities."[34] The potential for new identities unfolds from within the ambiguities inherent in the composite figure of the "dandy-aesthete," who yokes contradictory stereotypes of masculinity. To explain Bunthorne's remaining unmarried at the end of *Patience*, Denisoff proposes that he engages in an "indefinite deferral" of marriage, with his choice of Patience, an utterly inappropriate and unattainable object of affection, as his temporizing ploy. For Denisoff, a dandy-aesthete like Bunthorne might make himself popular with the ladies, but he steers clear of commitment, keeping his options open by suspending himself between one identity and another. Thus the figure of the dandy-aesthete hints at freedom to be gained by avoiding marriage altogether. According to this line of argument, Bunthorne is not denied marriage; he escapes it. Like Wilde's Bunburying hero in *The Importance of Being Earnest* (of whom Bunthorne is the most immediate ancestor), and like all the husbands in the serious family tradition, who temporarily escape domestic confinement, the dandy-aesthete manages to find pockets of relief from the strictures of compulsory domesticity.[35]

Vincent Lankewish focuses on the historical emergence of the homosexual at the end of the nineteenth century, only gradually becoming visible as a new type of social and sexual life.[36] Thus Lankewish treats Bunthorne as prefigural, regarding *Patience* as an early moment in the long process of the homosexual emerging from "the closet of representation."[37] In "No Patience for the Marriage Plot," he offers evidence from other writers at the time—Walter Pater, Gerard Manley Hopkins, John Addington Symonds— to demonstrate their shared desire to be acknowledged. Then, in a reading of *Zero Patience* (1993), John Greyson's film musical about the AIDS epidemic, Lankewish explores the retrospective reconstruction of their desire to emerge.[38]

Zero Patience imagines Sir Richard Francis Burton as the curator of a natural history museum in the present time. Burton, we will remember, was a nineteenth-century anthropologist, explorer, and translator, perhaps best known today for his conception of a "sotadic zone," which, he argued, contained a higher concentration of pederasty and homosexuality than did other places on the globe. In the film, true to his nineteenth-century taxonomic bent, Burton is building a "Hall of Contagion" that will feature Gaëton Dugas as Patient Zero, the supposed source of the AIDS epidemic. The film then narrates the erotic attraction that develops between Burton and Dugas, who returns from the dead in order to bring Burton out of the closet and to refute the concept of a "patient zero." Thus both Burton and Dugas emerge into clearer visibility—Burton from the constraints of an earlier time that supposedly prevented his full awareness of his own homosexuality and Dugas not only from the punitive misconception of him as "patient zero," but also, and more dramatically, from beyond the grave.

As Lankewish points out, *Zero Patience* asserts its connection to *Patience* with an allusion to "Gilbert Sullivan Pharmaceuticals," which is profiting from its production of the AIDS medication AZT, pricing it so high that most patients cannot afford to buy it. Thus the film casts Gilbert and Sullivan—and, by extension, *Patience*—as villains, implying that the opera's exclusion of Bunthorne from its conjugal festivities is another version of the historical failure to acknowledge the homosexual. It imagines the comic opera as an earlier pivotal moment in a story that continues to unfold. Both works raise a set of difficult questions about the contradictory effects of public and historical visibility. To be represented explicitly in popular culture means to be reductively typed, misrecognized, misunderstood, and marked out for possible punishment. Yet without visibility in representation—and in social life—there is no opportunity for recognition. The film recommends that we have "zero patience" to wait any longer for that recognition. Thus, Lankewish argues, *Patience* and *Zero Patience* represent two points in a long process that stretches from the late nineteenth century to the present day, a gradual emergence that is still in progress, entailing both suffering and hope.

Bunthorne, left alone with his lily at the end of *Patience*, now seems clearly legible as a moment in the emergence of a queer historiography. At this point, regardless of whether any particular reader or audience member perceives a homosexual subtext in the work, no good interpretation of *Patience* can fail to recognize its important place in the history of homosexuality, which emerged as a social identity and social type during the late nineteenth century, crystallizing into sharp visibility in the public punishment of Wilde during and after the trials of 1895.[39] As time went on and *Patience* became more popular, Bunthorne was increasingly associated with Wilde; by the late 1880s, the connection was fixed in popular representation, and it had gathered explicitly homosexual and homophobic significance.

The association was cinched tightly after the passage of the Criminal Law Amendment Act of 1885. The "Labouchère Amendment" to that act provided a larger catchment for the criminalization of homosexuality, instituting "gross indecency" instead of the narrower category of "sodomy" as the punishable crime. This change in the law prepared the way for the Wilde trials and for many other prosecutions before it.[40] Another wave of journalistic and legal reaction was precipitated by the Cleveland Street affair

(1889–1890), in which police arrested telegraph workers for serving as male prostitutes. By this time, some readers of *Punch* tacitly assumed a connection between *Patience* and homosexuality, as Denisoff has shown, for the magazine printed a parody of Bunthorne's patter song, "with acknowledgments to the Author of 'Patience'":

If you aim to be a Shocker, carnal theories to cocker is the best way to
  begin.
And every one will say,
As you worm your wicked way,
"If that's allowable for *him* which were criminal in *me*,
What a very emancipated kind of youth this kind of youth must be."[41]

The verse is somewhat garbled in both meter and message, but while most of its animus is directed against those who would aim to shock, it also strikes out against the difference in class that might make it allowable to hire a male prostitute, but not to be one. In any case, it offers clear evidence that by the late 1880s, a popular association of *Patience* with male homosexuality had emerged.

In *The Invention of Love* (1997), Tom Stoppard has reiterated, elaborated, repopularized, and reinterpreted the association for our time. Deeply informed by late-twentieth-century histories of late-nineteenth-century homosexuality, his play represents the historical emergence of the homosexual through the figures of A. E. Housman and Oscar Wilde. *The Invention of Love* is relevant to my argument not only because, like *Zero Patience*, it identifies two points in the history of homosexuality, but also because, again like *Zero Patience*, it directly alludes to *Patience* in doing so.

The action of Stoppard's play arises in the Oxford of the 1880s, when Housman went up, a period of internecine conflict between "the Aesthetes and the hairshirts." Housman's painfully divided life forms the center of interest for the play. On the one hand, he leads a conventional public life as a classical scholar; on the other, in private, he is a poet and a closeted homosexual. This painful self-division is directly attributed to the influence of the Oxford milieu, where "Greek love" is publicly discussed, but is legitimized only as an aspect of a good classical education.[42] As is usual in his work, Stoppard provides a densely researched background for the issues under his consideration. For example, at one point in the play, Benjamin Jowett explicitly mentions the reason for his famous disapproval of Walter Pater—Pater's indiscrete attachment to "the Balliol bugger," William Money Hardinge— a story that had only recently come to light when Stoppard was writing

The Invention of Love.[43] At another point, the Oxford dons exchange interesting tidbits of gossip about a new student, Oscar Wilde. Here Stoppard begins the process of representing Wilde's gradual public emergence in the 1880s. A generation younger than Housman, Wilde is not visible in act 1 of the play, but his reputation precedes his appearance on stage.

At the end of the play, both Housman and Wilde are waiting for death. By then, it is crystal clear that the argumentative structure of *The Invention of Love* juxtaposes the two figures as earlier and later moments in a development, with Wilde emerging only in the play's second half, against the background of Housman's life. One of them reticent and the other flagrantly expressive, one private and the other public, one in the closet and the other out—the play's two main characters embody its concern with the historical emergence of the homosexual through their opposed styles of "the invention of [homosexual] love."[44] Housman feels passionately, but cannot make his feelings part of his public identity. Even when a homosexual friend argues that "we aren't anything till there's a word for it," scholarly Housman objects to the word "homosexual" as a barbarism—half Greek and half Latin.[45] Wilde, on the contrary, is extravagantly outspoken. "A scholar is all scruple, an artist is none," he epigrammatically proclaims.[46] While Housman looks to the past, in both his poetry and his classical scholarship, Wilde looks to the future, aware of his position on the cusp of historical change: "I lived at the turning point of the world when everything was waking up new—the New Drama, the New Novel, New Journalism, New Hedonism, New Paganism, even the New Woman."[47]

Stoppard explicitly establishes *Patience* as part of the historical context early in act 2, when a small fragment appears as a play within the play. When Housman and Moses Jackson, the friend whom Housman silently loves, attend a performance of *Patience*, the figure of Bunthorne appears, singing a bit of the aesthete's patter song. Then, waiting for the train after the play, Housman and Jackson discuss what they have seen. Their responses differ considerably:

> JACKSON: Wasn't it magnificent? A landmark, Hous!
>
> HOUSMAN: I thought it was . . . quite jolly. . . .
>
> JACKSON: Quite jolly? It was a watershed! D'Oyly Carte has made the theatre *modern.*
>
> HOUSMAN (*surprised*): You mean Gilbert and Sullivan?
>
> JACKSON: What? No. No, the *theatre.* . . . The first theatre lit entirely by electricity! . . . D'Oyly Carte's new Savoy is a triumph.
>
> HOUSMAN: . . . [Y]ou're the only London theatre critic worthy of the name. "The new electrified Savoy is a triumph. The contemptible

flickering gas-lit St. James . . . the murky malodorous Haymarket . . . the unscientific Adelphi . . ."

JACKSON: But it was exciting, wasn't it, Hous? Every age thinks it's the modern age, but this one really is. Electricity is going to change every-thing. Everything![48]

Thus Stoppard makes it clear that *Patience* and the new Savoy Theatre represent modernity—in aesthetic, technological, and historical terms. Jackson is a practical, manly man, a sportsman and engineer, unlike Housman, so the scene humorously and poignantly captures their differences in temperament and viewpoint, as well as in gender and sexual style. Jackson's utilitarian perspective is meant to be charming and exuberant here, whereas it will become pernicious, anti-aesthetic, and homophobic, when he rejects Housman and sneeringly asks, with reference to Wilde, "What *use* is he to anyone?" Through his practical attitude, Jackson is aligned in the play with Henry Labouchère, both of them representing the philistine, middlebrow point of view. Labouchère reacts with savage professional jealousy to Carte's promotion of Wilde in America, protesting that "Oscar himself has never *done* anything."[49] In other words, the play carefully sets up an opposition between doing and being, practical accomplishment and other, less visible forces for change.

Jackson's remarks about the new lighting of the Savoy Theatre gain profundity later in *The Invention of Love*, when it becomes clear that the historical emergence of Wilde sheds a brighter, more public light on the sexuality that Housman wants to keep to himself. Wilde's particular invention of love, like the electric lighting of the Savoy Theatre, "is going to change everything." Thus the play's pairing of Housman and Wilde offers a form of dramatized historical thinking, with private and public, residual and emergent types playing off each other in detailed, personally embodied situations. When he first appears, Wilde willingly comes out, but later we are given to understand that he was forced into the public eye, much farther out than he wanted to go, by the punitive light of journalistic typing and juridical judgment—both of which entail the radical reduction of his real complexity of character and motivation.[50] In this respect, Stoppard's play examines the perils and rewards of visibility and powerfully shows that the creation of social types is an aesthetic and historical effect that is both inevitable and reductive.

Even though one moral of Stoppard's story seems to be that poignant, human individuality must fit in or suffer the consequences, the punitive pressure to conform is seen to have its positive effect. For the play uses the figure of Wilde to assert the superiority of being out, no matter what the consequences, in metaphors of brilliant fire and light. Wilde insists: "Better a fallen rocket than never a burst of light. . . . The blaze of my immolation threw its light into every corner of the land where uncounted young men sat each in his own darkness."[51] Thus the electric illumination of the Savoy Theatre is set up to prefigure Wilde's passionate, outré flaming-out.

But the play as a whole does not choose Wilde over Housman. Rather, more comprehensively, it stages a transitional situation in which two modes of homosexuality—and poetics—exist together, in mutual relation. When Wilde first appears on stage in act 2, he is reading aloud from *A Shropshire Lad*, tacitly identifying himself as heir to Housman's poetic genius. Thus *The Invention of Love* as a whole, like the poets' duet during the resolution of *Patience*, asserts both the opposition and the co-implication of aesthetic poetry and idyllic poetry, here represented by Wilde and Housman.

Through the artifice of character doubling, *The Invention of Love* makes it clear that Wilde is heir to Bunthorne as well, for the same actor plays both Bunthorne and Wilde.[52] In one magnificent production, when Wilde appears on stage for the first time, he steps out of the same box set—framed by garish electric lights—in which Bunthorne has appeared in the fragment of *Patience*.[53] Thus the play explicitly dramatizes the argument that Bunthorne prefigures Wilde both aesthetically and historically, in art and in life, one on stage and the other out in the world, one remaining within the frame and the other coming out. In *The Invention of Love*, Stoppard makes visible the historical emergence of Oscar Wilde from the precise place of "Reginald Bunthorne," each of them framed by a revolutionary new form of theatrical illumination.

Making Fun of Victorian Poetry

The opposition and co-implication of aesthetic and idyllic poetry forms the structure of the genre parody in *Patience*, which also pursues an analysis of changing gender norms. The genre parody was noticed immediately, when the astute reviewer for the *Illustrated London News* singled out *Patience* as the best of the parodies of aestheticism, because it offers "a travesty not only of the mere decorative craze, *but upon the form of literature* that is supposed to be held in high esteem by the ardent lovers of the beautiful in art."[54] This point, clearly articulated at the time, has been generally overlooked since then. Similarly, Gilbert's deep engagement with nineteenth-century poetry and poetics has been relatively unacknowledged.[55]

Patience takes "Victorian poetry" as a generic whole and divides it into two dominant subgenres: Reginald Bunthorne representing aesthetic poetry and Archibald Grosvenor, idyllic poetry. Simply to nominate and dramatize these as the two main currents in Victorian poetry makes for a brilliant analytic hypothesis. Two parallel scenes of reading highlight this structural opposition, when Bunthorne in act 1 and Grosvenor in act 2 perform their poetry for the adoring Aesthetic Maidens. Aesthetic and idyllic poetry, it turns out, advance distinct perspectives on Victorian forms of gender, and both are subject to parodic critique.

Before turning to the two scenes of reading, we should glance at the germ of *Patience* in "The Rival Curates" (1867), one of Gilbert's Bab Ballads.[56] In the ballad, two clergymen vie for the reputation of being the mildest and most insipid curate in the neighborhood. After writing a great deal of an opera libretto based on this premise, Gilbert abandoned it, for the Church was still off-limits, and he "felt . . . crippled at every turn by the necessity of protecting [himself] from a charge of irreverence."[57] Luckily for us, the clerical version of *Patience* survives in manuscript.[58] The name of the central clergyman, the Reverend Lawn Tennison, prefigures the parody of Victorian poetry to come, and the poet laureate remains an active object of parody in *Patience*.

"The Rival Curates" tells of Mr. Clayton Hooper, curate of Spiffton-extra-Sooper, and his rival, Reverend Hopley Porter, curate of nearby Asses-milk-cum-Worter. These amusing place-names suggest the degree of insipidity attributed to the curacy, an insipidity thoroughly entangled with conventions of gender and sexuality. Hopley Porter displays his competitive effeminacy by participating in the craft hobbies of his female parishioners (reminding us that the term "effeminate" described a man who sought the company of women before it indicated a feminine man). Clayton Hooper's defeat of Hopley Porter, however, owes to his militancy, for he dispatches minions to threaten Porter with assassination if he does not yield. Porter does yield, becoming a vulgar flirt, leering and winking "at every passing girl" (figure 6.11). This mock conversion to vulgar heterosexuality is depicted as the fulfillment of strong desires, hitherto disguised and suppressed. (Likewise, in act 2 of *Patience*, Bunthorne defeats his poetic rival, forcing him to yield "under compulsion" and to become the vulgar, "every-day young man" he has "long wished" to be.) Thus in "The Rival Curates," compulsory heterosexuality comes in for its share of a parody that is directed primarily against the clergy who would renounce or avoid it. While the conventionally heterosexual behavior of Hopley Porter is clearly characterized as "low," the mild, asexual bearing of Clayton Hooper suggests his association with High Church Anglicanism. Indeed, as Stedman argues, "the references to medieval

FIGURE 6.11 Hopley Porter converts to vulgar heterosexuality: "For years I've longed for some / Excuse for this revulsion; / Now that excuse has come— / I do it on compulsion!!!" Drawing by Bab [W. S. Gilbert] to accompany "The Rival Curates," *Fun*, October 19, 1867. (Collection of Fredric Woodbridge Wilson)

art and Early English belong as much to a caricatured [High Church] Oxford Movement as to a parodied Aesthetic one."[59]

Thus Reginald Bunthorne's "high aesthetic line" picks up where the High Church leaves off. In both clerical and aesthetic contexts, then, it makes sense for Bunthorne to counter vulgar jostling with high apostling:

> Though the Philistines will jostle, you will rank as an apostle in the high
>   aesthetic band,
> If you walk down Piccadilly with a poppy or a lily in your medieval hand.

Bunthorne hates his rival's "confounded mildness" and vows: "I will show the world I can be as mild as he. If they want insipidity, they shall have it. I'll meet this fellow on his own ground and beat him on it." When Lady Jane urges Bunthorne to "go to him and say to him with compliment ironical . . . 'Your style is much too sanctified—your cut is too canonical,'" we can feel the earlier clerical version still at work. During their wonderful duet, Bunthorne imagines telling Grosvenor off:

To doubt my inspiration was regarded as heretical—
Until you cut me out with your placidity emetical.

Gilbert's brilliant stroke of rhyming "heretical" with "emetical" connects the clerical to the aesthetic version, too, for Bunthorne's aesthetic poetry offers emesis as a metaphor for poetic expression in general.

Bunthorne introduces the reading of his poem "Oh, Hollow! Hollow! Hollow!" by calling it a "wild, weird, fleshly thing," inviting recollection of a controversy provoked ten years earlier, when Robert Buchanan attacked the Pre-Raphaelite poets—and Dante Gabriel Rossetti in particular—in his notorious essay "The Fleshly School of Poetry."[60] Buchanan's chief target was the open sensuality of Rossetti's poetry, especially his daring attribution of spiritual value to sexual love. According to Buchanan, Rossetti's poetry asserts "that the body is greater than the soul, and sound superior to sense." Thus Buchanan associates poetic sound with the lowly body, whereas he associates poetic "sense" (his word for content or meaning) with the higher faculties of the soul. From this ratio, he extrapolates a reflection on gender: "[T]he poet . . . must be an intellectual hermaphrodite, to whom the very facts of day and night are lost in a whirl of aesthetic terminology." He registers his fear of changing gender norms, while ostensibly focusing on poetic sound and sense, accusing the poet of treating "nasty" topics by obfuscating their meaning with beautiful sounds.

Buchanan also rants against certain stylistic features associated with Pre-Raphaelite medievalism, which seem to him mere "affectations" in poetic attitude, diction, and versification. He loathes faux-archaic half-rhyme and the ballad refrain, but he reserves particular scorn for the "habit of accenting the last syllable in words which in ordinary speech are accented on the penultimate." The libretto of *Patience* features every one of the poetic devices that Buchanan found objectionable. In their opening chorus, the lovesick Aesthetic Maidens sing a prototypical ballad refrain: "Ah, miserie!" And in the aesthete's famous patter song, Bunthorne teaches the audience how to perform the aesthetic pose by offering a veritable catalogue of the things Buchanan hated. As represented by Bunthorne, the aesthete prefers obscuratism to plain speaking and devotes himself to the past instead of the present. In addition to poetic diction and revivalist tastes in art, the aesthete's sexuality comes in for pointed innuendo:

Then a sentimental passion of a vegetable fashion must excite your languid spleen,
An attachment *à la* Plato for a bashful young potato, or a not-too-French French bean!

Although an extremely slow, "vegetable" love is familiar from Marvell's well-known heterosexual address "To His Coy Mistress," this parody emphasizes the supposedly asexual or homosexual preferences of the aesthete, for an "attachment *à la* Plato" could indicate either or both. Finally, Bunthorne's last words in the opera allude directly to Buchanan's attack, while his pose imitates that of the iconic du Maurier caricature of the aesthete gazing at a lily, refusing food in favor of aesthetic contemplation. Goading Buchanan's hatred of poetic archaism, Bunthorne not only accents the last syllable of "lily," but also archaically rhymes the word with "die":

> In that case unprecedented,
>   Single must I live and die—
> I shall have to be contented
>   With a tulip or li*ly*!

Thus, in the end, Bunthorne plays into the popular caricature of lily-loving aesthetic contemplation.

Exaggerating the stereotype, Bunthorne's poetry blends high aesthetic mannerisms with "nasty" innuendo about low bodily functions—lower even than the ones Buchanan had in mind. Before his reading of "Oh, Hollow! Hollow! Hollow!" he is "*seen in all the agonies of composition. The Ladies are watching him intently as he writhes. At last he hits on the word he wants and writes it down. A general sigh of relief.*" During his "*agonies of composition*," Bunthorne writhes like the "writhing maid" in the poem he will soon recite. Associating poetic composition with the bodily processes ignored by the caricature aesthete, he exults: "The poem is finished, and my soul had gone out into it. That was all. It was nothing worth mentioning, it occurs three times a day." Together with this allusion to digestion, the "*general sigh of relief*" emitted when he is finished links poetic composition to the bodily evacuation of its contents.

Of course, "Oh, Hollow! Hollow! Hollow!" is pretentious, dense, and nearly impenetrable. Half the humor inheres in its interpretive difficulty; but the other half employs a dirty joke to comment on gender. To prepare the Aesthetic Maidens, Bunthorne suggests an attitude of aesthetic contemplation: "To understand it, cling passionately to one another and think of faint lilies. (*They do so as he recites*)":

> What time the poet hath hymned
> The writhing maid, lithe-limbed,
>   Quivering on amaranthine asphodel,
> How can he paint her woes,

Knowing, as well he knows,
    That all can be set right with calomel?

When from the poet's plinth
The amorous colocynth
    Yearns for the aloe, faint with rapturous thrills,
How can he hymn their throes
Knowing, as well he knows,
    That they are only uncompounded pills?

Is it, and can it be,
Nature hath this decree,
    Nothing poetic in the world shall dwell?
Or that in all her works
Something poetic lurks,
    Even in colocynth and calomel?
                    I cannot tell.

Bunthorne's poetic style flies in the face of Buchanan's middlebrow desire for immediate meaning. Both poetic sound and specialized language obscure the sense, which can be grasped only by those who know that colocynth and aloe are botanical purgatives, while calomel is a chloride of mercury, all the "uncompounded" ingredients of emetic and laxative pills.[61] In other words, the poem poses a riddle about poetic content: What is contained in the body, is the result of digestion, and provides a "general sense of relief" when it is expressed from the body? Could the libretto be any clearer about the poem's excremental theme than to have the Maidens call it "fragrant! . . . precious! . . . nonsense"?

In one respect, Bunthorne's poem imagines a maiden who fails to recognize her "inner" feelings. She writhes, in what looks like erotic yearning, but instead is the suffering of constipation. The aesthetic poet knows what she does not know: the true meaning of her "woes." The poem reduces passionate feeling to low bodily necessity while transforming unmentionable bodily functions into beautiful, "poetic" language. Meanwhile, the scatalogical joke tacitly associates both poetry and romantic love with impacted excrement. Interpretation amounts to the difficulty of understanding the content of a beautiful, enigmatic form, represented by a woman's body.[62] But beautiful forms can lie; even this tried-and-true signifier can turn out to be hollow or, even worse, the opposite of hollow— yet a near equivalent—full of shit.[63] "Oh, Hollow!" imitates this deflating discovery, the "wail of the poet's heart on discovering that everything is commonplace." The "writing maid" does not understand her feelings, and in this we can see a parodic representation of one strand of Victorian gender ideology: the ignorance of bodily, especially sexual, feeling that is demanded of conventional femininity.

The difficulty of interpreting the poem mimics the body's difficulty in delivering itself of its content. And, indeed, that difficulty is a large part of the pleasure for those knowing members of the audience who get the joke. One major point of the poem's difficulty has to do with its sound effects. In this respect, it most especially parodies Swinburne, who was himself a great poetic parodist, especially of his own poetry, and precisely on this very point. Swinburne knew that his involved sonorities and grammatically shifting near-repetitions could make it difficult for readers to follow what his poems mean.[64] But Bunthorne's poem alludes to Swinburne's reputation for risqué content as well. When *Poems and Ballads* burst on the scene in 1866, it marked a sensation in the history of nineteenth-century poetic content; no one had published such sexually explicit poetry before, not even Rossetti. By the time *Patience* opened, everyone who knew anything about contemporary poetry would have known about Swinburne's shocking heterosexual, sadomasochistic, and homoerotic themes.

In the final analysis, the difficulty of Bunthorne's poem is due not only to its semantic obscurity and sound effects, but also to its overt refusal to be interpreted. The figure of "Nature" has definitely issued a decree, but what does it mean? Two absolutely contradictory, hypothetical positions are put forward. Either Nature has decreed that "Nothing poetic in the world shall dwell," or she has decreed that "in all her works / Something poetic lurks," even in the ingredients for a laxative pill. The poet's only first-person intervention comes at the end, when he admits that he "cannot tell" which of these alternatives is correct. In other words, the poem performs a reflexive and anguished uncertainty about the nature of poetry itself, a pure lyric refusal of simple content or meaning. Thus Bunthorne's poem is intensely "aesthetic," for it detaches art from any utilitarian, instrumental, or referential purpose.

For many decades before *Patience* was produced, attempts to express powerful feelings—and parodies of those attempts—had formed one main current of late-eighteenth- and nineteenth-century poetics. "Oh, Hollow!" bundles together these poetic movements, issues, and earlier parodies in one densely compacted place to suggest that high feelings of romantic yearning are prompted by low bodily functions. Making fun of absolutely contradictory caricatures of the aesthetes—their supposed desire to repress the demands of the body and their supposed desire to revel in bodily feeling—

Bunthorne's poem also raises several serious theoretical issues: the relation of form and content; the relative value of sound and sense; and the interpenetration of lyric, narrative, and moral impulses. In fact, "Oh, Hollow! Hollow! Hollow!" may be taken as a commentary on the relation between Romantic and Victorian poetry, one that makes fun of Romantic interiority and expressiveness in general. According to Bunthorne's poem, the "spontaneous overflow of powerful feelings" has been stopped; Romantic overflow has been supplanted by exaggerated Victorian reserve, its gushing evacuations succeeded by an equally problematic constipation.[65]

Now let us turn to Archibald Grosvenor's idyllic poetry, which comes in for its share of parody, too. His name alludes to the Grosvenor Gallery, which Sir Coutts Lindsay had opened in 1877 in London's fashionable Mayfair district. Like his namesake, Grosvenor claims to be "a trustee for Beauty." Initially associated with the Pre-Raphaelites and with Whistler (and drawing hostile reviews through both associations), the Grosvenor soon acquired a high cultural authority of its own. In both respects, by 1881 it was ripe for parodic deflation.[66] Highlighting his opposition to Bunthorne's "complicated state of mind," Grosvenor describes himself as the "Apostle of Simplicity." *Patience* makes it clear, however, not only that Grosvenor's simplicity is simplistic, but also that it is a pose, every bit as artificial as Bunthorne's aesthetic pose. According to *Patience*, the idyllic poet is not unaffected, merely affected in another style.

Identifying Grosvenor as an "idyllic poet" suggests a wide range of high and low poetic associations, stretching from the early to the late nineteenth century. Often said to derive its name from *eidyllion* (Greek for "little picture"), the idyll was taken to offer set pieces of the simple life.[67] Significantly, however, a debate about what counts as "simplicity" can be traced across the period. (And the parody of simplicity represented by Patience and Grosvenor is a latter-day participant in that long debate.) A scholarly interest in the Greek idyllists dates from the 1830s, but by the 1880s, idyllic poetry, no longer associated primarily with the classical past, was attempting to represent simplicity in the present, with a middlebrow moralism that favored domestic settings. The nineteenth-century English idyll became not so much a little picture as a little narrative. In the libretto for *Patience*, Gilbert adopted this later perspective, imagining idyllic poetry not as a learned form, inherited from classical antiquity, but as the form enjoyed by a low- or middlebrow reader such as Buchanan or Grosvenor.

Buchanan's reverence for Tennyson was the flip side of his hatred of Rossetti and Swinburne, and if we recall that the Reverend Lawn Tennison was to have been the main character in the clerical version of *Patience*, we should be able to deduce Tennyson's place in Victorian poetry, according to Gilbert. Tennyson was without doubt the chief reference point for the Victorian idyll, and the figure of Grosvenor is Gilbert's imitation of Buchanan's middlebrow tastes. The early form of the Tennysonian idyll dates from his 1842 volume, later titled *English Idyls, and Other Poems*.[68] However, audience members in 1881 most readily would have recalled Tennyson's *Idylls of the King* (1856–1885), in which the poet recasts the Arthurian cycle as a set of familiar, domestic narratives.[69] In a brilliantly scathing essay, Swinburne attacks Buchanan for his diatribe against "the fleshly school," implying that *Idylls of the King* would be just the sort of poetry that Buchanan might misread as a domestic novel about adulterous intrigue. Of course, Tennyson's *Idylls* were intended to bring the stories of King Arthur's court down to earth, preserving their "Early English" historical value while refocusing the narrative interest on their domestic drama. Swinburne shows what might happen if a reader of *Idylls of the King* looked for domestic prurience instead of Early English dignity.[70]

Browning published his two series of *Dramatic Idyls* in 1879 and 1880. Thus the idyll was still current coin when *Patience* opened in 1881. Tennyson privately deplored Browning's adoption of the term, for Browning was "invading [his] poetic terrain."[71] However, Coventry Patmore had appropriated the idyll, too, heightening its traditional association with domestic ideals, for the narrative portions of *The Angel in the House* (1854, 1862) were called "idyls" in the poem's early editions. Patmore has often been suggested as a model for Grosvenor because of his excessive mildness and "insipid amiability."[72] Patmore's High Church commitments should interest us as well. In *The Angel in the House*, those commitments abide, reinvested in the confidence, purity, and chastity of conjugal love between the allegorically named Felix and Honoria, perfect representations of graphic gender differentiation in the "serious family." Although he was a master prosodist, Patmore practiced a severe reserve with respect to his extraordinary metrical gift. Exquisite to the knowing few, his stanzas seemed to the many only to ring infinitesimal changes on a jog-trot tetrameter. Edmund Gosse, whose tastes were more aesthetic than idyllic, called Patmore the "laureate of the tea-table, with his hum-drum stories of girls that smell of bread and butter." Knowing Patmore's prosodic genius, Gosse complained of his self-restriction: "So brilliant and pungent a thinker has perhaps never been content so long to dwell on the very borderland of insipidity. . . . Dowered with a rare ear for metrical effect, . . . he has of set purpose chosen the most sing-song of English meters as the almost exclusive vehicle of his ideas."[73]

The metrical pattern of which Gosse complains is Grosvenor's, too—tetrameter, rather than the blank verse associated with the Tennysonian idyll. As we turn to Grosvenor's scene of reading, we should remember that his poetry is meant to be heard as the opposite of Bunthorne's aesthetic poetry: not "fleshly," but pure; not complicated, but simple; not lyrical, but narrative; not disinterested, but moralistic. Like Bunthorne, Grosvenor is a composite character, yoking together a parody of High Church mildness with a parody of Low Church self-righteousness. Stedman points out that the earliest version of *Patience* had Grosvenor reading from a "black-letter rubricated" tome, and she argues that without this prop the literary parody of his "tractlike verses" might be lost.[74] But his verses are "tractlike" not only because they might suggest Tractarianism, but also because they display a certain Low Church homiletic moralism that had been available to parody for a long time. (Think of the Reverend Brocklehurst's initial interaction with Jane Eyre, when he recommends that she read *The Child's Guide* for her improvement, itself a parody of the Reverend William Carus-Wilson's periodical the *Children's Friend*.) Like these simplistic tracts, poetry written for children makes its moral design—and its pedagogical purpose—risibly visible. So, too, do Grosvenor's poems.

"Here is a decalet—a pure and simple thing, a very daisy," Grosvenor announces to the Aesthetic Maidens, who have begged him to read. He admits: "To appreciate [the decalet], it is not necessary to think of anything at all." This blatant parallelism with Bunthorne's aesthetically "intense" instructions to the maidens emphasizes the parodic intent of what is to come:

> Gentle Jane was good as gold,
> She always did as she was told;
> She never spoke when her mouth was full,
> Or caught bluebottles their legs to pull,
> Or spilt plum jam on her nice new frock,
> Or put white mice in the eight-day clock,
> Or vivisected her last new doll,
> Or fostered a passion for alcohol.
> And when she grew up she was given in marriage
> To a first-class earl who keeps his carriage!

Grosvenor proudly proclaims that "there is not one word in that decalet which is calculated to bring the blush of shame to the cheek of modesty." Angela agrees: "Not one—it is purity itself." The joke cuts against excessive mildness and bourgeois rectitude, with its strict codes of feminine modesty.

Like the writhing maidens of Bunthorne's poem, the character of Patience parodies this exaggerated ideal. This sort of empty-headed purity, argues *Patience*, should be just as suspect as the aesthetic poet's beautifully dirty wail. Unlike Bunthorne's sonorous evacuation, Grosvenor's namby-pamby decalets are overloaded with childish, utilitarian content:

> Teasing Tom was a very bad boy,
> A great big squirt was his favourite toy;
> He put live shrimps in his father's boots,
> And sewed up the sleeves of his Sunday suits;
> He punched his poor little sisters' heads,
> And cayenne-peppered their four-post beds,
> He plastered their hair with cobbler's wax,
> And dropped hot halfpennies down their backs.
>   The consequence was he was lost to*ta*lly,
>   And married a girl in the *corps de bally*!

The pointed emphasis, in the penultimate line, on the penultimate syllable of "to*ta*lly" should convince us that Gilbert was enjoying his great skill in versification. The complex parody simultaneously makes fun of Grosvenor's putative lack of technical skill in versification (since he must distort the rhythm in order to achieve his rhyme); his class-inflected accent (for "totally" must rhyme with the Cockney pronunciation of "ballet"); and the aesthetic affectation of archaic pronunciation. In a deliciously low parody of a high aesthetic device, we have not a "li*ly*" forced to rhyme with "die," but an everyday cognate, as "to*ta*lly" twists to rhyme with "*bally.*"

Grosvenor's poems are distinctly middlebrow, a parody of simplistic moral design supporting conventional gender roles and the social status quo. Feminine docility is rewarded with an upwardly mobile marriage, while masculine high jinks are punished with a downwardly mobile one. Thus the parody turns against a sort of poetic justice that is not poetic at all, but novelistic. In other words, Grosvenor's poetry is not "aesthetic" because it is instrumental and moralistic in intent; nor is it even "poetry" because it is more like a novel (or the parody of a novel), with social rewards of upward and downward mobility being doled out on the marriage market. This parody of idyllic poetry's simple-mindedness links it to the character of Patience and prefigures her pairing with Grosvenor in the end. When Bunthorne decides to change his personality in order to attract Patience, he adopts these attitudes, alerting his audience to the opera's ironic interpretation of them: "Henceforth I am mildly cheerful. My conversation will blend amusement with instruction." He vows to modify his aestheticism until it becomes "the most pastoral kind." As he later sings,

> "High diddle diddle"
> Will rank as an idyll,
> If I pronounce it chaste!

This parodic comment on Grosvenor's idyllic poetry leads us to see the opera's critique of "every-day" attitudes that are seemingly vindicated, but are actually undercut in the end.

In this respect, the name that Gilbert chose for Colonel Calverley is a small detail that speaks volumes. The Colonel in *Patience* represents the middlebrow voice of common sense (as did Our Gallant Colonel in du Maurier's *Punch* cartoons and the military men in all the plays of the serious family tradition, including Burnand's *The Colonel*). His very name makes the connection between simplistic common sense and idyllic poetry. For Colonel Calverley is named after Charles Stuart Calverley, a well-known idyllist and parodist who participated in the second wave of the idyll craze, publishing his translations of Theocritus in 1869. But even during his idyllic days, and certainly after, he was best known for his brilliant poetic parodies, including the ode "To Beer," which is a pastiche parody of Keats's odes, and *The Cock and the Bull* (1872), a parody of Browning's *The Ring and the Book* (1868–1869). In a mere 129 lines, Calverley manages to include references to more than 100 specific passages from across the length of Browning's 21,000-line poem. This drastic act of reduction makes one point of the parody, which clearly implies that Browning's poem is exceptionally long-winded, but Calverley makes Browning's mannered representation of speech another point of his parodic barb.[75] Calverley made fun of the nineteenth-century ballad revivals, too, producing such powerfully concentrated insipidity as the following:

> The farmer's daughter hath soft brown hair;
> (Butter and eggs and a pound of cheese)
> And I met with a ballad, I can't say where,
> Which wholly consisted of lines like these. ("Ballad," ll. 21–24)

The parenthetical second line, repeated in each stanza throughout the poem, reduces the ballad refrain—and perhaps poetry in general—to a list of items on a shopping list (a point also made by the poets' duet in *Patience* ["When I go out of door"]).

Proponents of the simple-minded, idyllic mode are destined to prevail in this battle of the poetic genres. In any case, they are rewarded by the marriages that constitute the giddy conclusion of *Patience*. But this ending is itself parodic, for the sudden, hyperbolically multiplied marriages further undermine the ideal of domesticity that has been subjected to critique through its association with idyllic poetry. In the end, when Grosvenor reappears with his hair cut, wearing *"an ordinary suit of dittoes and a pot hat"* (a jacket with trousers in matching plaid and a derby), while the Aesthetic Maidens reappear wearing fashionable contemporary garb—as do the wives at the conclusion of plays in the serious family tradition—the audience can see that the social trend toward aestheticism has literally been redressed. These new, anti-aesthetic costumes throw aestheticism into the past, against the colorful relief of the present moment, but also indicate a distinct comedown in both class and brow-elevation level. Surely, then, the ultimate humor of *Patience* resides in the fact that parody has already hollowed out the representations of these triumphantly commonplace folk. Surely, in the end, "the wail of the poet's heart on discovering that everything is commonplace" still hangs in the air: "Oh, Hollow!"

7

Transforming the Fairy Genres

Women on Top in *Iolanthe*

L
ike *Patience*, both *Iolanthe; or, The Peer and the Peri* (1882) and *Princess Ida* play with changing gender norms and roles. While *Patience* raises the issue of the effeminate man, *Iolanthe* and *Princess Ida* turn their special attention to the masculine, or "strong-minded," woman.

The separation of the Chorus into Peers and Peris employs that formal device more wittily than ever before. On one level, this division stresses the opposition between the mortal and supernatural realms; on another level, the opposition is more specific, the argument more pointedly about gender. At this point in the collaboration, we would expect the Savoy Chorus to divide according to gender, but instead of parodically twisted oppositional types of masculinity and femininity—such as sentimental Pirates and Wards—the value of the opposition between Peers and Peris is more abstract. The Peers represent not only the parodic type of incompetent Peers, but also mortal man in general, while the Fairies represent woman in general, in many respects a higher form of being altogether. Like the Dragoon Guards of *Patience*, the Peers recall a form of masculinity that is already out of step with the times. Even after they engage in marriages with the Peers, marriages that are motivated by sexual desire as well as desire for rank, the Fairies are ascendant. Thus their marriages accomplish a funny exchange, for the Peers outrank the Fairies on earth, while the Fairies outrank the Peers absolutely, ontologically, in the end.

Indeed, the male and female Choruses literally come from different worlds, so the usual gender opposition in the Chorus is writ large, as cultural difference. True, in *Trial by Jury*, *H.M.S. Pinafore*, and *The Pirates of Penzance*, the genders are shown to be worlds apart, but in *Iolanthe* the separate realms are humorously literalized as Fairyland ("high") and parliamentary politics ("low"). This opera brilliantly transforms the "separate spheres" of Victorian gender ideology into two cultures, each operating according to its own distinct system of government and law (the Fairy Queen must enforce her "fairy laws," and the Lord Chancellor, in his own realm, "embod[ies] the Law"). Of course, the boundary drawn between these two cultures exists in order to be transgressed (plate 11). The two realms infiltrate each other, both in matters of government and in matters of love. After all, the play opens with the premise that they have already mixed, for Iolanthe has broken the most important fairy law—"every fairy must die who marries a mortal"—and given birth to a son. She has been banished by the Fairy Queen for her disobedience.

As we know, representations of gender have everything to do with genre (and vice versa). *Iolanthe* chiefly parodies the fairy extravaganza, but it is humorously situated in relation to other fairy genres as well. Although Terence Rees argues that *Thespis* was Gilbert and Sullivan's "sole excursion into the realm of mid-Victorian extravaganza,"[1] *Iolanthe* should be regarded as another—and an even greater—parody of the extravaganza tradition, including its inheritance from pantomime. While *Thespis* parodies the classical extravaganza, *Iolanthe* parodies the other dominant subgenre of extravaganza, fairy extravaganza, also launched by James Robinson Planché and Madame Vestris in the 1830s. *Iolanthe* exhibits all the dominant conventions of fairy extravaganza, including the establishment of two separate worlds: a realm of fantasy, Fairyland, which abuts on the real, metropolitan world of the present moment. Taking this generic premise and mapping its separate worlds onto the separate spheres, *Iolanthe* reminds us that extravaganza fairies are generically gendered feminine. The risqué suggestiveness of extravaganza is made explicitly sexual in *Iolanthe*, which imagines "marriage" between mortals and fairies. Thus Strephon, issue of the sexual union between Iolanthe and her mortal lover, is "half a fairy." Because of his mixed parentage, Strephon makes an appropriate go-between, so the Fairy Queen sends him to intervene in human law and male customary behavior by entering Parliament. His symbolic self-division is the occasion of much sexual innuendo, since he is a "fairy down to the waist," but "his legs are mortal." Like the separate realms of Fairyland and the mortal world, Strephon's body is zoned into high and low functions. In this parodic mixture, high functions seem to reign when Strephon enters Parliament, but low urges seem to take over when all the Fairies decide to marry mortals. In one last topsy-turvy reversal, however, everyone flies away to Fairyland. In the end, the reunion of Fairies and mortals is predicated on heterosexual attraction triumphing over gender separatism and cultural difference—an idea that will be reiterated, with an entirely different result, in *Princess Ida*.

Despite its assumption of an irrational, yet inevitable, heterosexual attraction between the Fairies and the humans, *Iolanthe* considers the possibility of female equality—or even female superiority. Furthermore, unlike in most traditional treatments of this topic, the women stay "on top" in the end, assimilating the human world into their higher regime. Focusing on that crucial figure of female power, the Fairy Queen, we will find in her the occasion to consider the large contralto character familiar in most of the Savoy operas. Savoy opera adapts and plays with the traditional Dame figure from pantomime to form a new gender parody. As we know, Gilbert and Sullivan ruled out cross-dressing in their productions after *Thespis*, arguing "on artistic principles [that] no man should play a woman's part and no woman a man's."[2] Thus they strategically mobilized the force of gender propriety to mark their own emerging genre, differentiating their work from the lower genres of burlesque. And yet, pantomime and extravaganza cross-dressing live on, especially in *Iolanthe* and *Princess Ida*, both strong examples of how older genre conventions can be felt, through parody, even when they are ostensibly absent. In the preposterous temporality of genre parody, the past can inhabit the present in a re-dressed form.

Fairy Genres

Victorian fairies served as a screen for projection, a vehicle of fantasy, a way of imagining. Indeed, "enthusiasm for the fairies swept all branches of the arts," as Carole Silver has demonstrated. According to Silver, this widespread enthusiasm reached its high point in the years between 1880 and 1910. Produced at the beginning of this span, *Iolanthe* thus takes its place as a central cultural text in the long Victorian reflection on the fairies.[3]

In one sense, fairies may be understood as a secularized, folk form of supernatural power. Thus their prominence in the nineteenth century participated in the general project of recasting divinity both more abstractly and closer to human terms. As Coleridge put it: "[F]rom my early reading of Faery Tales . . . my mind had been habituated *to the Vast*. . . . I know no other way of giving the mind a love of 'the Great' & 'the Whole.'"[4] Like animism or pantheism, belief in the fairies could endow the natural world with supernatural presence, for they were supposed to live nearby, in a nearly invisible parallel universe, and to influence human life for good or ill. In particular, their well-known mischievousness or downright malevolence could provide

an explanation for such human calamities as mental defect, physical defor-
mity, and infant mortality. But even this reduced sense of the supernatural
raised many doubts. Whether actually to believe in the fairies was an end-
lessly debated question in the nineteenth century, and Silver remarks that
the Victorians "waver[ed] between a somewhat outmoded but not abandoned belief . . . and an enlightened skepticism."[5] It was precisely this temporal sense of their passing away that made fairies susceptible to such a wide
range of nostalgic, romantic, humorous, and parodic treatments.

The costs of modernization—whether conceived as Enlightenment
demystification, technological progress, the spread of literacy, or industrialization and urbanization—were realized in fantasies that the fairies had
fled, emigrated, been exiled, or hidden themselves deeper in the earth. John
Aubrey famously wrote in 1686 that "the divine art of Printing and Gun-
powder have frighted away Robin-goodfellow and the Fayries," and by 1847,
when Jane Eyre laments that the fairies "were all gone out of England to
some savage country where the woods were wilder and thicker," her feeling is utterly conventional.[6] Silver argues that the disappearance of the fairies was a constituent part of their cultural construction, from "The Wife of
Bath's Tale" onward.[7] As a form of folk nationalism, then, fairies expressed
the anxiety that an essential organic connection to the land had been lost,
cut off by the advance of modern rationality. Imaginative visions of fairies surviving in remote nature and "outlandish" border zones, visible only
under certain special circumstances, provided an alternative to the modern
reality. Significantly, then, fairy lore accorded the fairies their own culture.
As Susan Stewart explains, "the fairy is depicted as a socialized being with
a culture (dress, ritual organization, economy, and authority structure) particular to fairydom."[8]

This fairy blend of nature and the supernatural resided in the deep pockets and outlying peripheries of the nation—away from the surface, away
from the cities. An ancient, primeval race, the fairies were intensely local,
regional, and rural. This sense of micro-difference within the macro-culture
allowed an ethnographic imagination to work not outside but within the
borders of the nation; the fairies served as a cultural other, internal to "Great
Britain," roughly from the time of its formation. That fairies survived longest
in the "border" countries (Ireland, Scotland, and Wales) affirms the primitive charm of these places, relative to the cosmopolitan center, while recollecting the fissures within a "Britain" that aims to be "Greater" than the sum
of its parts. Thus fairies provided a fantasy of indigenous belonging, their
lore thought to be the remnants of an oral culture that had long since been
re-created in literary form.[9] Old dames like Mother Goose are figures for

this collective urge to recollect the days (and tales) gone by. They are anthological memory banks, repositories of folk wisdom, and great storytellers.

Although British fairies were quintessentially regional and national, they were also significantly foreign, especially French and German.[10] Mother Goose herself was an early-eighteenth-century import from France, by way of the famous collection of Charles Perrault, *Histoires ou contes du temps passé, avec des moralités: Contes de ma mère l'Oye* (*Stories or Tales of Past Times, with Morals: Tales of Mother Goose*, 1697). As we can see in his title, looking back at *temps passé* was part of the fairy-tale form from its inception. At the same time, Madame d'Aulnoy collected her light, sophisticated tales in *Les contes des fées* (*Fairy Tales*, 1697) and *Contes nouveaux, ou Les fées à la mode* (*New Tales, or The Fairies in Fashion*, 1698). The more grisly tales collected by the Brothers Grimm (*Kinder- und Hausmärchen* [*Children's and Household Tales*], 1812) came much later and claimed direct access to authentic folk material, while the tales of Hans Christian Andersen, so important in the nineteenth century, were largely literary inventions. Late-nineteenth-century collections displayed the cultural eclecticism and anthological tendencies characteristic of the time, culminating in Andrew Lang's multivolume sequence of color-coded fairy books (1889–1910), just a bit later than *Iolanthe*.

In other words, the literary genre of the fairy-tale collection long predates and then accompanies the late-eighteenth- and nineteenth-century emphasis on folkloristic compilation. This is important in relation to the fairy extravaganza partly because its primary source material was found in French and English folk- and fairy tales. The first English fairy extravaganza, *Riquet with the Tuft* (1836), which James Robinson Planché modeled after the precursor genre, French *féerie* (fairy opera with ballet, popular in the eighteenth century), was based on a tale by Perrault, "Riquet à la houppe"; then, over the course of his career in Fairyland, Planché adapted many other tales from Madame d'Aulnoy. Moreover, unlike the lower burlesques, fairy extravaganza was itself anthological, mixing allusions to plot elements from many tales, collected together with authorial additions by an arch *pasticheur*. Savoy opera recollects these recollections. Thus fairies provided a useful figure for cross-cultural awareness, both inside and outside national boundaries, for adults and children, folklorists and scholars, the low- and the high-minded. When in the finale of act 1, the Fairies of *Iolanthe* boisterously offer Latin, Greek, and French "remarks," it is this pop-cultural eclecticism to which they jokingly refer.

But fairies also provided a screen for more intimate projections, a vehicle for relieving inhibitions, and a cover for all sorts of fantasies involving gender and sexuality. Although no scholar of Fairyland claims that all fairies are women, "fairy" was so generally associated with "woman" in the Victorian period—and, more specifically, with female sexuality—as to form the metaphorical basis for a cluster of euphemisms.[11] For example, to mention a "fairy form" was a respectable way to admire a beautiful female figure (as in Dr. Daly's admiration of Constance in *The Sorcerer*). By the same token, to name the site of domestic bliss the "fairy cottage" deftly bundled the cross-cultural implications of the separate spheres, the otherworldly character of the private realm, the gender of its tutelary spirit, and the sexual aspect of the spousal relation, made respectable by its domestication. In other words, these colloquial euphemisms bound together respectability and sexiness, without explicit acknowledgment.

Representational displacement into another realm altogether—Fairyland—permitted even greater explicitness, for Victorian fairies were much less inhibited than their human counterparts. One strain of fairy painting, a widespread genre during the Victorian period, makes their use for sexual fantasy especially clear. Often crowding the picture with "tiny, perfectly formed, naked and amorous bodies," fairy painting resembles the fairy extravaganza, which crowds the stage with bodies, especially female bodies (plate 12).[12] Yet in fairy painting, the fairy bodies were taken to be pristine, innocent, and natural. In attempting to explain why this overt sexuality went unremarked, Charlotte Gere concludes simply that the displacement to another world made it permissible; Susan Stewart agrees, arguing that the distance achieved through displacement accounts for the fairies' physical perfection in the first place; and Maureen Duffy maintains that these representations were "an attempt to desexualize . . . [what] the Victorians found so hard to handle."[13] In several senses, these fairies represented the obverse of the domestic, middle-class "angel in the house," for they are aggressively undomesticated. Yet like the angels—with whom they were often compared—fairies signified a certain spiritual superiority to heavy, solid, dense earthly things.

In the Victorian theater of extravaganza, where a certain kind of voluptuousness was ostentatiously on display, fairies most certainly were women. The refrain of one popular mid-Victorian music-hall song puts this assumption most clearly and simply:

> Oh the fairies, whoa the fairies!
> Nothing but splendour and feminine gender!
> Oh the fairies, whoa the fairies!
> Oh for the wings of a Fairy Queen!

As Lionel Lambourne points out, this chorus happily acknowledges "the frisson of sensuality which for centuries has been created by the fairies in the theatre."[14] Until the theater closed in 2005, this song was still sung as the anthem of the Players Theatre, Villiers Street, London, where a Victorian music-hall program was reenacted as a retro tourist entertainment, a popular signature of Victorian cultural heritage. "The politics of fairyland are never correct," as Lambourne reminds us.[15] But the fairy extravaganza self-consciously plays with this risqué suggestiveness, aiming to have it both ways, to be both knowing and innocent, both sensual and merely playful. In the Fairyland of extravaganza, the fantasy of childlike play joins the fantasy of sexual desire, in a realm where overt sexuality has been sublimated and made innocent again. We must remember, as we have seen in the discussion of *Thespis*, that extravaganza began as a high form of burlesque, developed in the 1830s by Planché at the Olympic Theatre under the management of Madame Vestris.[16] One of its chief generic purposes was to etherealize burlesque sexiness, the abundance of exposed flesh—legs, in particular—being of special interest. In many images of the period, fairies are represented simply as legs (plate 13).[17] The concluding tag of *The Pretty Druidess; or, The Mother, the Maid, and the Mistletoe Bough* (1869), Gilbert's burlesque of Bellini's *Norma* (1831), plays with this convention of sexual display:

> So for burlesque I plead. Forgive our rhymes;
> Forgive the jokes you've heard five thousand times;
> Forgive each breakdown, cellar-flap and clog,
> Our low-bred songs—our slangy dialogue;
> And, above all, oh, ye with double barrel—
> Forgive the scantiness of our apparel!

The women who portrayed burlesque fairies were not thought to be innocent; Tracy Davis has discussed in detail the ways their bodies were encoded for consumption.[18] But fairy extravaganza attempted to elevate this sexual display while preserving it in a general voluptuousness; Savoy opera further elevated, negated, and preserved it as well. The Savoy Chorus girls were not available for sexual liaisons, their costumes were proper, and the genre parody provided a certain humorous distance—and yet the mise-en-scène was often utterly voluptuous.

Planché adapted the fairy extravaganza from the French *féerie*, which he blended with English pantomime. Highly successful with a sophisticated and mixed audience, Planché's fairy extravaganzas were staged at least once a year and sometimes twice (at both Christmas and Easter) from the 1830s well into the 1860s. In English pantomime, the story is launched in the so-called Opening, a series of scenes structured around the fate of two lovers, whose union is opposed by her father, and around the struggle between two supernatural forces: an evil demon and a good fairy. As the plot unfolds, its threads are spun around a familiar fairy tale, nursery rhyme, folktale, or popular fiction. To emphasize their combat, the demon and the fairy are thematically coded as opposites; for example, in Gilbert's only pantomime, *Harlequin Cock Robin and Jenny Wren!* (1867), based on the theme of public sanitation, the good Spirit of Fresh Air opposes the Demon Miasma (see plate 2). The fairy protects the lovers, who always triumph in the end. At the moment of their triumph, the characters from the Opening are suddenly transformed into the main character types of the commedia dell'arte, who then engage in the raucous antics of the harlequinade, replete with chases, pratfalls, and tricks.

Fairy extravaganza refines its structural debt to pantomime by harking back to the elegant fairy tales of Perrault and Madame d'Aulnoy. Planché hoped to replace the reductive versions of the tales, known to English children through the pantomimes, with his own more accurate translations. He restored the wit, satire, parody, and arch "moral lessons" of the originals, all written with adults (more than children) in mind. But the French influence is felt mainly as a matter of tone, for the fairy extravaganza offers an original plot, tied less securely to any single fairy tale than is the pantomime. As Donald Roy points out, "in adapting [the French *féerie*] to English taste, Planché naturalized it so thoroughly as to make a lasting contribution to the English theater."[19] Like classical extravaganza, fairy extravaganza offers rhymed dialogue, lyrics set to familiar melodies, elaborate puns and word-play, burlesque cross-dressing, humorous anachronisms, and topical references to contemporary city life, culture, and politics.

The last convention is especially important for understanding *Iolanthe*. Although the action of the fairy extravaganza takes place in a fantasy realm, that realm is punctuated with scattershot references to the present-day urban world outside the theater. The juxtaposition of the two realms—Fairyland and contemporary London—facilitates an arch attitude toward both. As Roy points out, extravaganza's allusiveness and topicality presuppose an intelligent, intellectually inclined audience, ready to catch all sorts of allusions.[20] Most of all, fairy extravaganza indulges in a particular kind of voluptuous, lush, and fantastic spectacle that was enabled by developments in stage technology. In other words, Victorian Fairyland was very much a creation of industrial light and magic. Suspended on wires, in harnesses, and stabilized with counterweights or elevated on lifts, fairies could rise into the air; innovative traps and pulleys allowed for sudden appearances and disappearances; moving backgrounds made it possible for a suspended fairy to look as if she were flying forward, traveling through space. Filmy gauze drop cloths could create a hazy, otherworldy atmosphere, even the oxymoronic look of invisibility. Improvements in stage lighting throughout the nineteenth century contributed various forms of dazzling evanescence, from the "colored fire" traditional in extravaganza transformations to the radically new electric lighting at the Savoy Theatre beginning in 1881, the year before *Iolanthe* was produced. Act 2 of *Iolanthe* made use of this new light, for the Fairies sported coronets of glittering electric bulbs (figure 7.1).[21] Planché emphasizes the central importance of spectacle when he describes the characteristics of a good fairy extravaganza: "a plot, the interest of which is sustained to the last moment, and is not in the least complicated; a series of startling and exciting events, the action in which required no verbal explanation; and numerous opportunities for scenic display and sumptuous decoration."[22]

The transformation scene became increasingly important over the history of the fairy extravaganza. As the pantomime transforms the principal characters in the end, extravaganza transforms the stage itself, in a long, voluptuous unfolding of spectacular enchantment. The transformation scene gradually replaced the harlequinade, offering another sort of metamorphosis altogether—not to anarchic revelry, but to an etherealized realm of fantasy and beauty. Writing in 1881, about twenty years after the highwater mark of fairy extravaganza and one year before the production of *Iolanthe*, Percy Fitzgerald described the transformation scene:

[H]ow quietly and gradually it is evolved. First the 'gauzes' lift slowly one behind the other . . . giving glimpses of 'the Realm of Bliss', seen behind in a tantalizing fashion. Then is revealed a kind of half-glorified country, clouds and banks, evidently concealing much. Always a sort of pathetic and at the same time exultant strain rises, and is repeated as the changes go on. Now we hear the faint tinkle—signal to those aloft on 'bridges' to open more glories. Now some of the banks begin to part slowly, showing realms of light, with a few divine beings—fairies—rising slowly here and there. More breaks beyond and fairies rising, with a pyramid of these ladies beginning to mount slowly in the centre. Thus it goes on, the lights streaming on full, in every colour and from every quarter, in the richest effulgence. In some of the more daring efforts, the *femmes suspendues* seem to float in the air or rest on the frail support of sprays or branches or trees. While finally . . . the most glorious paradise of all will open, revealing the pure empyrean itself, and

FIGURE 7.1 In act 2 of *Iolanthe*, the Fairies wore headdresses adorned with electric lights. (Note the large Fairy Queen compared with the small Lord Chancellor.) Lithograph by "G. R.," for cover of the sheet music for *Iolanthe Lancers* (1882), arranged by Charles D'Albert. (Collection of Fredric Woodbridge Wilson)

some fair spirit aloft in a cloud among the stars, the apex of all. Then all motion ceases; the work is complete; the fumes of crimson, green, and blue fire begin to rise at the wings; the music bursts into a crash of exultation.[23]

Deeper and deeper spaces open on the stage, populated by a vast proliferation of seemingly weightless bodies. During the lengthy development of "the Realm of Bliss," the audience has time to revel in fantasy and bliss out.

That Gilbert worked within the tradition of extravaganza has been well recognized since the 1870s.[24] Planché considered Gilbert his only worthy successor.[25] During his transition from extravaganza to comic opera, however, Gilbert experimented with another fairy genre, the fairy comedy, which blends supernatural romance with psychological realism in order to comment on the foibles of modern life. Of Gilbert's five fairy comedies, *The Wicked World* (1873) is most relevant to *Iolanthe*, for it explicitly considers fairies in relation to human sexuality. Like fairy extravaganza, *The Wicked World* assumes the existence of two separate worlds: one sublunary and mundane, and the other a supernatural abode of the fairies. The absolute bliss of this particular Fairyland is predicated on the notion that fairies have never experienced "mortal love." In a topsy-turvy exchange, fairy emissaries go down to earth, while their earthly counterparts—mortal men—come up to Fairyland. Disastrous results ensue. The fairies fall in love with the men, experiencing all the attendant emotions of unsatisfied yearning, jealousy, anger, and dependence. In short, they are miserable (figure 7.2). The resolution returns everything to the status quo ante, reestablishing Fairyland and "the wicked world" as two separate realms, one chaste, and the other still plagued by "mortal love."

FIGURE 7.2 "Mortal love" gone wrong in Gilbert's *The Wicked World*. Engraving by D. H. Friston, in *Illustrated London News*, February 8, 1873. (Collection of Fredric Woodbridge Wilson)

Some reviewers recognized that *The Wicked World* deals with sexual matters, for there was a debate about whether it was "indecent"; Gilbert's habits of humorous sexual suggestion pressed against the edges of convention in this respect.[26] It seems clear that Gilbert was working out a way to manage a more overt consideration of gender and sexuality, which came to fruition within the topsy-turvy dynamics of Savoy genre parody. After considering *The Wicked World*, we will not miss hearing in the word "mortal" a euphemism for "sexual." Thus when Strephon describes himself as a "fairy down to the waist," but "mortal" below, the sexual innuendo should be easy to grasp. His entry into Parliament provides the occasion for a joke about a "fairy member" (not only an MP, but also the male instrument of "mortal love"). In other words, the Savoy operas inherited techniques of sexual suggestion from the fairy comedy as well as from the fairy extravaganza.

The fairy genres specialize in this ambivalent sexual insinuation, which plays with the complex and contradictory Victorian associations of "fairy" with "woman." It is not surprising that "woman" should be ambivalently understood at this time, as both spiritual and material, ethereal and sexual, for the separation of the gendered "spheres" in social life precipitated a cascade of fractures within the concept of the feminine (and the masculine, as we have seen in *Patience*). The dichotomies within the cultural construction of "woman"—high/low, rising/falling, spirit/body, ethereal/sexual, angel/demon, monster, or madwoman—have been an important focus, even the foundation of a methodology, in feminist studies of the Victorian period.[27] For decades, scholars have examined Victorian gender ideology, especially as it circulates around domesticity. The "angel in the house" was charged with keeping the domestic sphere safely separate from the world of work, money, sexuality, male rivalry, and male bonding. Segregation in social fact and splitting in cultural conception removed the spiritualized, domesticated woman from the worldly, "fallen" woman, whose transgression was in part her acknowledging her sexuality, in part her wandering outside the domestic sphere. The Victorian association of "woman" with "child" can be understood in this framework, too, for a woman's spiritual nature depended on her being kept in childlike innocence (or ignorance) of the wicked world outside the home.

In the figure of the fairy, these dichotomous cultural conceptions—the supernatural and the human, the spiritual and the fleshly, the ethereal and the sexual, the innocent domestic woman and the low actress who plays her on the stage—are tied together in one complex and contradictory knot. In other words, there is no better figure through which to view Victorian gender ideology as a contradictory, systematic formation.

Sometimes Victorian children were hired to play the fairies. In Charles Kean's famous productions of *A Midsummer Night's Dream* (1856) and *The Tempest* (1857), eight-year-old Ellen Terry was featured in the role of Puck and thirteen-year-old Kate Terry in the role of Ariel.[28] Kean's biographer, praising the "etherial [sic] essence" of Kate Terry in the role, acknowledged that "there have been Ariels in profusion, who could act and sing beyond the reach of critical censure, but they were full-grown voluptuous-looking females: no one could beguile himself into the delusion that they were anything less material and substantial."[29] Likewise, Theodor Fontane, writing for a German audience, commented on Ellen Terry, comparing her Puck with Robin Goodfellow and confessing that "the impression of her mere appearance was so considerable, that I could no longer contemplate a Puck with a full bosom and plump arms."[30] As Russell Jackson has argued, Victorian representations of fairies "wavered between two archetypes, the womanly and the childlike."[31] The figure of the fairy could hover along this spectrum, expressing the undifferentiated "puckishness" of prepubescent boys and girls; the promise of an inherent sexuality, soon to be expressed; or the fully sexualized voluptuousness of the mature female. Thus ambiguous as to their state of maturity and availability for sexual activity, fairies were similar to both the sexualized Victorian child and the childlike, desexualized Victorian gentlewoman.[32]

Significantly, however, the Fairies of *Iolanthe* are not ethereal. Their otherworldly power is overtly sexual and embodied by adult women who comfortably take themselves to be in charge. That *Iolanthe* is a genre parody may be seen in this humorous characterization of the Fairies, which supports the opera's twist on the story of fairy marriage and its complex characterization of the Fairy Queen. Cutting through the tight knot of Victorian gender ideology, *Iolanthe* provides a sympathetic portrait of a fully substantial, fully sexual "strong-minded woman."

Fairy Marriages

Iolanthe twists the popular fantasy of marriage between a human male and a fairy into its parody of fairy extravaganza. The germ of the opera appears in a Bab Ballad, "The Fairy Curate" (1873), which tells of a peculiar fairy marriage and its issue (figure 7.3):

> Once a fairy
> Light and airy

Married with a mortal;
    Men, however
    Never, never
Pass the fairy portal.
    Slyly stealing,
    She to Ealing,
Made a daily journey;
    There she found him,
    Clients round him
(He was an attorney).[33]

Their son, Georgie—like Strephon, half a fairy—grows up to become a curate. Gradually becoming more and more attracted to High Church ritual, Georgie shocks his fairy mama, who is more conventional in her religious practice. She begs Georgie to be more "unpretending" and "unaffected" in his worship. Georgie's Bishop, watching this interview between son and mother, mistakes her for a "Ballet miss." As in *Iolanthe*, the mother's agelessness makes her appear to the Bishop as a "hussy . . . [who] isn't two-and-

FIGURE 7.3 A fairy marriage. Drawing by Bab [W. S. Gilbert] to accompany "The Fairy Curate," *Fun*, July 23, 1870. (Collection of Fredric Woodbridge Wilson)

twenty!" Using this confusion of one sort of woman for another, the poem plays with various aspects of the figure of the fairy.

Like "The Rival Curates," which led to *Patience*, "The Fairy Curate" set the scene for *Iolanthe*. The idea that gender difference may be seen as cultural difference, already evident in the Bab Ballad, is hinted in the humorous premise that men can never cross the portal into Fairyland. This cultural difference is made even funnier by the inane specificity of Ealing, chosen to represent the sublunary world. Transposing the context of religion to that of gender and social class, and adopting the structural opposition suggested by the rhyme of "Peers" with "Peris," *Iolanthe* developed from this germ, relying, like "The Fairy Curate," on familiar associations with the fairy marriage for its humor. Carole Silver details the Victorians' interest in fairy brides, persuasively arguing that the many stories about fairy brides—and the many interpretations of these stories by Victorian folklorists—clearly encode issues of gender and social power being contested in the period.[34] Silver shows that the interest in fairy brides reached its zenith in the 1880s and 1890s, "when the debates on other issues pertaining to women . . . were also escalating."[35] Thus, its production falling squarely within this span, *Iolanthe* must be regarded as part of these conversations.

In Victorian folk- and fairy tales, marriage between humans and fairies is not propitious, to say the least. The most ancient fairy brides, the Irish "fairy queens," abandon their human mates without compunction.[36] Later romances between humans and various sorts of fairy—sylphs, naiads, undines, swan maidens—suggest that women are closer than men to wild nature; that they are powerful, independent, and difficult to tame; and that they must be confined and domesticated for orderly civilization to be established. Perhaps these stories bespeak a primordial yearning for union with nature, but, if so, that union is understood in a strikingly sexual sense. When conceived as animals, fairy brides are highly sexed, but when conceived as superior beings, they are hardly sexual at all.[37] In either case, they are overwhelmingly attractive, seductive, and compelling; as Maureen Duffy has argued, their bewitching irresistibility takes the irrationality of sexual desire—especially taboo sexual desire, such as adultery or incest—and imagines that the woman is intentionally alluring and entrapping the man.[38] Whether ethereal or bestial, however, the fairy bride is irreducibly "other," the denizen of another world, another culture, another system of laws. As Silver puts it, she "lived by her own code."[39]

Fairy brides can be captured or enraptured by a human male, but they cannot be kept. Both fairies and Amazons are "nonmonogamous, nonmaternal, outdoor creatures," everything the normative middle-class Victorian woman was not.[40] The fairy bride chafes against domesticity and can leave her marriage and her children if her husband violates the specific prohibition she laid down at the time of their union; his violation of her taboo renders her desertion intelligible and faultless. As Silver has shown, this arbitrary stipulation of a "fairy law"—not visiting her on Saturday, for example, or not dealing her "three causeless blows"—often reflects contemporary claims of women's rights within marriage (the rights to privacy and freedom from domestic violence), while fairy abandonment of husband and children suggests a consideration of the rationales for divorce.[41] Silver links the popularity of these stories to discourse on the "woman question," escalating from the 1860s to the 1890s, particularly on the origins of matrimony, the right to divorce, the passage of the Married Women's Property Acts, the rise of the "New Woman," and the widespread discussion of the "marriage question" in the 1880s and 1890s.[42] As she demonstrates, the story of the fairy marriage cleverly raises all sorts of issues about gendered inequalities of power: the meaning of marriage to women, their yearning for greater freedom, the nature of female sexuality, and even the dangerous idea that maternal feelings might not be "natural." In other words, the fairy bride provided a figure through which Victorians could engage both positive and negative attitudes toward the slowly growing independence of women within marriage.

Silver readily admits that the Victorians did not seem to recognize the critique of domesticity implicit in their stories of fairy brides. As often as not, the radical "otherness" of the fairy brides—their extraordinary power, their difficulty in tolerating marriage, their flight from motherhood—was deemed to be destructive and primitive. John Stuart-Glennie, in "The Origins of Matriarchy" and "Incidents of Swan-Maiden Marriage" (1891), made the strongest case for the ancient superiority of the female, but his theories were hotly debated and ultimately rejected.[43] In fact, many Victorian folklorists believed that the powerful women of the ancient past had been duly superseded in the modern world.[44]

These debates among Victorian folklorists represent one version of a well-recognized narrative in the field of cultural anthropology. Stories of ancient matriarchies in general are designed to justify and explain their eventual defeat and replacement by patriarchal culture. Thus the rule of women inevitably turns out to have been flagrant misrule. This "myth of matriarchy" makes female governance a topic of ridicule rather than an image of power.[45] Similarly, traditional cultures in western Europe foster cross-dressing rituals and carnival inversions of gender hierarchy, but only temporarily. Thus images and performances of "women on top" are the ne plus ultra of traditional social parody, especially when they involve men cross-dressing as women. Interpretations of these ritual performances almost always focus on how the temporary rule of women provides a cultural "safety valve," permitting relaxation of hierarchical norms in the service of their eventual reassertion, when women are again suppressed or, at the least, reiteratively defined as aberrant.

Since the publication of Natalie Zemon Davis's groundbreaking essay on symbolic sexual inversion, however, these ritual performances have widely been understood to be "multivalent." In other words, the practice of male-to-female cross-dressing does not unequivocally support the status quo, but, instead, the unruly, scary, or repugnant woman on top can be seen as energetic, lustful, intelligent, and strong. Even though they show women being ridiculed, these ritual performances also demonstrate the attractiveness of women in power; both the ridicule and the attraction are effective in the social world, after the ritual is over.[46] Michael McKeon has elaborated on these rituals in the formation of modern domesticity in seventeenth- and eighteenth-century England, showing that domestic "rule" became a figure for right and wrong practices in government.[47] The association of domestic with governmental rule is directly relevant to *Iolanthe* and to the Dame figure, whose male-to-female cross-dressing also stages the temporary misrule of "women on top." Classical extravaganza, for example, specializes in burlesques of the strong-minded woman, such as Francis Talfourd's *Alcestis; or, The Original Strong-Minded Woman* (1850) and Robert B. Brough's *Medea; or, The Best of Mothers, with a Brute of a Husband* (1856), in which the great burlesque actor Frederick Robson excelled in the title role.[48]

Working directly within this tradition of symbolic inversion, *Iolanthe* turns the conventional social parody on its head. In a parody of the usual gender parody, it presents women on top who stay on top, assimilating human males into their fairy culture, not vice versa. Like the sprightly yet ethereal fairies of Romantic ballet, the Fairies of *Iolanthe* are active in pursuit of their chosen human mates. To see them as parodic comments on Romantic ballet is to realize that they have been significantly rematerialized, since, perhaps more than any other fairy genre, Romantic ballet invested in the techniques of feminine etherealization that we have been examining.[49] Of course, these poignant stories of mysterious creatures and their humans—*La Sylphide* (1832), *Giselle* (1841), *Ondine* (1843), and *Swan Lake* (1877)—end tragically, but not before providing a high flight of fantasy on the subject of the seduction of men by the otherworldly feminine, made hyper-ethereal through the illusion of weightless floating effected by locomotion on point.

But the Fairies of *Iolanthe* are neither tragic nor ethereal; they are successfully seductive and material. The opening Chorus announces its parodic intent, for, like the gentlemen of Japan in the opening Chorus of *The Mikado*, these Fairies acknowledge their origins in art. They introduce themselves by pointing out how endless reiterations of a convention can unmoor behavior from reason and make it seem absurd: "Tripping hither, tripping thither, / Nobody knows why or whither." This opening directly parodies the inane fairy introductions in pantomime:[50]

> We are dainty little fairies,
>   Ever singing, ever dancing;
> We indulge in our vagaries
>   In a fashion most entrancing.
> If you ask the special function
>   Of our never-ceasing motion,
> We reply, without compunction,
>   That we haven't any notion!

Thus the Fairies of *Iolanthe* make fun of the typical, repetitive gender performances demanded of theatrical fairies. They are neither ignorant of their sexual feelings (as is the maiden in Bunthorne's poem "Oh, Hollow! Hollow! Hollow!") nor coy about them (as Princesses Nekaya and Kalyba are taught to be in *Utopia, Limited*). They are active and lustful, in control of Parliament and of the plot. By the end, the Fairies have "helped themselves, and pretty freely, too," to form their liaisons with the Peers. In *Iolanthe*, "this is what comes of women in politics," happy fairy marriages and a happy extravaganza hybrid of human and fairy law.

The Dame Figure and the Fairy Queen

In order to understand the full humor of *Iolanthe*'s argument about "women in politics," we must explore the figure of the Fairy Queen. Supernaturally powerful, she gets what she wants in the end, and, through her power, the entire company is translated to Fairyland. Yet the large contralto characters in Savoy operas have long been controversial. Without much critical examination, they are assumed to be grossly misogynistic representations of the middle-aged, unmarried, vain, desiring woman. Centering on the Fairy Queen, and moving outward to the other such characters in the Savoy canon—especially Ruth, Lady Jane, Katisha, and Lady Blanche—I want to engage this controversy, arguing that what we see in the Savoy operas is usually not the misogynistic figure itself, but a parody of that figure. Thus the

Savoy version of the Dame figure should be regarded afresh, perhaps even with an appreciative eye.

The Fairy Queen is partly based on the Dame figure of pantomime, a female role that was always played by a low-comic man. This pantomime tradition of male-to-female transvestism must be distinguished from the female-to-male crossed-dressed roles characteristic of burlesque and extravaganza. They return us to the dynamic of feminine etherealization and sexualization, for a crossed-dressed female was thought to etherealize her male role. At the same time, as Tracy Davis has shown, the cover of a male role (and costume) made female sexual display permissible, encoding it as "innocent" high jinks.[51] The sexy, insouciant actress—displaying her hour-glass figure, waist, and legs while playing the princes and noble young men of extravaganza and burlesque—succeeded in these parts by developing a special brand of pert bravado that rendered the sexual display "perfectly free from offense," as Dickens said of Marie Wilton.[52] Gilbert expressed a slightly different view in "What Is a Burlesque?" a Bab Ballad from 1868, in which he writes of the prince:

Beautiful curls,
Form like a girl's—
Figure, I mean,
Looks epicene.[53]

In other words, depending on the particular performance and the par-ticular spectator, these figures could seem to effeminize the male, mascu-linize the female, or hover somewhere in between (plate 14).[54] Later in the nineteenth century, translated to the music halls, cross-dressed actresses would emphasize the pert bravado more than the "epicene" effeminization; Vesta Tilly playing swells and toffs is the best example.[55] Reaching across a spectrum from elegant nobility to urban swagger that reflects the history of their theatrical genres, these figures represent one side of the female-to-male travesty role.[56]

Female-to-male cross-dressing was also deployed to embody masculine vulnerability or weakness. With "waif-fragility," attractive actresses played the mutes, victims, little boys, and "witless adolescents" of melodrama.[57] For example, Miss Scott played the outcast "dumb sailor boy" in Edward Fitz-ball's *The Inchcape Bell; or, The Dumb Sailor Boy* (1828), and many of Dick-ens's suffering male characters were performed by women. Mrs. Keeley was a famous Smike, while Maggie Brennan played Pip in Gilbert's own version of *Great Expectations* (1871). Effeminized by definition, these weak male characters made masculine vulnerability graphic, yet unthreatening, when played by a woman. And, of course, as we have seen, female cross-dressing etherealizes the male role, emphasizing innocence and virtue (figure 7.4).

The Dame figure represents the other tradition in Victorian theatrical transvestism. Burlesque as well as pantomime—the two precursors of extravaganza—feature the Dame. For example, Frederick Robson famously starred in Robert Brough's burlesque of the Italian actress Adelaide Ristori's Medea. His *Medea; or, The Best of Mothers, with a Brute of a Husband* was billed as "a conjugal lesson . . . an awful warning to every single individual." Very much like Katisha in *The Mikado*, Brough's Medea coyly admits, "I fear I'm rather vicious"; but Robson endowed her with a certain tragic grandeur, even though her dagger turns into a jester's bauble in the end (figure 7.5).[58] In 1882, the same year as *Iolanthe* was produced, Robert Reece's burlesque *Little Robin Hood* portrayed Maid Marian as a strong-minded woman:

MARIAN:
  These are the good old days (folks may abuse 'em),
  When girls have muscles, and know how to use 'em.
ROBIN:
  Strong-minded women, as a rule, are hated.
  You're simple, dear, and yet so-fist-icated![59]

The cross-dressed comic man also figures in nonburlesque drama to embody a stereotype of the "masculine" woman. Many of Dickens's older women characters were played this way. Robert Keeley appeared as Sairy Gamp in a production of *Martin Chuzzlewit*; William Atwood doubled as Uriah Heep and Miss Mowcher in one version of *David Copperfield*, while Henry Widdicombe doubled as Miss Mowcher and Mr. Micawber in another.[60] But the Dame figure is most important in pantomime. Sometimes she represents the crone-like wise woman who has access to oral culture. Mother Goose, Mother Shipton, and Mother Bunch are good examples of this sort of Dame, as is Widow Twankey, launched in the pantomime *Aladdin* (1861). Most often, however, the Dame is an earthy, grotesque caricature, specializing in maternal obstruction or unwelcome instruction, prudery, or prurience. This character type is middle-aged or older, large or fat, plain or downright ugly, bad-tempered or cruel, nagging or shrewish, and always vain, with an exaggerated love of makeup and fine dress. Often the role focuses on her sexual desire, which is portrayed as particularly ridiculous. In other words, the Dame figure, like the princes of extravaganza and the waifs of melodrama, condenses and encodes cultural conceptions of both gender and sexuality.

FIGURE 7.4 Carrie Burton as Phoebe Farleigh cross-dressed as a virtuous Tar in Edward Solomon's *Billee Taylor; or, The Reward of Virtue* (1880), a nautical comic opera. Cabinet photograph by Marc & Schlum (New York, 1881). (Collection of Fredric Woodbridge Wilson)

FIGURE 7.5 Frederick Robson as Medea, a Dame figure, in Robert Brough's *Medea; or, The Best of Mothers, with a Brute of a Husband.* (Harvard Theatre Collection, Houghton Library)

This figure of the masculine woman is centrally important in *Patience*, *Iolanthe*, and *Princess Ida*, although it also appears earlier and later in the Savoy canon; indeed, the tradition of Savoy Dames is as old as the collaboration itself. From reviews in periodicals, we know that Venus in *Thespis* was "fair, fat, and forty."[61] And, as we have seen, the "elderly, ugly daughter" from the *Trial by Jury* backstory is a grotesque example of the type, but the misogyny directed at her is ascribed to the Judge and the male network of power represented by the judicial system. The woman too unattractive to be desired in her own right is used to emphasize the Judge's unscrupulous ambition and lack of disinterestedness; he colluded with her father just as he colludes with the Defendant, and thus the "nature" of privileged male desire continues to reassert itself, while being subjected to critique. In other words, even where the misogyny is so obvious, the figure is more complicated than the image alone would suggest.

Jane Stedman was the first to analyze the relevance of the Dame figure to the Savoy canon.[62] The argument of her groundbreaking essay is based on the distinction between the Dames of Savoy opera and the Dame figure of pantomime, although she does not press far enough toward the recognition that the Savoy Dames are parodies of the pantomime Dames. Stedman argues, correctly, that most of the Savoy Dames are not wholly unattractive; that they are never directly insulted, as the Dame figure in pantomime is; and that they often marry well. In short, she maintains that the Savoy operas move this figure away from "Dame" and toward a realistic representation of "woman." But I see this figure differently.

Little Buttercup in *H.M.S. Pinafore* is explicitly attractive, an object of male desire; as Captain Corcoran says, she is "the rosiest, the roundest, and the reddest beauty in all Spithead." If it were not for her melodramatic "revealings" and the formative mistake she made while still a nursemaid, she could hardly be regarded as a Dame at all. Ruth in *The Pirates of Penzance* offers a more complex turn on the Dame figure. Her nursemaid's mistake, like Buttercup's, is attributed to stupidity; more important, her sexual desire for Frederic is disturbing. After his angry rejection of her advances, however, she is rehabilitated by the plot and gamely joins the slapstick interplay between Pirates and Police in act 2, becoming herself a cross-dressed pirate in most productions. Ruth establishes the pattern for the central Savoy Dames: a middle-aged woman, definitively past her prime, attempts to woo a man who is distinctly not interested; yet by the end of the opera, she will have demonstrated a good-spirited, comforting, and comradely loyalty that turns out to have its own attractions. Nevertheless, each of the Savoy Dames from *Pirates* to *The Mikado* focuses on one or more aspects of the traditional Dame figure: Ruth's desire for Frederic is unseemly; Lady Jane is stubborn, aging, and "massive," an old maid among the other, nubile Aesthetic Maidens; the Fairy Queen is lustful, super-powerful, and controlling; Lady Blanche is ambitious and overly intellectual; and Katisha is frighteningly jealous and vengeful.

In *Patience*, however, Lady Jane more than holds her own. She begins as the spokeswoman of an absurd aestheticism, but her character deepens over the course of the opera. She is not fickle like the other maidens, who desert Bunthorne for the next fashionable trend, personified by Grosvenor. Although in act 1, her steady devotion is simply irritating, an obstacle to Bunthorne's preoccupation with Patience, in act 2 her loyalty and camaraderie aid him in fending off the competition. The wonderful duet in which they imagine what Bunthorne might say to Grosvenor ("So go to him and say to him") testifies to this transformation. However, at the opening of act 2, her loyalty is still being ridiculed as an element of the Dame's exaggerated self-confidence. I think it is fair to say that the ridicule is tempered with poignancy, when Lady Jane meditates on her own "ripe" charms, "already decaying." Even though this scene, perhaps more than any other, has been used to argue for the misogyny of the entire Savoy canon, it has also been relished. The stage directions position Lady Jane "*leaning on a violoncello,*" which is surely meant to epitomize her full female figure (figure 7.6). In the recitative, she indulges in self-pity well designed to evoke memories of the stereotypical Dame figure:

> Sad is that woman's lot who, year by year,
> Sees, one by one, her beauties disappear,
> . . .
> Reduced, with rouge, lip-salve, and pearly grey,
> To "make up" for lost time as best she may!

Her song then dilates on the inevitable losses (of hair, of good complexion, of gaiety, of vision) and the unwelcome gains brought about by aging:

> Fading is the taper waist,
>   Shapeless grows the shapely limb,
> And although severely laced,
>   Spreading is the figure trim!
> Stouter than I used to be,
>   Still more corpulent grow I—
> There will be too much of me
>   In the coming by and by!

FIGURE 7.6 Rosina Brandram as Lady Jane with her cello in *Patience*. Photograph in *The Sketch*, December 5, 1900. (Collection of Fredric Woodbridge Wilson)

Of Alice Barnett, who created the role, one critic wrote that the part is "written up ostentatiously to her wealth of physical development." Although this scene has been called "distasteful" and "in the cruellest taste,"[63] I disagree. In an opera that makes fun of the notion of selfless feminine love, Lady Jane is active and self-interested. She does not end as an old maid, but catches the biggest matrimonial fish of them all, shedding her loyalty to Bunthorne and throwing him over for the Duke. That concluding plot twist turns on her role as parody Dame figure, since the Duke chooses her because she is plain and, he reasons, deserves a break. Surely that should be enough to alert us to the parodic nature of this use of the Dame figure, especially since the Duke himself, like the Peers in *Iolanthe*, is no particular prize, except for his rank. The ineffectual man locks together perfectly with the active and powerful woman, two sides of one joke.

Within the context of *Iolanthe*, weight is the opposite of ethereal weightlessness, and the "substantial" woman is the pointed opposite of the conventional, fairy-like feminine. This is the context for the Duke's sexist joke against Lady Jane: "Has he succeeded in transfiguring *you*? Good old Bunthorne!" She takes all this in stride. When Bunthorne makes fun of her for not conforming to the type of the feminine ("A pretty damozel *you* are!"), she proudly replies: "No, not pretty. Massive" (figure 7.7).[64] This remark clearly turns against the ridicule typically heaped on the Dame with its own oppositional claim, aggressively owning the charge that was supposed to have been insulting. Bunthorne soon calls her, instead, "a fine figure of a woman," appreciating her attributes for what they are. Like Lady Jane, the Fairy Queen also throws her weight around. As she proudly puts it: "I see no objection to stoutness, in moderation."

Katisha in *The Mikado* is the most imposing Dame of them all—a truly awesome figure, proud that she is "tough as a bone with a will of her own." She is described in the dramatis personae as "*an elderly Lady*," although that characterization contributes not only to the parody of the Dame, but also to the opera's satire on Victorian restraint, since "in Japan girls do not arrive

FIGURE 7.7 Lady Jane: "No, not pretty. Massive." Detail from *Illustrated London News*, June 18, 1881. (Collection of Fredric Woodbridge Wilson)

at years of discretion until they are fifty." The humor of her strong-minded-ness is clear upon her introduction, for she interrupts the Mikado himself, asserting her position as "daughter-in-law elect." Often played by a huge diva, Katisha can be electrifying, exciting, even terrifying. She enters *"melo-dramatically"* at the end of act 1, furious with her "perjured lover," Nanki-Poo, and threatening to reveal his true identity as the son of the Mikado.[65] The entire cast tries to *"sing Japanese words, to drown her voice,"* yet her powerful voice soars above the ensemble. Katisha, too, famously asserts the attractiveness of her kind: "I am an acquired taste—only the educated palate can appreciate *me.*" Not her face, but her "left shoulder-blade is a miracle of loveliness." Again, this absurd boast should surely alert us to the fact that this is a parody, as should Katisha's self-pointed moral: "Learn, then, that it is not in the face alone that beauty is to be sought." The figure of Katisha is certainly multivalent, in Natalie Zemon Davis's sense of that word, on the one hand ridiculing the coy flirtatiousness of the older woman, just as a Dame figure would be ridiculed, but, on the other, offering an image of thrilling, indeed massive, female power and a protest against namby-pamby femininity. Emphasizing the figure's multivalence, Katisha conveys her power in the form of coy flirtation ("And you won't hate me because I'm just a teeny-weeny wee bit blood-thirsty, will you?") another sure sign of parody at work. Ko-Ko soon joins her defense of aging, in their wonder-ful duet, whose burden asserts that their "tastes are one." True, he has little choice, but he accepts his fate with good-natured grace. With some ner-vousness, always in the process of being dispelled, they celebrate the idea that "there is beauty in extreme old age" and that a maiden will "last a good deal longer when she's tough."[66]

Lady Jane, the Fairy Queen, and Katisha represent the great phase of the Savoy Dame figure, when the wit of the parody is operating perfectly in tan-dem with the operas' meditations on gender. After Katisha, there is a falling off. Indeed, before Katisha, Lady Blanche in *Princess Ida* is the worst of the Savoy Dames: schoolmarmish, pseudo-intellectual, prudish, unsympathetic to the wishes of the young—an altogether forbidding, unlikable figure of instruction.[67] Audrey Williamson calls her "not only detestable but a crash-ing bore."[68] Nor is Lady Blanche rehabilitated by the plot, even though she gets her wish to become the head of the university in Ida's place. Her tak-ing over is a bad omen for the future of the women's university, which the libretto continues to trivialize by ridiculing Blanche. The problem with the figure of Lady Blanche is that it was conceived under the aegis of burlesque. In other words, Lady Blanche is not a Savoy parody of the Dame figure; she *is* a Dame figure.

After *The Mikado*, Dame Hannah, Dame Carruthers, the Duchess of Plaza-Toro, Lady Sophy, and Baroness von Krakenfeldt continue to ring their individual changes on the figure of the strong-minded woman, but none of them is as articulately parodic of the Dame figure they inhabit as are the greatest Savoy Dames. Dame Hannah begins as a spinster aunt and becomes a parody of the beset woman of melodrama. Sexual abduction of an elderly woman is meant to be a joke; no one would want to "carry her off" and despoil her "blameless womanhood." In her efforts to fend off her abduction, she characterizes herself as a "tiger-cat" and invites a knife fight with the challenge "let the best man win." Her very small knife is perhaps a distasteful physical slight, and the history of low-comic transvestism certainly can be detected behind the old woman put in a sexual position. Nevertheless, the plot restores her to an earlier maidenhood and her true love in the end.

After Dame Hannah, the parodic allusion to the pantomime Dame diminishes considerably. Dame Carruthers is grisly, but she does not assume the character of the Dame until the terrible scene near the end of *The Yeomen of the Guard*, when Sergeant Meryll is forced to marry her to buy her silence. The Duchess of Plaza-Toro is bossy, but humorous. Lady Sophy is positively benign, though prudish. And Baroness von Krakenfeldt is mainly a great foil for both Rudolph and Julia Jellicoe, miserly yet born to be a lady, while Julia is only acting the part. She performs the *brindisi* with rare gusto, as if "the Gilbertian contralto came back for a final tipsy turn."[69]

The full use of the Dame figure may well have diminished in response to pressure from Sullivan, who famously grew to hate it. I would be inclined to argue that he was underestimating its parodic complexity (and therefore that this is another element of the Gilbert and Sullivan legend, like the story of the lozenge plot, that calls for critical reevaluation). However, the preponderance of critical response over the years has agreed with Sullivan's view. In the late nineteenth century, the idea that these are characters of gross misogyny began to be taken as simple fact. In 1892, George Bernard Shaw mentioned "the inevitable old woman brought on to be jeered at simply because she was old," as if the matter were settled.[70] Stedman details the further development of what she calls the "myth of Gilbert's cruelty" during the twentieth century: Sir Arthur Quiller-Couch thought him "thoroughly caddish"; Louis Kronenberger found his treatments "faintly pathological"; Edmund Wilson adduced "a streak of vulgar cruelty" with "a tendency to rely on formula"; even Isaac Goldberg mentioned his "cruel treatment of aging woman-kind." Hesketh Pearson—like David Eden, more recently—taking a psychoanalytic view, found that these figures show his "dislike for his mother." The Savoy Dames "began to be taken *sui generis*," as if Gilbert had invented the type, rather than receiving it and twisting it to his own purposes.[71]

Those purposes are parodic. Gilbert did not invent the Dame figure, but received it from the traditions of earlier genres and changed it. Since parody must imitate its object in order to criticize it, the parody can easily be mistaken for that object. We should not make the mistake of reading the Savoy Dames straight.

It would be pointless to deny the element of misogyny expressed by the figure of a fat, middle-aged, vain, and flirtatious woman, which is as old as Greek and Roman comedy, as new as *Big Momma's House* (2000). To insist that these characters are deeply conventional is not to say that they are unobjectionable. However, more than enough signs show that the Savoy Dames do not simply replicate the conventional figure but reproduce it within a context of parodic critique. Thus they establish their distance from the Dame figure of pantomime, emphasizing not only the conventional familiarity of that figure from the past, but also its very pastness. Parody represents conventional figures *as* conventional, bound to a past that is in the process of being revised in the present. In other words, the Savoy Dame is context-specific, and the pat assumption that the Savoy representations of the Dame—or of women in general—are simply misogynistic is itself historical as well, the result of a failure to recognize the parody. Why did this failure in interpretation come about? My guess is that the influence of realism took its toll on the public appreciation of nonrealistic theatrical genres.

The humor of the Savoy Dames is not realistic, although realism is not entirely irrelevant either, for the social world outside the theater has been refracted through the lens of social types. In this sense, the Savoy Dame comments on gender relations in the real world, but also on currently circulating types and caricatures. Thus *Iolanthe*—like *Patience, Ruddigore,* and *Utopia, Limited*—offers a range of feminine types. As *Patience* gives us a Chorus of mindless followers of fashion, an ingénue who is correctly feminine (innocent to the point of stupidity), and a strong-minded woman, *Iolanthe* gives us a Chorus of Fairies who are conscious of the conventional behavior expected of them yet are breaking away from it, an ingénue who is the object of all masculine desire, a very young-looking mother, and a supernaturally powerful Fairy Queen. To perceive the array of feminine types helps us to understand the Savoy Dame as part of a system of relations. Both Stedman and Andrew Crowther argue, as I do, that the Savoy Dame is meant to be a comment on Victorian norms of femininity. Stedman insists that these characters "satirize the premium . . . placed on youthful beauty" and give the audience "relaxation from that idealization of Woman which was at least a public tenet of the age." For his part, Crowther claims that the middle-aged women are "deliberate reactions against the cliché ideal of the 'angel in the house' and with their fierceness, frustration and anger they are much more real than any of the fantasy heroines of Dickens." Although their tendency toward misogyny has to be acknowledged, he continues, "their power remains undeniable."[72]

As we have seen, the divided Chorus sets out particular stereotypes of masculinity and femininity in a systematic structure, and parody works on the full range of these types: on the ingénue every bit as much as the Dame, on Patience as much as Lady Jane, on the stolid, old-fashioned manly man as much as the effeminate poet. To see the Savoy Dame afresh, we must position her in the context of a Savoy parody of gender arrangements in general. These "arrangements" are systematic, the two genders envisioned as the interlocking parts of a binary structure, open to parodic inversion. On several levels, the structure of *Iolanthe* presents this system and its inversions: the topsy-turvy world of women controlling politics, with Fairies over Peers; the masculine assertiveness of the Fairy Queen; and the structural relation of the Fairy Queen to the Lord Chancellor, her "massive" presence comically relieved by a smaller, capering man.[73]

In addition to taking part in this systematic gender parody, the Savoy Dame is parodic on her own. If the Dame figure of pantomime is already a gender parody (an inversion of conventional feminine behavior), the Dame of Savoy opera is a parody of that parody. She is not conventionally feminine, but she is not precisely masculine either; she hovers somewhere in between, a layered figure. Although the Savoy Dame is played by a woman, everyone in the nineteenth-century audience could have remembered the cross-dressed figure of the pantomime Dame and could have recognized the allusion to—and the parodic overturning of—a specific history of theatrical cross-dressing. In other words, the Savoy Dame alludes to cross-dressing without actually cross-dressing. She is a woman impersonating a man who is impersonating a woman—a layered performance of gender. Gilbert used a similar strategy in *The Gentleman in Black* (1870, with music by Frederic Clay), in which the souls or psyches of Hans and Otto are exchanged and inhabit each other's bodies. The role of Hans was played by a woman, and thus after the exchange, the audience saw and felt the layered representation of a woman playing a man inhabited by another man's soul. So, too, in the Dame figure, pantomime and extravaganza cross-dressing—its fantasy quotient, its sexual titillation, its power—can be preserved even after having been ruled out.

Thus the Savoy parodies of masculinity, femininity, and systematic gender arrangements in general took their place among all the other projects of denaturalizing gender in Victorian fin-de-siècle culture. As a way out of or around the binary system of gender, the limits of inversion would soon be clearly expressed in sexology, which attempted to press beyond heterosexuality, but could theorize a "third sex" only through inversion; the sexological types of the invert were the feminine man and the masculine woman. Thus the Savoy operas can be evaluated as a part of this historical trend, but they go further, with their layered figures and inversions of previous inversions, showing once again that, however perdurable it may be, gender is nonsensical. *Iolanthe* tries to get at the absurdity of gender by crossing the real world with Fairyland, using this fundamental feature of extravaganza. Indeed, the figure of the Fairy Queen operates as the switch point between the two worlds within the play and as the switch point between the play and the world outside the theater. Thus the Fairy Queen must be seen as a reference to the real world of social types and as a recollection of genres and conventions that both register and help to create these social types, reminding us that both social types and theatrical, generic types are equally cultural artifacts.

Significantly, a woman really was "on top" in Victorian England. Queen Victoria fit herself to the roles of domestic woman and powerful monarch, becoming a complex icon of proper gender behavior for women as well as its very opposite. While some historians and critics have suggested that Victoria was perceived as a "docile wife and mother rather than a forceful potentate," others have claimed that she used her public domesticity as a canny political strategy, playing with (rather than being played by) the reigning gender ideology.[74] Adrienne Munich argues persuasively that the Dame figures in Savoy opera "glow in the light emanating from their real-life muse on her throne."[75] Isaac Goldberg also notices this potential allusion: "A year after [Gilbert's] birth a woman was on the throne. To the rule of the bourgeois was added the rule of the petticoat." Goldberg continues, "[A]s I have sat before one of the Savoy operettas, with their recurrent types of the all-too-fleshly, all-too-unmarried, predacious female, I have thought that I could see a malicious reference to the Queen."[76] Goldberg does not pursue an analysis of this thought, but Munich does. As she points out, Benjamin Disraeli called Victoria "the Fairy Queen," with a pointed reference to Edmund Spenser's *Faerie Queene* (1590, 1596).[77]

Moreover, argues Munich, the character of the Savoy Dame refracts the figure of the queen in a particular way, as "queen of a certain age"—that is, "a menopausal woman at the height of her power, a woman on the edge—of domesticity, of middle age, of unfemininity."[78] Munich reads Lady Jane's lament

("Spreading is the figure trim!") as a sly commentary on Queen Victoria, whose girth in 1882 was increasingly a topic of popular humor. In her interpretation, the comic denigration of the monarch's body also alludes to her vast empire, spreading around the globe.[79] Furthermore, the conventional lustfulness of the Dame figure serves as a focus for lampoons of Queen Victoria's supposed widowed and middle-aged erotomania: her extravagant mourning for Prince Albert and her well-known affection for John Brown.[80] Thus the woman's desire for power was ridiculed in both public and private senses, inextricably linked. To Queen Victoria as muse, the Savoy operas pay "modified homage."[81]

The Fairy Queen not only points to the real world outside the theater, but also bundles together parodic recollections of a wide variety of performance traditions, roles, texts, and genres. This is as it should be in a parody of the fairy extravaganza, which pointedly blends allusions to fairy tale, folklore, literature, art, and music with references to topics and features of the metropolis. Thus the Fairy Queen, her pastiche allusiveness emphasizing the overdetermination of her figure, calls attention to the genre parody. She recalls not only the Dame figure, but also the good fairy of pantomime, whose power helps the lovers overcome obstacles to their union. This aspect of her character is on display in the opening scene, when Iolanthe emerges from the stream, weeds in her hair, and is pardoned by her queen (figure 7.8). In the original production of *Iolanthe*, the Fairy Queen was dressed in Wagnerian garb, with a helmet and metal corselet like Brünnhilde's and a spear like Wotan's. This costume characterized her great power while signaling the opera's parody of Wagner (figure 7.9). Sullivan did not admire Wagner (with the exception of *Die Meistersinger* [1868]), and for this scene he invented a wonderful mock-heroic suggestion of Wagnerian portentousness. Iolanthe emerges from the bottom of the stream to a parody of the Rhine Maidens' music from *Das Rheingold* (1869), and the Fairies' wailing just before the plot's resolution, when again it seems that Iolanthe has broken fairy law, is similarly allusive: "Aiaiah! Aiaiah! / Willahalah! Willaloo!"

As a genre, the fairy extravaganza is deeply involved in genre parody. One great example of this fascination with genre comes from a scene in Planché's *The Good Woman in the Wood* (1852), when the Fairy Fragrant conveys Dame Goldenheart to the "'Cabinet des Fées,' whose shelves are lined with fairy tales . . . including 'stage editions.'"[82] In other words, this extravaganza embeds within it a little library of its sources, including references to both fairy-tale collections and stage adaptations. Just so, the Fairy Queen in *Iolanthe* represents a densely sedimented textual and performance history, made clear during the climax of act 1—perhaps the greatest ensemble build-up in the entire Savoy canon—when the Peers and the Lord Chancellor are

FIGURE 7.8 Jessie Bond as Iolanthe, rising from the stream in her weeds to be forgiven by the Fairy Queen. Cabinet photograph by Elliott & Fry (London, 1882). (Collection of Fredric Woodbridge Wilson)

suddenly made to understand the Fairy Queen's power. In response, the Lord Chancellor ruefully sings:

> A plague on this vagary,
> I'm in a nice quandary!
>   Of hasty tone
>   With dames unknown
> I ought to be more chary;
> It seems that she's a fairy
> From Andersen's library
>   And I took her for
>   The proprietor
> Of a Ladies' Seminary!

In other words, he took her for the familiar repressive female figure in social life, whereas her character is more overtly drawn from "Andersen's library."

FIGURE 7.9 Alice Barnett as the Fairy Queen, dressed in Wagnerian helmet, breastplate, and spear. Cabinet photograph by Elliott & Fry (London, 1882). (Wikimedia Commons)

At this point, the Fairy Queen becomes a recollection of generic signs, a bundle of allusions to social life and literary or theater history: to Queen Victoria and, through her nickname, to Spenser and his Fairy Queen; to a Wagnerian mythic heroine; to both the good fairy and the Dame figure from the pantomime tradition; to the older woman with access to fairy lore (like Mother Goose); and to "The proprietor / Of a Ladies' Seminary." Like the surrogate mother or nursemaid, the last figure portrays social repression as a woman.[83] But she is characterized this way from the point of view of the Lord Chancellor, a frightened, male, "puny mortal" at this particular moment in the plot.

"Then away we go to Fairyland"

Iolanthe ends with a transformation of the extravaganza transformation scene, the ultimate sign of its genre parody. When the Fairy Queen gives her final command, suddenly *"Wings spring from shoulders of* PEERS," signaling their transformation. Fairyland overcomes the mundane world, with all the liberating promise of a flight from reality. And yet, as we have seen, the two worlds have been joined, in a happy revision of the fairy marriage. Humans, Fairies, and half-fairies all exuberantly rejoice:

> Happy are we—
> As you can see,
> Every one is now a fairy!
> . . .
> We will arrange
> Happy exchange—
> House of Peers for House of Peris!

This "happy exchange" also involves the hybridization of human and fairy law, brought about by the combined executive powers of the Fairy Queen and the Lord Chancellor. In this case, the usual hyper-logical Savoy resolution makes fun of human law. If the "subtleties of the legal mind are equal to the emergency," they amount to the immediate transformation of fairy law into its very opposite by the addition of one word: "[E]very Fairy must die who *don't* marry a mortal." Thus the subtleties of the legal mind are identical to its absurdities.

With one last joke about the uselessness of representative Peers—they may as well be transformed into fairies, for, as Lord Mountararat puts it, "I really don't see what use *we* are down here"—the Fairy Queen announces the transformation. It is a brilliant stroke to juxtapose the obsolescence of the aristocratic male with the triumph of the female realm. Again, as in *Patience*, we are treated to the social parody of an old-fashioned masculinity, "dating from the Flood," yet the joke is on the Fairies, too, for being attracted to human rank and status. The Fairy Queen's desire for Private Willis is funny in precisely this respect; although he is attractive physically, he ranks beneath her, another representative type of old-fashioned masculinity: "I don't think much of the British soldier who wouldn't ill-convenience himself to save a female in distress." Thus we have both high and low representations of class-bound masculinity, and in this way *Iolanthe* deftly intertwines its arguments about class and gender.

In claiming that *Iolanthe* "linked the radical threat to the House of Lords and the first manifestations of female politics," Lionel Lambourne is correct,[84] but only if we understand that both "threats" are treated with full approval. The opening-night audience recognized the humor.[85] Making fun of the House of Peers, Lord Mountararat expresses the national version of his individual incapacity:

> The House of Peers throughout the war,
>> Did nothing in particular,
>>> And did it very well.

Here he applauds the Peers for being outworn, residual historical formations, just as *Iolanthe* takes them to be. His song is not represented as a "radical threat," but as an easily received view.

Like the Aesthetic Maidens in *Patience*, the Fairies are attracted to traditional masculinity after all. The critique is tacit: even supernaturally strong-minded women will succumb to heterosexual desire. If the Lord Chancellor is "susceptible," so are the Fairies. Even the Fairy Queen (especially the Fairy Queen), with her hilariously salacious self-control—another Savoy dig at Victorian respectability in matters of sex and gender—yields to sexual desire. Significantly, however, the story ends with women still "on top." These Fairies are not domesticated. Indeed, the opposite is true, for their husbands are translated into their realm.[86] This is "what comes of women in politics," for the Fairies helpfully rid the nation of its moribund House of Peers.

8

War Between the Sexes

Princess Ida

Like *Iolanthe*, *Princess Ida; or, Castle Adamant* (1884) raises the question of female equality, although it does so in quite a different tone and to quite a different purpose. The scene is set in a fairy-tale microcosm, distanced in time and place from the real world, a "medieval" realm of royal families, castles, and tournaments. In *Iolanthe*, Fairies and humans, women and men figuratively inhabit separate cultures and have their different powers, governments, and systems of law. Asking what "comes of women interfering in politics," *Iolanthe* delivers a proto-feminist answer. Extending *Iolanthe*'s implication that women and men inhabit different worlds, *Princess Ida* asks a more radical question: What if women were to establish a separate culture of their own—not figuratively, but literally? The answer that *Princess Ida* gives is problematic. To say the least, the opera envisions the necessary renunciation of feminist separatism in favor of conventional gender arrangements. In addition, its relation to parody is confused and unclear.

Like the poem by Tennyson on which it is based, *Princess Ida* offers a just-so story that rationalizes Victorian gender conventions, but its rationale is more conservative even than Tennyson's (which is saying a lot). *Princess Ida* confirms conventional gender as the expression of natural instinct, heterosexual attraction, and the need for the biological reproduction of the species. While *Patience* and *Iolanthe* make fun of conventional types of masculinity and femininity, *Princess Ida* makes fun of the very idea that conventional gender could be changed or transcended. *Patience* explores changing gender norms, even though it ends with a comic reinstatement of the everyday, and *Iolanthe* ends with women "on top," but *Princess Ida* justifies the reproduction of the status quo. Placing thematic concerns with higher education for women and with biological evolution side by side, *Princess Ida* offers a fable of maturation: young people become mature men and women by embracing conventional gender roles. These issues—oriented around the burlesque convention of cross-dressing—are already present in *The Princess: A Medley* (1847–1851), the long poem by Alfred, Lord Tennyson, on which the Savoy opera is modeled.

More than a decade before *Princess Ida*, Gilbert wrote a burlesque version, *The Princess* (1870), from which *Princess Ida* eventually derived. Both works are explicitly parodic, in the common sense of that term, for they are founded on the poem by Tennyson, whose gender and genre politics have long been a matter of critical dispute. In all three works, one by Tennyson and two by Gilbert, gender and genre are central issues. Thus there are "three Princesses," all of which must be taken into account in order to explain the odd mixture of tones in *Princess Ida*.[1] If *The Princess* is a burlesque of Tennyson's poem, *Princess Ida* is a revision of *both* earlier works, establishing a higher seriousness than the burlesque while still offering itself as a "Respectful Perversion" of Tennyson.

As in *Iolanthe*, allusions to cross-dressing in *Princess Ida* preserve the memory of past theatrical conventions while elevating them within the newer form. Even though Gilbert and Sullivan disliked cross-dressing, they used the memory of it to their advantage. In *Princess Ida*, however, elevating the tone does not solve the problems endemic to the "three Princesses," for all are troubled by the relations among gender, genre, and parody, and each work makes that trouble its central theme. The changing role of transvestism in each of the "three Princesses" will help us to focus on those troubling relations.

Tennyson's *Princess* makes the obvious point that conventions of dress signify distinctions in gender, but at first the poem seems to be using its episodes of cross-dressing to query those distinctions; Princess Ida's hauteur, intellectualism, and "masculine" willingness to wage war seem admirable at first, while the Prince's "weird seizures," difference from his violently misogynistic father, and cross-dressing seem to be signs of an equally admirable embrace of a certain effeminacy. Yet in the end, as the result of a war against the female citadel, Ida and the Prince are forcibly returned to their properly gendered spheres. Within this framework, Gilbert takes the significance of cross-dressing further than Tennyson did. As in Tennyson's poem, the young men dress as women to penetrate the walls of Castle Adamant, but in both of Gilbert's versions, Ida's brothers also undress, taking off their armor piece by piece, to show their incomplete inhabitation of the masculine warrior role that has been prescribed for them. For a moment, it seems clear that martial masculinity is no more "natural" than traditional femininity. In the end, however, neither cross-dressing nor undressing indicates an evolution of gender. Instead, "natural instinct," heterosexual attraction, and the need to create "Posterity" return Hilarion and Ida to their conventionally gendered positions.

Tennyson's "Strange Diagonal"

The burlesque element in *Princess Ida* is not Gilbert's invention, for it is already apparent in Tennyson's *The Princess*. For that reason, we must look at the poem in order to understand how it provides a framework for the opera's treatment of gender and genre. When we return to *Princess Ida*, we will see how *The Princess* complicates, undermines—and perhaps dooms to failure—some of the tried-and-true Savoy strategies of gender and genre parody.

At the time of the poem's publication, Princess Ida was "readily recognizable as a contemporary phenomenon," a representation of the "strong-minded woman" whose self-assertion and aspiration to equality were widely understood to threaten the clear differentiation of the sexes.[2] Charles Kingsley's comments are typical. He argued that Tennyson "shows us the woman, when she takes her stand on the false masculine ground of the intellect, working out her own moral punishment, by destroying in herself the tender heart of flesh."[3] Even though Tennyson's poem is more complex than Kingsley's moralistic account would suggest, it does conclude with Ida's choice of domesticity. While most Victorian reviewers praised Ida's conversion to feminine feeling and heterosexual attraction in the end, most contemporary critics praise, instead, Tennyson's vision of women's higher education in the poem's first half. On the other side of the gender divide, most Victorian critics regarded the Prince as "unpleasantly effeminate,"[4] while none responded to his prediction that in the future men may become more feminine while women may become more masculine, thus reaching a balance of gendered traits in both sexes that would permit true partnership. Indeed, the poem is notable for its ambivalence, in which can be seen the slow historical process of changing gender norms, beyond the poem's conservative ending.

Tennyson's *The Princess* is a frame tale, whose frame opens at the estate of Sir Walter Vivian, on the day of an outdoor fête for tenants and the "neighboring borough," in the Victorian present. Amusements for "the people" include games and amateur scientific exhibitions, "so that sport / Went hand in hand with science." This Victorian fantasy of happy class relations sponsored by noblesse oblige leads directly into the central tale of Princess

Ida and her university, set in a fairy-tale feudal past. Thus the frame and its tale suggest a certain relation of past to present, as well as a middlebrow wish for scientific explanation that appears throughout *The Princess* and will issue in the joke about "Darwinian Man" in *Princess Ida*. On the day of the fête, young Walter Vivian and six of his friends, visiting from college, decide to narrate the story of the princess. The plan is hatched when the young men amble to the Gothic ruins of the estate, along with a sedate maiden aunt and Lilia, who is pointedly characterized as "wild with sport, / Half child, half woman." Her position on the verge of womanhood marks her special significance to the frame. Among the ruins, the group encounters the broken statue of Sir Ralph, an ancient Vivian ancestor. Lilia playfully drapes the statue with rosy orange silk. Thus the story unfolds under the sign of burlesque cross-dressing.

Under the auspices of this totemic "feudal warrior lady-clad," the young men idealistically recall Ralph's wife, who "drove her foes with slaughter from her walls," thus invoking another transgressive figure of inversion, the warrior woman, as a counter to the "feudal warrior lady-clad." But young Walter relegates the warrior woman to the distant past; patting Lilia on the head, he asks, "Where . . . lives there such a woman now?" Lilia bristles with indignation and fiercely advances the feminist argument from socialization, while outlining her dream of a women's college:

> Quick answered Lilia: 'There are thousands now
> Such women, but convention beats them down;
> It is bringing-up; no more than that.
> You men have done it—how I hate you all!
>   . . . I wish I were
> Some mighty poetess, I would shame you then,
> That love to keep us children! O, I wish
> That I were some great princess, I would build
> Far off from men a college like a man's
> And I would teach them all that men are taught;
> We are twice as quick!' And here she shook aside
> The hands that play'd the patron with her curls.

In other words, it is Lilia's proto-feminist frustration, ambition, and desire that catalyze the telling of the tale, as she shakes away Walter's attempt to patronize her.

Alluding to musical form, Tennyson's poem bills itself, in its subtitle, as *A Medley*. There are several ways to understand this claim—all of them relevant to *Princess Ida*. For one thing, the tonal shifts in the poem must be rationalized or justified somehow, for the tale is told chiefly in an elevated vein of high seriousness, while its frame opens and closes in burlesque; thus the tonal relation between the frame and the tale is, to put it mildly, vexed.[5] In a related sense, "medley" refers to the generic mixture of the poem. The form of narration, based on the chain stories the young men once told during Christmas vacation, allegorizes the poem's generic mixture:

> We forged a sevenfold story. Kind? What kind?
> Chimeras, Crotchets, Christmas solecisms;
> Seven-headed monsters, only made to kill
> Time by the fire in winter.

Perhaps the narrator protests too much. John Westland Marston thought so, writing for the *Athenaeum* soon after the poem's publication, when he argues that this "consciousness of an eccentric plan can scarcely excuse it." He criticizes the "discordant nature of its elements," protesting that the poem's "different parts refuse to amalgamate. They are derived from standards foreign to each other," among which conflicting standards he mentions "genial satire and tragic emotion, lecture rooms and chivalric lists, modern pedantry and ancient romance."[6] As Herbert Tucker puts it, the poem displays "a finicky narrative apparatus that diffuses authorial responsibility for the plot as thoroughly as possible."[7] This, then, is a winter's tale, with Ralph (the "feudal warrior lady-clad") its tutelary genius and Lilia ("half child, half woman") its mistress of ceremonies.

In addition, the "medley" of tones and genres must be understood as a function and an effect of gender, since the blank verse narrated by the men is punctuated by lyrics sung by the women. (Tennyson's form—of narrated action intermittently interrupted by lyric—should remind us, by the way, of ballad opera, burlesque, and comic opera.) The songs are explicitly meant to be subservient, "to give . . . breathing space" to the narrators between the segments of their story. But many critics have discovered that they are neither as incidental nor as subservient to the story as the narrator makes them out to be; instead, they often occur "at an odd or even subversive angle to what is manifestly supposed to be going on."[8] Thus the form of the work is explicitly based on gender, while its plot provides an allegory to rationalize the gendered division of labor typical to the poem's Victorian present time. Like the "myth of matriarchy," which we examined in relation to *Iolanthe*, the powerful, self-sufficient community of women exists in order to be demolished, to show why a patriarchal order must unseat and replace it.[9]

In the frame and in the tale, the war between the sexes is seen both as a matter of burlesque and as a highly serious matter. In response to Lilia's demand for a women's college, the young men imagine how much better college would be with "prudes for proctors, dowagers for deans, / And sweet girl-graduates in their golden hair." Lilia quarrels with their tone: "That's your light way; but I would make it death / For any male thing to peep at us." In other words, their sentimentalized, sexist view of co-education prompts Lilia to imagine an even more radical female separatism. While Lilia and the maiden aunt want a grave and solemn story, the young men banter. Walter proposes:

'Take Lilia, then, for heroine,' clamor'd he,
'And make her some great princess, six feet high,
Grand, epic, homicidal; and be you
The prince to win her!'

In their different ways, both the main male narrators and Lilia regard the separation of women from men as a matter of life and death.

Not only the opening frame of the story, but the plot depends on burlesque cross-dressing. The Prince opens by displaying a certain effeminacy, describing his hair ("like a girl") and the trancelike states into which he falls from time to time.[10] His "weird seizures" are the result of a family curse that seems to encode the psychological fallout from a strictly gendered family, for his mother was as "mild as any saint," while his father is distant, hierarchical, authoritarian, unaffectionate, judgmental, and pedantic. It is this patriarch who wants to go to war against the women, to eradicate their university and force Ida to marry his son. His horrifying violence is matched by the kinder (but still dismissive) misogyny of Ida's father, Gama, who blames Ida's defection on "two widows" who "fed her theories . . . that with equal husbandry / The woman were an equal to the man." Thus is Lilia's explanation of gendered socialization displaced and blamed on the older women, cast as feminist rabble-rousers. Despite men who "love to keep [them] children," these two widows preach that girls must grow up, "lose the child, assume / The woman." The questions will be: What is the correct way to grow up? What does a mature woman do?

Within this context of paternal hostility to Ida's project, the Prince formulates his plan to enter the all-female university with his friends by dressing as women:

A thought flash'd thro' me which I clothed in act,
Remembering how we three presented Maid,
Or Nymph, or Goddess, at high tide of feast,
In masque or pageant at my father's court.

Thus the plan to cross-dress is explicitly developed not only as a suitor's way of coming into the presence of his beloved, but also as a response to the antifeminist positions of the two fathers. The act of cross-dressing is hardly superficial, in other words, for it expresses the Prince's largely unconscious effeminization in relation to the fathers.

Soon after the young men arrive, Lady Psyche—one of the female professors at Ida's university—expounds her theory of evolution. From the nebular hypothesis, she moves on to the arrival of "the monster, then the man," who evolves from barbarian to civilized. Her retelling of planetary and human history, from a woman's perspective, includes the "legendary Amazon . . . emblematic of a nobler age." Like the young men in the frame, who contemplate Ralph's warrior wife, Psyche looks back to a time when women were stronger, more heroic, more masculine—a powerful civilizing force. Although she believes that woman is distinctly superior to man at the present time, Psyche's prophetic vision of the future involves equality, mutuality, and gender teamwork. Significantly, it is during the exposition of her evolutionary theory that she recognizes her brother, one of the Prince's cross-dressed friends. The titillating exposure of the cross-dressed men involves several stages and burlesque double entendres, culminating with Cyril's singing a "tavern-song," Princess Ida's fall into the river, and the Prince's rescue of her. In other words, the discovery of the cross-dressed men creates a great deal of chaos—in the story and in the poem. This is the turning point of the plot, after which the poem begins its rationalization for the failure of the women's university.

Marking this turn, the poem's "Interlude"—another allusion to theatrical and musical form—clearly registers the danger of the men's transgressive invasion. Lilia sings a song of martial fervor, demanding war, "like one that wishes to change / The music." And, indeed, the music does change. Her song apostrophizes a woman whose man is away at war, where he is inspired to fight by the memory of the domestic happiness awaiting him at home; his victory against the foe depends on the vision of "his brood about [her] knee." Like Mabel in *The Pirates of Penzance*, Lilia assumes the persona of the martial woman, sending men off to fight, rather than the woman warrior of the imaginary feudal past. Her song is at odds with her previous plan, for she demands that the women in the story fight for what they believe; yet after this interlude, the story is no longer driven by Lilia's desire. The women do not fight, and from now until its end, the poem falls apart, divorcing itself from its initial premises and taking apart Princess Ida's visionary university as well. Ida will have a change of heart and will capitulate to—indeed, in the end, will desire—conventional femininity.

How does the poem bring about this dénouement? The war against Ida's Castle Adamant provides the occasion. And in Tennyson's *Princess*—unlike either of Gilbert's versions—the Prince falls in battle. When Princess Ida sees how badly wounded he is, "Her iron will was broken in her mind." She is fully conscious of her "fall" into femininity. Considering the process of her feminization, Ida links tone, class, and gender when she notes that feeling "drags [her] down / From [her] fixd height" to the "soft and milky rabble of womankind."[11] Shockingly, Ida has kidnapped Psyche's baby daughter and has begun to grow attached to her, unaware of what this new feeling might be. When the Prince falls in battle, Ida transfers her nascent maternal feelings to him, finding comfort in the activities of nursing. In a ghastly transformation, the disorder of the war gives way to an explicitly gendered order. With the "fair college turn'd to hospital," "a kindlier influence reigned," and all the women are more beautiful for going "to and fro . . . with angel offices": "Like creatures native unto gracious act, / And in their own clear element they moved." This, of course, is a description of the familiar figure of the "angel in the house," although she operates in a hospital. Convalescing under Ida's care, the Prince compares himself to "infants in their sleep." While he is thus infantilized, Ida falls in love with him, in a conventional Victorian plot in which the man must be weakened so that the strong woman may embrace him. He recovers, of course, and begs for a kiss, which seals their union, from his point of view: "My spirit closed with Ida's at the lips," while "her falser self slipt from her like a robe, / And left her woman." For us, the metaphor is notable. The masculinized woman is re-dressed and put to rights, her essential feminine nature finally expressed, as nakedness. Like the Prince and his friends, although of course in reverse, Ida has been figuratively in disguise as a man, and her true womanhood can be revealed only when she takes off the robe of her "falser self."

The poem then knuckles down to the work of explaining Ida's conversion. In part, she rationalizes it to herself; in part, the Prince persuades her; but in part, as Tucker has shown, the change is understood to take place outside the realm of consciousness. The poem makes this point through its form, especially the role played by the last intercalated lyric. While reading "a volume of the poets of her land" to the fallen Prince, Ida softens. Tucker's analysis of "Come down, O maid, from yonder mountain height" shows in detail how that lyric condenses and recapitulates the narrative's main thrust, which calls for the high aims of feminist separation to be brought down to earth. With promises of happiness, the lyric exhorts the maid to "come down . . . for Love is of the valley."[12] Ida's acceptance of gender, previously portrayed as a "fall," now becomes a voluntary comedown. Crucially, "Come down, O maid," sonically prefigures the story's closure, when the Prince makes his proposal:

> . . . Indeed I love thee; come,
> Yield thyself up; my hopes and thine are one.
> Accomplish thou my manhood and thyself;
> Lay thy sweet hands in mine and trust to me.

These are the last words of the framed tale (which will be truncated in both of Gilbert's versions and transferred to the voice of Ida).

The masculinized female must become "woman" in order to bestow manhood on the man. Man cannot be man without the woman to reproduce him; after providing this office, the woman's role is to trust him for guidance. The Prince himself outlines the correctly differentiated and systematic form of gender relations:

> Henceforth thou hast a helper, me, that know
> The woman's cause is man's; they rise or sink
> Together . . .
> For woman is not undevelopt man,
> But diverse. Could we make her as the man,
> Sweet Love were slain; his dearest bond is this,
> Not like to like but like in difference.
> Yet in the long years liker must they grow;
> The man be more of woman, she of man;
> He gain in sweetness and in moral height,
> . . .
> She mental breadth, nor fail in childward care,
> Nor lose the childlike in the larger mind;
> Till at the last she set herself to man,
> Like perfect music unto noble words.

An explicit argument against the "manly" woman, this is as clear a statement of Victorian concepts of sexual difference and gender relations as one could ever hope to find. Perhaps "in the long years liker must they grow," but for now, they must be clearly "diverse," yet "rise or sink / Together." In other words, there is a catch in this vision of mature mutuality, and it is related to cross-dressing. For the idea that the "woman's cause is man's" suggests not only that the man will fight for the woman's cause, but also that he will take the woman's part—that is, take it away from her. As Elaine Showalter points out, the cross-dressed man often signifies this substitution, in which a man is seen to play the woman better than a woman could do; the feminist agenda is less threatening when pronounced by a man.[13]

Thus the Prince's vision of mutuality is explicitly based on sexual difference. If woman were "as the man," then heterosexual attraction, or "Sweet Love," would be "slain." This argument positions marriage and childbearing as the peak of maturity. But maturity for a woman is contradictory, for she should not "fail in childward care, / Nor lose the childlike in the larger mind." Thus the feminist theory propounded by the "two widows" has been turned upside down, their message reversed, for "lose the child, assume / The woman" has become have a child, yet remain one. The assumption is clear that Ida will learn to recapitulate the Prince's angelic mother, who has, after all, reproduced the Prince in her own image. Thus what is made to look like a compromise between equal man and woman is really a recapitulation of the status quo, and Tennyson's attempt to obfuscate (with the Prince's "nor equal nor unequal") does nothing to change this basic structure.

After the tale has been told, we are returned to the frame, where even Walter Vivian is disappointed, saying of the princess, "I wish she had not yielded!" As Tucker puts it, "Marital and social bonds are accepted, but not the acceptance itself, not quite."[14] In the closure of the frame, the narrator returns to his discussion of mixed genres and tones. In other words, disappointment about the resolution of the story slides directly into disappointment about the uneasy mix of tones and genres, and most readers, accordingly, have regarded the "Conclusion" as an apology for the shortcomings of the poem. Since the tonal territory has been divided along strict gender lines from the beginning, perhaps it is not surprising to find the narrator blaming the tale's disappointing ending on the women, whose songs and "silent influence . . . drove us . . . to quite a solemn close." In other words, while the women claim that male banter keeps them down, the men claim that female solemnity brings them down, and now everyone is "down," feeling deflated at the recognition of culture's relentless reproduction of its norms.

Looking back on the incomplete success of the poem, the main narrator summarizes: the men wanted a "sort of mock-heroic gigantesque," but the women "had ever seem'd to wrestle with burlesque." And though Princess Ida in the framed tale is "true-heroic—true-sublime," the narrator reasons that the poem could not be wholly serious "with such a framework." In the midst of this "feud between the mockers and the realists," the narrator claims that he has worked out a compromise formation, moving, as he says, "betwixt them both, to please them both . . . in a strange diagonal." But he admits that this strategy may have failed, "maybe neither pleased myself nor them." In the narrator's discomfort with his own "strange diagonal," a residual critique of conventional gender remains detectable. In this respect, the closing of the frame is suggestive, since it features the undressing of the cross-dressed statue. The poem pans outward to assume a cosmic perspective:

> Last little Lilia, rising quietly,
> Disrobed the glimmering statue of Sir Ralph
> From those rich silks, and home well-pleased we went.

How truly "well-pleased" has already been subjected to question, and the fault lines within that "we" have been severely felt. Lilia's quiet, conclusive gesture suggests her understanding that the play of gender and genre is over. Cross-dressing an artifactual representation of the past has done nothing to change the reproduction of gender relations in the present. Telling the story under the aegis of cross-dressing does nothing to change the story.

Burlesquing *The Princess*

Gilbert staged his burlesque *The Princess* at the Olympic Theatre in 1870, a year before his first collaboration with Sullivan.[15] Technically, then, *The Princess* is not part of the Savoy canon. Yet, in an important sense, it *is* part of the Savoy canon, for the libretto for *Princess Ida* reproduces much of its dialogue, almost verbatim. Thus *Princess Ida* will struggle in its own "strange diagonal," which veers between its burlesque dialogue and its operatic reframing.

Billed as "A Whimsical Allegory (Being a Respectful Perversion of Mr. Tennyson's Poem)," *The Princess* is composed of five scenes, played without a break (like most burlesques). Its blank verse is out of the genre's ordinary way (although not unheard of), since most burlesques revel in their rhymed couplets. Puns in abundance riddle the play texts of burlesque, and *The Princess* exhibits its fair share of groaners. As usual in burlesque, the intercalated lyrics are set to the music of familiar tunes (in this case, from Offenbach's *La Périchole* [1868] and *Le pont des soupirs* [*The Bridge of Sighs*, 1861], Rossini's *The Barber of Seville* [1816], Auber's *Manon Lescaut* [1856], and others).

Most important for our purposes, all the parts for young men were played by women, as was conventional in burlesque—not only the three romantic leads (Hilarion, Cyril, and Florian), but also Ida's brothers (Arac, Guron, and Scynthius) (figure 8.1). This casting convention utterly changes the dynamics of the cross-dressing episode in the plot.

A year before the production of *Princess Ida*, Gilbert explained that he had "endeavored so to treat [Tennyson's poem] as to absolve [himself] from a charge of willful irreverence."[16] Perhaps Gilbert's demurral should be seen in the light of a retrospective disavowal, very much like the narrator's conclusion of the poem. Max Keith Sutton argues that *The Princess* is not primarily a parody, but used Tennyson's original "not as a target but as a frame for satire upon the question of equality between the sexes."[17] However, keeping in mind that parody does not necessarily attack its precursor, we can see several respects in which Gilbert does parody both the form and the themes of Tennyson's poem. Most obviously, the blank verse directly imitates Tennyson's meter; if taken as an allusion to Tennyson, a burlesque in blank verse (instead of the usual rhymed couplets) would have been amusing, mock-heroic on the very face of things. Although Tennyson's poem is a generic

FIGURE 8.1 Women playing men playing women: female-to-male cross-dressing in Gilbert's burlesque *The Princess*. Engraving by D. H. Friston, in *Illustrated London News*, January 20, 1870. (Wikimedia Commons)

"medley," the tale is meant to be "high," and therefore Gilbert's general shift to burlesque is a good example of parodic deflation overall.[18] Several particular burlesque features—numerous puns and faux-shocking wordplay, allusions to Shakespeare, and a kind of casual, swaggering misogyny and misanthropy—characterize *The Princess*. In other words, Gilbert's play is a parody of one particular work, not a genre parody, although it skillfully *uses* a particular genre, burlesque, to perform its take on Tennyson's poem. As we have seen, the poem also sports with burlesque, and its overall structure—blank verse interrupted by lyrics—bears such a striking resemblance to that of ballad opera, burlesque, extravaganza, and comic opera (all of which are punctuated by lyrics) that one might wonder if Gilbert recognized this relation and performed his own clever reading of Tennyson's mixed form.

Several changes to the characters, plot, themes, and form of cross-dressing suggest that Gilbert did critically evaluate the poem. The exaggeration of some figures and the comic inversion of others is one sure sign. For example, Gilbert named the prince Hilarion, with perhaps an allusion to *Giselle* (1841), but with surely a suggestion of the play's intended hilarity. (Tennyson did not name his Prince.) Hilarion's father, Hildebrand, is a parody of the pantomime tyrant, according to Jane Stedman.[19] Gama, Ida's father, already grotesque in Tennyson's poem ("a little dry old man . . . not like a king"), is, in the burlesque version, "a twisted monster—all awry," a "monkey head" with a stinging tongue. In a punning allusion to Hamlet's comparison of his father to his uncle ("Hyperion to a satyr"), the play compares Gama's sharp tongue to a periodical well known for its sharp criticism ("Hyperion to a Saturday Review"). Ida's brothers, exaggeratedly warlike in Tennyson's original, shy away from combat in Gilbert's version, rather like the Police in *The Pirates of Penzance*.

Changes made to the plot further indicate a parodic critique of Tennyson's poem. I will give only the four main examples. First, the debate in Tennyson's *Princess* about whether women should or should not be "childlike" is diverted in Gilbert's *Princess* into the stock idea of the baby engagement. True, Ida was betrothed as a child of eight in the original poem, but in the burlesque she is betrothed "at the extremely early age of one." Imagining his wife, Hilarion admits that it "Seems strange that she / Should have become a woman." Instead of defending Ida's project to his anti-feminist father, as he does in the poem, Hilarion diverts himself into a long riff on his baby wife, "all bib and tucker, frill and furbelow." It is clear that Gilbert enjoyed this plot device in its own right (see also *Patience* and *The Gondoliers*), but in *The Princess* he used it purposively, to avoid the touchy issue of sexual or gender maturation.

PLATE 1 For a decade before collaborating with Sullivan, Gilbert wrote comic journalism for *Fun*, the chief rival to *Punch*. Illustration by Alfred Concanen, for cover of
the sheet music for *Fun Quadrilles* (1865), composed by F. Lancelott. (The Pierpont
Morgan Library, New York. The Gilbert and Sullivan Collection)

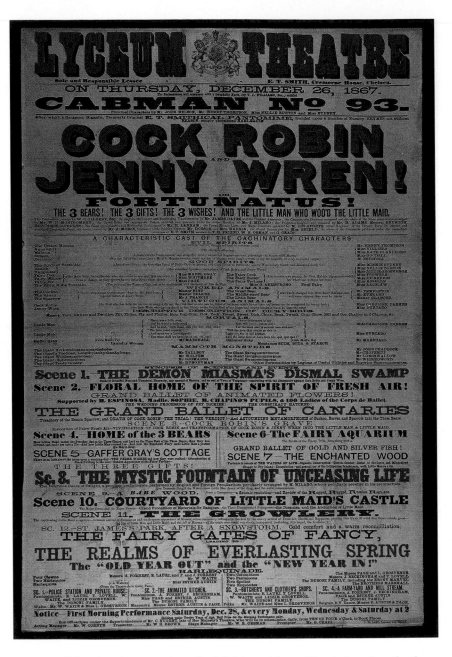

PLATE 2 Gilbert's only pantomime, *Cock Robin and Jenny Wren!*—based on the theme of public sanitation—featured the opposition of the Demon Miasma and the Spirit of Fresh Air. Playbill for Lyceum Theatre, December 26, 1867. (The Pierpont Morgan Library, New York. The Gilbert and Sullivan Collection)

PLATE 3 The Chorus of Sisters, Cousins, and Aunts is watched by the Chorus of Sailors on the other side of the stage. Lithograph by Alfred Concanen, for poster for the first production of *H.M.S. Pinafore* (1878). (The Pierpont Morgan Library, New York. The Gilbert and Sullivan Collection)

PLATE 4 "There! What do you think of that?" Nellie Farren's costume for her role as Ganem in Robert Reece's burlesque *The Forty Thieves* (1880) displays her famous figure. Illustration by Jack, for "Society" Bijou Portraits. (Collection of Fredric Woodbridge Wilson)

PLATE 5 In a parody of the extravaganza transformation scene (*top*), the Judge's bench becomes a wedding cake, while in a parody of the minstrel line (*bottom*), the Defendant is backed up by the Chorus of Jurors. Cover of the sheet music for *Trial by Jury Waltz* (1875), arranged by Charles D'Albert. (Collection of Fredric Woodbridge Wilson)

PLATE 6 "Very good, then, we will proceed at once to the Incantation." Poster for the Savoy Theatre revival of *The Sorcerer* (1884). (The Pierpont Morgan Library, New York. The Gilbert and Sullivan Collection)

PLATE 7 Visual parody through the adaptation of a burlesque pun: "The Merry Merry Maiden and the Tar." Lithograph by Currier & Ives (New York, 1879). (Collection of Fredric Woodbridge Wilson)

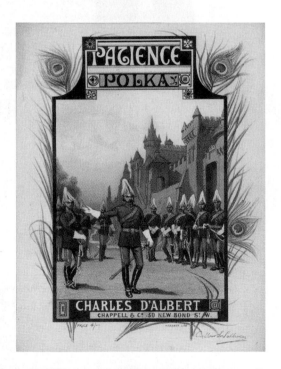

PLATE 8 Dragoon Guards as exaggeratedly upright, manly men. Cover of the sheet music for *Patience Polka* (1881), arranged by Charles D'Albert. (Collection of Fredric Woodbridge Wilson)

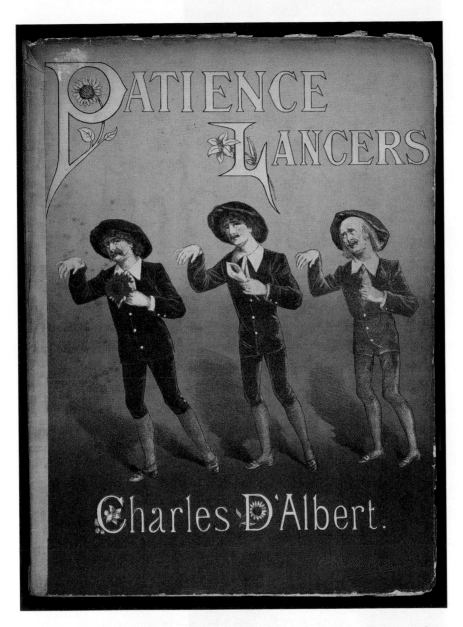

PLATE 9 Dragoon Guards attempt to pose as aesthetes. Cover of the sheet music for *Patience Lancers* (1881), arranged by Charles D'Albert. (The Pierpont Morgan Library, New York. The Gilbert and Sullivan Collection)

PLATE 10 Aesthetic teapot: (*top, center*) both sides of the teapot, showing isomorphic male and female aesthetes displaying the "crooked wrist"; (*bottom*) on the bottom is inscribed "Fearful consequences, through the laws of Natural Selection and Evolution, of living up to one's Teapot." Teapot, Royal Worcester Porcelain Company (1881). (The Pierpont Morgan Library, New York. The Gilbert and Sullivan Collection)

PLATE 11 The Fairy Queen and the Fairies outside the Houses of Parliament, in a scene from act 2 of "Gilbert and Sullivan's Latest Comic Opera." Poster printed by J. G. Hyde (New York, 1884). (Harvard Theatre Collection, Houghton Library)

PLATE 12 Naked bodies crowd Sir Joseph Noel Paton's fairy painting *The Reconciliation of Oberon and Titania* (1847). (By permission, National Gallery of Scotland, Edinburgh [Bridgeman Art Library])

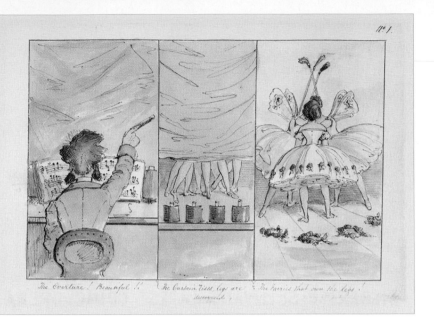

PLATE 13 Taking a part for the whole: stage fairies represented by female legs. "The Overture! Beautiful!! / The Curtain rises, legs are discovered / The Fairies that own the legs!" First page of Alfred Crowquill [Alfred Henry Forrester], "Pantomime, as It Was, Is and Will Be" (ca. 1848). (MS Thr 26, Harvard Theatre Collection, Houghton Library)

PLATE 14 Female-to-male cross-dressing: Louisa Fairbrother as Abdallah in the pantomime *The Forty Thieves*. Lithograph by John Brandard, after J. W. Child (1845). (Harvard Theatre Collection, Houghton Library)

MAY·YOU·HAVE·A·QUITE·TOO·HAPPY·TIME·

PLATE 15 Varieties of Victorian Japonisme: (*top*) James Abbott McNeill Whistler's Peacock Room (1876–1877; highbrow); (*bottom right*) blue-and-white willow-pattern china (ca. 1850; middle- to highbrow); (*bottom left*) Christmas card linking Japanese screen with aesthetic diction ("quite too") and iconic teapot (ca. 1880; middle- to lowbrow). (Bridgeman Art Library)

PLATE 16 Feminine self-division: "A heart that does not know its mind." Rose Maybud is torn between the suits of Dick Dauntless and Robin Oakapple. Advertisement for the touring production of *Ruddigore* (1887). (The Pierpont Morgan Library, New York. The Gilbert and Sullivan Collection)

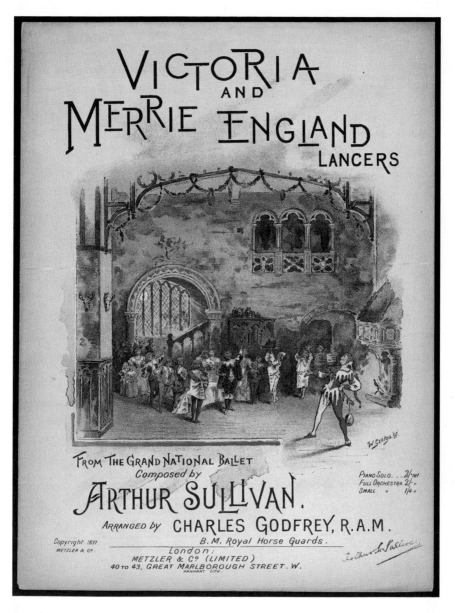

PLATE 17 A popular figure of national nostalgia, "Merrie England" was associated with Queen Victoria in Sullivan's "Grand National Ballet." Lithograph by W. George, of scenes from the ballet, for cover of the sheet music for *Victoria and Merrie England Lancers* (1897), arranged by Charles Godfrey. (The Pierpont Morgan Library, New York. The Gilbert and Sullivan Collection)

PLATE 18 Fantasy Venice. Poster for the touring production of *The Gondoliers* (1889). (The Pierpont Morgan Library, New York. The Gilbert and Sullivan Collection)

PLATE 19 Commercial appropriation of *The Mikado*: American trading cards (ca. 1885) advertise Thomson's Patent Glove Fitting corsets (*top*) and the "Mikado" stove, "Dedicated to His Majesty . . . Grand Dictator of the Realm of Japan" (*bottom*). (The Pierpont Morgan Library, New York. The Gilbert and Sullivan Collection)

PLATE 20 Commercial
parody on *The Mikado*:
cover of Ed J. Smith,
The Capitalist; or,
The City of Fort Worth
(The Texas Mikado) (1888).
(Collection of Fredric
Woodbridge Wilson)

PLATE 21 H. W. McVickar,
cover of D. Dalziel, *A*
Parody on Iolanthe (1883),
"Respectfully dedicated to
the conductors of the
Chicago & Alton Railroad."
(Collection of Fredric
Woodbridge Wilson)

Second, Gilbert reworked the relation between love and war. In the poem, war is a serious threat from early on; in the burlesque, Hilarion plans to wage a war of courtship, "to storm / Their eyes and hearts, and not their citadel." Later in the plot, Hildebrand's siege of Castle Adamant is itself a mock war, to be fought with battalions of baritones and tenors, photographs and valentines, robes of French design, waltzing bachelors, and five hundred toilet tables equipped with mirrors. Hildebrand inanely describes this siege of seduction to the tune of "Largo al factotum" from *The Barber of Seville* (for example, "Oh, flatter your fairy / Ever unwary / Tickle it, ah!" and so forth). Matters of life and death in the poem are reduced to flirtation, and the war between the sexes is reduced to a tourney of three on three. If Hilarion wins, Arac himself—who is Ida's great champion in the poem—will force her to marry the prince. But the most shocking change is that Hilarion *does* win. He does not fall in battle; thus he is not weakened, needs no nursing, and the play consequently leaves no time or space for Ida's interior conversion. Of course, interiority is hardly the point in burlesque, and the suddenness of the resolution is perhaps meant to be funny.

Hilarion's proposal to Ida is harsh, although meant to be flattering and inviting: "Woman has failed you utterly, try man." A safety valve is built into this proposal, for Ida may return to Castle Adamant if she grows "a-weary of the Prince." (Of course, it is assumed that she will not return, but this burlesque critique of marriage does allow for the woman's point of view.) Above all, Ida has the last words in this version. They are a direct quotation from the Prince's last words in the poem, minus his ultimate direct appeal to gender: "Accomplish thou my manhood and thyself." Ida yields immediately to her "fate" and turns over the university to Lady Blanche. Thus her embrace of a domestic future is more strongly expressed than in the poem; although the idealistic sentiment of the conservative ending is undercut by a few closing burlesque jokes, made by the fathers, Ida herself is not ambivalent:

"We will walk the world
Yoked in all exercise of noble end!
And so through those dark gates across the wild
That no man knows! Indeed, I love thee—Come!"

Gayden Wren argues, with respect to *Princess Ida*, which ends in the same way, that Ida's "Come!" is "a call to action," whereas the Prince's "Come!" in Tennyson's poem is merely "a cajoling inducement to surrender."[20]

Third, Gilbert made the evolutionary argument simpler and more explicit, turning it into a joke while retaining a serious point. Psyche explains,

> . . . the grand hypothesis,
> That as the Ape is undeveloped Man
> So man is undeveloped Woman.

Since the term "undeveloped" bears such a crucial weight in Tennyson's ending, I would take this change as a sign of parody. As it will be in *Princess Ida*, the analogy between evolution of the species and evolution of the sexes is firmly connected to the play of cross-dressing, and it will be further elaborated in the great novelty number "A Lady fair, of lineage high" (known as "The Lady and the Ape") in *Princess Ida*.

Fourth, Gilbert pressed the thematic significance of cross-dressing further than did Tennyson, allowing it to expand its importance within the hospitable generic context of burlesque. After all, cross-dressing was a convention of nineteenth-century burlesque, known at the time as "leg theater."[21] *The Princess* contains six cross-dressed roles; thus the stage picture is often composed entirely of female bodies (see figure 8.1). Burlesque female-to-male cross-dressing generates several effects: masculinity is softened and "etherealized"; sexual jokes have an entirely different significance; and, finally, when the young men (played by women) decide to dress in women's robes in order to penetrate the walls of Castle Adamant, the play of cross-dressing becomes complex and layered, an example of what Marjorie Garber calls "double drag."[22] Like the complication in the figure of the Savoy Dame—who may be seen, figuratively, as a woman playing the part of a low-comic man playing a woman—these cross-dressed invaders are clearly women, who are playing men playing women. The gender and sexual confusion is funny, titillating, and even thought provoking, for it permits a complex audience response, composed of inestimable combinations of identification and desire on the part of both male and female spectators.[23] Gilbert surely understood that cross-dressing could be seductively and productively deployed in a genre whose conventions support it, and he made the best of this point of comparison between Tennyson's poem and burlesque.

The burlesque, not unexpectedly, exaggerates the sexual innuendo inherent in the idea of women playing men dressed in women's clothes. For example, in Scene Second, when the young men are trying on the women's academic robes and plotting their cross-dressed invasion, their song is meant to be pert and sexy, "showing an inch of ankle—so!" Or, for example, in their initial interview, Psyche speaks to them as if they were women, asking them to swear to love their fellow students and never to marry any man. Their compliance in her radical feminist exclusivity contains a heavy dose of nudge-nudge, wink-wink, based on the idea that they are played by women (who would marry a man), but are playing men (who would not). Yet, visually, they are women promising to love other women. They humbly admit that they are "homely ladies," based on the idea that they are playing men. Yet, visually, they are not homely, but beautiful and sexy. The cross fire in these layers of cross-dressing humor can be intense at times. For example, when Princess Ida shows an interest in knowing whether the prince is handsome ("And is the booby comely?"), Hilarion replies:

> Pretty well.
> I've heard it said that if I dressed myself
> In Prince Hilarion's clothes (supposing this
> Consorted with my maiden modesty),
> I might be taken for Hilarion's self.

In this exchange, a man in woman's clothes (played by a woman) imagines himself a woman dressing in man's clothes. Keeping track of these layered gender identities becomes difficult, and that difficulty is a large part of the point, when the intellectual humor of cross-dressing goes along with its studied titillation.[24]

Always bawdy, Cyril pursues Hilarion's line of thinking, claiming that the three ladies are "inseparables," that they all love the prince, and that "he loves [them] sincerely in return." Thus the camaraderie of male bonding is facilitated by heterosexual fantasy. Then, again, the disguised prince and his female persona supposedly have ridden the same horse. When the princess asks whether "she" has ridden "astride," she conjures the image of a woman straddling a horse, while Cyril projects the image of the prince and his female look-alike wearing the same clothes and getting tipsy in the same company. All this leads to Cyril's major outburst, which is here called a "laughing song." Featuring a man reading for the bar, who gets diverted into a sexual dalliance, the song teases its audience by refusing to answer the question: "And what d'you think he told her?" What is not said is left to the imagination of the audience, thus implying that its content is too risqué to get past the censor—or to be uttered in polite company (which the audience for burlesque was decidedly not). After the song, Cyril lights a cigarette, surely even then a token of the sexual relaxation that has been conjured. At this point, Ida falls into the water, is rescued, and dismisses them pointedly and scathingly: "Begone! men in women's clothes!"

The burlesque *Princess* also features a scene of Gama taunting the young men dressed in women's clothes. He insults Hilarion's manhood and begs the "young ladies" to flirt with Hildebrand. In retaliation, the prince is provoked into asserting his manhood ("My sword is long and sharp!"), at which point Gama ridicules him as a virago and a termagant. Then, making fun of them as "pretty ones," Gama praises his own manly sons and incites their combat. In other words, his taunting takes the form of sexual harassment, when he treats the cross-dressed men as young women, and the form of intimidating misogyny, when he treats them as older, masculine women; back and forth, the cross fire goes, the figurative object shifting rapidly from one kind of denigrated woman to another. And in addition to the burlesque misogyny, one can detect the homoerotic and homophobic interest in this treatment of "men in women's clothes."[25]

We must remember that the company consisted almost entirely of women; only Gama, Hildebrand, and four minor characters were played by men. While capitalizing on the full range of sexual suggestiveness, in other words, burlesque keeps its eye on the female form. Gilbert proceeded with his usual intense interest in genre, using the plot to investigate the burlesque fascination with women. Affording an almost revue-like vista of woman-hood to the gaze, Ida's university puts different kinds of "woman" on display. (This tendency would be extended and made explicit in *Princess Ida* with Hilarion, Cyril, and Florian's song about types of womanhood: "cold and stately," "frank and simple," "coyly blushing." The song's refrain offers a good statement of carefree burlesque connoisseurship: "Haughty, humble, coy or free, / . . . Every maid is the maid for me!")

If Tennyson's *Princess* analyzes "instinct in the toils of culture,"[26] Gilbert's *Princess*, like *Princess Ida*, focuses almost entirely on instinct, supposed to be entirely heterosexual. The resolution turns, as does *Princess Ida*'s, on the conundrum about "Posterity."[27] Still focused on her feminist project, Ida claims that if she carried out her scheme, "Posterity / Would bow in grati-tude!" But Hildebrand asks:

If you enlist all women in your cause,
. . .
. . . "How
Is this Posterity to be provided?"

The closing song, set to a melody by Offenbach, celebrates men and women, masculine and feminine, all finally straightened out. In this song, voice reg-isters clearly signify a notion of gender grounded in biological sex; no matter how bodies are dressed, the voice reveals the truth of gender. Gilbert would press this point even further in *Princess Ida*. For now, hero and heroine are finally singing together, and the conventional romantic pairing of their voices makes a fine figure for the return to conventional gender:

> Singers know
> How sweetly at a piano
> A tenor and soprano
>   Together sound.
>
>   This will show
> That men and women verily
> Can get along more merrily
>   Together bound.

Princess Ida and "Darwinian Man"

Like *The Princess*, *Princess Ida* is "A Respectful Perversion" of Tennyson's poem, but this time the perversion was billed as "Operatic" rather than "Whimsical." Indeed, Sullivan's score moved closer to the music of grand opera than had the score of any other collaboration so far.[28] As Leslie Baily puts it, *Princess Ida* intends to be "highbrow."[29] Its three acts and blank-verse dialogue, altogether anomalous in the Savoy canon, together with the usual attention to sumptuous sets and beautiful costumes, make it clear that the production aimed high indeed (figure 8.2).[30] But the dialogue, taken largely from *The Princess*, sits uneasily in its new framework. Its burlesque provenance can be keenly felt, to the detriment of the work as a whole.

In the first instance, however, the importance of that new framework should not be underestimated. The lyrics were new, and they both elaborate the dramatic structure and recontextualize the burlesque dialogue by intensifying themes that are only implicit in the burlesque version. The lyrics also productively interrupt the burlesque banter with their range of moods. (For example, after the men cross-dress, the lyric interruption of "The world is but a broken toy" comes out of nowhere and shifts the mood forcefully, or after the exposure of the women's ridiculous inability to wage war, Princess Ida realizes that she is alone and laments her failed project in the moving lyric interruption of "I built upon a rock.") More important still, Sullivan's original music makes the definitive difference in shifting the genre. *Princess Ida* cannot be called a burlesque, despite its burdensome burlesque residue, yet an uneasy disparity remains between the words and the music in this

FIGURE 8.2 The "high" medieval set of *Princess Ida*. Illustration by D. H. Friston (engraved by H. Werdmuller), in *Illustrated Sporting and Dramatic News*. (Collection of Fredric Woodbridge Wilson)

comic opera. The clash of tones between the dialogue and its frame seems oddly reminiscent of that in Tennyson's poem, but in reverse, since in *Princess Ida* burlesque blank-verse dialogue was reframed to a higher purpose, whereas in Tennyson's poem, an elevated blank-verse tale was embedded in a burlesque framework. Thus, oddly, although *The Princess* is a parody, *Princess Ida*, reframing and revising the parody, moves closer to the poem in its form.

The high quality of the music was widely praised. The reviewer for the *Musical Times* approved: "[B]y general consent the Music . . . shows yet further progress towards that intellectual standard which should be the goal of every earnest composer." He praised Sullivan's "masterly use of the orchestra" in particular, asserting his superiority in this respect to all foreign composers of light comic opera. The reviewer also recognized Sullivan's musical genre parodies, insofar as he noted the "felicitous reproductions of old world rhythms and cadences."[31] William Beatty-Kingston of the *Theatre* added that the Savoy Chorus was better than the chorus in any Continental opera house. The music in *Princess Ida* is as different in overall mood and conception from that in *Iolanthe* as that opera's is from the score of *Patience*.[32] As Audrey Williamson notes, Sullivan inventively experimented with chromaticism in *Princess Ida* (as he had experimented with leitmotifs in *Iolanthe*).[33]

The libretto was found lacking, however. While Gilbert's imagination frequently worked through revisions of his own ideas, particularly germs from the Bab Ballads, he had never recycled an entire play, and this decision drew many negative comments.[34] Other complaints were heard as well: *Princess Ida* was too long; act 2, especially, was disproportionately long, leaving no natural place for the intermission. Worse still, some reviewers, like Edmund Yates, writing in the *World*, found it "desperately dull," while others called it "clumsy," "tedious," and "tiring."[35] In short, despite its wonderful music, *Princess Ida* was not a success. It played for only ten months, when, showing "signs of dropping," it was replaced by a revival of *The Sorcerer* as a stopgap measure while the next opera was being prepared.

Princess Ida exposes the fault lines that had been present from the beginning in Tennyson's poem. The frame does not entirely fit the tale. Perhaps the contemplation of gender dynamics in *Patience* and *Iolanthe* prompted Gilbert to reach back into the early 1870s, when not only *The Princess* but also two of his fairy comedies involved communities of women who leave the larger world behind.[36] At that time, his treatments of the "woman question" had protested against the sexual double standard, defending the fallen woman and suggesting that the man should share the blame, at the very least. Thus, as Andrew Crowther points out, his ridicule of the women's college in *Princess Ida* seems to demonstrate a logical inconsistency.[37] Perhaps it represents a misreading of Tennyson's poem, for if Gilbert took Tennyson to be making a feminist argument, he might have planned the anti-feminism of *Princess Ida* as a parodic inversion. But this seems unlikely, since most nineteenth-century readers easily recognized Tennyson's Princess Ida as a representation of the "She-man" (as Ida was called in *Howitt's*).[38] Ida, Charles Kingsley wrote, has "all the peculiar faults of woman and none of the peculiar excellences of man."[39]

As we have seen with respect to *Patience*, the middlebrow appetite for ridicule of abnormal gender performances seems to have been insatiable. In George du Maurier's cartoons for *Punch*—always a good indicator of these attitudes—the theme persisted through the 1870s and 1880s. His anti-aesthetic cartoons, as we have seen, attack both effeminate men and masculine women, focusing especially on the idea that aestheticism stood in the way of marriage, family, and reproduction. Likewise, and for the same reasons, he disparages higher education for women. Some cartoons make fun of the supposedly intellectual woman for being unsexed—or, alterna-tively, starved for sex. For example, "Terrible Result of Higher Education of Women" depicts Miss Hypatia Jones, "Spinster of the Arts," who chats with a male companion about the fact that young men may be fine to look at, but women with higher educations want to marry older men for their good con-versation.[40] (The clear implication is that these spinsters cannot have, do not want, or should not want sexual attractiveness in a mate.) Other cartoons point up the impossibility that women can be genuinely intellectual. In "The Higher Education of Women," Jessica, a supposedly intelligent woman, is asked whether she happened to see a star shower. "No," she replies, "but it couldn't have been much, for there are no stars missing."[41] This sort of humor may have been conventional enough in journalistic genres, but uncannily similar attitudes may be found in serious medical discourse, where women's supposed incapacity for difficult intellectual work was attributed to physical limitation. Furthermore, such scholarly work was thought to draw energy away from the proper exercise of reproduction.[42] In a wide range of popular, professional, and esoteric discourses, women who asserted equality were taken to be aggressively claiming superiority, a will to domination, or a destructive wish to obliterate sexual difference, refuse heterosexuality, and damage the family.[43]

All these attitudes are on view in *Princess Ida*, where a "Woman's college [is portrayed as the] maddest folly going!" In Tennyson's poem, the Prince defends Ida's feminist project, but in *Princess Ida*, Hilarion makes her aims sound silly:

They intend to send a wire
    To the moon—to the moon;
And they'll set the Thames on fire
    Very soon—very soon.

In Cyril's voice, this ridicule turns ugly when, singing of things that cannot be done, he rhymes "the little pigs they're teaching / For to fly" with "the niggers they'll be bleaching, / By and by."[44] The idea of women in charge immediately suggests hen-pecked emasculation; the crowing is done "by an accomplished hen," while (with recourse to a burlesque pun) "the mails . . . are driven (as males often are / In other large communities) by women." Those "accomplished hens," the female dons, are portrayed as especially ridiculous. When Lady Psyche lists what should be read for a degree in clas-sics, the superficiality of the list format—funny almost everywhere else in the Savoy operas—falls flat because it is made the vehicle for a misogynist slur. Likewise, the old joke about the classics being risqué and therefore unsuitable for women readers, which was humorous enough when it poked fun at English prudery in *Thespis*, falls flat in *Princess Ida*, where it is meant to show feminine squeamishness even in the female don.

In other words, *Princess Ida* ridicules, from the very beginning, the utopian vision of the women's university, which in Tennyson's poem is vividly and sympathetically portrayed (until it is abolished). In *Princess Ida*, the women's aims are regarded as, at best, naïve and self-contradictory, and, at worst, hypocritical. For example, Lady Blanche's fierce competitiveness belies the feminist intention to share knowledge without competition, while the Amazonian servants, the Daughters of the Plough, belie the feminist intention to abolish class distinctions. (The Daughters of the Plough also figure in Tennyson's poem, where they play a more dignified part in the action.) All the other traditional anti-feminist stereotypes are trotted out: feminists have no sense of humor; they talk too much; their thinking falls short of rationality; and they hate men. As Lady Psyche teaches:

Man will swear and Man will storm—
Man is not at all good form—
Man is of no kind of use—
Man's a donkey—Man's a goose—
Man is coarse and Man is plain—
Man is more or less insane—
Man's a ribald—Man's a rake—
Man is Nature's sole mistake!

Lady Blanche is even harsher, sternly dealing out absurd punishments: to one girl for having brought chessmen into the female precincts of Castle Adamant, to another for having sketched a perambulator. Her "reasoning" powers are entirely self-interested; her lecture on "Abstract Philosophy" advances all three of its hypotheses ("The Is, the Might Be, and the Must") to assert that she will replace Ida as head of the university. In the heat of battle, when Blanche discourses on "the Needful" and "the Superfluous," her pseudo-philosophical speech encodes mere prudish dither about female dress codes.

Even Ida's own argument about the superiority of woman is a parody of feminine illogic:

Man, whose brain is to the elephant's
As Woman's brain to Man's—(that's rule of three),—
Conquers the foolish giant of the woods,
As Woman, in her turn, shall conquer Man.

That evolutionary argument will become important later in the opera, but after its proudly logical assertion (with its silly citation of the "rule of three"), her logic degenerates. Woman excels in math, because household math, equal to every feminine occasion, can prove that two and two make three or five. Woman excels in diplomacy, for a diplomat can wheedle a monarch, but a woman can wheedle the diplomat. Woman excels in social interaction, for men would rather spend time with a woman than with other men. Woman excels in argument: "Why, tyrant Man himself admits / It's waste of time to argue with a woman!" If women do not succeed in conquering men, she concludes, they will punish men by no longer caring how they look. In other words, Ida is ridiculed for being "strong-minded" *and* for not being strong-minded.

Princess Ida lacks the usual Gilbertian play with genres and stereotypes. Since the strong-minded woman was an entrenched stereotype by 1884, one would have expected a parody of it, and this topsy-turvy version does make fun of conventional femininity. But, as Jane Stedman argues, "it was [Gilbert's] habit to show the fallacious or absurd bases of what his contemporaries took seriously. Yet the subject of a female college offered no real fallacy in itself, while a great many Victorian males took it anything but seriously." As she points out, one reviewer complained that "in a burlesque one expects everything to be topsy-turvy, whereas Tennyson's world was topsy-turvy to begin with."[45] Although the opera had—and still has—its staunch defenders, many critics have claimed that *Princess Ida* was simply out of tune with its times. What may have been funny in 1870 was no longer funny in 1884. Queen's College, London, the first institution of higher education for women, had been established in 1847, the year Tennyson published *The Princess*. A movement on behalf of higher education for women had gathered strong momentum since the 1860s, and the first women's colleges at Cambridge and Oxford were established as a result: Girton College in 1869, Newnham College in 1871, and Somerville Hall and Lady Margaret Hall in 1878. Westfield College, which some have cited as the model for Castle Adamant, opened in London in 1882. By the time *Princess Ida* premièred two years later, the ridicule of higher education for women seemed distinctly out of date.[46] But the failure of the dialogue has as much to do with genre as with historical timing. In its burlesque setting, the misogynist jokes could have been understood as conventional, since burlesque aims to be politically incorrect. In that generic setting they are, at least, legible as jokes; in their new generic setting, they are not so clearly legible.

After all this has been said, several features in *Princess Ida*'s libretto deserve praise. The new lyrics add to characterization and plot, as Savoy lyrics always do, and several songs make a burlesque caricature more amusing as a character. Gama's patter song in act 1 ("If you give me your attention, I will tell you what I am"), another in the series of autobiographical self-revelations, is a good example. (As Isaac Goldberg points out, "the upward skip from the second to the seventh of the scale, at the words 'such a disagreeable man,' with the climax on 'disagreeable,' is one of Sullivan's deftest touches" of musical wit.)[47] Similarly, Ida's brothers' lyrics make their characterizations amusing, since they engage in the parody of dense, old-fashioned masculinity that we have seen before in *Patience* and *Iolanthe*:

> We are warriors three,
> > Sons of Gama, Rex.
> Like most sons are we,
> > Masculine in sex.
> . . .
> Politics we bar,
> > They are not our bent;
> On the whole we are,
> > Not intelligent.

The song's wonderful musical setting swirls behind the words' stolidity. Like the Police with their "Tarantara!" in *The Pirates of Penzance*, the Dragoon Guards singing about their uniforms in *Patience*, and the Peers parading about in *Iolanthe*, these masculine types are childish,

> . . . longing for the rattle
> > Of a complicated battle—
> For the rum-tum-tum
> Of the military drum
> > And the guns that go boom! boom!

One might want to suggest that *Princess Ida* intends a critique of masculinity in both men and women. But Ida's brothers offer what the female characterizations do not: a successfully funny inversion of type. In act 3, when they are expected to fight, they cower and hesitate, taking off the costume of the manly warrior. It seems that they are overdressed in masculinity:

> This helmet, I suppose,
> Was meant to ward off blows,
>   It's very hot,
>   And weighs a lot,
> As many a guardsman knows,
> So off that helmet goes.

As Williamson points out, this song engages in a parody of Handel in order to emphasize the mock-heroic lyrics.[48] Piece by piece, they strip off their armor, taking off the cuirass, the brassets, and the leg pieces (whose name they cannot remember), while dilating knowingly, like Major-General Stanley, on not knowing the specialized jargon of the military past. Undressing signifies their shedding of an expected martial masculinity (figure 8.3).

FIGURE 8.3 Martial masculinity undermined by Princess Ida's brothers. Lithograph by "G. R.," for cover of the sheet music for *Princess Ida Lancers* (1884), arranged by Charles Coote. (Collection of Fredric Woodbridge Wilson)

Even more brilliant than these witty characterizations is the thematic linkage of the undressing of Ida's brothers to the cross-dressing of their three counterparts, both of which represent forms of emasculation. Much commentary has focused on the idea that Gilbert and Sullivan broke their own rule against cross-dressing in *Princess Ida*, but that is not precisely the case, since the rule applied to actors and actresses, not to characters, for whom cross-dressing is an element of the plot (and in academic robes, at that, which cover up their princely tights and doublets). Nevertheless, as in *Iolanthe*, the cross-dressing alludes to a convention that had been ruled out as a matter of genre, and thus preserves the memory of it even under erasure.

In the burlesque *Princess*, as in Tennyson's *Princess*, the cross-dressing is part of an explicitly premeditated plot to invade Castle Adamant. In *Princess Ida*, however, Hilarion and his friends stumble into their transvestism, get caught at it, and then get caught up in it. While playfully trying on the collegiate robes of "lady undergraduates," Florian and Cyril engage in the salacious cross-gender fantasy that they are seeking sanctuary behind the walls of the university in penitence for "deeds there's no undoing." In other words, they raise and enjoy the fantasy of female sexual misconduct. This prompts them to try on—figuratively speaking—the whole range of feminine types: "Haughty, humble, coy, or free." Suddenly, they are interrupted at their play by Princess Ida and forced to maintain the masquerade. Thus their cross-dressing is accidentally achieved and its illicitness is disavowed, even though the scene is framed with sexual implication. On the spot, Hilarion improvises the story that they are three female students who wish to join the university, and the scene then becomes loaded with burlesque byplay: they forget to curtsey; they claim to be "homely ladies"; they laugh heartily and are "unseemly in their mirth"; they revel in the suggestive double meanings made possible by the princess's seeking their promise to "love" their fellow students and never to marry any man. And so, frequently reminding us that they are men, "the plunge is taken" and "willy-nilly, [they are] maidens now."

In a further integration of thematic material, Gilbert linked the opera's evolutionary argument more firmly with the idea of cross-dressing than he had in *The Princess*. For it is within the context of male-to-female cross-dressing that Lady Psyche sings her song about "Darwinian Man." Like the "Junction Song" in *Thespis* and the fable of "The Magnet and the Churn" in *Patience*, "A Lady fair, of lineage high" ("The Lady and the Ape") offers a little embedded allegory of the work as a whole. As in *Thespis*, the frame around the song makes this intention clear, for it is provoked by Psyche's discovery of her brother dressed as a woman. The young men attempt to divert her with their teasing banter, trivializing her position as a don (and an adult) by reminiscing about her pedantic nature as a child. Like Lilia in Tennyson's poem, Psyche tries to shake off their patronizing jests. Explaining why the women have "renounce[d] mankind," she propounds her theory of evolution:

> We are all taught, and, being taught, believe
> That Man, sprung from an Ape, is Ape at heart.

Lady Psyche's novelty song then tells the story of an ape who fell in love with a maiden, but the maiden rejected his advances (figure 8.4). In an attempt to "rise in the social scale" so that he might pursue her, the ape shaved his bristles and dressed up as a man. Thus the young men's dressing as women is directly linked to the ape's dressing up to "ape" man. The displacement of gender and class issues within this interspecies scenario is clear enough. Through an explicit question—Can an ape imitate (and therefore become) a man?—other implicit questions are also raised: Can men imitate (and therefore learn to be) women? Can the lower classes "rise in the social scale" by dressing up and imitating their betters? The song answers these questions in the negative; in this little fable, biological essence trumps socialization. Gender and class are biologically determined. The moral of the story is that the ape remained "the apiest Ape that ever was seen":

FIGURE 8.4 "Darwinian Man." Drawing by Bab [W. S. Gilbert] to accompany "The Lady and the Ape," in *Songs of a Savoyard* (1891). (Collection of Fredric Woodbridge Wilson)

And to start in life on a brand-new plan,
He christened himself Darwinian Man!
 But it would not do,
 The scheme fell through—
For the Maiden fair, whom the monkey craved,
 Was a radiant Being,
 With a brain far-seeing—
While a Darwinian Man, though well-behaved,
At best is only a monkey shaved!

The theme of evolution first figures prominently in Tennyson's *Princess*, also in the context of cross-dressing, as we have seen. In the poem, Psyche's argument emphasizes the potential of man to improve. First monster, then savage barbarian "crushing down his mate," in the future man might be capable of an equitable, mutual relation between the sexes. Psyche's purpose in setting forth her evolutionary theory is very high indeed, nothing less than "the secular emancipation . . . of half this world." In this vision, the utopian feminist future, the great "to-be," will rise on the bones of past barbarism. In *Princess Ida*, however, the utopian feminist "to-be" has devolved into Lady Blanche's ambitious "must" and Lady Psyche's jaunty comparison between man and ape. In Tennyson's version of Psyche's theory, culture emerges from nature to drive further evolution; but in *Princess Ida*, nature is all.

In Tennyson's poem, female maturity is signified by the desire for a child— or an infantilized man—to care for. But in Gilbert's versions, female maturity is signified by heterosexual attraction. "The Lady and the Ape" diverts this point briefly into burlesque banter. But directly after the song comes the revelation of feminine "nature." In *Princess Ida*, as in Tennyson's *Princess*, Melissa is the chief spokeswoman for an essential heterosexuality. She has never seen a man, and yet she is immediately attracted. The ape's bristles would be no impediment to winning this maiden, for Melissa is fascinated by the marked features and hard chin of the male; she very much likes his beard. Rapturously, she discovers that men are "quite as beautiful as women are! / *As* beautiful, they're infinitely more so!" she exclaims, reveling in her discovery of graphic sexual difference. Then follows the quintet in which Psyche, Melissa, and the three young men nail down the message. Melissa sings:

My natural instinct teaches me
 (And instinct is important, O!)
You're everything you ought to be,
 And nothing that you oughtn't, O!

This paean to nature ponders how "The woman of the wisest wit / May sometimes be mistaken, O!" Princess Ida has been wrong, it seems. The song's refrain ("The truth is found—the truth is found!") refers to the truth of heterosexual attraction. Taking his hint from *The Princess*, Gilbert used the metaphor of voice registers to signify the power of biological sex to trump any social attempt to disguise or deny it. Melissa tries to conceal the identities of the cross-dressed young men from her mother, but Lady Blanche immediately penetrates the disguise, not by seeing, but by hearing that "Two are tenors, one is a baritone!" Even when visual signs break down, the fundamental sound of sexual difference will inevitably come out. On this, the resolution of the opera will turn.

Cross-dressing, in other words, both frames and provokes Melissa's discovery of sexual difference. Deepening the opera's debate between nature and culture, Melissa asks in fascinated amazement if they really are young men, and Florian answers that they "hope by dint of study to become, / In course of time, young women." But, of course, like the ape's attempt to become a man, "it will not do." Men cannot "evolve" into women by cultural means, whether through dress or education, nor do they really want to. The implication is clear: neither should women attempt to "evolve" into men through dress or education. Like the Dragoon Guards in *Patience*, who are so essentially masculine that they cannot assume the poses of effeminate aesthetes, Hilarion and his friends cannot remain disguised in female dress. As surely as masculine beauty will attract Melissa, masculine barbarity will burst out. Their burlesque antics and double entendres are only the prelude to Cyril's outburst, here called a "kissing-song," which he attributes to Hilarion. The song praises reticent and "blushing" roses as opposed to "bold and gay" sunflowers and hollyhocks, concluding that womanly "shame-a" sets his heart "aflame-a!" In other words, conventional feminine modesty provokes male lust; outspoken women, with their tongues that go "clang-a," are not sexually attractive. In all three versions, Cyril's song may be read as an eruption of ungoverned masculinity; in its extreme form, masculinity may be crude, but it is irrepressible. And Cyril's outburst is the immediate cause of the disruption of Ida's university. In all three versions, it is after Cyril's song that Ida falls into the stream and must be rescued, the "men in women's clothes" are arrested or expelled, and the walls of the castle are breached by Hildebrand's forces.

During the ensuing war between the sexes, act 3 relentlessly pursues the essential nature of gender. The Girl Graduates are meek and terrified: "Do not hurt us, if it please you! . . . Maids are we—maids are we!" Whatever martial bravery they may have learned would now be only an act or a disguise, and they simply cannot put it on. Just as men may dress as women but cannot "by dint of study" become women, women cannot by dint of study learn to wage war. The very idea of dressing more lightly in order to keep the limbs free for fighting provokes Lady Blanche's hysterically abstract discourse about dress impropriety; the "lady surgeon" will cut off limbs and heal wounds only "in theory," not in practice; the lady fusiliers will not carry their guns, for fear they might go off; the military band fakes sick and will not play; and Lady Psyche falls back on thoroughly conventional, feminine means of fighting, recommending eyes that flash their rage and tongues that blow up the enemy.

This war between the sexes is not the serious war of Tennyson's poem. Instead, Hilarion bases his confidence on his own heterosexual attractiveness: "[W]e will use no force her love to gain, / Nature has armed us for the war we wage!" But his idea of "Nature" includes culture, specifically the art of courtship, for he will be armed with "expressive glances," "pops of Sillery," "sweet urbanity," "such frivolity," "verbal fences," and "ballads amatory." Even the prince's violently anti-feminist father, who would like to "storm the lady" rather than "sue politely," refuses to negotiate "to fit the wit of a bit of a chit." (The staccato of this itchy rhyme might have been funny, if it reflected a parody of Hildebrand's patriarchal anti-feminism, but unfortunately it simply sounds like the general anti-feminism of the rest of the dialogue.) The brilliant scene of Ida's brothers undressing also emphasizes the parodic deflation of serious war while making its point about gender, too.

As in Gilbert's *Princess*, Hilarion wins the battle. Ida yields to him (and to their fathers).[49] Everything happens too fast, and the conclusion is incompletely rationalized, to say the least. But unlike other sudden endings in the Savoy operas, this one is not funny, nor does it turn on a genre parody. In the end, the maiden will marry the ape after all. As in *The Princess*, Hildebrand poses the question that resolves the plot:

> But pray reflect—
> If you enlist all women in your cause,
> And make them all abjure tyrannic Man,
> The obvious question then arises, "How
> Is . . . Posterity to be provided?"

Perhaps it is meant to be amusing when Ida, who has thought of so much else, replies "I never thought of that!" and quickly yields to her "fate." Unlike *Iolanthe*, which offers a parodic inversion of the "myth of matriarchy," *Princess Ida* sticks closely to that myth, providing a justification for patriarchal rule. Volunteering to become an experimental subject for female scientific mastery ("mould us as you will"), Hilarion uses the supposed evolutionary inferiority of men as an argument for women returning to normal gender relations; the masculine posture of being "grosser clay" returns the feminine to her "divine" status. As in the episode of cross-dressing, the prince adopts a subservient position in order to restore his dominance.

Lady Blanche will take over the university, which will continue, albeit under the (mis)rule of an overly ambitious, overly abstract, pseudo-intellectual woman. Blanche is not a parody of the Dame figure, as we have seen, but an example of that figure of denigration, signaled in part by her being insulted to her face. As in *The Princess*, an odd misogynistic series of burlesque insults prepares for the famous last words. First Gama insults his own daughter through her mother, posing the conundrum about posterity yet again:

> Consider this, my love, if your mamma
> Had looked on matters from your point of view
> (I wish she had), why where would you have been?

This casual, parenthetical slur against his wife implies that Gama wishes that Ida had never been born. Especially gratuitous since it comes at the end, this outburst of burlesque humor is redoubled in the misogynistic horror that Blanche might "discourse for hours" on the subject. Princess Ida herself puts Lady Blanche down.

Then she turns to Hilarion to apologize for her "error," exhorting him to their future noble partnership by quoting the end of Tennyson's *Princess*. In what Alan Fischler calls an "unblushing endorsement of Nature's dictates," "a genuflection to the sex drive,"[50] the opera ends:

> It were profanity
> For poor humanity
> To treat as vanity
>   The sway of Love.

If *Iolanthe* shows that women can remain on top, *Princess Ida* shows that they cannot. But the failure of *Princess Ida* is due to its genre trouble as much as to its gender trouble. *Iolanthe* launches a successful parody of fairy extravaganza, but *Princess Ida* merely reproduces the conventions of burlesque, framing them within the context of comic opera.

Part III. Cultures

9

Estrangement and Familiarity

The Mikado

The plots of *Iolanthe* and *Princess Ida* use gender to represent graphic cultural difference; masculine and feminine realms are radically distinct, each operating under its own system of law. This consideration of the separate spheres, as if they were actually separate cultures, was not entirely new, for it was prefigured in *Trial by Jury* and *H.M.S. Pinafore*, when the female Choruses of Bridesmaids and of Female Relatives sweep into the male precincts of courtroom and ship. But the examination of gender in *Iolanthe* and *Princess Ida* does point directly toward the late Savoy operas, most of which focus on culture as such: English culture, of course, but also other cultures, cultural difference, and the encounter between cultures. Thus the focus on gender as culture prepares the way for the cross-cultural thinking of the late Savoy operas, beginning with *The Mikado; or, The Town of Titipu* (1885). If in earlier operas, gender difference could represent cultural difference, now cultural difference is sometimes used to represent gender difference. With this shift in emphasis, in other words, the focus on gender is not forgotten.

From the beginning, Savoy opera was engaged with the question of what it meant to be English. Even before Gilbert and Sullivan settled into their formula, *Thespis* twists the English classical extravaganza together with the French opéra bouffe, in parody versions that work toward a specifically English critique and a specifically English genre. *The Sorcerer*, then, makes its quintessential Englishness felt when the magical love potion is served from a teapot. *H.M.S. Pinafore* humorously examines the "customary attitudes" that make the Jolly Jack Tar recognizable as a type and pokes fun at English pride in national identity, as if it were chosen "in spite of all temptations /

To belong to other nations." *The Pirates of Penzance*, too, clearly revolves around peculiarly English institutions, with its arch concluding homage to the queen and the peerage. David Cannadine, who has written brilliantly on the history of the rise and fall of Savoy opera as a national institution, nevertheless underestimates the degree to which parody is a formative force in the operas' self-conscious Englishness.[1] The operas were self-reflexively and parodically involved in marking their place within national culture all along. But, as John Wolfson has pointed out, the later operas increasingly have non-English settings: Venice and Barataria in *The Gondoliers*; a South Sea island in *Utopia, Limited*; and a small, middle European duchy, roughly German, in *The Grand Duke*.[2] Even *The Yeomen of the Guard* can be seen in this light, if we take into account its setting in the sixteenth century, for England's mythic past is represented with all the markings of cultural difference.

After *The Mikado*, the genre was fully formed, and the dynamic of genre parody would no longer structure the coherence of the whole—except in *Ruddigore* and, to some extent, *The Grand Duke*. In addition, the gendered, divided Chorus would receive less emphasis as a structuring principle in the late operas.[3] But we must remember that Gilbert and Sullivan's critical thinking about gender led directly to their late concern with culture. In *The Mikado* and after, the operas turn outward in order to reflect on the interior. They look at English culture through an ethnographic mirror.

"The Town of Titipu"

At the time of its first production, no one thought that *The Mikado* was meant as a serious representation of Japan. Reviewers fully registered, without confusion or ambivalence, the opera's intent to make fun of English culture. The reviewer for the *Monthly Musical Record* expressed this awareness succinctly: "[T]hough nominally Japanese, the allusions are more or less thinly veiled sarcastic references to our native institutions and peculiarities."[4] Nevertheless, the cultural politics of the opera's reception have raised questions ever since. For example, *The Mikado* was censored in 1907 before the state visit of Crown Prince Fushimi of Japan. Several members of Parliament spoke out against this measure, some alluding to the "Gilbertianism" of the real-life situation. Its music played widely all the while the play was prohibited, even on Japanese warships, providing a sort of musical commentary on the absurd situation. One distinguished Japanese journalist, asked to view and evaluate a performance of the opera, noted that the representation was an utter fantasy, nothing like Japan, but the ban continued for six weeks nevertheless.[5] In our own time, this issue has again come to the fore, as some productions of *The Mikado* have been met with protests about its putatively trivializing—or even racial—slurs against Japanese culture.[6]

Again, we come up against the problems of recognition raised by parody, problems that become even more vexed and delicate within a cross-cultural framework. Because parody must imitate its object, it can be mistaken for a straight representation. What happens when parody imitates its object in disguise, in costume, in masquerade? In *The Mikado*, for example, English culture, the object of the parody, is represented not through a twisted imitation or exaggeration of English ways, but through a projection or displacement of them. The strangeness of the opera's fictive "Japan"—as most viewers of *The Mikado*, then and now, have understood—then turns its mirror to reflect England. Thus *The Mikado* presents an autoethnographic project, through which English culture is defamiliarized, yet remains familiar: a fantasy culture where genteel respectability is so important that one could be executed for flirting, where bureaucracy's various departments have proliferated to the point of absurdity, and where a legal fiction could cause something that has not been done to be "as good as done."[7] The bizarre legal code of Titipu, a brilliant invention, reminds the opera's audiences that from an outsider's perspective, any culture can seem absurd—and this perspective can be taken on the home culture, too. Cultural conventions, utterly taken for granted by an insider, are thus best illuminated under an estranging light.

So *The Mikado* parodies English ways. But how do we know? One clue is that the "gentlemen of Japan" in the opening Chorus of Nobles make it clear that they derive from art, not from life: "On many a vase and jar— / On many a screen and fan," they "figure in lively paint." In this sense, the characters acknowledge that they have sprung to life from collected artifacts and that the Japanese setting of the opera is literally a façade, a "screen" in several senses of the term: a screen that divides one space from another while it connects them; a screen that conceals while it reveals; and a screen onto which an image can be projected. On this Japanese screen, a twisted vision of England is projected. When the gentlemen of the Chorus accuse the audience of thinking that they "are worked by strings, / Like a Japanese marionette," they make the point that the customs of other cultures look oddly compulsive and nonsensical from an insular point of view, and they proceed to educate the Savoy audience ("You don't understand these things: / It is simply Court etiquette"), teaching a little lesson in cross-cultural awareness that also cuts against the difference between high and low culture.

There are many other clues to this intent in the text, remarks that could be made only from an English point of view. My own particular favorite is

Ko-Ko's way of disclaiming all knowledge of Nanki-Poo's true identity: "It might have been on his pocket-handkerchief, but Japanese don't use pocket-handkerchiefs! Ha! ha! ha!"[8] These effects can also be felt in the music—in the way the Lord High Executioner's entrance music echoes "A Fine Old English Gentleman," for example, or the way Nanki-Poo carries "*a native guitar*," but sings distinctly English songs. Of course, the point of view of Ko-Ko's famous patter song, the "little list" of "society offenders who might well be underground, / And who never would be missed," is quintessentially Victorian. In Titipu (unlike on the island of Utopia in *Utopia, Limited*), no actors and actresses come on the scene in English dress, to enact an encounter between two cultures. Partly because everyone *looks* "Japanese," we can deduce that no one is "really" Japanese.

Although we are clearly not in Japan, touches of visual authenticity seduce the gaze and destabilize the reflexive reference to England. This devotion to the realism of the spectacle is evident in *Trial by Jury* and *H.M.S. Pinafore*, where the cross between fantasy and realism heightens the absurdity. From *The Mikado* on, however, visual splendor heightens the fantasy instead of the absurdity (and for that reason, it has been criticized).[9] The gorgeous Japanese-style costumes were elaborately fashioned of fabric from Liberty & Company, known at the time for its history of trading in Japanese artifacts. Some costumes were antiques, imported from Japan. The ensemble was trained in authentic Japanese gestures, especially in the celebrated fan work of the Chorus of School-girls. To achieve that aura of authenticity in body language, Gilbert famously consulted the inhabitants of the Japanese Village in Knightsbridge, who were brought in to instruct the cast. That rehearsals had been conducted under the auspices of real Japanese people was announced in the program, and several reviewers mentioned this preparation in their reviews. But Jessie Bond, the popular Savoy ingénue, whose role as Pitti-Sing catapulted her into stardom, pushed against the Japanese idiom by using both her body and her costume to reassert the joking English point of view; she had her obi made twice as big as those of the other two little maids and waggled it ostentatiously behind her.

Language, often an explicit focus of cross-cultural forces in Savoy opera, contributes to the cross fire of authenticity and estrangement. The idea that "foreign" languages sound absurd dovetails nicely with the opera's defamiliarization of customs, gestures, and body language. At the end of act 1, when the Chorus attempts to drown out Katisha's revelation that Nanki-Poo is the son of the Mikado, they sing Japanese words: "Oh ni! bikkuri shakkuri to! oya! oya!" Although these words really are Japanese, they are strung together nonsensically; as Earl Miner points out, they may be freely rendered as "You devil! with fright, with hiccups! hey! hey!"[10] Nevertheless, their opacity lends an air of estranging authenticity. In addition, "The March of the Mikado's Troops" (Miya sama) evokes a mysterious, other-cultural pomp. "Miya sama" was a relatively recent composition at the time of Sullivan's use of it, written in 1867/1868 during the Meiji Restoration as an aid to conscripts with little training, who had to learn to march in step.[11] Miner offers a translation, in order to disprove the rumor that the song is obscene. Admitting that the text is corrupt, he argues that it probably means something like this:

> Honored prince, Honored prince
> What does this mean—
> This business of fluttering
> About before the ladies?
> Hey nonny, nonny, nonny, hey![12]

In other words, "Miya sama" is a real Japanese song, with a nonsense refrain.[13] Sullivan probably got the music from A. B. Mitford, author of the well-known *Tales of Old Japan* (1871).

After Sullivan went to see Mitford, Paul Seeley explains, he began to show a Japanese influence in the music, "thinking more in pentatonic or near-pentatonic phrases and motifs."[14] Thus the music—as well as the costumes, gestures, and language—offers its authenticating Japanese touches. The reviewer for the *Monthly Musical Record* mentioned "the 'local colouring' which might be expected in a work dealing with a people whose musical scale is divided into twenty-three portions instead of our chromatic thirteen." (He regarded Japanese harmony as "barbaric," so was pleased that it "has been sparingly used.") The same reviewer pointed out that these Japanese motifs take their place within Sullivan's characteristically encyclopedic reference to European musical styles, "of Balfe, Bishop, Gounod, Weber, Verdi, Bellini, Offenbach, or even of Sullivan's other songs," making it clear that the European multicultural pastiche was appreciated even before the addition of musical elements from farther afield.[15]

The generic allusiveness in the music is embodied in Nanki-Poo's self-introduction, "A wandering minstrel I," in which his character comes forward as an anthology of English song styles—sentimental, patriotic, nautical. Like a songbook collection, Nanki-Poo has something for every occasion, and this song demonstrates the Savoy operas' self-consciousness about genre parody in the music. Alluding to a phrase from *Hamlet* in "A thing of shreds and patches," Nanki-Poo harks back to the burlesque tradition (substituting "thing" for "king") while resuscitating Shakespeare's own allusion to the figure of Vice from the ancient mysteries, who was dressed in the ragged king's disguise. But in *The Mikado*, to be "A thing of shreds and patches, / Of ballads, songs and snatches," is to be composed of bits and pieces of various musical styles, recollected together, each available at a moment's notice. In this sense, Nanki-Poo becomes a figure for the Savoy operas' music in general. Carl Dahlhaus makes a similar point: "[W]hen, at the opening of *The Mikado*, the emperor's son, disguised as a minstrel, offers in succession a sentimental ballad, a bombastic patriotic anthem, and a sailor's chantey for no particular reason and with no relation to the dialogue, the scene is turned into a parody of Savoy opera itself, which thrives on stylistic quotation."[16]

If Nanki-Poo's song—like the faux-Japanese setting—suggests that national identity can be "put on" and "taken off" (like a costume, like a burlesque parody), then at a certain point it must be stressed that it is precisely *English* national identity that most often travels far and wide. Within the context of empire, any place can suddenly turn into, or turn out to be like, England. This, indeed, is one of James Buzard's chief arguments in his exploration of the effect of empire on the development of an autoethnographic perspective in Victorian fiction. Although neither the anthropological concept of "culture" (the term for a complex and systematic whole) nor the anthropological concept of "cultures" (the term, in the plural, that stresses their difference from one another) had been explicitly formulated in the nineteenth century, these perspectives were coming into focus.[17] Buzard shows the major Victorian novelists—Dickens, Charlotte Brontë, Eliot—practicing with the dynamic interplay of "inside" and "outside" viewpoints, each interrupting the other. Through their autoethnographic work, Victorian novels "disorient" the fantasy of British universalism.

The late Savoy operas playfully take up these ideas as well. If earlier attitudes about the British Empire had fostered a palpable ethnocentrism—even the belief that British values could or should be universalized—by the late nineteenth century, that bluff confidence was being questioned. Certainly, the Savoy operas make several attempts to provide "inside" and "outside" viewpoints simultaneously, showing English customs not as ideal standards, ready for export, but as one odd variation among the customs and cultures of the globe. Never going so far as to propose a full-fledged cultural relativism, they do make English culture seem quite off-center. In almost all the late Savoy operas, especially *Utopia, Limited*, "the empire looks back"; they are concerned with either the clash of cultures or the dynamic of global cultural exchange. If English culture can go anywhere, while the artifacts of other nations are easily imported and displayed in the metropolitan centers of Great Britain, then what results is a confusing mixture of cultures, very well exemplified by the town of Titipu.[18]

Ever since the Great Exhibition of 1851, an expanding culture of exhibition played a significant role in the British assimilation of things Japanese. The Japanese Village in Knightsbridge is a perfect example of Victorian culture attempting to exhibit not only things, but also practices, from another culture. A sort of ethnographic theme park, the Japanese Village was established in Humphrey's Hall in 1885, absolutely contemporaneous with (and invoked as an important influence on) *The Mikado*. (In the opening-night program, the management of the Savoy Theatre acknowledged "the valuable assistance afforded by the DIRECTORS AND NATIVE INHABITANTS OF THE JAPANESE VILLAGE, KNIGHTSBRIDGE.")[19] A fully active village of some hundred people inside a purpose-built iron-and-glass exhibition hall, the Japanese Village included five streets of houses and shops; a Buddhist temple; niches for craftsmen making textiles and pottery, carving wood, and working with metal and lacquer; demonstrations of wrestling, martial arts, and Kabuki theater; and a fully functioning tea garden (figures 9.1 and 9.2). In other words, the Japanese Village offered the theatrical display of a miniaturized facsimile of Japan within the confines of England.[20] That is why when the Mikado asks Ko-Ko for Nanki-Poo's address, he answers, "Knightsbridge."

The Japanese Village was not the only significant attempt to import Japan to England. Indeed, *The Mikado* offers a parody of Victorian culture's fascination with all things Japanese. In this sense, *The Mikado* is most closely related to *Patience*, not only because it also parodies a current English craze, but also because the vogue for things Japanese was a strong element in aestheticism. Thus by the end of the nineteenth century, Oscar Wilde could jokingly assert—with his own critique of the English point of view—that Japan is nothing but an exotic English fantasy: "In fact the whole of Japan is a pure invention. There is no such country, there are no such people. . . . [T]he Japanese people . . . are simply a mode of style, an exquisite fantasy of art." Like Jean Des Esseintes, the hero of Joris-Karl Huysmans's *À rebours* (*Against the Grain*, 1884), who painstakingly prepares for a trip to England, only to abandon his plan in favor of imaginary travel, aided by reading Dickens, Wilde plays with the idea that "if you desire to see a Japanese effect, you will not behave like a tourist and go to Tokio. On the contrary, you will stay at home and steep yourself in the works of certain Japanese artists."[21] Gilbert's and Wilde's aesthetic use of "Japan" should be distinguished from the Orientalism described by Edward Said,[22] for they make fun of an insular, absorptive projection of Japan as a cultural "other." When the cultural other fails to be wholly other, we have tourism, not anthropology, and imaginary

FIGURE 9.1 Exhibitions at the Japanese Village, Knightsbridge. *Illustrated London News,* February 21, 1885. (Collection of Fredric Woodbridge Wilson)

FIGURE 9.2 "Afternoon Tea at the Japanese Village, Knightsbridge." *Graphic*, March 13, 1886. (Collection of Fredric Woodbridge Wilson)

tourism at that.[23] In an attempt to have it both ways—using Japan as an exotic pretext while not only overtly acknowledging that it is doing so, but also displaying an implied critique of English ethnocentrism—*The Mikado* gives this fantastic place an invented name.

This is the "entertainment" of difficult ideas about customs, manners, and cultural signs—an exercise in reading a foreign semiotic system while acknowledging that reading can fall into self-centered fantasy. This is the junction where a "fascination with Japan" merges with a "fascination with that fascination, that is, to the beginnings of a critical engagement with Britain's own orientalist practices."[24] In the process of engaging the unfamiliar, we see the distortions involved in making it familiar. On most levels, the mind-boggling aspects of this enterprise are, of course, no joke. But *The Mikado* raises serious questions within its silly framework, establishing a duck-rabbit or M. C. Escher sort of aesthetic play with the double perspective of cross-cultural awareness, in which background and foreground are mobilized against each other to the point of dizziness. Its fantastic blending loosens the "reality" of both places simultaneously. Here and there, our culture and theirs, England and Japan are blended through parodic double coding. Thus the setting of *The Mikado* is both Japanese and English—and therefore, it is neither. That, finally, is the point: to create a fantasy realm between the two, the absurd site of their crossing: "the Town of Titipu."

Victorian Japonisme

The Mikado stages a "parody of [Victorian] Japonisme."[25] In this respect, *The Mikado* is closely allied to the parody of aestheticism in *Patience*, since Japanese artifacts were a central element in the eclectic collection of cultural signs that characterize aesthetic high culture. Indeed, Miner humorously suggests that "aestheticism seems to have been composed of two parts of medievalism and one of Orientalism," while Toshio Watanabe devotes a long chapter to "Japanese art as medieval art."[26] That confusion of categories is the sign of aesthetic recollection, for late-nineteenth-century English aestheticism mixed Japanese, Gothic (medieval), early Italian (Pre-Raphaelite), and "Queen Anne" styles.[27] When Lady Jane describes the "cobwebby grey velvet, with a tender bloom like cold gravy," she emphasizes just this mixture of styles: if the Dragoon Guards' uniforms were "made Florentine fourteenth-century, trimmed with Venetian leather and Spanish altar lace, and surmounted with something Japanese—it matters not what—[they] would at least be Early English!" In this ludicrous compendium, eclecticism itself is on display. "It matters not what" the Japanese things actually are, and the culminating touch is the preposterous suggestion that this collection of styles signifies "Early English."

Thus *The Mikado* looks back at *Patience*, in which the vogue for all things Japanese had first been made an object of derision. As we will recall, the recitative introduction to the aesthete's patter song includes Bunthorne's confession that he does "*not* long for all one sees / That's Japanese," although he goes on to instruct would-be aesthetes to "convince 'em, if you can, that the reign of good Queen Anne was Culture's palmiest day." Similarly, when the two poets sing their list of identifying traits, objects, and venues, Bunthorne calls himself

> A Japanese young man,
> A blue-and-white young man,
> Francesca da Rimini, miminy, piminy,
> *Je-ne-sais-quoi* young man!

Again, the odd compendium of Japanese and Pre-Raphaelite motifs, gathered together with a casual French tag ("I-don't-know-what"), makes the point that "Japanese" is only one element in an eclectic collection of objects, places, times, and languages.

But in *The Mikado*, the focus is not on cultural pastiche but on the Japanese element in particular. Using the Orient as a screen for national projection and reflection was not new, but it did take a new form in the latter half of the nineteenth century. As many critics have pointed out, the widespread interest in things Japanese succeeded vogues for Chinese art and poetry in the seventeenth and eighteenth centuries, and for the Oriental tale in the eighteenth and early nineteenth centuries. Considered as a genre, the Oriental tale is notable for its use of cultural difference to establish an outsider's perspective on England.[28] But Victorian Japonisme was specific to the second half of the nineteenth century, after Japan was opened to trade with the West in 1853/1854. Serious Victorian engagement with Japanese art and artifacts dates from the 1850s and 1860s; by the time of *The Mikado*, it had become a craze. As Miner puts it, "the country remains strange, but the very strangeness was familiar."[29]

The legendarily original moment of nineteenth-century Japonisme occurred in 1856 at a print shop in Paris, when Félix Bracquemond became fascinated with the first volume of Hokusai's *manga* (1814). Thus the cultural circulation of things Japanese began with wood-block prints, primarily in the form of *ukiyo-e* (pictures of the floating world), from *ukiyo*, the Buddhist term for "the floating world," which refers both to the fleeting nature of mortal existence and to contemporary urban zones of pleasure and relaxation. The French word for European borrowings from Japanese art, *japonisme*, was not coined until 1872, by Philippe Burty, "to designate a new field of study—artistic, historic, and ethnographic."[30] In other words, the term is broadly inclusive, indicating not only a set of urban fashions, attitudes, and objects, but also a field of scholarship and art production. But before the word was coined, the phenomenon had reached England; the International Exhibition of 1862 in London was the crucial turning point.[31] This exhibition brought together the largest display of Japanese art and artifacts seen in Europe until that time, demonstrating the ethnographic passion for collecting things in order to convey the strangeness of another culture. In addition to prints and illustrated books, the exhibition featured sixty-seven types of paper, specimens of timber, "imitation leather, a straw raincoat, wooden clogs . . . an umbrella, a paper lantern, oilpaper cloth, a wooden pillow, surgical instruments and medicines." The central emphasis was on the "industrial arts": "textiles, ceramics, lacquerware, ivory carvings, enamelwork," screens, porcelain, raw silk and cocoons, cabinetwork, and metalwork, the last including both jewelry and weaponry.[32] Along with the

Exhibition Universelle of 1867 in Paris, to which Japan contributed for the first time, the International Exhibition of 1862 determined that most forms of Japanese art and craft were circulating by the 1870s.[33]

James Abbott McNeill Whistler, unquestionably the most important early figure in the development of English Japonisme, illustrates the conjunction between collecting artifacts and producing "high" art. He brought the vogue from France to England in both respects. Almost all his paintings dating from 1862 to 1870 display the influence of Japanese pictorial art and begin to be signed with his stylized butterfly "chop." Dante Gabriel Rossetti soon entered into a friendly rivalry with Whistler as a collector of things Japanese, and his paintings of the mid-1860s and early 1870s show the Japanese influence as well. Many other aesthetes, including Edward Burne-Jones and William Morris, were known as Japanophile collectors. Oscar Wilde famously decorated his rooms at Oxford with Hokusai prints and blue-and-white china, which he felt he must struggle to "live up to." Thus expert collecting was joined by an amateur, decorative eclecticism, with commodified and collected objects coming to advertise a personal identity, to become "interior" decoration, in both senses of the term. Curio shops all over London and Paris catered to this popular taste. Liberty & Company (then known as Farmer and Rogers of Regent Street and popularly called the Oriental Warehouse) opened in London in 1862.[34] Blue-and-white willow-pattern china became not only a staple of middle-class homes, but also a staple allusion in Victorian literature.[35] The relation of *The Mikado* to this craze is well documented. For example, the reviewer for *Harper's New Monthly Magazine* characterized the opera's setting as "the very world of 'willow pattern' china," while Rutland Barrington, who created the role of Pooh-Bah, called the poses of the Chorus of Nobles "Japanese plate attitudes" (plate 15).[36]

Thus—as in *Patience*—high art and market capitalism are inextricably bound. International trade and consumption participated in building popular cross-cultural awareness.[37] But the high-culture tradition had its own versions as well. Whistler delivered his lecture "Ten O'Clock" on February 20, 1885, just a few weeks before *The Mikado* opened in London. In his talk, he famously compared ancient Greek and Japanese art, with a vatic pronouncement that "the story of the beautiful is already complete—hewn in the marbles of the Parthenon—and broidered, with the birds, upon the fan of Hokusai—at the foot of Fusiyama."[38] Walter Pater had advanced this sort of comparativist idea in his preface to *The Renaissance*, arguing that beauty cannot be defined in the abstract; to the aesthetic critic, "all periods, types, schools of taste, are in themselves equal."[39] In this sort of thinking, we can detect the gradual replacement of a stadial scheme of history (and art history)—which emphasizes chronological development from primitive to civilized—with a spatial, cross-cultural scheme in which cultures distant in time and space can be more neutrally compared, each appreciated on its own terms.[40] This sort of cultural comparison makes the stand on "art for art's sake" possible; form, not content, is the artist's aim and the critic's. Thus in his highly Paterian essay "The English Renaissance of Art," Wilde praises Japanese art for freeing itself from the intellect and devoting itself to pure pictorialism. In this way, the Japanese influence contributed to the development of modernism, by helping to free art not only from "the intellect," but also from illusionistic representation and varieties of realism.[41]

As part of its parody of Victorian Japonisme, *The Mikado* also recollects, recirculates, and parodies stereotypes of the Japanese. Some of them were appreciative, viewing Japan as a peaceable, intelligent, and civilized ancient culture, with dignified ceremonial manners and behavior. But the popular image was complex and contradictory, for some stereotypes were trivializing or denigrating, imagining the Japanese as diminutive, puppet-like, quaint, and jolly, on the one hand, but proud and cruel, on the other. As with the Dame figure, the spectator should imagine that these stereotypes are being inhabited and transformed rather than simply replicated. In other words, *The Mikado* knowingly presents cultural stereotypes as themselves artifactual, part of a genre parody. Through its masculine stereotypes, we can see "Japanese" governmental absurdity proffering the familiar Savoy figure of male professional self-division, consummately represented in Pooh-Bah, whose "identity" is humorously fractured among the various competing departments he represents. Pooh-Bah recycles the character of Baron Factotum, the "Great-Grand-Lord-High-Everything" from James Robinson Planché's *The Sleeping Beauty in the Wood* (1840).[42] And the central conception of the Mikado derives from the conventional pantomime tyrant, perfectly adapted to a parodic Orientalism.[43]

Japanese femininity was a particular object of fascination, stereotyped as elaborately courteous, submissive, sexually alluring, and available. Highly improper to British eyes, but exquisitely proper within her own cultural codes, the figure of the geisha suggests that gender and sexual behavior are determined more by culture than by biological essence, while permitting sexual voyeurism under the cover of cross-cultural curiosity. Interestingly enough, the fascinating Japanese courtesan does not figure in *The Mikado*, but instead we have playful School-girls and the towering Katisha. In other words, both the diminutive and the cruel Japanese stereotypes have been fitted to their English setting, through the opera's examination of femininity. Reviewers at the time of the first production seemed especially sensitive to gender distinctions and their abrogation, one complimenting the three little maids' charming "kitten-like antics," while others complained that the costumes "obliterate[d] the natural distinctions between the sexes." Another critic waxed on about the supposed effeminacy of the Japanese male, citing "the half-feminine courtesy and softness which belong to the cultivated male in the Land of the Rising Sun."[44]

Indeed, the impact of Victorian Japonisme is most forcibly registered on the stage.[45] Earl Miner, among others, argues that *The Mikado* solidifies both a vogue and a genre.[46] Before *The Mikado*, the first known play based on Japanese prints, *L'île de la demoiselle* (1863) by the French artist Zacharie Astruc, was "a fifteen-act play about love and honor, betrayal and banishment, wherein the Mikado's pardon leads to a happy ending." Although Astruc's play was never performed, it was widely read.[47] The 1870s brought many works of Japanese-inspired musical theater, most notably *La princesse jaune* (1872) by Camille Saint-Saëns. In that work, a Japanese painting comes to life, which suggests not only the derivation of life from art, as in *The Mikado's* opening Chorus, but also the genre of the tableau vivant, or "living picture," whose conception would inform *Ruddigore*.

But *The Mikado* was a watershed, after which Japanese theater became a mania. From 1885 until the 1930s, "not a month passes . . . without some journal carrying mention of a Japanese play or an article either on pseudo-Japanese plays or on the real Japanese drama."[48] Like Japanese pictorial art, Japanese drama (both Kabuki and Noh) exerted an important influence on modernist aesthetics. But the chief thread of popular representation was most influenced by *Madame Chrysanthème* (1887), a novel by Pierre Loti, which tells the story of a French naval officer's hiring of a temporary Japanese "wife," whom he later leaves. Unlike her later avatars, Miss Chrysanthemum is a mercenary figure; nevertheless, her tale consolidated popular taste for this plot, and the story of the abandoned Japanese "wife" became an important theatrical subgenre. In Edwin Arnold's *Adzuma; or, The Japanese Wife* (1893), the innocent Adzuma is murdered, caught up within a fierce male rivalry. *The Geisha* (1896) by Sidney Jones (with a libretto by Owen Hall and lyrics by diverse hands) makes simpler use of the stereotypes: a Jolly Jack Tar meets a geisha, but does not marry her, for the language barrier stands in their way. (Carte deplored *The Geisha*, regarding its tremendous commercial success as evidence of the public's devolving taste for the simplistic fun of musical comedy, the successor genre to Savoy opera.) In addition to these popular examples, of course, the same complex of cultural concerns issues most famously in Giacomo Puccini's *Madame Butterfly* (1905), based on a play by David Belasco (which was itself based on a story by John

Luther Long). Again, the Japanese "wife" is abandoned, but because of her child and her suicide, the plot assumes a tragic modality that still performs a cross-cultural critique, insofar as Pinkerton's casual sexual appropriation and abandonment is seen to be analogous to American cultural imperialism.

This vogue has continued in our own day, after being interrupted during and after World War II. Stephen Sondheim's *Pacific Overtures* (1976, with a libretto by John Edgar Weidman) explicitly acknowledges its place as heir to *The Mikado*, especially in "Please Hello," a parody of the Gilbert and Sullivan patter song. Set at the moment when Admiral Matthew Perry's black ships arrive and Japan is forcibly opened to the West, *Pacific Overtures* seizes on the generic story but unfolds it from the Japanese point of view. Sondheim's title ironically refers to American overtures across the Pacific, anything but pacific in intent. Again, gender and sexuality are central to the representation of imperial appropriation and cross-cultural (mis)understanding. In "Welcome to Kanagawa," several girls are brought forward to make the visitors "comfortable," while in "Pretty Lady," two American soldiers mistake a beautiful Japanese woman for a geisha and are attacked by a samurai for their mistake. As in traditional Japanese theater, all the parts are played by men, until the end. David Henry Hwang's *M. Butterfly* (1988) carries forward the idea that gender and sexuality serve to represent national identity and vice versa—and that theatrical transvestism activates a different set of gendered significances in the cross-cultural encounter. Thus both Sondheim and Hwang take a post-*Mikado* tradition and, using its conventional stereotypes, bend it to a serious critique of the nationally differentiated stereotypes of gender and sexuality.

But *Topsy-Turvy* (1999), Mike Leigh's wonderful film about the making of *The Mikado*, argues that many of these concerns are implicit in *The Mikado* itself, especially when it is considered within its ambient culture. Thus *Topsy-Turvy* serves not only as critical commentary on *The Mikado*, but also as a work of serious scholarship, both historical and autoethnographic. Just as Tom Stoppard's *The Invention of Love* (1997) focuses on particular significances of *Patience*, so *Topsy-Turvy* focuses on particular significances of *The Mikado*. One important strand of the film's argument is about the relation among national conventions, gender, and genre.

In a thoughtful set piece of cross-culturalism, the film re-creates the Japanese Village in Knightsbridge. Gilbert's wife, Kitty, insists that they visit it, because "the whole of London will be going." The scene presents Victorian exhibition culture as an estranging confusion of people and objects: "*fans, pots, vases, boxes, etc.*," a woman working a spinning wheel, a calligrapher, a dancer with a fan, a singer playing the shamisen, a martial arts demonstration of two kendo fighters, and a Kabuki drama. Gilbert is clearly fascinated. When they stop at the traditional Japanese teahouse, Gilbert and Kitty comment on the strange green tea.[49] The language barrier—and the attempt to overcome it—adds to the estrangement, for the Gilberts are unable to understand the Japanese waitress when she demands "sixerpen prea." Kitty translates, after having discerned that the waitress is speaking English, whereupon Gilbert gives her the nickname "Miss Sixpence Please." In this exchange, we observe the Gilberts' cross-cultural curiosity mixing with their casual English condescension, especially as their amusement leads to his cultural appropriation. But, clearly, Gilbert has been moved by the strange spectacle. Later, when a souvenir Japanese sword falls from the wall of Gilbert's study, he is shocked into his inspirational conception of *The Mikado*. At least, so would biographical legend have it.[50] The scene is beautifully done in *Topsy-Turvy*. Gilbert's eyes begin to gleam, and the camera pans closer and closer, until suddenly it cuts to the finished production, which seems to have sprung directly out of his twinkling eyes.

But the film's sensitivity to the complexities of Victorian cross-cultural awareness makes itself most saliently felt in its treatment of gender. I will mention only three scenes. In one, the principal male actors in the original production of *The Mikado* lunch together at a metropolitan restaurant soon after General Charles Gordon was killed by the Mahdi's troops at Khartoum. Their conversation turns to a debate about cross-cultural differences in the conception of masculine honor in battle. Rutland Barrington (who created the role of Pooh-Bah) insists that the Mahdi has not played fair. In response, George Grossmith (Ko-Ko) engages in a riff of parodic racism, in order to make the point that Barrington's critique is launched from an ignorant English attitude, which would imagine that "the Hottentot in the desert doesn't play cricket . . . he is as yet hardly able to walk upright, don't you know."[51] Then Durward Lely (Nanki-Poo) reminds his companions that the English militia killed fifty-six families on the Isle of Skye in 1882, thus making two nationally self-reflexive points: the English do not play fair, either, and the nation is internally divided.

Juxtaposed scenes in the ladies' and gentlemen's dressing rooms show that national styles of femininity and masculinity (unsurprisingly) depend on Victorian standards of respectability. In these scenes, both Jessie Bond (Pitti-Sing) and Durward Lely fret about the Japanese costumes they are expected to wear. From an English point of view, they are immodest and indecent, for they do not permit a corset to be worn underneath. She fears for her reputation, while he worries that he will miss the extra diaphragmatic support for his singing voice. Thus we are entertained by variously gendered forms of English fastidiousness, which prevent Bond and Lely from freely assuming the costumed look of the other culture. The ladies' costumier proposes that the obi replace the missing corset, helping to create the shape of a pinched waist (and Bond adopted this "foreign" item to her comic advantage, waggling it behind her like a bustle, as we have seen). Lely, appalled that his minstrel costume is so short that he must show his calves, and assuming a stance of outraged dignity, asks the men's costumier: "May I draw your attention to the fact . . . that I am not actually a Japanese peasant?" At this juncture, Gilbert intervenes, with a point about theatricality: "No, you're a Scotch actor who's taking the part of a Japanese prince who is pos-ing as an itinerant minstrel." Gilbert deflates Lely's pretentions with a point about genre: "[T]his is not grand opera in Milan. It is merely low burlesque in a small theatre on the banks of the River Thames." High-minded concerns for gender propriety have no business in this genre.

A rehearsal for the number "Three little maids from school are we" advances the analysis of the relation among nationality, gender, and genre. In this scene, "Miss Sixpence Please" and other denizens of the Japanese Village teach the three actresses who will play Yum-Yum, Peep-Bo, and Pitti-Sing to act Japanese-feminine. Throughout the scene, gender is shown to be a set of culturally relative, conventional performances; but through its consideration of gender, the scene launches a critique of racist trivializations of "the Oriental" in Victorian burlesque. In the end, because cultural sign systems are conditioned by genre, the scene suggests that prejudiced representations may be malleable, subject to change along with the fluctuating formation of genres. Thus the carefully crafted middle way of Gilbert and Sullivan's genre—lower than high art and grand opera, but higher than low burlesque—bears within itself the power to loosen entrenched stereotypes.

Johnny D'Auban, the choreographer, represents those who are caught up in older-style theatrical conventions for representing "Oriental" manners. When meeting the Japanese women, he *greets them with 'Chinese' bows.* Likewise, his proposed choreography has the three little maids toddling along rhythmically with their heads bobbing from side to side, their elbows akimbo, and their palms held together in an attitude of prayer. In other words, as the stage directions make clear, "*Their gestures are very much in the pantomime 'Chinky Chinese' mode.*" The Japanese ladies are shocked. After many attempts to negotiate the language barrier, Gilbert manages to direct them to show his actresses how to move and gesture correctly. D'Auban watches, but does not understand:

D'AUBAN: I do beg your pardon, Mr. Gilbert, but I appear to have missed the point somewhat.

GILBERT: That is the very effect I need.

D'AUBAN: And what effect exactly is that?

GILBERT: Did you not see what they did?

D'AUBAN: Yes, they walked downstage . . .

GILBERT: They walked downstage *in the Japanese manner*.

D'AUBAN: They walked downstage in the Japanese manner *because they are Japanese*.

GILBERT: Exactly; and that is precisely why they are here.

D'AUBAN: Our three little maids are not Japanese—however, they are very funny.

GILBERT: No funnier, however, than they would be if they all sat down on pork pies.

(*Loud mirth from all.*)

D'AUBAN: Young feller-me-lad, Mr. Gilbert, sir. I've arranged terpsichore—Chinese, Japanese, everybody-wash-your-knees—for pantomime, burlesque and the ballet, for many a season, always to great acclaim.

GILBERT: D'Auban, this is not burlesque, this is an entirely original Japanese opera.[52]

Again, the film emphasizes both the tight relation between gender and nationality, showing that there is no "natural" form of femininity, and the importance of genre as a context for the interpretation of gender performance. Of course, we are meant to notice that Gilbert contradicts his earlier argument, when he ordered Lely to come down off his high horse by saying that *The Mikado* is not grand opera but "merely low burlesque." In this scene, Gilbert claims the opposite: that *The Mikado* represents a higher genre, "an entirely original Japanese opera." Both assertions are correct. Taken together, Gilbert's two seemingly contradictory assertions pinpoint the parodic middle ground that Savoy opera means to occupy.

Laboriously, the Japanese women teach the three actresses how to use their fans, and the long time spent on this lesson makes it all the more thrilling when the film suddenly cuts to the relevant scene in the finished production of *The Mikado*. Yum-Yum, Peep-Bo, and Pitti-Sing come downstage "in the Japanese manner," and they begin to flash and snap their fans. The scene ends with "*the three actresses . . . in the famous pose*." However stereotypical the three little maids may look to us now, the film makes the point that their body language was carefully crafted to be more authentic and more respectful than what had passed for "the Japanese manner" in the theater until then. *Topsy-Turvy* places Victorian theatrical conventions of gender representation within a complex cross-generic framework that argues for a long evolution of cross-cultural thinking and representation that continues to this day.

10

Mixing It Up

Gothic and Nautical Melodrama in *Ruddigore*

rilliant in its conception, *Ruddigore; or, The Witch's Curse* (1887) is nevertheless flawed, as many critics over the years have pointed out. In no other Savoy opera is the genre parody so overt, however, and thus for my argument, *Ruddigore* is very important. It offers a parody of melodrama in general, as Earl Bargainnier points out—stage directions frequently call for things to be done *"Melodramatically"*—but it also attends to several specific subgenres, parodying supernatural melodrama, village or seduction melodrama, and nautical melodrama, by turns.[1] This strategy is one foundation of the opera's humor, which revels in the great variety of melodramatic conventions clashing and pulling in different directions. In other words, the opera's composite parody of several subgenres of melodrama is intellectually coherent, even though it produces a certain amount of intentionally humorous incoherence in performance. After its pyrotechnically exuberant appearance in *Ruddigore*, genre parody would become less central to the Savoy operas, at least until *The Grand Duke*.

The practice of using the divided Chorus to organize the Savoy operas' arguments about gender also would diminish after *Ruddigore*, which displays a strong reminder of this powerful device in its encounter between the Professional Bridesmaids and the Bucks and Blades. A wonderful example of the double Chorus, as well as the Chorus divided according to gender types, the Bridesmaids sing first, welcoming the "gentry." Then, playing to type, the Bucks and Blades announce that they intend to dally with the village maidens. When they are

> . . . thoroughly tired
> Of being admired
> By ladies of gentle degree,

they yearn for the "prettiness rural" that would teach them to become the "slaves" of "Amaryllis . . . Chloe and Phyllis." The Bridesmaids, in turn, sing of their boredom with local "sons of the tillage" and "people of lowly degree." This scene of cross-class attraction, in other words, is staged as a particular sort of sexual encounter, conventional in seduction melodrama, in which rakish gentlemen engage with village maidens, but only "for the moment." Thus when the Bridesmaids' welcome is sung against the rakish intentions of the Bucks and Blades, in the double Chorus, a point is made that speaks to the opera's concerns with both gender and genre. The divided and doubled Chorus embodies—and makes audible—the fact that these groups fit together as two aspects of the conventional seduction plot, like moth and flame. This focused opposition is brief, however; the Bucks and Blades play no real part in the plot, and this double Chorus soon becomes merely one more element in the rampant parody of melodrama. In the work overall, the male and female Choruses are not distinctly organized as a gender opposition. Even though the characterization of the women as Professional Bridesmaids makes its point about gender conventions, the male Choruses of Officers, Ancestors, and Villagers never bring a gendered opposition into focus, except in this scene with the Bucks and Blades.

Billed as an "Entirely Original Supernatural Opera," *Ruddigore* subordinates its other genre parodies to an overarching concern with gothic melodrama. Its original title, *Ruddygore*, made this debt even clearer, leaning toward the charnel house rather than the epistemological or spiritual questions raised by ghostly matters.[2] In serious studies of the gothic, *Ruddigore* is usually relegated to a footnote or an aside, but its parody of gothic conventions is intelligently comprehensive.[3] Specific targets of parody include a witch's curse on an aristocratic family; disturbances in the family's lineage; the Picture Gallery, which represents the past of the family; and the plot of "bad Baronets," dastardly deeds, guilt, remorse, and reform. Within the framework of the witch's curse on the Murgatroyds, the opera's teeming blend (and clash) of genre parodies is organized through the relationship between Sir Ruthven Murgatroyd (in disguise as Robin Oakapple) and Richard (Dick) Dauntless, his foster brother, a sailor deployed on the *Tom-Tit*, a sloop. Their rivalry for the hand of Rose Maybud structures the romance plot, while Robin/Ruthven's efforts to escape the Murgatroyd family curse, correlatively, are based in large part on his wish to marry Rose. Although gothic melodrama predominates overall, most of act 1 is devoted to setting up this romantic triangle, one of whose points is the parody of nautical melodrama.

The clash between gothic and nautical idioms is clearly meant to be the foundation of the humor of *Ruddigore*. To take the most flagrant example: Sir Ruthven/Robin threatens Rose in the lingo of an old-fashioned gothic seducer: "Soho! My pretty one! In my power at last!" In this conventional threat, an evil aristocrat attempts to gain power over a virtuous village girl. But the threat is immediately countered, when Dick produces a Union Jack. "Here is a flag which none dare defy," he proclaims, and "(*all kneel*)."[4] The "glorious rag" is completely out of place as a weapon against the rapacious gothic aristocrat. Of course, the joke is that the display of the flag comes from another subgenre altogether, nautical melodrama. Gothic and nautical were the two major subgenres of early melodrama, as we have seen. Although the two can be—and often are—found together in the same work, Gilbert shows the logical absurdity of their integration. That the spatial setting is "the fishing village of Rederring (in Cornwall)" announces the joke.

The temporal setting of *Ruddigore*, "early in the 19th century," is likewise significant in terms of genre, for at that time, the blending of nautical and gothic melodrama was common. Edward Fitzball's *The Inchcape Bell; or, The Dumb Sailor Boy* (1828) serves as a good example (as does Fitzball's version of *The Flying Dutchman* [1826]). The first two scenes of *The Inchcape Bell* are nautical and gothic by turns, the latter set in "*a Gothic room of the castle, . . . [where] the portraits of a lady and a child [are] hanging up.*" The "dumb sailor boy" of the play's subtitle turns out to be that child, of course, mute because of the abuse he has suffered, in the conventional way of early melodrama. Conventional, too, for these powerless youths, his part was played by a cross-dressed young woman. A veritable treasure trove for exemplifying the mixture of gothic and nautical conventions, this play clearly juxtaposes the degeneration of the aristocracy, the suffering of the underclass, and the exploits of a benevolent Tar. In *The Inchcape Bell*, he takes the form of a captain in the "Preventive Service" who, like Dick Dauntless in his "Revenue sloop," is a guardian of the nation's "duties"—in the double sense of moral obligations and import taxes—against smugglers and other trade outlaws. Furthermore, the villainous smuggler's accomplice in *The Inchcape Bell* turns out to be the aristocrat's illegitimate son, born of a poor and humble maiden who trusted him and whom he seduced and abandoned. The illegitimate son, "the outcast," is called Guy Ruthven. Thus early-nineteenth-century melodrama often depended on a wild mixture of melodramatic purposes, as does *Ruddigore*, and it is against this wild mixture that Gilbert took aim.

Ruthven is the conventional name of an aristocratic vampire in nine-teenth-century literature and theater. First portrayed by Lady Caroline Lamb in *Glenarvon* (1816), Lord Ruthven began as a Byronic hero; then, in John William Polidori's famous short story "The Vampyre" (1819), Lord Ruthven becomes a vampire. Written as a contribution to the legendary ghost-story competition, which also eventuated in Mary Shelley's *Frank-enstein* (1818), Polidori's story was inspired by a fragment about vampires by Byron (and was originally attributed to him). The derivation of the English vampire from the Byronic hero is significant, and many Ruthvens followed, especially in the theater. In James Robinson Planché's *The Vam-pire; or, The Bride of the Isles* (1819–1820), the role of Ruthven, Earl of Marsden, was played by T. P. Cooke, the famous nautical actor (creator of the role of William in Douglas Jerrold's *Black-Ey'd Susan; or, All in the Downs* [1829]). A Lord Ruthven also appears in Heinrich Marschner's opera *Der Vampyr* (1828), which may have influenced the Incantation Scene in *The Sorcerer*. By the time Alexandre Dumas *père* published *The Count of Monte Cristo* (1844–1846), the countess calling Edmond Dantès by the name Lord Ruthven can easily be recognized as a cross-cultural allusion. But perhaps most widely known of all was Dion Boucicault's *The Vampire: A Phantasm* (1852), in which the author played the title char-acter.[5] Not until 1897, with the publication of Bram Stoker's novel, did Count Dracula overshadow Lord Ruthven with another characterization. In other words, Ruthven is like many other Savoy summations of long fig-ural traditions in popular culture (the benevolent Jolly Jack Tar in *H.M.S. Pinafore*, for example, or the aesthete in *Patience*). The notion of an aristo-crat, Ruthven Murgatroyd, disguised as a simple villager, Robin Oakapple, links a joke on vampire gothic to the opera's parodies of seduction, nauti-cal, and domestic melodrama.

The nautical elements in *Ruddigore*, while subsidiary, are blatant enough to be hilarious at times. The character of Dick Dauntless turns the melodra-matic Tar inside out, accomplishing a very different parody than the one focused through the character of Ralph Rackstraw in *Pinafore*. The audience must deduce that Ralph is an exaggeration of the virtuous, benevolent Tar; but Dick, like the outspoken sailor he is, proclaims his generic affiliation, reveling in its conventions. In his self-description, he is "a jolly Jack Tar," and he regards Rose as a "smart little . . . neat little, sweet little,"

> . . . bright little, tight little,
>   Slight little, light little,
>   Trim little, prim little craft!

Although *Pinafore* uses very little nautical metaphor, just enough to drop the hint, Dick peppers his speech with "sartinly," "d'ye see," and other conventional nautical jargon.[6] Unlike Ralph, whose speech is mostly unmarked, showing that he is a candidate for upward mobility, Dick uses vulgar pronunciations ("ax") and bad grammar ("you did *not* ought"). Unlike Ralph, parodic through the exaggeration of the idealized Tar's conventional virtues, Dick is the de-idealized Tar, a parodic inversion of the virtuous Tar: roving, unfaithful, given to drink and swearing, and tattooed up to the shoulder. (Thus he harks back to an earlier characterization of the Tar, before nautical melodrama idealized the character.) He is disreputable, but he is most truly "jolly," and he can dance a hornpipe. Durward Lely, who created the role of Dick Dauntless, was a huge hit dancing to Sullivan's wonderful hornpipe music.

The character of Dick Dauntless also facilitates a parody of the automatic and ungrounded patriotism of nautical melodrama. In his cameo number, "I shipped, d'ye see, in a Revenue sloop," Dick narrates an encounter between his English ship and a French frigate. He is clearly an unreliable narrator, for the idea of a compassionate, "marciful" Revenue sloop, sparing the frigate because the French are so pitiably inferior, is ridiculously overweening, since the English would clearly be overmatched in this confrontation. (A frigate is a warship, while a sloop is only a small sailboat with one mast.) In this song, Dick engages in a blazon of derogatory terms for the French—the "darned Mounseer," the "poor Parley-voo," "Froggee," and so forth—displaying the seamy underside of English nationalism and patriotism. His anti-French sentiment involves the imputation of effeminacy: "to fight a French fal-lal— it's like hittin' of a gal! / It's a lubberly thing for to do." In Dick's view, not only are the French weak and effeminate, but their ways are suspiciously homosocial: "I'll wager . . . they kissed each other's cheek / (Which is what them furriners do)." Clearly, assumptions about gender and sexuality enter into the cross-cultural confrontation. But the thrust of this humor is not against the French, but against common English prejudice and the scurrilous, stupid forms it takes. Bargainnier helpfully calls this "reverse jingoism," for "while enthusiastically praising the British Navy, the song actually describes a cowardly retreat."[7] Dick's ungrounded assertion of British superiority shows the dense, unthinking side of the conventional Jolly Jack Tar.

The visual wit of the opera's genre parody is its tour de force. Even more clearly than *H.M.S. Pinafore*, *Ruddigore* takes up the joke on melodrama's principle of physiognomic legibility. Sir Despard Murgatroyd, for example, is so much the caricature of a melodramatic villain that "*All the Girls express their horror [and] as he approaches them they fly from him, terror-stricken.*" He tells us exactly how to interpret his look and sound. His song in act 1 pokes fun at how very easy it is to read him:

> Oh, why am I moody and sad?
>
> . . .
>
> And why am I guilty and mad?
>
> . . .
>
> Because I am thoroughly bad!
>
> . . .
>
> Oh, why am I husky and hoarse?
>
> . . .
>
> It's the workings of conscience, of course.
>
> . . .
>
> And huskiness stands for remorse.

The rhymes are funny, linking "hoarse" with "remorse" and emphasizing the conventionality of it all ("of course"), the stock melodramatic assumption that guilt will show itself in the visage ("You'll see it at once in my face"), a subset of the interpretive faith that appearances are readable in general.

Thus the melodramatic transformations that take place between act 1 and act 2 show up as humorously and exaggeratedly visual jokes. When Robin must reassume his role as Sir Ruthven, the "bad Baronet," he appears suddenly changed, "*wearing the haggard aspect of a guilty roué.*" Correlatively, Old Adam Goodheart, Robin's loyal servant, has been transformed from the "good old man" of domestic melodrama into the "wicked steward" of the evil aristocrat. The parody of Adam's servile devotion allows for necessary exposition, for the "good old man" cannot but speak out: "[A]s we are here alone, and as I belong to that particular description of good old man to whom the truth is a refreshing novelty, let me call you by your own right title once more! . . . Sir Ruthven Murgatroyd! Baronet! Of Ruddigore!"[8] They enter "*melodramatically*" and speak, throughout the following scenes, "*melodramatically*" as well.

The clever chiasmic plot structure depends on this visual joke about melodramatic visual recognition. As good has suddenly been transformed into an exaggeration of melodramatic evil, so villainy has been transformed into an exaggeration of good. When the curse is transferred to Ruthven, Despard suddenly looks like rectitude personified. Now he adores Mad

Margaret (whom he disliked while he was accursed and "bad"), and both are dressed in Methodist garb. This joke on the melodramatic transformation scene depends not on the revelation of a secret, as at the end of *Pinafore*, but, as at the end of *The Pirates of Penzance*, on the sudden reform of a criminal or villain. Making fun of abrupt changes in identity, these transformations also focus on upward and downward mobility. In act 2, Despard, formerly the "bad Baronet," acts resolutely lower middle class, stressing his affiliation with Dissenting sectarianism.

Along with these transformations in character, the scene shifts from village to castle, where the visual logic of physiognomic legibility is writ large in the family Portrait Gallery.

Living Pictures

At the end of act 1, a stage direction stipulates that Robin "*falls senseless on the stage. Picture.*" The stage direction "*Picture*" refers to the tableau that ended almost every act of a melodrama (and many other nineteenth-century theatrical genres as well). The stage convention of the tableau undergirds the famous setting of act 2, which takes place in the Picture Gallery of Ruddigore Castle, when the family portraits "*are seen to have become animated.*"

Related to the several Victorian genres involving poses and attitudes, tableaux vivants provided a form of middle-class home entertainment in which ordinary people dressed up, took on roles, and posed in a scene familiar to their audience. But tableaux were equally intertwined with the history of nineteenth-century theater, especially melodrama, where they ranged from the sentimental and domestic to the supernatural and terrifying. In every kind of tableau, however, a pause in the dramatic action and a shift in the representational register—from action to stillness, from sound to silence— alerted the audience members to the demand that they read and interpret the picture. Especially interesting in light of the ever-increasing pictorialism of the Victorian stage in general was the tableau "realization," in which actors and actresses suddenly froze into an imitation of a well-known work of art. The most famous use of this convention in melodrama occurs in *The Rent Day* (1832) by Douglas Jerrold, which opens on a realization of the painting of the same name by David Wilkie, dating from 1807. Act 1 then closes on a realization of a related painting by Wilkie, *Distraining for Rent* (1815).[9] Since it depended for its effect on audience recognition, the realization offers cultural evidence of a widespread new form of visual literacy that linked the history of art to the proliferation and circulation of images in the popular press since the 1830s. The development of photography, of course, formed a huge chapter in this history.

The pictorialism of the Victorian stage reached its apogee in Squire and Marie Bancroft's management of the Haymarket Theatre, beginning in 1880, when they transformed the proscenium arch into a gigantic gilt picture frame by extending it across the bottom as well as the sides and top of the stage. Their spectacular gesture merely made explicit the nine-teenth-century history of shrinking the wings and forestage, coalescing that development into one grand summary visual statement. Indeed, the box set, with which Madame Vestris had experimented as early as the 1830s at the Olympic Theatre, became, during the Bancrofts' management of the Prince of Wales's Theatre, the basis for the "cup-and-saucer" or "drawing-room" society comedies of T. W. Robertson. The picture-frame stage, the box set, and the so-called fourth wall, which these conventions established, laid the groundwork for nineteenth-century stage realism. A detailed history of stage realism is beyond the boundaries of this study, but suffice it to say that these developments were profound, for when dramatic representation is arranged as a composition, oriented in planar fashion against the "fourth wall," it separates the audience from the drama, now delimited as a pictorial work of art. The tableau is a microcosmic representation of the increasingly pictorial nature of the Victorian stage itself.

In gothic melodrama, the tableau promotes a particular form of ek-phrasis. Not only can the tableau create suspense, but it can cause art and life to become fruitfully confused. Think of the frozen body of a character fixated with terror or the mutually frozen stares of two characters in the throes of recognition. Now think of a ghost, an apparition, or a dead person coming into visibility in the rear of the stage. In nineteenth-century theater, these effects are perhaps most familiar from Dion Boucicault's *The Corsican Brothers* (1852) and Leopold Lewis's *The Bells* (1871). In the latter, when the tableau of the dead Jew begins to move, a still picture is invested with all the horror of the dead coming back to life, the past coming back to haunt the present. Similarly, family portraits hanging in a gothic castle always sug-gest that the dead are still, in some sense, alive, if only in representation. Like a ghost hovering over present-day complications, a single portrait is a reminder of sin or sorrow that took place before the opening of the drama, conditioning its plot. Or, in the portrait gallery, a series of pictures repre-sents the entire lineage of an aristocratic family. Family portrait galleries make it possible for the history of the family not only to appear in static, visual form, but to be enclosed within the house (which then takes on a slightly allegorical significance as the House). In this respect, a suddenly moving picture represents a revival of the family's past. Of course, that is why the parody of this genre convention in *Ruddigore* is so witty, for just as the baronets step out of their picture frames and come back to life, gothic melodrama is being revived through its parodic rendering.

Before his collaboration with Sullivan, Gilbert wrote a number of plays for the Gallery of Illustration, founded and managed by Thomas and Priscilla German Reed. In our context, the name of their theatrical venue is itself significant, related to both the increasing pictorialism of Victorian theater and the Victorian culture of exhibition. Their claim that the theater was merely a "gallery of illustration" allowed the Reeds to evade various popular forms of anti-theatricality. In one of his best pieces for the Gallery of Illustration, *Ages Ago: A Musical Legend* (1869), Gilbert experimented with the comic potential of the living picture.[10]

The scene of *Ages Ago* is set in the *"Picture Gallery in Glen-Cockaleekie Castle,"* and the plot involves the strangely discontinuous inheritance of that castle, whose title deed can be found only once every hundred years. While its human inhabitants sleep, the castle's portrait gallery comes to life. Lady Maud (painted in the fifteenth century) steps from her frame, looks around her, and fails to recognize the people in the later pictures:

> Am I in the world? And if so, where in the world am I? (*Looking round.*) A picture gallery! Oh, of course, *our* picture gallery. But the pictures. I don't know them. . . . They were not here when I died. Died? Then I'm dead! . . . Then I suppose I'm a ghost! My own ghost! . . . I wonder how my portrait has kept? . . . Let me see, where did it hang? (*Walks up to frame.*) Why the picture's gone. . . . But I came from there just now! I remember distinctly coming from that frame. Then I'm only a picture. Well, I'm glad I'm not a ghost.[11]

After this riff on the gothic equation of portraits and ghosts, other "living pictures" join Lady Maud, engaging in complex flirtations and intrigues. The confusion of art and life takes a particularly Gilbertian turn, involving couples of widely disparate "ages"—with a pun on "ages," for the age of each "living portrait" is determined both by the historical age in which the subject was painted and by the chronological age of the subject at the moment of being painted (figure 10.1). Thus, for example, Lady Maud, who was painted at age seventeen in the fifteenth century, is both younger and older than Lord Carnaby Poppytop, who was painted at age sixty-five in the eighteenth century—and who is attracted to her. If "his grandmama is seventeen, / And he is sixty-five," his situation suggestively combines an old

FIGURE 10.1 Family portraits from various historical periods come to life, step out of their frames, and argue in Gilbert's *Ages Ago: A Musical Legend*, presented at the Gallery of Illustration. Engraving by D. H. Friston, in *Illustrated London News*, January 15, 1870. (Collection of Fredric Woodbridge Wilson)

man's lust for a young woman, the fantasy and horror of regression at the hands of a grand maternal figure, and the threat of incest—all concerns that Gilbert would reprise in the Savoy operas. As in *The Pirates of Penzance* and *Iolanthe*, these issues are deflected by the absurd hyper-logic involved in the numerical play on ages.

Thus the title, *Ages Ago*, alludes to the supernatural ambience of gothic castles and their ghosts, but it also raises complex questions of historical priority and lineage. "Ages" are properties of both persons and historical epochs, and in Gilbert's comic play, aided by the magic of fantasy, they are all mixed up, "living" at the same time and competing for a priority that involves erotic power more than chronological sequence. Who will "marry" whom, thus determining the future of the family lineage? In the end, the middle-aged Dame Cherry Maybud enables Lady Maud to join her age-mate, and she successfully flirts with Lord Carnaby Poppytop herself. (Thus Dame Cherry is a good example of a benign middle-aged Dame figure.) Gilbert's engagement in this parody of gothic melodrama is complex, for both plots—the inheritance of the castle and the erotic intrigues among the living pictures—are resolved by a legal document. Dame Cherry places the title deed on the table, to be discovered when the sun rises; the frame of the story closes; and the living characters in the present awake to find the deed, an uncanny gift from the past. Thus problems of linear inheritance are settled at the same time that the transgressive erotic energies of the past are sorted out and put to rest. The living pictures return to their frames as the story closes, celebrating "the very purpose for which [they had] been revived."

In productions of *Ruddigore*, unfortunately, the scene of the family pictures coming to life often does not work as well as in *Ages Ago*. The stagecraft is usually not up to the challenge of achieving the full effect of the mystery, surprise, horror, and humor. Perhaps, though, the problem rests partly with the music, which is spooky and somber rather than dynamic and frightening. Of the different moods of "supernatural" music, Sullivan's choice was perhaps not the best; "Painted emblems of a race" is funereal, although the pace picks up a bit in "When the night wind howls in the chimney cowls" (which could have been a patter song if set at a different tempo, in a different mood). Somehow the whole scene drags, even though the idea is brilliant. The apparition of Sir Roderic attempts to persuade us of a theoretical humor: "We spectres are a jollier crew / Than you, perhaps, suppose!" As a stage picture about living pictures, however, the scene works brilliantly (figure 10.2).

In other words, *Ruddigore* takes advantage of the generic history of the living picture, literalizing it within the Picture Gallery of Ruddigore Castle. After the living pictures step out of their frames, the dialogue between Sir Ruthven/Robin and Sir Roderic's picture turns on several pointed jokes about the confusion of art and life, before losing energy in the discussion of whether Robin is actually perpetrating the daily crime that was mandated by the witch's curse. In the end, the logic whereby Sir Roderic is returned to life should remind us of the concluding logic of *The Mikado*; Roderic's being "practically alive" is like Nanki-Poo's being "practically . . . dead." He returns from art to life. Through a familiarly absurd Savoy hyper-logic, the ghost has been revived.

Gender, Madness, and Patter

At the Mad Hatter's tea party, Alice begins to suspect that everyone in Wonderland is mad, and later, the Cheshire Cat confirms her discovery that "we're all mad here." Likewise, in *Ruddigore*, Mad Margaret exclaims: "[T]hey are all mad—quite mad! . . . They sing choruses in public. That's mad enough,

FIGURE 10.2 Revival in the Picture Gallery of Ruddigore Castle: "Painted emblems of a race / All accurst in days of yore, / Each from his accustomed place / Steps into the world once more." Engraving by Percy Macquoid, in *Graphic*, January 29, 1887. (Collection of Fredric Woodbridge Wilson)

I think!" While at first her remark may seem simply a self-reflexive allusion to the form of the comic opera—the counterpart, one might say, of Ralph Rackstraw's "I know the value of a friendly chorus" in *H.M.S. Pinafore*—it offers a thematic hint as well. They *are* all mad, in one way or another.

Yet madness seems to be particularly attendant on being female. Central female characters include the neurotically insipid and hyper-correct Rose; the spinsterish Dame Hannah, hysterically defending her virginity; and Margaret, the seduced, abandoned woman gone totally mad. In other words, feminine gender positions are starkly differentiated in *Ruddigore*, but all are determined by the range of relations to the Victorian marriage plot. Given the characterization of the female Chorus as Professional Bridesmaids, it would not be too far-fetched to argue that the opera considers how the pressure to marry, or the failure to do so, might drive a woman mad. Clearly, the naïve, absurdly virtuous girl is destined to marry, although the rules of gender and courtship entangle her in absurdity. Her character is triangulated against two others who have been disappointed in love. Outside marriage, it seems that the scripts of gender allow for only hysterical defensiveness, on the one hand, and full-blown lunacy, on the other. Together with the Chorus, Rose, Hannah, and Margaret offer a comment on the limited spectrum of roles available for women.[12] (A similar structural effect is evident in *Patience*, where female possibility is parsed among the blindly adoring Aesthetic Maidens, the naïve Patience, and the strong-minded Lady Jane.) As Bargainnier points out, each of the three main female characters in *Ruddigore* may be seen as a parody of the heroine of melodrama: the innocent village maiden, the abducted virgin, and the woman gone mad from loss of love.[13] Thus, through the lens of *Ruddigore*, we can remember that melodrama itself scrupulously attends to the pressures related to gender.

The genre parody is not only figural, but a matter of plot structure as well, for Rose is positioned as the central focus of rivalrous male desire, also made the butt of parody. Rose's identity as a character revolves around her nubile potential; like Josephine in *Pinafore*, but in an altogether different tone, Rose acts out the psychomachia of the marriage choice. The libretto cleverly reinforces her destiny to be married by weaving her name into the lyrics. At the very opening of the opera, addressing Rose, the Chorus of Professional Bridesmaids associates her with the feminine waiting game: "Is anybody going / To marry you to-day?" Unlike Rose, who clearly will be chosen, Mad Margaret, reflecting on the fact that she was not chosen ("To a garden full of posies"), figures herself as a violet who is not picked: "For he gathered for his posies / Only roses—only roses!" In other words, the explicit foundation and parody of the marriage plot inheres in the name of the Rose.[14]

All along, the Chorus of Professional Bridesmaids, always "on duty" to promote marriage, emphasizes the opera's hyperbolic, parodic focus on this gendered pressure. They are annoyingly repetitive. Driven almost to distraction in act 1, Robin tries to silence them: "Hold your tongues, will you! . . . Will you be quiet! Go away!" This is one of the best of the Savoy characterizations of femininity, signaling an awareness not only of the social pressure, but also of genre, for the multiple marriages at the end of most Savoy operas are themselves a parodic commentary on the conventional ending of comedy. *Ruddigore*, too, ends with multiple marriages, each couple representing a different taste in marital bliss. But despite the happy ending, the social practices surrounding marriage are subjected to critique throughout the opera.

Like Patience, the character of Rose Maybud makes fun of the simple village maiden. Her name recalls other good girls, the orphan Rose Maylie in *Oliver Twist* (1838) and Mary Maybud, the heroine of J. T. Haines's *My Poll and My Partner Joe* (1835), a well-known nautical melodrama. Like Maggie

Macfarlane in Gilbert's *Engaged* (1877), she studies hard to seem like "a varra, varra gude girl," but she always has her eye on her own advancement. In the character of Rose, Gilbert "rips apart the doll-like heroine of melodrama," with her "unbelievable propriety, . . . unconscious priggishness, and . . . simpleminded stupidity."[15] She is a parody inversion of that virtuous figure, a "brazen little gold-digger," one of Gilbert's "sugared minxes," a sentimental heroine "slyly turned the wrong side out."[16]

As an infant, Rose was hung in a plated dish cover to the knocker of a workhouse door, with only a change of baby linens and an etiquette book.[17] In other words, she is an orphan, that quintessential figure of novelistic and melodramatic narrative. But Gilbert turns the character in a different direction than he did in *The Pirates of Penzance*, where the hint of illegitimacy floats in the background. Rose's attachment to the etiquette book may be seen as a substitute for the parental guidance she never had. "Little wonder," she says, "if I have always regarded that work as a voice from a parent's tomb." Here the parody of feminine conduct books, proliferating in the period, abuts on some canny psychological analysis. But the psychological point is never allowed to become poignant. Rose's "hallowed volume" was "composed . . . by no less an authority than the wife of a Lord Mayor." Thus parental, institutional, religious, and governmental authority are bundled under the sign of a great middle-class pettiness, with the psychological potential tipped toward a parody of the genres devoted to feminine socialization. When Rose worries about petty offenses—like eating peas with a knife, using a pocket comb in public, pointing, whispering, hinting, or speaking before being spoken to—the opera makes fun of excessive attention to the rules of etiquette while defamiliarizing them and making them seem absurd cultural rituals. The class issue is highlighted in the idea of a village girl in training to be "ladylike." Rose speaks in an old-fashioned biblical (King James) diction, thee-ing and thou-ing and adding "-eth" to her verbs: "It may be that he drinketh strong waters which do bemuse a man, and make him even as the wild beasts of the desert!" Thus her language, through which she means to indicate her innocence and high-mindedness, does the opposite, signaling her pretentious self-consciousness. She displays a minute attention to rank, status, and wealth (as she compares the "lowly mariner" with the "tiller of the land," for example). The joke, of course, is on female socialization and the genres of instruction that mediate it, especially the conduct books and Sunday schools, founded in 1811 as a means to instruct the poor.[18]

Rose with her etiquette book forms one of Gilbert's clearest representations of the absurdities of female enculturation (the other being the exhibition of the two young princesses in *Utopia, Limited*). Going by the book makes Rose incapable of sincere, "heartfelt" feeling. Thus, although clearly destined to marry, she veers from man to man all through act 1, crazily dissociated, embodying an exaggerated and highly gendered form of social-ized self-division. (As we have seen, Savoy opera consistently examines self-division in terms of gender; while masculine self-division usually results from assuming a professional role, which inevitably clashes with individual desire, feminine self-division is usually caused by the demand to perform correct gender behavior.) Rose carries her self outside herself, searching for her actions and feelings in the etiquette book, which she also obsessively consults for advice about how to interpret the "moral worth" of those she encounters in everyday life. There is a subtle gender critique in the humor-ous paradox that her flightiness derives from her inculcated innocence and inexperience. Like Patience and the "writhing maid" in Bunthorne's poem, Rose has been educated to a studied ignorance of her own feelings, which she cannot recognize because, strictly speaking, she has none; they are out-side her, in the etiquette book, written by culture at large.

Her words in the trio "In sailing o'er life's ocean wide" proclaim the diffi-culties of having "a heart that does not know its mind," another parody of the feminine psychomachia we observed of Josephine in *H.M.S. Pinafore* (plate 16). When Rose turns from Dick to Robin, she explains in song:

> Ten minutes since my heart said "white"—
> > It now says "black."
> It then said "left"—it now says "right"—
> > Hearts often tack.

Ruddigore drives hard at the idea of dissociation between heart and mind, which results in what can be called the joke about the talking heart. The whole of act 1 revolves around the idea of the heart telling the character what to do, as if it were external to the self and its body. If someone loved her, Rose sings to Hannah, "My heart would point him out to me / And I would point him out to you." This form of socialized self-division is a mild and ordinary form of madness. Dick, like Rose, suffers from it; we know they are meant to be analogous in this respect, because all through the scene when he listens to his heart, "a-dictatin' to me like anythink," she madly consults her etiquette book. Like Rose, he speaks only rote-learned, hackneyed senti-ments, which parody the manly eloquence familiar in nautical melodrama.

Significantly, it is just after the trio sung by Dick, Robin, and Rose that Mad Margaret enters for the first time, suggesting a relation between Rose's separation of heart and mind and Margaret's madness. Margaret is, of

FIGURE 10.3 Jessie Bond as Mad Margaret in act 1 of *Ruddigore*. Cabinet photograph by Barraud (London, 1887). (Collection of Fredric Woodbridge Wilson)

course, the most flagrantly and conventionally mad of all the characters. As the stage direction announces: *"She is wildly dressed in picturesque tatters, and is an obvious caricature of theatrical madness"* (figure 10.3). Her scena is a wonderful parody of an operatic mad scene, its allusiveness designed to sweep from Donizetti's *Lucia di Lammermoor* (1835) to Ambroise Thomas's *Hamlet* (1868)—but especially designed to recall the latter, in a generalized parody of the bel canto styles of Donizetti and Bellini. The playful flute accompaniment adds a conventionally "mad" musical touch:

Cheerily carols the lark
  Over the cot.
Merrily whistles the clerk
  Scratching a blot.

This particular juxtaposition of natural and petty-professional imagery indicates one way the English can go mad. But Margaret's madness is a matter of gender, too. Her mind wanders amid riddles, allusions, and memories; she feels motherless as well as "love-lonely"—"abandoned" in several senses of the word. Both sad and mad, she wants to pinch Rose because the object of her own affections "gathered . . . only roses." That she is singing even plays into the caricature, for madwomen like Ophelia sing their distracted fragments of folk song and introspection, even in nonmusical theater. Margaret's mental wandering presses the parody, for she cannot remember her song: "The cat and the dog and the little puppee / Sat down in a—down in a—in a—." The cure for her distraction will be the reformation of the villain, of course, but melodrama's sudden and retroactive changes in identity are themselves mad, as we have seen.

In act 2, Margaret emerges transformed, wearing a change of clothes to show it. Re-dressed in plain black Dissenting garb, she and Despard now parody the plot of reformation (figure 10.4); they have become district visitors and spend their time dancing "blameless dances" and turning "respectable capers." But Margaret is still mad, on the verge of hysterics at every moment. However, like Rose's, Margaret's madness has a Method(ism) in it. In one respect, Rose displays too much method and Margaret too little. Yet in another sense, the opposite is the case, for Rose is flighty and unmoored, while Margaret attempts to be ultra-methodical in act 2. The hint that this change in behavior may entail a parodic critique

FIGURE 10.4 Rutland Barrington and Jessie Bond as Despard Murgatroyd and Mad Margaret in act 2 of *Ruddigore*, after their transformation. Cabinet photograph by Barraud (London, 1887). (Collection of Fredric Woodbridge Wilson)

of Methodism occurs early in the libretto, when Dame Hannah wonders if Robin might suit her, since he "combines the manners of a Marquis with the morals of a Methodist." The silly, obsessive alliteration on the *m* makes a stuttering joke of the methodically careful moral self-inspection of the "simple folk." (Coming up again in *The Gondoliers*, the Methodism of the monarch of Barataria suggests that Gilbert was still searching for a way to make fun of evangelical Christianity.) Conversion itself—like reform, like melodramatic transformations in identity—is somewhat absurd from a hyper-logical point of view. It seems impossible (and therefore absurd) that Mad Margaret would now be a district visitor, that Despard would now do penny readings "not remarkably entertaining," and that together they "rule / A National School." Their new devotion to social institutions of welfare, inflected by evangelical Christianity, amuses through its graphic difference from what they were before. Despard compliments Margaret for being so "orderly, methodical, neat" and for having her "emotions well under control." But even while expressing her gratitude to him for their new, calm, and "unimpassioned" life, Margaret threatens to burst out "(*Wildly*)" with her hyperbolic gratitude and affection. "Pray restrain yourself," he says, adding, in one of the best lines of the opera, "a district visitor should learn to eschew melodrama."

Margaret crazily asks for a device to "recall me to my saner self," a "word that teems with hidden meaning," and the word they bathetically settle on is "Basingstoke." Like an incantation in reverse, this word subdues spirits instead of raising them. As Jane Stedman points out, this is "a parody of the 'thrilling word' of melodrama, the word which, uttered by a mysterious character, could cause another to blench at the terrible significance of which only the two were aware."[19] Adrienne Munich correctly points to an "affectionate misogyny" in this scene. Crazed by thwarted desire, like many theatrical madwomen, Margaret is wild, wanton, extravagant, fearful, pitiful, disorderly, and subject to fits; but she suffers from "curable erotomania," for marriage supposedly tames her. Yet her hysteria keeps threatening to burst out. Munich argues that the humor of the "Basingstoke" mantra "identifies pacification with a middle-class Victorian town." Identifying Margaret's symptoms with the menopausal "Queen of a Certain Age," Victoria, Munich argues that her "other climacteric symptoms are disciplined not in the madhouse but in the suburbs."[20]

As Robin and Dick triangulate around Rose for the trio about self-division in act 1, Robin and Despard triangulate around Margaret for the famous patter-trio in act 2: "My eyes are fully open to my awful situation." In this song, patter hovers on the verge of madness. The patter-trio presents a manic force, the powerful feeling that threatens to spill over or burst out and refuses to be contained. As it stands, *Ruddigore* has no patter song for an individual singer,[21] but throws the force of its thematics of madness into the patter-trio, notable, among other reasons, for its rhyming of "idyll" and "indiwiddle" and for its refrain, which comments self-consciously on its own form. Each of the verses contributes deftly to the ongoing characterizations; Margaret, for example, describes herself as "a little mad and generally silly." But if she were not mad, she would have made brilliant points:

> On the subject I shall write you a most valuable letter,
> Full of excellent suggestions when I feel a little better,
> But at present I'm afraid I am as mad as any hatter,
> So I'll keep 'em to myself, for my opinion doesn't matter!

After each verse, the other two echo the last line, and then the refrain, sung by all, repeats the word "matter" with maniacal frenzy: "Her opinion doesn't matter, matter, matter, matter, matter!"

Not only Margaret, but the whole "awful situation" is mad. Despard tells Robin that he, Robin, is responsible for Despard's bad deeds, for legally he was the "bad Baronet," and the mad situation of self-division across bodies links into the frenzy of the song. But, as we have seen, patter as a genre often expresses forms of social madness. Earlier, in our discussion of *The Sorcerer*, we saw that patter served the market, since it was practiced by street vendors hawking their wares as well as by chairmen in music halls, who diverted their audiences between acts, distracting them from the fact that nothing was happening and keeping them in their seats. Thus patter illustrates the uses of distraction for control of modern consumers. In the same vein, patter reveals the necessity for—and the pretense of—professional expertise (as in John Wellington Wells's song in *The Sorcerer* and Major-General Stanley's song in *The Pirates of Penzance*), a fragmentary sort of modern "knowledge," put together for the purpose of selling the expert. Like this fragmentary knowledge, like a page of newspaper—or a page of *Punch* or *Fun*—patter suggests the pieced-together, pastiche quality of popular culture, its relentless circulation of superficial information (as in the "receipt for the popular mystery" and the "residuum" it creates in *Patience*). Similarly, patter is used to convey the odd associations that characterize mental processes, especially the seemingly nonsensical associations of dreams (as in the Lord Chancellor's "Nightmare Song" in *Iolanthe*). It is the perfect vehicle for conveying madness as well as dream work, and thus patter is strongly linked both to the efflorescence of nonsense verse in the Victorian period and to the emergence of psychoanalysis. Like the Cheshire Cat, Sigmund Freud would illuminate the ways "we're all mad here." But Savoy patter focuses especially on socially determined forms of madness in daily life. As expressed in the "Junction Song" in *Thespis*, patter suggests the manic, mechanical quality of modern work, the rapid acceleration of modern life, the exhaustion of having to keep going, and the maddening effort to keep up. Like other feats of rote learning and recitation (whether in school or in church), the patter song bespeaks a wide range of excesses in modern discipline that might drive one mad, repression leading to repeated outbursts like Margaret's. In such situations, as Isaac Goldberg points out, rapid repetition drains words of their significance.[22]

An elocutionary tour de force in which culture meets carnival, Savoy patter is stuffed as full as a Victorian sofa, yet pretends to be empty. Thus *Ruddigore*'s patter-trio is profoundly self-reflexive about the superficiality of patter itself; it is patter about the genre of patter, sound ostensibly trumping meaning while revealing its own sense. Driven by sound—rhythm, rhyme, and other sonic repetitions, rattled off at a breakneck pace—this late Savoy patter aggressively and mechanically disavows its own significance:

> This particularly rapid, unintelligible patter
> Isn't generally heard, and if it is it doesn't matter!

The repetition of the word "matter" between the verses, if performed well, sounds like mad muttering, sotto voce: "It really doesn't matter, matter, matter, matter, matter!" Of course, it *does* matter. And it *is* matter, a dense residuum deriving from, diverting us from, and then returning us to the material conditions of social life. Patter conceals while revealing what's the matter.

11

The Past Is a Foreign Country

The Yeomen of the Guard

The *Yeomen of the Guard; or, The Merryman and His Maid* (1888) is anomalous in several important respects. First, it is serious, but humor plays its part. Although farfetched, its plot adheres to standards of human probability, as Gilbert and, especially, Sullivan understood that concern. Because of his objections to the "lozenge plot," Sullivan was relieved—on Christmas Day of 1887—to hear the story of the new piece. In his diary, the composer wrote that he was "immensely pleased with it. Pretty story, no topsy-turvydom, very human and funny also."[1] As Isaac Goldberg points out, sympathizing with Sullivan's point of view, Gilbert had "thrown off the incubus of inversion."[2] From my point of view, this entailed losses as well as gains in the plot, but the losses are offset by the sweeping, driving, moving coherence of the music. (One could even say that the plot is a quintessential opera plot, displaying holes and dropped threads rather than the rigorous internal consistency so typical of the earlier Savoy operas.)[3] *The Yeomen of the Guard* was the favorite of both its authors, "because each beheld in it a partial fulfillment of what he considered his higher aims."[4] For Gilbert, *Yeomen* reached closer to serious drama; for Sullivan, it reached closer to grand opera than did their previous collaborations.

Second, then, *The Yeomen of the Guard* is operatic. With no qualifying adjective on the title page of the libretto, *The Yeomen of the Guard* announces itself simply as "A New and Original Opera."[5] Indeed, it approaches grand opera in format, in the special English tradition of Michael Balfe and Vincent Wallace. As contemporary reviewers pointed out, this "genuine English opera" might be seen to herald the "prospect of a school of English opera."[6] Thus *Yeomen* stretches even the boundaries of Gilbert and Sullivan's own particular genre, "native English comic opera," for although it is punctu-ated by humorous situations and lyrics, it is not precisely "comic," except in the strictly technical sense that it ends with marriage. Its seriousness is underscored by the fact that Gilbert urged the cutting of the first comic song in order not to interrupt the momentum of the opening, which, as he put it, was *"tearful . . . serious and martial . . . grim . . . [and] sentimental in character."*[7]

Third, *The Yeomen of the Guard* treats the issue of genre in a nonparodic way, as do most of the later operas (except *Ruddigore* and *The Grand Duke*), although it does use and mix genres self-consciously. The romance plot depends on a family melodrama, with the villainous relative, Sir Clarence Poltwhistle, having caused Colonel Fairfax to be imprisoned for sorcery, so that he might succeed to the estate if Fairfax should die unmarried. (In addition to the villain, this set of complex conditions for inheritance, sim-ply "given" and not explained, is the perfect precondition of a melodramatic plot.) The delayed reprieve of Fairfax, too, is the quintessential stuff of melo-drama. Robert Hall Jr. points out that the plot of imprisonment and reprieve imitates the classic "rescue opera, a post-Revolutionary precursor of melo-drama."[8] The other main terms of our argument about genre, burlesque and extravaganza, might at first seem to be missing from *Yeomen*. But at least two critics have argued that Jack Point personifies an older form of humor, the tired burlesque humor that Gilbert had become famous for replacing.[9] If so, then elements of both melodrama and extravaganza are still present in the work.

The reviewer for *Punch* was not alone in noticing the plot's similarity to Edward Fitzball's libretto for Wallace's *Maritana* (1845). Elsie Maynard's marriage to the imprisoned Fairfax seems clearly to imitate the wedding of a blindfolded gypsy girl to a condemned man in *Maritana*. But, as Gold-berg points out, the critic might have mentioned that the situation is as old in English theater as John Gay's *The Beggar's Opera* (1728). Reginald Allen quotes one reviewer who even suggested that *Yeomen* might be regarded as a subtle attempt at parody, were it not so serious.[10] Based on the play *Don César de Bazan* (1844) by Adolphe d'Ennery, *Maritana* also was adapted as an opera by Jules Massanet (1872), so the story was familiar. In this chain of adaptations, in other words, we can observe the familiar dynamic we have seen so often in relation to the Savoy operas, many of which are based on extremely familiar plots, specifically to emphasize—usually to parody—their familiarity. For example, as we have seen, *Patience* plays within the serious family tradition, while the particularly English intoxication of *The Sorcerer* can be appreciated only in relation to the long tradition of magical-elixir narratives. A delicious humor is gained by positioning a contemporary work within and against a long succession of models, each one copied and revised from all those that precede it. In other words, by 1888, the plot of *Maritana* had achieved the status of this sort of conventional plot; it was familiar, popular, and up for grabs, specifically because it had been adapted many times. The idea that this dynamic amounts to simple copying shows little understanding of its purposes; instead, its allusiveness humorously calls attention to convention. *Yeomen*'s subtlety about genre may be seen in the same light.

In any case, Gilbert "plagiarized" mainly from his own work, especially from the Bab Ballads and *The Mikado*. Like *The Yeomen of the Guard*, the Bab Ballad "Annie Prothero, a Legend of Stratford-Le-Bow" (1868) tells a story of near-execution and reprieve. Likewise, the idea of Annie pitching woo with a Public Headsman prefigures the odd romance of Phoebe Meryll and Wilfred Shadbolt. The notion that lovers might chat about whatever comes closest to hand is amusing when the topics seized on are public execution and torture; indeed, Wilfred declares that Phoebe's "allusions to [his] professional duties are in doubtful taste." Furthermore, in both the Bab Ballad "To Phoebe" (1865), and *Yeomen*, the woman intelligently schemes her way out of the man's attempt at entrapment. "Were I thy bride," sung by Phoebe to Wilfred, reverses the situation in the ballad, in which a young man tells Phoebe what he *would* say to her, if he loved her, before the poem ends with his abrupt confession that he does *not* love her.[11] But *The Yeomen of the Guard* owes most to *The Mikado*, turning the figures of the wandering minstrel and the public executioner in an entirely new direction. Moreover, in both works, a hastily contrived marriage turns into a serious one, and an elaborate lie is spun about the hero having been killed.[12]

Fourth, *The Yeomen of the Guard* is the only Savoy opera that does not open with the Chorus. Instead, it begins with Phoebe Meryll alone on stage, at her spinning wheel, singing her melancholy solo, "When maiden loves, she sits and sighs." Soon, however, an exquisite double Chorus sets a more familiar opening tone. As in *Ruddigore*, the plot and the thematic structure do not depend on the gendered opposition of the divided Chorus, which appears only at the beginning of act 2. Otherwise, the Chorus represents the general populace.[13] The double Chorus in act 1 emphasizes the character of the Tower warders, who are wistful, in "this the autumn of [their] life," yet are still "under orders" and willing to "face a foreign foe, / As in days of long ago." A similarly grand effect is achieved toward the beginning of act 2, when the Yeomen's "stout music" resonates against the "mockery of the Tower women." Thus a gendered opposition does come into play when the women taunt the men for having let Fairfax escape: "Warders are ye? / Whom do ye ward?" Against their derision, the Yeomen offer their diligent, rapid, and rhythmic searching for the escaped prisoner: "Up and down, and in and out."

Fifth, the thematic argument of *The Yeomen of the Guard* is less centrally dedicated to gender issues than are the story lines of the previous Savoy operas. But the marriage plot in general is under critique, as it is in *Ruddigore*. In paired numbers, Fairfax compares marriage to captivity ("Free from his fetters grim"), while Elsie likens it to a tomb ("Strange adventure"). Adventitious as it is, theirs will be the only happy marriage in the end. The multiple marriages so typical of a Savoy conclusion appear even more than usual to be a matter of chance, not character, in this opera. Not even the central match, between Fairfax and Elsie, seems entirely sympathetic. The lucky fact that Elsie falls in love with the man to whom she is already married forms a conventional part of the lover-in-disguise plot; Elsie and Fairfax do not know each other, so his testing of "her principles," which reveals her inclination toward "Leonard Meryll," seems ungrounded. Elsie sells herself into marriage, and her sick old mother, a hastily offered rationalization, never again appears in the plot to make Elsie's mercenary motives plausible. Meanwhile, Jack Point thinks of Elsie as his "promised bride," but there has been no indication that she agrees. Thus, early on, Jack is to Elsie as Wilfred is to Phoebe, an unaccepted lover.

The pairing of Phoebe Meryll and Wilfred Shadbolt has long caused consternation. Despite his lighthearted wish to be a jester—his two duets with Jack Point, "Hereupon we're both agreed" and "Like a ghost his vigil keeping," show this side of his character—Wilfred is grotesque; one must watch with discomfort the scene of Phoebe flirting with him in order to steal his keys. As Audrey Willliamson remarks, there is something of Dickens's Quilp about him. Both the Dickens of *The Old Curiosity Shop* (1841) and the Gilbert of *The Yeomen of the Guard* seem insufficiently aware of the darker suggestions being made through these leering, goblin-like figures.[14] Phoebe's agreement to entertain Wilfred's suit is so implausible that its forced nature is emphasized in the plot; Phoebe engages herself to Wilfred in order to buy his silence. True, the libretto suggests that she continues to manipulate him, providing a last-minute loophole for her when she promises to marry him in "in a year—or two—or three, at the most." Surely, we are meant to take the hint that she will engineer her own rescue beyond the closure of this rescue opera.

Similarly, Sergeant Meryll's capture by Dame Carruthers is distasteful. Gilbert slips up badly with this careless use of the Dame figure, so expertly deployed in other Savoy operas. At first, Dame Carruthers seems to be the grim spokeswoman for the Tower itself, a powerful role; her devolution into Sergeant Meryll's nemesis, sudden and revolting, turns her into a husband-chasing "old meddler." Like Lady Blanche, Dame Carruthers is the Dame figure used straight, with all its punishing potential. But in the more serious context of *The Yeomen of the Guard*, the effect is more jarring than in *Princess Ida*, where Blanche is a burlesque figure throughout. Why, in any case, should both Merylls be so unhappily paired? To explain the strange, mixed mood of the libretto, Hall interprets it as Gilbert's critical satire of his own "tomfoolery" and happy endings, "the bitterest of all satire, that of a man mocking his own work."[15] This is an extreme view, with which I do not agree. Instead, pairings of Phoebe with Wilfred and Sergeant Meryll with Dame Carruthers bolster the grim, bracing seriousness of the opera's themes. The distinction between the heart and the hand, which both Phoebe and Sergeant Meryll make, does not humorously extenuate the distastefulness of their engagements, as it was surely meant to do; rather, it contributes to the opera's critique of the marriage plot.

Yet the music is so beautiful—and so strongly dramatic—that it makes up, with its grand sweep and intense coherence, for anything missing in the libretto. A good example of this force occurs in Elsie's recitative and song, "'Tis done! I am a bride!" One soon forgets the circumstances under which she has married, when swept away by the passionate musical figures swirling behind "Though tear and long-drawn sigh / Ill fit a bride." That song bespeaks the sadness of entrapment for women, whether with or without marriage, raising the question of marriage to an existential level, on a par with Fairfax's question: "Is life a boon?" Individual moments of musical brilliance are too many to name, but we might single out the sinuous, winding woodwind introduction to "I've jibe and joke," the lighthearted pizzicato accompaniments in "Were I thy bride" and "Free from his fetters grim," and the hushed, hymnal aura of the Chorus's admiration for "Leonard Meryll": "'Tis ever thus!" The pace of musical development is perhaps the opera's greatest strength. Despite the English form, alternating dialogue and musical numbers, the overarching momentum is Verdian or even Wagnerian in its grand scope and coherence, and not only because the leitmotif, adumbrated in *Iolanthe*, is even more consistently deployed in *Yeomen*.[16]

The overture to *The Yeomen of the Guard*, like that to *Iolanthe*, written in sonata form, is more carefully arranged than are Sullivan's usual last-minute anthologies (which he often turned over to other orchestrators). Its opening statement and closing preparation for the coda are especially effective. The overture opens with the Tower motif in the woodwinds and brasses; only fourteen instruments—flutes, oboes, cornets, horns, clarinets, and trom-

The Yeomen of the Guard;

OR,

THE MERRYMAN AND HIS MAID.

FIGURE 11.1 The Tower motif from the overture to *The Yeomen of the Guard*, arranged for piano by J. H. Wadsworth. (Collection of Fredric Woodbridge Wilson)

bones—are used to create a huge, stately, sonorous effect, as if the Tower itself were striding forward or suddenly being raised up from nothing, like the mythic structure it is meant to be (figure 11.1). Gervase Hughes praises the musical characterization of the Tower, which hovers over the opera like a brooding presence.[17] Commenting on Sullivan's remarkable tendency, in musical characterization, to focus on general types or social groups, Hughes argues that the score of *The Yeomen of the Guard* is "even more remarkable," because "Sullivan achieved an *impersonal* characterisation, for the spirit of the grim old Tower indefinably pervades the music from the first bar of the overture to the final *dénouement*."[18] Taken up by Dame Carruthers ("When our gallant Norman foes"), the Tower motif then reappears at the beginning of the finale to act 1. The second subject, "when a wooer goes a-wooing," also modulates throughout the overture, and thus the two motifs announce the tension in the plot between the intractable forces of history and power represented by the Tower, on the one hand, and the romance plot, on the other.

The "Early English" touches in the music emphasize the opera's thematic concern with the history of the nation. Using musical history to underscore national history, *The Yeomen of the Guard* gestures to the origins of the madrigal in sixteenth-century Italy and England. Sullivan had been working up to the "Strange adventure" quartet with the madrigals in *The Mikado* and *Ruddigore*.[19] The partially unaccompanied bridal trio in the act 2 finale ("'Tis said that joy in full perfection / Comes only once to womankind"), while not precisely a madrigal, has an Early English feel in its polyphonic texture. The Early English elements in the music—together with Early English elements in the setting and plot—raise intensely interesting critical questions. For *The Yeomen of the Guard* has often been called nostalgic, uncritically evocative of a deep national past. But it would be more accurate—and more revealing— to think of the Early Englishness of the opera as autoethnographic, an attempt to reflect on English identity by imagining an earlier phase in its development. In one sense, nostalgia is the very opposite of parody, for nostalgia regards the past as better than the present, whereas parody regards past forms as outworn, humorous, and in need of revisionary critique in the present. But in *Yeomen*, no golden haze obscures the grim aspects of the national past. The particular founding moment of the Norman Conquest provides a bracing interpretation of the history of England as a history of invasion, conquest, and cruelty—all represented by the Tower of London. Moreover, this retrospective view involves the autoethnographic recognition that "Great Britain" was *made* over time. The lineage from its Anglo-Saxon past to its nineteenth-century present has been broken by invasion, and long before the Acts of Union, the nation was already a complex, internally divided whole, formed in the clash of cultures.

In another sense, however, nostalgia is dialectically related to parody—its structural twin, although its opposite in intent—for, like parody, nostalgia establishes a graphic difference between past and present. After historical difference has been asserted, the past can be projected as if it were another place or culture. In other words, the achievement of historical distance has its aesthetic consequences. As does *The Mikado*, *The Yeomen of the Guard* looks into the mirror of another culture in order to learn about its own. In this opera, however, the "other" culture is the deep past of England itself. Thus *The Yeomen of the Guard* is as clearly autoethnographic as *The Mikado*. The past is a foreign country.[20] With one eye on the Tower of London and the other on the Merryman and His Maid, the opera looks at two sides of the history of England, one high and the other low, one involving the history of conquest and the other the history of theater.

"When our gallant Norman foes made this merry land their own"

All the Savoy operas are intent on their Englishness. *Thespis* and *The Sorcerer* imagine particularly English forms of intoxication to supplant French opéra bouffe; *H.M.S. Pinafore* and *The Pirates of Penzance* spoof nautical melodrama to make fun of rote-learned patriotism; *Iolanthe* pits a band of Fairies against a passel of Peers; *Princess Ida*, like *Ruddigore*, is set in a mythical past. But *The Yeomen of the Guard* takes the mythical past of England seriously, looking back to the founding moment in the Norman Conquest and the establishment of the Tower of London. According to this view, "Merrie England" is not very merry.

The retrospective characterization of "Merrie England" conjures an idyllic location in a vague mythical time between the Middle Ages and the industrial revolution. According to Ronald Hutton, the imaginative projection of "Merrie England" can be dated between the late fourteenth and early sixteenth centuries.[21] But the nineteenth century brought a resuscitation of this fantasy as a literary topos, owing not only to the felt need to respond to the industrial revolution, but also to the revivalist interest in literary and intellectual movements that predated industrialization. The excavation of traditional elements in the culture of "Great Britain," for the literary creation of a usable past, is a familiar strain in Romantic and Victorian literature. We have examined this function of folk- and fairy tales in the discussion of *Iolanthe*, but in *The Yeomen of the Guard*, the focus is on re-creating a fantastic version of the historical record. The nineteenth-century idea of "Merrie England," in other words, is both a part of this strain of Romantic historicism and a defensive (and often conservative) response to recent historical events: the American and French Revolutions, the Napoleonic Wars, and profound industrial changes to the landscape. Especially in the last respect, the yearning for a simpler, earlier world in the English countryside became an object of literary and cultural concern. In his essay "Merry England" (1819), William Hazlitt popularized the term for the nineteenth century.[22] But that essay was only one among many dilations on traditional rural pastimes. William Cobbett's *Rural Rides* (1822–1826) and Dickens's *The Pickwick Papers* (1836–1837) celebrate traveling by coach in the years before the coming of the railways. From late Coleridge to Thomas Carlyle's *Past and Present* (1843), evocations of the olden days served various argumentative agendas.

The trope of "Merrie England" was durable across the nineteenth century in music and theater as well as literature. Barry Cornwall's poem "Hurrah for Merry England" was set to music in 1861 and 1880.[23] Sullivan's own *Victoria and Merrie England* (1897)—ballet music composed for the Diamond Jubilee—consists of seven historical vignettes, including a scene of "Ancient Britain" and two of Victoria in the present time (plate 17). Soon after finishing the score for *The Yeomen of the Guard*, Sullivan started work on *Ivanhoe* (1891), a grand opera with a libretto by Julian Sturgis. Soon after the turn of the century, Edward German's comic opera *Merrie England* (1902) was produced at the Savoy Theatre. In other words, the re-creation of "Merrie England" was a long-lasting endeavor, involving as much invention as historical retrospection. The popular Christmas carol "God Rest You Merry, Gentlemen," can serve as an example. Printed in both broadsheet and chapbook in the late eighteenth century, it was anthologized in William B. Sandys's *Christmas Carols Ancient and Modern* (1833). But after appearing in Dickens's *A Christmas Carol* (1843), it was definitively granted an ancient lineage and taken to be an artifact of oral folk culture.[24] In fact, the celebration of Christmas itself was an offshoot of the popularization of "Merrie England," advanced immeasurably by its literary avatar, *A Christmas Carol*. Like Christmas, a number of traditions were "invented" in the nineteenth century.[25]

Needless to say, the cultural politics surrounding the aim of returning in the imagination to "Merrie England" have always been complex. In the nineteenth century, the concept appealed to both conservatives (like Carlyle) and progressives (like William Morris in *News from Nowhere* [1890]). In some instances, conservative and radical views would blend. For example, in *The Condition of the Working Class in England in 1844*, Friedrich Engels takes the concept seriously, when he writes that "the very name of 'Merry England' has long since been forgotten, because the inhabitants of the great manufacturing centers have never heard from their grandparents what life was like in those days." However, in a famous footnote on the "philanthropic Tories" (who called themselves the "Young England" movement), he protests that their hope for "a restoration of the old 'Merry England' with its brilliant features and its romantic feudalism . . . is of course unattainable and ridiculous, a satire upon all historic development." Yet he acknowledges that their "good intention, the courage to resist the existing nature of things . . . and the vileness of our present condition, is worth something anyhow." And then he goes on to praise Carlyle's demand for the "organization of labour."[26] Lately, the concept has been attributed largely to a conservative agenda, but in the nineteenth century it was still very much alive as an argumentative tool available to all positions on the conservative–progressive spectrum.[27]

The attention paid in the Savoy operas to the preposterousness of returning to "Early English" styles is familiar from the parody of aestheticism in *Patience*, where Lady Saphir's remark to Colonel Calverley—"Oh, be Early English ere it is too late!"—reveals the superficial side of such attempted revivals. So, too, does Bunthorne's advice to those who would pose as aesthetes: "[C]onvince 'em, if you can, that the reign of good Queen Anne was Culture's palmiest day." In *Iolanthe*, Lord Mountararat looks back to an idealized past "When Britain really ruled the waves— / (In good Queen Bess's time)." He employs nostalgia for a parodic aim, to show that the House of Peers was then and is still useless. Thus parody can use nostalgia for its own purposes, too. But after the jocular medievalism of *Patience* and *Princess Ida*, *The Yeomen of the Guard* takes the vague period of "Early English" somewhat straight.

Situating its action in the sixteenth century, *The Yeomen of the Guard* is ostentatiously "historical," not only in its setting but also in its inclusion of a historical figure, the only one in the Savoy canon. Sir Richard Chol-mondeley directed the Tower from 1513 to 1524.[28] Other historical touches include the arquebus[29] and the archaic dialogue—thee-ing and thy-ing, mayst-ing and wilt-ing—which attempts to convey a sense of the history of the English language. It is hard to forget, however, that this diction is associated with Rose Maybud in *Ruddigore*, a parody of the hyper-virtu-ous village girl. As in *The Sorcerer*, where the sounds of love in the making are particularly English folk sounds ("Eh but oi du loike you!"), *Yeomen* could have done more with the history of the language; given the opera's attention to the Norman Conquest, it might have made sense to empha-size the influx of French terms and the appreciation of "the English" as a polyglot people, both linguistically and culturally. Since it is set in the six-teenth century, *The Yeomen of the Guard* could also have taken advantage of the Tudor myth of a golden age. But its focus on the Tower of London and the Norman Conquest turns instead to a grim moment in national history. The Tower serves as metonymy of the English past as a history of unjust torture and execution, while the Norman Conquest, although bracingly praised by Dame Carruthers, recalls an invasion, after all. With respect to the olden days, in other words, the important thing to keep in mind about *The Yeomen of the Guard* is that its portrait of "Merrie Eng-land" is hardly idyllic.

Thus the opera chooses to memorialize not a vague golden age, but a par-ticular history. Dame Carruthers clearly does not subscribe to the popular seventeenth- and eighteenth-century protest against the "Norman yoke," but, alluding to the concept of "Merrie England," she celebrates the Conquest:

> When our gallant Norman foes
>   Made our merry land their own,
>   And the Saxons from the Conqueror were flying,
>   At his bidding it arose,
>   In its panoply of stone,
>   A sentinel unliving and undying.

Describing the opening of the opera to Sullivan, Gilbert called Dame Car-ruthers's song "*grim in character.*"[30] She looks back to the establishment of the Tower of London by William the Conqueror in 1078 and, before that, to the violent conquest by the Normans, beginning in 1066 with the death of Edward the Confessor and the Battle of Hastings. This total usurpation of the Anglo-Saxon aristocracy and Church hierarchy was a turning point in the his-tory of the nation, to say the least. In particular, we should note that England was founded in a clash of cultures. In this sense, the national past is, quite literally, a foreign country.

The Tower is stony and "insensible," impenetrable and unsusceptible to persuasion, "Though a queen to save her head should come a-suing." But although it is characterized as impersonal, it broods, as many have pointed out, over the opera like a personified presence; indeed, in Dame Carruthers's song, it gains a voice and "speaks" of its "duty" in a grisly refrain:

> "The screw may twist and the rack may turn,
> And men may bleed and men may burn,
> O'er London town and its golden hoard
> I keep my silent watch and ward!"

Proud of its lack of mercy for the "flower of the brave," Dame Carruthers praises the Tower for taking "little heed of aught / That comes not in the measure of its duty."

Refusing a too-easy nostalgia for the English past, the tone of *The Yeomen of the Guard* is autumnal and melancholy, on the one hand, but cruel and bracing, on the other. We might say that it displays a blend of "restorative nostalgia" and "reflective nostalgia," Svetlana Boym's terms for two purposes to which nostalgia can be bent: one that regrets the destruction of a "homeland," while the other understands that we cannot return to the past.[31] Dame Carruthers emphasizes the symbolic nature of the Tower and its history, again anthropomorphizing its visage: "There's a legend on its brow." Just before Dame Carruthers's imposing song, Phoebe Meryll makes the point in another mood, comparing the Tower to "a cruel giant in a fairy-tale, [who] must be fed with blood, and that blood must be the best and bravest in England, or it's not good enough for the old Blunderbore." To this, Dame Carruthers snaps: "Silence, you silly girl."

Phoebe was born in the old keep; she is identified with it—and imprisoned by it—every bit as much as Dame Carruthers is. In fact, her metaphor of ingestion by a "cruel giant in a fairy-tale" emphasizes the role of the Tower to contain (arms, treasure, the Crown Jewels) and imprison (the long line of royal prisoners and high-ranking nobles). Into this contained space (and space of containment) come the strolling players. In a perfect example of the Savoy "invasion motif," they come from the outside in, to mix "quips and cranks" with the grimness of the Tower's inhabitants. Together with its nostalgic, but bracing, representation of a monumental national past that is both mythical and historical, *The Yeomen of the Guard* attends to the past of folk culture, through the story represented by its subtitle, *The Merryman and His Maid.* The Tower may seem like a hermetically sealed microcosm,[32] but it is not impermeable, for into this world come Jack Point and Elsie Maynard. Into this monument to a particular national past, in other words, come the representatives of a particular theatrical past.

The Merryman and His Maid

In nineteenth-century theater, the figure of the strolling player often represents an older day of rural freedom, thus activating nostalgia about the nation by evoking an unregulated folk theatricality that flourishes outside the theater. The figure of the jester, however, usually signifies a particular connection to power. The jester's oddly twinned or shadow-like relation to the king (or nobleman) who employs him bespeaks both loyalty and subversion, for the jester's joking and riddling style, radical innocence, and sometimes madness enable critical commentary to be delivered obliquely. The tradition of the jester effectively ended with the Civil War, and it was not revived after the Restoration, so by the nineteenth century, traditional jesting was identifiable as pre-puritanical. In other words, the figures of the strolling player and the jester look back to a time before the Licensing Act of 1737 codified laws against itinerant actors and cast them as "rogues" and "vagrants."

Other plays of the 1880s recall this particular theatrical past, showing its contemporary interest. The Jarvis family of itinerant actors in George Robert Sims's urban melodrama *The Lights O' London* (1881) represents this typical form of theatrical nostalgia very well.[33] They have named their son Shakespeare Jarvis, in order to emphasize the prodigious powers of this "infant feenonynom." (His character was also another opportunity for the male adolescent to be played by a cross-dressed actress.) An idealized jack-of-all-trades who can play any part, this "Shakespeare Junior" helps Mrs. Jarvis write the dramas, like a present-day revival of his namesake. Needless to say, the ingenuity of this infant phenomenon is crucial to the melodramatic resolution of the play. In the end, the hero and heroine look forward to "what a pleasant life it will be roaming from place to place with the Jarvises, free and without fear," all over the countryside, where they long to travel "beyond the London lights." Through the Jarvis family, theatrical itinerancy becomes the vehicle for the return to the pastoral landscape of the past. That past triumphs over the urban realism of *The Lights O' London,* where, as in *The Yeomen of the Guard,* we can see that modernity produces its usable pasts.

FIGURE 11.2 George Grossmith as Jack Point. Cabinet photograph by Barraud (London, 1888). (Collection of Fredric Woodbridge Wilson)

The character of Jack Point should be seen in this light, as both Early English and specifically Shakespearean (figure 11.2). Certainly, *The Yeomen of the Guard* was thought to be Shakespearean when it opened—"There is a Shakespearean halo about the whole," wrote the reviewer for the *Morning Post*—and the setting of the opera was Elizabethan before it was Tudor.[34] Critics have disagreed about the particular Shakespearean valence of Jack Point, some claiming that he is based on a particular Shakespearean character, and others arguing against any such influence whatever.[35] The strongest links can be made to Shakespeare's domestic fools, Touchstone in *As You Like It* and Feste in *Twelfth Night*. Like Feste, Jack is philosophical, "wise enough to play the fool." Like Touchstone, he is anti-idealistic, stressing the natural, mortal prevalence of folly. Feste is peripatetic and must talk his way out of being dismissed, and Jack entertains that possibility, too, in "A private buffoon is a light-hearted loon." His moods of "melancholy mumming" seem to allude to Feste's melancholy, and it is not a stretch to say that his riddling wit, with its arcane, proverbial turns, leans toward liminal, critical fooling (as in *King Lear*, for example).

In one sense, Jack Point may be regarded as a figural parody of the whole group of Shakespearean clowns, fools, and jesters. More than twenty years earlier, Gilbert had created a parody jester for an issue of *Fun* (see plate 1). His parody review *Gemma di Vergy; or, The Wild Harper of the Twelve Trees* (1865) makes fun of a contemporary play's ludicrous efforts to create an "early Welsh" setting, and the character of the jester is part of its preposterous attempt to revisit an imaginary past. Jumbles, the jester, speaks "*sarcastically*" and makes the same point over and over again: "It is thou that art the fool, and even I, JUMBLES, the poor jester, am the wise man." As Isaac Goldberg points out, "Jumbles the Jester" is the heir of Jaques, Touchstone, and Autolycus and is certainly "the Gilbertian brother of Jack Point."[36]

Less a critique than a pastiche of allusions, Jack Point suggests a type, or a jumble of types. In the same sense that Ralph Rackstraw is a parody of the Jolly Jack Tar, Jack Point alludes to a long history of jesters; the humor of these characterizations derives from the way they subtly exaggerate the tradition. Thus when Jack recites his qualifications to the Lieutenant, he exaggerates the capacities of his "pretty wit": "I can be merry, wise, quaint, grim, and sardonic, one by one, or all at once; . . . I know all the jests—ancient and modern—past, present, and to come." It is in this context that we should understand his reference book, "The Merrie Jestes of Hugh Ambrose," not as evidence that Jack plagiarizes others' work, but as evidence that he is derivative in another way, placing himself in a long tradition. Naturally, as we should have come to expect by now, that tradition is a bit frayed and outworn, characterized by much repetition and revision over the years and thus susceptible to parody. Thus it is funny when he refers to the joke about jokes being identifiable by number, consulting the book for "No. 7863," or when he offers to share the sources of his jokes with Wilfred Shadbolt. Jack Point has every reason to fear, as he sings in act 2, that a "sharp" listener might exclaim, "I have known that old joke from my cradle!"

Yet in another sense, Jack Point's poignancy exceeds his parody. At their entrance, Elsie and Jack, down on their luck, are being harassed by an angry crowd:

> Here's a man of jollity,
>> Jibe, joke, jollify!
> Give us of your quality,
>> Come fool, follify!

In this scene, Elsie is threatened with sexual molestation, and Jack uses his wit to defend her. The two strolling players desperately need money for Elsie's sick mother ("we have come here to pick up some silver to buy an electuary for her"), and though this plot thread is soon dropped, it is meant both to prove that Elsie is a good girl and to rationalize the otherwise pre-posterous marriage "for an hour" to a man whom she has never seen and who is about to die. After this point in the plot, Jack's sensitivity to his own harassment, not Elsie's, dominates his character. But before that twist turns the plot toward its chief direction, Jack and Elsie perform the "singing farce of the Merryman and His Maid" to pacify the angry crowd.

The celebrated song that ensues, "I have a song to sing, O!" derives its inspiration from the chantey "I'll sing you one, O!" in which the initial statement is met with a question: "What is your one, O?" or "What is your song, O?" Like its predecessor, Jack and Elsie's song accumulates all pre-vious responses in each new response to that question. Gervase Hughes compares this aspect of the song's structure with the configuration of "The Twelve Days of Christmas," while others have pointed out its similarity to the nursery rhyme "This is the house that Jack built."[37] The verses of Jack and Elsie's song always end with the same melancholy description of the forlorn love, "Who sipped no sup, and who craved no crumb, / As he sighed for the love of a ladye." This point echoes its precursor's refrain: "One is one and all alone and ever more shall be so." Thus both songs build their call-and-response structure toward a vision of loneliness in the end.

The role of this song in the structure of *The Yeomen of the Guard* is similar to that of the novelty songs in earlier operas—the "Junction Song" in *Thes-pis*, "The Magnet and the Churn" in *Patience*, and "The Lady and the Ape" in *Princess Ida*. Although its tone differs considerably from these earlier examples, the song clearly represents a miniature, moralized encapsulation of the overall plot. Gilbert, however, turns this one to dramatic advantage by making it a red herring. The song leads us to believe that its last verse predicts the outcome of the story—that Elsie will be rejected by a noble lover and then beg for the love of Jack Point—but the very opposite hap-pens. Although Fairfax does seem to invite the song's scorn for the "peacock popinjay, bravely born," Elsie marries him instead of "begg[ing] on her knees, with downcast eyes / For the love of the merryman, moping mum." On this twist depends the "tragic" conclusion of the opera, when Jack softly sings a reprise of "I have a song to sing, O!" that registers his terrible disappoint-ment. In the end, the merryman *"falls insensible at [her] feet,"* for the maid will not, after all, be his.

Whether Jack dies or just faints at the end of *The Yeomen of the Guard* has been a crux of discussion for years, even though the answer cannot be established in the text and thus should properly be ruled out as a ques-tion for serious discussion.[38] The best answer is that given by J. M. Gordon, who purported to have it from Gilbert himself: "The fate of Jack Point is in the hands of the audience, who may please themselves whether he lives or dies."[39] The Christian overtones of his agonized protest at the end ("Oh thoughtless crew! Ye know not what ye do!") may seem a bit over the top, especially since Jack has displayed his unpleasant side more than once. But when his small voice, halfway between speech and song, comes to the fore amid the general jubilee, it is affecting. The performance tradition for this figure has been particularly rich. Henry Lytton's interpretation emphasized the sentimental, "with its weak, cracked voice, trembling hands, touching last gesture of kissing a lock of Elsie's hair, and death-white face." Both Lytton and Martyn Green established the tradition of Jack Point fondling a jester's doll's head on his folly stick, which emphasizes the theatrical self-reflectiveness of the piece, as well as of the character, for it suggests that Jack Point's only real friend is this typified, iconic representation of himself.[40]

In any case, as many have pointed out, Jack Point's merryman is hardly merry. His name, of course, alludes to the punch line of a joke, as well as to the sharp attack of a knife-like instrument. In other words, like the Tower of London aspect of the plot, the "merryman and his maid" aspect is braced by grimness, not only in the melodramatically cruel way that Fairfax toys with and "tests" Elsie, but, most of all, in the figure of Jack Point, whose biliousness, frustration, and selfishness never fail to surprise. For many years, Jack was idealized in the commentary on Gilbert and Sullivan.[41] More recently, however, he has been savagely de-idealized, with every critic pointing out his failings. Most held against him is his selfish response when Elsie finds that she has perhaps been yoked for life to an unknown husband. At that point, he thinks only of himself: "Oh woe is *me*, I rather think!" Again, though, I believe we can steer a better course if we think of the character as a parodic amalgamation of the characteristics of the traditional jester, often biting and melancholy, sarcastic and self-centered.

Goldberg praises the characterization inherent in the musical introduction to "I've jibe and joke / And quip and crank": "[W]ith flute and bassoon here [Sullivan] has painted Jack Point before the merry-andrew opens his mouth; he has betrayed the care at the root of his humor; he has introduced us to his exotic claims."[42] The ensuing song, "I've wisdom from the East and from the West," offers a tripping sing-song—a kind of modified patter—in which Jack lays out his philosophy of jesting. His aims are aggressive, as Freud tells us jokes often are; he wants to "wither" an upstart and set a braggart "quailing." That the butt's "merry laugh" is hollow, barely covering the "echo that is grim," emphasizes this aggression. But, as is traditional with his kind, he asserts the meaning behind the mask, the "grain or two of truth among the chaff." In addition, he asserts the traditional purpose of using humor for educational purposes. The point may hurt, but it is good for us; and since it is distasteful, "he who'd make his fellow-creatures wise / Should always gild the philosophic pill!"

Importantly, his songs emphasize the problems of professional labor. In this respect, Jack Point and Wilfred Shadbolt are paired characters, or foils, since Wilfred, although Head Jailer and Assistant Tormentor, harbors the dream of being a jester. Their duets, "Hereupon we're both agreed" and "Like a ghost his vigil keeping," are fabulous, both depending on the relation of jester and would-be jester. Wilfred's ambition to become a lighthearted jester sets off the defining force of profession; he is entrapped in the profession of entrapping. The irony of Phoebe complimenting his wit, saying that "the anecdotes of the torture-chamber are the prettiest hearing," drives home this point. But the pairing of Wilfred and Jack around their common ambition to be funny sets off the professional entrapment of Jack Point as well. For a "salaried wit" is a kind of contradiction in terms, similar in the effect of its oxymoronic wit to a "professional sorcerer"; both must do for a living something that seems more properly to be a mysterious gift or spontaneous talent. Jack Point's patter song, "Oh! a private buffoon is a light-hearted loon," unfolds the "rules" that jesters "must observe, if they love their profession." Unlike the "professional sorcerer," who must hawk his wares on the market, the "private buffoon" has one employer, whose individual quirks determine his working conditions. He must know his audience and design his humor accordingly, for different spectators will have different tastes and standards—some prudish and particular, some stupid, some sharp. Gilbert makes room for social commentary here, activating the Victorian resonance of a "family fool" who must not tell jokes "imported from France." But the main point is the paradoxical predicament of being "paid to be funny" in the first place. The song's concluding fantasy, that the buffoon's "wife ran away with a soldier that day," shows that it is not only the butt of the joke, but the joker himself whose laughter is hollow:

> It's a comfort to feel,
>   If your partner should flit,
> Though *you* suffer a deal,
>   They don't mind it a bit—
> They don't blame you—so long as you're funny!

This verse turns the song into a meditation on the sentimental suffering of those who must act for a living, especially those who must be funny, and it prefigures Jack's extravagant suffering at the end.[43]

Jack Point has often been interpreted as a surrogate for Gilbert.[44] To the extent that this might be so, it is not a flattering self-portrait, although Gilbert often acknowledged and even prided himself on his irascible temperament. Arguing that there is no evidence for the autobiographical association, Jane Stedman ventures that it suggests "a man who wants to return to serious drama, but who cannot."[45] But I would argue, instead, that the salience of Gilbert's relation to Jack is not autobiographical, but figurative. Gilbert's characterization of Jack represents a complex attachment to an earlier time in English theater, an attachment that is both nostalgic and parodic— nostalgic in the sense that the itinerancy of the strolling player recalls an earlier, more carefree time, but parodic in the sense that Jack both rings the changes on the traditional jester figure and ups the ante of its sarcasm and biliousness. This complex attitude toward the theatrical past is characteristic of the Savoy operas, with their "affectionate" parody and their avid recollection of bygone figures, plots, jokes, and genres.

The prime evidence for my view of Jack is that he becomes funnier when we regard him this way, as a figure full of outworn jokes. One aspect of this interpretation would stress the idea that Jack represents the old burlesque and extravaganza jokes that Gilbert supplanted; this is Harley Granville-Barker's point of view.[46] But the other aspect of this interpretation is that Jack represents the good things about old jokes—the groan factor of their sheer familiarity, the pleasure in recognizing their chain of conventionality. Like the joke about the strawberry mark, Jack's jokes are already known. We do not even have to be told the punch line in order to be amused, as we can see when Jack offers his "best conundrum" ("[W]hy a cook's brain-pan is like an overwound clock") without its solution. Like Alice in Wonderland, struggling with a riddle ("Why is a raven like a writing-desk?"), it is not the solution but the zany form of the joke itself that is funny. Instead of seeing Jack Point as a mask for Gilbert, it would be more rewarding—and, I think, more accurate—to see that Gilbert identified with the jester tradition as a past form of theater.

12

Imaginary Republicanism

The Gondoliers

The action of *The Gondoliers; or, The King of Barataria* (1889) takes place in two picturesque, imaginary locations, both like and unlike England. For Victorians who would recall John Ruskin's assertion that the Doge's Palace is "the central building of the world,"[1] Venice, the setting of act 1, was a sublime city of the imagination, a near-mythical repository of great art and architecture, a symbol of the Venetian Gothic poised at its moment of perfection. (According to Ruskin, Venice provided a warning to England, too; in his opening comparison of Venice with Tyre, he adumbrates the "Fall" that might await England's "domination.") The setting of act 2 is the imaginary island nation of Barataria, through which the opera hints at English insularity and the peculiarities of English governance. Thus the opera moves from England to Venice, and from Venice to Barataria, the name of the island invented by Miguel de Cervantes in 1605, when Don Quixote awards its governorship to Sancho Panza, in recognition of his faithful service. Since Sancho Panza might be seen as an idealized, traditional, and literary representative of "the people," Barataria is well cast as the setting for a farcical meditation on republicanism.

For several reasons, Venice also makes a good setting for the opera's scattershot byplay with the idea of republicanism. The long history of the independent Republic of Venice gives plenty of scope for a general "republican" theme while placing the theme securely in the past. And yet the independence of Venice was also of fairly recent memory, for after the unification of Italy, consummated finally in 1866, a regionalist movement promoted the revival of the Republic of Venice as a culture with its own traditions and language. Perhaps in the background of *The Gondoliers* is the suggestion that the struggle to unite fiercely independent nation-states as the nation of Italy forms a reflection of the formation of "Great Britain" from its component parts. But the dating of the opera in 1750 makes the suggestion of the latter days of the Republic of Venice more salient than the evocation of nineteenth-century politics. It would probably be stretching a point to imagine that the shadow of projection may have been aimed at the state of England in 1889, although the recent proliferation of republican clubs suggests otherwise. But far and away the most important effect of the Venetian setting, in any case, is its collection of Venetian props and costumes; its establishment of an exotic, other world; and its tone or atmosphere, the "sunny" disposition of this fantastic southern setting, its difference from the cold north, its suggestion of satisfied desire (plate 18).[2]

The Italianate music makes the opera's sunny disposition explicit. Sullivan relished the idea of an opera set in Venice. To the extent that *The Gondoliers* involves genre parody, the parody is of Italian opera in general, with perhaps a whiff of Venetian carnival in the background; but if so, this is parody of the most affectionate kind, all homage and little critique. Yet there is humor in the stylistic allusiveness when, for example, another great "dilemma" quartet, "In a contemplative fashion," recalls and tops "A nice dilemma" from *Trial by Jury*. The close Neapolitan harmonies of the two tenor *gondolieri* deliver the Italian flavor on its demotic side. This musical allusiveness is echoed in the opening scene by the phrase dropping of the *gondolieri* and *contadine*, who remind their audiences constantly of their nationality by speaking tourist Italian: rhyming "*dolce far niente*" with "*contradicente*," "ben venuti" with "our duty," and "carissimi" with "umilissimi," "bellissimi," and "eccellentissimi."

The Gondoliers is the last great Savoy success. Gayden Wren describes it as a masterpiece that also shows the signs of dissolution.[3] The opera played to an ecstatic response in England, running longer than any Savoy opera except *H.M.S. Pinafore*, *The Mikado*, and *Patience* (although it was not popular in the United States, where the New York press quipped that it should be called the "Gone Dollars").[4] One mark of its popularity was a royal command performance on March 6, 1891, the first performance at Windsor Castle since the death of Prince Albert thirty years earlier.[5] Queen Victoria followed along in the program, tapping her foot with enjoyment at the jaunty reference to a "right down regular Royal Queen" (figure 12.1). But the signs of dissolution can be detected, especially in the incompletely unified plot, whose pacing sometimes drags. George Bernard Shaw felt that *The Gondoliers* marked the moment when "the Savoy operas became machine-made."[6] His is a minority view, for most reviewers have found the music wonderful enough to support the seriously flawed libretto. But Shaw does have a point about the libretto.

FIGURE 12.1 The royal command performance of *The Gondoliers* at Windsor Castle. Engraving by Walter Wilson, in *Illustrated London News*, March 14, 1891. (Collection of Fredric Woodbridge Wilson)

For our consideration of gender, genre, and parody, *The Gondoliers* has less to offer than do any of the other Savoy operas. In this regard, it is most notable for its Italian musical styling, its parody of republicanism and limited-liability companies as social and legal formations, and its own slightly generic quality—that is, its return to the main line of Gilbert and Sullivan comic opera after the operatic ambitions of *The Yeomen of the Guard*. One has only to think of the difference between the revelation of identity at the end of *H.M.S. Pinafore* and the revelation of identity that forms the resolution of *The Gondoliers*—similar in so many respects—to appreciate the importance of genre parody when it is working powerfully. The disclosure that Luiz is the real heir to the throne of Barataria is comparatively superficial, conventional without the added depth of significant genre implications.

The focus of *The Gondoliers* on republicanism continues the Savoy operas' obsession with forms of multiplicity within identity, present in Gilbert's thought and plotting from the first. We have traced his fixation on social and professional forms of self-division, usually engendered in male characters by professional roles and in female characters by behavioral norms of femininity. When Thespis worries about the difficulties of being a manager, when the Lord Chancellor regrets that he "is a man of two capacities, and they clash," and when Pooh-Bah revels in his many functions and roles, the plot is exploring the various forms of masculine social self-division. When Josephine agonizes over her marriage choice and when Rose Maybud consults her etiquette book, the libretto is pondering the various forms of feminine social self-division. The obsession with self-division merges sometimes into a consideration of collectivities and the individuals that compose them, as when Frederic proclaims to the Pirates, "individually I love you all . . . but collectively I look upon you with . . . disgust."

Both republicanism and the limited-liability company allowed Gilbert to think about the flip side of internal division: the constitution of a superordinate or corporate entity that can be conceived of, and legally treated as, an individual. The last three Savoy operas focus tenaciously on the idea of the legal fiction that makes such aggregate identities possible. In *The Gondoliers*, this thread is braided through the consideration of republicanism and the twinning of the *gondolieri* in the role of king; in both *The Gondoliers* and *Utopia, Limited*, it twines around the notion of capitalist incorporation; in *The Grand Duke*, like *Thespis*, it is joined to the examination of the irreducible theatricality of all social roles and the idea of a legal fiction whereby several individuals sequentially occupy the role of the Grand Duke. The connection between republicanism and the limited-liability company (as two forms of aggregate identity) could have been the key to a coherence that the plot of *The Gondoliers* never seems to achieve. Instead, the satire of republicanism is directed mostly toward its supposedly absurd commitment to equality, parodied as the demand for absolute equivalence (rather than social equality). Thus the opera does not capitalize on a potential formal analogy that could have been developed between republicanism and incorporation, even though its mathematical, hyper-logical attention to making one from two, or one from many, suggests such a consistency on the level of form. The theme song of this aspect of the plot is certainly "Replying, we sing / As one individual," which hits both themes: the relation between the one and the many and the belief that "all shall equal be."

Republicanism as False Conundrum

How can two (or more than two) become one? This is the question that links the several themes and scenes of action in *The Gondoliers*. First, how can two *gondolieri* rule Barataria as one monarch? This is the central joke of the opera, a joke at the expense of republican equality, a joke drawn out as a reductio ad absurdum, as if to prove that equality itself is a logical absurdity. Second, how can a group of directors form one entity (a company) that is then represented by one person, the Duke of Plaza-Toro? And since both the Duke and the Duchess personify the company—or front for it—marriage comes into this meditation on corporate entities formed from the hypothetical union of individuals.

Indeed, marriage is established from the beginning as a test case of the "unity" of two in one, but it is not explicitly knit into the thematics of the opera until later. In the long opening scene, the Choruses of *contadine* and *gondolieri* act out a fundamental dance of heterosexual attraction, although there is none of the pointed gender opposition that we have come to expect from the divided Chorus. Instead, the male and female cohorts are divided, but absolutely devoted to compatibility, and there is about twenty minutes of music while the *gondolieri* choose their wives through a choreographed game of blindman's buff. Love is blind, but through blind chance two become one; two pairs of two become one pair of married pairs. Only later can this opening scene of marriage be recognized as part of the opera's meditation on identity. Toward the end of the opera, the quintet opening the finale makes this point explicit:

> O moralists all,
>   How can you call
> Marriage a state of unitee,
> When excellent husbands are bisected,
>   And wives divisible into three?

The idea that marriage is a form of legal fiction could be better integrated with the serious considerations of republicanism and company formation, but instead the idea is floated with an ease that keeps anything from becoming weighty. When Marco and Giuseppe Palmieri depart from Venice to become the king of Barataria, at the end of act 1, their song is a motto for the libretto's lack of firm direction: "We know not where, and we don't much care, / Wherever that isle may be."

The plot structure is bifurcated, and the two parts sit uneasily together. As Gaydon Wren has pointed out, *The Gondoliers* is really two operas "stitched together, operating side by side with very little overlap." Taking the cue of the opera's title and subtitle, he calls the first "The Gondoliers" and the second "The King of Barataria," suggesting that each part represents one of the collaborators; according to this argument, Sullivan's generous, genial sentiment characterizes the plot of the two *gondolieri*, while Gilbert's satirical grotesqueries are embodied in the Plaza-Toros.[7] In fact, the dialogue commences and the libretto properly begins, breaking the long introductory musical sequence, only when the Plaza-Toros arrive. The two plots are linked by Don Alhambra del Bolero, the Grand Inquisitor, who hid the prince of Barataria in Venice long ago. He disrupts the marriages of the *gondolieri* and *contadine*, providing the conflict that opens the story, and thus it is to him that the Plaza-Toros apply to find their daughter's past and future husband. Although not sufficiently characterized, Don Alhambra is the linchpin of the plot.

Even though this divided and improbably united structure seems uneasy, it does mirror the opera's obsession with the uneasy division and multiplication of identity. *The Gondoliers* tests the possibility that identity can be shared (as both *gondolieri* will serve as the one king of Barataria) or divided (as Tessa protests against being married to a "vulgar fraction"). As marriage and this strange monarchy balance two against one, republican government and company capitalism juggle the one and the many. The witty, rhyming enjambments "sequel / Re" and "Equal- / Ly" in the Duchess's song about the Plaza-Toros' marriage embodies the difficulties of binding together two as one—whether the two are *gondolieri* serving as one king or people joined in the bonds of matrimony.

All the pairs are already formed at the beginning of the opera, however, eliminating this structural principle of comic suspense. It only remains to be discovered who is the king of Barataria, but that man (whoever he may be) is married to Casilda. True, a modicum of suspense inheres in the notion that either Tessa or Gianetta may be cheated of a husband. But surely, by the time of this twelfth collaboration, the audience for Gilbert and Sullivan's opera would have expected a story that ends happily; surely, after *The Yeomen of the Guard*, the audience would have been glad to be humored again in this way. The infant marriage, the baby switching, the appearance of the mother/nurse figure, and the revelation of Luiz's royal birth are familiar elements of Savoy plotting (in *H.M.S. Pinafore*, *Patience*, and *Princess Ida*); each is common in traditions and genres outside Savoy opera as well, although the parody is more scattershot than focused in *The Gondoliers*. So many clues are given in the first half of act 1 that any attentive audience member, familiar with Gilbert and Sullivan, can see the general drift of how the plot will unfold. To this extent, the generic quality of a Gilbert and Sullivan opera shows all too well; to this extent, Shaw was right.

The Gilbert and Sullivan commentary tradition has often taken the opera's reflections on division and unity as an exercise in generic self-reflection, reading *The Gondoliers* as self-referential in two respects. First, it has often been taken to represent the differences that had troubled the relationship between the collaborators before its composition, during the so-called cipher quarrel. Protesting that he felt like a "cipher in the theatre," Sullivan had provoked Gilbert into an exaggeratedly wounded response. According to this line of reasoning, the diplomatic resolution—"If we meet, it must be as master and master"—eventually offered by Gilbert is figured in the plot and form of the libretto to *The Gondoliers*. That the opera opens with nearly twenty minutes of uninterrupted music and no dialogue prefigures the centrality of the music throughout; in general, *The Gondoliers* has more music than usual (its vocal score is the longest) and, like the elaborately choreographed opening sequence, the wonderful dance numbers—cachucha and gavotte—offer extended music free from word setting. All these features have been understood as Gilbert's concession to Sullivan's demand that his music be given more scope.[8] Thus the *gondolieri* who would be king are often said to be like Gilbert and Sullivan themselves, joined to one purpose, and, correlatively, *The Gondoliers* seems to reflect on the difficulties involved in its own composition.[9] Although this may seem to be a far-fetched (or too theoretical) reading now, it was clearly felt to be apt at the time the opera was produced. A cartoon from *Punch* pictures Gilbert and Sullivan as grumbling monarchs united on one throne (figure 12.2).

Second, like *Thespis*, Gilbert and Sullivan's first collaboration, and like *The Grand Duke*, their last, the structure of *The Gondoliers* is the result of a production history that suggests the difficulties of forming and maintaining a theatrical company. Jessie Bond, the great Savoy soubrette, who created the role of Tessa, recorded in her autobiography the consternation caused by the departure of George Grossmith from the D'Oyly Carte Opera Company. (Her own departure would soon cause a similar crisis.) The solution, according to Bond, was the decision to "have an opera . . . in which there shall be no principal parts. No character shall stand out more prominently than another." In other words, "we all shall equal be."[10] In this interpretation, Gilbert transferred the personnel problems of governing the Savoy company to the political problems of governing a country, and then deflected the seriousness of that theme through the familiar Savoy plot devices of identity confusion, infant betrothal, and baby switching.[11]

Regardless of the reason, Gilbert did take the notion of universal equality and converted it into a false conundrum: if everyone is "equal," then everyone is alike, and if that's the case, maybe no one is "anybody." The abolition of rank is taken to imply utter equivalence of individuals. Actually

" Once upon a time there were two Kings."

FIGURE 12.2 Two *gondolieri* as one king taken as a representation of the collaboration between Gilbert and Sullivan. E. J. Wheeler, "Once upon a time there were two Kings," *Punch*, January 4, 1890. (Reproduced with permission of Punch, Ltd., www .punch.co.uk)

more a play on words than a real conundrum, this issue is not at all on a par with the more interesting question of how two (or more) can become one. Like so much of this opera, the idea had been with Gilbert for a long time. Max Keith Sutton offers an example from Gilbert's days with *Fun*, when, writing pseudonymously as Snarler, he protested that "everybody is somebody, except your Snarler, who (it would seem) is Nobody."[12] Elsewhere concerned with the forces that fracture identity, in *The Gondoliers* Gilbert seems to treat individuality itself as a mere legal fiction.[13] Thus the question of identity is linked—by the slenderest thread—to the question of republicanism, through this confusion of equality with exact equivalence. In this respect, the libretto of *The Gondoliers* does have some satirical and parodic bite, but it is relegated to a small part of the opera's length, as Audrey Williamson points out, becoming apparent only toward the end of act 1 and then disappearing again halfway through act 2.[14]

The Gondoliers looks at republicanism from two angles, one much more interesting than the other. On the one hand, republicanism suggests considerations of multiplicity and integrity (many united as one) or of divided loyalties and the "vulgar fractions" of human beings that result. On the other hand, republicanism suggests the logical limits of social equality, and Gilbert seems to have made no advances in his thinking about this topic since the "Junction Song" in *Thespis* conservatively purported to show the necessity of social hierarchy. An important residue of Chartism, republicanism—in the form of republican clubs—had flourished in the 1870s. From 1871 to 1874, many clubs were established, showing that the movement for workers' rights was still active, long after the defeat of the Charter in 1848. Indeed, these clubs have been credited with keeping the movement alive.[15] But the libretto does not make this cultural context explicit; if reference to the republican clubs is intended, it is subtle indeed. To the extent that an attitude can be detected, it is a strikingly conservative one— more the kind of middlebrow hostility found in *Punch* than a more serious literary response to republican ideas.[16] As one critic points out, late Victorian satirists frequently devoted themselves to minimizing the seriousness of working-class republicanism.[17] So, too, in *The Gondoliers*, the *gondolieri* begin as workingmen with republican convictions, but offered the chance for one of them to become a king, they suddenly throw over their anti-monarchical and republican principles. As Giuseppe puts the rationalization: "Well . . . there are kings and kings. When I say that I detest kings, I mean I detest *bad* kings." They welcome the chance to give preferment to their friends in court, and they make those who perform low jobs into "Lord High" this and that (in a pointed recollection of Pooh-Bah's bureaucratic greed in *The Mikado*). Inconsistently, though, they pitch into the other side of the topsy-turvy equation, helping with the menial tasks of dressing their valet, writing letters for their private secretary, and seeing no reason why a Lord High Chancellor should not play leapfrog with his own cook. (Earlier, tellingly, "Dook" rhymes with "Cook.") However, the plot never really turns on the republican convictions of the *gondolieri* or their abolition of class and rank. In other words, the opera raises a serious question—What would it be like if "all shall equal be?"—in a decisively unserious way.

Socially, logically, and sociologically, *The Gondoliers* presses toward the reductio ad absurdum of ideals of equality. When Giuseppe explains to the Grand Inquisitor that "the Monarchy has been re-modelled on Republican principles," he extends his point in a bureaucratic direction: "All departments rank equally, and everybody is at the head of his department." This is what provokes Don Alhambra to sing "There lived a King, as I've been told," a novelty song pointedly reminiscent of "I once knew a chap who discharged a function" from *Thespis*. The "moral" of both stories is the same: some hierarchical system must be observed, or chaos will ensue:

> The end is easily foretold,
> When every blessed thing you hold
> Is made of silver, or of gold,
> > You long for simple pewter.
> When you have nothing else to wear
> But cloth of gold and satins rare,
> For cloth of gold you cease to care—
> > Up goes the price of shoddy.
> . . .
> In short, whoever you may be,
> To this conclusion you'll agree,
> When every one is somebodee,
> > Then no one's anybody!

The worth of persons, equated with social status, is made equivalent to the value of goods on the market. Cynical and pseudo-logical, this song is the culmination of the opera's satire on republicanism. But the general spirit of these questions are taken up and carried further by the Plaza-Toros (and even further by *Utopia, Limited*).

Thus even though it is undeveloped, the underlying coherence of the plot of *The Gondoliers* can be found in the way the forms of marriage, republicanism, monarchy, and company capital may be seen to overlap. Gilbert's omni-directional satire, although more superficial than usual, does carry a point, however. For the satire on republicanism is balanced by an equal-opportunity satire on monarchy and a semi-profound joke about the contradiction between the two. We can see a bit of autoethnographic critique, focused mainly on the absurdity of conjoining republicanism and monarchy—an absurdity that refers to Great Britain's own unusual system. But the autoethnographic critique is blunted by marked autoethnographic homage; the antimonarchical humor comes out blatantly, but it is made inconsequential, the fact of its studied inoffensiveness demonstrated by its choice as Queen Victoria's command performance. *Utopia, Limited* would consider another island in which England might mirror itself and its government. Thus Barataria—the namesake island of Sancho Panza's reward—becomes the name of a fantasy land where one can experience "A monarchy that's tempered with / Republican Equality."

The Duke of Plaza-Toro, Limited

In the Duke and Duchess of Plaza-Toro, we encounter another thematic satire on the decline of the aristocracy, combined with a parody of the legal form of the limited-liability company. The Peers in *Iolanthe* are represented as useless and outworn, yet in the song "Blue Blood," they beg for sympathy with their plight. And a similar humor presides over the wonderful gavotte in *The Gondoliers*, "I am a courtier grave and serious," which focuses on the elaborate precision demanded by aristocratic body language, in order to display just the right amount of "high" distinction from those beneath, yet just the right amount of noble benevolence and condescension as well. While Marco and Giuseppe try to "combine a pose imperious / With a demeanor nobly bland" and "Take an attitude not too stately, / Still sufficiently dignified," the gavotte proceeds at its humorously measured pace, beautifully emphasizing the choreographed attitudes and poses involved in court behavior, one of Gilbert's favorite topics from *The Mikado* on. The socially residual role of faded nobility, in *"pompous but old and faded clothes,"* is made an object of both parody and sympathy.

Most important, the Duke of Plaza-Toro is a sellout, for his fading fortunes have prompted him to form himself into a limited-liability company:

> Although I am unhappily in straitened circumstances at present, my social influence is something enormous; and a Company, to be called the Duke of Plaza-Toro, Limited, is in course of formation to work me. An influential directorate has been secured, and I shall myself join the Board after allotment.

Casilda wonders whether, as queen of Barataria, she might be called on at some point to put her father "in process of liquidation," and her mother chimes in, with a torturous pun on winding a clock and dissolving a limited-liability company, to agree that if the speculation should fail, it might be necessary to "wind him up." Making the expected conservative joke (or joke on conservatism), Casilda is especially disgusted that he is a public company: "[I]t's so undignified—it's so degrading!" Her mother's response, that he does not follow fashions, but leads them, provides the introduction for the Duke's signature song, which proves, on the contrary, that he is no leader at all. The song emphasizes his cowardice, while its refrain rattles off the rhymes in a martial rat-tat-tat:

In enterprise of martial kind,
    When there was any fighting,
He led his regiment from behind—
    He found it less exciting.
But when away his regiment ran,
    His place was at the fore, O—
        That celebrated,
        Cultivated,
        Underrated
          Nobleman,
The Duke of Plaza-Toro!

To earn his living, the Duke of Plaza-Toro pretends to have selfless motives to "help unhappy commoners, and add to their enjoyment." In the duet "Small titles and orders," the Duke and Duchess explain how they will help, by arranging small honors for the commoners and appearing at their ceremonial dinners, always for remuneration. Like Pooh-Bah's, their "high" position is directly supported by monetary tokens of appreciation for a wide range of functions: "Foundation-stone laying"; speech spinning at charity dinners; escorting and "whitewashing" ladies of dubious propriety; playing cards at parties; sponsoring dressmakers, cheap tailors, and patent medicines; and sitting on the directorates of "several Companies bubble." In short, the Duke explains, the best bait for swindles is to "trot out a Duke or a Duchess."

That "Companies bubble" were often launched with little more authority than a sponsoring duke or an aristocratic directorate had long provided a topic of ridicule. As Mary Poovey has shown, mid-nineteenth-century England boasted the most permissive company law in the world. The absurd ease with which a limited-liability company could be established (and then liquidated) became a matter of parody soon after the comprehensive Companies Act of 1862 was passed. Dickens published several long treatments of the new rules for speculation and company flotation in *All the Year Round* between 1863 and 1865, including Charles Reade's *Hard Cash* (1863) and three series of articles by Malcolm Ronald Laing Meason. Poovey foregrounds Meason's parodic piece describing the flotation and liquidation of the fictional Bank of Patagonia, a limited, joint-stock bank that the narrator conjures out of thin air and then cynically winds up, profiting at both ends of the transaction.[18] But the familiarity of this parodic butt is no obstacle to its enjoyment; as we have repeatedly seen, the traditional, even old-hat nature of an object of parody only makes it more valuable in the Savoy aesthetic. Rather than going into the absurdities of the limited-liability company, however, *The Gondoliers* floats the idea of a gullible public still fixated on the old-fashioned authority of a fading aristocracy. Thus *The Gondoliers* prepares the way for the much more profound parody of *Utopia, Limited,* in which corporate capitalism and limited liability are explicitly correlated with cultural colonialization.

13

Capitalism and Colonialism

Utopia, Limited

U topia, Limited; or, The Flowers of Progress (1893), an anti-colonialist, anti-capitalist comic opera, takes aim at the English attitudes involved in imperial domination and makes the explicit argument that an alliance of capitalism and bureaucracy is the driving force behind empire. The opera stages a parodic version of the colonial encounter, when a tiny South Sea island nation, humorously named Utopia, actively courts its own cultural colonization. The Utopians invite a delegation of English bureaucrats, the Flowers of Progress, to instruct them in English dress, behavior, and forms of social organization. Thus *Utopia, Limited* opens with the flagrantly absurd reversal of colonial resistance. Mr. Goldbury, a Company Promoter, one of the Flowers of Progress, recommends the incorporation of Utopia as a joint-stock company, under the provisions of limited liability. Trouble ensues, of course, showing that the union of colonialism and corporate capitalism is precisely what transforms Utopia into "Utopia, Limited."

The graphic cultural difference between Utopia and England is expressed visually in the difference between acts 1 and 2, which take place, respectively, in a Utopian palm grove and in the throne room of the Utopian palace after it has been "Anglicized completely."[1] A wholesale costume change signals this cultural transformation. The "native Utopian dress" of the Maidens is coded for its loose and sexy freedom from restraint, at once suggesting "Oriental" eroticism and "natural" innocence, while the indigenous costume of King Paramount seems to represent a mythic foreign barbarity, simultaneously idealized and trivialized (figures 13.1 and 13.2). In different ways, each gender specific, these costumes bespeak contradictory attitudes toward the cultural other, desire (of the women) juxtaposed with defensive denigration

FIGURE 13.1 Utopian Maidens at the opening of act 1 of *Utopia, Limited*, "lying lazily about the stage and thoroughly enjoying themselves in lotus-eating fashion." Cabinet photograph by Alfred Ellis (London, 1893). (The Pierpont Morgan Library, New York. The Gilbert and Sullivan Collection)

FIGURE 13.2 Rutland Barrington as King Paramount in "native Utopian dress" in act 1 of *Utopia, Limited*. Cabinet photograph by Alfred Ellis (London, 1893). (The Pierpont Morgan Library, New York. The Gilbert and Sullivan Collection)

(of the men). Both extremes carefully locate this South Sea island in the realm of fantasy. The English court costumes of act 2 re-dress the Utopians in elaborately realistic indications of profession, rank, and status (for the men) and up-to-the-minute fashionableness (for the women). They were designed with care as meticulous (and produced at an expense as exorbitant) as that taken with the Japanese costumes for *The Mikado*—and to like purpose, for they served, autoethnographically, to exhibit the "native dress" of English royalty, aristocracy, and the professions. From the estranging point of view of the Utopian, English dress seems absurdly restrictive. King Paramount, uncomfortable in his new clothes, sheepishly asks: "It's not a practical joke, is it?" Indeed it is a joke, one that takes English dress codes as a metonymy for the sweeping limitations expressed in the opera's title.

This cultural contrast was to have included a linguistic dimension that now exists only in residual form. At one point, Gilbert planned that "the piece may begin with a very short dialogue in Utopian." Of course, he went on to say, the Utopian language would be "mere gibberish." Then an official would inform the Utopians that their language had been forbidden at court, and henceforth only English might be spoken.[2] This plan was abandoned, perhaps because it would have expressed, too explicitly, the violence of cultural colonization; but it can still be detected in the scraps of Utopian that remain in the finished libretto. In the finale to act 1, for example, the Chorus welcomes the Flowers of Progress with shouts of "Ulahlica! Ulahlica! Ulahlica!" These remnants of a "native" tongue suggest, at some points, the imitation of an unspecified African language and, at others, a parody of Wagnerian mytho-heroic declamation. Even their residual presence hints, in a strangely displaced way, at the barely suppressed fury of the colonized, for Tarara, the Public Exploder, a figure of anarchism absurdly formalized into a bureaucratic department, expresses his wrath in the native tongue of the Utopians: "Lalabalele molola lililah kalabalele poo!"[3]

The plot of *Utopia, Limited* follows directly from the governmental concerns of *The Gondoliers* and leads to those of *The Grand Duke*. After experiments with republicanism, the Utopians have found an ideal government in "Despotism tempered by Dynamite," for the office of the Public Exploder is meant to limit the king's power. Although King Paramount is a kind and proper monarch, a "Society" newspaper, the *Palace Peeper*, reports on his scandalous immorality. No one realizes that the king writes those reports himself, under pressure from his power-hungry advisers. Under their watchful eyes, with the society press as their tool, this monarch must be quite respectable (like the monarchy in England). Utopia is a peculiarly limited monarchy even before it becomes a limited company, and it will return to being another sort of limited monarchy in the end.

In other words, the cultural differences between Utopia and England are emphasized because the point, in the end, depends on their confusion and conflation. After all, English actors and actresses are acting like South Sea islanders who learn to act English. The lack—or disappearance—of stable differences between home and abroad, between national identity and the fantasy of an altogether different culture, creates autoethnologic absurdity in *Utopia, Limited*. The ethnographic gaze is turned outward and then reflected back toward the home culture, as it was in *The Mikado*, but with a more pointed set of epistemological and cross-cultural questions, from the English point of view: What might we look like to them? Can they learn to act like us? Should they? Can English culture really survive its translation elsewhere? Should English culture go abroad, transforming the world into an image of England? These are the questions that subtend the cultural politics of representation in this autoethnographic mirror.[4]

Princess Zara returns to Utopia from her study at Girton College, prompting the cultural colonization of the kingdom. This cosmopolitan cultural exchange casts Zara as a sort of missionary, and thus her characterization seems in part to offer a correction to the scathing portrait of female higher education promulgated in *Princess Ida*. As the Utopian Vice-Chamberlain explains, with mock-heroic grandeur:

> His Majesty's eldest daughter, Princess Zara, who left our shores five years since to go to England—the greatest, the most powerful, the wisest country in the world—has taken a high degree at Girton, and is on her way home again, having achieved a complete mastery over all the elements that have tended to raise that glorious country to her present pre-eminent position among civilized nations!

The absurdly hyperbolic praise of England continues when Zara imports the English Flowers of Progress, those "six Representatives of the principal causes that have tended to make England the powerful, happy, and blameless country which the consensus of European civilization has declared it to be." As if it were featured in one of James Robinson Planché's dramatic revues, this pageant of English bureaucratic institutions displays one representative type after another for humorous scrutiny, including a Lord Chamberlain, who aims to purify the court and the stage; a County Councilor, who aims to purify the city streets and the music halls; and Captain Sir Edward Corcoran, K.C.B., who has been knighted since we last saw him and who duly trots out the "What never? Well, hardly ever!" joke from *H.M.S. Pinafore*.[5] Addressing these "wanderers from a mighty State," Zara begs them to "teach us how to legislate." Following Zara's lead, all the Utopians fast become "Anglo-maniacs."

Chief among the Flowers of Progress, Mr. Goldbury, the Company Promoter, recommends the reform of the island nation in accordance with the principle of limited liability. "No scheme's too great and none too small / For Companification!" Mr. Goldbury exults. "Utopia's much to big for one small head— / I'll float it as a Company Limited!" No one understands what he means, so Mr. Goldbury explains:

Some seven men form an Association
    (If possible all Peers and Baronets),
They start off with a public declaration
    To what extent they mean to pay their debts.
That's called their Capital: if they are wary
    They will not quote it at a sum immense.
The figure's immaterial—it may vary
    From eighteen million down to eighteenpence.
        I should put it rather low;
        The good sense of doing so
Will be evident at once to any debtor.
        When it's left to you to say
        What amount you mean to pay,
Why, the lower you can put it at the better.
. . .
They then proceed to trade with all who'll trust 'em,
    Quite irrespective of their capital
(It's shady but it's sanctified by custom);
    Bank, Railway, Loan, or Panama Canal.
You can't embark on trading too tremendous—
    It's strictly fair, and based on common sense—
If you succeed, your profits are stupendous—
    And if you fail, pop goes your eighteenpence.
        Make the money-spinner spin!
        For you only stand to win,
And you'll never with dishonesty be twitted,
        For nobody can know,
        To a million or so,
To what extent your capital's committed!
. . .
If you come to grief, and creditors are craving

(For nothing that is planned by mortal head
    Is certain in this Vale of Sorrow—saving
        That one's Liability is Limited),—
Do you suppose that signifies perdition?
    If so you're but a monetary dunce—
You merely file a Winding-Up Petition,
    And start another Company at once!
        Though a Rothschild you may be
        In your own capacity,
    As a Company you've come to utter sorrow—
        But the Liquidators say,
        "Never mind—you needn't pay,"
So you start another Company to-morrow!

The privilege of limited liability, a Victorian invention, is the crux of modern company law. In its critique of limited liability, this song focuses on provisions for disguising the accountability to risk of the company directors (and thus for passing that risk on to the shareholders). The beginning of the association is "a public declaration / To what extent they mean to pay their debts," which Albert Borowitz calls "one of the finest working definitions of corporate capital, at least from the point of view of the creditors."[6] As Mr. Goldbury's song makes clear, the limitation of liability allows for trade on a vast scale, since "you only stand to win." Finally, the process of liquidation, or "winding-up," allows for the closure of the venture—again, without strict accountability.

Perhaps Gilbert was moved to this satire by international events, such as the Panama Canal scandal (indicated in the song), which had broken earlier in 1893, or by national events, such as the Glasgow Bank fraud case of 1878, both of which Borowitz suggests as contexts for interpretation. Perhaps his sensitivity derived from his own experience of company capitalism and his recent struggles with Sullivan and Carte. The famous "carpet quarrel," from which the three collaborators had only recently recovered, was specifically a disagreement about the precise contractual provisions on profit sharing in the Savoy Theatre. Maybe, too, as John Wolfson claims, Gilbert was disgusted by Carte's scheme to "float" a renovation of the Royal English Opera House as the Palace Theatre of Varieties.[7] Many contexts have been advanced to explain Gilbert's interest in the absurdities of incorporation, but the most telling evidence is the general pervasiveness of commentary on this question and the sheer number of possible reasons that have been adduced. For although the Chorus claims that the "Joint Stock Company's

Act of Sixty-Two" was an "invention new," when it offers "the only choral tribute to a corporation statute" in all of opera history[8]—

> All hail, astonishing Fact!
>> All hail, invention new—
> The Joint Stock Company's Act—
>> The Act of Sixty-Two!—

in fact, in 1893, the act of 1862 was not at all an "invention new."

The principles of the joint-stock company had existed in England since the mid-sixteenth century and had been prevalent since the eighteenth. What was new in the nineteenth century was the principle of limited liability. Limited liability was not instituted by the act of 1862, which only consolidated its provision, but had been established in 1856, with five subsequent statutes and elaborated procedures for liquidation.[9] The alliance of capitalism and the state was especially not new, for the granting of trade concessions and "exclusive rights" of trading within certain areas to certain companies had been practiced for centuries, accompanied by protests and satires against such setups.[10] If we appreciate the length and depth of this history, we can see that Gilbert chose to parody a feature of the social realm that was as venerable, in its own way, as the magical elixir to the literary realm. Again, the originality of a parody depends on widespread recognition of its object, not on the object itself being original or even specific. When the Utopians hail the act as "invention new," in other words, we should hear the irony, clearly introduced in the first verse of the song:

> Let's seal this mercantile pact—
>> The step we ne'er shall rue—
> It gives whatever we lacked—
>> The statement's strictly true.

Modern forms of finance and credit had accelerated the pace of capital accumulation, however, and these developments were inextricable from the growth of empire. As Mary Poovey has shown, "by 1862 England had the most permissive company law in the world." Furthermore, commentary on the links among speculation, company law, and colonial expansion had circulated ever since the consolidation of limited liability between 1844 and 1862.[11] To demonstrate this cultural awareness, Poovey presents Laurence Oliphant's "Autobiography of a Joint-Stock Company (Limited)," a fictionalized account of a well-known financial scandal, told from the first-person point of view of "an abstract being," and Malcolm Ronald Laing Meason's articles on the fictional Bank of Patagonia, whose story shows the narrator cynically profiting during both incorporation and winding-up.[12] Meason's critique focuses on the same issues that Gilbert chose to highlight: the ease with which the company could be launched, the absurd limitation of liability, and the awareness that colonial expansion both "depended on and exposed" these manipulations of capital. In the prospectus that Meason's narrator prepares for his investors, he offers both philanthropic and missionary rationales, and ends by claiming that his venture has the full support of "the most influential native chiefs."[13] Poovey points out that this humor "brings the earliest rationales for colonialization— philanthropy and missionary conversion—into alignment with the latest, most explicitly economic rationale." Together, they form an ideological knot, parodied by Meason, that binds the profit motive to the tacit assumption of cultural superiority on the part of the English.

Gilbert seized on the principle of limited liability as a topical link with which to join ethnographic, colonial, and national dimensions of the plot with the opera's anti-capitalist burden; with this expedient, however, he made a powerful economic argument. The setting of *Utopia, Limited* thus alludes equally to the late-nineteenth-century addition to the British Empire of several islands in the South Pacific and to the notorious South Sea Bubble of 1720. These associations are made clear through the funny consequences of "companification" developed in act 2. King Paramount's stereotypically evil and controlling advisers, now turned greedy entrepreneurs, have "contracted to supply the entire nation with a complete English outfit." Thus the change in costume, which already signifies cultural colonization, results explicitly from rapacious, monopolistic trading. Upping the ante, when the Utopians receive bills for their "English outfits," they refuse to pay, for each of them has individually incorporated as a limited-liability company and can "plead liability limited to a declared capital of eighteenpence, and apply to be dealt with under the Winding-up Act—as in England."

This reductio ad absurdum is profoundly funny, for never in the history of rationalizations for the limitation of liability would it ever have been suggested that it could be applied democratically. The whole point of the privilege is to endow powerful capitalist interests with even more expansive power, to facilitate trading on an ever more extravagant scale, and to detach risk from individual directors by allowing both the capital accumulation and the liability to "float" intangibly free from the personal finances of any member of the association. As Mr. Goldbury explains, when describing the failure of a venture:

> Though a Rothschild you may be
> In your own capacity,
> As a Company you've come to utter sorrow.

Long obsessed with the humor of the modern and artificial separation of "capacities," as we have repeatedly seen, Gilbert turned, in the last three Savoy operas, from a focus on various forms of self-division within an individual to a consideration of large structures. For like a republic, as imagined in *The Gondoliers*, a "company" is the topsy-turvy opposite of several "capacities" at war within the same person—since it establishes a putatively superordinate "body" (*corpus*) of commerce by the artificial association of "some seven men" or more, for the purposes of capital accumulation.

In this respect, the analogy the opera draws between the limited-liability company and the nation becomes quite haunting: like a modern corporation, the nation itself is an imaginary "association" of disparate elements, not an "identity." This aspect of the nation troubles the close of *Utopia, Limited*, as we shall see. Entertaining the fairly radical notion that what it really means to be "Anglicized completely" is to be incorporated and protected for trade under the privilege of limited liability, the opera's argument is clear: this instrument of company law exists in order to favor the rich and to assist England in evading its "corporate" responsibilities, the state is already tantamount to a limited-liability company, and capitalism hinders the utopian potential of the nation. King Paramount, in recitative, expresses his doubts:

> Well, at first sight it strikes us as dishonest,
> But if it's good enough for virtuous England—
> The first commercial country in the world—
> It's good enough for us.
> . . .
> And do I understand you that Great Britain
> Upon this Joint Stock principle is governed?

Mr. Goldbury replies: "We haven't come to that, exactly—but / We're tending rapidly in that direction." Inspired by mimetic desire, King Paramount enthusiastically embraces the plan, hoping to outpace even Great Britain, by becoming the first country to be registered under the "Joint Stock Company's Act of Sixty-Two." No longer Utopia, his nation now becomes Utopia, Limited.[14]

In act 2, the autoethnographic intentions of *Utopia, Limited* become even clearer. The principles of company capitalism have been hyperbolically extended to every man, woman, and child in Utopia, and, signifying the cultural colonization of Utopia, everyone is now costumed in English dress. Three scenes in the opera provide graphic illustrations of the ethnographic gaze turned back on England: in act 2, the Cabinet Council is represented in the style of the Christy Minstrels, and the elaborately staged first "Drawing-Room" reenacts, with scrupulously realistic detail, Queen Victoria's receptions; in act 1, the two younger princesses are exhibited in the public square as consummate examples of correct feminine behavior, on the English model. Thus the opera focuses on genres of English cultural theatricality, displacing them through the fantasy that Utopians are learning to act English.

In the scene of the "first Utopian Drawing-Room," every detail of the entrance of the English royal household, the royal family, and the court, as well as every detail of the presentation of the debutantes, was followed "practically as at Buckingham Palace" (figure 13.3). Rutland Barrington, who created the role of King Paramount, reported that Gilbert hired a "lady professor of deportment" to attend the rehearsals and teach the actors precisely how to bow, the actresses how to handle their trains, and everyone how and where to walk. No expense was spared in the lavish authenticity of the spectacle. (Both hiring an authenticating coach—to teach the replication of an unknown culture—and spending a fortune on the spectacle recall the production strategies used for *The Mikado*.) The production costs reached an astonishing £7200, of which more than £5000 went for costumes, accessories, and "hand-props."[15] The ceremony unfolds very slowly, and at the end, King Paramount summarizes grandly: "This ceremonial our wish displays / To copy all Great Britain's courtly ways." Despite its pomp and dignity, the representation included one jokey innovation: a "cup of tea and . . . plate of mixed biscuits." According to all accounts, this little dig at the reputed discomfort of a real-life drawing room was soon taken seriously, and the cup of tea and plate of mixed biscuits were adopted in all good humor as an improvement by the real-life royal family. Thus did Savoy opera play its own small part in the continuing invention of tradition.

As Reginald Allen points out, this scene prefigures a later genre of musical theater, the costume spectacle, in which the unfolding plot is suspended during a lengthy sequence of visual splendor, music, and dance.[16] In *Utopia, Limited*, there is no dancing, but the precisely choreographed movement

FIGURE 13.3 The "first Utopian Drawing-Room" in act 2 of *Utopia, Limited*. (Collection of Fredric Woodbridge Wilson)

of court pageantry. And, in fact, an analysis of court behavior as a form of theater is familiar in Savoy opera; one is reminded of "I am a courtier grave and serious" from *The Gondoliers* and the "gentlemen of Japan" from *The Mikado*, who explain that their puppet-like movement is "simply Court etiquette." George Bernard Shaw registered the particular sort of pleasure derived by the spectators of this drawing-room pageantry. "I cannot vouch for its verisimilitude," he wrote, "as I have never, strange as it may appear, been present at a Drawing Room; but that is exactly why I enjoyed it, and why the majority of the Savoyards will share my appreciation of it."[17] As Shaw's comment suggests, no doubt many in the audience enjoyed being virtually present in a place from which they would normally be excluded. The ethnographic mirror turns outward toward the audience, to reveal difference *within* the home culture, showcasing class hierarchy even while it is being temporarily transcended in this virtual, spectacular access to the interior of the palace. Furthermore, as David Cannadine has argued, in the last decades of the nineteenth century, "every royal occasion was also an imperial occasion, designed to conceal and render acceptable the novelty of a mass society at home as well as a formal empire abroad."[18]

The scene was "played straight, not as a comic travesty of Queen Victoria's receptions."[19] Nevertheless, we should keep in mind that English-looking aristocrats and members of the royal household were being played by South Sea island "natives." Both humor and critical inquiry lie at the heart of this conjunction of autoethnography, spectacle, and the idea of colonial mimicry as a powerful response to cultural imperialism.[20] If the acquisition of "culture" may be reduced to a theatrical performance, there is the possibility, within this cross-cultural framework, of uncertain slippage between identities. King Paramount's anxious questions—"[T]his is all right? It's not a practical joke, is it?"—aim the critique back toward the repressive restrictions of "cultured" English behavior, but the dynamic of colonial mimicry hovers nearby.

The best representation of this critical anxiety appears in the wonderful scene of the Cabinet Council, which is paired structurally with the "Drawing-Room" in order to drive home the autoethnographic point. Just before the "Drawing-Room" scene, King Paramount calls the Flowers of Progress together and asks to be taught the proper procedures for an English Cabinet Council. Lord Dramaleigh, the Lord Chamberlain, suddenly directs the Flowers of Progress to draw their chairs into the familiar semicircle, *like Christy Minstrels*," as the stage directions make clear (figure 13.4). The king, who assumes the central position as interlocutor, again displays his nervousness—"You are not making fun of us? This is in accordance with the practice at the Court of St. James?"—to which Lord Dramaleigh replies: "Well, it is in accordance with the practice at the Court of *St. James's Hall* [emphasis added]." This exchange, with its sudden downshifting of cultural reference, is a parody of minstrel dialogue that names the venue where the Christy Minstrels (and many other minstrel acts) performed in London. The metatheatrical analogy between the Court of St. James and St. James's Hall rewrites the opera's overarching confusion between England and Utopia, this time briefly foregrounding the issue of race and performance.[21]

Minstrel shows had been a popular genre of musical theater in London since the late 1830s and the 1840s. By the 1890s, they had significantly influenced other forms of burlesque.[22] Like the native English burlesque and music-hall traditions, this first indigenous American genre of musical theater involved takeoffs on other popular genres, comic skits, female impersonation, and songs. But its dominant convention was blackface masquerade, enabling white actors to impersonate black male and female slaves, former slaves, and urban "swells." Minstrels and "Ethiopian Delineators" were often billed as a variety of the ethnographic exhibition, a pretense that

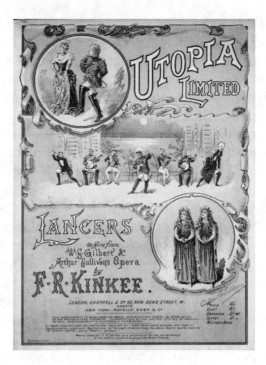

FIGURE 13.4 The Cabinet Council convening, in the style of the Christy Minstrels (*middle*). Cover of the sheet music for *Lancers on Airs from Utopia, Limited* (1893–1894), arranged by F. R. Kinkee. (Collection of Fredric Woodbridge Wilson)

may explain, in part, why minstrel shows were received as highly respectable, educational entertainments.[23] For example, the press advertisement for the inaugural appearance in London, in 1843, of the Virginia Minstrels announces an "exhibition" or "a true copy of Ethiopian life" and promises a portrait of "the sports and pastimes of the Southern slave race of America."[24] Alternately slapstick and sentimental, these performances were, of course, rife with racial stereotypes and caricatures.

In the context of *Utopia, Limited*, this complex allusion to the former American colony and its internalized cultural other, "the Southern slave race," creates a sort of imperialist *mise en abîme*. The Flowers of Progress did not appear in blackface; instead, their minstrel scene shows that *Utopia, Limited* is conscious of being itself a sort of whiteface masquerade, in which the "natives" learn to act English. In other words, the allusion to blackface takes its place beside other forms of masquerade in this opera, as if race could be put on and taken off as easily as a costume, theatrical genre, or national identity. Staging an impersonation of a genre of impersonation, a burlesque of a genre of burlesque, this scene demonstrates the Savoy dynamic of using lower genres as a resource and recollecting them within the higher framework of comic opera. As in burlesque, seriously critical implications are raised, only to be deflected, for once again the more profound and dangerous questions about imperial domination are turned back toward the parody of English institutions.

Originally, the scene opened with some "nigger dialogue" between King Paramount, as interlocutor, and Mr. Blushington, of the County Council, on the bones; this dialogue was cut before opening night.[25] Still, King Paramount dances a breakdown and sings along. Accompanying themselves on bones and tambourine, while in their minstrel lineup as Cabinet Council, the Flowers of Progress sing a wonderful number that always brought down the house. "Society has quite forsaken all her wicked courses," a parody of a minstrel song, opens to the tune of "Johnny Get Your Gun," a plantation song similar to the Northumbrian folk song "The Keel Row."[26] The song boisterously celebrates social improvements that have *not* in fact been made in England. Thus, supposedly, in Utopia, the streets are clean, the slums have been eradicated, "poverty is obsolete and hunger is abolished," the court and stage have been purified, titles are now given to literary men, and the peerage has been remodeled "on an intellectual basis." The autoethnographic reflection hits home as King Paramount describes improvements and the Chorus claims that they will soon be made in England; thus, within the premise of this song, England must look to Utopia as a model for its own reform. The refrain, repeated three times in the course of the song, makes this point clear:

> It really is surprising
> What a thorough Anglicizing
> We have brought about—Utopia's quite another land;
> In her enterprising movements,
> She is England—with improvements,
> Which we dutifully offer to our mother-land!

The rhyme of "mother-land" with "another land" emphasizes the cross fire of perspectives within this ethnographic mirror.

English national culture is represented not only by the Flowers of Progress, however, but also by figures of English-style femininity. As in *H.M.S. Pinafore* and *The Mikado*, gender is a subset of national identity; as in *Pinafore* and *Ruddigore*, gender is a performance of socialized, learned behavior. While Princess Zara is off at Girton, receiving her higher education in English ways, her younger sisters, Nekaya and Kalyba, are being schooled at home by Lady Sophy, the proper English governess hired to "finish" them. Like Mrs. General in *Little Dorrit* (1855) and Miss Prism in *The Importance of Being Earnest* (1895), Lady Sophy is "that blameless type of perfect womanhood," who has "Respectability enough for Six." In other words, she is the latest Savoy incarnation of woman as enforcer of propriety. Although she is compulsively conscientious, however, she is benign for the most part. But her cultural role as theatrical production manager of proper gender behavior is not seen as benign. She has socialized the two princesses to perform an exhibition in the public square, "from ten to four without a pause," to display the actions of proper English girls during courtship (figure 13.5).

The two young princesses, whose twinship emphasizes their uniform replication of rote behavior, go through the "poses" of exaggerated reticence and theatrical modesty "like clockwork toys." Their modesty, clearly a form of exhibitionism, should provoke laughter at the contradiction in terms:

FIGURE 13.5 The public exhibition: Lady Sophy and her "finished" pupils, Princesses Nekaya and Kalyba, illustrate proper feminine behavior during courtship. Cabinet photograph of Rosina Brandram, with Emmy Owen and Florence Perry, by Alfred Ellis (London, 1893). (The Pierpont Morgan Library, New York. The Gilbert and Sullivan Collection)

English girls of well-bred notions
Shun all unrehearsed emotions.
    English girls of highest class
    Practice them before the glass.

With a lecturer's wand, Lady Sophy points out the salient aspects of being "brought up on the English scheme," while the princesses act out, in perfect unison, their "well-known blush—[their] downcast eyes / [Their] famous look of mild surprise." The Chorus, acting as surrogate for the audience, exclaims:

See how they blush, as they've been taught,
    At this publicity unsought!
How English and how pure!

Perfect femininity must act as if it does not solicit the gaze while reveling in its vocation to be looked at. Using the theatrical attitude to emphasize a social critique, this scene hammers home the point that gender is learned through repeated performance, and—as usual in Savoy opera—that the internalization of proper gender behavior prevents straightforward, natural feeling.

In addition, the exhibition format shows that the populace should be instructed, through the example of these paragons. The crowd of spectators takes notes and snaps Kodak photographs to record the lesson.[27] Analogous to Rose Maybud's etiquette book in *Ruddigore*, the cultural institution of public exhibition is identified as a theatrical genre of social control, with the governess serving as dramatic director. The autoethnographic critique in *Utopia, Limited*, in other words, includes its awareness that Victorian exhibition culture played an important role in the processes of imperialism: as Englishness was diffused around the world, internalized representations of other cultures were imported into England, marking the unequal cross-cultural exchange. Thus this scene links the opera's argument about gender to its argument about colonialism—as well as to its argument about capitalism, for courtship is explicitly recognized as a "business" venture. As in Gilbert's *Engaged* (1877), the financial underpinnings of one particular form of incorporation, marriage, recruit the forces of business to support an endless reproduction of the social status quo.

If Princesses Nekaya and Kalyba represent English femininity *in malo*, Princess Zara represents English femininity *in bono*. *Utopia, Limited* offers the parody of gender propriety in act 1 in order to overturn it in act 2, with a song that points the opera toward its conclusion. Sung by Mr. Goldbury, the Company Promoter, "A wonderful joy our eyes to bless" offers a paean to "the bright and beautiful English girl," who represents the opposite of the two clockwork princesses. Decidedly not diminutive, she is a strapping girl of "eleven stone two / And five foot ten in her dancing shoe!" Her comeliness is "magnificent." She hunts, plays cricket and lawn tennis, bicycles, golfs, punts, rows, swims, plays music, sings, and dances tirelessly. Strong and active, she engages in particularly English pursuits; indeed, the song is full of the specialized jargon of English national sports, especially foxhunting and cricket.

True English femininity does not show "mock-modesty" or "the conscious blush and the downcast eye," but is unpretentious, straightforward, "hale and healthy," and utterly natural (like a "beautiful bird," a "mountain rill," a "floating feather"). Again, perhaps the character of Princess Zara is meant to redress *Princess Ida*'s dismissal of higher education for women, for even though a certain amount of parody resides in the idea that a Girton degree might issue in the sort of wholesale approval of English institutions that Zara displays, she is not an object of figural parody. Perhaps, too, "the bright and beautiful English girl" responds to the "Girl of the Period" debates, which had been occupying the periodical press since Eliza Lynn Linton's controversial essay by that name. Published in 1868, the essay launched an extremist attack on the modern girl, the "revolting daughter" (in the slang of the time) who rebels against conventional gender propriety by devoting herself to immodest fashions, garish makeup, fun, and luxury. A "fast," selfish, unfeeling, anti-domestic girl, this bad imitation of the demimondaine does not please men, Linton argued: "All men . . . prefer the simple and genuine girl of the past, with her tender little ways and pretty bashful modesties, to this loud and rampant modernization."[28] Linton's entire argument took place within a nationalistic context ("We prided ourselves as a nation on our women"), measuring the good English girl against French, Italian, American, and German girls. As an ideal figure, "the bright and beautiful English girl" of *Utopia, Limited* seeks to occupy a sane middle ground; neither the mechanically correct young princesses nor Linton's domestic idealization of the past, she represents a new figure of natural, national virtue:

Go search the world and search the sea,
Then come you home and sing with me
There's no such gold and no such pearl
As a bright and beautiful English girl!

This song provokes the conversion of Princesses Nekaya and Kalyba, who suddenly gain access to their own more natural femininity. After his song, Mr. Goldbury encourages their individualism: "Be nobody else but *you*." Thus it is the capitalist who liberates the younger princesses to that most

paradoxical of moral injunctions: act naturally. Then comes a further paradox as the capstone of Mr. Goldbury's argument: when you become unique,
you will then be the perfect representative of a type:

> Your character true unfurl;
>> And when it is ripe,
>> You'll then be a type
> Of a capital English girl.

Within the context of this opera, I believe we must hear the pun in "capital."

Multicultural Ambivalence

The conversion of the two young princesses to a more natural style of gendered behavior begins the pervasive liberation that prepares for the comic
ending of *Utopia, Limited*. One by one, happy couples stop pretending,
confess their desires, throw off restraints, and pair off, dancing wildly. King
Paramount defies his evil advisers; Lady Sophy invites "some demon power"
to "quell [her] over-conscientious heart." In her fifteenth year, under the
influence of "fairy lore," she vowed to marry only a "spotless King." In the
end, King Paramount proves that he is that blameless king, finally refuting
the slander that was written about him in the *Palace Peeper* by confessing
that he wrote it himself, under compulsion.

Against the opera's uneasy backdrop of national, imperial, and capitalist politics, the usual mass pairings seem an especially weak resolution. But despite
the darkness of the political analysis, a multicultural joy pervades the ending.
Although they look superficially alike (and, due to the costume change for act
2, they all look English), the happy couples are all mixed couples, half Utopian
and half English. Thus *Utopia, Limited* presents an opportunity for a novel
sort of production in our own day, a critical multiculturalist or a postcolonial
production that would emphasize the hybridity of contemporary, postcolonial, and global culture.[29] This would require no updating, for the suggestion
is in the original text. The happiness of these couples is predicated on an intimate, natural form of mixing England with its colonies, a situation in which
prudish England relaxes a bit, while Utopia continues to imitate English ways.

The logic of the conclusion is a bit torturous (like the ending of *Thespis*),
with its insistence that the imitation of England has caused everything to
become too perfect and, therefore, imperfect—for without the usual problems, business has come to a standstill. In a parody of colonial resistance, the

Utopians finally call for the expulsion of the "hated Flowers of Progress." When the natives get restless, however, a further dose of anglicization turns out to be the cure. Suddenly, Princess Zara remembers the one thing needful: "Government by Party," which will cyclically undo all the reforms that the Flowers of Progress have brought about. The opera veers wildly from its earlier focus; no longer capitalism, but now party politics is the root problem. The hint of colonial unrest is deflected into a now-bitter critique of home institutions and empire; English culture is riddled with misery masquerading as prosperity, and England communicates its particular forms of misery "abroad" in the name of progress. The dialogue closes on this note, with a lame attempt to make a joke of it all: King Paramount proclaims that "Utopia will no longer be a Monarchy Limited, but, what is a great deal better, a Limited Monarchy!"

This closing affirmation feels forced and precipitous. The finale, in the guise of a patriotic hymn to the greatness of Great Britain, raises directly some of the anxieties that float tacitly throughout *Utopia, Limited*. Expressing the hope that England might live up to its ideals, potential, and reputation, the song admits a doubt—a doubt that speaks particularly of the paradoxes of incorporation:

> Oh, may we copy all her maxims wise,
>   And imitate her virtues and her charities;
> And may we, by degrees, acclimatize
>   Her Parliamentary peculiarities!
> By doing so, we shall, in course of time,
>   Regenerate completely our entire land—
> Great Britain is that monarchy sublime,
>   To which some add (but others do not) Ireland.

The curtain falls on a repetition of the refrain, expressing a clear anxiety about whether "the nation" really *is* "all she professes to be."[30] An even greater concern comes to light in the parenthetical mention of Ireland, an allusion to the fierce struggle for Home Rule at this time. The parentheses, like a frame, deftly reenact the status of Ireland, both included and excluded from the union. This anxiety strikes deep, not only because of its painful topicality, but also because it expresses profound unease about the corporate identity of "Great Britain" itself. What does the nation include, and what does it exclude? And what is its proper relation to its colonies? For the colonies might suggest not only those distant and exotic lands, which most easily lend themselves to luxurious fantasy, but also those lands so close to home as to be a painful reminder of—indeed (perhaps), a very part of—home itself.

14

Continental Recollections

The Grand Duke

The *Grand Duke; or, The Statutory Duel* (1896) returns to the metatheatrical framework of *Thespis*, and thus the sequence of Savoy operas comes full circle, ending with another topsy-turvy takeover by a theatrical company. We can detect a certain humorous deflation over time, for in 1896, the acting troupe is no longer led by a mythic figure, the titular spirit of drama, but by Ernest Dummkopf (earnest stupid-head), while the sphere of action comes down from the heights of Mount Olympus to a small middle European duchy. As in *Thespis*, however, the members of the company struggle incessantly among themselves; as in *Thespis*, they demonstrate the absurdities that arise when personal identity alienates itself in order to play a part. But the metatheatrical analogy that compares a theater with the state government—already present in *Thespis*—is turned toward a more serious, cross-cultural purpose in *The Grand Duke*. Ernest makes the analogy early on, confident that "the man who can rule a theatrical crew . . . can govern this tuppenny State!"

In both book and music, *The Grand Duke* revels in excess, chance, and the centrifugal force at work during the process of theatrical production. If *Ruddigore* offers a composite parody of the various subgenres of melodrama, then *The Grand Duke* goes even further into composite parody, offering a wild mix of English and European genres and styles—from Shakespeare to classical extravaganza, from opéra bouffe to melodrama. Since the Dummkopf troupe prepares *Troilus and Cressida*, the totem of English drama is humorously translated into a Continental context and performed in Greek dress by actors and actresses who are supposedly German. But Shakespeare turns out to be a mere pretext for genre recollection of a particularly unruly kind. The formal dynamic of "recollection," always a part of Savoy genre formation, is taken to its extreme in this opera, so much so that *The Grand Duke* becomes an allusive collection of genres and styles, anthological in its scope, but like a grab bag in its feel.

If, as Fredric Jameson would have it, parody stripped of its critical edge might better be called pastiche, we should nevertheless remember that pastiche in both its senses—the generalized imitation of a theatrical, literary, or musical style, and the mix of disparate elements set in one performance framework—was an active genre in its own right in nineteenth-century musical theater. The first sense of the term emphasizes derivation; in this sense, pastiche is similar to parody but "blank."[1] The second sense of the term, however, emphasizes amalgamation; in this sense, pastiche is similar to medley, quodlibet, or potpourri—all forms of citational variety. The Italian word *pasticcio* originally referred to a pie containing bits and pieces of this and that, mixed and baked. Adopted by English and first used of painting, the term "pasticcio" soon came to denote "a dramatic . . . vocal work whose parts have been wholly or partly borrowed from existing works by various composers." While this is not an accurate description of *The Grand Duke*—for Sullivan's music is original, and its overarching sequence forms a strong compositional whole—the idea of pastiche does get at the anthological allusiveness of the opera, the way that compositional coherence can "result from the clever arrangement of . . . parts."[2] We might see this dimension of the last Savoy opera as both a summa and a transformation of the nineteenth-century culture of adaptation and variety, or as both a summa and an extreme example of the dynamics of Savoy genre formation.

In *The Grand Duke*, a teeming stew of genre parodies establishes the swirling texture of the work—although neither "genre" nor "parody" quite grasps the giddy feel of this form. So, for example, "Shakespeare" does not name a genre, but does name a venerable English tradition—at once literary, dramatic, theatrical, and historical. The nineteenth century treated Shakespeare with equal parts bowdlerization and bardolatry, with a few signal attempts at historically informed performance to vary the tone. James Robinson Planché, who has figured in this study until now as the preeminent extravaganza writer of the nineteenth century, was also a great historian of costume and setting, a sort of archaeologist of the theatrical past and, especially, of Shakespeare. Burlesque and extravaganza preserved Shakespeare in another way—piecemeal. Like the nineteenth-century extravaganza writers before him, Gilbert, to say the least, was hardly overawed by Shakespeare's cultural authority. One legendary anecdote particularly characterizes his attitude. At the Garrick Club one evening, Gilbert was baiting a group of Shakespeare lovers about the Bard's obscurity. "Take this passage, for example," he said. "'I would as lief be thrust through a quickset hedge, as cry "Plosh" to a callow throstle.'" One of his listening adversaries protested that the passage was perfectly clear. It meant that the speaker would rather be scratched all over in a thorny bush than disturb the bird at its song. "What play is that from?" he asked. Gilbert answered, "No play. I made it up. And jolly good Shakespeare it is, too!"[3]

In "The Art of Parody," published in *Fun* early in his career, under the pseudonym A Trembling Beginner, Gilbert explicitly purports to be writing a "remarkably clever parody on the melancholy Jaques's speech in *As You Like It*."[4] The parody roughly follows Jaques's elaboration of the seven ages of man, inanely twisting it around the topic of "Sea-sickness." Leaning on sonic equivalents both minutely close yet excruciatingly far-fetched, the parody turns out to be not of Shakespeare, but of the genres of burlesque and extravaganza, with their egregiously complicated puns. By convention, those genres italicized their puns in play text, playbill, and dramatis personae, so as to alert the reader to their presence. Gilbert parodies that genre convention by italicizing the explanatory notes to his parody of Jaques's speech:

> When first he's in for't,
> Mouthing and choking, hear him curse his qualms.
> Then as he lies recumbent, him you catch ill (*satchell, you know*)
> With whining mourning (*morning, you will remember, in the original*)
>   face, weeping like hail (*creeping like snail*) . . .

And so forth, ending with the "useful dose . . . / Which he drunk—drank ("*For his shrunk shank.*" *Observe how close is my parody, and at the same time, how natural*)." Of course, the sonic equivalences in burlesque are anything but "close" and "natural." This example well illustrates Gilbert's particular "art of parody," which presses through a particular work toward a generic impact. From the pen of A Trembling Beginner, we can see the instinct to make something new out of the old, as well as to parody more than one genre at the same time.

Gilbert's consummate Shakespeare parody, *Rosencrantz and Guildenstern: A Tragic Episode in Three Tableaux*, was first performed in 1891.[5] A sort of metadramatic retelling of *Hamlet*, from the point of view of the minor players, this version imagines that Claudius once wrote a five-act tragedy, "Gonzago," which had proved a total flop because his audience mistook it for a farce; angry at his lack of success on the stage, Claudius has decreed that anyone who causes the play to be performed will be sentenced to death. So it almost goes without saying that this is the play that Hamlet directs the players to perform. The play's pastiche of "Shakespearean" blank verse sometimes breaks into prose and sometimes into the jingling couplets of burlesque. Rosencrantz and Guildenstern repeatedly interrupt Hamlet at his soliloquizing; one of them plays a hornpipe on Hamlet's flute; and the play within the play turns out to be written in iambic tetrameter, like Grosvenor's simple-minded decalets in *Patience*. At the end, to help Hamlet avoid the death sentence, Ophelia proposes that he be dispatched to "Engle-land," to join that "cultured race—compared with whom / We are but poor brain-blind barbarians." In her speech, of course, we hear the germ of *Utopia, Limited*.

In all this, Gilbert followed a genre of Shakespeare parody widespread in the nineteenth-century theater, which Richard Schoch has explored in detail. Since Shakespeare stands for the authority of England's theatrical past, he explains, Shakespeare burlesques were directed against "the pomposities of official Shakespearean culture." Their parodic deflation could be aimed simultaneously at pretension, officialdom, and respectability, on the one hand, and the bardolatry that made hash of Shakespeare's plays in nineteenth-century revivals, on the other. As we have seen, individual audience members could catch each burlesque allusion or not, and still enjoy the play; so in this respect, Shakespeare allusions operate very much like classical allusions in classical extravaganza. However, far more middle-class audience members knew their Shakespeare then than they do now, so they could be depended on to get the jokes. Thus the humor offers "the disconcerting reality of the familiar made absurd," very much in line with Savoy humor.[6]

In *The Grand Duke*, however, Shakespeare is treated as one iconic sign among many, a token that can be taken up and tossed off. Indeed, the only real reason for having the Dummkopf troupe prepare a performance of *Troilus and Cressida* is to get them into Greek costumes for act 2—and, more important, to signal that classical extravaganza is part of the parodic mix. Thus allusions to Shakespeare and Aristophanes blend the authority of the English theatrical past with both classical Greek theater and English classical burlesque.[7] All these references are filtered through the lens of Continental styles, past and present. Surely Rutland Barrington, as Ludwig playing "Agamemnon in a Louis Quatorze wig," represents the zany principle of this composite, while the women's costumes were sexy and luxurious in the mode of extravaganza (figures 14.1 and 14.2). Their pairing is similar to that of King Paramount and the Utopian Maidens, parodic male against sexually explicit female.

FIGURE 14.1 Rutland Barrington as Ludwig playing King Agamemnon in a "Louis Quatorze wig" in act 2 of *The Grand Duke*. Photograph in *Sketch*, 1896. (Collection of Fredric Woodbridge Wilson)

FIGURE 14.2 Ilka von Palmay as Julia Jellico in act 2 of *The Grand Duke*. Photograph in *Sketch*, 1896. (Collection of Fredric Woodbridge Wilson)

To highlight its parody of classical extravaganza, *The Grand Duke* offers a mocking display of classical erudition, exaggeratedly pedantic in the conventional way.[8] Ludwig's song near the beginning of act 2 announces this element of the genre parody: "At the outset I may mention it's my sovereign intention / To revive the classic memories of Athens at its best." Admitting that the actors will need "a course of quiet cramming" to pull it off, Ludwig rattles off a list of Greek terms that he associates with the management of a theater—"*choreutae . . . choregus . . . oboloi . . . drachmae* . . . Kalends"— all of them jokingly set against their modern counterparts (for example, "hyporchematic" is parenthetically translated as "ballet-operatic"). In the second verse, in some longer Greek phrases, he compares classical and modern styles of eating and drinking, with a winking, knowing fondness for present customs: "And we modern Saxons know a trick worth two of that, I think!" Finally the song turns to consider "Dionysiac or Bacchic" revels, with a sly eagerness to entertain the risqué that is typical of both French opéra bouffe and English extravaganza:

> Then came rather risky dances (under certain circumstances)
>> Which would shock that worthy gentleman, the Licenser of Plays,
> Corybantian mani*ac* kick—Dionysiac or Bacchic—
>> And the Dithyrambic revels of those undecorous days.
> . . .
> Yes, on reconsideration, there are customs of that nation
>> Which are not in strict accordance with the habits of our day,
> And when I come to codify, their rules I mean to modify,
>> Or Mrs. Grundy, p'r'aps, may have a word or two to say.
> . . .
> They wore little underclothing—scarcely anything—or nothing—
>> And their dress of Coan silk was quite transparent in design—
> Well, in fact, in summer weather, something like the "altogether."
>> And it's *there*, I rather fancy, I shall have to draw the line!

Although elaborately clever, this sort of humor was very old by 1896. The double critique—of indecency and English respectability—that seems so sharp in *Thespis* is all but buried under the torrent of conventional, hyperbolic pedantry and recycled old jokes (including a cross-cultural joke about handkerchiefs like that in *The Mikado*). That the list of Greek terms is meant in the spirit of extravaganza pedantry is made clear in a confidential aside to the audience. Ludwig admits:

At this juncture I may mention
   That this erudition sham
Is but classical pretension,
   The result of steady "cram.":
Periphrastic methods spurning,
To this audience discerning
I admit this show of learning
   Is the fruit of steady "cram."!

To some extent, Ludwig's confession could be taken as a metaphor for the plot construction of *The Grand Duke*, also "the fruit of steady 'cram.,'" in both the Victorian and the contemporary senses of the term. Not only is the erudition patently superficial and jokey, "got up" for the immediate purpose, but, like the plot, it is stuffed full of material—overstuffed, in fact, like a huge Victorian sofa. I would tend to praise, rather than blame, the opera for this quality, however. In order to enjoy *The Grand Duke*, one must submit to the growing absurdity, as more and more plot elements are maniacally added; this last Savoy opera provides a great example of parodic recollection taken to the nth degree.

As in *Thespis*, the parody of classical extravaganza is joined to a parody of opéra bouffe in *The Grand Duke*. As in *Thespis*, the specific parody of one opéra bouffe by Jacques Offenbach suggests a parody of the genre as a whole. The Savoy opera's very title announces its parody of Offenbach's work, through its explicit allusion to *La grande-duchesse de Gérolstein* (*The Grand Duchess of Gerolstein*, 1867). (In act 1, Julia Jellicoe, who is seeking the role of the Grand Duchess, admits that it is "a very good part in Gerolstein.") But the plot of that hit is turned upside down in gendered terms in *The Grand Duke*. No longer does one Grand Duchess rove among several objects of her affection, as she does in Offenbach's opera; in *The Grand Duke*, four women vie for the role of the Grand Duchess. This multiplication of potential Grand Duchesses offers a hyperbolic parody of Offenbach's singular one. Furthermore, *La grande-duchesse de Gérolstein*'s already parodically inflated location, in Steis-Stein-Steis-Laper-Bottmoll-Schorstenburg, is parodically deflated in *The Grand Duke*, for act 1 takes place in the public square of Speisesaal (refectory, or dining room) in the fictional grand duchy of Pfennig Halbpfennig.[9]

The mixture of genres becomes hilarious with the entrance of the delegation from Monte Carlo, late in act 2. After three other women have made their claims known, one can hardly believe that yet another claimant to the title of Grand Duchess of Pfennig Halbpfennig has entered the plot. Form following content, the scene might suggest the chaos of a pantomime harle-quinade or the beginning of an extravaganza transformation. Instead of the "cut and dried formality" they had been promised, Ludwig treats the delega-tion from Monte Carlo to a "wild yell" and a "reckless dance," announced by the sound of a gong. Grand punctuation in any case, the gong reaches back to early-nineteenth-century popular theater. Gilbert specified a gong to be struck at the end of *Trial by Jury*, to signal that work's concluding parody of a transformation scene. I would guess that the allusion, easily caught in 1875, may not have been as easily recognized in 1896, and we had best imagine that its reference to earlier genres remains implicit.

All the characteristic bouffe topoi tumble over one another in *The Grand Duke*: the celebration of intoxication, and the threat that risqué dress, behav-ior, or sexual topics might come to the fore. Yet all are humorously twisted and deflated by the poverty-stricken miserliness of Grand Duke Rudolph and Baroness von Krakenfeldt. This is bouffe indulgence on a budget, Continental permissiveness self-consciously undercut. Nevertheless, a topsy-turvy tipsi-ness results: water turns into wine, wild dances are danced, and the threat of multiple bigamies is entertained. In *The Grand Duke*, the *brindisi* ("Come, bumpers—aye, ever-so-many") is not pointedly anglicized, as it is in *The Sor-cerer*, but remains very French, for even though the Baroness hopes to drink "at somebody else's expense," the wine celebrated is "Pomméry seventy-four." Likewise, the "Roulette Song" ("Take my advice—when deep in debt") has a French refrain and compares the "cosmic game" of roulette to a course of woo-ing. If "the little ball's a true coquette" who cannot make up her mind among suitors, then the song is risqué not only for its celebration of gambling, but also for its sexual innuendo. Perhaps a further indecent suggestion may be detected in the choice of *Troilus and Cressida* as the play the actors are prepar-ing to present, for the Victorians found the play too explicit to be performed; if so, it functions primarily to suggest sexual impropriety without enacting it.

Finally, in this grand mix of genres, *The Grand Duke* stages a cameo appearance of melodrama (structurally very much like the cameo appear-ances of minstrelsy in *Trial by Jury* and *Utopia, Limited*). Julia's monodra-matic number modulates through several intense emotions, culminating in melodrama's conventional "Remorse! Remorse!" Thus the diva exhibits her "notion of a first-rate part," but although she describes the genre of her per-formance as "high-class art," audiences were likely to recognize its reference to over-the-top melodramatic plots and acting styles.

The music, too, is elaborately recollective, comprehending the Euro-pean past and present, in stylistic registers both high and low. In this sense, *The Grand Duke* represents a magnificent summation by Sullivan of international styles in nineteenth-century music, like an anthology compiled on the very eve of modernism. As Jonathan Strong puts it:

> In *The Grand Duke*, one might see Sullivan as bidding farewell to a century of classical *opéra bouffe*, a form traceable back through Offenbach and Johann Strauss to the earlier French vaudeville, now augmented with touches of the grander operatic tradition drawn from Weber and Rossini and Donizetti. Sullivan was heir to that tradition, and as it began to break apart by 1896, he offered this last compendium.[10]

"Compendium" is precisely the right word. Gilbert's plot may seem to be a grab bag, but Sullivan's music lends the opera an urbane, cosmopolitan aura. The Sullivan of *The Grand Duke* is a "continentalized Sullivan," writes Richard Traubner.[11] From one point of view, "the Continent" serves as a generalized cultural other, fully assimilated; the style of Sullivan's music performs its mastery of a collection of styles. Strong provides a helpful (and heady) detailing of the elements of this compendium: the French galop at the height of the Bacchanal; the Provençale dance for the entrance of the Prince and Princess of Monaco; the *café chantant* "Roulette Song"; Julia's Italian operatic scena ("I have a rival! Frenzy-thrilled"); the Baroness's *brindisi*; the Wagnerian march; the Viennese waltz duet; the polonaise in the finale to act 1 ("But stay, your new-made court"); the habanera for the Grand Duke and the Baroness; and, most magnificent of them all, the Greek chorus "Opoponax! Eloia!" As Strong points out, if the English madrigal and the Irish jig are added to the list, *The Grand Duke* represents "all Europe, with Ireland thrown in!'"[12]

Unfortunately, some critics at the time felt that Gilbert and Sullivan were parodying themselves. The reviewer for the *Musical Standard*, picking up on the statutory duel's creation of a "legal 'ghoest'" (so spelled and so pronounced to rhyme with "lowest"), wrote that *The Grand Duke* was merely "a 'ghoest' of Gilbert and Sullivan opera." Pointing out that the authors had repeated many familiar tricks, he judged that "they have studied their former selves."[13] Thus to some contemporary spectators, the proliferation of parodies seemed counterproductive; instead of registering the critical difference within parodic repetition, they saw merely the repetition. But other reviewers understood the point of the opera's compendious allusiveness. Although the work as a whole was not successful (only 123 performances), the music was praised by most critics and was generally thought much better than the libretto. In fact, the score was lauded specifically for its genre parody; for example, the reviewer for the *Musical Standard* particularly liked the "wonderful bit of musical humour—an exact copy of the regulation operatic quintet" (which another reviewer compared with "the regulation mad-rigal").[14] As in 1871, responding to *Thespis*, some reviewers thought that the allusiveness of the music would render it impenetrable to its audience. The critic for the *Graphic*, for example, argued that the "vulgar chansonette of the Parisian music hall" and the Greek chorus were "a little above the heads of the audience."[15] I doubt it. The Savoy operas had educated their audiences to understand this sort of humor. And, besides, the libretto offers many hints to guide an understanding of the music's humorous allusiveness. Bestowing the name Dr. Tannhäuser on the Notary is the most blatant of them all.

Metatheatrical Government, Identity, and Gender

Two plot threads interweave to make a mighty tangle: the Dummkopf troupe's conspiracy to take over Pfennig Halbpfennig, including the statutory duel, and the infighting among the members of the acting troupe about who will play which role, including the intrigue among claimants to the title of Grand Duchess. Indeed, some threads are left hanging, even in the end, but there is much to admire even so.[16]

The overstuffed plot is grounded, most obviously, in its topsy-turvy inver-sion. Even before the statutory duel, the Dummkopf troupe plans a coup, signaling to one another by the cryptic sign of eating a sausage roll. *Utopia, Limited*, with its character of the Public Exploder, also makes fun of anar-chism, a matter of rising concern in the late nineteenth century. But in both works, the theme remains peripheral to the plot.[17] Relegating anarchism to a mere "topic" may seem shocking, although the mainstream of burlesque topicality works in exactly this way, with glancing references to the most serious political events and concerns, tossed off and rapidly abandoned. Scattershot suggestions about state government abound, but they scarcely add up. The metatheatrical analogy loosely connects them, working in both directions: theater is like government, but government is like theater, too.

As in *Thespis*, a theatrical company represents the ne plus ultra of difficult management, and the man who can "rule" a troupe of actors can rule any-thing, including a "tuppeny State." The particular "tuppeny State" in ques-tion, Pfennig Halbpfennig, rapidly becomes a metaphor for Europe:

Oh, the man who can drive a theatrical team,
With wheelers and leaders in order supreme,
Can govern and rule, with a wave of his fin,
    All Europe, with Ireland thrown in![18]

The fantasy of throwing Ireland into the composition of Europe suggests, on the one hand, that Ireland is a problem that might best be gotten out of the way (a risky suggestion, handled much more deftly at the end of *Utopia, Limited*) and, on the other hand, that the constitution of "Europe" has been, and is, both conceptually and politically difficult. Without a coup, but after the statutory duel, the actors take over the government of Pfennig Halbpfennig, and Ludwig ascends to the role of stage manager *and* Grand Duke.

But, as Max Keith Sutton points out, Grand Duke Rudolph has been acting like a stage manager all along.[19] Like *The Gondoliers* and *Utopia, Limited*, this opera stresses the role-playing and ceremony that mark the governing classes. The passing of Rudolph's snuffbox and handkerchief through the ranks of the Chamberlains, before being presented, by the most senior Chamberlain, to the Grand Duke, not to mention his public courtship in the marketplace, designed to increase the value of his real estate, demonstrate the theatricality of government-as-usual, as well as the relation between government and the market economy. In a somewhat tedious scene, Gilbert overworks his parody of bureaucracy by giving Rudolph a chain of functionaries, beginning with a Chamberlain and devolving through Vice- and Assistant Vice-Chamberlains, all the way down to Acting Temporary Sub-Deputy Assistant Vice-Chamberlain. This chain of surrogation develops the idea that bureaucratic subordinates acting on behalf of those higher in the hierarchy constitute an important form of acting, a displacement of identity and power very much like the legal fiction that constitutes the statutory duel. Likewise, the Prince of Monte Carlo enters with "a good useful working set of second-hand nobles." His retinue of "supernumeraries," who have been "engaged from the Theatre Monaco," for with "a brilliant staff a Prince should make a show," are "rigged out in magnificent array" by a "very well-known costumier." These actors perform a higher social class than their own, for they are actually "wealthy members of the brewing interest"; they must remain silent, for they "break . . . grammar's laws"; and they must keep their gloves on, for "their nails are not presentable." In other words, this scene demonstrates the role-playing necessary for upward mobility—an idea common to the Savoy operas, as we have seen. The Prince teaches them the attitudes necessary to perform their roles:

> You needn't say anything, but let your gestures be in accordance with the spirit of the conversation. . . . Affability! (*attitude*). Submission! (*attitude*). Surprise! (*attitude*). Shame! (*attitude*). Grief! (*attitude*). Joy! (*attitude*).

Unlike the "customary attitudes" assumed by the Sailors on board the *Pinafore*, these poses are explicitly theatrical; unlike the Dragoon Guards attempting to act like aesthetes, these faux-nobles can assume the correct postures.

The legal fiction that the statutory duel activates launches another form of acting as surrogation. As we have seen, the idea of someone being "practically . . . dead," which permits the resolution of *The Mikado*, is echoed by the idea of someone being "practically alive," which permits the resolution of *Ruddigore*. Fascinated by the logical conundrums that could be engendered by a legal fiction, while pondering the opera that would become *The Grand Duke*, Gilbert became interested in the possibility of someone coming back from the dead—not, as in *Ruddigore*, the return of a ghost, but the return of the actual person after having been declared legally dead. John Wolfson adduces the evidence of a fan letter from Bertram Ellis in Keene, New Hampshire, who urged Gilbert to consider the hypothetical situation of a man resuscitated after "Electrical execution" (that is, execution by the electric chair). Ellis dilated on the difficulties that would ensue for the man's legal, financial, and marital status: Could the dead man resume his living identity? Must he discharge his former debts and obligations? Would he still be married? As Wolfson points out, Gilbert "pasted Mr. Ellis's letter on the first page of the plot-book for *The Grand Duke*."[20] Other sources include "The Duke's Dilemma" (1853), a story published in *Blackwood's Edinburgh Magazine*, and a musical by H. B. Farnie and Alfred Murray based on that story, *The Prima Donna* (1889), which had originally been titled *The Grand Duke*. Those plots feature a poverty-stricken duke and a set of actors who fill in for his courtiers, thus hiding his impecunious status from the princess he wants to woo. Having successfully courted her, her fortune restores his own.[21]

Thus, in other words, *The Grand Duke* gives the long Savoy meditation on divided or multiple identities yet another twist. If *The Gondoliers* asks whether two can become one, *The Grand Duke* asks whether one role can be occupied by two (or more) persons. The legal fiction instituted by the statutory duel is the linchpin of this conundrum. According to the law of the statutory duel, he who draws the higher card wins, while the other dies a "civil death" and becomes "a legal 'ghoest.'" In other words, "civil death," although a mere fiction, empties the role of its actor and installs another, who assumes the powers and privileges of the role along with the personal obligations of the original player. As in *Thespis*, the analysis of social role-playing takes place through the separation of the role from the person who inhabits it. Thus it is that Ludwig may (or may not) be married to four women, two by virtue of his former identity as an actor and two by virtue of his new identity as the Grand Duke. Like Thespis, then, Ludwig is a substitute ("acting") ruler of an inverted order. The role of the Grand Duke is both emptied and divided in two. (For that reason, it is surprising that Gilbert did not pun on "duel" / "dual.") Furthermore, in this topsy-turvy world, law is represented, in all its absurdity, by a game of chance.

As we have seen, in both *The Gondoliers* and *Utopia, Limited*, questions about the constitution of identity are also directed at nations, nation-states, and other governmental entities. In the last three Savoy operas, Gilbert was clearly thinking about the changing world map, as smaller governments were taken up into larger wholes. *Utopia, Limited* quite explicitly addresses the formation of the British Empire, while *The Gondoliers* and *The Grand Duke* allude to the unifications of Italy and Germany (and, as we have seen, *The Grand Duke* also considers the constitution of "Europe"). These are forms of superordinate union, like "Great Britain," also a matter of explicit concern in both *Utopia, Limited* and *The Grand Duke* through their allusions to Ireland. The relative insignificance of the duchies after the unification of Germany is reminiscent of the residual Republic of Venice after the unification of Italy, a context for *The Gondoliers*. In both places, dusty, old-fashioned cultures persisted in time, and the memory of fragmentation and multiplicity hovered within the unified nation of the late-nineteenth-century present. Attention to the formation of superordinate governmental entities—and the internal fragmentation that continued—represents the continuation of the Savoy meditation on internally self-divided individuals.

Both "The Duke's Dilemma" and *The Grand Duke* make fun of the sheer number of small duchies, electorates, and principalities, as well as the relative impotence of their petit royalty. Although the poverty of Grand Duke Rudolph (like that of the Duke of Plaza-Toro) drives the plot and his culture is humorously old and outworn, Rudolph need not be played as a comic old man, exhausted and decrepit. His querulousness comes not from his age, or even from his miserliness, but from the effeteness associated with his high-ranking, but largely ineffectual, role. He should be played as a young, fin-de-siècle representative of old-fashioned, European petit royalty, as imagined from a late-nineteenth-century English perspective.[22] Having considered the decline of the English aristocracy many a time (most notably in *Iolanthe*), Savoy opera now turned its attention to that of the Continental aristocracy. Thus this cross-cultural "fun" at the expense of a small and powerless imaginary duchy carries its own autoethnographic point, which may be felt particularly in the linguistic humor.

The residents of Pfennig Halbpfenning were supposed to have been speaking German. What we have, then—and this is important to remember, as a part of the opera's metatheatrical wit—is English actors and actresses playing German actors and actresses, who are playing several parts in the plot by turns: political conspirators, jealous members of an acting company, and members of the cast of *Troilus and Cressida*. Only Julia Jellicoe is supposed to be English. Ilka von Palmay, a beautiful Hungarian soprano who spoke with a heavy accent, created the role of this sole English member of the Dummkopf acting troupe. Thus, when she spoke, the audience would hear her middle European accent, while a joke would be made about her impenetrable "English" accent; meanwhile, all the other actors and actresses, speaking perfectly unaccented English, were fictionally taken to be speaking German. Clearly, her role was written this way—and the linguistic joke developed this way—to accommodate Palmay and to work her particular star power into the plot.[23] But because the role of Julia is so blatantly rationalized (and nationalized) in the libretto, we can also see the spotlight trained on the cosmopolitan invasion of a quintessentially English company.[24] In this last collaboration of Gilbert and Sullivan, concern with what it means to be English is focused through (and reduced to) one linguistic joke, although it is a meaningful one, since it turns on the autoethnographic consideration of England in relation to continental Europe. Their mutual infiltration is suggested by Ernest, when he proposes to Julia: "We will fly to your native land, and I'll play broken-English in London, as you play broken-German here!"

This linguistic play returns us to the metatheatrical consideration of social roles, especially those related to nationality, class, and gender. *The Grand Duke* is the culmination of the long examination of the social roles of everyday life in the Savoy operas. Sutton sees this point, arguing that the chief import of the work is "the way social roles can obscure a person's sense of identity, especially as the individual shapes his personality to fit his role."[25] Citing Matthew Arnold's "The Buried Life" (1852) and Dickens's characterization of John Wemmick in *Great Expectations* (1860–1861), he shows that self-alienation was an acknowledged topic of the time.[26] As we have seen, however, attention to this insight extends along the entire sequence of Savoy operas, all of which stress that social roles are theatrical, their performance is perceived as a social demand, the process of socialization is like learning a part, and the experience of playing a social role precipitates a sense of internal self-division—experienced by men in their playing of professional roles and by women in their playing of gender roles. Both masculinity and femininity are explicitly shown to be contradictory productions in the theatricality of everyday life.[27]

This modern awareness of social roles is intensified in *The Grand Duke*, which explicitly links it to class and gender. Thus Baroness von Krakenfeldt expresses scorn for Julia's attempt to play the part of a Grand Duchess, disclosing her aristocratic belief that only birth can prepare one for an aristocratic role; a lower-class actress would not be up to the part. Julia, though, believes herself equal to any part. Sutton argues that there is nothing at all—no personal identity—outside Julia's prowess as an actress and the roles she might be given to play, no "unrehearsed emotion."[28] Yet a personal identity *is* projected in her ambitious determination to choose the roles that she would like to perform. Her wish to play—that is, to be—the Grand Duchess amounts to a parody of the middle-class person dead set on upward mobility, while her analysis of the variety of ways she could play "the wife" amounts to a critique of gender ideology. As a wife, she could play one of two roles: a "hoity-toity vixenish virago" or "a tender, gentle, submissive, affectionate . . . child-wife . . . a wife who regards her husband's slightest wish as an inflexible law." Ludwig, her manager-director, who might also become her husband, tries in vain to direct her toward the latter choice, with full acknowledgment that the "timid tender / Feminine gender" is, in his view, best represented by the "innocent *ingenoo*," clearly the butt of parody:

> Now Julia, come,
> Consider it from
>> This dainty point of view—
> A timid tender
> Feminine gender,
>> Prompt to coyly coo—
> Yet silence seeking,
> Seldom speaking
>> Till she's spoken to—
> A comfy, cosy,
> Rosy-posy
>> Innocent *ingenoo*!
>> The part you're suited to—
>> (To give the deuce her due)
>> A sweet (O, jiminy!)
>> Miminy-piminy,
>> Innocent *ingenoo*!

The critique obviously depends on the notion that gender is a theatricalized social role. The ensemble offers a limited set of roles, as if to exaggerate the limited set of available roles in social life as well as the theatricality of social roles.

Ludwig knows that Julia can act the part of the "innocent *ingenoo*" if she chooses to do so, but Julia does not so choose. Instead, she would like to exercise her "high dramatic sense" in "situations tragic— / Undeniably intense." Here a wonderful genre parody lends force to this gender parody, focused on who will rule—who will choose the roles and cast the types—within a marriage. Brilliantly, *The Grand Duke* focuses Julia's ambition through a formal parody of melodrama. In "I have a rival! Frenzy-thrilled," she declaims, thus fulfilling the operatic sense of "melodrama" as well as alluding to the popular Victorian "platform melodrama," in which a performer recited, sometimes to music.[29] But her set piece is even more recognizable as a parody of melodramatic histrionics, the plots of sensation novels, and the mad scenes of grand opera. In other words, the sort of woman she will play involves a choice of genre as well as a choice among the ensemble stereotypes prescribed and available for inhabitation.

The debate between Ludwig and Julia—about whether she will be forced into the role of ingénue or whether she will play the sensational diva—is comparable in some respects to Margaret's mad scene in *Ruddigore*. Provoked into showing off her high dramatic prowess by Ludwig's wish that she play "the innocent *ingenoo*," Julia very "*dramatically*" goes through the heightened, careening emotions of a sensation heroine—first discovering that she has a rival, then tracking down that rival and strangling her, and finally feeling terrible remorse. The heights of her melodramatic remorse are deflated when she discovers that her imagined rival is actually her lover's aunt, but once again she rallies and winds up "*shuddering*" her way into a full-fledged mad scene, gazing on the lifeless form of her rival:

Then, mad—mad—mad!
    With fancies wild—chimerical—
Now sorrowful—silent—sad—
    Now hullaballoo hysterical!
       Ha! ha! ha! ha!
But whether I'm sad or whether I'm glad,
    Mad! Mad! Mad! Mad!

Her repetition of "Mad!"—not manic, like patter, but uttered with rising hysteria—reaches a crescendo, and then she comes down, restoring the plangency with which she began, calmly singing a framing commentary on her own performance:

This calls for the resources of a high-class art,
And satisfies my notion of a first-rate part!

As in *Ruddigore*, madness is coded female; as in *Ruddigore*, female madness derives from disappointment in love. But while Mad Margaret was
abandoned and sad, Julia plays a more active heroine, the bad-mad heroine
of sensation novels such as Mary Elizabeth Braddon's *Lady Audley's Secret*
(1862), who gains plenty of agency by playing self-interested parts. Mad
Margaret is supposed to have been suffering real madness, whereas Julia's
madness, assumed as a theatrical role, serves her own ambition. These two
parodies of scripted female madness work differently, in other words. In
one, madness indicates female dependence, while in the other, madness
indicates transgressive female strength—but both refer their performances
to the genres of music, theater, and literature through which female roles
are delineated.

Anachronism

The temporal dynamic of parody brings fragments of the past into the present with preposterous effects. Set, like *The Gondoliers*, in 1750, *The Grand
Duke* revels in bits and pieces from other times. Examples of anachronism
abound: Alfred Nobel had not invented dynamite, nor had William Morris
designed his famous wallpapers, although both are referenced; anarchism
was not a notable concern in 1750, although all the late Savoy operas are
interested in cultural unrest. Aestheticism, as we know, became a steady
reference point after *Patience*. In *The Grand Duke*, however, the point seems
to be eclecticism itself. The opera's disorderly jumble of ages and styles purports to be grounded in topsy-turvydom:

In the period Socratic every dining room was Attic
    (Which suggests an architecture of a topsy-turvy kind).

That groan-worthy pun—pure burlesque—returns to extravaganza's use of
that device, which previous Savoy collaborations had transcended. But the
topsy-turvy inversion yields to a wild mix of genres and styles—each raised
ever so lightly and then tossed away—creating an anarchic, anachronistic
blend. Past genres enter the swirl, where they are not used structurally or
consistently, or remembered nostalgically, but appear with a ribald, zany

disregard, in which Shakespeare's drama turns out to be Greek and a classical Greek king sports a "Louis Quatorze wig." On the level of the plot, Ludwig in his wig represents the threadbare actor who must be able to play any part at a moment's notice, as well as the haphazard quality of a small troupe's theatrical wardrobe, collections of things, of shreds and patches. As a metatheatrical comment on the level of form, Ludwig in his Greek costume and French wig represents the grab bag aspect of *The Grand Duke*, which joins anachronism to historical pastiche.

In a sense, the opera points up the absurdity of revival itself. The Dummkopf troupe sets itself a patently impossible task: "Old Athens we'll exhume!" With effects as complex as the legal fiction produced by the statutory duel, the exhumation of the past creates a temporal patchwork, with more than one era competing for precedence and responsibility. Exhumation is not grisly, gory, or scary, but there is a hint of decomposition in the play of genres. And the theme of historical revival is echoed in the plot of the "statutory duel." As a "spectre appalling," with his "voice from the tomb" and his "stern supernatural diction," Ernest inspires Julia only with "*affected terror*," and they dance off in different directions. A funny specter, a merely "technical bogey," Ernest's absurd resuscitation suggests the absurdity of reviving past genres and traditions. As in Gilbert's *Ages Ago: A Musical Legend* (1869), the "ages" are mixed up, not as a function of ghosts, as in that earlier entertainment, but as a function of theatrical presentation.

The real organizational principle of the plot is not the topsy-turvy inversion, but the temporal separation assumed between act 1 and act 2. A wholesale costume change marks the graphic difference between the acts, as it does in *Ruddigore* and *Utopia, Limited*. But in *The Grand Duke*, the difference between act 1 and act 2 creates a version of the "rehearsal" structure, hypothetically separating two phases of theatrical staging and showing the actors both before they act and while they are acting (a rich field for reflection, since, of course, we know that they are acting all along). Some visual sign would help to separate these temporal stages, and Strong suggests that a stage on the stage might remind audiences of the governing structure of the play within the play.[30] Indeed, the original production seems to have used such a device (figure 14.3). Showing the audience the actors' awareness that they are acting, which has signaled bad acting since the time of Denis Diderot,[31] is the whole point in act 2, which should be an extravaganza of chaos.

Gilbert attempted to build that awareness into the text, in an almost shocking moment of metatheatrical reflexiveness. Just before the finale to act 1, Ludwig asks, "How shall we summon the people?" and Rudolph

FIGURE 14.3 The set for act 2 of *The Grand Duke*, with a stage on the stage illustrating the rehearsal structure of the plot. Illustration by Holland Tringham, in *Illustrated London News*, March 14, 1896. (Collection of Fredric Woodbridge Wilson)

answers: "Oh, there's no difficulty about that. Bless your heart, they've been staring at us through those windows for the last half-hour!" Although Savoy opera is not known for breaking the fourth wall, this exchange offers a jarring (and exciting) moment of modernist self-consciousness. We should remember, however, that extravaganza's tradition of direct addresses to the audience had broken it, before the convention of the fourth wall was solidly established. Thus can the old tradition be reinvented as if it were new and the casual abrogation of the distinction between the representation and the audience be reunderstood as "breaking the fourth wall." This example well illustrates the preposterous temporality of re-creation.

Indeed, critics have detected other modernist elements in *The Grand Duke*. Sutton, agreeing with John Bush Jones, finds the opera decadent and then suggests a much more tantalizing idea: that it is "perhaps a deliberate parody" of perversion at the time of Oscar Wilde's *Salomé* (1893), for it piles on the decadent themes: nausea, amorality, necrophilia.[32] But these very features can also be explained by the Savoy operas' indebtedness to extravaganza and opéra bouffe, with their generic fondness for nose thumbing, risqué sexuality, and intoxication. Perhaps the sausage rolls, eaten by the conspirators as a secret sign of their alliance, allude to the sausages of the pantomime harlequinade, updating a traditional form of theatrical anarchy and making it a sign of modern anarchism. Sutton also emphasizes the modern, deflated tone of the ending, arguing that "the last word before the finale should be spoken as a most laconic, Brechtian, 'hurrah.' The flimsy artifice on which the plot is founded disappears in a flash, as at the end of *Alice in Wonderland*, when she asserts the imaginary nature of her tormenters, who are 'nothing but a pack of cards.'"[33] The comparison is apt, since the plot of *The Grand Duke*, too, turns on a pack of cards; as Ludwig jokes, attempting to explain Rudolph's absence, "[H]e died of pack-of-cardiac affection." One must only hope that the audience remembers extravaganza punning, so as to recognize this parody of it.

The tendency to read the opera as a modernist artifact is mistaken in its emphasis, however. *The Grand Duke* is quintessentially late Victorian, a recollective summation of Victorian theater practice. It does not lead to modernist drama in the sense that it overturns its own generic practice for another, but it leads to modern drama precisely because it so densely weaves its awareness of the long history of Victorian theatrical genres. As we must recall, parody is not a modern mode, but it is a *modernizing* one. In *The Grand Duke* can be easily seen the modernizing momentum of parody.

As in *Thespis*, so in *The Grand Duke*, there is no transformation at the end, but a return to the beginning.[34] The reestablishment of order does not signify renewal, but the reproduction of the status quo. When the Notary, Dr. Tannhäuser, clarifies the legal form of the statutory duel, it turns out that the Ace is the lowest card—not the highest—in the deck, and this "arbitrary re-reading of the Law flips everything back to where it started."[35] Unlike the Lord Chancellor's addition of one little word that absolutely negates the previous rule of law in *Iolanthe*, this clarification by the law's functionary simply reinterprets existing law, providing a pat ending to a topsy-turvy premise. Thus it is significant that *The Grand Duke* is the only one of the Savoy operas to close with its opening music, as Strong has pointed out.[36] For those of us who have followed the evolution of Savoy opera, this closing of the circle is both anticlimactic and uncanny. In so many ways, *The Grand Duke*, by pressing forward into extremity, also turns back the clock. For those of us who appreciate the preposterous temporality of parody, however, even this extreme re-creation can be savored.

After Gilbert and Sullivan

The Momentum of Parody

The collaboration between Gilbert and Sullivan ended after 1896, when the last Savoy Opera, *The Grand Duke*, had an unsuccessful run. By then, both a genre and a tradition had been firmly established. Following performance traditions set by Gilbert and Sullivan themselves, the D'Oyly Carte Opera Company attempted to maintain strict control of the performance style, disallowing departures of any kind. As we have seen, American and provincial English touring companies were better off when they could offer a stable and recognizable product with very high production values.

After the deaths of Arthur Sullivan and Richard D'Oyly Carte (in 1900 and 1901, respectively), the D'Oyly Carte Opera Company mounted a series of revivals of the operas, beginning in 1906. Unfortunately, the production values were allowed to slip. Although he directed some of the revivals, Gilbert feuded publicly with the management's casting choices, annoyed that he had not been consulted and furious that the productions had been done "shamefully on the cheap."[1] William Schwenck Gilbert died in 1911, and the effort to cut costs continued to ride roughshod over production values throughout the early twentieth century. The adoption of the so-called unified set was a particularly egregious moment in the production history of the Savoy operas. Designed to make touring easier and cheaper, one set framework was employed, with modifications, for all the operas. For most spectators worldwide, then, the look of a D'Oyly Carte production was standardized and cheapened—although it was also, certainly, made even more recognizable. The tradition, in other words, was a very valuable piece of cultural capital, owned by the D'Oyly Carte Opera Company and willingly preserved by devoted fans. After the demise of the originating triumvirate, the history of Savoy opera reveals the tension between devoted fidelity to the original productions and various allowances of departure from that authority. "Devotion" and "fidelity" are not idle metaphors in this case. Taking the original productions as a canon, the company treated them as an inheritance that had to be kept in the family, as cultural capital for reinvestment and eventually as national heritage.[2]

But the Savoy operas were used for purposes other than their own, even from the beginning. Spinoff products, like the aesthetic teapot (see plate 10), served as souvenirs that might also carry a parodic hint. Then, too, companies far removed from the realm of theater and the arts piggybacked on the enormous success of Savoy opera, using familiar Savoy figures to advertise their wares. Trading cards abounded, such as those depicting the three little maids to advertise Thomson's Patent Glove Fitting corsets and "gentlemen of Japan" to advertise the "Mikado" stove, dedicated to the "Grand Dictator of the Realm of Japan" (plate 19).[3] "The Gilbert and Sullivan Legacy," an exhibition of holdings from the Harvard Theatre Collection, displayed several commercial spinoffs that must be considered as parodies, produced especially in the United States to advertise everything from soap to cities. For example, the pamphlet *Rymes from Ye Playe of "Pynafore"* (1879), published by Enoch Morgan and Sons, the maker of Sapolio Soap, contains "Sapoli-o-lic Selections from E.M.S. Pinafore" ("E.M.S" for Enoch Morgan and Sons), with parody lyrics written anonymously by Bret Harte. One parody of *The Mikado* was a kind of real-estate gambit that "extolled the commercial prospects of Fort Worth, Texas" (plate 20). Most elaborate of all, the lavish "Railroad parodies" were beautifully produced and illustrated full parodies of *Patience*, *Iolanthe*, *Princess Ida*, and the Bab Ballads, written in praise of the Chicago and Alton Railroad (plate 21).

Meanwhile, the Savoy performance tradition was disseminated worldwide by an avid amateur movement that surely has no equal in theater history. The devotees' fidelity to the performance tradition was supported by the D'Oyly Carte Opera Company, which circulated hand-copied, semi-official prompt books that taught schoolchildren and club members around the globe the exact bit of stage "business" appropriate for every stage turn. Legendary anecdotes about the Savoy actors—and about Gilbert and Sullivan themselves—added to the amateurs' feeling of being rewarded for their dedication by being deeply in the know. The fan-based dissemination of these stories has sometimes encouraged more anecdotage than critical reflection—but the transmission of the legendary anecdotes kept up a lively popular interest in the collaboration.[4]

The copyrights in the libretti did not expire until December 31, 1961, fifty years after Gilbert's death. (The copyrights in the music had expired in 1950, but because a full production of any opera needs the libretto, the operas were not truly in the public domain until 1961.) When the time for the copyrights to expire rolled around, there was a great deal of agitation about what would happen to the performance tradition. And, indeed, change did come. For almost sixty years, the world has been treated to—or has suffered through, depending on your point of view—many updated versions of the operas, many "concept" productions, and a great deal of commentary about what makes a good and faithful reproduction of the original or, on the contrary, what constitutes the desecration of a sacred object. Needless to say, the quality of each new production has to be evaluated in its own right.[5]

But my point is that both sides of this debate will, and must, continue to circulate, for both parody and tradition building are incorporated into the logic of not only genre in general, but this genre in particular. Parody, as we will recall, is the negative moment in tradition building. Perhaps it would be most accurate to say that both aspects of the genre's logic continue to operate—both its conservative remembering and tradition building and its progressive turning away from the past, toward a continually updated present. Thus genre parody continues to produce tradition, and tradition is susceptible to genre parody, in turn. In the world of Gilbert and Sullivan, arguments about fidelity to or transgression against the tradition have become a part of the tradition itself.

A revival is not a parody, but the purposive intent to bring a production back to life must always go a bit awry. Since every production—indeed, every performance—is a singular event, "anything in the way of an actual revival must always be impossible."[6] This brings revival interestingly close to parody, insofar as both imitate and diverge from an original that is never fully reproducible. On the spectrum from imitation to critique, a revival is a reproduction that adheres more closely to imitation, while a parody emphasizes changes, shifts, and critique; but both operate with the impossibility of exact reproduction in the background. Moreover, this is the same paradoxical (and productive) tension that regulates the concept of genre itself, which coheres through recognizable conventions but also supports and mandates novelty through further mixing, twisting, and revision of its norms. Rupert D'Oyly Carte, who assumed the management of the family company in 1913, explained his attitude toward this question:

I have always kept a strict watch on any suggested changes to the words and music, but decor is a different thing. As years pass the public's sense of style changes remarkably. Appreciation of colour changes. Even the very shape of our women has changed! Dresses and shapes and colours which were once thought beautiful are now thought dowdy. It is this subtle change in public taste which necessitates periodic redressing of the operas.[7]

Amusingly, in light of one of the concerns of this book, "the very shape of our women" is Carte's most specific marker of changing public taste, along with a vaguer attention to color schemes and costumes. But he importantly distinguished between the words and music, on the one hand, and the "decor," on the other—the spirit and the body of the Savoy operas. The body can be allowed to change, while the spirit remains the same. But this is easier said than done, when what is wanted is revival, not the revelation of the operas as the undead.

Eventually, production standards became standardization, the formula began to seem formulaic, and the operas became a heritage phenomenon. In this respect, the story of the formation of a genre yields to the story of Gilbert and Sullivan themselves being considered as "generic." Easily recognized, the genre could be treated as a recipe, "museum" performances could become a tourist phenomenon (which everybody had to see, whether or not they liked it), and "a D'Oyly Carte production" could be received as an outmoded performance style. The genre of "Gilbert and Sullivan" then became susceptible to the logic and momentum of genre parody—which is to produce further parody. This moment cannot be dated, because it is a part of the logic of the genre itself; parody begins as soon as the genre begins to form. Indeed, the operas parody themselves overtly, as when Major-General Stanley can "whistle all the airs from that infernal nonsense *Pinafore*."

As well as revival, updating—changing topical references, songs, or whole productions to make them more up-to-date—is built into the genre of Gilbert and Sullivan opera, as it is in the burlesque and extravaganza traditions.[8] A blatant acknowledgment of the investment in absolute currency, updating is a special case of parody's ambivalent attachment to both the ever-receding past and the ever-modernizing present. Adapting themselves to the immediate concerns of contemporary audiences, certain songs in the Savoy repertory are especially open to new verses or revisionist lyrics made to fit the changing issues of new times and new places. Examples of this, especially on the Web, are innumerable.

It is but a tiny step from updating stanzas to updating whole songs—a practice most people would unhesitatingly call "parody." Ian Bradley devotes a chapter of his most recent book to the widespread parodies of Gilbert and Sullivan, discussing many examples and describing John Cannon's collection of parodies, "almost certainly . . . the largest in the world." Using that collection, he is able to show, with numerical evidence, what we may have already guessed, that "I am the very model of a modern Major-General" from *The Pirates of Penzance* is the most parodied song, with Ko-Ko's "I've got a little list" from *The Mikado* a close second.[9] Both have been adapted to every conceivable use by groups that want to identify and characterize various types of contemporary social life—whether to appreciate and identify with them or to sing out a trenchant critique. Ko-Ko's song is particularly versatile, for it explicitly invites its own updating by every audience member. Complaining about bad politicians, the song suddenly pretends to be conveying an inside joke—a secret parody of specific statesmen—but it is also a snarling general parody of the censorship of the English stage, since the Examiner of Plays would not allow explicit political satire of prominent contemporary figures:

> And apologetic statesmen of a compromising kind,
> Such as—What d'ye call him—Thing 'em-bob, and likewise—Never-mind,
> And 'St— 'st— 'st— and What's his name, and also You-know-who—
> The task of filling up the blanks I'd rather leave to *you*.

This address to "*you*" brings home the mandate to continue updating to every spectator, from the "now" of Gilbert and Sullivan to the "now" of whenever *you* are watching *The Mikado* (or reading this book).

Updating whole operas provokes a set of even more vexed questions, although they are essentially the same question we have been investigating. The Federal Theatre Project's *Swing Mikado* (1939); *The Hot Mikado* (1939), starring Bill "Bojangles" Robinson; Harold Rome's "Red Mikado" (1939), a sketch in the revue *Pins and Needles*, produced by the International Ladies' Garment Workers' Union; George S. Kaufmann's *Hollywood Pinafore, or The Lad Who Loved a Salary* (1945); *Der Yiddisher Pinafore* (1952); even Jonathan Miller's "Black and White" *Mikado* (2003), which places the action in a seaside spa during the flapper era—all these productions have, more or less, been taken as homage. Peter Sellars's Japanese-gangster *Mikado* (1983), Ken Russell's *Princess Ida* (1992), and Joseph Papp's centenary production of *The Pirates of Penzance* (1980) at the Delacorte Theater in Central Park, though, have been subjected to more skepticism. Are they revivals or parodies? Argument will always rage within Gilbert and Sullivan circles, for this very question is definitive—and even constitutive—of the field, determined by the momentum of genre parody. To debate this point is one important part of the attempt to understand Gilbert and Sullivan. The tendency to modernize and the tendency to recollect—both are extensions of the logic of the genre we call "Gilbert and Sullivan." In our debates on this point, we continue the tradition.

This deeply coherent set of tensions also accounts for the variety of uses to which the Savoy operas may be put, when they are used as references in other cultural texts. This dynamic has been mobilized ever since the operas were current phenomena. In George Gissing's *The Odd Women* (1893), attending a Gilbert and Sullivan opera is the height of urban modernity and highly familiar at the same time. In Evelyn Waugh's *Brideshead Revisited* (1945), Gilbert and Sullivan are used to mark a nostalgic remembrance of the past. In the film *Chariots of Fire* (1981), a short scene from *The Mikado* provides a retro period detail. And in the "Cape Feare" episode of *The Simpsons* (1993), the allusions to Gilbert and Sullivan first make fun of government bureaucracy and then parody the devoted zaniness of fans like Side Show Bob. In all these works, the reference to Gilbert and Sullivan is to a piece of iconic Victoriana, remembered in fragments in the present to assert the modernity of the book or film, whether by differentiating itself from or asserting its continuity with Gilbert and Sullivan. Thus fragmentary allusion goes beyond parody, revival, and updating of "the thing itself," and the momentum becomes a principle of historical consciousness, while the tradition becomes a part of the contemporary moment.

Notes

Introduction

1. Richard D'Oyly Carte brought them together in 1875 for *Trial by Jury*. But Gilbert and Sullivan had collaborated once before, on *Thespis* (1871), under the auspices of John Hollingshead at the Gaiety Theatre. See chapters 1 and 2.
2. The best biography is Arthur Jacobs, *Arthur Sullivan: A Victorian Musician*, 2nd ed. (Portland, Ore.: Amadeus Press, 1992). Also excellent is Michael Ainger, *Gilbert and Sullivan: A Dual Biography* (Oxford: Oxford University Press, 2002).
3. Jane W. Stedman, *W. S. Gilbert: A Classic Victorian and His Theatre* (Oxford: Oxford University Press, 1996) p. 23, and *W. S. Gilbert's Theatrical Criticism* (London: Society for Theatre Research, 2000), passim, but especially pp. 33–52.
4. Stedman, *W. S. Gilbert*, p. 13.
5. *The Bab Ballads by W. S. Gilbert*, ed. James Ellis (Cambridge, Mass.: Belknap Press of Harvard University Press, 1970).
6. Isaac Goldberg, introduction to W. S. Gilbert, *New and Original Extravaganzas*, ed. Isaac Goldberg (Boston: Luce, 1931), p. xvii.
7. *Gilbert Before Sullivan: Six Comic Plays by W. S. Gilbert*, ed. Jane W. Stedman (Chicago: University of Chicago Press, 1967).
8. *Original Plays* is dated 1876, but actually was released in 1875. See Stedman, *W. S. Gilbert*, p. 135.
9. W. S. Gilbert, *Original Plays*, 4 vols. (London: Chatto & Windus, 1922–1924), and *Plays by W. S. Gilbert: The Palace of Truth, Sweethearts, Princess Toto, Engaged, Rosencrantz and Guildenstern*, ed. George Rowell (Cambridge: Cambridge University Press, 1982).
10. "Parody," *Westminster Review* 62 (1854): 95–115.
11. "Parody," pp. 96–100.
12. Margaret A. Rose, *Parody: Ancient, Modern, and Post-Modern* (Cambridge: Cambridge University Press, 1993), p. 19. For Rose's detailed discussion of the history of debates on the etymology of "parody," see pp. 6–19.

13. The quoted compendium of meanings for *para-* in ancient Greek usage is taken from Fred W. Householder Jr., "ΠΑΡΩΙΔΙΑ," *Classical Philology* 39, no. 1 (1944): 1–9, quoted in Rose, *Parody*, p. 8; see also pp. 48–50. On the ambivalences of *para-* and its relation to the German critical tradition of distinguishing between *Beigesang* (a song sung alongside another) and *Gegengesang* (a song sung in opposition to another), see Margaret A. Rose, *Parody/Meta-Fiction: An Analysis of Parody as a Critical Mirror to the Writing and Reception of Fiction* (London: Croom Helm, 1979), pp. 33–34.

14. Other rhetorics of temporality include history (Mark Phillips, "Histories, Micro- and Literary: Problems of Genre and Distance," *New Literary History* 34 [2003]: 211–29; "Distance and Historical Representation," *History Workshop Journal* 57 [2004]: 123–24; and *"To Bring the Distant Near": Historical Distance and the Shaping of the Past* [New Haven, Conn.: Yale University Press, forthcoming]), autobiography (Jean Starobinski, "The Style of Autobiography," in *Autobiography: Essays Theoretical and Critical*, ed. James Olney [Princeton, N.J.: Princeton University Press, 1980], pp. 236–67), and allegory (Paul de Man, "The Rhetoric of Temporality," in *Blindness and Insight: Essays in the Rhetoric of Contemporary Criticism* [1971; reprint, Minneapolis: University of Minnesota Press, 1983], pp. 187–228).

15. Yes, parody can be both conservative and progressive in the political senses of those terms as well. But that dimension of their significance depends entirely and absolutely on this temporal structure.

16. "The subversive force of parody is equivalent to its constructive force," as Joseph A. Dane puts it, in a formulation that intends "subversive" in a purely descriptive, structural sense (*Parody: Critical Concepts Versus Literary Practices, Aristophanes to Sterne* [Norman: University of Oklahoma Press, 1988], p. 8). Perhaps most familiar these days in Theodor Adorno, this kind of negative dialectic was also common in the nineteenth-century critical tradition—in Walter Pater, for example, who wrote, describing Leonardo's disciplined progress through negation, that "the way to perfection is through a series of disgusts" (*The Renaissance: Studies in Art and Poetry* [London: Macmillan, 1910], p. 103).

17. Max Keith Sutton, *W. S. Gilbert* (Boston: Twayne, 1975), p. 88; Rose, *Parody*, pp. 47–48. Among the essays comparing Gilbert with Aristophanes, see Walter Sichel, "The English Aristophanes," pp. 69–110, and Edith Hamilton, "W. S. Gilbert: A Mid-Victorian Aristophanes," pp. 111–34, both in *W. S. Gilbert: A Century of Scholarship and Commentary*, ed. John Bush Jones (New York: New York University Press, 1970).

18. On "now-disappeared performances" and "the terminology of 're' in discussions of performance," see Elin Diamond, introduction to *Performance and Cultural Politics*, ed. Elin Diamond (New York: Routledge, 1996), especially p. 2.

19. Marvin Carlson makes this point about *H.M.S. Pinafore* in "He Never Should Bow Down to a Domineering Frown: Class Tensions and Nautical Melodrama," in *Melodrama: The Cultural Emergence of a Genre*, ed. Michael Hays and Anastasia Nicolopoulou (New York: St. Martin's Press, 1996), pp. 147–51.

20. Writing for *London Society* in 1868, Gilbert excoriated the popular nostalgia for childhood, saying that its supposed happiness lay merely "in its total irresponsibility, its incapacity to distinguish between right and wrong, its general helplessness,

its inability to argue rationally, and its having nothing whatever upon its half-born little mind,—privileges which are equally the property of an idiot in a lunatic asylum" (quoted in Stedman, *W. S. Gilbert*, p. 7).

21. Stephen Jay Gould, "The True Embodiment of Everything That's Excellent: The Strange Adventure of Gilbert and Sullivan," *American Scholar* 69, no. 2 (2000): 35–49.

22. George Levine, *The Realistic Imagination: English Fiction from Frankenstein to Lady Chatterley* (Chicago: University of Chicago Press, 1981). Michael McKeon stresses the difference between ancient and modern conceptions of genre as well, when he points out the piety that epic literature displays toward tradition, rather than the modernizing leveling of values; the result is not unity but the inexhaustible critical reflection and doubling within the object (*Theory of the Novel: A Historical Approach* [Baltimore: Johns Hopkins University Press, 2000], p. 317). Compare Levine's argument about realism, which is not only descendentalizing and secularizing, but also in an important sense "antiliterary" or even "antigeneric" in its thrust (*Realistic Imagination*, pp. 11–12).

23. Thus Derrida's "law of genre" ("genres must not be mixed; you must not mix them") is valued only in its deconstruction, and thus the supposedly postmodern "blurring" of genres is actually a much older phenomenon, not specific to postmodernism at all. See Jacques Derrida, "The Law of Genre," *Glyph* 7 (1980): 176–232.

24. Some critics restrict the term "parody" to those works that make fun of one specific work, while others admit general parodies, sometimes using "pastiche" or "burlesque" to indicate genre parodies. But "genre parody" is a better term, not only because I want to focus on the theoretical point, but also because in nineteenth-century theater history, the term "burlesque" must be reserved for a specific form of theatrical parody. For a good discussion of these related terms, see Rose, *Parody*, pp. 54–99.

25. Stedman, *W. S. Gilbert*, 72–73.

26. Fredric Woodbridge Wilson, "W. S. Gilbert and the Past," pp. 10–11 (lecture delivered at the Harvard College Library, Cambridge, Mass., February 13, 2001; the second of three lectures—"The Gilbert and Sullivan Legacy"—presented on the occasion of "The Gilbert & Sullivan Operas: A Centenary Exhibition," Harvard Theatre Collection / Pusey Library, November 22, 2000–April 13, 2001).

27. On this point, see Richard Schechner, *Between Theater and Anthropology* (Philadelphia: University of Pennsylvania Press, 1985) and *Performance Theory*, rev. ed. (New York: Routledge, 2004).

28. "Parody."

29. The theoretical and practical development of the concept of "cultural formations" is, in general, a legacy of the cultural-materialist inflection of early British cultural studies. According to Raymond Williams, for example, "[W]hat then emerges as the most central and practical element in cultural analysis is what also marks the most significant cultural theory: the exploration and specification of distinguishable cultural formations" ("The Uses of Cultural Theory," *New Left Review*, no. 158 [1986]: 29). See also Michael Bérubé, ed., *The Aesthetics of Cultural Studies* (Malden, Mass.: Wiley-Blackwell, 2004).

30. See Caroline Levine, "Strategic Formalism: Toward a New Method in Cultural Studies," *Victorian Studies* 48 (2006): 625–57, and, in response, Herbert F. Tucker, "Tactical

Formalism: A Response to Caroline Levine," *Victorian Studies* 49 (2006): 85–93, and Carolyn Dever, "Strategic Aestheticism: A Response to Caroline Levine," *Victorian Studies* 49 (2006): 94–99.

31. Quoted in Arthur Lawrence, *Sir Arthur Sullivan: Life Story, Letters, and Reminiscences* (Chicago: Stone, 1900), p. 85. For another discussion of Gilbert's innovations in the Chorus, see Stedman, *W. S. Gilbert*, pp. 219–20.

32. William Cox-Ife, *W. S. Gilbert: Stage Director* (London: Dobson, 1977), pp. 70–81, and *Training the Gilbert and Sullivan Chorus* (London: Lowe & Brydone, 1953).

33. W. S. Gilbert, *Dulcamara! or, The Little Duck and the Great Quack*, in *New and Original Extravaganzas*, p. 9.

34. As Stedman rightly notes in *W. S. Gilbert*, p. 220. See also Sutton, *W. S. Gilbert*, p. 88.

35. Jane W. Stedman, "W. S. Gilbert: His Comic Techniques and Their Development" (Ph.D. diss., University of Chicago, 1956).

36. The Savoy operas will treat this topos of parody again in *Iolanthe* and *Princess Ida*. See chapters 7 and 8.

37. In the Savoy operas, cross-dressing is used for the characters (such as the young men in *Princess Ida* dressing as Girl Graduates) but is not used for the roles (such as a woman playing a prince or a man playing the Dame). For more on cross-dressing, see chapters 1 and 7.

38. Kathy Fletcher, "Planché, Vestris, and the Transvestite Role: Sexuality and Gender in Victorian Popular Theatre," *Nineteenth Century Theatre* 15, no. 1 (1987): 9–33.

39. On "natural acting" in the nineteenth century, see Lynn M. Voskuil, *Acting Naturally: Victorian Theatricality and Authenticity* (Charlottesville: University Press of Virginia, 2004).

40. Andrew Goodman, *Gilbert and Sullivan at Law* (Rutherford, N.J.: Fairleigh Dickinson University Press, 1983), p. 41.

41. On Gilbert's attention to steady work and good pay for women, see Tracy C. Davis, "The Savoy Chorus," *Theatre Notebook* 44, no. 1 (1990): 26–38, and *Actresses as Working Women: Their Social Identity in Victorian Culture* (New York: Routledge, 1991), pp. 65–67. When the Choristers' Union was formed in 1893, Gilbert became the first (and honorary) president.

42. On the late-nineteenth-century "denaturalization" of gender norms and roles, see Kathy Alexis Psomiades, *Beauty's Body: Femininity and Representation in British Aestheticism* (Stanford, Calif.: Stanford University Press, 1997); Talia Schaffer and Kathy Alexis Psomiades, eds., *Women and British Aestheticism* (Charlottesville: University Press of Virginia, 1999); Talia Schaffer, *The Forgotten Female Aesthetes: Literature and Culture in Late-Victorian England* (Charlottesville: University Press of Virginia, 2000); and Dennis Denisoff, *Aestheticism and Sexual Parody, 1840–1940* (Cambridge: Cambridge University Press, 2001). See also Jonathan Loesberg, "Fin de Siècle Work on Victorian Aestheticism," *Victorian Literature and Culture* 29, no. 2 (2001): 521–34.

43. For authoritative views on "the sex/gender system," see Rayna Reiter, ed., *Toward an Anthropology of Women* (New York: Monthly Review Press, 1975).

44. Gervase Hughes, *The Music of Arthur Sullivan* (New York: St. Martin's Press, 1960), p. 131.

45. Quoted in Reginald Allen, ed., *The First Night Gilbert and Sullivan: Containing Complete Librettos of the Fourteen Operas, Exactly as Presented at Their Première Performances; Together with Facsimiles of the First-Night Programmes* (New York: Heritage Club, 1958), p. 208.

46. A discussion on SavoyNet among Steve Lichtenstein, Derrick McClure, and Chris Webster exposes, as well, the similarities between "O wandering one!" and "Sempre libera" and "Amami, Alfredo, amami" from *La Traviata*. See http://diamond.boise-state.edu/gas/pirates/discussion/3–2.html#wandering, especially section 3.4.1.

47. Anthony Tommasini, "That Gilbert and Sullivan Maiden with Mission and Erudition," *New York Times*, January 7, 2008.

48. According to Carl Dahlhaus, "The fairy music in *Iolanthe* . . . is not simply a Mendelssohn parody, although it can certainly be appreciated on that level. . . . Rather, its purpose is to suffuse a magical fairy-tale aura fractured but not smothered by irony, an aura without which Gilbert's daring dramaturgical construct would be nothing but a mechanism spinning idly in a void" (*Nineteenth-Century Music*, trans. J. Bradford Robinson [Berkeley: University of California Press, 1989], p. 235).

49. "Music. Savoy Theatre.—'Princess Ida.' By Gilbert and Sullivan," *Athenaeum*, January 12, 1884, 63.

50. Hughes, *Music of Arthur Sullivan*, p. 143.

51. Hughes, *Music of Arthur Sullivan*, pp. 143, 141.

52. Hughes, *Music of Arthur Sullivan*, p. 143.

53. Jeffrey Shandler, in discussion at the Center for Critical Analysis of Contemporary Culture, Rutgers University (March 2002); Anna Russell, *How to Write Your Own Gilbert and Sullivan Opera*, compact disc, Sony Masterworks, MDK 47252.

54. Andrew Crowther, *Contradiction Contradicted: The Plays of W. S. Gilbert* (Madison, N.J.: Fairleigh Dickinson University Press, 2000), p. 189.

55. Robyn Warhol-Down, personal communication, April 2008, in which she also discusses the example of "Ah, leave me not to pine." For an excellent elaboration of the claims of affect, see Robyn R. Warhol, *Having a Good Cry: Effeminate Feelings and Pop-Culture Forms* (Columbus: Ohio State University Press, 2003).

1. *Thespis*

1. The exception is Terence Rees, whose *Thespis: A Gilbert and Sullivan Enigma* (London: Dillon's University Bookshop, 1964), is indispensable. He uses evidence from periodical reviews to establish omissions in the text.

2. For one example of the usual dismissal, see Gayden Wren, *A Most Ingenious Paradox: The Art of Gilbert and Sullivan* (Oxford: Oxford University Press, 2001). Wren perceives "no thematic resonance" and claims that "*Thespis* [is not] about anything" (pp. 29, 46). I argue against the prevailing opinion that "*Thespis* offers only the faintest opportunity to see the emerging Gilbert & Sullivan" (p. 25). Alan Fischler, too, underestimates the importance of the early collaborations in *Modified Rapture: Comedy in W. S. Gilbert's Savoy Operas* (Charlottesville: University Press of Virginia, 1991), pp. vii–ix.

3. This pun on "younger son" shows Gilbert's engagement with plot conventions of the novel.

4. Rees, *Thespis*, pp. 15–16; Edith Hall, "Classical Mythology in the Victorian Popular Theatre," *International Journal of the Classical Tradition* 5, no. 3 (1999): 336–66; Isaac Goldberg, *The Story of Gilbert and Sullivan; or, The "Compleat" Savoyard* (New York: Simon and Schuster, 1928), p. 146; Jane W. Stedman, *W. S. Gilbert: A Classic Victorian and His Theatre* (Oxford: Oxford University Press, 1996), p. 95.

5. Rees, *Thespis*, p. 92.

6. Quoted in Reginald Allen, ed., *The First Night Gilbert and Sullivan: Containing Complete Librettos of the Fourteen Operas, Exactly as Presented at Their Première Performances; Together with Facsimiles of the First-Night Programmes* (New York: Heritage Club, 1958), p. 6.

7. Quoted in Goldberg, *Story of Gilbert and Sullivan*, p. 143. Later, as we shall see in chapters 7 and 8, *Iolanthe* and *Princess Ida* allude broadly to particular forms of theatrical transvestism.

8. Quoted in Allen, ed., *First Night Gilbert and Sullivan*, p. 6, and Rees, *Thespis*, p. 13.

9. Pantomime, unlike burlesque and extravaganza, was intended for a mixed audience of children and adults. The Gaiety's opening-night offering was an opera burlesque by Gilbert, *Robert the Devil; or The Nun, the Dun, and the Son of a Gun* (1868), a parody of Giacomo Meyerbeer's *Robert le diable* (1831). This demonstrates not only Gilbert's marketable popularity at the time, but also the importance of opera burlesque and extravaganza for the later development of English comic opera.

10. Both burlesque and extravaganza are themselves forms of parody. In nineteenth-century England, the term "burlesque" indicated the mock-heroic deflation of a particular work belonging to a higher tradition of literature or music. James Robinson Planché distinguished between "burlesque" and "extravaganza" by noting whether the work parodied a specific work or diffused itself among many familiar stories (*The Recollections and Reflections of J. R. Planché* [London: Tinsley, 1872], paraphrased in Hall, "Classical Mythology," p. 340). These related genres are known for conventional forms of sexual display, although extravaganza is more refined. Later (especially American) burlesque exaggerates the risqué sexual content, using an episodic, vaudevillian format, thus influencing the current colloquial understanding of the term. See also Richard W. Schoch, introduction to *Victorian Theatrical Burlesques*, ed. Richard W. Schoch (Aldershot: Ashgate, 2003), pp. xii–xviii.

11. Donald Roy, introduction to *Plays by James Robinson Planché*, ed. Donald Roy (Cambridge: Cambridge University Press, 1986), p. 10. Steven Connor examines this aspect of Charles Mathews's performance style in *Dumbstruck: A Cultural History of Ventriloquism* (Oxford: Oxford University Press, 2000), pp. 265–89. This focus on the multiple roles encompassed in one acting body will become an obsession in the Savoy operas.

12. Gilbert's debt to Planché is well known. See, especially, Harley Granville-Barker, "Exit Planché—Enter Gilbert," in *The Eighteen-Sixties: Essays by Fellows of the Royal Society of Literature*, ed. John Drinkwater (Cambridge: Cambridge University Press, 1932), pp. 102–48. My point, however, is a more general one, for the influence of extravaganza as a genre was more culturally pervasive than the debt of one singular author to another could signify.

13. "A Gossip with Meyer Lutz," *Era*, July 22, 1893, p. 9, quoted in Stedman, *W. S. Gilbert*, p. 95.
14. Hall mentions most of these familiar elements in "Classical Mythology," p. 363.
15. Swinburne's "pagan" speaker in "Hymn to Proserpine" (1866) bitterly addresses the new god: "Thou hast conquered, O pale Galilean; the world has grown grey with thy breath." The poem bears the poignant subtitle "(After the Proclamation in Rome of the Christian Faith)." Walter Pater's central character in *Marius the Epicurean* (1885) experiences the historical rise of the Christian era, displacing the pantheistic religion of his rural youth. In *Father and Son* (1907), Edmund Gosse looks back on the intolerance and condescension toward "the pagan gods" practiced by the dissenting sect of his childhood. For poetic arguments that align southern climates with the past and northern climates with the present, see Matthew Arnold, "Dover Beach" (1867) and "Stanzas from the Grande Chartreuse" (1855). Nietzsche, Pater, and Vernon Lee wrote about "the gods in exile," displaced from their original southern habitats to northern lands (where, like the gods in *Thespis*, they must bundle up against the cold).
16. Although *Götterdämmerung* was not performed until 1875, it provides an important touchstone for *Thespis*, which Leslie Baily calls a "comic Twilight of the Gods" (*The Gilbert and Sullivan Book* [London: Spring Books, 1952], p. 111). Goldberg, too, makes this association in *Story of Gilbert and Sullivan*, pp. 146–47.
17. For example, in *Das Leben Jesu* (*The Life of Jesus*, 1835), David Friedrich Strauss focuses on the biography of a historical personage rather than on an incarnation of godhead; Ludwig Feuerbach interprets "the essence of Christianity" as an anthropological principle of reverence for the ritual performances of everyday life; Auguste Comte and George Eliot imagine a "religion of humanity."
18. Gilbert repeatedly tiptoed up to this verboten topic, as I will show in my readings of *The Sorcerer* and *Patience*. See chapters 3 and 6.
19. According to Fischler, "The deities of *Thespis* have become so outmoded and remote from mankind that they must be replaced by mortal agents; their status, in other words, is not much different from that which was accorded the Christian God in the post-Darwinian Victorian mind" (*Modified Rapture*, p. 52).
20. Elizabeth Burns, *Theatricality: A Study of Convention in the Theatre and in Social Life* (New York: Harper & Row, 1972), especially pp. 1–8.
21. Hall, "Classical Mythology," pp. 338–39, and passim. I am greatly indebted to her analysis on this point. For more detail on the changing face of classical education at this time, see Christopher Stray, *Classics Transformed: Schools, Universities, and Society in England, 1830–1960* (Oxford: Oxford University Press, 1998), and Christopher Stray, ed., *Oxford Classics: Teaching and Learning, 1800–2000* (London: Duckworth, 2008).
22. Hall, "Classical Mythology," pp. 350–51.
23. Hall, "Classical Mythology," p. 336.
24. Hall, "Classical Mythology," pp. 345–46, 355.
25. Planché, *The Golden Fleece*, in *Plays by James Robinson Planché*, p. 147.
26. Hall, "Classical Mythology," pp. 352–54.
27. For reviews making this point, see Rees, *Thespis*, pp. 26, 58. Writing in 1889, George Bernard Shaw took this as given in "Gilbert and Offenbach," in *Shaw on Music*, ed. Eric Bentley (New York: Doubleday, 1955; New York: Applause Books, 1983), p. 202.

28. Max Keith Sutton, *W. S. Gilbert* (Boston: Twayne, 1975), pp. 83, 133n.3. Andrew Crowther compares *Thespis* and *Orphée aux enfers* in *Contradiction Contradicted: The Plays of W. S. Gilbert* (Madison, N.J.: Fairleigh Dickinson University Press, 2000), pp. 71–72.

29. Rees, *Thespis*, pp. 36–37.

30. Surely, Planché's single-person Chorus in *The Golden Fleece* influenced the creation of the figure of Public Opinion in Offenbach's *Orphée aux enfers*. He, too, is a single figure who serves as a parody of the Greek Chorus. In other words, English extravaganza influenced Offenbach, just as Planché, in developing the genre of extravaganza, had been influenced by the pre-Offenbachian spectacles of French *féerie*.

31. Wren, *Most Ingenious Paradox*, p. 27.

32. Quoted in Stedman, *W. S. Gilbert*, p. 130. This was said of the relation between Offenbach's *La Périchole* (1868) and *Trial by Jury*, which played on a double bill at the Royalty Theatre in 1875.

33. On this point, see Kathy Fletcher, "Planché, Vestris, and the Transvestite Role: Sexuality and Gender in Victorian Popular Theatre," *Nineteenth Century Theatre* 15, no. 1 (1987): 9–33.

34. Many critics have pointed out that Mercury prefigures the bureaucratic multiplicity and self-division of Pooh-Bah in *The Mikado*. See, for example, Goldberg, *Story of Gilbert and Sullivan*, p. 150.

35. Rees, *Thespis*, pp. 41–42.

36. Jon McKenzie most effectively expands performance theory to include the discipline of workplace performance in *Perform or Else: From Discipline to Performance* (New York: Routledge, 2001).

37. We know that this reference was widely grasped by contemporaries, because it appears in the Duke of Sutherland's obituary notice in the *Times* in September 1892. See Andrew Goodman, *Gilbert and Sullivan at Law* (Madison, N.J.: Fairleigh Dickinson Press, 1983), pp. 171–72.

38. *Pall Mall Gazette*, quoted in Rees, *Thespis*, p. 64. Rees speculates that this "new instrument" was a pair of blocks covered in sandpaper, whose swishing, grating sound was subsequently much used in the music hall.

39. Quoted in Rees, *Thespis*, pp. 40, 64.

40. In his comic journalism, Gilbert frequently describes the difficulty of mounting a coherent theatrical production, due to the number of competing forces in charge. See, for example, "A Stage Play," his satirical piece for *Tom Hood's Comic Annual* (1873), and "A Hornpipe in Fetters," in *Era Almanack and Annual* (1879).

2. *Trial by Jury*

1. The Licensing Act of 1737 had specifically forbidden any impersonation of the Crown or its agents. *The Happy Land* (1873), Gilbert's pseudonymous political parody of his own *The Wicked World* (1873), had recently been censored for precisely this offense: its impersonations of Prime Minister William Gladstone; Acton Ayrton, of the Office of Works; and Robert Lowe, Chancellor of the Exchequer. So we may

be certain that Fred Sullivan's makeup intentionally displayed its provocation. See Ellwood P. Lawrence, "'The Happy Land': W. S. Gilbert as Political Satirist," *Victorian Studies* 15, no. 2 (1971): 164–72.

2. The suit against the Tichborne Claimant precipitated two of the longest trials in English history, during which he became the focus of a radical popular movement in the 1870s and 1880s. In 1874—the year before the staging of *Trial by Jury*—the Claimant was sentenced to fourteen years in prison. See Rohan McWilliam, *Popular Politics in Nineteenth-Century England* (New York: Routledge, 1998), pp. 69–70.

3. Andrew Goodman, *Gilbert and Sullivan at Law* (Madison, N.J.: Fairleigh Dickinson University Press, 1983), pp. 62–63.

4. Quoted in Arthur Lawrence, *Arthur Sullivan: Life Story, Letters, and Reminiscences* (Chicago: Stone, 1899), p. 107. See also Goodman, *Gilbert and Sullivan*, pp. 61–62.

5. *Times* (London), March 29, 1875, quoted in Leslie Baily, *The Gilbert and Sullivan Book* (London: Spring Books, 1952), pp. 127–28.

6. Quoted in Jane W. Stedman, *W. S. Gilbert: A Classic Victorian and His Theatre* (Oxford: Oxford University Press, 1996), p. 130.

7. W. S. Gilbert, "Trial by Jury—An Operetta," *Fun*, April 11, 1868, in *The Bab Ballads by W. S. Gilbert*, ed. James Ellis (Cambridge, Mass.: Belknap Press of Harvard University Press, 1970), pp. 157–59. The original publication in *Fun* parodied legal discourse more explicitly, rhyming "Trial-la-law" with arcane legal abbreviations that also seem to mimic a nonce system of musical notation (*ca. sa., fi. fa.*).

8. Stedman, *W. S. Gilbert*, p. 155.

9. Audrey Williamson, *Gilbert and Sullivan Opera: A New Assessment* (New York: Macmillan, 1953), p. 29. Ian Bradley offers an autoethnographic interpretation, for he stresses "the quaint customs of English legal procedure," as well as the popular English joke of attributing a general madness to England (*The Complete Annotated Gilbert and Sullivan* [Oxford: Oxford University Press, 1996], p. 4).

10. Gilbert, *Bab Ballads*, p. 340.

11. I intentionally allude to Gayle Rubin's influential formulation of the "sex/gender system" in "The Traffic in Women: Notes Toward a Political Economy of Sex," in *Toward an Anthropology of Women*, ed. Rayna Reiter (New York: Monthly Review Press, 1975), pp. 157–210.

12. Fredric Woodbridge Wilson, *An Introduction to the Gilbert and Sullivan Operas: From the Collection of the Pierpont Morgan Library* (New York: Pierpont Morgan Library, in association with Dover, 1989), pp. 28–29. Wilson points out the parody of the minstrel show in his caption.

13. Promptbook for *Trial by Jury*, p. 4b, opposite p. 5, W. S. Gilbert Papers, vol. 22, Add. MSS 49310, British Library, London.

14. Recent work on blackface minstrelsy focuses on relations of class, race, and gender. See Eric Lott, *Love and Theft: Blackface Minstrelsy and the American Working Class* (New York: Oxford University Press, 1993), and W. T. Lhamon Jr., *Raising Cain: Blackface Performance from Jim Crow to Hip Hop* (Cambridge, Mass.: Harvard University Press, 1998). The most comprehensive treatment of minstrelsy in England is Michael Pickering, *Blackface Minstrelsy in Britain* (Aldershot: Ashgate, 2008).

15. Isaac Goldberg, *The Story of Gilbert and Sullivan; or, The "Compleat" Savoyard* (New York: Simon and Schuster, 1928), p. 173.

16. Isaac Goldberg, quoted in Andrew Crowther, *Contradiction Contradicted: The Plays of W. S. Gilbert* (Madison, N.J.: Fairleigh Dickinson University Press, 2000), p. 77.

17. Rubin, "Traffic in Women"; Eve Kosofsky Sedgwick, *Between Men: English Literature and Male Homosocial Desire* (New York: Columbia University Press, 1985).

18. This flirtatiousness is even more emphatically represented in the 1884 revival. See Bradley, *Complete Annotated Gilbert and Sullivan*, pp. 26, 28, 30, 34.

19. J. L. Austin famously uses the "I do" of the marriage ceremony as his exemplary case of performative language in *How to Do Things with Words* (Cambridge, Mass.: Harvard University Press, 1962). For a critique, see Andrew Parker and Eve Kosofsky Sedgwick, introduction to *Performance and Performativity* (New York: Routledge, 1995).

20. Susie L. Steinbach, "The Melodramatic Contract: Breach of Promise and the Performance of Virtue," *Nineteenth Century Studies* 14 (2000): 11–12.

21. That the suit for breach of promise euphemistically covered a more risqué topic was emphasized in the 1990 Bournemouth production of *Trial by Jury*, featuring "an obviously pregnant Angelina" (Bradley, *Complete Annotated Gilbert and Sullivan*, p. 5).

22. Martha Vicinus, "'Helpless and Unfriended': Nineteenth-Century Domestic Melodrama," in *When They Weren't Doing Shakespeare: Essays on Nineteenth-Century British and American Theatre*, ed. Judith L. Fisher and Stephen Watt (Athens: University of Georgia Press, 1989), pp. 174–86.

23. Kristin Leaver argues that seduction melodrama displays the shift from public issues of class relations to private issues of gender relations in "Victorian Melodrama and the Performance of Poverty," *Victorian Literature and Culture* 27, no. 2 (1999): 443–56.

24. This is the thesis of Steinbach, "Melodramatic Contract," p. 12.

25. Goldberg, *Story of Gilbert and Sullivan*, p. 169.

26. According to Steinbach, "Defense counsels in breach of promise cases often complained that juries were far too sympathetic to pretty faces" ("Melodramatic Contract," p. 3).

27. Steinbach, "Melodramatic Contract," p. 10.

28. Steinbach presents clear evidence that the comparison between the courtroom and the theater was a commonplace in contemporary discussions of breach of promise in "Melodramatic Contract," especially p. 14.

29. I am indebted for the information in this paragraph to Susie L. Steinbach, "Promises, Promises: Not Marrying in England, 1780–1920" (Ph.D. diss., Yale University, 1996), pp. 234–41.

30. For the story of May Fortescue and Lord Garmoyle, see Goodman, *Gilbert and Sullivan*, pp. 41–42.

31. For *Trial by Jury*'s debt to *The Pickwick Papers*, see Goodman, *Gilbert and Sullivan*, pp. 165–66.

32. In *The Old Curiosity Shop* (1840–1841), when Dick Swiveller determines to drop his courtship of Sophie Wackles, he does so with the cautious reminder to himself

that he has given her no cause to sue for breach of promise. In the same novel, Sally Brass pursues an action for breach. Similarly, Miss Ruggs, the daughter of Doyce and Clennam's legal adviser in *Little Dorrit* (1855–1857), achieves financial independence as the result of a successful suit for breach of promise.

33. Goodman, *Gilbert and Sullivan*, p. 59. To my knowledge, no one but Goodman has discussed the parody of the suit for breach of promise.

34. For a description of the extravaganza transformation scene, see chapters 1 and 7.

35. Wilson makes these points in *Introduction to the Gilbert and Sullivan Operas*, pp. 28–29.

36. Promptbook for *Trial By Jury*, p. 14.

37. Bradley, *Complete Annotated Gilbert and Sullivan*, pp. 36–38; Stedman, *W. S. Gilbert*, p. 209. Although the extravaganza transformation scene does derive from the pantomime harlequinade tradition, this is not a harlequinade—as Gayden Wren presupposes in *A Most Ingenious Paradox: The Art of Gilbert and Sullivan* (Oxford: Oxford University Press, 2001), p. 24—but another genre's version of sudden transformation.

3. *The Sorcerer*

1. Isaac Goldberg first calls it "the Gilbert and Sullivan formula," in *The Story of Gilbert and Sullivan; or, The "Compleat" Savoyard* (New York: Simon and Schuster, 1928), p. 197.

2. I draw on the description given by Fredric Woodbridge Wilson in "The Gilbert and Sullivan Legacy" (three lectures presented on the occasion of "The Gilbert & Sullivan Operas: A Centenary Exhibition," Harvard Theatre Collection / Pusey Library, November 22, 2000–April 13, 2001).

3. Benedict Anderson, *Imagined Communities: Reflection on the Origin and Spread of Nationalism* (London: Verso, 1983).

4. See, for example, Ruth A. Solie, "No 'Land Without Music' After All," *Victorian Literature and Culture* 32, no. 1 (2004): 261–76. This review essay considers fourteen recent works in the field of nineteenth-century English music.

5. On relations between exhibitions and operatic spectacle, see Edward W. Said, "The Empire at Work: Verdi's *Aida*," in *Culture and Imperialism* (New York: Knopf, 1993), pp. 111–32.

6. Tracy C. Davis, *The Economics of the British Stage, 1800–1914* (Cambridge: Cambridge University Press, 2000), pp. 110–11.

7. Richard D'Oyly Carte to W. S. Gilbert and Arthur Sullivan, April 8, 1880, quoted in Leslie Baily, *The Gilbert and Sullivan Book* (London: Spring Books, 1952), p. 125.

8. Arthur Sullivan to Richard D'Oyly Carte, June 5, 1877, reproduced in Baily, *Gilbert and Sullivan Book*, p. 141. This agreement provided a financial incentive for Gilbert and Sullivan to produce good work. But it also struck a blow against the culture of adaptation from elsewhere, especially from the French. In other words, the nationalistic thrust of this genre formation was by no means only a formal matter.

9. For more on this inconvenient first theater, see Goldberg, *Story of Gilbert and Sullivan*, p. 188; Jane W. Stedman, *W. S. Gilbert: A Classic Victorian and His Theatre* (Oxford: Oxford University Press, 1996), p. 152; and Colin Prestige, "The Early Operas' First Home," *Gilbert & Sullivan Journal*, May 1951, pp. 223–24.

10. Richard D'Oyly Carte to an unknown nobleman (from whom Carte sought investment capital), 1877, quoted in Goldberg, *Story of Gilbert and Sullivan*, pp. 185–87.

11. Arthur Sullivan to Alan Cole, November 22, 1877, quoted in Reginald Allen, ed., *The First Night Gilbert and Sullivan: Containing Complete Librettos of the Fourteen Operas, Exactly as Presented at Their Première Performances; Together with Facsimiles of the First-Night Programmes* (New York: Heritage Club, 1958), p. 50. Others joined in Sullivan's excitement. Sims Reeves, a famous tenor of the day, wrote to Sullivan that he was looking forward to "something that will astonish the nations, and make the teeth of the furreneers gnash" (quoted in Baily, *Gilbert and Sullivan Book*, p. 128).

12. Goldberg, *Story of Gilbert and Sullivan*, p. 197.

13. *Rutland Barrington: A Record of Thirty-five Years' Experience on the English Stage; By Himself*, with a preface by Sir William S. Gilbert (London: Grant, 1908), quoted in Goldberg, *Story of Gilbert and Sullivan*, p. 191.

14. The "Italian opera" was cut, but it bears mentioning, for it displays the parodic dynamic of genre formation.

15. "Mario" was the name of a famous "Italian" (that is, English) singer whom Carte had managed during his earlier days as an impresario and agent. The anecdote is in Walter J. Wells, *Souvenir of Arthur Sullivan* (London: Newnes, 1901), quoted in Baily, *Gilbert and Sullivan Book*, p. 144.

16. Mike Leigh, *Topsy-Turvy* (London: Faber and Faber, 1999), pp. 36–37. See also Stedman, *W. S. Gilbert*, pp. 207–9.

17. Quoted in Baily, *Gilbert and Sullivan Book*, p. 138.

18. The parodic dynamic is more complex still, for *L'elisir d'amore* adapts a prior story, Eugène Scribe's farcical libretto for Daniel Auber's *Le philtre* (1831), and Scribe, in turn, takes off on an Italian play, *Il filtro* (1830), by Silvio Malaperta. In other words, Donizetti's opera might be said to elevate the farcical Auber version, while disenchanting the early legend of Tristan and Isolde.

19. On the domestication of tea in the Victorian period and on tea as the "national beverage," see Julie E. Fromer, "'Deeply Indebted to the Tea-Plant': Representations of English National Identity in Victorian Histories of Tea," *Victorian Literature and Culture* 36, no. 2 (2008): 531–47.

20. Ian Bradley, *The Complete Annotated Gilbert and Sullivan* (Oxford: Oxford University Press, 1996), p. 80; Fromer, "Deeply Indebted to the Tea-Plant," p. 533.

21. W. S. Gilbert, "An Elixir of Love," in *The Lost Stories of W. S. Gilbert*, ed. Peter Haining (London: Robson Books, 1982), pp. 17, 106–24.

22. Frank Rahill, *The World of Melodrama* (University Park: Pennsylvania State University Press, 1967), p. 127.

23. Bradley, *Complete Annotated Gilbert and Sullivan*, pp. 100–102.

24. Rahill also comments on the affinity of Weber's music with melodrama, especially the creation of eerie suspense in "that memorable shiver of the violins accompany-

ing the deeper tones of the clarinet and the sinister pounding of the drums" (*World of Melodrama*, p. 127).

25. It was greatly reduced in the 1884 revision. See Gervase Hughes, *The Music of Arthur Sullivan* (New York: St. Martin's Press, 1960), p. 150, and Baily, *Gilbert and Sullivan Book*, p. 144.

26. On the importance of the *brindisi* to operetta, see Bradley, *Complete Annotated Gilbert and Sullivan*, p. 1174.

27. Bradley, *Complete Annotated Gilbert and Sullivan*, p. 80.

28. "One owl" (that is, unattributed), quoted in Goldberg, *Story of Gilbert and Sullivan*, pp. 199–200.

29. A record of Dodgson's approach to Sullivan, which is both shy and arrogant—or perhaps simply unaware of the fact that a composer of Sullivan's stature could not be solicited—may be found, along with Sullivan's curt reply, in Baily, *Gilbert and Sullivan Book*, pp. 136–37.

30. Charles Dodgson, "The Stage and the Spirit of Reverence," *Theatre*, June 1, 1888, quoted in Goldberg, *Story of Gilbert and Sullivan*, p. 200.

31. Andrew Goodman claims that Gilbert satirized two "pet hates" in *The Sorcerer*: the clergy and the snobbery of the country "petty bourgeoisie" (*Gilbert and Sullivan at Law* [Madison, N.J.: Fairleigh Dickinson University Press, 1983], p. 172). On the contrary, I find that *The Sorcerer* is tender toward both.

32. Quoted in Allen, ed., *First Night Gilbert and Sullivan*, p. 48.

33. This story is told in many sources, but my version is taken almost verbatim from Stedman, *W. S. Gilbert*, pp. 152–53. See also Baily, *Gilbert and Sullivan Book*, p. 143.

34. Stedman, *W. S. Gilbert*, p. 155; quoted in Allen, ed., *First Night Gilbert and Sullivan*, p. 48; Goldberg, *Story of Gilbert and Sullivan*, p. 196.

35. Gayden Wren, *A Most Ingenious Paradox: The Art of Gilbert and Sullivan* (Oxford: Oxford University Press, 2001), p. 47, figs. 5.1–5.3 (pp. 37–39).

36. Edith Hall, "Classical Mythology in the Victorian Popular Theatre," *International Journal of the Classical Tradition* 5, no. 3 (1999): 346, 355. She gives examples of songs that list Jove's love affairs with mortals, songs that race the audience through a fast panorama of classical history and myth, and songs that list classical authors.

37. On the monopolylogues, see Steven Connor, *Dumbstruck: A Cultural History of Ventriloquism* (Oxford: Oxford University Press, 2000), pp. 266–69.

38. Goldberg also mentions Samuel Arnold's *Enraged Musician* (1788), in *Story of Gilbert and Sullivan*, pp. 197–98.

39. Henry Mayhew, *London Labour and the London Poor*, ed. Victor Neuburg (London: Penguin, 1985), p. 9

40. Discussing the catalogue form in relation to Oscar Wilde, Neil Bartlett argues that it serves at once as a register of modern consumerism and of addictive, erotic yearning, in *Who Was That Man? A Present for Mr. Oscar Wilde* (London: Serpent's Tail, 1988), pp. 175, 184, 182.

41. Goldberg, *Story of Gilbert and Sullivan*, p. 198n.6.

42. Compare the opening of *The Pretty Druidess; or, The Mother, the Maid, and the Mistletoe Bough* (1869), Gilbert's parody of Vicenzo Bellini's *Norma* (1831) (which turns on the inanity of repeatedly rhyming "chatting," "tatting," and "ratting"), with

La Vivandière; or, True to the Corps (1867), his parody of Gaetano Donizetti's *La fille du régiment* (*The Daughter of the Regiment*, 1840) ("I'm familiar with the clatter of her chatter chatter chatter"), in W. S. Gilbert, *New and Original Extravaganzas*, ed. Isaac Goldberg (Boston: Luce, 1931), pp. 153–54, 66.

43. For more on patter, see chapter 10.

44. Northrop Frye uses *The Mikado* to illustrate art rather than savagery in his discussion of ritual human sacrifice and comic "playing at sacrifice" (quoted in Max Keith Sutton, *W. S. Gilbert* [Boston: Twayne, 1975], pp. 95–96).

45. The reference to "Oromanes" earlier in the libretto is a version of "Ahrimanes," the Zoroastrian personification of evil. The "Abudah chests" (also mentioned there) derive from a pseudo-Persian fairy tale; Abudah was a merchant in Baghdad, haunted by a hag who appeared from a box in his chamber and told him to seek Oromanes. See Bradley, *Complete Annotated Gilbert and Sullivan*, pp. 68, 108.

46. In *The Sorcerer*, *Faust* can be clearly seen operating as an intertext. Compare Gilbert's story "An Elixir of Love," in which Baylis "had sold himself to the Devil at a very early age" and therefore "had become remarkably proficient in all kinds of enchantment" (p. 109). For the evasive use of "Hades," see Audrey Williamson, *Gilbert and Sullivan Opera: A New Assessment* (New York: Macmillan, 1953), p. 52.

47. From the license copy, discussed in Bradley, *Complete Annotated Gilbert and Sullivan*, pp. 100–102.

48. The figure of Ahrimanes was to have been doubled by the actress playing Lady Sangazure, Mrs. Howard Paul, veiled in black. Stedman argues that "the scene was sensibly deleted" (*W. S. Gilbert*, p. 154). Perhaps she felt this way because it would have transgressed Gilbert's rule against cross-dressing.

49. Stedman, *W. S. Gilbert*, p. 154.

4. *H.M.S. Pinafore*

1. James Robinson Planché, *The Camp at the Olympic* (1853), in *Plays by James Robinson Planché*, ed. Donald Roy (Cambridge: Cambridge University Press, 1986), pp. 187–88.

2. The best account of English melodrama is still Michael R. Booth, *English Melodrama* (London: Jenkins, 1965).

3. Douglas Jerrold, *Black-Ey'd Susan*, in *Nineteenth Century Plays*, ed. George Rowell (Oxford: Oxford University Press, 1953), pp. 1–43.

4. Quoted in V. C. Clinton-Baddeley, *The Burlesque Tradition in the English Theatre After 1660* (London: Methuen, 1952), p. 99.

5. J. S. Bratton describes this structural conjunction of family and nation in "British Heroism and the Structure of Melodrama," in *Acts of Supremacy: The British Empire and the Stage, 1790–1930*, ed. J. S. Bratton, Richard Allen Cave, Breandan Gregory, Heidi J. Holder, and Michael Pickering (Manchester: Manchester University Press, 1991), pp. 18–61.

6. Jane Moody argues that Jerrold's dénouement is self-consciously ironic, "mock[ing] the sheer contingency of melodramatic justice" (*Illegitimate Theatre in London,*

1770–1840 [Cambridge: Cambridge University Press, 2000], pp. 105–6). See also Matthew Kaiser, "Ludicrous Politics: Nautical Melodrama and the Degradation of Law," in *Leeds Centre Working Papers in Victorian Studies*, ed. Martin Hewitt (Leeds: Leeds Centre for Victorian Studies, University of Leeds, 2001), vol. 4, pp. 71–80.

7. Marvin Carlson calls the ending of *Black-Ey'd Susan* "quite worthy of Gilbert and Sullivan," in "'He Never Should Bow Down to a Domineering Frown': Class Tensions and Nautical Melodrama," in *Melodrama: The Cultural Emergence of a Genre*, ed. Michael Hays and Anastasia Nikolopoulou (New York: St. Martin's Press, 1996), p. 155.

8. Peter Brooks describes melodrama as "radically democratic, striving to make its representations clear and legible to everyone . . . the principal mode for uncovering, demonstrating, and making operative the essential moral universe in a post-sacred era" (*The Melodramatic Imagination: Balzac, Henry James, Melodrama, and the Mode of Excess*, 2nd ed. [New Haven, Conn.: Yale University Press, 1995], p. 15).

9. Jane W. Stedman, *W. S. Gilbert: A Classic Victorian and His Theatre* (Oxford: Oxford University Press, 1996), p. 157.

10. Adrienne Munich, *Queen Victoria's Secrets* (New York: Columbia University Press, 1996), p. 113.

11. Donald Roy, introduction to *Plays by James Robinson Planché*, p. 29.

12. By the time of *Pinafore*, the pantomime was widely felt to be in decline, its harlequinade having been largely replaced by the extravaganza transformation scene.

13. Clinton-Baddeley, *Burlesque Tradition*, p. 117; Eileen E. Cottis, "Gilbert and the British Tar," in *Gilbert and Sullivan: Papers Presented at the International Conference Held at the University of Kansas in May 1970*, ed. James Helyar (Lawrence: University of Kansas Libraries, 1971), p. 34. See also Leonard R. N. Ashley, "Gilbert and Melodrama," in *Gilbert and Sullivan*, ed. Helyar, pp. 1–6.

14. Ian Bradley, *The Complete Annotated Gilbert and Sullivan* (Oxford: Oxford University Press, 1996), p. 120. Compare *Ruddigore*'s characterization of Dick Dauntless: "a better hand at turning-in a dead-eye don't walk the deck!"

15. Clinton-Baddeley traces Jolly Jack Tar as far back as the costumed singers of sea songs in early-eighteenth-century music houses, in "The Jolly Jack Tar Joke," in *Burlesque Tradition*, pp. 97–107; Bratton traces the figure back even farther, to the medieval mystery plays, in "British Heroism," pp. 33–34. See also Cottis, "Gilbert and the British Tar," pp. 33–42, and Charles Napier Robinson, *The British Tar in Fact and Fiction* (London: Harper, 1909).

16. Cottis calls the Tar "a sort of Noble Savage in whiteface" ("Gilbert and the British Tar," p. 33).

17. Bratton, "British Heroism," p. 34.

18. "Sketches of Stage Favourites: Mr. T. P. Cooke," *Illustrated London News*, October 15, 1853, p. 319, quoted in Bratton, "British Heroism," pp. 42–43.

19. Clinton-Baddeley, *Burlesque Tradition*, p. 102.

20. Other parodies are detailed in Clinton-Baddeley, *Burlesque Tradition*, pp. 104–7.

21. Captain Frederick Marryat, *Mr. Midshipman Easy* (Ithaca, N.Y.: McBooks Press, 1998).

22. Although Frederick Fox Cooper's *Black-Eyed Sukey; or, All in the Dumps*, a burlesque of *Black-Ey'd Susan*, was performed in 1829, the same year as its object and

model, it parodied only the village elements of the melodrama, not the nautical ones. On the nautical burlesques of the 1860s, see Clinton-Baddeley, *Burlesque Tradition*, pp. 106–7, and Cottis, "Gilbert and the British Tar," pp. 33–34, 42.

23. F. C. Burnand, *The Very Latest Edition of Black-Eyed Susan; or, The Little Bill That Was Taken Up*, in *Victorian Theatrical Burlesques*, ed. Richard W. Schoch (Aldershot: Ashgate, 2003), pp. 101–49. Burnand was Gilbert's friend and rival; thus his nautical burlesque was undoubtedly known by Gilbert. See also Michael Slater, "The Transformations of Susan," *Theatre Notebook* 50, no. 3 (1996): 146–75.

24. The parody of nautical melodrama in *Pinafore* preserves the memory of nautical melodrama at the present time, as noted in Cottis, "Gilbert and the British Tar," p. 42, and Carlson, "He Never Should Bow Down," p. 137.

25. Clinton-Baddeley, *Burlesque Tradition*, p. 107.

26. Bratton comments on the Tar's divided language in "British Heroism," pp. 33, 39.

27. On the man of feeling, see Michael McKeon, "Historicizing Patriarchy: The Emergence of Gender Difference in England, 1660–1760," *Eighteenth-Century Studies* 28, no. 3 (1995): 314.

28. Percy Fitzgerald, *Principles of Comic and Dramatic Effect* (London, 1870), quoted in Richard W. Schoch, introduction to Burnand, *Very Latest Edition of Black-Eyed Susan*, p. 98.

29. *The Bab Ballads by W. S. Gilbert*, ed. James Ellis (Cambridge, Mass.: Belknap Press of Harvard University Press, 1970), pp. 284–86, 361.

30. Cottis, "Gilbert and the British Tar," p. 38.

31. Kirsten Gram Hölmstrom, *Monodrama, Attitude, Tableaux Vivants: Studies on Some Trends of Theatrical Fashion, 1770–1815* (Stockholm: Almquist and Wiksell, 1967).

32. On the dissolving views, see Isobel Armstrong, *Victorian Glassworlds: Glass Culture and the Imagination, 1830–1880* (Oxford: Oxford University Press, 2008), pp. 258–65, 272–316.

33. Bratton, "British Heroism," pp. 51–59. He calls Jack Tar "the most powerful instrument of imperialist ideology on the nineteenth-century stage" (p. 33).

34. Bratton discusses the use of the music halls for raising patriotic sentiment, detailing the history of working-class jingoism from 1901 onward, in "British Heroism," pp. 20, 60n.7.

35. G. W. Hunt, "Macdermott's War Song," in *The Illustrated Victorian Songbook*, ed. Aline Waites and Robin Hunter (London: Michael Joseph, 1984), pp. 95–98, 180–84. Hunt had used "by jingo" in an earlier song for George Leybourne (1868), but G. H. Macdermott's song popularized the phrase.

36. Quoted in Waites and Hunter, eds., *Illustrated Victorian Songbook*, p. 182.

37. The curious practice, at various Gilbert and Sullivan festivities, of singing this song "straight," as if it were a straightforward patriotic anthem, never ceases to amaze me.

38. A heroine caught between two lovers was recognized as humorously conventional at the time, according to Clinton-Baddeley, *Burlesque Tradition*, p. 43. In fact, *Pinafore*'s subtitle, *The Lass That Loved a Sailor*, is itself a stock phrase for this situation. Cottis points out that a melodrama written in 1841 by E. R. Lancaster was called *Ruth; or, The Lass That Loved a Sailor*, in "Gilbert and the British Tar," p. 40.

39. The structure is most comprehensively analyzed in Eve Kosofsky Sedgwick, *Between Men: English Literature and Male Homosocial Desire* (New York: Columbia University Press, 1985).

40. Recitative was long taken to be an affected element in Italian opera. In John Gay's *The Beggar's Opera* (1728), for example, the Beggar promises that he has "not made [his] Opera throughout unnatural, like those in vogue; for I have no Recitative."

41. On appointments of the middle-class home and the invention of "antiques," see Charlotte Gere and Lesley Hoskins, *The House Beautiful: Oscar Wilde and the Aesthetic Interior* (Aldershot: Lund Humphries, in association with the Geffrye Museum, 2000), pp. 102–3, 114–36.

42. Quoted in Leslie Baily, *The Gilbert and Sullivan Book* (London: Spring Books, 1952), p. 149.

43. For more on this, concerning Bunthorne's relation to Oscar Wilde, see chapter 6.

44. Quoted in Waites and Hunter, eds., *Illustrated Victorian Songbook*, p. 182.

45. Samuel Butler, *The Way of All Flesh* (New York: Modern Library, 1998), p. 301.

46. Quoted in Bradley, *Complete Annotated Gilbert and Sullivan*, p. 134.

47. By the early nineteenth century, this form of sociological explanation was common in both conservative and liberal arguments. For example, Thomas Carlyle complains in "Signs of the Times" (1829) that the rise of environmental explanation is an example of "Mechanism" and "Unbelief": "For it is the 'force of circumstances' that does everything; the force of one man can do nothing." In "On the Logic of the Moral Sciences," book 6 of *A System of Logic* (1843), John Stuart Mill most clearly explicates and synthetically resolves the central paradox in liberal philosophy: on the one hand, environment determines character; on the other, character can determine itself. With thanks to George Levine and Kristie Allen on this point.

48. Leonard Manheim, "Strephon's 'Tipsy Lout': To Cut or Not to Cut," in *Gilbert and Sullivan*, ed. Helyar, pp. 107–11.

49. Andrew Goodman, *Gilbert and Sullivan at Law* (Madison, N.J.: Fairleigh Dickinson University Press, 1983), pp. 167–68.

50. This point is frequently made. See, for example, Cottis, "Gilbert and the British Tar," p. 40. Azucena is "lily" in Spanish, while Buttercup is a plainer, more English flower.

51. Jill C. Matus, "Wet Nursing, Infanticide and Baby-Farming," in *Unstable Bodies: Victorian Representations of Sexuality and Maternity* (Manchester: Manchester University Press, 1994), pp. 157–67. I am indebted to Matus's work for my overview of these issues.

5. *The Pirates of Penzance*

1. Andrew Goodman, *Gilbert and Sullivan at Law* (Madison, N.J.: Fairleigh Dickinson University Press, 1983), pp. 204–5.

2. The story of the rise and fall of the Comedy Opera Company is best told in Goodman, *Gilbert and Sullivan*, pp. 65–99.

3. This warning had no legal standing and was itself conventional (compare the *Nickleby* Proclamation, a three-page warning with similar intent that Dickens issued in 1838, a

few weeks before *Nicholas Nickleby* began its serial publication), but it shows their early awareness of the problem, as Goodman points out in *Gilbert and Sullivan*, p. 204.

4. Goodman, *Gilbert and Sullivan*, pp. 202–14; John Russell Stephens, *The Profession of the Playwright: British Theatre, 1800–1900* (Cambridge: Cambridge University Press, 1992), pp. 84–115, especially pp. 106–10, 113.

5. Stephens, *Profession of the Playwright*, p. 84.

6. Quoted in Stephens, *Profession of the Playwright*, p. 89.

7. Print copyright itself was a complex, unevenly developing work in progress. See David Saunders, *Authorship and Copyright* (New York: Routledge, 1992), pp. 122–48.

8. Stephens, *Profession of the Playwright*, pp. 105–15.

9. Novelists were caught up in this tangle differently from playwrights. They hurried to adapt their novels, sometimes even before serialization was complete (*Nicholas Nickleby* [1838–1839] provides a good example). In a measure structurally similar to the copyright performance, novelists were obliged to record a preemptive dramatic version of their work at Stationers' Hall in order to forestall hack adaptors and pirate-managers from staging their own versions.

10. Stephens, *Profession of the Playwright*, p. 113.

11. Stephens, *Profession of the Playwright*, p. 104. Meredith McGill takes up these transatlantic issues from the American perspective in *American Literature and the Culture of Reprinting, 1834–1853* (Philadelphia: University of Pennsylvania Press, 2003). Within the American "culture of reprinting," the accusation of "piracy" only serves to signal that an English perspective is being taken.

12. Quoted in Arthur Lawrence, *Sir Arthur Sullivan: Life Story, Letters, and Reminiscences* (Chicago: Stone, 1900), pp. 130, 129, 140. Goodman uses the phrase "memory pirates" in *Gilbert and Sullivan*, p. 207.

13. Quoted in Stephens, *Profession of the Playwright*, p. 108; italics added.

14. Colin Prestige, "D'Oyly Carte and the Pirates: The Original New York Productions of Gilbert and Sullivan," in *Gilbert and Sullivan: Papers Presented at the International Conference Held at the University of Kansas in May 1970*, ed. James Helyar (Lawrence: University of Kansas Libraries, 1971), pp. 113–48.

15. Another round of struggle with the American pirates would take place five years later, around the production of *The Mikado*. See Stephens, *Profession of the Playwright*, pp. 108–9, and Goodman, *Gilbert and Sullivan*, pp. 208–12.

16. Jane Moody, *Illegitimate Theatre in London, 1770–1840* (Cambridge: Cambridge University Press, 2000), p. 4.

17. Vincent J. Liesenfeld, *The Licensing Act of 1737* (Madison: University of Wisconsin Press, 1984), pp. 9–13.

18. The complexities within each of these generalizations deserve acknowledgment. Michael Booth, for example, claims that working-class audiences were more concerned with propriety than were their West End counterparts, in *Theatre in the Victorian Age* (Cambridge: Cambridge University Press, 1991), p. 146. See also John Johnston, *The Lord Chamberlain's Blue Pencil* (London: Hodder & Stoughton, 1990), p. 29.

19. Moody, *Illegitimate Theatre*, p. 17.

20. Moody, *Illegitimate Theatre*, pp. 19–22.

21. "Red fire"—made from strontia, shellac, and chlorate of potash—was originally man-

ufactured as a military explosive. Moody interprets the significance of the blow-up scene as "the collapse of legitimate genres such as sentimental comedy as ideological models for the dramatisation of a modern nation" (*Illegitimate Theatre*, p. 28).

22. Moody, *Illegitimate Theatre*, p. 18.
23. Moody, *Illegitimate Theatre*, pp. 10–47.
24. Moody, *Illegitimate Theatre*, pp. 16–17.
25. The legal right of the Lord Chamberlain, through his Examiner of Plays, to license (and therefore to censor) any play performed on the stage "for hire" was not abolished until the Theatres Act of 1968.
26. Moody, *Illegitimate Theatre*, pp. 6, 10.
27. Ian Bradley, *The Complete Annotated Gilbert and Sullivan* (Oxford: Oxford University Press, 1996), p. 190.
28. J. S. Bratton, "British Heroism and the Structure of Melodrama," in *Acts of Supremacy: The British Empire and the Stage, 1790–1930*, ed. J. S. Bratton, Richard Allen Cave, Breandan Gregory, Heidi J. Holder, and Michael Pickering (Manchester: Manchester University Press, 1991), p. 40. Kristie Allen unfolds the connection between nautical melodrama and slavery in "'Confound the Pirates!' Nautical Melodrama and the Anti-Slave Trade in the Making of the British Nation State," *Nineteenth Century Studies* (forthcoming). The discourse on the lash shows up in *H.M.S. Pinafore* in the song about the "cat."
29. Sentimental robbers are common in the burlesque tradition, according to V. C. Clinton-Baddeley, *The Burlesque Tradition in the English Theatre After 1660* (London: Methuen, 1952), p. 89.
30. Bradley reminds us that the setting of act 1 of *The Pirates of Penzance* was originally planned as "a cavern by the sea-shore" (*Complete Annotated Gilbert and Sullivan*, p. 192). Eileen E. Cottis points out that Cornwall is the legendary site of piracy in England in the seventeenth century, in "Gilbert and the British Tar," in *Gilbert and Sullivan*, ed. Helyar, pp. 40–41. Its location in Cornwall makes Penzance more suggestive of a borderland with a real history of piracy.
31. *Les brigands; Opera bouffe en trois actes par H. Meilhac et Ludovic Halévy, musique de Jacques Offenbach, l'adaption anglaise par W. S. Gilbert* (London: Boosey, 1871). George Bernard Shaw discusses *Les brigands* as an ancestor of *Pirates*, including musical indebtedness to Offenbach, in "Gilbert and Offenbach" (1889), in *Shaw on Music*, ed. Eric Bentley (New York: Doubleday, 1955; New York: Applause Books, 1983), p. 202.
32. Another example is Félix Pyat's *The Brigand and the Philosopher* (1834), which "presented speculators on the Stock Exchange as no better than highway robbers" (Daniel Gerould, "Melodrama and Revolution," in *Melodrama: Stage Picture Screen*, ed. Jacky Bratton, Jim Cook, and Christine Gledhill [London: British Film Institute, 1994], p. 187).
33. *Les brigands*, trans. Gilbert, pp. 8, 10.
34. Bradley, *Annotated Gilbert and Sullivan*, p. 220.
35. Goodman, *Gilbert and Sullivan*, pp. 173–74.
36. Bradley mentions this suggestion, but does not think that it plays a part in the character of the Major-General, in *Annotated Gilbert and Sullivan*, p. 230.
37. On the two Stanleys, see Bradley, *Annotated Gilbert and Sullivan*, p. 220.

38. Shaw, "Gilbert and Offenbach," p. 204. Oscar Wilde's *The Importance of Being Earnest* (1895) should also be noted in this respect, with its implied critique of earnestness.

39. Richard W. Schoch argues that the audience was not meant to follow and understand, but to succumb to the hilarity of the puns' sonic conversion of language into nonsense, in introduction to *Victorian Theatrical Burlesques*, ed. Richard W. Schoch (Aldershot: Ashgate, 2003), pp. xxvi–xxviii.

40. Natalie Zemon Davis, "Women on Top: Symbolic Sexual Inversion and Political Disorder in Early Modern Europe," in *The Reversible World: Symbolic Inversion in Art and Society*, ed. Barbara A. Babcock (Ithaca, N.Y.: Cornell University Press, 1978), pp. 147–90.

41. Adrienne Munich, *Queen Victoria's Secrets* (New York: Columbia University Press, 1996), p. 119.

42. The ridicule of sexual desire on the part of the middle-aged woman is an element of the stereotypical Dame figure, which is discussed in chapter 7.

43. Ruth cross-dressed as a pirate alludes to another conventional figure of pirate lore, the woman who goes to sea in disguise as a man. On female pirates and warrior women, see Marjorie Garber, *Vested Interests: Cross-Dressing and Cultural Anxiety* (New York: Routledge, 1992), pp. 181–82.

44. The standard works are Barry R. Burg, *Sodomy and the Pirate Tradition: English Sea Rovers in the Seventeenth-Century Caribbean* (New York: New York University Press, 1995), and Hans Turley, *Rum, Sodomy, and the Lash: Piracy, Sexuality, and Masculine Identity* (New York: New York University Press, 2001).

45. Hakim Bey, "Pirate Utopias," in *T.A.Z: The Temporary Autonomous Zone, Ontological Anarchy, Poetic Terrorism* (New York: Autonomedia, Anti-Copyright, 1985, 1991), available at http://www.hermetic.com/bey/taz_cont.html.

46. Michael Warner, "Irving's Posterity," *English Literary History* 67 (2000): 798n.46.

47. On chatter, see chapter 3.

48. On pirates and cross-dressing, see Garber, *Vested Interests*, pp. 179–81.

49. Male parental surrogation frequently foregrounds the uncle. For a study of this category in the Victorian period, see Eileen Cleere, *Avuncularism: Capitalism, Patriarchy, and Nineteenth-Century Culture* (Stanford, Calif.: Stanford University Press, 2004). She argues that the figure of the uncle represents a schism both in the traditional father-centered family and in paternalist philosophy more generally. See also Eve Kosofsky Sedgwick, "Tales of the Avunculate: *The Importance of Being Earnest*," in *Tendencies* (Durham, N.C.: Duke University Press, 1993), pp. 52–72.

50. Bradley, *Annotated Gilbert and Sullivan*, p. 216.

51. Laura Peters, *Orphan Texts: Victorian Orphans, Culture and Empire* (Manchester: Manchester University Press, 2000), pp. 16, 23, 28, and passim.

52. Fictional figures of orphans and wards may be seen as Victorian transformations of the foundlings and bastards analyzed by Marthe Robert, who uses Freud's theorization of the "family romance"—the fantasy of noble parentage—to interpret the history of the novel as a genre, in *Origins of the Novel*, trans. Sacha Rabinovitch (Bloomington: Indiana University Press, 1980). She divides the family romance into two temporal phases of the narcissistic demand for recognition: the first, when the subject imagines that he or she was left as a foundling; and

the second, when the subject imagines that he or she is the illegitimate child of a noble father.

53. Cottis, "Gilbert and the British Tar," pp. 40, 34, 36.

54. On the circulation of fraudulent orphan narratives, see Lydia Murdoch, *Imagined Orphans: Poor Families, Child Welfare, and Contested Citizenship in London* (New Brunswick, N.J.: Rutgers University Press, 2006), especially pp. 12–42, on melodrama and popular representations of poor children as orphans; and Seth Koven, *Slumming: Sexual and Social Politics in Victorian London* (Princeton, N.J.: Princeton University Press, 2004), pp. 6–45.

55. Allen, "Confound the Pirates!"

56. Michael Booth offers many examples in "Soldiers of the Queen: Drury Lane Imperialism," in *Melodrama: The Cultural Emergence of a Genre*, ed. Michael Hays and Anastasia Nicolopoulou (New York: St. Martin's Press, 1996), p. 6. Cottis, too, provides examples, pointing out the "magical powers of the Union Jack, when waved at appropriate moments," and making the connection to *The Pirates of Penzance* ("Gilbert and the British Tar," pp. 37–38).

57. Munich, *Queen Victoria's Secrets*, p. 119. For a discussion of Munich's analysis of representations of the queen in Savoy operas, see chapter 7.

58. Cottis, "Gilbert and the British Tar," p. 41.

6. Patience

1. In this book, however, I have followed the standard practice of using the term "Savoy operas" to refer generically to the entire series of comic operas by Gilbert and Sullivan.

2. Fredric Woodbridge Wilson, "Richard D'Oyly Carte and the Future" (lecture delivered at the Harvard College Library, Cambridge, Mass., April 3, 2001; the third of three lectures—"The Gilbert and Sullivan Legacy"—presented on the occasion of "The Gilbert & Sullivan Operas: A Centenary Exhibition," Harvard Theatre Collection / Pusey Library, November 22, 2000–April 13, 2001).

3. Tracy C. Davis, *The Economics of the British Stage, 1800–1914* (Cambridge: Cambridge University Press, 2000), pp. 110–11.

4. On electric lighting as a metaphor for modernity, see Wolfgang Schivelbusch, *Disenchanted Night: The Industrialization of Light in the Nineteenth Century* (Berkeley: University of California Press, 1995), and Tom Stoppard, *The Invention of Love* (New York: Grove Press, 1997).

5. For a more detailed analysis of Lady Jane, along with other Savoy parodies of the Dame figure, see chapter 7.

6. Jane W. Stedman, *W. S. Gilbert: A Classic Victorian and His Theatre* (Oxford: Oxford University Press, 1996), p. 181.

7. *Illustrated London News*, June 18, 1881, p. 598. In the 1880s, sunflowers were considered "old-fashioned" garden flowers, associated with the Queen Anne Revival, while lilies had "Art Catholic" associations, as Colin Cruise has shown in "Versions of the Annunciation: Wilde's Aestheticism and the Message of Beauty," in *After the*

Pre-Raphaelites: Art and Aestheticism in Victorian England, ed. Elizabeth Prettejohn (Manchester: Manchester University Press, 1999), pp. 167–87. Cruise traces the link between the aesthetes, their symbolic flowers, and the developing codes of homosexuality. See also Neil Bartlett, "Flowers," in *Who Was That Man? A Present for Mr. Oscar Wilde* (London: Serpent's Tail, 1988), pp. 39–59.

8. Percy Fitzgerald, "Mr. Gilbert's Humour," *Theatre*, December 1, 1881, p. 340.

9. Stedman adduces other precursors in addition to the two I discuss here, in *W. S. Gilbert*, p. 182.

10. As we have seen in chapter 5, the question of originality is always vexed within the Victorian context of adaptation and parody. In this particular case, however, Gilbert may have feared allegations of plagiarism. Stedman quotes from a disingenuous letter in which Gilbert mentions his almost finished libretto for *Patience*, so that Albery might not later conclude that it was "suggested" by his play (*W. S. Gilbert*, pp. 288–89).

11. The aesthete's names pointedly prefigure those of Lambert Strether (Henry James, *The Ambassadors*, 1903) and Basil Hallward (Oscar Wilde, *The Picture of Dorian Gray*, 1890), while recalling Walter Pater's "The School of Giorgione" (*The Renaissance*, 1873).

12. F. C. Burnand, *The Colonel*, ed. Anton Kirchhofer, pp. 53–56 (copyright 2004), transcribed from Add. MSS 53248 C. (Lic. 19), Lord Chamberlain's Files, British Library, London, available at http://www.xix-e.pierre-marteau.com/ed/colonel/transcript.html.

13. Morris Barnett, *The Serious Family: A Comedy in Three Acts*, French's Standard Drama, no. 79 (New York: Samuel French, 1849; facsimile repr., Ann Arbor: Scholarly Publishing Office, University of Michigan Library, n.d.).

14. Kirchhofer quotes Burnand's report that Squire Bancroft urged him to "bring the piece 'up to date.'"

15. Michael Ainger, *Gilbert and Sullivan: A Dual Biography* (Oxford: Oxford University Press, 2002), pp. 50–51. See also Stedman, *W. S. Gilbert*, pp. 11–22, quote on p. 15.

16. Oscar Wilde to George Grossmith, n.d. [in Grossmith's letter album, Pierpont Morgan Library], quoted in Stedman, *W. S. Gilbert*, p. 183.

17. Jeff Nunokawa reads *The Importance of Being Earnest* for its "light desire" and its "late-Victorian climate of manufactured and manipulable passion" (*Tame Passions of Wilde: The Styles of Manageable Desire* [Princeton, N.J.: Princeton University Press, 2003], p. 44). Eve Kosofsky Sedgwick argues that the play displaces the usual ideological control by "the name of the Father" ("Tales of the Avunculate: The Importance of Being Earnest," in *Tendencies* [Durham, N.C.: Duke University Press, 1993], pp. 52–72). Both Nunokawa (p. 45) and Sedgwick (p. 72) note the collapse, at the end of the play, back into the ideology of the "serious family."

18. Richard Kelly, *The Art of George du Maurier* (Brookfield, Vt.: Ashgate, 1996). I am especially indebted to part 2 of this study, "Society Pictures."

19. Ed Cohen, "Posing the Question: Wilde, Wit and the Ways of Man," in *Performance and Cultural Politics*, ed. Elin Diamond (London: Routledge, 1996), p. 41. Cohen also points out that the popular hostility to the aesthete contributes to the production of normative masculinity.

20. Burnand, *Colonel*, p. 54.

21. Cohen makes this argument in "Posing the Question," pp. 35–47.

22. On the supposed unhealthiness and effeminacy of the aesthetes, see J. B. Bullen, *The Pre-Raphaelite Body: Fear and Desire in Painting, Poetry, and Criticism* (Oxford: Clarendon Press, 1998), especially pp. 149–216.

23. Linda Dowling notes that in the latter half of the nineteenth century, observers and critics frequently associated the decadent and the New Woman, the dandy and the suffragist, as inextricably related forms of deviation from an established, family-driven order, in "The Decadent and the New Woman in the 1890's," *Nineteenth-Century Fiction* 33, no. 4 (1979): 434–53. For a different take on these issues, see Anne Anderson, "'Fearful Consequences . . . of Living Up to One's Teapot': Men, Women, and 'Cultchah' in the English Aesthetic Movement c. 1870–1900," *Victorian Literature and Culture* 37 (2009): 219–54.

24. For another example of nationalistic teapot humor in a Savoy opera, see chapter 3.

25. Quoted in Jane W. Stedman, "The Genesis of *Patience*," in *W. S. Gilbert: A Century of Scholarship and Commentary*, ed. John Bush Jones (New York: New York University Press, 1970), p. 311n.8.

26. According to Max Beerbohm, "Perhaps aestheticism, as a social foible, would not have outlasted 1880 if George Du Maurier had not so persistently and so deftly satirised it, week by week, in the pages of 'Punch.' In which case posterity's debt to Du Maurier is even greater than we knew. 'Patience' would not have been written but for him" ("A Note on 'Patience,'" [p. 2] [unpaged pamphlet written on the occasion of a revival of *Patience* (London, 1918)], collection of Fredric Woodbridge Wilson).

27. Fitzgerald, "Mr. Gilbert's Humour," p. 340.

28. Beerbohm, "Note on 'Patience,'" [p. 1].

29. James Abbott McNeill Whistler, *The Gentle Art of Making Enemies* (1890), quoted in Kelly, *Art of George du Maurier*, p. 241.

30. Cohen, "Posing the Question," p. 42.

31. *New York Tribune*, January 3, 1883.

32. Cohen, "Posing the Question." As Cohen acknowledges, Wilde's powerful critique of bourgeois respectability is also explained in Regenia Gagnier, *Idylls of the Marketplace: Oscar Wilde and the Victorian Public* (Stanford, Calif.: Stanford University Press, 1986). Gagnier opposes "the dandy" to "the gentleman," arguing that the dandy represents a critique of middle-class gender ideology.

33. Dennis Denisoff, *Aestheticism and Sexual Parody, 1840–1940* (Cambridge: Cambridge University Press, 2001), p. 2.

34. Dennis Denisoff, "The Comic Promiscuity of W. S. Gilbert's Dandy-Aesthete," in *Mapping Male Sexuality: Nineteenth-Century England*, ed. Jay Losey and William D. Brewer (Madison, N.J.: Fairleigh Dickinson University Press, 2000), p. 133. A later version of this essay appears as "Gigolo Economics: W. S. Gilbert and the Market Value of Parodic Promiscuity," in *Aestheticism and Sexual Parody*, pp. 56–70.

35. Denisoff, *Aestheticism and Sexual Parody*, pp. 235–37. He also discusses the relation of Gilbert's *Engaged* and *Patience* to Wilde's most famous play (pp. 243–47). See also Rita Felski, "The Counterdiscourse of the Feminine in Three Texts by Wilde, Huysmans, and Sacher-Masoch," *PMLA* 106, no. 5 (1991): 1094–1105. Her argument tends in the opposite direction from Cohen's and Denisoff's, tracing the relation of the

dandy-aesthete to representations of women and contending that although identification with the feminine seems to have destabilized conventional bourgeois masculinity, in the end it reinscribed the binary system of gender even more insistently.

36. Vincent Lankewish analyzes the historical emergence of the figure of the homosexual in relation to the Victorian discourse on male–male marriage plots and the correlative refusal of those plots by the single queer aesthete in "Seeing Through the Marriage Plot: Queer Visionaries in Victorian Literature" (book manuscript).

37. The concept and term is in Ed Cohen, "Writing Gone Wilde: Homoerotic Desire in the Closet of Representation," *PMLA* 102, no. 5 (1987): 801–13.

38. Vincent Lankewish and Carolyn Williams, "To Those Who Wait: *Patience*, Patient Zero, *Zero Patience*" (paper presented at the conference of the Northeast Victorian Studies Association [NVSA], Queen's University, Kingston, Ontario, April 2002).

39. Like Cohen in "Writing Gone Wilde," I am arguing that although *Patience* is not explicitly homosexual in its content, it became an important part of the historical emergence of the homosexual as a social identity. As Cohen puts it elsewhere, "Rather than *being* a novel about 'homosexuality,' Wilde's novel was an integral part of the *processes whereby 'homosexuality' came to be*" ("Posing the Question," p. 44). The full and complex history of the emergence of the homosexual is beyond the scope of this book. The late nineteenth century remains pivotal as the moment when the social identity was typed and named, although much recent scholarship argues for an earlier scene of emergence. Eve Kosofsky Sedgwick offers an exemplary study, focusing on the historical rise of compulsory identification through the binary system of hetero- and homosexuality, in *Epistemology of the Closet* (Berkeley: University of California Press, 1990).

40. Ed Cohen, "Legislating the Norm: From 'Sodomy' to 'Gross Indecency,'" in *Talk on the Wilde Side: Toward a Genealogy of a Discourse on Male Sexualities* (New York: Routledge, 1993), pp. 103–25. The increase in the number of prosecutions for homosexuality beginning in the mid-1880s is illustrated in H. G. Cocks, *Nameless Offences: Homosexual Desire in the Nineteenth Century* (London: Tauris, 2003), chart on p. 30. See also Charles Upchurch, *Before Wilde: Sex Between Men in Britain's Age of Reform* (Berkeley: University of California Press, 2009).

41. Quoted in Denisoff, *Aestheticism and Sexual Parody*, p. 239. The association gained strength in the early decades of the twentieth century. In *The Art of Being Ruled* (1926), for example, Wyndham Lewis quotes from *Patience* in order to parody male–male homosexuality. See Lesley Higgins, *The Modernist Cult of Ugliness: Aesthetic and Gender Politics* (New York: Palgrave Macmillan, 2002), pp. 83–85.

42. The situation was much more complex, with homosexuality emerging *through* the Oxford discourse on the classics, as shown in Linda Dowling, *Hellenism and Homosexuality in Victorian Oxford* (Ithaca, N.Y.: Cornell University Press, 1996).

43. Tom Stoppard, *The Invention of Love* (New York: Grove Press, 1997), p. 21. Stoppard draws on historical data gathered by Billie Andrew Inman, "Estrangement and Connection: Walter Pater, Benjamin Jowett, and William M. Hardinge," in *Pater in the 1990s*, ed. Laurel Brake and Ian Small (Greensboro, N.C.: ELT Press, 1991), pp. 1–20.

44. This is not the only interpretive sense of the play's title, but it is the only one I will focus on.

45. Stoppard, *Invention of Love*, p. 91.
46. Stoppard, *Invention of Love*, p. 96.
47. Stoppard, *Invention of Love*, pp. 96–97.
48. Stoppard, *Invention of Love*, pp. 52–53; italics added.
49. Stoppard, *Invention of Love*, pp. 55, 58; italics added.
50. On the anathematic "typing" of Wilde in the newspaper coverage of the trials, see Ed Cohen, "Typing Wilde: Construing the 'Desire to Appear to Be a Person Inclined to the Commission of the Gravest of All Offenses,'" in *Talk on the Wilde Side*, pp. 126–72.
51. Stoppard, *Invention of Love*, p. 96.
52. For casting of the English and American premieres, see Stoppard, *Invention of Love*, pp. ix–x.
53. The production was at the Wilma Theater, Philadelphia (2000, dir. Blanka Zizka). For more details, see Carolyn Williams, "Two East Coast Productions of Tom Stoppard's *The Invention of Love*," *Pater Newsletter*, no. 43 (2001): 14–22.
54. "Patience; or, Bunthorne's Bride," *Illustrated London News*, June 18, 1881, p. 598; italics added. The reviewer for the *Times* echoed the point, praising the "clever parody of certain tricks and mannerisms of modern poetry" (quoted in Stedman, "Genesis," p. 309).
55. Audrey Williamson's short discussion of the "rivalry in poetic styles" is a signal exception (*Gilbert and Sullivan Opera: A New Assessment* [New York: Macmillan, 1953], p. 84).
56. *The Bab Ballads by W. S. Gilbert*, ed. James Ellis (Cambridge, Mass.: Belknap Press of Harvard University Press, 1970), pp. 120–21, 333–34.
57. W. S. Gilbert, "Author's Note," in *Patience; or, Bunthorne's Bride* (New York: Doubleday, Page, 1902), p. vi.
58. W. S. Gilbert, *Patience* (manuscript), W. S. Gilbert Papers, British Library, London. This clerical version is transcribed in Stedman, "Genesis," pp. 290–310.
59. Stedman, "Genesis," p. 308.
60. Thomas Maitland [Robert Buchanan], "The Fleshly School of Poetry: Mr. D. G. Rossetti," *Contemporary Review* 18 (1871): 334–50.
61. This would have been widely known. See Roy Porter, *The Greatest Benefit to Mankind: A Medical History of Humanity* (New York: Norton, 1997), pp. 266–69, 674–75. According to Porter, "Calomel (mercurous chloride) appeared in every physician's bag throughout the nineteenth century, and was an active ingredient in the 'blue pills' prominent in nineteenth-century English therapeutics" (p. 266). With thanks to Ann Jurecic for her guidance.
62. For the definitive study of this trope in British aestheticism, see Kathy Alexis Psomiades, *Beauty's Body: Femininity and Representation in British Aestheticism* (Stanford, Calif.: Stanford University Press, 1997).
63. Harry G. Frankfurt has discussed the connections between shit and bullshit, as well as their oppositional relation to aesthetic form: "Is [the bullshitter's] product necessarily messy or unrefined? The word *shit* does, to be sure, suggest this. Excrement is not designed or crafted at all; it is merely emitted, or dumped. It may have a more or less coherent shape, or it may not, but it is in any case certainly

not *wrought*" (*On Bullshit* [Princeton, N.J.: Princeton University Press, 2005], pp. 21–22).

64. Of Swinburne's self-parodies that focus especially on sound obscuring sense, see especially "Poeta Loquitur" and "Nephilidia" (1880). John Bush Jones notes that Bunthorne echoes Swinburne's rhythms, in "In Search of Archibald Grosvenor: A New Look at Gilbert's *Patience*," in *W. S. Gilbert*, ed. Jones, pp. 245–47.

65. For a longer version of this argument, including the role of the Spasmodic and Della Cruscan poets, as well as more discussion of the excremental metaphor, see Carolyn Williams, "Parody and Poetic Tradition: Gilbert and Sullivan's *Patience*," *Victorian Poetry* 46, no. 4 (2008): 375–403.

66. For commentary on the hostile reviews, see Bullen, *Pre-Raphaelite Body*, pp. 202–3.

67. John Addington Symonds, "The Idyllists," in *Studies of the Greek Poets*, 3rd ed. (London: Black, 1893), vol. 2, pp. 244–45, 258, 248. With thanks to Jason Rudy.

68. Taking his cue from the fact that Tennyson calls them "*English* idyls," Herbert F. Tucker examines their "domesticating tactics," showing that they insistently speak from, of, and to a common, national life, in "In England: Arts of the Joiner in the Domestic Idylls," in *Tennyson and the Doom of Romanticism* (Cambridge, Mass.: Harvard University Press, 1988), pp. 270–345.

69. The evolution of *Idylls of the King* spans the years 1842 to 1885. In other words, the project was current for a very long time, certainly when *Patience* was produced.

70. Algernon Charles Swinburne, "Under the Microscope," excerpted in *The Broadview Anthology of Victorian Poetry and Poetic Theory*, ed. Thomas J. Collins and Vivienne J. Rundle (Peterborough, Ont.: Broadview, 1999), pp. 1329–48.

71. Linda H. Peterson, "Domestic and Idyllic," in *A Companion to Victorian Poetry*, ed. Richard Cronin, Alison Chapman, and Antony H. Harrison (Oxford: Blackwell, 2002), p. 53.

72. Jones, "In Search of Archibald Grosvenor," pp. 247–51. Jones also suggests that Swinburne's parody of Patmore, "The Person in the House," published in his anonymous *Heptalogia; or, The Seven Against Sense* the year before *Patience* was produced, may have influenced Gilbert.

73. *Athenaeum*, June 12, 1886, p. 771.

74. The clerical version of *Patience* included the stage direction "absorbed in his folio [words crossed out] / *black-letter, rubricated*" (quoted in Stedman, "Genesis," p. 304).

75. For more detail, see Williams, "Parody and Poetic Tradition," pp. 394, 400.

7. *Iolanthe*

1. Terence Rees, *Thespis: A Gilbert and Sullivan Enigma* (London: Dillon's University Bookshop, 1964), p. v.

2. Gilbert recalled their decision in an address to the O. P. Club in 1906. Quoted in Sidney Dark and Rowland Grey, *W. S. Gilbert: His Life and Letters* (London: Methuen, 1923), p. 194.

3. Carole G. Silver, *Strange and Secret Peoples: Fairies and Victorian Consciousness* (New York: Oxford University Press, 1999), pp. 4–6. She cites Michael R. Booth, who pointed out that "the acceptance and rapid growth of fairyland as fit subject matter for literature, painting and the stage from the 1820's to the 1840's and its survival at least until the First World War is one of the most remarkable phenomena of nineteenth-century culture" (*Victorian Spectacular Theatre, 1850–1910* [London: Routledge & Kegan Paul, 1981], p. 36).

4. Quoted in Stella Beddoe, "Fairy Writing and Writers," in *Victorian Fairy Painting*, ed. Jane Martineau (London: Merrell Holberton, 1997), p. 29.

5. Silver, *Strange and Secret Peoples*, p. 32.

6. Quoted in Beddoe, "Fairy Writing and Writers," p. 23.

7. Silver, *Strange and Secret Peoples*, pp. 9, 15, 185–212. Silver argues that the final departure of the fairies was caused by their extreme popularity, which, along with the Victorian cult of childhood, reduced fairy otherness to mere decoration and relegated the fairy story, formerly addressed to adults, to the nursery.

8. Susan Stewart, *On Longing: Narratives of the Miniature, the Gigantic, the Souvenir, the Collection* (Durham, N.C.: Duke University Press, 1998), pp. 111–12.

9. Kevin Pask, "The Fairy Way of Writing" (manuscript). For a discussion of the elite invention of the folk, see Peter Burke, "The 'Discovery' of Popular Culture," in *People's History and Socialist Theory*, ed. Raphael Samuel (London: Routledge & Kegan Paul, 1981), pp. 216–26.

10. Silver has suggested that the resurfacing of the fairies in the late eighteenth century responded in part to the fairy lore of France and Germany with "a sense that fairies . . . were part of England's precious heritage" (*Strange and Secret Peoples*, p. 10). Jennifer Schacker, tracing the emergence of fairy-tale collections as popular reading (in the 1820s through the 1850s), argues that they became the basis of a widespread mediation of transnational as well as intranational relations, in *National Dreams: The Remaking of Fairy Tales in Nineteenth-Century England* (Philadelphia: University of Pennsylvania Press, 2003), p. 11.

11. The sense of "fairy" later began to shift, to become an American slang reference to a certain effeminate delicacy and fastidiousness attributed to homosexual men. This redefinition was surely influenced by theatrical culture and probably began earlier than current scholarship, which usually pinpoints the 1890s, would suggest. See "Fairy," in *Encyclopedia of Homosexuality*, ed. Wayne R. Dynes (New York: Garland, 1990), vol. 1, p. 384. More work on the role of the theatrical fairy genres in establishing this usage is necessary.

12. David Mayer, "Supernumeraries: Decorating the Stage with Lots (& Lots & Lots) of Live Bodies," in *Ruskin, the Theatre, and Victorian Visual Culture*, ed. Anselm Heinrich, Katharine Newey, and Jeffrey Richards (New York: Palgrave Macmillan, 2009), pp. 154–68.

13. Charlotte Gere, "In Fairyland," in *Victorian Fairy Painting*, ed. Martineau, p. 68; Stewart, *On Longing*, pp. 11–12; Maureen Duffy, *The Erotic World of Faery* (London: Hodder and Stoughton, 1972), pp. 287–97. Duffy also comments on the convention of crowding the picture with a "Bosch-crowd" of tiny bodies (p. 294).

14. Lionel Lambourne, "Fairies and the Stage," in *Victorian Fairy Painting*, ed. Martineau, p. 47.

15. Lambourne, "Fairies and the Stage," p. 47.

16. For the distinction between burlesque and extravaganza in the nineteenth century, see chapter 1, n. 10.

17. For similar but more explicitly sexualized representations of fairies than those in plate 13, see Lambourne, "Fairies and the Stage," pp. 46, 53. The illustrations are from the *Days' Doings*, characterized as "an erotic magazine" in Tracy B. Davis, *Actresses as Working Women: Their Social Identity in Victorian Culture* (London: Routledge, 1991), p. 116. For a great picture of burlesque fairies, in their sexually explicit costumes, see Richard W. Schoch, *Not Shakespeare: Bardolatry and Burlesque in the Nineteenth Century* (Cambridge: Cambridge University Press, 2002), p. 72.

18. Davis, *Actresses as Working Women*, pp. 105–36.

19. Donald Roy, introduction to *Plays by James Robinson Planché*, ed. Donald Roy (Cambridge: Cambridge University Press, 1986), p. 12.

20. Roy, introduction to *Plays by James Robinson Planché*, p. 16.

21. Reginald Allen, ed., *The First Night Gilbert and Sullivan: Containing Complete Librettos of the Fourteen Operas, Exactly as Presented at Their Première Performances; Together with Facsimiles of the First-Night Programmes* (New York: Heritage Club, 1958), p. 174. Reviewing opening night, William Beatty-Kingston in the *Theatre* approvingly described the "self-lighting fairies with electricity stored somewhere about the small of their backs."

22. Quoted in Roy, introduction to *Plays by James Robinson Planché*, p. 14.

23. Percy Fitzgerald, *The World Behind the Scenes*, quoted in Russell Jackson, *Victorian Theatre: The Theatre in Its Time* (Franklin, N.Y.: New Amsterdam, 1989), p. 193.

24. Harley Granville-Barker, "Exit Planché—Enter Gilbert," in *The Eighteen-Sixties: Essays by Fellows of the Royal Society of Literature*, ed. John Drinkwater (Cambridge: Cambridge University Press, 1932), pp. 102–48.

25. Roy, introduction to *Plays by James Robinson Planché*, p. 31.

26. Dennis Denisoff, *Aestheticism and Sexual Parody* (Cambridge: Cambridge University Press, 2001), p. 238.

27. Focusing on sexuality rather than gender, Freud famously discusses the neurotic male's splitting of Madonna and whore. In *A Room of One's Own* (1929), Virginia Woolf first used the figure of Coventry Patmore's "angel in the house" to name the patriarchal enforcement of female domestication. Works in nineteenth-century feminist studies that take up the cultural splitting of the feminine include Sandra M. Gilbert and Susan Gubar, *The Madwoman in the Attic: The Woman Writer and the Nineteenth-Century Literary Imagination* (New Haven, Conn.: Yale University Press, 1979); Nina Auerbach, *Woman and the Demon: The Life of a Victorian Myth* (Cambridge, Mass.: Harvard University Press, 1982); and Mary Poovey, *The Proper Lady and the Woman Writer: Ideology as Style in the Works of Mary Wollstonecraft, Mary Shelley, and Jane Austen* (Chicago: University of Chicago Press, 1984). The opposition between "the angel in the house" and "the strong-minded woman" was propounded in Elizabeth Helsinger, Robin Lauterbach Sheets, and William Veeder, "The Angel and the Strong-Minded

Woman," in *The Woman Question: Society and Literature in Britain and America, 1837–1883*, vol. 3, *Literary Issues* (Chicago: University of Chicago Press, 1989), pp. 79–110.

28. For a photograph of Ellen Terry as Puck, see Lambourne, "Fairies and the Stage," p. 42. To some extent, this was not a Victorian innovation, for in 1767, eleven-year-old Sarah Kemble (later Mrs. Siddons) played Ariel in Roger Kemble's production of John Dryden and William Davenant's version of *The Tempest*. And the practice was not consistent, for in William Macready's production of 1838, Priscilla Horton, the most famous Ariel of the nineteenth century, seemed both ethereal and sensual; after all, she was twenty years old.

29. J. W. Cole, *The Life and Theatrical Times of Charles Kean, F.S.A.* (1859), quoted in Russell Jackson, "Shakespeare's Fairies in Victorian Criticism and Performance," in *Victorian Fairy Painting*, ed. Martineau, p. 43.

30. Quoted in Jackson, "Shakespeare's Fairies," p. 42.

31. Jackson, "Shakespeare's Fairies," p. 39.

32. On the sexualized Victorian child, see James Kincaid, *Child-Loving: The Erotic Child and Victorian Culture* (New York: Routledge, 1992).

33. *The Bab Ballads of W. S. Gilbert*, ed. James Ellis (Cambridge, Mass.: Belknap Press of Harvard University Press, 1970), pp. 287–89, 361–62.

34. Silver, *Strange and Secret Peoples*, pp. 89–116.

35. Silver, *Strange and Secret Peoples*, p. 89.

36. Silver, *Strange and Secret Peoples*, p. 95.

37. Silver, *Strange and Secret Peoples*, pp. 100–101. See also Barbara Fass Leavy, *In Search of the Swan Maiden: A Narrative on Folklore and Gender* (New York: New York University Press, 1994).

38. See, for example, Duffy, *Erotic World of Faery*, pp. 21–22, 34, 73–75.

39. Silver, *Strange and Secret Peoples*, p. 90.

40. Silver, *Strange and Secret Peoples*, p. 93.

41. Silver, *Strange and Secret Peoples*, pp. 102–3. On fairy wives and the imposition of taboos, see also Katharine Briggs, *The Vanishing People: Fairy Lore and Legends* (New York: Pantheon, 1978), p. 145.

42. Silver, *Strange and Secret Peoples*, p. 93.

43. Silver, *Strange and Secret Peoples*, pp. 97–99.

44. On scholarly debates that defend or discredit the notion of an ancient matriarchy, see Silver, *Strange and Secret Peoples*, pp. 94–105.

45. Joan Bamberger, "'The Myth of Matriarchy': Why Men Rule in Primitive Society," in *Woman, Culture, and Society*, ed. Michelle Zimbalist Rosaldo and Louise Lamphere (Stanford, Calif.: Stanford University Press, 1974), pp. 263–80. See also Cynthia Eller, *The Myth of Matriarchal Prehistory: Why an Invented Past Will Not Give Women a Future* (Boston: Beacon Press, 2000).

46. Natalie Zemon Davis, "Women on Top: Symbolic Sexual Inversion and Political Disorder in Early Modern Europe," in *The Reversible World: Symbolic Inversion in Art and Society*, ed. Barbara A. Babcock (Ithaca, N.Y.: Cornell University Press, 1977), pp. 147–90. Adrienne Munich also uses Davis in her discussion of Gilbert and Sullivan, in *Queen Victoria's Secrets* (New York: Columbia University Press, 1996), pp. 113–14.

47. Michael McKeon, *The Secret History of Domesticity: Public, Private, and the Division of Knowledge* (Baltimore: Johns Hopkins University Press, 2005), pp. 171–72.

48. Munich mentions Talfourd's and Brough's burlesques, along with the story of Venus and Adonis, sometimes read as a story of the seduction of a young man by an experienced woman, in *Queen Victoria's Secrets*, p. 229n.13. See also William Davenport Adams, *A Book of Burlesque, Sketches of English Stage Travestie and Parody* (London: Henry, 1891).

49. Davis, *Actresses as Working Women*, especially pp. 108–31. See also Tracy C. Davis, "The Actress in Victorian Pornography," in *Victorian Scandals: Representations of Gender and Class*, ed. Kristine Ottesen Garrigan (Athens: Ohio University Press, 1992), pp. 99–133.

50. Jane W. Stedman gives a good example: "Hither, hither, hither, hither, / Trip, fairies, hither, trip, trip," etc. (*W. S. Gilbert: A Classic Victorian and His Theatre* [Oxford: Oxford University Press, 1996], p. 194).

51. Jackson, "Shakespeare's Fairies," pp. 38–41; Davis, *Actresses as Working Women*, pp. 108–15.

52. Quoted in Jane W. Stedman, "From Dame to Woman: W. S. Gilbert and Theatrical Transvestism," in *Suffer and Be Still: Women in the Victorian Age*, ed. Martha Vicinus (Bloomington: Indiana University Press, 1972), p. 26.

53. Gilbert, *Bab Ballads*, p. 218.

54. It is precisely the latter potential—the "category crisis" that disrupts the binary oppositions to which sex and gender are usually reduced—that Marjorie Garber emphasizes as the primary characteristic of cross-dressing in *Vested Interests: Cross-Dressing and Cultural Anxiety* (New York: Routledge, 1992).

55. On Vesta Tilly's cross-dressed persona, see Martha Vicinus, "Turn-of-the-Century Male Impersonation: Rewriting the Romance Plot," in *Sexualities in Victorian Britain*, ed. Andrew H. Miller and James Eli Adams (Bloomington: Indiana University Press, 1996), pp. 187–213.

56. The gender-bending performances evoke complex possibilities for identification and desire, on the part of both male and female audience members, according to Vicinus, "Turn-of-the-Century Male Impersonation," and Kathy Fletcher, "Planché, Vestris, and the Transvestite Role: Sexuality and Gender in Victorian Popular Theatre," *Nineteenth-Century Theatre* 15, no. 1 (1987): 9–33.

57. Stedman, "From Dame to Woman," p. 21.

58. Robert B. Brough, *Medea; or, The Best of Mothers, with a Brute of a Husband* (London: Thomas Hailes Lacy, 1856); Mollie Sands, *Robson of the Olympic* (London: Society for Theatre Research, 1979), pp. 77–78.

59. Quoted in Stephanie L. Barczewski, *Myth and National Identity in Nineteenth-Century Britain: The Legends of King Arthur and Robin Hood* (Oxford: Oxford University Press, 2000), p. 198.

60. Stedman, "From Dame to Woman," p. 22.

61. Quoted in Rees, *Thespis*, p. 43.

62. Stedman, "From Dame to Woman," 20–37.

63. Audrey Williamson, *Gilbert and Sullivan Opera: A New Assessment* (New York: Macmillan, 1953), pp. 98, 89, 93.

64. The caricature of Lady Jane in the *Illustrated London News* takes the full hourglass figure, epitomized by the cello, and makes it simply fat, thus flattening the parody.

65. Munich has pointed out Katisha's representation of "the vengeful soul of the older woman abandoned for a younger one" (*Queen Victoria's Secrets*, p.124).

66. Katisha's song about the "beauty in the bellow of the blast" was originally meant for Lady Jane in *Patience*. See Jane W. Stedman, "The Genesis of *Patience*," in *W. S. Gilbert: A Century of Scholarship and Commentary*, ed. John Bush Jones (New York: New York University Press, 1970), pp. 297, 314n.46.

67. I say "long before" Katisha, because the character was originally formulated for Gilbert's *The Princess* (1870), a burlesque version of Tennyson's long poem *The Princess: A Medley* (1847–1851).

68. Williamson, *Gilbert and Sullivan Opera*, p. 125.

69. Jonathan Strong, "Remarks to the Valley Light Opera" (paper presented at the spring meeting of the Valley Light Opera, Amherst, Mass., 2001), p. 7.

70. George Bernard Shaw, "Gilbert, Sullivan and Others," in *Shaw on Music*, ed. Eric Bentley (New York: Doubleday, 1955; New York: Applause Books, 1983), p. 213.

71. Quoted in Stedman, "From Dame to Woman," p. 36; David Eden, *Gilbert and Sullivan: The Creative Conflict* (Madison, N.J.: Fairleigh Dickinson University Press, 1989). Indeed, Gilbert did *not* like his mother, but this is not relevant to my argument, which is figural, not biographical.

72. Stedman, "From Dame to Woman," pp. 34, 26; Andrew Crowther, *Contradiction Contradicted: The Plays of W. S. Gilbert* (Madison, N.J.: Fairleigh Dickinson University Press, 2000), p. 139.

73. The misogynistic uses to which the dual figure of the huge woman and the tiny man was put are discussed in Tracy C. Davis, *The Economics of the British Stage, 1800–1914* (Cambridge: Cambridge University Press, 2000), pp. 273–306.

74. Silver, *Strange and Secret Peoples*, p. 99. For this debate within studies of Queen Victoria, see Adrienne Munich and Margaret Homans, *Remaking Queen Victoria* (Cambridge: Cambridge University Press, 1997).

75. Munich, *Queen Victoria's Secrets*, p. 113.

76. Isaac Goldberg, "W. S. Gilbert's Topsy-Turvydom," in *W. S. Gilbert*, ed. Jones, p. 140. Lambourne also makes this connection in "Fairies and the Stage," pp. 52–53.

77. Munich, *Queen Victoria's Secrets*, pp. 116, 230n.78.

78. Munich, *Queen Victoria's Secrets*, p. 113.

79. Munich, *Queen Victoria's Secrets*, pp. 187–210.

80. Munich, *Queen Victoria's Secrets*, pp. 105–9, 161–64.

81. Munich, *Queen Victoria's Secrets*, pp. 125–26. She goes on to argue that these grotesque caricatures of the powerful woman are envisioned from the point of view of an infantilized male (pp. 111–13, 115), reminding us of Dorothy Dinnerstein's (*The Mermaid and the Minotaur: Sexual Arrangements and Human Malaise* [New York: Harper & Row, 1976]) and Nancy Chodorow's (*The Reproduction of Mothering: Psychoanalysis and the Sociology of Gender* [Berkeley: University of California Press, 1978]) theoretical explanations of misogyny: the gendered division of labor that continues to reinstate women as caregivers of infants instills—in male and female children alike—the fear of mother and of being infantilized as adults (p. 230n.16).

82. Roy, introduction to *Plays by James Robinson Planché*, pp. 27–28.
83. This "figure of instruction, repressive and reproving" is "a stand-in for the Victorian nanny" (who, herself, is a stand-in for the mother) (Munich, *Queen Victoria's Secrets*, pp. 126, 114).
84. Lambourne, "Fairies and the Stage," p. 52.
85. The opening procession of Peers, "cloaked and gartered and coroneted, is the most absurd thing conceivable," said the reviewer for the *Advertiser*, while the *Era* agreed: "Nothing could be better of its kind than the pompous blustering and mock-heroic march that ushers in the procession" (quoted in Allen, ed., *First Night Gilbert and Sullivan*, p. 174).
86. In this respect, then, I disagree with Munich, who argues that marriage is a ritual taming (*Queen Victoria's Secrets*, pp. 115–17, 121–22), and with Silver, who argues that *Iolanthe* participates in the general Victorian effort to denigrate "female power and separation" (*Strange and Secret Peoples*, p. 93).

8. *Princess Ida*

1. I refer to Gayden Wren's organization of the "three Princesses" at the American part of the Buxton Festival of 1996, held in Philadelphia, where a reading of Tennyson's *The Princess* was followed first by a performance of Gilbert's *The Princess* and then by a performance of *Princess Ida*.
2. Elizabeth K. Helsinger, Robin Lauterbach Sheets, and William Veeder, "The Angel and the Strong-Minded Woman," in *The Woman Question: Society and Literature in Britain and America, 1837–1883*, vol. 3, *Literary Issues* (Chicago: University of Chicago Press, 1989), p. 94. They date the negative caricature from 1854 (p. 92).
3. [Charles Kingsley], "Tennyson," *Fraser's* 42 (1850): 250.
4. [Kingsley], "Tennyson," quoted in Helsinger, Sheets, and Veeder, "Angel and Strong-Minded Woman," p. 96.
5. The relation between the frame and the tale has been a critical crux since the poem's publication. Recent views include Eve Kosofsky Sedgwick, "Tennyson's *Princess*: One Bride for Seven Brothers," in *Between Men: English Literature and Male Homosocial Desire* (New York: Columbia University Press, 1985), pp. 118–33; Herbert F. Tucker, "*The Princess*: Muffled Like the Fates," in *Tennyson and the Doom of Romanticism* (Cambridge, Mass.: Harvard University Press, 1988), pp. 351–76; Donald E. Hall, "Reading Tennyson Reading Fuller Reading Tennyson: The Anti-Feminism of *The Princess*," in *Fixing Patriarchy: Feminism and Mid-Victorian Male Novelists* (New York: New York University Press, 1996), pp. 44–62; and Jason Rudy, "Telegraphing *The Princess*," in *Electric Meters: Victorian Physiological Poetics* (Athens: Ohio University Press, 2009), pp. 58–69.
6. [John Westland Marston], *Athenaeum*, January 1, 1848, pp. 6–8, in *Tennyson: The Critical Heritage*, ed. John D. Jump (London: Routledge & Kegan Paul, 1967), pp. 168, 171, 167.
7. Tucker, *Tennyson and the Doom of Romanticism*, p. 351.
8. Sedgwick, *Between Men*, p. 132. In addition, see Rudy, who argues that "dis-linked" parts of the tale are connected through the lyrics, whereby "brief flashes

of lyric intimacy" become "the relay points . . . of a network" (*Electric Meters*, p. 63).

9. See chapter 7.
10. Hallam Tennyson stressed that the seizures emphasize the Prince's "*comparative want of power*" (quoted in Hall, *Fixing Patriarchy*, p. 54; italics added).
11. Ida's contempt for other women has been evident all along, and her top–down feminism, like the aristocratic ideology of the frame, creates the major fault line within the poem's coherence, as Sedgwick points out in *Between Men*, pp. 126–29.
12. For his reading of "Come down, O maid," see Tucker, *Tennyson and the Doom of Romanticism*, pp. 371–76. He argues that the dispossession enacted in lyric, in contest with the idyllic narrative, produce the political unconscious, whereby "the muffled violence of . . . entrenched power" comes to seem an individual choice.
13. Elaine Showalter, "Critical Cross-Dressing: Male Feminism and the Woman of the Year," in *Men in Feminism*, ed. Alice Jardine and Paul Smith (New York: Methuen, 1987), p. 123. Showalter's argument is cited in connection with *The Princess* by Hall, *Fixing Patriarchy*, p. 46, and in connection with cross-dressing in general by Marjorie Garber, *Vested Interests: Cross-Dressing and Cultural Anxiety* (New York: Routledge, 1992), pp. 5–9. Garber argues that the fluctuating construction, deconstruction, and reconstruction of gender defines the work of culture itself. For our purposes, Adrienne Munich puts the point most succinctly and categorically, when she claims that in *Princess Ida* the "transvestite roles serve the cause of male supremacy" (*Queen Victoria's Secrets* [New York: Columbia University Press, 1996], p. 111). Hall links the Prince's final words to the young men's cross-dressing, in *Fixing Patriarchy*, pp. 56–57.
14. Tucker, *Tennyson and the Doom of Romanticism*, p. 376.
15. W. S. Gilbert, *The Princess*, in *Original Plays*, 1st ser. (London: Chatto & Windus, 1922), pp. 133–69.
16. W. S. Gilbert, "An Autobiography," *Theatre*, April 1883, pp. 217–34.
17. Max Keith Sutton, *W. S. Gilbert* (Boston: Twayne, 1975), p. 68, following a reviewer in the *Graphic*, November 26, 1870, p. 523.
18. At this time, the term "burlesque" implied ridicule of a particular work. See chapter 1, n. 10. Richard W. Schoch understands burlesque travesty in two senses: as a matter not only of theatrical cross-dressing but also of the form itself, "a play self-consciously 'dressed up' as another play," a revised version that has been "redressed" or corrected, as if in "comic misquotations" (introduction to *Victorian Theatrical Burlesques*, ed. Richard W. Schoch [Aldershot: Ashgate, 2003], p. xiii).
19. Jane W. Stedman, *W. S. Gilbert: A Classic Victorian and His Theatre* (Oxford: Oxford University Press, 1996), p. 229.
20. Gayden Wren, *A Most Ingenious Paradox: The Art of Gilbert and Sullivan* (Oxford: Oxford University Press, 2001), p. 153.
21. John Hollingshead, quoted in Stedman, *W. S. Gilbert*, p. 222.
22. Garber, *Vested Interests*, p. 177.
23. Kathy Fletcher, "Planché, Vestris, and the Transvestite Role: Sexuality and Gender in Victorian Popular Theatre," *Nineteenth-Century Theatre* 15, no. 1 (1987): 9–33.
24. Compare the situation in Gilbert's *The Gentleman in Black* (1870), which Jane W. Stedman calls "a kind of intellectual transvestism" ("From Dame to Woman: W. S.

Gilbert and Theatrical Transvestism," in *Suffer and Be Still: Women in the Victorian Age*, ed. Martha Vicinus [Bloomington: Indiana University Press, 1972], p. 27).

25. As Schoch has shown, the audience for burlesque was "fast" and loose, largely a "bachelor sub-culture" (introduction to *Victorian Theatrical Burlesques*, p. xxxiv). He reminds us, too, that in 1870, the year in which Gilbert wrote *The Princess*, Ernest Boulton and Frederick William Park were arrested for cross-dressing as they came out of a burlesque. This famous scandal—along with the Cleveland Street affair of 1889/1890 (chap. 6)—both repressed and helped to consolidate a homosexual sub-culture in the years before the trials of Oscar Wilde (pp. xxxiv–xxxv).

26. Tucker, *Tennyson and the Doom of Romanticism*, p. 357.

27. This conundrum also appears in the prologue to Gilbert's play *The Wicked World* (1870), written in the same year as the burlesque *Princess*.

28. *Princess Ida* is the best and most operatic of the collaborations, according to Wren, *Most Ingenious Paradox*, pp. 154, 158–59, and Audrey Williamson, *Gilbert and Sullivan Opera: A New Assessment* (New York: Macmillan, 1953), pp. 135–38. (The other main contender for this honor is *The Yeomen of the Guard*.)

29. Leslie Baily, *The Gilbert and Sullivan Book* (London: Spring Books, 1952), p. 250.

30. William Beatty-Kingston, writing for the *Theatre*, praised the production for displaying "among the most beautiful pictures ever exhibited on any stage." Said the reviewer for the *Sportsman*, "[T]he girls were dressed with a quaint richness, suggesting Portia after a visit to Swan and Edgar's" (quoted in Reginald Allen, ed., *The First Night Gilbert and Sullivan: Containing Complete Librettos of the Fourteen Operas, Exactly as Presented at Their Première Performances; Together with Facsimiles of the First-Night Programmes* [New York: Heritage Club, 1958], p. 206). On the elaborate sets and expensive armor, see Stedman, *W. S. Gilbert*, p. 204, and Williamson, *Gilbert and Sullivan Opera*, p. 137.

31. *Musical Times*, February 1, 1884, pp. 79–80. This high opinion of the music and orchestration was echoed by the music critic of the *Sunday Times*, Herman Klein, quoted in Allen, ed., *First Night Gilbert and Sullivan*, p. 208.

32. Isaac Goldberg, *The Story of Gilbert and Sullivan; or, The "Compleat" Savoyard* (New York: Simon and Schuster, 1928), p. 300.

33. Michael Ainger, *Gilbert and Sullivan: A Dual Biography* (Oxford: Oxford University Press, 2002), p. 226; Williamson, *Gilbert and Sullivan Opera*, pp. 130–32.

34. Williamson, *Gilbert and Sullivan Opera*, p. 120.

35. Quoted in Allen, ed., *First Night Gilbert and Sullivan*, p. 207.

36. Andrew Crowther, *Contradiction Contradicted: The Plays of W. S. Gilbert* (Madison, N.J.: Fairleigh Dickinson University Press, 2000), pp. 26, 138.

37. Crowther, *Contradiction Contradicted*, pp. 138–39.

38. Quoted in Helsinger, Sheets, and Veeder, "Angel and Strong-Minded Woman," p. 94.

39. [Kingsley], "Tennyson," quoted in Helsinger, Sheets, and Veeder, "Angel and Strong-Minded Woman," p. 95.

40. George du Maurier, "Terrible Result of Higher Education of Women," *Punch*, January 24, 1874, p. 38.

41. George du Maurier, "The Higher Education of Women," *Punch*, December 22, 1877, p. 279, in Richard Kelley, *The Art of George du Maurier* (Brookfield, Vt.: Ashgate, 1996).

42. Angélique Richardson quotes Grant Allen's "Plain Words on the Woman Question" (1889), in which he warns that "emancipation would leave a woman a 'dulled and spiritless epicene automaton'" and that "healthy girls who embarked upon higher education ('mannish training') became unattractive and unsexed; 'both in England and America, the women of the cultivated classes are becoming unfit to be wives or mothers. Their sexuality (which lies at the basis of everything) is enfeebled or destroyed'" (*Love and Eugenics in the Late Nineteenth Century* [Oxford: Oxford University Press, 2003], pp. 42–43). The idea found its footing in Henry Maudsley, "Sex in Mind and Education," *Fortnightly Review*, April 1874, pp. 466–83. See also Joan N. Burstyn, *Victorian Education and the Ideal of Womanhood* (New York: Rowman & Littlefield, 1980), especially pp. 84–98. According to Burstyn, "Undue brain activity had a sterilising effect on both sexes, claimed [Edward H.] Clarke, but its influence was 'more potent' upon women, because the physiological effort of reproduction was far greater for them than for men" (p. 94).

43. Depictions of masculine women bonding with other women intensified the threat, and female political assertiveness was frequently taken as a sign of aberrant sexuality, as Martha Vicinus has shown in "Fin-de-Siècle Theatrics: Male Impersonation and Lesbian Desire," in *Borderlines: Genders and Identities in War and Peace, 1870–1930*, ed. Billie Melman (London: Routledge, 1998), pp. 163–92. Thus the disparaging of higher education for women often barely concealed an incipient homophobia, even before the explicit description of lesbianism in late-nineteenth-century sexology.

44. On the Victorian usages and valences of the word "nigger," see Michael J. Pickering, "White Skin, Black Masks: 'Nigger' Minstrelsy in Victorian England," in *Music Hall: Style and Performance*, ed. J. S. Bratton (Milton Keynes: Open University Press, 1986), pp. 70–91. This trope ("The niggers they'll be bleaching / By and by") has a long history. "To wash a blackamoor white," according to Ephraim Chambers's *Cyclopaedia* (1741) (and, no doubt, to many other sources), meant "a fruitless undertaking." Srinivas Aravamudan refers to Chambers and discusses this trope in *Tropicopolitans: Colonialism and Agency, 1688–1804* (Durham, N.C.: Duke University Press, 1999), pp. 1–4.

45. Stedman, *W. S. Gilbert*, p. 203.

46. Williamson comments that "in essentials [it was] out-moded even when it first appeared" (*Gilbert and Sullivan Opera*, p. 121). The topic was no longer topical. She also points out that the supposed timidity of women in wartime could hardly have been topical, either, when Florence Nightingale and the Crimean War were still active memories (pp. 121–22).

47. Goldberg, *Story of Gilbert and Sullivan*, p. 296.

48. Williamson, *Gilbert and Sullivan Opera*, pp. 124–25.

49. Wren claims that *Princess Ida* does not particularly focus on gender, since both men and women of the younger generation must break with the older generation, in *Most Ingenious Paradox*, pp. 152–54. But in my view, that purported break turns out to be a repetition, and it has everything to do with gender.

50. Alan Fischler, *Modified Rapture: Comedy in W. S. Gilbert's Savoy Operas* (Charlottesville: University Press of Virginia, 1991), pp. 58, 108–9.

9. *The Mikado*

1. David Cannadine, "Gilbert and Sullivan: The Making and Un-Making of a British 'Tradition,'" in *Myths of the English*, ed. Roy Porter (Cambridge: Polity Press, in association with Blackwell, 1992), pp. 12–32. This is an excellent essay. As will be clear by now, however, I disagree with Cannadine's attribution of "unabashed patriotism" to the operas. The Savoy operas are not "a paean of praise to national pride and to the established order" (pp. 27, 19), but a humorous, parodic critique of them.

2. John Wolfson, *Final Curtain: The Last Gilbert and Sullivan Operas* (London: Chappell, in association with Deutsch, 1976), pp. 11–14. There is also the Sicilian setting of *The Mountebanks* (1892, with music by Alfred Cellier) and the Danish setting of *His Excellency* (1894, with music by Osmond Carr). Wolfson argues that these far-flung settings allowed Gilbert's antimonarchical arguments to come more fully to the fore.

3. Although focusing neither on genre nor specifically on a periodization of the Savoy collaborations, Jane W. Stedman implies her understanding of the last six operas as a phase of development by having titled one of her chapters "The Mikado and After," in *W. S. Gilbert: A Classic Victorian and His Theatre* (Oxford: Oxford University Press, 1996), pp. 221–38.

4. *Monthly Musical Record*, May 1, 1885, p. 103. G. K. Chesterton agreed: "The cannon had been fired point-blank at us. . . . I doubt if there is a single joke in the whole play that fits the Japanese. But all the jokes . . . fit the English" (quoted in Sidney Dark and Rowland Grey, *W. S. Gilbert: His Life and Letters* [London: Methuen, 1923], p. 101).

5. Leslie Baily, *The Gilbert and Sullivan Book* (London: Spring Books, 1952), pp. 390–92. For another version of the story, see John Johnston, *The Lord Chamberlain's Blue Pencil* (London: Hodder & Stoughton, 1990), pp. 42–45. Johnston presents evidence, to the contrary, that Crown Prince Fushimi critically compared making fun of the Mikado with making fun of King Edward VII, although he claimed, "To say that the Japanese are offended by *The Mikado* would be using too strong a term" (p. 44).

6. For a more recent example of a controversial production at Occidental College, thoughtfully described, see Morgan Pitelka, "On Japanophilia: Collecting, Authenticity, and Making Identity," June 2007, DiscoverNikkei, http://www.discovernikkei .org/forum/en/node/1709 (accessed April 15, 2009). On "yellowface minstrelsy," see Joseph McLaughlin, "'Figure(s) in Lively Paint': *The Mikado*, Yellowface Minstrelsy, and Aestheticist Orientalism" (manuscript). McLaughlin treats "yellowface minstrelsy" (as well as blackface minstrelsy) as a nexus of cultural mixing and exchange, a place to explore "hybridized types of metropolitan modernity" and the confusion of class, national, racial, sexual, and gender identities evoked by theatrical performances of these hybridized types.

7. Richard A. Kaye sees in the prohibition on flirting a spoof of Darwin's thinking about sexual selection, in *The Flirt's Tragedy: Desire Without End in Victorian and Edwardian Fiction* (Charlottesville: University Press of Virginia, 2002), pp. 95, 108–9. Flirtation came to the fore as a topic in the late nineteenth century, he argues, at a time "in the history of social relations when masculine and feminine roles are undergoing radical transformations" (p. 33). To illustrate the prevalent attitudes against flirting, Kaye

quotes from the conduct books of Sarah Stickney Ellis (pp. 23–24). But Jeff Nunokawa explores the use of "the figure of Japan" to produce a late-nineteenth-century "safer passion" characterized by artfulness and control, in *Tame Passions of Wilde: The Styles of Manageable Desire* (Princeton, N.J.: Princeton University Press, 2003), p. 47.

8. The handkerchief could be seen as an exemplary English object, along the lines of John Plotz's argument in *Portable Property: Victorian Culture on the Move* (Princeton, N.J.: Princeton University Press, 2008).

9. Edward Ziter, *The Orient on the Victorian Stage* (Cambridge: Cambridge University Press, 2003). His focus is not a critique of *The Mikado*, but a discussion of the nonreflective role of "authenticity"—"real sets," geography, and race" (pp. 1–21)—in spectacular Oriental settings.

10. Earl Miner, *The Japanese Tradition in British and American Literature* (Princeton, N.J.: Princeton University Press, 1958), p. 56. Arthur Jacobs argues that it was a children's song, in *Arthur Sullivan: A Victorian Musician*, 2nd ed. (Portland, Ore.: Amadeus Press, 1992), p. 203.

11. Paul Seeley, "The Japanese March in 'The Mikado,'" *Musical Times*, August 1985, p. 455. The best discussion of the Meiji Restoration as a context for imperial Britain's attraction to Japan is Joseph McLaughlin, "The 'Japanese Village' and the Metropolitan Construction of Modernity," RaVoN, no. 48, November 2007, http://www.erudit.org/revue/ravon/2007/v/n48/017441ar.html (accessed December 11, 2009).

12. Miner, *Japanese Tradition*, p. 57. Seeley translates it: "Prince! Prince! What is it that flutters there in front of your horse?" ("Japanese March in 'The Mikado,'" p. 455). A second verse, not reproduced in *The Mikado*, answers this question: "That—don't you know—is the Brocade Standard, the symbol of our orders to defeat the Emperor's foe."

13. Ian Bradley continues the case for obscenity, originated by the British composer Thomas Dunhill, arguing that *tokoton* is a slang word for "the finish," with a possibly sexual connotation, in *The Complete Annotated Gilbert and Sullivan* (Oxford: Oxford University Press, 1996), p. 320.

14. Seeley pinpoints particular musical phrases that introduce the opening chorus and the oboe countermelody in "The sun whose rays," in "Japanese March in 'The Mikado,'" p. 456. Jacobs notes that Sullivan's diary records his visit to Mitford, in *Arthur Sullivan*, p. 203.

15. *Monthly Musical Record*, May 1, 1885, pp. 103–4.

16. Carl Dahlhaus, *Nineteenth-Century Music*, trans. J. Bradford Robinson (Berkeley: University of California Press, 1989), p. 236.

17. James Buzard, *Disorienting Fiction: The Autoethnographic Work of Nineteenth-Century British Novels* (Princeton, N.J.: Princeton University Press, 2005). Buzard traces the development of cross-cultural awareness within the nation—in regional literatures—showing that it then moved outward to comprehend relations between the nation and its external others. See also Brad Evans, *Before Cultures: The Ethnographic Imagination in American Literature, 1865–1920* (Chicago: University of Chicago Press, 2005).

18. In a chapter on *Bleak House* as "metropolitan autoethnography," Buzard focuses on the paradoxical result that "anywhere's nowhere" within the imperial desire to export English culture, in *Disorienting Fiction*, pp. 105–56. The Savoy operas focus

on its opposite, the overstuffed Victorian effect of import and theatrical staging: "everywhere's here."

19. Facsimile included with Reginald Allen, ed., *The First Night Gilbert and Sullivan: Containing Complete Librettos of the Fourteen Operas, Exactly as Presented at Their Première Performances; Together with Facsimiles of the First-Night Programmes* (New York: Heritage Club, 1958).

20. The best work on the Japanese Village—and exhibition practices more generally, as they relate to *The Mikado*—is McLaughlin, "'Japanese Village' and Metropolitan Construction of Modernity."

21. Oscar Wilde, "The Decay of Lying," in *The Critic as Artist: Critical Writings of Oscar Wilde*, ed. Richard Ellmann (Chicago: University of Chicago Press, 1969), pp. 315–16. See also Roland Barthes, "Faraway," in *Empire of Signs*, trans. Richard Howard (New York: Hill and Wang, 1982), p. 3. Nunokawa helpfully juxtaposes these two theorists (*Tame Passions of Wilde*, pp. 50–52) and adduces an example from Rudyard Kipling's *From Sea to Sea and Other Sketches* (1900) that stresses the relation of this form of imaginary travel to exhibition culture: "It would pay us to establish an international suzerainty over Japan . . . to put . . . the whole Empire in a glass case and mark it, *Hors Concours*, Exhibit A" (quoted on p. 48).

22. Edward W. Said, *Orientalism* (New York: Pantheon, 1978).

23. Buzard, *Disorienting Fiction*, p. 307.

24. McLaughlin, "'Japanese Village' and Metropolitan Construction of Modernity," par. 13. He is discussing *Punch*'s representations of reverse colonialism, such as the cartoon "An English Village from a Japanese Point of View," *Punch*, January 24, 1885, p. 47. As he does, I am claiming this awareness for *The Mikado*.

25. Yoko Chiba argues for this interpretation in "'Japonisme': East-West Renaissance in the Late Nineteenth Century," *Mosaic* 31, no. 2 (1998): 7.

26. Miner, *Japanese Tradition*, p. 54; Toshio Watanabe, *High Victorian Japonisme* (Bern: Peter Lang, 1991), pp. 166–210. McLaughlin points out that this confusion was facilitated by the stereotype of Japan as a culture "stuck in the Middle Ages" ("'Japanese Village' and Metropolitan Construction of Modernity," par. 1).

27. Indeed, Japonisme was influential in the transition from the massive high Victorian Gothic Revival to the lighter, vernacular "Queen Anne" style. Drawing on the work of Mark Girouard, Watanabe stresses "the Japaneseness of Queen Anne" (*High Victorian Japonisme*, pp. 176, 174–78, 189–95).

28. For an excellent overview, see Alan Richardson, introduction to *Three Oriental Tales* (Boston: Houghton Mifflin, 2002).

29. Watanabe focuses on the 1850s and 1860s in his excellent *High Victorian Japonisme*; Miner, *Japanese Tradition*, p. 34.

30. Quoted in Chiba, "'Japonisme,'" p. 2.

31. In "'Japonisme,'" Chiba argues, though, that English Japonisme began even earlier, with the Great Exhibition of 1851, where some Japanese objects were displayed.

32. Watanabe, *High Victorian Japonisme*, pp. 89–91.

33. Chiba, "'Japonisme,'" pp. 2–3.

34. On curio shops, see Watanabe, *High Victorian Japonisme*, pp. 94–98; on Liberty's, see Alison Adburgham, *Liberty's: A Biography of a Shop* (London: Allen & Unwin, 1975).

35. Patricia O'Hara, "'The Willow Pattern That We Knew': The Victorian Literature of Blue Willow," *Victorian Studies* 36 (1993): 421–42. The willow pattern—depicting a Chinese story, contributing to the "Japanese" craze, and appearing on porcelain designed and manufactured in England—was already popular in 1851 at the time of the Great Exhibition, as this essay's amusing epigraph from Francis Talfourd and W. P. Hale's play *The Mandarin's Daughter* (1851) makes clear, with its own cross-cultural humor.

36. *Harper's New Monthly Magazine*, February 1886, p. 476; quoted in Allen, ed., *First Night Gilbert and Sullivan*, p. 237.

37. Victorian "thing theory" is more complex than I have presented it here. For a good overview, see John Plotz, "Can the Sofa Speak? A Look at Thing Theory," *Criticism* 47, no. 1 (2005): 109–18. And for a great example of theory in practice, see Elaine Freedgood, *The Ideas in Things: Fugitive Meaning in the Victorian Novel* (Chicago: University of Chicago Press, 2006).

38. James Abbot McNeill Whistler, *The Gentle Art of Making Enemies: As Pleasingly Exemplified in Many Instances, Wherein the Serious Ones of This Earth, Carefully Exasperated, Have Been Prettily Spurred on to Unseemliness and Indiscretion, While Overcome by an Undue Sense of Right*, 3rd ed. (1890; New York: Putnam, 1904), p. 159.

39. Walter Pater, *The Renaissance: Studies in Art and Poetry* (1873; London: Macmillan, 1910), p. x.

40. It is on this principle that Watanabe distinguishes some Victorian Japonisme from Said's form of Orientalism, arguing that the superiority, not inferiority, of Japanese culture was the grounding assumption, in *High Victorian Japonisme*, p. 246.

41. For a list of the influential qualities of Japanese art, see Chiba, "'Japonisme,'" p. 3.

42. Donald Roy, introduction to *Plays by James Robinson Planché*, ed. Donald Roy (Cambridge: Cambridge University Press, 1986), p. 31.

43. Stedman, *W. S. Gilbert*, pp. 226–32. Gilbert wrote that "he has no more actuality than a pantomime king" (quoted in Dark and Grey, *W. S. Gilbert*, p. 101).

44. *Monthly Musical Record*, May 1, 1885, p. 104; William Beatty-Kingston, in *Theatre*, quoted in Allen, ed., *First Night Gilbert and Sullivan*, p. 239; *Academy*, March 21, 1885, p. 231.

45. Chiba, "'Japonisme,'" pp. 1–20.

46. Miner, *Japanese Tradition*, p. 57.

47. Chiba, "'Japonisme,'" p. 6.

48. The word "mania" was used at the time. "The Japs," *Theatre*, October 1, 1885, mentions "the mania for Japanese pieces" (quoted in Miner, *Japanese Tradition*, pp. 55, 57). For a discussion of many of these works, see pp. 57–61.

49. I have always felt that *The Mikado* misses a great opportunity by not playing with the Japanese tea ceremony, which could have allowed for cross-cultural byplay around the customs associated with the English national drink. McLaughlin discusses the Japanese ceremony of "Teaism" as a "religion of aestheticism," quoting Kakuzo Okakura's *The Book of Tea* (1906), in "'Japanese Village' and Metropolitan Construction of Modernity," par. 2.

50. This is an origin myth that persists in scholarship on Gilbert and Sullivan, and McLaughlin debunks it, showing that Gilbert could not have visited the Japanese Village in time for it to be an inspiration for *The Mikado*, in "'Japanese Village' and Metropolitan Construction of Modernity," par. 7.

51. Mike Leigh, *Topsy-Turvy* (London: Faber and Faber, 1999), pp. 68–69.

52. Leigh, *Topsy-Turvy*, p. 92.

10. *Ruddigore*

1. Earl F. Bargainnier, "*Ruddigore*: Gilbert's Burlesque of Melodrama," in *Gilbert and Sullivan: Papers Presented at the International Conference Held at the University of Kansas in May 1970*, ed. James Helyar (Lawrence: University of Kansas Libraries, 1971), pp. 7–16. He clearly recognizes the genre parody: "*Ruddigore*'s plot is original; that is, Gilbert burlesques the type rather than a specific work" (p. 8).

2. In response to many objections about the indelicacy of *Ruddygore*, the title was changed eleven days after the opening. See Reginald Allen, ed., *The First Night Gilbert and Sullivan: Containing Complete Librettos of the Fourteen Operas, Exactly as Presented at Their Première Performances; Together with Facsimiles of the First-Night Programmes* (New York: Heritage Club, 1958), p. 304.

3. Marshall Brown, *The Gothic Text* (Stanford, Calif.: Stanford University Press, 2004), p. 62.

4. V. C. Clinton-Baddeley discusses the burlesque patriotic joke, "to which . . . the English have so long been addicted" (*The Burlesque Tradition in the English Theatre After 1660* [London: Methuen, 1952], pp. 76–77).

5. For a good history of the English vampire, see Nina Auerbach, *Our Vampires, Ourselves* (Chicago: University of Chicago Press, 1997).

6. Richard's locutions are specifically parodic: "sartinly" alludes to Long Tom Coffin from James Fenimore Cooper's *The Pilot* (1824), while "D'ye see?" derives from Tobias Smollett. See Eileen E. Cottis, "Gilbert and the British Tar," in *Gilbert and Sullivan*, ed. Helyar, pp. 34–35.

7. Bargainnier, "*Ruddigore*," p. 13. On French indignation at this song, see Ian Bradley, *The Complete Annotated Gilbert and Sullivan* (Oxford: Oxford University Press, 1996), p. 674. Akin to indignation at *The Mikado*, on behalf of the Japanese, this is another place to see that the double edge of parody cuts particularly sharply in a cross-cultural setting.

8. On the "good old man" of melodrama, see Michael Booth, *English Melodrama* (London: Jenkins, 1965), pp. 30–32.

9. Martin Meisel, *Realizations: Narrative, Pictorial, and Theatrical Arts in Nineteenth-Century England* (Princeton, N.J.: Princeton University Press, 1983), pp. 148–54.

10. W. S. Gilbert, *Ages Ago*, in *Gilbert Before Sullivan: Six Comic Plays by W. S. Gilbert*, ed. Jane W. Stedman (Chicago: University of Chicago Press, 1967), pp. 81–106.

11. Gilbert, *Ages Ago*, p. 90.

12. Adrienne Munich interprets the women's roles as three reactions to male aggression: "Mad Margaret's wild frustration; Rose Maybud's seductiveness; Dame Han-

nah's meek, nervous victimhood" (*Queen Victoria's Secrets* [New York: Columbia University Press, 1996], pp. 3, 120). Her argument supports mine.

13. Bargainnier, "*Ruddigore*," p. 9.

14. The groundbreaking study is Nancy K. Miller, *The Heroine's Text: Readings in the French and English Novel, 1722–1782* (New York: Columbia University Press, 1980). For the "marriage plot" in its Victorian setting, see Joseph Boone, *Tradition Counter Tradition: Love and the Form of Fiction* (Chicago: University of Chicago Press, 1989).

15. Bargainnier, "*Ruddigore*," p. 14.

16. Audrey Williamson, *Gilbert and Sullivan Opera: A New Assessment* (New York: Macmillan, 1953), pp. 168, 5.

17. Rose's discovery hanging in a dish cover on the workhouse door surely was another Gilbertian influence on Oscar Wilde's *The Importance of Being Earnest*, whose hero was found as a baby in a handbag in the left-luggage office at Victoria Station.

18. Gilbert directed Rose to be utterly un-self-conscious and sincere in her consultation of the book, according to Percy Fitzgerald, *The Savoy Opera and the Savoyards* (London: Chatto & Windus, 1899), quoted in Bargainnier, "*Ruddigore*," p. 179n. On the proliferation of conduct books, see Mary Poovey, *The Proper Lady and the Woman Writer: Ideology as Style in the Works of Mary Wollstonecraft, Mary Shelley, and Jane Austen* (Chicago: University of Chicago Press, 1984), and Sarah Stickney Ellis, *The Women of England: Their Social Duties and Domestic Habits* (London: Fisher, 1839), *The Daughters of England: Their Position in Society, Character, and Responsibilities* (London: Fisher, 1842), *The Wives of England: Their Relative Duties, Domestic Influence, and Social Obligations* (London: Fisher, 1843), and *The Mothers of England: Their Influence and Responsibility* (London: Fisher, 1844). On the foundation of the Sunday schools in 1811 with Dissenting Church backing, see Herbert Schlossberg, *The Silent Revolution and the Making of Victorian England* (Columbus: Ohio State University Press, 2000), p. 207.

19. Jane W. Stedman, "W. S. Gilbert: His Comic Techniques and Their Development" (Ph.D. diss., University of Chicago, 1956), quoted in Bargainnier, "*Ruddigore*," p. 11.

20. Munich, *Queen Victoria's Secrets*, pp. 121–22. Munich also argues that Margaret's deference to Despard is a parody of Queen Victoria's excessive deference to Prince Albert.

21. *Ruddigore* gave a patter song to Robin in act 2—two versions, in fact—but they were cut. For the texts of both versions, see Bradley, *Complete Annotated Gilbert and Sullivan*, pp. 732–34.

22. Isaac Goldberg, *The Story of Gilbert and Sullivan; or, The "Compleat" Savoyard* (New York: Simon and Schuster, 1928), p. 198. For more on the patter song, see chapter 3.

11. *The Yeomen of the Guard*

1. Quoted in Reginald Allen, ed., *The First Night Gilbert and Sullivan: Containing Complete Librettos of the Fourteen Operas, Exactly as Presented at Their Première Performances; Together with Facsimiles of the First-Night Programmes* (New York: Heritage Club, 1958), p. 307.

2. Isaac Goldberg, *The Story of Gilbert and Sullivan; or, The "Compleat" Savoyard* (New York: Simon and Schuster, 1928), p. 363.

3. For a detailed account of the plot's shortcomings, see Audrey Williamson, *Gilbert and Sullivan Opera: A New Assessment* (New York: Macmillan, 1953), pp. 201–10.

4. Goldberg, *Story of Gilbert and Sullivan*, p. 370.

5. Almost all the other Savoy operas emphasize their special generic status as "Nautical Comic," for example, or "Fairy," "Japanese," or "Supernatural" opera. Allen makes this point in *First Night Gilbert and Sullivan*, p. 309.

6. Allen, ed., *First Night Gilbert and Sullivan*, p. 312.

7. Quoted in Allen, ed., *First Night Gilbert and Sullivan*, p. 308.

8. Robert A. Hall Jr., "The Satire of *The Yeomen of the Guard*," in *W. S. Gilbert: A Century of Scholarship and Commentary*, ed. John Bush Jones (New York: New York University Press, 1970), p. 225n.22. He gives the examples of Beethoven's *Fidelio* (1805) and Luigi Cherubini's *Les deux journées, ou Le porteur d'eau (The Two Days, or The Water Carrier,* 1799). On the relation between opéra comique and the political and tragic themes of the rescue operas, see Carl Dahlhaus, *Nineteenth-Century Music*, trans. J. Bradford Robinson (Berkeley: University of California Press, 1991), p. 65.

9. Harley Granville-Barker, "Exit Planché—Enter Gilbert," in *The Eighteen-Sixties: Essays by Fellows of the Royal Society of Literature*, ed. John Drinkwater (Cambridge: Cambridge University Press, 1932), pp. 147–48, cited in Hall, "Satire of *The Yeomen of the Guard*," pp. 221, 224n.14.

10. Allen, ed., *First Night Gilbert and Sullivan*, p. 312.

11. *The Bab Ballads of W. S. Gilbert*, ed. James Ellis (Cambridge, Mass.: Belknap Press of Harvard University Press, 1970), pp. 200–203, 61.

12. Goldberg, *Story of Gilbert and Sullivan*, pp. 359, 363–64, 369.

13. Goldberg, *Story of Gilbert and Sullivan*, p. 369.

14. Williamson, *Gilbert and Sullivan Opera*, p. 217. Gayden Wren mentions Wilfred Shadbolt's erotic sadism, in *A Most Ingenious Paradox: The Art of Gilbert and Sullivan* (Oxford: Oxford University Press, 2001), p. 215.

15. Hall, "Satire of *The Yeomen of the Guard*," p. 223.

16. For debates on this point, see Williamson, *Gilbert and Sullivan Opera*, pp. 223–26. She interprets Sullivan's mature style as a blend of Wagnerian and early English influences (p. 226).

17. On Sullivan's use of the sonata form, see Gervase Hughes, *The Music of Arthur Sullivan* (New York: St. Martin's Press, 1960), pp. 138–39; on the opening Tower motif, see p. 97.

18. Hughes, *Music of Arthur Sullivan*, pp. 143, 141.

19. Williamson compares the musical effects of "Bim-a-boom" in the quartet "Strange adventure" with the "Fal-la" refrain in *Ruddigore*, in *Gilbert and Sullivan Opera*, p. 219.

20. Thus I have taken David Lowenthal's title slightly, but not entirely, out of context: *The Past Is a Foreign Country* (Cambridge: Cambridge University Press, 1999).

21. Ronald Hutton, *The Rise and Fall of Merrie England: The Ritual Year, 1400–1700* (Oxford: Oxford University Press, 1994).

22. William Hazlitt, "Merry England," in *Lectures on the English Comic Writers* (London: Taylor and Hessey, 1819).

23. Barry Cornwall, *English Songs and Other Small Poems* (London: Chapman and Hall, 1851), pp. 101–2.

24. William Sandys's edited volume, *Christmas Carols Ancient and Modern* (London: Richard Beckley, 1833), was presented as a collection of folk carols from the fifteenth to the seventeenth century, but we now know that he composed some of the carols.

25. Examples of the relatively recent institution of traditions that are then imagined to have much older roots are offered in Eric Hobsbawm and Terence Ranger, eds., *The Invention of Tradition* (Cambridge: Cambridge University Press, 1992).

26. Friedrich Engels, *The Condition of the Working Class in England in 1844* (New York: Cosimo, 2008), pp. 293–94.

27. Patrick Wright, *On Living in an Old Country: The National Past in Contemporary Britain* (London: Verso, 1985). Under the term "deep England" movement, the viewpoints of Wright and Angus Calder have been grouped together and criticized for their idealization of the English past.

28. Ian Bradley discusses the historical Sir Richard Cholmondeley in *The Complete Annotated Gilbert and Sullivan* (Oxford: Oxford University Press, 1996), p. 772.

29. Bradley, *Complete Annotated Gilbert and Sullivan*, p. 830.

30. Quoted in Allen, ed., *First Night Gilbert and Sullivan*, p. 308.

31. Svetlana Boym, *The Future of Nostalgia* (New York: Basic Books, 2002). Her introduction discusses the chief critical objections to nostalgia ("Taboo on Nostalgia?" pp. xiii–xix). See also Nicholas Dames, *Amnesiac Selves: Nostalgia, Forgetting, and British Fiction, 1810–1870* (Oxford: Oxford University Press, 2003).

32. This is the view of Wren, *Most Ingenious Paradox*, p. 208.

33. George Robert Sims, *The Lights O' London*, in *The Lights O' London and Other Victorian Plays*, ed. Michael Booth (Oxford: Oxford University Press, 1995), pp. 104–70.

34. Quoted in Williamson, *Gilbert and Sullivan Opera*, p. 227, and Jane W. Stedman, *W. S. Gilbert: A Classic Victorian and His Theatre* (Oxford: Oxford University Press, 1996), p. 251. The original intention was to give *Yeomen* a modern setting and a burlesque treatment, but Gilbert decided to make it "a romantic and dramatic piece, and to put it back into Elizabethan times" (Bradley, *Complete Annotated Gilbert and Sullivan*, quoted in Wren, *Most Ingenious Paradox*, p. 343).

35. On Touchstone from *As You Like It*, see Andrew Goodman, *Gilbert and Sullivan at Law* (Madison, N.J.: Fairleigh Dickinson University Press, 1983), p. 171. For Williamson's evaluation of Jack Point in relation to all the Shakespearean figures, see *Gilbert and Sullivan Opera*, pp. 209–10

36. Goldberg, *Story of Gilbert and Sullivan*, p. 359.

37. Hughes, *Music of Arthur Sullivan*, pp. 143–44. See also Goldberg, *Story of Gilbert and Sullivan*, p. 367.

38. The history of this question—whether Jack Point faints or dies—is given in Stedman, *W. S. Gilbert*, p. 252. Compare Hans Sachs's loss of Eva in Wagner's *Die Meistersinger* (1868), which Sullivan thought the finest comic opera ever written.

39. Quoted in Wren, *Most Ingenious Paradox*, p. 207.

40. Williamson, *Gilbert and Sullivan Opera*, pp. 208, 230–31.

41. Hall, "Satire of *The Yeomen of the Guard*," p. 220.

42. Goldberg, *Story of Gilbert and Sullivan*, p. 369.

43. Compare the sad, jealous clown in Ruggero Leoncavallo's opera *Pagliacci* (*Clowns*, 1892)—a jealous husband in a troupe of commedia dell'arte strolling players in the nineteenth century—whose character recalls that of sixteenth-century Italian commedia, as well as Pierrot, the French variant of the prototypical sad clown.

44. For a compendium of such views, see Hall, "Satire of *The Yeomen of the Guard*," p. 220. Sometimes this attribution occurs along with the customary idealization, such as in Goldberg's view that Jack is "Gilbert's spiritual testament . . . his apologia for the art of the professional comic" (*Story of Gilbert and Sullivan*, p. 364).

45. Stedman, *W. S. Gilbert*, p. 252. David Eden claims, however, that Gilbert said the character of Jack Point contained his "real self." In his reading of *The Yeomen of the Guard*, Eden marshals biographical evidence and speculation about Gilbert's possible disappointed love for Euphrosyne Parepa (later Parepa-Rosa) in order to argue for the identification of Gilbert with Jack Point, in *Gilbert and Sullivan: The Creative Conflict* (Madison, N.J.: Fairleigh Dickinson University Press, 1989), pp. 53, 109–20.

46. Granville-Barker, "Exit Planché—Enter Gilbert," pp. 147–48.

12. *The Gondoliers*

1. John Ruskin, *The Stones of Venice*, vol. 2 (1853), in *The Works of John Ruskin*, ed. E. T. Cook and Alexander Wedderburn (New York: Longmans, Green, 1903), vol. 9, pp. 38–39. The Doge's Palace is also the central building of the Renaissance, which Ruskin despised.

2. On Venice as a particular site for the nineteenth-century fantasy, see Tony Tanner, *Venice Desired* (Cambridge, Mass.: Harvard University Press, 1992), and Jonah Siegel, *Haunted Museum: Longing, Travel, and the Art-Romance Tradition* (Princeton, N.J.: Princeton University Press, 2005), pp. 58–59.

3. In some respects, *The Yeomen of the Guard* is "not a new beginning but an end," "less an innovation than a culmination," most striking not in "how different [it] is from its predecessors" but in "how little it resembles its successors" (Gayden Wren, *A Most Ingenious Paradox: The Art of Gilbert and Sullivan* [Oxford: Oxford University Press, 2001], p. 202).

4. Leslie Baily, *The Gilbert and Sullivan Book* (London: Spring Books, 1952), p. 347.

5. On this performance, see George Rowell, *Queen Victoria Goes to the Theatre* (London: Elek, 1978), pp. 94, 107–8, 138. Among his discussion of many other command performances, Richard W. Schoch does not discuss this one in *Queen Victoria and the Theatre of Her Age* (Basingstoke: Palgrave Macmillan, 2004).

6. George Bernard Shaw, "Sturgis and Sullivan," in *Shaw on Music*, ed. Eric Bentley (New York: Doubleday, 1955; New York: Applause Books, 1983), p. 196.

7. Wren, *Most Ingenious Paradox*, p. 230.

8. Audrey Williamson analyzes the musical heritage of the cachucha in *Gilbert and Sullivan Opera: A New Assessment* (New York: Macmillan, 1953), pp. 252–53. For one version of the "cipher quarrel," see Jane W. Stedman, *W. S. Gilbert: A Classic Victorian and His Theatre* (Oxford: Oxford University Press, 1996), 257–62.

9. Wren gives his account of the "cipher quarrel" in *Most Ingenious Paradox*, pp. 228–30. He further argues that the three last operas involve self-reference (p. 228).

10. Jessie Bond, *The Life and Reminiscences of Jessie Bond, the Old Savoyard (as Told to Ethel MacGeorge)* (London: Bodley Head, 1930).

11. John Wolfson makes a similar argument about *The Grand Duke*—that its plot reflects and comments on difficulties within the D'Oyly Carte Opera Company—in *Final Curtain: The Last Gilbert and Sullivan Operas* (London: Chappell, in association with Deutsch, 1976), pp. 83–91.

12. Snarler [W. S. Gilbert], "Out of Town Talk," *Fun*, August 26, 1865, p. 141, quoted in Max Keith Sutton, *W. S. Gilbert* (Boston: Twayne, 1975), p. 30.

13. For a discussion of law and character, see Alan Fischler, *Modified Rapture: Comedy in W. S. Gilbert's Savoy Operas* (Charlottesville: University Press of Virginia, 1991), especially pp. 76–81.

14. Williamson, *Gilbert and Sullivan Opera*, pp. 237–43.

15. Christopher Rumsey, *The Rise and Fall of British Republican Clubs, 1871–1874* (Oswestry: Quinta Press, 2000). See also Margot Finn, *After Chartism: Class and Nation in English Radical Politics, 1848–1874* (Cambridge: Cambridge University Press, 1993).

16. Stephanie Kuduk Weiner, *Republican Politics and English Poetry, 1789–1874* (New York: Palgrave Macmillan, 2005).

17. The jacket of Rumsey, *Rise and Fall of British Republican Clubs*, is illustrated with a cartoon from the April 8, 1871, issue of *Punch*. Titled "A French Lesson," it depicts a dignified, iconic female representation of France ready to strike, with her fist, a scruffy lout carrying a hammer and a rolled-up broadside labeled "Republicanism." Her words to him, given in the caption, are, "Is *that* the sort of thing you want, you little idiot?" Social chaos, perhaps even war, is visible in the vague background.

18. Mary Poovey, "Speculation and Virtue in *Our Mutual Friend*," in *Making a Social Body: British Cultural Formation, 1830–1864* (Chicago: University of Chicago Press, 1995), pp. 155–81. Her discussion of Malcolm Meason is on pp. 160–64.

13. *Utopia, Limited*

1. Reproductions of hand-colored photographs of the ravishing sets by Hawes Craven may be seen in John Wolfson, *Final Curtain: The Last Gilbert and Sullivan Operas* (London: Chappell, in association with Deutsch, 1976), following p. 102. For contemporary comments on these sets "of bewildering splendour," see Reginald Allen, ed., *The First Night Gilbert and Sullivan: Containing Complete Librettos of the Fourteen Operas, Exactly as Presented at Their Première Performances; Together with Facsimiles of the First-Night Programmes* (New York: Heritage Club, 1958), pp. 378–79.

2. W. S. Gilbert, plot book for *Utopia, Limited*, facing p. 6, The Pierpont Morgan Library, New York, The Gilbert and Sullivan Collection.

3. Wolfson suggests a connection between the Utopians' "raging gibberish" and the name of King Lobengula of Matabeleland, who had been sent a conciliatory deputa-

tion of First Life Guards a few years before the production of *Utopia, Limited*, in *Final Curtain*, p. 58n.

4. Unlike earlier melodrama, which was often characterized by imperialist patriotism, "late-century . . . imperialist drama [was] largely concerned . . . with rebellion in the colonies, and with asserting Britain's power and fitness to rule subject peoples" (Michael Booth, "Soldiers of the Queen: Drury Lane Imperialism," in *Melodrama: The Cultural Emergence of a Genre*, ed. Michael Hays and Anastasia Nikolopoulou [New York: St. Martin's Press, 1996], p. 6).

5. Extravaganza topicality often broaches serious political issues, in its glancing way. For example, the Ogre Ravagio in James Robinson Planche's *The Bee and the Orange Tree; or, The Four Wishes* (1845) is clearly a personification of industrial capitalism, while *The Seven Champions of Christendom* (1849) surveys the unrest in Europe; although it seems "smug and chauvinistic . . . to modern taste," the revue was a huge success (Donald Roy, introduction to *Plays by James Robinson Planché*, ed. Donald Roy [Cambridge: Cambridge University Press, 1986], pp. 15, 20).

  Besides this appearance of Captain Corcoran, another Savoy self-reference to the Mikado of Japan occurs when Lady Sophy urges King Paramount to slay the scribbler who is writing lies about him in the *Palace Peeper*, for that would mean that he would have to slay himself.

6. Albert I. Borowitz, "Gilbert and Sullivan on Corporate Law," *American Bar Association Journal* 59 (1973): 1278.

7. For accounts of the Panama Canal scandal and the Glasgow Bank fraud case, see Borowitz, "Gilbert and Sullivan on Corporate Law," pp. 1280–81. For accounts of the "carpet quarrel," see Isaac Goldberg, *The Story of Gilbert and Sullivan; or, The "Compleat" Savoyard* (New York: Simon and Schuster, 1928), pp. 386–90, and Leslie Baily, *The Gilbert and Sullivan Book* (London: Spring Books, 1952), pp. 323–32. For the story of the Royal English Opera House (later the Palace Theatre), see Wolfson, *Final Curtain*, pp. 23–24.

8. Borowitz, "Gilbert and Sullivan on Corporate Law," p. 1278.

9. For the provisions of the acts of 1856 and 1862, see Borowitz, "Gilbert and Sullivan on Corporate Law." For the history of the joint-stock company, see Fernand Braudel, *The Wheels of Commerce: Civilization and Capitalism*, vol. 2, *Fifteenth to Eighteenth Century* (New York: Harper & Row, 1982), pp. 433–55, especially pp. 439–42.

10. Braudel, *Wheels of Commerce*, pp. 453–54.

11. Mary Poovey details the sequence of this legislation, from the Registration Act (1844), through the Limited Liability Act (1855) and the Joint Stock Companies Act (1856), to, finally, the comprehensive Companies Act (1862), in *Making a Social Body: British Cultural Formation, 1830–1864* (Chicago: University of Chicago Press, 1995), pp. 156–57.

12. Laurence Oliphant, "The Autobiography of a Joint-Stock Company (Limited)," *Blackwood's Edinburgh Magazine*, July 1876, in *The Financial System in Nineteenth-Century Britain*, ed. Mary Poovey (New York: Oxford University Press, 2003), p. 355; Poovey, *Making a Social Body*, pp. 155–81, with the discussion of Malcolm Meason on pp. 160–64.

13. Poovey, *Making a Social Body*, pp. 161–62.

14. For an expanded version of this argument, see Carolyn Williams, "*Utopia, Limited*: Nationalism, Empire, and Parody in the Comic Operas of Gilbert and Sullivan," in *Cultural Politics at the Fin de Siècle*, ed. Sally Ledger and Scott McCracken (Cambridge: Cambridge University Press, 1995), pp. 221–47.

15. Allen, ed., *First Night Gilbert and Sullivan*, pp. 379–80.

16. Allen, ed., *First Night Gilbert and Sullivan*, p. 379.

17. George Bernard Shaw, *Music in London, 1890–1894*, vol. 28 of *The Collected Works of George Bernard Shaw*, Ayot St. Lawrence ed. (New York: Wise, 1931), p. 66.

18. David Cannadine, "The Context, Performance, and Meaning of Ritual: The British Monarchy and the 'Invention of Tradition,' c. 1820–1977," in *The Invention of Tradition*, ed. Eric Hobsbawm and Terence Ranger (Cambridge: Cambridge University Press, 1983), p. 124.

19. Allen, ed., *First Night Gilbert and Sullivan*, p. 379.

20. On colonial mimicry, see Homi Bhabha, "Of Mimicry and Man: The Ambivalence of Colonial Discourse," *October* 28 (1984): 124–34.

21. Ian Bradley has collected a fascinating array of critical responses to the scene of the Cabinet Council, in *The Complete Annotated Gilbert and Sullivan* (Oxford: Oxford University Press, 1996). For the allegation that the idea had been plagiarized from F. C. Burnand's burlesque *The Very Latest Edition of Black-Eyed Susan; or, The Little Bill that Was Taken Up* (1866), which features a court-martial in the form of a minstrel show, see p. 1050.

22. The best accounts of the adaptation of the minstrel show to an English setting are J. S. Bratton, "English Ethiopians: British Audiences and Black-Face Acts, 1635–1865," *Yearbook of English Studies* 11 (1981): 127–42, and Michael Pickering, "White Skin, Black Masks: 'Nigger' Minstrelsy in Victorian Britain," in *Music Hall: Performance and Style*, ed. J. S. Bratton (Milton Keynes: Open University Press, 1986), pp. 70–91. Michael Pickering's *Blackface Minstrelsy in Britain* (Aldershot: Ashgate, 2008), the definitive scholarly account of this subject, was published too late to be fully assimilated into this study .

23. Other explanations are given in Bratton, "English Ethiopians," and Pickering, "White Skin, Black Mask."

24. William Torbert Leonard, *Masquerade in Black* (Metuchen, N.J.: Scarecrow Press, 1986), p. 232.

25. It is reproduced in Bradley, *Complete Annotated Gilbert and Sullivan*, pp. 1048–50.

26. Bradley quotes George Bernard Shaw's lavish praise for this number, in *Complete Annotated Gilbert and Sullivan*, p. 1050.

27. George Eastman launched the Kodak camera in 1888, according to Bradley, *Complete Annotated Gilbert and Sullivan*, p. 990.

28. Quoted in Elizabeth Helsinger, Robin Lauterbach Sheets, and William Veeder, "Eliza Lynn Linton and 'the Girl of the Period,'" in *The Woman Question: Society and Literature in Britain and America, 1837–1883*, vol. 1, *Defining Voices* (Chicago: University of Chicago Press, 1989), pp. 104, 112.

29. On racial mixture and intermarriage, and the reading of culture through allegorical marriages, see James Buzard, *Disorienting Fiction: The Autoethnographic Work of Nineteenth-Century British Novels* (Princeton, N.J.: Princeton University Press,

2005), p. 297–98. The differences between "natives" and English can be bridged through "allegorical unions," in what Buzard calls "boundary-work" (p. 300).

30. Max Keith Sutton also calls attention to the production of anxiety in "a decade of imperial self-importance" (*W. S. Gilbert* [Boston: Twayne, 1975], p. 116).

14. *The Grand Duke*

1. Fredric Jameson's notion of pastiche as "blank parody" (neutralized, nonintentional, normless) is developed in "Postmodernism and Consumer Society," in *The Anti-Aesthetic: Essays on Postmodern Culture*, ed. Hal Foster (Port Townsend, Wash.: Bay Press, 1983), pp. 111–25, and "Postmodernism, or the Cultural Logic of Late Capitalism," *New Left Review* 146 (1984): 53–92. A strong argument can be mounted against what Margaret Rose calls Jameson's "willful redefinition of pastiche as postmodern" (*Parody: Ancient, Modern, and Post-Modern* [Cambridge: Cambridge University Press, 1993], pp. 220–32). Certain practices now usually associated with the "postmodern" are common in late-nineteenth-century variants.

2. Reinhard Strohm, "Pasticcio," in *The New Grove Dictionary of Music and Musicians*, ed. Stanley Sadie (London: Macmillan, 1980), vol. 14, pp. 288–89; Richard Traubner, "Pasticcio and Zarzuela, Italy and Russia," in *Operetta: A Theatrical History* (Oxford: Oxford University Press, 1983), pp. 423–29.

3. Quoted in Clifton Fadiman and André Bernard, eds., *Bartlett's Book of Anecdotes* (New York: Little, Brown, 2000), pp. 236–37. In other sources, Gilbert is quoted as having said "Pooh" or "Posh" rather than "Plosh." The anecdote contains the hint of a Tennyson parody as well—specifically of line 17 of "Claribel: A Melody," in *Poems, Chiefly Lyrical* (1830): "The callow throstle lispeth."

4. A Trembling Beginner [W. S. Gilbert], "The Art of Parody," *Fun*, September 9, 1865, p. 169.

5. W. S. Gilbert, *Rosencrantz and Guildenstern: A Tragic Episode in Three Tableaux*, in *Original Plays*, 3rd ser. (London: Chatto & Windus, 1923), pp. 75–89.

6. Richard W. Schoch, *Not Shakespeare: Bardolatry and Burlesque in the Nineteenth Century* (Cambridge: Cambridge University Press, 2002), pp. 6, 28.

7. Max Keith Sutton, "The Significance of *The Grand Duke*," in *Gilbert and Sullivan: Papers Presented at the International Conference Held at the University of Kansas in May 1970*, ed. James Helyar (Lawrence: University of Kansas Libraries, 1971), pp. 223–24.

8. For the conventions of classical allusion in classical extravaganza, see chapter 1. Like the mixture of bouffe and extravaganza humor, *The Grand Duke*'s mixture of French and Greek (with imaginary German thrown in) intends to delight a connoisseur audience, as it did in the finale to act 1 of *Iolanthe*.

9. The duchy's name refers to an ancient monetary unit in Germany, the pfennig, devalued since the introduction of the gold mark in 1873 (1 mark = 100 pfennig), and thus it announces the opera's focus on impecuniousness and excessive thrift.

10. Jonathan Strong, "Remarks to the Valley Light Opera" (paper presented at the spring meeting of the Valley Light Opera, Amherst, Mass., 2001), p. 2. I owe a great deal to Jonathan Strong in general, but especially in this chapter.

11. Traubner, *Operetta*, p. 182.

12. Strong, "Remarks," pp. 8–9.

13. Quoted in Reginald Allen, ed., *The First Night Gilbert and Sullivan: Containing Complete Librettos of the Fourteen Operas, Exactly as Presented at Their Première Performances; Together with Facsimiles of the First-Night Programmes* (New York: Heritage Club, 1958), p. 415; Audrey Williamson, *Gilbert and Sullivan Opera: A New Assessment* (New York: Macmillan, 1953), p. 273.

14. Quoted in Williamson, *Gilbert and Sullivan Opera*, p. 273.

15. *Graphic*, March 14, 1896, quoted in Max Keith Sutton, *W. S. Gilbert* (Boston: Twayne, 1975), p. 112.

16. Williamson offers the strongest critique of the plot, in *Gilbert and Sullivan Opera*, p. 269.

17. David Weir, *Anarchy and Culture: The Aesthetic Politics of Modernism* (Amherst: University of Massachusetts Press, 1997).

18. A "lost song" from *The Grand Duke*, "The Stroller's Song," compares a monarch to an actor, as pointed out by John Wolfson, *Final Curtain: The Last Gilbert and Sullivan Operas* (London: Chappell, in association with Deutsch, 1976), pp. 85–88. It was replaced by "Ernest's Song," which also considers how hard it is to manage a theatrical troupe.

19. Sutton, "Significance of *The Grand Duke*," p. 223.

20. Wolfson, *Final Curtain*, pp. 68–69. This particular plot book reposes in the W. S. Gilbert Papers, British Library, London.

21. Wolfson carefully analyzes the changes Gilbert wrought on these sources, in *Final Curtain*, pp. 69–78.

22. Strong, "Remarks," p. 7; Jonathan Strong, conversations with the author.

23. Wolfson helpfully explains the effect on the plot of the casting of Ilka von Palmay, in *Final Curtain*, pp. 68, 78.

24. Wolfson advances an intriguing theory that Gilbert may have intended a satire on the "German" line of the British monarchy. Julia Jellicoe's "Anglo-German dyslexia," as Wolfson calls it, could have been inspired by two Victorias: "a German-speaking Queen in England and an English-speaking Queen in Germany" (*Final Curtain*, p. 81). Although Wolfson senses a muffled critique of Queen Victoria in the opera, I would argue, instead, that Gilbert had been examining the polyglot nature of English culture from the beginning of his collaboration with Sullivan.

25. Sutton, "Significance of *The Grand Duke*," p. 222.

26. Sutton, "Significance of *The Grand Duke*," pp. 221–28.

27. Sutton does emphasize the importance of the "professionals, who sink their identities in their public roles and become, in a comic sense, hollow men" ("Significance of *The Grand Duke*," p. 225). He points out that the professional man abounds in Gilbert's work. See also chapter 3.

28. Sutton, "Significance of *The Grand Duke*," p. 222. Unlike the Lord Chancellor in *Iolanthe*, Julia has not even the residual sense of a "private self with whom she can carry on debates" (p. 225).

29. This specific genre is used only once in the Savoy operas, as Ian Bradley points out in *The Complete Annotated Gilbert and Sullivan* (Oxford: Oxford University Press,

1996), p. 1160. On the popularity of Victorian monodramatic melodrama (declaimed text set to musical accompaniment or introduced and concluded with music), see David Mayer, "Parlour and Platform Melodrama," in *Melodrama: The Cultural Emergence of a Genre*, ed. Michael Hays and Anastasia Nicolopoulou (New York: St. Martin's Press, 1996), pp. 211–34. For a longer history of monodrama, from Rousseau's *Pygmalion* (1762) to Tennyson's *Maud* (1855), see A. Dwight Culler, "Monodrama and the Dramatic Monologue," *PMLA* 90 (1975): 336–85.

30. Strong conversation, October 2008.
31. Denis Diderot, "The Paradox of the Actor," in *Selected Writings on Art and Literature*, trans. and ed. Geoffrey Bremner (Harmondsworth: Penguin, 1994), pp. 98-158.
32. Sutton, "Significance of *The Grand Duke*," pp. 221, 228nn.3, 4, citing John Bush Jones, "Gilbert and Sullivan's Serious Satire: More Fact than Fancy," *Western Humanities Review* 21 (1967): 219, and Barbara W. Tuchman, *The Proud Tower: A Portrait of the World Before the War, 1890–1914* (New York: Macmillan, 1966).
33. Sutton, "Significance of *The Grand Duke*," p. 228. Sutton also compares *The Grand Duke* with Anton Chekhov's *The Seagull* (1896) and Franz Kafka's *The Trial* (1925) (pp. 224, 226–27).
34. Alan Fischler argues that this conclusion "entirely reverses the pattern of the transformation found in pantomime and extravaganza" (*Modified Rapture: Comedy in W. S. Gilbert's Savoy Operas* [Charlottesville: University Press of Virginia, 1991], p. 66).
35. Sutton, "Significance of *The Grand Duke*," p. 224.
36. Strong, "Remarks," pp. 6–7.

After Gilbert and Sullivan

1. Quoted in Jane W. Stedman, *W. S. Gilbert: A Classic Victorian and His Theatre* (Oxford: Oxford University Press, 1996), p. 326.
2. A wonderful history of the phenomenon is David Cannadine, "Gilbert and Sullivan: The Making and Un-Making of a British 'Tradition,'" in *Myths of the English*, ed. Roy Porter (Cambridge: Polity Press, in association with Blackwell, 1992), pp. 12–32.
3. Fredric Woodbridge Wilson, *An Introduction to the Gilbert and Sullivan Operas: From the Collection of the Pierpont Morgan Library* (New York: Pierpont Morgan Library, in association with Dover, 1989), p. 62. Using the three little maids to advertise a corset is meant to be especially funny, since the actresses did not wear corsets under their Japanese costumes. See chapter 9.
4. Ian Bradley, *Oh Joy! Oh Rapture! The Enduring Phenomenon of Gilbert and Sullivan* (Oxford: Oxford University Press, 2005), pp. 115–42.
5. Cannadine credits Gilbert and Sullivan with having been "theatrical innovators so deliberate and so successful that they might almost be called revolutionaries" ("Gilbert and Sullivan," p. 13). However, their innovative quality was obscured in the process of the Savoy operas' becoming a national institution, he argues, emphasizing the deleterious effects of "tradition" (pp. 24–28). Thus, for Cannadine, the expiration of the copyrights has enabled the operas to be "emancipated from the thralldom of British 'tradition'" (p. 29). Bradley, though, admittedly with tongue in cheek, refers

to them as "the sacred texts," while enjoying many revisions of the canon (*Oh Joy! Oh Rapture!* p. ix and passim).

6. Walter Pater, writing not about performance, but about poetry, in "Aesthetic Poetry," in *Selected Writings of Walter Pater*, ed. Harold Bloom (Columbia: Columbia University Press, 1974), p. 196.

7. Quoted in Fredric Woodbridge Wilson, "Richard D'Oyly Carte and the Future" (lecture delivered at the Harvard College Library, Cambridge, Mass., April 3, 2001; the third of three lectures—"The Gilbert and Sullivan Legacy"—presented on the occasion of "The Gilbert & Sullivan Operas: A Centenary Exhibition," Harvard Theatre Collection / Pusey Library, November 22, 2000–April 13, 2001).

8. Richard W. Schoch, "The Art of the Topical," in introduction to *Victorian Theatrical Burlesques*, ed. Richard W. Schoch (Aldershot: Ashgate, 2003), pp. xx–xxii. Planché's use of this device is well known. For examples, see Donald Roy, introduction to *Plays by James Robinson Planché*, ed. Donald Roy (Cambridge: Cambridge University Press, 1986), pp. 14–15.

9. Bradley, *Oh Joy! Oh Rapture!* pp. 159–78. For the numerical evidence, see p. 160.

Index

Numbers in italics refer to pages on which illustrations appear.

Behn, Aphra, 130
"Behold the Lord High Executioner"
(*Mikado*), 24
Belasco, David, 268
bel canto style, 289
Bellini, Vincenzo, 25, 129, 193, 259, 289,
383n.42
Bells, The (Lewis), 281
Benedict, Julius, 76
Bey, Hakim, 139
Bickerstaff, Isaac, 76, 104
Big Momma's House (film), 214
bildungsroman, 11, 142
Billy Budd (Melville), 107
Bishop, Sir Henry Rowley, 259
"Black and White" *Mikado* (Miller), 369
Black-Ey'd Susan (Jerrold), 97, 99–101, 105,
108, 277, 385nn.7,22
Black-Eyed Sukey (Cooper), 385n.22
Blackwood's Edinburgh Magazine, 355
Blanchard, Edward, 37
Blanche, Lady (*Princess Ida*), 204, 209, 212,
235, 243, 249–52, 298
Bleak House (Dickens), 142, 407n.18
"Blue Blood" (*Iolanthe*), 322
Boileau, Nicolas, 38
Bond, Jessie: as Iolanthe, *218*; as Mad
Margaret, *289, 290*; as Pitti-Sing, 258,
270–71; as Tessa, 318
Bon Gaultier (William Edmonstoune
Aytoun and Theodore Martin), 8
Book of Tea, The (Okakura), 409n.49
Booth, Michael, 388n.18, 391n.56, 397n.3
Borowitz, Albert, 330
Boucicault, Dion, 277, 281
Boulton, Ernest, 404n.25
Bowles, Thomas Gibson, 106
Box and Cox (Morton), 2, 15
Boym, Svetlana, 304, 413n.31
Bracquemond, Félix, 265
Braddon, Mary Elizabeth, 360
Bradley, Ian, 72, 83, 141, 368–69, 379n.9,
389n.30, 407n.13, 420n.5
Brandram, Rosina: as Lady Jane, *210*; as
Lady Sophy, *339*; as Ruth, *138*

Bratton, J. S., 105, 385n.15, 386nn.26,33,34
Brecht, Bertold, 363
Brennan, Maggie, 205
bricolage, 133
Brideshead Revisited (Waugh), 370
Brigand and the Philosopher, The (Pyat),
389n.32
Brigands, Les (Offenbach), 13, 44, 131–32,
143, 389n.31
"British Tar, The" (Gilbert), *111*
"British Tar is a soaring soul, A" (*Pinafore*),
26, 109–10, 112, 113
Brittania (Mallett), 104
Brontë, Charlotte, 130, 260
Brooks, Peter, 385n.8
Brothers Grimm, 191
Brough, Robert B., 203, 206, 400n.48
Brown, John, 217
Brown, Mrs. Cimabue (du Maurier), 156,
157
Browning, Robert, 182, 185
Brünnhilde (*Rheingold*; Wagner), 217
Buchanan, Robert, 177–79, 181–82
Bucks and Blades, Chorus of (*Ruddigore*),
23, 274–75
Buddhism, 265
"Bumboat Woman's Story, The" (Gilbert),
108
Bunthorne, Reginald (*Patience*), 133, 204;
as aesthetic poet, 11, 152–53, 157, 159,
175–86, 288, 302; Grossmith as, 156;
Lady Jane and, 209–11; patter song of,
159–60, 171, 172, 177, 264; sexuality of,
167–73; Wilde and, 165–67, 169, 174
bureaucracy: capitalism and, 325–26, 328;
divided function and, 22, 49, 52, 109;
hierarchies of, 90, 102, 106, 320–21,
354; as incompetent, 16, 94, 101, 115,
129, 133; parody of, 40, 106–9, 121, 257,
267, 354, 370
"Buried Life, The" (Arnold), 357
burlesque: cross-dressing in, 194, 205,
223–25, 227, 233, *233*, 236–38, 404n.25;
double entendre in, 228, 250; extravaganza and, 38, 193, 203, 345–46,

burlesque (*continued*)
376n.10; as lower genre, 189, 191, 212,
223, 271–72, 336, 338; misogyny in,
234, 238, 245, 252; nautical themes
and, 13, 106–7, 108, 131, 385n.22; patter
tradition in, 91; as precursor genre, 18,
206, 239–40, 259, 311; puns in, 143, 232,
234, 242, 346, 360, *plate 7*; racism in,
270–71; rhymed couplets in, 18, 38, 107,
232–33, 233; as risqué, 237, 376n.10;
theater tradition and, 14, 21, 35–36, 60,
373n.24, 389n.29, 410n.4; topicality of,
91, 353, 368; travesty in, 4, 35, 47, 205,
336, 376n.10, 403n.18
"*burletta* rule," 127
Burnand, F. C., 2, 15, 44, 106–8, 154–57,
185, 386n.23
Burne-Jones, Edward, 266
Burstyn, Joan, 405n.42
Burton, Carrie, 207
Burton, Sir Richard Francis, 169–70
Burty, Philippe, 265
Butler, Samuel, 117
Buzard, James, 260, 407nn.17,18
Byron, George Gordon, Lord, 130, 277
Byron, H. J., 155

Cabinet Council (*Utopia*), 334, 336, 337,
417n.21
Calder, Angus, 413n.27
Calliope (Daphne; *Thespis*), 47, 48
Calverley, Charles Stuart, 185
Calverley, Colonel (*Patience*), 156, 160, 185,
302
Cannadine, David, 256, 335, 406n.1, 420n.5
Cannon, John, 368–69
cantata, 55, 56, 60
capitalism: as corporate, 93, 166, 315–17,
324–25, 330–34, 416n.5; D'Oyly Carte
Opera Company and, 39, 49, 53;
empire and, 6, 266, 340–43; limited
liability and, 327, 329–30
Capitalist, The (The Texas Mikado) (Ed J.
Smith), *plate 20*
Carlson, Marvin, 385n.7

Carlyle, Thomas, 301, 302, 387n.47
Carroll, Lewis, 11, 84, 383n.29
Carruthers, Dame (*Yeomen*), 213, 297–99,
303–4
Carte, Richard D'Oyly: "carpet quarrel"
and, 330; collaboration and, 1, 4, 56,
77–78, 371n.1; death of, 365; piracy and,
122–25; theater management and, 21,
151–52, 382n.15; Wilde and, 165, 173. *See
also* D'Oyly Carte Opera Company
Carte, Rupert D'Oyly, 367–68
Carus-Wilson, William, 183
Casilda (*Gondoliers*), 317, 322
Castle Adamant (*Princess Ida*), 223, 229,
235–36, 243–44, 247
Cellier, Alfred, 79, 406n.2
censorship, 11, 126–28, 175, 237, 256, 369,
378n.1, 389n.25
Cervantes, Miguel de, 312
chantey, 260, 308
Chaplin, Charlie, 53
Chariots of Fire (film), 370
Charity (Gilbert), 3, 68
Charles II (king of England), 126
Chartism, 320
chatter songs, 23, 94, 109, 139, 140, 383n.42.
See also patter
Chekhov, Anton, 420n.33
Cherubini, Luigi, 412n.8
Cheshire Cat (*Alice's Adventures in Won-
derland*; Carroll), 284, 293
Chesterton, G. K., 406n.4
Chiba, Yoko, 408nn.25,31
Children's Friend (journal), 183
Chodorow, Nancy, 401n.81
Cholmondeley, Sir Richard, 303
choreography: Chorus and, 17–19; in
Gondoliers, 27, 315–20, 322; in *Mikado*,
271; in *Pinafore*, 110; in *Thespis*, 52; in
Utopia, 334–35
Choristers' Union, 374n.41
Christianity, 40–41, 85
Christmas Carol, A (Dickens), 301–2
Christmas Carols Ancient and Modern
(Sandys), 301, 413n.24

Christy Minstrels, 334, 336

Clark, Edward H., 405n.42

Classical Dictionary (Lemprière), 39, 46

classical extravaganza, 37, 188, 194, 255, 344, 350, 418n.8; English comic opera and, 33–54, 347, 349; strong-minded woman and, 203. *See also* extravaganza; fairy extravaganza

Clay, Frederic, 3, 130, 215

Cleveland Street affair, 170–71, 404n.25

Clinton-Baddeley, V. C., 106, 107, 385n.15, 386n.38, 389n.29, 410n.4

Cobbett, William, 301

Cock and the Bull, The (Calverley), 185

Cockburn, Sir Alexander, 55, 62, 134

Coelina (Pixérécourt), 142

Cohen, Ed, 158, 165, 168

Coleridge, Samuel Taylor, 108, 189, 301

Colonel, The (Burnand), 154–56, 185

colonialism, 134, 323–43, 408n.24, 416n.4

"Come, bumpers—aye, ever-so-many" (*Grand Duke*), 351

comedietta, 3

"Come down, O maid" (Tennyson), 229–30, 403n.12

Comedy Opera Company, 78, 122–23

"Coming Race, The" (du Maurier), 163, *163*

commedia dell'arte, 35, 52, 194, 414n.43

Companies Act (1862), 323

Comte, Auguste, 377n.17

Condition of the Working Class in England in 1844, The (Engels), 302

confession: of Bunthorne, 159, 264; of Defendant (Edwin), 59–60; of Learned Judge, 61–63, 88–89, 133; of Little Buttercup, 98, 119, 146, 208; of Ludwig, 349–50; in melodrama, 5, 101; of Ruth, 147

Congreve, William, 104

consumerism, 89, 93, 115, 266, 292, 383n.40, 409n.37

contadine, Chorus of (*Gondoliers*), 316–17

Contes des fées, Les (*Fairy Tales*; Madame d'Aulnoy), 191

Contes nouveaux (*New Tales*; Madame d'Aulnoy), 191

Cooke, T. P., 105, 277

Cooper, Frederick Fox, 385n.22

Cooper, James Fenimore, 130, 410n.6

copyright performance, 123–24

Corcoran, Captain (*Pinafore*; *Utopia*), 108, 119–21, 135, 208, 328, 416n.5

Cornwall, Barry, 301

Corsair, The (Byron), 130

Corsican Brothers, The (Boucicault), 281

costumes: of aesthete, 157, 164, 166, *167*, 186; cultural clues and, 270–71, 342, 347, 360–61; cultural transformation and, 325–26, 332; in extravaganza, 35–36, 37; gender and, 19, 25, 27, 246–47; in *Mikado*, 258–59, 268, 270–71, 420n.3; in Savoy opera, 75, 193, 239; uniform and, 152, 159, 245, 264. *See also* cross-dressing

Cottis, Eileen, 147, 385n.16, 386n.38, 389n.30, 391n.56

Counsel for the Plaintiff (*Trial*), 59, *63*, 71

Count of Monte Cristo, The (Dumas), 277

County Councilor (*Utopia*), 328, 338

courtship: absurdity of, 4, 68–70, 235, 251, 285, 339–40, 354; behavior and, 46, 64, 154–56, 168, 354, 380n.32

Covent Garden Opera, 79, 126

Cox and Box (Sullivan), 2, 15, 44

Craven, Hawes, 415n.1

Crimean War, 405n.46

Criminal Law Amendment Act (1885), 170

Cross, J. T., 99

cross-dressing: in burlesque, 194, 205, 223–25, 227, 233, *233*, 236–38; criminality of, 404n.25; Dame figure and, 203, *207*, 236, 374n.37; in extravaganza, 20, 48–49, 130, 189, 194, 205–6, 215; female-to-male, *207*, 233, *233*, 236, 276, 305, *plate 14*; gender and, 22, 202–3, 269; Gilbert and, 189, 205, 215, 384n.48; in pantomime, 205–6, 213, 215, *plate 14*; in *Princess* (Tennyson), 228,

cross-dressing (*continued*)
231–32; in *Princess Ida*, 27, 223, 247–48,
250–52, 403nn.13,24; in productions
of Dickens, 205–6; re-dressing and,
189, 229; Ruth and, *138*, 208, 390n.43;
in *Thespis*, 20, 35–36, *36*, 47–49, 189;
undressing and, 223–24, 232, 246–47,
251. *See also* costumes
Crowther, Andrew, 28, 214–15, 241
Cyril (*Princess Ida*), 228, 233, 237–38, 242,
247, 250

Dahlhaus, Carl, 260, 375n.48
Daly, Dr. (*Sorcerer*), 82, 84–85, 96, 192
Dame figure: cross-dressing and, 203,
207, 236, 374n.37; Dame Carruthers as,
213, 279–99, 303–4; Dame Cherry as,
283–84; Dame Hannah as, 213, 285–86,
288, 291, 410n.12; Fairy Queen as, 189,
204–19; Katisha as, 204, 209, 211–12,
267; Lady Blanche as, 204, 209, 212;
misogyny and, 204–15, 252, 297–98,
390n.42, 401n.81; in pantomime, 4,
189, 205, 208, 213–19; in *Patience*, 204,
209–12, 216–17; Ruth as, 204, 208–9
Dane, Joseph A., 372n.16
Daniel Deronda (Eliot), 111
Daphne (*Thespis*), 47, *48*
Darwin, Charles, 160, 406n.7
"Darwinian Man" (Gilbert), 50, 225, 239–52,
248
D'Auban, Johnny, 271–72
Daughters of the Plough (*Princess Ida*), 243
d'Aulnoy, Madame, 191, 194
Dauntless, Dick (*Ruddigore*), 275–78, 288,
291, 410n.6, *plate 16*
David Copperfield (Dickens), 206
Davis, Natalie Zemon, 203, 212
Davis, Tracy, 193, 205
Deadeye, Dick (*Pinafore*), 98, 102–4, *103*,
106, 110
deadpan acting style, 7, 20, 28, 76
"deep England" movement, 413n.27
Defendant (Edwin; *Trial*), 55, 57–64,
69–71, 73, 160, 208, *plate 5*

"Defendant's Song" (*Trial*), 27, 59–60
deflation: humor and, 10, 33–42, 61, 76, 85,
90, 351; parody and, 38, 181, 234, 251,
271, 344, 347
Defoe, Daniel, 130
Delacorte Theater (New York), 369
democratization, 13, 42–43, 49, 82, 90,
385n.8
Denisoff, Dennis, 168–69, 171
D'Ennery, Adolphe, 295
Dent, John, 127
Derrida, Jacques, 373n.23
Deux aveugles, Les (*The Two Blind Men*;
Offenbach), 44
Deux journées, Les (*The Two Days*; Cheru-
bini), 412n.8
Devil's Elixir, The (Fitzball), 83
Diana (Nicemis; *Thespis*), 34, 47–48, *48*
Dibdin, Thomas J., 130, 147
Dickens, Charles: breach of promise in
works of, 68–69, 380n.32; characters
of, 106, 205–6, 215, 286, 297, 339, 357,
380n.32; English society and, 260–61,
301, 357; theater productions of,
205–6
Diderot, Denis, 142, 361
dilemma ensemble, 25, 71, 313
Dimond, William, 130
Dinnerstein, Dorothy, 401n.81
"Disastrous Result of Beautymania" (du
Maurier), *153*
Disraeli, Benjamin, 216
Distraining for Rent (Wilkie), 280
Dodgson, Charles. *See* Carroll, Lewis
Dolaro, Selina, 56, 72, *73*
domesticity: Amazons and, 201, 228, 243;
"angel in the house" and, 182, 192, 198,
215, 229; fairies and, 192–93, 201–3, 221;
gendered behavior and, 216, 224, 271,
287, 340–41; illegitimacy and, 136–47;
melodrama and, 100–101, 106–9, 139,
277–80; of Victorian gender ideology,
22, 100, 154–56, 169, 186, 198, 235
Don César de Bazan (D'Ennery), 295
Don Giovanni (Mozart), 96

18; Casilda in, 317, 322; *contadine* Chorus in, 316, 317; Don Alhambra del Bolero in, 317, 320–21; Duchess of Plaza-Toro in, 213, 316–17, 322–23; Duke of Plaza-Toro in, 316–17, 322–23, 356; as ethnographic mirror, 256, 291, 312–24; Gianetta in, 317, 320; Gilbert's libretto for, 313, 315–20; Giuseppe Palmieri in, 316, 320, 322; *gondolieri* Chorus in, 27, 315–20; Grand Inquisitor in, 317, 320; "I am a courtier grave and serious" in, 322, 335; Luiz in, 314, 317; Marco Palmieri in, 316, 322; Methodism in, 291; republicanism in, 312–16, 319–21, 327, 415n.17; as self-reflexive, 317–18; "Small titles and orders" in, 323; Sullivan's music for, 313, 316, 318, 323; Tessa in, 317–18; "There lived a King, as I've been told" in, 320

Goodheart, Old Adam (*Ruddigore*), 279

Goodman, Andrew, 69, 120, 122, 381n.33, 383n.31

Good Woman in the Wood, The (Planché), 217

Gordon, Charles, 270

Gordon, J. M., 308

Gosse, Edmund, 182–83, 377n.15

gothic melodrama, 25, 96–97, 274–77, 281–83. See also *Ruddigore*

Gothic style, 225, 264, 312, 408n.27

Götterdämmerung (Wagner), and *Thespis*, 41, 377n.16

Gould, Stephen Jay, 12

Gounod, Charles, 24, 259

governess, 142, 339–40

Grand Duke; or, The Statutory Duel, The (1896), 26, 318, 344–64, 418n.9; Baroness von Krakenfeldt in, 213, 351–52, 357; Chorus in, 352–53; "Come, bumpers—aye, ever-so-many" in, 351; Dr. Tannhäuser in, 353, 363; Dummkopf troupe in, 344, 347, 353, 357, 361; Ernest Dummkopf in, 344, 357, 361; "Ernest's Song" in, 419n.18; as genre parody, 274, 295; Gilbert's libretto for, 352–53,

357; "I have a rival! Frenzy-thrilled" in, 352; Julia Jellicoe in, 213, *348*, 350–53, 357–61, 419n.28; Ludwig in, 347, *348*, 349–51, 355–56, 361, 363; "Opoponax! Eloia!" in, 352; as recollective, 352, 361, 363; resolution in, 355; "Roulette Song" in, 351–52; as self-reflexive, 344, 356, 361, 415n.11; statutory duel in, 352–55, 361–63; "The Stroller's Song" and, 419n.18; Sullivan's music for, 345, 351–52

Grande-duchesse de Gérolstein, La (*The Grand Duchess of Gerolstein*; Offenbach), 350

Grand Inquisitor (*Gondoliers*), 317, 320

grand opera: *brindisi* in, 83, 213, 351–52; Italian style of, 38, 76, 78–79, 289, 387n.40; parody of, 10, 18, 21, 24–25, 81–82, 83, 95–96, 271, 289–90, 382n.14; *Princess Ida* as, 239–41, 404n.28; Sullivan and, 2, 239–41, 294, 301, 352, 404nn.28,31; *Yeomen* as, 294, 314

Granville-Baker, Harley, 311

Graphic (periodical), 353

Great Exhibition (1851), 261, 408n.31, 409n.35

Great Expectations (Dickens), 51, 205, 357

Greek drama, 10, 18, 347, 361

Green, Martyn, 309

Gretchen (Gilbert), 85

Greyson, John, 169

Grossmith, George, 116, 318; as Bunthorne, 156; as Jack Point, *306*; as Ko-Ko, 270; as Major-General Stanley, 134; as Sorcerer, 78–79, 85–88, *87*

Grosvenor, Archibald (*Patience*), 152, 175–86, 209, 347

Grosvenor Gallery, 181

"Hail, Poetry" (*Pirates*), 130

Haines, J. T., 102, 147, 286

Hale, W. P., 409n.35

Halévy, Ludovic, 131

Hall, Donald, 402n.5

Hall, Edith, 42–43, 91

Hot Mikado, The, 369

Housman, A. E., 171–74

"How beautifully blue the sky" (Pirates), 23

Howe, Richard, 105

Hughes, Gervase, 22, 26–27, 299, 308

humor: deflation and, 10, 33–42, 61, 76, 85, 90, 351; as risqué, 33, 44–47, 56, 60

Humphrey's Hall, 261

"Hurrah for Merry England" (Cornwall), 301

Hutton, Robert, 301

Huysmans, Joris-Karl, 261

Hwang, David Henry, 269

hymns, 2, 298, 343

"Hymn to Proserpine" (Swinburne), 377n.15

"I am a courtier grave and serious" (Gondoliers), 322, 335

"I am so proud" (Mikado), 22

"I am the very model of a modern Major-General" (Pirates), 94, 122, 133, 292, 368, 369

Ibsen, Henrik, 135

Ida, Princess (Princess Ida), 29, 212, 233–37, 241, 245–46, 250–51

identity: as corporate, 6, 314–19, 322, 333, 336–38, 343; as divided, 99–101, 169, 172, 267, 286, 355; in group, 91, 152; as hidden, 5, 119–21, 136, 142, 147, 212, 258–59, 314; as national, 76, 113, 128, 255, 260, 269, 300, 328; as performance, 3, 120, 344, 354–58; socialization and, 27, 135–36, 142, 170, 394n.39; transformation and, 85, 279–80, 290, 290–91

idyllic poetry, 152, 174–86

Idylls of the King (Tennyson), 182, 396n.69

"If you give me your attention" (Princess Ida), 245

"If you want a receipt for that popular mystery" (Patience), 160

"I have a rival! Frenzy-thrilled" (Grand Duke), 352

"I have a song to sing, O!" (Yeomen), 308

"I know the value of a kindly chorus" (Pinafore), 27

Île de la demoiselle, L' (Astruc), 268

"I'll sing you one, O!" (chantey), 308

Illustrated London News, 154, 174

"Impartial Statement in Black and White, An" (du Maurier), 160, 162

imperialism: America and, 337; of Britain, 112–13, 335, 386n.33, 407n.11, 416n.4; capitalism and, 325; colonialism and, 134, 332; as cultural, 260, 269, 335–38, 340, 343, 408n.21. See also Englishness; nationalism; patriotism

Imperial Theatre, 123

Importance of Being Ernest, The (Wilde), 156, 169, 339, 390n.38, 411n.17

Incantation Scene (Sorcerer), 82–83, 85–86, 88, 95, 277

incest, 46–47, 137–38, 140, 201, 283

Inchcape Bell, The (Fitzball), 142, 205, 275

"Incidents of Swan-Maiden Marriage" (Stuart-Glennie), 202

infant marriage, 12, 234, 317–18

"Infernal Chorus" (Orphée aux enfers; Offenbach), 45

International Exhibition (1862), 265, 266

Interpretation of Dreams, The (Freud), 93

intoxication: of extravaganza, 363; in opéra bouffe, 82, 300, 351, 363; in Sorcerer, 75, 79–85, 94, 295, 300; in Thespis, 44–45, 54, 81, 300; in Trial, 71

Invention of Love, The (Stoppard), 171–74, 269

inversion: in extravaganza, 35, 40–41, 44–45, 49, 54, 57, 72; as gendered, 22, 163, 202–3, 215, 225, 234, 241, 251; in Grand Duke, 360–61; in Iolanthe, 22, 215–16; in Patience, 163; in Pinafore, 108; in Pirates, 132–33; of social hierarchy, 14, 294; socialization and, 5–8, 11–16, 57–58, 74, 95, 132, 320; in Trial, 57, 69, 74; of type, 108, 132, 245, 278, 287

Iolanthe (Iolanthe), 188, 218

Iolanthe; or, The Peer and the Peri (1882), 118, 187–221, 283, 366, plate 11; "Blue Blood" in, 322; cross-dressing in, 247;

"Pretty Lady" (*Pacific Overtures*; Sond-
heim), 269
Prima Donna, The (Farnie and Murray),
355
Prince (*Princess*; Tennyson), 223–24,
227–31, 235, 242, 403nn.10,13
Prince of Wales's Theatre, 281
Princess, The (Gilbert), 3, 223–40, *233*,
244–49, 418n.3
Princess, The (Tennyson), 3, 44, 222–52,
402n.5
Princesse jaune, La (Saint-Saëns), 268
Princess Ida (Russell), 369
Princess Ida; or, Castle Adamant (1884),
222–52, 317, 366, 405n.49; "A Lady
fair, of lineage high" in, 236, 247;
Castle Adamant in, 223, 229, 235–36,
243–44, 247; cross-dressing in, 27,
223, 247–48, 250–51, 374n.37, 403n.13;
Cyril in, 228, 233, 237–38, 242, 247,
250; Dame figure in, 204, 209, 212;
"Darwinian Man" in, 50, 225, 239–52,
248; "Do not hurt us, if it please you"
in, 250; English culture and, 189, 255,
300, 302; evolution in, 235–36, 244,
247–49, 252; feminism in, 29, 225–43,
249, 251, 403n.11; Florian in, 233, 238,
247, 250; Gilbert's libretto for, 27, 29,
212, 232, 241, 245; Girl Graduates in,
250, 374n.37; as grand opera, 239–41,
404n.28; Hilarion in, 224, 233–38, 242,
247, 250–52; Hildebrand in, 234, 237–
38, 250; "If you give me your attention"
in, 245; King Gama in, 223, 227, 234,
237–38, 245, 252; Lady Blanche in, 204,
209, 212, 235, 243, 249–52, 298; Lady
Psyche in, 228–29, 235–36, 242–43,
247–49, 251; patter song in, 245; "Posterity" theme in, 238, 251–52; Princess
Ida in, 29, 212, 233–37, 241, 245–46,
250–51; resolution in, 231, 235, 238, 250,
251; strong-minded woman in, 187,
208, 224, 244, 250; Sullivan's music
for, 24, 238–41, 245, 404nn.28,31; "The
Lady and the Ape" in, 236, *248*, 308;

"This helmet I suppose" in, 25, 27;
women's education and, 225, 227–29,
235, 238, 241–46, 250–52, 341
Princess Toto (Gilbert), 130, *131*
Prism, Miss (*Importance of Being Earnest*;
Wilde), 339
Procter, Adelaide, 2
professionalism: of Bridesmaids, 19–20,
23, 55–57, 102, 255, 274–75, 285–86; of
executioner, 296; guilds and, 88, 89;
of jester, 310; loss of identity and, 357,
419n.27; modernization and, 94, 96; of
Pirates, 131–32, 135; self-division and,
49–52, 135, 288, 314–15; of Sorcerer, 13,
82, 85–91, 292
Psyche, Lady (*Princess Ida*), 228–29,
235–36, 242–43, 247–49, 251
psychoanalysis, 65, 197, 213, 227, 287;
Freud and, 11, 93, 293, 390n.52
psychomachia, 115, 286, 288
Puccini, Giacomo, 268
Punch (periodical), 2, 8, 86, 116, 292;
cartoons in, 318, 415n.17; on Cleveland
Street affair, 170–71; du Maurier's cartoons in, 156–58, 160–64, 185, 241
puns: in burlesque, 143, 232, 234, 242, 346,
360, *plate 7*; English humor and, 43,
322, 341, 390n.39; in extravaganza, 38,
143, 194, 363; Gilbert and, 39, 53, 62, 89,
107, 144; as principle of plot, 135–36,
143–45, 376n.3
Purse, The (Cross), 99
Pyat, Félix, 389n.32
Pygmalion (Shaw), 120
Pygmalion and Galatea (Gilbert), 3

quartet, 25, 71, 299, 313, 412n.19
Queen Anne style, 264, 302, 408n.27
Queen's College, 244
Quiller-Couch, Sir Arthur, 213

Rackstraw, Ralph (*Pinafore*), 27, 91, 98–121,
105, 135–36, 277–78, 285, 307
Rahill, Frank, 83, 382n.24
"Railroad" parodies, 366

Ruthven Murgatroyd in, 275–76, 279, 284; Sullivan's music for, 26, 278, 284, 289, 299, 412nn.16,19; tableau vivant in, 268; transformation in, 279–80, *290*, 290–91

Ruddigore Castle (*Ruddigore*), 280, 284, *285*

Rudy, Jason, 402nn.5,8

Rural Rides (Cobbett), 301

Ruskin, John, 312, 414n.1

Russell, Anna, 27

Russell, Ken, 369

Ruth (*Pirates*), 136–40, *138, 140*, 147, 204, 208–9, 219, 390n.43

Ruth; or, The Lass That Loved a Sailor (Lancaster), 386n.38

Rymes from Ye Playe of "Pynafore" (advertising pamphlet), 366

Sadler's Wells, 98

Said, Edward, 261, 409n.40

Sailors, Chorus of (*Pinafore*), 17, 22–23, 97–98, 104–10, 113–14, 355, *plate 3*

sailors, sentimentalization of, 97–98, 104–10

Saint-Saëns, Camille, 268

Salomé (Wilde), 362

Sancho Panza (*Don Quixote*; Cervantes), 312, 321

Sandow, Eugen, 111–12

Sandys, William, 301, 413n.24

Sangazure, Lady (*Sorcerer*), 82, 96, 384n.48

Santley, Kate, *131*

Saphir, Lady (*Patience*), 302

Sapphire Necklace, The (Sullivan), 2

satire: Gilbert and, 316–17, 319, 331–32, 419n.24; parody and, 4, 6, 15, 55, 164, 194; as political, 61, 315, 319–22, 330–31, 343, 369; as social, 55, 61, 76, 84, 233, 298, 302; as Victorian, 45, 121, 211–12, 226

Savoy operas: American piracy of, 6, 122–26, 388nn.11,15; autobiographical lyrics in, 11, 61–63, 69, 245; characteristics of, 28–29, 75–76; choreography in, 17–19, 52, 110, 271, 316, 318, 322, 334–35; collaboration on, 1–4, 28–29, 33–36, 56, 77–78, 371n.1, 406n.3; Continental views and, 79–85, 344–47, 353–56; copyrights and, 122–26, 367, 420n.5; as cultural critique, 1, 6, 16–17, 255–73, 407n.18; divided Chorus in, 17–23, 27, 75–76, 102, 109, 187, 215, 256; double Chorus in, 22–23, 274–75, 296; formula for, 5, 75–76, 213, 255, 294, 317, 368, 381n.1; genre recollection and, 344–45, 352, 361, 363, 373n.24; "Gilbert and Sullivan Legacy" and, 366; Gilbert's paternalism and, 21, 68, 334, 374n.41; hyper-logic of, 135, 220, 283–84, 291, 315; invasion motif of, 19, 200, 300–304; marriage plot and, 167–68, 275–76, 285, 295–99, 308; "Merrie England" topos and, 300–305; as mock-heroic, 25, 38, 217, 233, 246, 328, 402n.85; as novel genre, 4–6, 82, 271, 272; parodies of, 366, 368–69; performance tradition of, 27, 53, 94, 365–70, 420n.5; precursor genres of, 2, 4–10, 128, 296; production values of, 5–7, 36, 56–57, 75–76, 239, 334, 404n.30, 407n.9; propriety and, 44–49, 76, 79, 139, 193, 198, 243; revivals of, 241, 361–62, 365–70; special effects in, 5, 72, 82–83, 95–96, 194–96; stage rights to, 123–24; stage sets of, 20, 39, *240*, 281, 325, 334, *335, 362*, 365, 415n.1; theater tradition and, 4–5, 9–10, 17, 26, 334. *See also* D'Oyly Carte Opera Company; English comic opera; genre parody

Savoy Theatre, 1, 77, 151–52, 172–74, 261, 330

Scarron, Paul, 38

Schiller, Friedrich, 129

Schoch, Richard, 136, 347, 390n.39, 403n.18, 404n.25

School-girls, Chorus of (*Mikado*), 258, 267

Scott, Sir Walter, 130, 147

Scribe, Eugene, 382n.18

Seagull, The (Chekhov), 420n.33

secularization, 40–43, 85, 94–95

Sedgwick, Eve Kosofsky, 402n.5, 403n.11

seduction melodrama, 23, 55–57, 65–68, 274–77, 285, 380n.23

Seeley, Paul, 259, 407n.14

Sellars, Peter, 369

Sensation Novel, A (Gilbert), 3

sentimentalization: of pirates, 129–30, 132–33, 136, 143–46, 187, 389n.29; of sailors, 97–98, 104–10

Serious Family, The (Barnett), 154–55

serious family tradition, 152–66, 182, 185–86

Seven Champions of Christendom, The (Planché), 416n.4

sexuality: double standard and, 61, 68–69, 241; of fairies, 187–89, 191–93, 197–98, *plates 12, 13*; flirting and, 257, 406n.7; illegitimacy and, 136–47; reproduction and, 222, 232–33, 241–42, 401n.81, 405n.42; sexual inversion and, 203, 215; transgressions of, 44–50, 137–38, 140, 201, 238, 283. *See also* femininity; gender; masculinity

Shadbolt, Wilfred (*Yeomen*), 296–98, 307, 310, 412n.14

Shakespeare, William: allusions to, 234, 290, 307, 344, 351, 357, 361; theater history and, 234, 259, 306, 344, 345–47, 361

Shandler, Jeffrey, 27

Shaw, George Bernard, 4, 120, 135, 213, 313, 317, 335, 389n.31

Shelley, Mary, 277

Sheppard, Jack, 129

Sheridan, Richard Brinsley, 4

Showalter, Elaine, 231, 403n.13

Shropshire Lad, A (Housman), 174

"Signs of the Times" (Carlyle), 387n.47

Silver, Carol, 189–90, 201–2, 397n.10, 402n.86

Simpsons, The (television show), 370

Sims, George Robert, 305

"Six-Mark Tea Pot, The" (du Maurier), 160, *161*

Sleek, Aminadab (*Serious Family*; Barnett), 154

Sleeping Beauty in the Wood, The (Planché), 267

"Small titles and orders" (*Gondoliers*), 323

Smith, Horace, 8

Smith, James, 8

Smith, W. H., 116–17, *117*, 134

Smollett, Tobias, 104, 410n.6

social class: inequalities of, 98–104, 128, 320; role-playing and, 47–52, 120–21, 335, 354–58; theater culture and, 6, 22, 26–27, 40, 42–43, 151; upward mobility and, 107, 114–21, 143, 184, 248, 278, 354

socialization: circumstance and, 114, 118, 120–21, 136–37, 387n.47; inversion and, 5–8, 11–16, 57–58, 74, 95, 132, 320; metatheatrical critique and, 11, 16, 52–53, 57–59, 336, 344, 353–63; mutuality and, 228, 231, 249; serious family tradition and, 152–66, 182, 185–86; status quo and, 184, 197, 203, 222, 232, 340, 363

social problem plays, 3, 21, 68

social roles: court behavior and, 322, 325–26, 334–36; as theatrical, 56, 110, 120–21, 159, 168, 315, 354–60

"Society has quite forsaken all her wicked courses" (*Utopia*), 338

"Soldiers of the Queen" (Booth), 391n.56

solos, 22–23, 296

Somerville Hall, 244

Sondheim, Stephen, 269

Sophy, Lady (*Utopia*), 213, *339*, 339–40, 342, 416n.5

Sorcerer (John Wellington Wells; *Sorcerer*), 82, 85–91, *87*, 95, 292, *plate 6*

Sorcerer, The (1877), 1, 75–96, 114, 241, 303, *plate 6*; Ahrimanes in, 95, 384nn.45,48; Alexis Pointdextre in, 82, 90, 95, 96; *brindisi* in, 83, 351; Constance Partlet in, 82, 96, 192; Dr. Daly in, 82, 84–85, 96, 192; Gilbert's libretto for, 82, 95; Incantation Scene in, 82–83, 85–86, *88*, 95, 277; intoxication in, 75, 79–85, 94, 295, 300; John Wellington Wells in, 82, 85–91, *87*, 95, 292, *plate 6*; Lady

Sangazure in, 82, 96, 384n.48; magic elixir in, 13, 75, 79–82, 85–86, 104, 296; patter song in, 88, 292; "red fire" in, 95, 96; reformation in, 83; Savoy formula in, 5, 75–76, 381n.1; Sir Marmaduke Pointdextre in, 82, 96; teapot in, 3, 13, 79, 81–83, 85–86, 255

South Sea Bubble, 332

Sparkeion (*Thespis*), 34, 46–47, *48*

Spenser, Edmund, 216, 219

Sportsman (periodical), 404n.30

Stanley, Henry Morton, 134

Stanley, Major-General (*Pirates*), 22, 115, 132–34; as illegitimate authority, 137, *140*, 140–48, 246; patter song of, 94, 122, 133, 292, 368, 369

Stanley, Sir Frederick, 134

"Stanzas from the Grande Chartreuse" (Arnold), 377n.15

statutory duel, 352–55, 361–63

Stedman, Jane: on Dame figure, 208, 214–15; on development of Savoy operas, 57, 406n.3; on invasion motif, 19; on Jack Point, 311, 413n.38; on *Patience*, 153, 175–76, 183; on *Princess Ida*, 234, 244, 403n.24; on *Sorcerer*, 86, 384n.48; on "thrilling word" of melodrama, 291

Steinbach, Susie, 64, 67–68, 380nn.26,28

Stephens, John Russell, 123–24

stereotypes: as cultural, 269, 271–72, 332, 337, 408n.26; historical context of, 11, 15–16

Stewart, Susan, 190, 192

St. James Theatre, 81, 173, 336

Stoker, Bram, 277

Stoppard, Tom, 168, 171–74, 269

"Strange adventure" (*Yeoman*), 297, 299, 412n.19

Strauss, David Friedrich, 377n.17

Strauss, Johann, 352

Strephon (*Iolanthe*), 188, 198, 200

"Stroller's Song, The" (*Grand Duke*), 419n.18

strolling players, 304–5, 307, 311, 414n.43

Strong, Jonathan, 352, 363

strong-minded woman: Fairy Queen as, 187, 199, 221; Katisha as, 211–12; Lady Jane as, 152, 214–15, 286; Lady Psyche as, 228; Princess Ida as, 224, 229, 244; Savoy Dames as, 213, 401n.81; stereotype of, 203, 206, 244, 250, 398n.27, 402n.83

Stuart-Glennie, John, 202

Stupidas (*Thespis*), 35

Sturgis, Julian, 301

Styx, John (*Orphée aux enfers*; Offenbach), 44

Sullivan, Arthur, 72; "carpet quarrel" and, 330; Carroll and, 84, 383n.29; Carte and, 1, 4, 56, 77–78, 122–25, 268, 371n.1; "cipher quarrel" and, 318; collaboration and, 1–4, 28–29, 33, 35–36, 232; contrapuntal technique of, 22–23; death of, 2, 365; depictions of, *73*, 318, *319*; *Gondoliers* and, 313, 316, 318, 323; *Grand Duke* and, 345, 351–52; grand opera and, 2, 239–41, 294, 301, 313–14, 352, 404nn.28,31; hymns of, 2, 298, 343; *Iolanthe* and, 241, 298; knighting of, 2; lozenge plot and, 3, 79–80, 82, 213, 294; *Mikado* and, 2, 26, 212, 258–60, 299, 407n.14; mock-heroic music of, 25, 217, 402n.85; musical genius of, 24–29; *Patience* and, 24, 174–75, 186, 209, 241; *Pirates* and, 22–24, 28, 94; *Princess Ida* and, 24, 238–41, 245, 404nn.28,31; reputation of, 1–2, 24–29, 38, 44, 56, 78, 170; *Ruddigore* and, 26, 278, 284, 289, 299, 412nn.16,19; *Trial* and, 55–56; Wagner and, 25, 217, 413n.38; *Yeomen* and, 2, 26, 294, 297–99, 309–10, 314, 404n.28. *See also individual works*

Sullivan, Fred, 55, 378n.1

Sulpizio, Sergeant (*La Vivandière*; Gilbert), 14

"Sun whose rays are all ablaze, The" (*Mikado*), 28–29

supernatural melodrama, 3–4, 82–83, 85, 95–97, 274, 277

GENDER AND CULTURE

A Series of Columbia University Press

. . . .

Nancy K. Miller and Victoria Rosner, Series Editors